OFFENDER REHABILITATION AND TREATMENT
Effective Programmes and Policies to Reduce Re-offending

Edited by

James McGuire

Department of Clinical Psychology, University of Liverpool, UK

JOHN WILEY & SONS, LTD

Other Wiley Editorial Offices

John Wiley & Sons Inc., 111 River Street, Hoboken, NJ 07030, USA

Jossey-Bass, 989 Market Street, San Francisco, CA 94103-1741, USA

Wiley-VCH Verlag GmbH, Boschstr. 12, D-69469 Weinheim, Germany

John Wiley & Sons Australia Ltd, 33 Park Road, Milton, Queensland 4064, Australia

John Wiley & Sons (Asia) Pte Ltd, 2 Clementi Loop #02-01, Jin Xing Distripark, Singapore 129809

John Wiley & Sons Canada Ltd, 22 Worcester Road, Etobicoke, Ontario, Canada M9W 1L1

Library of Congress Cataloging-in-Publication Data

Offender rehabilitation and treatment : effective programmes and policies to reduce
re-offending / edited by James McGuire.
      p.   cm.—(Wiley series in forensic clinical psychology)
   Includes bibliographical references and index.
   ISBN 0-471-98761-1 (cased)—ISBN 0-471-89967-4 (pbk.)
   1. Prisoners—Mental health services.   2. Recidivism—Prevention.   3. Prisoners—Mental
health services—Great Britain.   4. Recidivism—Great Britain—Prevention.   I. McGuire, James.
II. Series.
   RC451.4.P68 O35   2002
   365'.66—dc21   2002071303

British Library Cataloguing in Publication Data

A catalogue record for this book is available from the British Library

ISBN 0-471-98761-1 (cased)
      0-471-89967-4 (paper)

Typeset in 10/12 pt Palatino by TechBooks, New Delhi, India
Printed and bound in Great Britain by Biddles Ltd, Guildford and King's Lynn
This book is printed on acid-free paper responsibly manufactured from sustainable forestry
in which at least two trees are planted for each one used for paper production.

OFFENDER REHABILITATION
AND TREATMENT

WILEY SERIES IN
FORENSIC CLINICAL PSYCHOLOGY

Edited by

Clive R. Hollin
Centre for Applied Psychology, The University of Leicester, UK

and

Mary McMurran
School of Psychology, Cardiff University, UK

COGNITIVE BEHAVIOURAL TREATMENT OF SEXUAL OFFENDERS
William L. Marshall, Dana Anderson and Yolanda Fernandez

VIOLENCE, CRIME AND MENTALLY DISORDERED OFFENDERS:
Concepts and Methods for Effective Treatment and Prevention
Sheilagh Hodgins and Rüdiger Müller-Isberner (*Editors*)

OFFENDER REHABILITATION IN PRACTICE:
Implementing and Evaluating Effective Programs
Gary A. Bernfeld, David P. Farrington and Alan W. Leschied (*Editors*)

MOTIVATING OFFENDERS TO CHANGE:
A Guide to Enhancing Engagement in Therapy
Mary McMurran (*Editor*)

THE PSYCHOLOGY OF GROUP AGGRESSION
Arnold P. Goldstein

OFFENDER REHABILITATION AND TREATMENT:
Effective Programmes and Policies to Reduce Re-offending
James McGuire (*Editor*)

CONTENTS

ABOUT THE EDITOR

James McGuire is a Reader in Clinical Psychology and Programme Director of the Doctorate in Clinical Psychology at the University of Liverpool, UK. He obtained his first degree in psychology at the University of Glasgow, his PhD in psychology from the University of Leicester based on cross-cultural research carried out in Hong Kong, and obtained an MSc in Clinical Psychology at the University of Leeds. He has previously held posts at the University of Edinburgh and University College London, and was for a time self-employed as a training consultant. He is a Chartered Clinical and Forensic Psychologist and carries out assessment of offenders for criminal courts and Mental Health Review Tribunals. He has conducted research in prisons, probation services, adolescent units and secure hospitals on aspects of the effectiveness of treatment of offenders and related topics. His recent work has included assessment of self-control of aggression in young offenders, and development and evaluation of social problem-solving training programmes. At present he is engaged in research projects funded by the Home Office Research, Development and Statistics Directorate, HM Prison Service, the Youth Justice Board, and the High Security Psychiatric Hospitals Commissioning Board. He is also involved in a range of consultative work with criminal justice agencies, has served on a number of advisory panels in this field in the United Kingdom and Canada, was co-organiser of the 'What Works' series of conferences and is the author or editor of eleven books and over seventy other publications.

LIST OF CONTRIBUTORS

Anthony R. Beech

School of Psychology, University of Birmingham, Edgebaston, Birmingham B15 2TT, UK

Charles M. Cleland

Principal Research Associate, National Development and Research Institutes Inc., 71 West 23rd Street, 8th Floor, New York, NY 10010, USA

Francis T. Cullen

Department of Criminal Justice, University of Cincinnati, 792 Mannington, Cincinnati, Ohio 45226, USA

Tom Ellis

Institute of Criminal Justice Studies, University of Portsmouth, Ravelin House, Museum Road, Portsmouth PO1 2QQ, UK

David P. Farrington

Institute of Criminology, University of Cambridge, 7 West Road, Cambridge CB3 9DT, UK

Vincente Garrido

Faculty of Psychology and Education, University of Valencia, 46010 Valencia, Spain

Paul Gendreau

Centre for Criminal Justice Studies, University of New Brunswick, PO Box 5050, Saint John, New Brunswick E2L 4LS, Canada

Claire Goggin

Centre for Criminal Justice Studies, University of New Brunswick, PO Box 5050, Saint John, New Brunswick E2L 4L5, Canada

The late Professor Arnold P. Goldstein

Center for Research on Aggression, School of Education, 805 S. Crouse Avenue, Syracuse, New York 13244-2280, USA

Donald A. Gordon

Department of Psychology, Ohio University, 200 Porter Hall, Athens, Ohio, 45701, USA

Clive R. Hollin

Centre for Applied Psychology, University of Leicester, University Road, Leicester LE1 7RH, UK

Douglas Lipton

Lipton Consulting, 8 Appletree Lane, East Brunswick, NJ 08816, USA

Ruth Mann

HM Prison Service, Offending Behaviour Programmes Unit, Abell House, John Islip Street, London SW1P 4LH, UK

James McGuire

Department of Clinical Psychology, University of Liverpool, Whelan Building, Liverpool L69 3GB, UK

Mary McMurran

School of Psychology, Cardiff University, PO Box 901, Cardiff CF10 3YG, UK

Paul E. Mullen

Victoria Institute of Forensic Mental Health, Monash University, PO Box 266, Locked Bag 10, Rosanna, Victoria 3085, Australia

Mario Paparozzi

Department of Law and Justice, College of New Jersey, PO Box 7710, Ewing, NJ 08628, USA

Frank S. Pearson

Senior Project Director, National Development and Research Institutes Inc., 71 West 23rd Street, 8th Floor, New York, NY 10010, USA

Santiago Redondo

Department of Personality, Assessment and Psychological Treatment, Faculty of Psychology, University of Barcelona, Passeig de la Vall d'Hebron, 171, 08035 Barcelona, Spain

Mary Nômme Russell

School of Social Work and Family Studies, University of British Columbia, 2080 West Mall, Vancouver, British Columbia V6T 1Z2, Canada

Julio Sánchez-Meca

Department of Basic Psychology and Methodology, Faculty of Psychology, Universidad de Murcia (Campus Universitario de Espinardo), Apartado 4021, 30080 Murcia, Spain

Brandon Welsh

Department of Criminal Justice Studies, University of Massachusetts at Lowell, 1 University Avenue, Lowell, MA 01854, USA

Jane Winstone

Institute of Criminal Justice Studies, University of Portsmouth, Ravelin House, Museum Road, Portsmouth PO1 2QQ, UK

Dorline Yee

Senior Research Associate, National Development and Research Institutes Inc., 71 West 23rd Street, 8th Floor, New York, NY 10010, USA

SERIES EDITORS' PREFACE

ABOUT THE SERIES

At the time of writing it is clear that we live in a time, certainly in the UK and other parts of Europe, if perhaps less so in areas of the world, when there is renewed enthusiasm for constructive approaches to working with offenders to prevent crime. What do we mean by this statement and what basis do we have for making it?

First, by "constructive approaches to working with offenders" we mean bringing the use of effective methods and techniques of behaviour change into work with offenders. Indeed, this view might pass as a definition of forensic clinical psychology. Thus, our focus is the application of theory and research in order to develop practice aimed at bringing about a change in the offender's functioning. The word *constructive* is important and can be set against approaches to behaviour change that seek to operate by destructive means. Such destructive approaches are typically based on the principles of deterrence and punishment, seeking to suppress the offender's actions through fear and intimidation. A constructive approach, on the other hand, seeks to bring about changes in an offender's functioning that will produce, say, enhanced possibilities of employment, greater levels of self-control, better family functioning, or increased awareness of the pain of victims.

A constructive approach faces the criticism of being a "soft" response to the damage caused by offenders, neither inflicting pain and punishment nor delivering retribution. This point raises a serious question for those involved in working with offenders. Should advocates of constructive approaches oppose retribution as a goal of the criminal justice system as a process that is incompatible with treatment and rehabilitation? Alternatively, should constructive work with offenders take place within a system given to retribution? We believe that this issue merits serious debate.

However, to return to our starting point, history shows that criminal justice systems are littered with many attempts at constructive work with offenders, not all of which have been successful. In raising the spectre of success, the second part of our opening sentence now merits attention: that is, "constructive approaches to working with offenders *to prevent crime*". In order to achieve the goal of preventing crime, interventions must focus on the right targets for behaviour change. In addressing this crucial point, Andrews and Bonta (1994) have formulated the *need principle*:

> Many offenders, especially high-risk offenders, have a variety of needs. They
> need places to live and work and/or they need to stop taking drugs. Some
> have poor self-esteem, chronic headaches or cavities in their teeth. These are
> all "needs". The need principle draws our attention to the distinction between
> *criminogenic* and *noncriminogenic* needs. Criminogenic needs are a subset of an
> offender's risk level. They are dynamic attributes of an offender that, when
> changed, are associated with changes in the probability of recidivism. Non-
> criminogenic needs are also dynamic and changeable, but these changes are not
> necessarily associated with the probability of recidivism. (p. 176)

Thus, successful work with offenders can be judged in terms of bringing about
change in noncriminogenic need *or* in terms of bringing about change in criminogenic need. While the former is important and, indeed, may be a necessary precursor to offence-focused work, it is changing criminogenic need that, we argue,
should be the touchstone in working with offenders.

While, as noted above, the history of work with offenders is not replete with
success, the research base developed since the early 1990s, particularly the meta-
analyses (e.g. Lösel, 1995), now strongly supports the position that effective work
with offenders to prevent further offending is possible. The parameters of such
evidence-based practice have become well established and widely disseminated
under the banner of "*What Works*" (McGuire, 1995).

It is important to state that we are not advocating that there is only one approach
to preventing crime. Clearly there are many approaches, with different theoretical
underpinnings, that can be applied. Nonetheless, a tangible momentum has grown
in the wake of the "*What Works*" movement as academics, practitioners, and policy
makers seek to capitalise on the possibilities that this research raises for preventing
crime. The task now facing many service agencies lies in turning the research into
effective practice.

Our aim in developing this Series in Forensic Clinical Psychology is to produce
texts that review research and draw on clinical expertise to advance effective work
with offenders. We are both committed to the ideal of evidence-based practice
and we will encourage contributors to the Series to follow this approach. Thus, the
books published in the Series will not be practice manuals or "cook books": they will
offer readers authoritative and critical information through which forensic clinical
practice can develop. We are both enthusiastic about the contribution to effective
practice that this Series can make and look forward to continuing to develop it in
the years to come.

ABOUT THIS BOOK

In 1995 we were instrumental in bringing about the publication, through John
Wiley and Sons, of James McGuire's edited text *What Works: Reducing Reoffending*.
We knew at the time that this was an important book because it drew together so
many connected strands to form a compendium on the state of the art at that time.
It is not a surprise that the book has been successful and many of the chapters
widely cited in the literature. Further, as we knew it would!, the "What Works"
ideal has become a major force in forensic work in the UK in both prisons and the

community. In a rapidly changing field, the time since the publication of *What Works: Reducing Reoffending* has seen a great deal of movement in both theory and practice in the assessment and treatment of offenders (Hollin, 2001). The current practice agenda is very much concerned with issues of implementation and evaluation of work with offenders, as seen in another book in this Series edited by Bernfeld, Farrington, and Leschied (2001). At the forefront of conceptual thinking are issues concerned with connection of the What Works ideas with treatment for "specialist offenders", such as mentally disordered offenders and sex offenders, and with broader criminological thinking (Crow, 2001).

These practical and conceptual concerns are reflected in the contents of this book, again collected and edited by James McGuire, which offers a companion to the earlier text. There is much to take from this book, but perhaps there are three matters of particular note. First, there is the welcome return of theory as a topic for discussion. The findings of the meta-analyses heralded an upsurge in practice which has not been matched by a similar consideration of theoretical issues. Several of the chapters here begin to make welcome moves in that direction. Second, the growing sophistication regarding the economic analysis of the effects of treatment. In is very much a part of current thinking that interventions must show themselves to be effective in economic as well as human terms. This is not a level of analysis that should cause concern: there is little doubt that effective work with offenders will pay its own way and more. Finally, the willingness of psychologists to engage in wider debates about social policy on the basis of sound research evidence and strong practice. These matters are set, one might venture, to become the issues over the next few years, after which we'll ask James to do the third book!

Clive Hollin and Mary McMurran

REFERENCES

Andrews, D. A., & Bonta, J. (1994). *The psychology of criminal conduct*. Cincinnati, OH: Anderson Publishing.

Bernfeld, G. A., Farrington, D. P., & Leschied, A. W. (Eds). (2001). *Offender rehabilitation in practice: Implementing and evaluating effective programs*. Chichester: John Wiley & Sons.

Crow, I. (2001). *The treatment and rehabilitation of offenders*. London: Sage Publications.

Hollin, C. R. (Ed). (2001). *Handbook of offender assessment and treatment*. Chichester: John Wiley & Sons.

Lösel, F. (1995). Increasing consensus in the evaluation of offender rehabilitation? *Psychology, Crime, & Law, 2*, 19–39.

McGuire, J. (ed). (1995). *What works: Reducing reoffending*. Chichester: John Wiley & Sons.

PREFACE

There is a widely shared view that we live in an era of *evidence-based practice* in which the direction of public policy in many fields should be informed by relevant research. On one level it may seem odd that things could ever have been otherwise. But the process of translating research findings into an interpretable form, in which their potential implications can be clearly and consistently discerned, is far from easy. The debate continues over whether "EBP" is a passing fashion or here to stay. In challenging its rise to prominence, some commentators raise the deeper question of what precisely constitutes evidence. The best research is usually considered to be that in which as many as possible of the operating variables are controlled. Paradoxically, the greater a researcher's success in achieving this, so the argument runs, the less relevant the findings are for practice. The cleanest, best-designed studies are conducted in conditions quite unlike those that are found in applied settings. So the more rigorously designed an investigation, the more it appears distant from the "real world" and lived experience of people where, among other things, acts of crime occur. Difficulties of this kind have led some to reject the concept of social science as a valid or meaningful approach to inquiry.

This book is founded on the view that research can be an enormously valuable resource in helping to solve human problems. In addressing the issue of how it can be applied in criminal justice I hope it will take the subject matter one step (or more) forward from where it currently stands. The book contains several chapters summarising the findings of recent large-scale, systematic reviews of intervention studies. It is also designed to explore a number of unresolved issues within those fields, to present findings and ideas relevant to them and to explore questions that to date have remained unanswered.

There is an important and useful distinction between three levels of prevention to reduce crime. The first is called *primary prevention*. It is usually of a long-term nature, in which resources are invested in designated ways in certain areas (such as high crime neighbourhoods) to improve the overall life opportunities of families and developing children. Alternatively it may consist of situational strategies such as target hardening, increased security or surveillance or other environmental measures. *Secondary prevention* has a slightly different objective: it is focused on recognised "at risk" populations, such as children who are truanting from school or experimenting with drugs, to prevent involvement in delinquency. *Tertiary prevention*, focused on adjudicated offenders (those already convicted of crimes), is the familiar terrain of those who work in penal services such as prisons, probation and youth justice.

Each of these levels is addressed in the present book. While most chapters focus on the third level, that of criminal justice or correctional services, material is also included on long-term developmental prevention (Chapter 5), and on interventions to ensure that low-level aggression does not escalate into more serious problems (Chapter 6). Several other chapters identify a variety of levels on which crime reduction strategies could be targeted, for example through evolving models of the links between alcohol and violent crime (Chapter 8). Many chapters also shift emphasis away from work centred exclusively on individuals, to interventions that focus on family, community, and other systemic or contextual factors.

The book is divided into three sections. The first consolidates and reinforces what is known at present, and includes three new meta-analytic reviews published here for the first time. In the opening chapter, I summarise findings on the impact of two general approaches to crime prevention at the tertiary level, one based on deterrence or criminal sanctions, the other based on delivery of organised services including structured programmes. The chapter also incorporates an overview of a total of 30 large-scale reviews carried out in this field to date. In Chapters 2 and 3 Douglas Lipton, Frank Pearson, Charles Cleland and Dorline Yee outline two sets of findings from the CDATE project. This is the largest single systematic review yet undertaken of the field of offender rehabilitation, the findings of which have been available so far only as conference papers and are keenly awaited in published form. The CDATE researchers here present findings within two of the categories of intervention they examined: therapeutic communities and cognitive-behavioural programmes; their review of the latter is the largest yet published on this type of rehabilitation programme. Following this, Santiago Redondo, Julio Sánchez-Meca and Vicente Garrido, who have for some years been collating studies of intervention with offenders in European countries, describe the most recent findings from that research, and place it in the context of findings from other reviews. In a different domain, David Farrington and Brandon Welsh then examine the findings from evaluation of long-term developmental prevention programmes. These authors have also recently turned their attention in a methodical way to the question of cost-effectiveness of these and other services. While the number of studies reported in this area remains small, the authors have found benefit–cost ratios to be positive, demonstrating another return from this kind of work. As governments and other agencies are under constant pressure to provide the most cost-efficient modes of service, studies of this kind are increasingly important.

Part II of the book has a more specific focus on selected problem areas in work with offenders, and on certain kinds of intervention used within the field. Two chapters address work done primarily with younger offenders and pay close attention to family and other social influences. The late Arnold Goldstein made an unrivalled contribution to the understanding and reduction of aggressive behaviour through both individual and systemic approaches. In Chapter 6 he discusses the nature of low-level aggression, and reviews evidence concerning how to prevent its intensification into more serious forms, by integrative approaches particularly in schools and in the community. Following this Don Gordon reviews evidence concerning the importance of working with families of young offenders, and presents key guidelines for such engagements. In particular, he outlines work on programmes such as *Functional Family Therapy* and *Parenting Wisely* and the accumulating evidence for their effectiveness.

In Chapter 8, Mary McMurran provides what, in my view, is the clearest formulation available to date of the seemingly impenetrable nexus of links between alcohol, aggression and violence. Development of an integrative model also yields valuable suggestions for intervention and the outcomes of some of these are reviewed. The following chapter, by Mary Russell, addresses some of the intricacies of the problem of domestic violence, placing it in a society-wide context in which a fundamental contributory factor resides in male attitudes towards women. Comparatively few studies have demonstrated the possibility of reducing spousal abuse, and the focus on attitude change is likely to be seen as an essential element of any successful approach to this issue. The final two chapters in this section turn attention to other groups of offenders who have been the subject of considerable research activity. Anthony Beech and Ruth Mann, leading researchers in the study of sexual offending, summarise key findings of the work that has been done to date. Equally important, they highlight the questions that should now be addressed for this specialised area of work to be able to advance further forward. Finally, Paul Mullen, internationally known for his psychiatric research on serious offences committed by people with severe mental disorders, reviews the evidence on the links between the two; and to the extent that it can be achieved in such a complex field, offers clarity where all too often confusion reigns.

Part III of the book turns our attention to aspects of practice and policy in criminal justice services. To act most effectively on the findings of treatment–outcome research, a central issue is the need to focus on individual assessment, particularly of static and dynamic risk factors (or "risks and needs"). Considerable mystification surrounds the meaning and implications of these terms and in Chapter 12 Clive Hollin presents a clearly written overview of the major themes in this area, the issues at stake, and the advantages and disadvantages of some of the most widely used instruments. The final two chapters of the book grasp the nettle of how best to disseminate and apply results concerning "what works" or is likely to work to reduce offender recidivism. In the adoption of evidence-based practice there are numerous unresolved problems over how to transfer the knowledge gained from research to everyday, practical settings while ensuring quality control of the work that is subsequently done. Such a task continues to pose major challenges and has sometimes given rise to heated debates.

In Chapter 13 Tom Ellis and Jane Winstone outline how findings from a survey of probation services were used to inform major departures in practice and policy in England and Wales towards the end of the 1990s. The scale and pace of these innovations have not been without their critics, and the authors express some reservations about the process and direction of the shift. These disputes underpin the assertion of a number of commentators on this area that the issue of programme implementation has been comparatively neglected in offender work. As Paul Gendreau, Claire Goggin, Francis Cullen and Mario Paparozzi show in the final chapter of the book, there are several kinds of gaps to be bridged in this respect. But there are also many other areas of knowledge on which it would be possible to draw when considering how to apply research findings in the "real world". Nevertheless, supposedly experienced expert advisers and development consultants all too often fail to draw on them. To close the book in a highly entertaining intellectual *tour-de-force*, Professor Gendreau and his colleagues offer an indispensable insight and practical lessons to invigorate more effective pursuit of these goals.

I am very grateful to all the contributors to this volume for allotting the time and expending the effort needed to prepare chapters of such high quality. Trying to marshal an evidence base in a multifaceted field of research with close links to practice and public policy, intertwined with political and ethical controversies, is an extremely daunting task. I don't think anyone has either understated the complexities or overstated their conclusions. The final text in every case is a product of methodical work and careful and measured reflection. I also thank Lesley Valerio, of John Wiley and Sons, for patiently steering this work to its conclusion; and Michael Coombs, former commissioning editor, for giving original shape to the project. Finally, I thank my partner Sheila Vellacott, and our daughters Emma and Jenny, for your marathon reserves of tolerance, love and support.

January 2002   James McGuire

PART I

RESEARCH FINDINGS

Chapter 1

INTEGRATING FINDINGS FROM RESEARCH REVIEWS

JAMES McGUIRE

Dept. Of Clinical Psychology, University of Liverpool, UK

From an historical perspective, those who live in the world's prosperous industrial economies have never been as safe as they are today. Broadly speaking, infant mortality has dropped and life expectancies have risen to levels that would have been unimaginable to prior generations. Many of the common dangers that plagued and distressed our predecessors have been eradicated or are for the most part controlled within manageable limits. Yet these societies still feel conscious of a number of seemingly ever-present threats. One of the most frequently discussed and acutely felt is the fear of crime.

As would be expected, the frequency and severity of this problem varies considerably between different countries (Newman, Bouloukos & Cohen, 2001), as does the subjectively experienced fear of it (Mayhew & White, 1997). Considerable effort has been expended in searching for methods of reducing its prevalence, and in responding to those who are known to have broken the law in ways that will make them less likely to do so again.

This book is focused on that problem and on steadily accumulating evidence that solutions to it can be found. It is concerned with the increasingly firm consensus regarding the prospects of achieving reductions in rates of re-offending. It takes as its starting-point the finding that "... offender rehabilitation has been, can be and will be achieved. The principles underlying effective rehabilitation generalize across far too many intervention strategies and offender samples to be dismissed as trivial" (Gendreau & Ross, 1987, p. 395). However, both research and practice in this field have moved beyond the basic question of "what works" and the influences that may contribute to that. The focus is now upon more complex questions of what works when, where, and with whom; and why the various combinations of such elements form the patterns that they do.

The objective of the present chapter is to provide a context for the book as a whole by consolidating the current position regarding the evidence that has accumulated

---

Offender Rehabilitation and Treatment: Effective Programmes and Policies to Reduce Re-offending. Edited by James McGuire.
© John Wiley & Sons, Ltd.

to date and its relationship to practical and policy considerations. To accomplish this, the chapter is divided into three sections. The first will consider what has been learned about punishment—which remains the dominant response, in almost all societies, to citizens who break the law. The second is to collate the findings of available large-scale reviews of research on constructive alternatives to it. The third is to illustrate selected aspects of that process in action, and to identify some of the key issues that arise in translating research findings into practical steps.

BEHAVIOUR CHANGE STRATEGIES

Behavioural psychologists have traditionally drawn a distinction between two broad strategies for altering patterns of behaviour, with particular reference to the reduction of some type of activity agreed to be socially undesirable; in this case, criminal recidivism (Goldiamond, 1974; and see McGuire, 2000a).

Eliminative strategies are based on the expectation that a problem behaviour will be suppressed by linking it to negative consequences for the individual. In behaviour modification, examples of such procedures include punishment, aversive conditioning, and response cost. In criminal justice decisions this is represented by deterrence-based sentences or punitive sanctions. They entail, for example, fines, and restriction of liberty to varying degrees including the use of custody, surveillance, shock incarceration or the imposition of demanding physical regimes. These are, of course, based on a long pedigree of ideas reaching back to the utilitarian philosophers of eighteenth-century Europe. Such ideas are assumed to enjoy wide popular support among the lay public, and to appeal to 'common sense' (see Chapter 14 by Paul Gendreau and his colleagues for a critique of the usefulness of that concept). There is thought to be a parallel between everyday experience of pain or discomfort and the use of judicial punishments.

Constructional strategies are based, by contrast, on the proposal that reduction of socially undesirable behaviour can be more effectively achieved through the building of new repertoires of action that effectively replace it. Rather than making the immediate consequences of an act unpleasant, in a constructional system effort is directed towards increasing the frequency of alternative behaviours by which an objective can be reached, and which may be incompatible with the problem behaviour. This can be accomplished through various behavioural methods, such as skills training, attitude change, education, employment and other forms of intervention.

Using this distinction as a framework, let us review the evidence concerning the outcomes of the respective approaches we have just defined.

DETERRENCE-BASED INTERVENTIONS

A declared intention underpinning the sentencing process is that it should alter criminal behaviour by attempting to manage its consequences. This is the core of what is variously called the *utilitarian* or *consequentialist* approach to crime and punishment (Walker, 1991). It is founded on the idea that legal sanctions will have an impact on those so dealt with.[1]*

---

* Notes are presented at the end of the chapter

Deterrence is conceptualized in a number of ways with an important distinction usually being made between its *specific* and *general* forms (Gibbs, 1986). The first refers to the influence of punishment on the individual made subject to it; the second to the wider impact this is assumed to have on others. Penologists also recognize that in considering the probable impact of punishments, their subjective or perceptual features are more important than their objectively defined characteristics. Stafford and Warr (1993) argued that the distinction between specific and general deterrence is difficult to sustain in other than broad and abstract terms. In everyday reality for most actual and potential offenders, there is likely to be a complex interplay between individual and general deterrent effects.

It is a traditional expectation of sentencing practices that they should deter individuals from committing crimes, but how well founded are such expectations? Several types of evidence are potentially relevant to the question of whether deterrent measures in criminal justice have an impact on recidivism.

Imprisonment and Crime Rates

At any one time, only a small fraction of those committing crimes in society is apprehended and punished. Yet the public visibility of this process is held to act as an indirect deterrent for the remainder of the population, including those likely to offend. If general deterrence operates to an extent that justifies its central position in society, there should be some association between the activity of the criminal justice system and the total amount of crime.

The broadest (though possibly weakest) kind of evidence pertaining to this comes from studies of the relationship between the number of persons incarcerated in a society and its general rate of recorded crime. For example, where opportunities have been available to monitor recorded levels of crime across periods when rates of incarceration were steadily changing, no clear relationship materializes (Zimring & Hawkins, 1994, 1995). This emerges particularly in studies of, and projections based upon, the increased use of incarceration in parts of the United States (Greenwood et al., 1996).

The deterrence hypothesis can also be tested at a specific or individual level. Do those offenders who are caught and punished respond to the experience by desisting from further criminal activity? Studies of the impact of imprisonment and other types of sanction, based on official statistics, do not show any unambiguous link between the severity of penalties (e.g. prison versus community sentences) and recidivism outcomes. Rates of reconviction following different types of court sentences, whether of a custodial or non-custodial nature, are remarkably similar (Kershaw, Goodman & White, 1999; Lloyd, Mair & Hough, 1994). Using specially developed prediction scales, follow-up studies of those dealt with in different ways by courts suggest that most offenders' likelihood of re-offending is little influenced by the sentences imposed on them. Judged at least by their subsequent behaviour, they appear impervious to the effects of criminal sanctions (McGuire, 2002).

Furthermore, recent research has failed to establish any relationship, in a direction that would be predicted by deterrence theory, between lengths of prison sentences and rates of recidivism. Gendreau, Goggin and Cullen (1999) have systematically reviewed this area in a report for the Solicitor General of Canada. The research group reviewed 23 studies yielding 222 comparisons of groups of offenders (total sample size, 68 248) who spent more time (an average of 30 months) versus less time (an average of 17 months) in prison. The groups were similar on a series of five risk factors. Contrary to what would be predicted by deterrence theory, offenders who served longer sentences had slight increases in recidivism of 2–3%. There was a small positive correlation between sentence length and subsequent rates of re-conviction.

Capital Punishment

Research on the most extreme of sanctions—capital punishment—has failed to find that the availability of this option has any clear suppressant effect on rates of the most serious crimes. In a global survey conducted for the United Nations, Hood (1996) was able to compare separate countries, or their internal member states, which fell into a number of discrete categories according to their pattern of usage of capital punishment over a 40-year period. Some were *retentionist*, in that they retained the use of the sentence throughout that time; others were *abolitionist*. Some practised execution for part of the period, but then abolished it. Others, notably a number of American states, had a period when execution was not used (as a result of a US Supreme Court ruling) but following which its use was restored. Analysis of the data for rates of serious crimes such as homicide under these different jurisdictions yielded no evidence that capital punishment was associated with reductions in their occurrence. The expected effects of capital punishment in suppressing rates of homicide or violent crime have proved elusive, even when comparisons have been made between roughly equivalent localities differing only in their usage of it (Cheatwood, 1993), or where we might have expected a general deterrent effect to be amplified through the publicity given to executions (Stack, 1993).

Enhanced and Intermediate Punishments

During the 1970s, the proclaimed failure of education, training or psychotherapy to have their intended impact on criminal recidivism has been associated with a shift towards a more punitive stance in a number of legislatures. Particularly in the United States, from that decade onwards there was a progressive shift towards harsher punishments and "turning up the heat" on offenders (Byrne, Lurigio & Petersilia, 1992; Shichor & Sechrest, 1996). At an institutional level such sentences included the use of boot camps and shock incarceration. In the community, intensive supervision, surveillance, random drug testing, curfews and various permutations of each were tried and tested.

Primary studies and evaluations of 'enhanced' and intermediate punishment therefore flourished during the 1980s and 1990s as the usage of these types of sanction became more widespread. These are not controlled trials but studies of the criminal justice system at work in which sanctions were compared with standard punishments or 'business as usual' within it. Often, the participants in the harsher forms of treatment were selected on a voluntary basis. Analysis of outcomes in such studies is made difficult by the fact that, although severity of punishment was escalated, there were additional elements of education, counselling and other provisions in certain instances.

Several large-sample, multi-site studies were conducted of these types of intervention, including both community-based intensive surveillance projects (Petersilia & Turner, 1993) and institutionally-based sanctions (MacKenzie & Souryal, 1994). Mackenzie, Wilson and Kider (2001) have recently reported a review of 29 evaluative studies of correctional boot camps. The mean effect size expressed as an odds ratio was 1.02, "...indicating an almost equal odds of recidivating between the boot camps and comparison groups" (2001, p. 130). On the basis of their review these authors concluded that "...in our overall meta-analysis of recidivism, we found no differences between the boot camp and comparison samples...the results of this systematic review and meta-analysis will be disappointing for many people...boot camps by themselves have little to offer as far as moving offenders away from criminal activities" is concerned (pp. 137, 139). These findings paralleled those obtained earlier from British studies on the evaluation of 'short sharp shock' Detention Centre regimes (Thornton et al., 1984).

Other meta-analytic reviews subsuming criminal sanctions within a wide range of approaches to intervention have typically found deterrence-based programmes to have zero or negative effect sizes (Andrews et al., 1990; Lipsey, 1992, 1995). Specialized meta-analyses of the relevant literature on community-based intermediate punishments have also drawn negative conclusions regarding the impact of enhanced punishments (Gendreau et al., 2001; Gendreau et al., 1993).

Controlled Studies of Deterrence

A possibly more robust approach is to examine deterrence effects when these have been directly manipulated, and there are several published reviews of this field. Sherman (1988) has reviewed studies in which the effect of deterrence practices has been evaluated using randomized designs. Of 21 studies included in Sherman's review, 14 found no differences in recidivism between experimental and control samples. In five studies, increased severity of penalties resulted in increased recidivism. Only two studies showed any impact of punitive sanctions and in one of these studies this effect was observed only in some sub-samples and not across the experimental group as a whole.

The most comprehensive attempt to catalogue the potential impact of punitive sanctions as specific deterrents was undertaken by Weisburd, Sherman and Petrosino (1990) who compiled a *Registry* of randomized experiments. This provides details of a series of 68 studies published between 1951 and 1984 involving random allocation to different levels of criminal justice sanction. The definition of the word "sanction" was very broad and encompassed both added levels of intervention in terms of prison, probation or parole, as well as other experiments in which treatments were included in traditional sanctioning procedures. Of the 68 studies examined, 44 reported no differences between experimental and control samples, while only two showed apparently better outcomes for interventions that could be construed as genuinely more punitive. In neither case did the authors report statistical significance and the conclusions drawn were based solely on apparent trends in the data. In the remaining 22 experiments, rates of recidivism, parole violation or other similar outcomes favoured experimental over control groups. However, in all the latter studies, the increased "sanction" consisted of provision of individual counselling, participation in group treatments, such as social skills training, or other forms of intervention that entailed sanctioning only in the respect that participation was non-voluntary.

Behavioural Research

Punishment-based techniques can be effective as a means of changing behaviour, though only providing certain conditions are met. A number of authors (e.g. Axelrod & Apsche 1983) have summarized the circumstances necessary to make punishment achieve its optimum effects. For it to work at all it should be unavoidable—i.e. there should be no escape from it. Its impact is a function of time and level of severity: the more speedily administered (celerity) and the higher the strength, the greater will be its impact. Finally, it is more likely to work when the individual can resort to alternative behaviours for pursuing a desired goal.

These conditions are however unlikely to be realized adequately in the complex, real-world environment of the criminal justice system, or in the lifestyle of many offenders. First, only a very small fraction of criminal behaviour results in punishment. For the United Kingdom, the available data suggests that the probability of being sent to prison for a crime is approximately 1 in 300 (Home Office, 1993). Second, when punitive sanctions are administered, this typically occurs weeks or months after the occurrence of the offence. Third, court sentences are graded on a scale of severity (the "tariff"), yet this bears only a fairly loose and uncertain relationship to the seriousness of crimes (Fitzmaurice & Pease, 1986). Finally, given the goal-directed nature of much crime and the limited personal resources and life circumstances of many persistent offenders, it is unlikely that many alternative courses of action are readily available to them. In all these respects, official punishment departs markedly from the required parameters of an effective "aversive conditioner".

This question was addressed systematically by Moffitt (1983) who examined whether findings from laboratory research can be extrapolated to the more loosely controlled circumstances of criminal justice services. Although Moffitt concluded that "... awareness of the principles of punishment may be of use to the deterrence theoretician" (1983, p. 154), the cumulative evidence merely attests to the difficulty of applying punishment in correctional settings in ways that approximate to those required for it to work.

Self-report Studies

Some investigators have focused on the reactions of individuals arrested and then punished for crimes, inviting them to comment on the extent to which their experience of the process may be likely to deter them from future offending. Other researchers have focused more closely on patterns in individuals' thinking in the period immediately prior to committing offences. Some of this work has been based on interviews with offenders during which they have been asked to describe their offending behaviour in some detail.

Klemke (1982) conducted a self-report survey of shoplifting by juveniles, but found little evidence of deterrence in preventing repeated acts of shoplifting by this age group. While only a small proportion of those arrested was apprehended a second time, a far higher portion admitted to further acts of theft. Conversely, while a proportion may have been deterred, other factors such as increasing age and maturation may also have explained desistance.

Most individuals are presumably aware in general terms of the possibility of being apprehended and punished should they break the law. However, studies of several different types of offence indicate that such a prospect is not in the forefront of their thinking in the moments prior to embarking on a criminal act. This clearly applies in the case of offences that result from strong feelings of anger or aggression leading to acts of violence, and also where offending is associated with substance abuse. Findings from a number of studies based on interviews, or *in vivo* observational work, suggest that prior to committing an offence most individuals are preoccupied with the execution of the act rather than deliberation upon or fear of consequences should they be caught (Carroll & Weaver, 1986; Light, Nee & Ingham, 1993; Morrison & O'Donnell, 1994). They may be in difficulty for some other reasons, experiencing stressors, crises or dysphoric moods (Zamble & Quinsey, 1997). Hence, would-be law-breakers are not for the most part in what Walker (1991, p. 15) called "deterrable states of mind".

Dimensions of Deterrence Effects

In certain circumstances specific deterrence can be shown to achieve its objectives. This is more likely when individuals have a great deal to lose; or where the risks of being caught are perceived as higher, or uncertain, rather than merely minimal. Borack (1998) has described the impact of random drug testing in the US Navy. Under conditions in which a randomly selected 20% of personnel were subjected to urinalysis per 30-day period, a suppressant effect on drug use of 56.5% was obtained. Large-scale piloting of random breath testing in Australia has shown that it can lead to reduced rates of vehicle accidents (Henstridge, Homel & Mackay, 1997). Von Hirsch and colleagues (1999) have reviewed evidence that manipulation of the perceived uncertainty of punishment can have marginal deterrent effects. By contrast, evidence of achieving effects by varying the severity of punishment remains exceedingly weak.

Where individuals perceive themselves as having little or nothing to lose, deterrence is much less likely to have any discernible effect. In a study of the impact of criminal sanctions on homeless street youths, Baron and Kennedy (1998, p. 30) concluded that "...perceptions of sanctions differ depending upon one's position in the social structure". These very different studies illustrate the reverse poles of a continuum of deterrence effects. While for the naval personnel described by Borack (1998) there was a great deal at stake, the opposite was true for homeless, economically deprived young males.

Thus I am not arguing here that deterrence never "works". In all likelihood, within any sample of offenders there will be a proportion for whom it does. Even were that never the case, there are sound justifications for the restraint of persons who are doing serious or repeated harm to others or to themselves. However, given that the use of punishment is regarded as the cornerstone of criminal justice, some fraction of the available evidence would surely provide clear indications of deterrent effects.

From a sociological perspective it may well be that punishment serves other symbolic functions in society, related to group cohesion, shared morality or civil governance. Perhaps it is important to avoid falling into what Garland has called "...the trap of thinking of it solely in crime-control terms" (1990, p. 20). Nevertheless some philosophers have argued that whether or not punishment can be justified is at least partly an empirical question (Farrell, 1985). If crime-control is an alleged purpose of punishment, then the paradox of its continued use alongside evidence that it fails to serve that purpose merits systematic inquiry. Honderich argued that punishment could be justified if it were, among other things, "economically preventive of offences"; or if it secured "...the reduction of distress at an economical rate" (1976, pp. 176, 181). Based on all the findings reviewed here, punishment does not reduce, and may well worsen, the problem which it is designed to cure. The conclusion reached by Gibbs (1986, p. 122) appears as valid today as when first written: "The bulk of findings indicate that offenders are not deterred when punished. More precisely, numerous researchers have reported either that recidivism is greater for offenders who have been punished the most severely or that there is no significant relation between punishment severity and recidivism." Reviewing evidence from controlled trials Sherman concurred: "The prevailing wisdom that punishment deters the future crimes of those punished is contradicted by the majority of the experimental evidence...the most frequent finding from randomized experiments is that sanctions make no difference" (1988, p. 86).

META-ANALYSES OF OUTCOME STUDIES

Given the evidence just reviewed, it is unfortunate that when during the 1970s proclamations were made regarding the "failure of treatment", and that "nothing works", the main direction taken by criminal justice agencies was to resort to greater use of punishment. As many authors have since agreed, those conclusions were inaccurate. A large quantity of evidence has now accumulated showing that interventions can reduce offender recidivism. A crucial element in bringing about recognition of this has been the use of methods of statistical review or meta-analysis in detecting and consolidating trends across the findings of large numbers of primary outcome studies.

Some method of integrating the findings from different research studies was initially developed by Karl Pearson as long ago as 1904 (Glass, 1976). Glass, McGaw and Smith (1981) used the method to resolve the long-standing dispute over the hypothesized relationship between class size and the educational attainment of young people. It is now an article of British government policy to reduce the size of classes (or pupil–teacher ratio).[2] Systematic review, often employing meta-analytic techniques, has meanwhile become an engine of progress in many fields of inquiry. The largest expansion in such activity has been in the field of healthcare, where the international *Cochrane Collaboration* set standards for research synthesis and acted as a central register for ongoing reviews and as holder of databases of outcome studies. In a parallel development, the *Campbell Collaboration* has now been established to work towards integration of research findings in the fields of educational, social and criminological interventions. In coming years there are likely to be significant advances made due to the activities if the *Campbell Crime and Justice Group* (Farrington & Petrosino, 2001).

Interpreting Outcome Studies and Large-scale Reviews

Where the results of research purportedly show that an intervention has been successful in reducing recidivism, there are many interpretative hurdles to be overcome before that conclusion can be endorsed. The following are some of the issues to be considered.

Research Design Limitations

The quality of research in outcome studies of criminal justice interventions has been much lamented. Factors that detract from what is conventionally accepted as sound experimental design include: the non-equivalence of comparison groups; the limited length of follow-up in many studies; small size of participant samples, furnishing limited statistical power and restricting statistical conclusion validity. The latter may be worsened by levels of attrition at post-test or follow-up phases. It has also been argued that positive outcomes are frequently a product of selection effects: offenders participating in programmes change mainly because they are motivated to do so (Simon, 1998). Furthermore, when attempting to review studies, general conclusions can be difficult to draw. Although cumulatively the number of primary studies in this field is fairly large, when meta-analysed the number of studies in any given category may be fairly small (Lösel, 2001).

To address these problems, in some reviews schemes have been developed for coding design quality in the analyses (e.g. Lipsey, 1992; Lipton et al., 1997; and see chapters 2–5 of the present book). Such a system has also been introduced in other studies using traditional narrative or tabulation approaches (MacKenzie, 1997).

One of the key advantages of meta-analysis of course is that the methodology allows account to be taken of many types of variations between primary studies. For example, the key outcome variable of recidivism has been defined in different ways using re-arrest rates, police contacts, parole violation, or re-conviction. By converting these divergences into a common effect-size metric, such variations can be absorbed in an integrative analysis.

Publication Bias

In the normal course of events, findings of research studies are communicated in academic journals, government reports, or other outlets. It is widely known that some biases operate within this and that studies obtaining nil effect sizes may be less likely to be submitted or accepted for publication than those with statistically significant effects. The two main remedies for this are first, to make every possible effort to locate unpublished studies; and to compute the file-drawer or fail-safe *n*, that is, the number of unpublished studies with zero or negative effect sizes that would be needed to undermine an observed positive mean effect size in published research.

Internal versus External Validity

Another problem is the tension between internal and external validity in research studies. *Internal validity* refers to the extent to which we can justifiably infer that a relationship between two variables within a research study is causal; this implies that other potentially explanatory variables have been controlled. *External validity* by contrast refers to the extent to which any such relationship can be generalized across different populations, places or times (Cook & Campbell, 1979). In field research, these two requirements often compete against each other (Robson, 1993). The more tightly controlled are the variables allowing clear conclusions to be drawn within a study, the less likely it is that the findings can be generalized to other populations, times and settings.

Efficacy Versus Effectiveness

Even where studies satisfactorily meet research design criteria another difficulty arises. This is illustrated in disputes from an adjacent specialist field. In the early 1990s, the American Psychological Association instigated a major review of the effectiveness of psychological therapies for mental health problems. The findings of this review led to the publication of a series of proposals concerning *empirically supported treatments* (Chambless & Hollon, 1998; Dobson & Craig, 1998). In this field there has been a general advance from the finding that several types of therapy work (Lambert & Bergin, 1994) to a more exact delineation of "what works for whom" (Roth & Fonagy, 1996), or what works best for which types of problem (Department of Health, 2001; Nathan & Gorman, 1998). The obstacle remains, however that the strongest types of evidence judged in purely scientific terms, such as randomized controlled trials, are often the least suitable for informing practical settings (Persons, 1991; Persons & Silbersatz, 1998). Finely tuned research studies with specially selected samples are usually conducted in conditions quite unlike those that operate in everyday clinical settings.

This is sometimes known as the "efficacy" versus "effectiveness" debate. Findings that an intervention works based on a well-designed clinical trial (efficacy) tell us little or nothing about whether it will do so when tested in the more challenging location of the "revolving-door" hospital or neighbourhood clinic (effectiveness).

At the same time, with reference to outcome studies in criminal justice this problem may be less acute. By virtue (if that is what it may be called) of their reputedly poorer research designs, studies in this field may actually be more applicable in the overcrowded prison or hard-pressed probation office: because it is in these sites that many initial studies are actually carried out.

Lipsey (1999) has identified the same problem in discussing the difference between "demonstration" and "practical" programmes and has urged that there be much more research on the latter. Typically, evaluations of such programmes yield effect sizes lower than those found in the former. Well-researched interventions are usually allocated extra resources such as more intensively trained staff. Bridging the gap to the ordinary, hectic, cluttered, real-world service setting poses a major outstanding problem in taking forward the evidence-based practice agenda.

Meta-analytic Reviews of Interventions with Offenders

Table 1.1 summarizes findings from a total of 30 meta-analytic reviews published between 1985 and 2001, in chronological order of appearance, showing the designated review field, the number of outcomes subsumed in each and the mean effect sizes so obtained.[3]

In several instances, the number of studies or research reports reviewed does not correspond to the number of outcome effects used to calculate the mean effect size. In some cases, published studies contained more than one investigation. For example, 10 of the 111 studies reviewed by Garrett (1985) examined the effects of more than one treatment, so producing a total of 121 effect size tests. Conversely, in other reviews not all studies that were located included recidivism as a dependent (outcome) variable. In the second review listed, by Gensheimer, Mayer, Gottschalk and Davidson (1986), 13 out of 44 studies that were found had no control sample and entailed pre-post comparisons only. Table 1.1 does not include the findings of Lipton and his colleagues, or by Redondo and his colleagues, reported in Chapters 2, 3 and 4 of the present book.

The majority of the meta-analyses, and the primary studies on which they are based, originate from the United States or Canada, and are focused on interventions with younger offenders (juveniles in the age range 14–17 and young adults aged 18–21). However, some reviews have dealt exclusively with European studies, and the largest review so far (the CDATE meta-analysis) includes studies from countries in many parts of the world.

The overwhelming majority of the primary studies deals with male offenders. In Lipsey's (1992, 1995) meta-analysis, only 3% of published studies focused exclusively on samples of female offenders. A recent review by Dowden and Andrews (1999a) was designed to counter-balance this and explore whether similar patterns of effects as found with men would emerge from studies with women offenders. While many primary studies report data concerning the proportions of offenders from different ethnic groups, the pattern of this is inconsistent and it is not often coded in meta-analyses.

General Findings

A first general finding shown across all meta-analyses is that the impact of "treatment" that can be defined in numerous ways is, on average, positive.[4] That is, it results in a reduction in recidivism in experimental relative to comparison samples. This contradicts the previously widely held expectation that little or nothing could be done to decrease offending behaviour among convicted offenders of whatever age (Hollin, 1999, 2001a; Lösel, 2001).

Secondly, however, the mean effect taken across a broad spectrum of treatment or intervention types is relatively modest. It is estimated on average to be

Table 1.1 A summary of meta-analytic reviews of tertiary prevention

Source	Number of computed outcomes (k)	Mean effect size (ES)	Descriptive information
Garrett (1985)	Total k = 121; 34 on recidivism	+0.18	Survey of 111 studies conducted in the period 1960–1984, describing residential treatment programmes for juvenile offenders. Cumulatively, 13 055 individuals were involved in the studies (mean age 15.8). Just under 50% of studies had random allocation or matched group designs. Reports effects of programmes on adjustment in institutions and community, in addition to recidivism outcomes. Largest ES for recidivism were obtained from life-skills and behavioural programmes.
Gensheimer et al. (1986)	31	+0.26 weighted mean ES	Reviewed 44 studies of diversion schemes for young offenders (mean age 14.6 years) published in the period 1967–1983; 43% entailed random allocation. Of these studies, 31 involved comparisons between experimental and control groups with a combined sample size of 10 210. There were highly significant relationships between numbers of contact hours and outcome effect sizes.
Mayer et al. (1986)	17	+0.33 weighted mean ES	A review of studies of the effects of interventions based on social learning principles published 1971–1982. A set of 34 studies yielded 39 effect sizes but only 17 were controlled experimental studies with recidivism as an outcome variable. Positive effect sizes were shown for behavioural, recidivism and attitude change measures.
Gottschalk et al. (1987a)	61	+0.22	Addressed the impact of community-based programmes for young offenders. From an initial pool of 643 research studies, 163 were extracted; 38% involved random assignment. For recidivism as an outcome variable cumulative sample size = 11 463. However, confidence intervals for most ES reported also included zero; authors interpreted positive findings cautiously.
Gottschalk et al. (1987b)	14	+0.25	Focused on behavioural programmes for young offenders. From the same database as employed in the preceding review, 25 studies were identified yielding 30 tests of treatment effects; 40% employed random assignment; however, only 14 addressed recidivism as the outcome variable.

Study	N	Effect size	Description
Lösel & Koferl (1989)	16	+0.12	A study of the impact of German "socio-therapeutic" prison regimes designed for serious, recidivistic adult offenders. Patterns of effects were studied among 16 studies evaluating 11 prisons operating such regimes. A main focus of the review was the association between regime characteristics and recidivism outcomes.
Whitehead & Lab (1989)	50	+0.13	A review of juvenile offender treatment studies published in the period 1975–1984. The majority dealt with diversion programmes. A wide range of effect sizes was noted with few positive results, though strict limits were set concerning what was regarded as constituting a significant finding (ES > 0.2).
Andrews et al. (1990)	154	+0.10 $d = 0.53$ for "appropriate" treatment	Subjected a series of 154 outcome effects from studies with both adult and juvenile offenders to analysis. Studies were classified according to the extent to which the respective interventions adhered to principles of correctional intervention derived from earlier research. The pattern of findings supported the hypothesis that services which applied the principles of "human service" (risk, need and responsivity) produced larger effect sizes than those which did not.
Izzo & Ross (1990)	46	Cog > non-cog 2.5/1	Review designed to compare offender programmes with and without cognitive training elements. Rather than computing a mean effect size, the authors reported the ratio of relative effectiveness of the two types of programme.
Roberts & Camasso (1991)	46	Range +0.06 to 0.81 (No mean ES given)	Review of treatment programmes for young offenders published between 1980 and 1990. The mean age of the samples studied was 15.1 years; some interventions were targeted on offenders in the 9–12 age range and entailed primary prevention.
Lipsey (1992, 1995)	397	+0.10	Largest published meta-analytic review encompassing 443 studies of treatment of offenders in the age range 12–21; 65% of the studies obtained positive ES findings. Significant positive ES obtained for multi-modal, behavioural and skill-oriented programmes; negative effect sizes for deterrence-based interventions; conflicting evidence on employment-focused programmes dependent on agency setting.

continues overleaf

Table 1.1 (*continued*)

Source:	Number of computed outcomes (*k*)	Mean effect size (ES)	Descriptive information
Hall (1995)	12	+0.12	Integrated findings from studies of the treatment of sexual offenders, both adolescent and adult. For this meta-analysis only 12 studies were located, with a total sample size of 1313. There was a wide range of types of sexual offence. The mean effect size was +0.12. The author calculated the "file drawer" sample size as 88.
Wells-Parker et al. (1995)	215	8%–9%	Remedial interventions with offenders convicted of driving while intoxicated. Multi-modal interventions combining education, psychotherapy or counselling and probation follow-up had the most positive effects in reducing drink–drive recidivism and alcohol-related accidents. Some single modalities used alone had negative effect sizes (psychotherapy and AA).
Gendreau & Goggin (1996)	138	0.00	Meta-analytic review focused exclusively on effects of deterrence-related procedures. Integrated results from 138 outcome studies focused on intermediate punishment or "smart sentencing" (use of enhanced punishment, surveillance, random drug-testing, intensive probation supervision and other criminal sanctions or court-mandated procedures).
Pearson, Lipton & Cleland (1997)	822	No mean ES given	Unpublished report given as a conference presentation. Part of a larger review known as the Correctional Drug Abuse Treatment Effectiveness (CDATE) project. Final project includes 1500 studies (see Lipton et al., Chapters 2 and 3 of the present volume).
Redondo, Garrido & Sánchez-Meca (1997)	57	+0.12	Integrative survey of studies conducted in European countries between 1980 and 1993; 49 studies were included, based on a total sample of 7728 participants. Mean ES for behavioural (0.23) and cognitive-behavioural (0.26) programmes were each double that for programmes as a whole.

Study	Effect size	Number	Description
Lipsey & Wilson (1998)	Institutions: +0.10 Community: +0.14	200	Studies of treatment of serious, persistent young offenders (age range 14–17); located 117 studies of community-based interventions; 83 based in institutions. Approximately half of the studies were randomized controlled trials. ES were computed in a number of ways: findings shown are "observed" ES. Numerous interaction effects were noted in the data. Largest and most consistent effects across settings were obtained with interpersonal skills training; for institutions, teaching family homes; for community, structured individual counselling and behavioural programmes.
Alexander (1999)	+0.10	79	A review of outcome studies of interventions with sex offenders published between 1943 and 1996; cumulative sample size 10 988. The results were analysed by age, offence type, setting, and treatment type. Included range of method/design quality. Recidivism rates generally low; positive treatment effects found for most categories of sexual offences against children but no differences observed for rapists.
Dowden & Andrews (1999a)	Not applicable	24	A review to test the hypothesis that principles of "human service" (risk, need and responsivity), which have emerged from meta-analyses in studies of male offenders, applied to women offenders also. The authors located 6 studies yielding 45 tests, 24 on samples composed exclusively of female offenders, confirming that similar trends appeared for female as for male offender samples.
Dowden & Andrews (1999b)	+0.09	229	A study of outcomes of interventions with young offenders; 134 primary studies; effect sizes ranged from −0.43 to +0.83. Supplementary analyses reported effect sizes associated with different treatment targets, distinguished criminogenic and non-criminogenic targets and tested hypotheses regarding "human service principles" in design of services.
Gallagher et al. (1999)	$d = +0.43$	25	Review of treatment of sex offenders; 22 studies. Most used cognitive-behavioural methods; only two employed random allocation; most reported positive ESs. Mixed results obtained for chemical/hormonal treatments; largest observed ES in a single study (for surgical castration) thought to be compounded by motivational factors. *continues overleaf*

Table 1.1 (*continued*)

Source:	Number of computed outcomes (k)	Mean effect size (ES)	Descriptive information
Polizzi, MacKenzie & Hickman (1999)	13	No mean ES given: ES range from −0.23 to +0.70	A review of 21 studies of treatment of sex offenders dealing with interventions in both prison and community settings. Only 13 of the studies met acceptable design criteria; 50% showed effect sizes in favour of treatment. Four of the six studies showing positive treatment effects used cognitive-behavioural methods. Effect sizes were larger in community settings. Research did not allow any conclusions to be drawn about specific types of sexual offending.
Redondo, Sánchez-Meca & Garrido (1999)	32	$d = +0.24$ $r = +0.12$	Second meta-analysis of European programmes focused solely on recidivism. Highest ES obtained were for behavioural and cognitive-behavioural programmes; ES were higher with juvenile offenders. Largest ES noted were with violent offenders and larger effect sizes for community than institutional programmes.
Dowden & Andrews (2000)	52	+0.07	A review of studies focused on reduction of violent recidivism; 34 studies were located yielding 52 tests; 30% of the comparisons were based on young offender samples. CI for the mean ES does not include zero; mean ES for deterrence-based interventions just below zero; for "human service interventions", mean ES +0.19. Highly significant correlation (0.69) found between ES and number of criminogenic needs targeted.
Petrosino et al. (2000)	9	−0.01	Review of randomized experimental evaluations of "scared straight" programmes, including visits by youth to prisons, meetings with adult prisoners, education and confrontational sessions in institutions. Conclusion drawn that their net effects were either negligible or potentially harmful.
Wilson, Gallagher & MacKenzie (2000)	53	Odds ratio: 1.52	Meta-analysis of 33 studies of educational, vocational training and allied programmes for adult offenders. Highest effect sizes for post-secondary education programmes (OR 1.74), corresponding to respective recidivism rates for comparison and intervention groups of 50% and 37%; lowest for a mixed group of multi-component studies (1.33). Differences due to methodological variables were non-significant.

Wilson & Lipsey (2000)	22	+0.18	Review of 28 studies of "wilderness challenge" or outdoor-pursuit programmes for young offenders. Of 60 effect size tests, 22 focused on recidivism. Positive effects sizes were associated solely with intensity of physical exercise and inclusion of distinct therapeutic components.
Gendreau et al. (2001)	140	0.00	Comparison between effect sizes for institutional and community sanctions and respective control samples. Total sample $n = 53614$. Reviewed studies of intensive supervision, arrest, fines, restitution, boot camps, scared straight, drug testing and electronic monitoring. Only fines yielded a small effect in reduced recidivism. All other interventions were associated with zero effects or marginally increased recidivism.
Lipsey, Chapman & Landenberger (2001)	14	Odds ratio: 0.66	Review of cognitive-behavioural programmes: only studies with relatively strong randomised (8) or quasi-experimental (6) designs were included. The mean effect size represents a recidivism rate for participants approximately two-thirds of that for control samples. Larger effect sizes were found for "demonstration" than for "practical" programmes.
MacKenzie, Wilson & Kider (2001)	44	Odds ratio: 1.02	Review of evaluations of correctional boot camps. Applied detailed assessment of design quality, 19 (43%) studies were judged to be methodologically solid. Wide range of effect sizes noted; 9 studies favoured boot camps, 8 favoured comparison conditions, 17 obtained no difference. The only factor associated with the positive effect sizes was presence of an after-care component for adult programmes.

approximately 9 or 10 percentage points (Lösel, 1995). But note that this is across all types of intervention, including criminal sanctions that have been shown to have zero or negative effect sizes. If these studies were excluded from the overall calculation, the mean effect for remaining treatments would be higher than observed.

Given its apparently unexceptional overall scale the question inevitably arises as to whether this finding has any meaningful policy significance. Rosenthal (1994) among other authors has drawn attention to an important distinction between *statistical* and *practical* significance. The mean effect sizes obtained, while typically small to mid-range, compare reasonably well with those found in other fields. Indeed some healthcare interventions that are generally regarded as producing worthwhile benefits have lower mean effect sizes. Others with mean effects only marginally higher are the object of considerable public investment (Lipsey & Wilson, 1993; McGuire, 2002).

Most reviewers however regard the average effect size as a fairly misleading figure in conveying the impact of interventions with offenders. All studies have found substantial variability in outcomes depending on a range of other factors, and most researchers are agreed that this variability is of much greater interest than the average finding in itself. There are, of course, several sources of the variation observed in outcome effects, including the type of design used in evaluation studies (Lösel, 2001).

One principal implication of this is that there is no single solution to the problem of offending behaviour or to the attempt to help individuals to reduce its frequency or severity. No single approach can be designated a panacea or "magic bullet". Methods that work well in one context, with one selected sample, may work less well in others. Decisions regarding the approach best adopted in a given setting for a given group therefore need to take a number of factors into account.

Bearing this caveat in mind, there is nevertheless a general accord among the reviews on a number of key points. The findings of the fairly large number of outcome studies now available are sufficiently consistent and robust for certain conclusions to be permissible regarding what is likely to contribute to effectiveness.

Ineffective Approaches

We saw earlier that the use of deterrence-based interventions has most frequently been shown to have non-existent or negative effects on subsequent recidivism. There are also several other approaches that receive little or no support as effective interventions from the evaluation research that is available.

They include vocational training activities without associated links to real prospects of employment, which are also associated with increased recidivism (Lipsey, 1992, 1995) though the number of studies relevant to this finding is fairly small. There are conflicting results for wilderness or outdoor challenge programmes which have yielded mainly weak or absent effects, unless they include high-quality training or therapeutic elements (Lipsey, 1992, 1995; Lipsey & Wilson, 1998; Wilson & Lipsey, 2000). The average outcome for so-called "scared straight" programmes is a slight increase in recidivism (Gendreau et al., 2001) and some authors have declared them to be potentially damaging (Petrosino, Turpin-Petrosino &

Finckenhauer, 2000). For young offenders, there is little support for the use of milieu therapy in institutional settings (Lipsey & Wilson, 1998) though there may be more positive evidence regarding this type of intervention with adults (see Lipton et al., Chapter 2 of the present volume).

Certain targets of change, though they may be deemed valuable for other purposes, are not promising as a focus in programmes designed to reduce offending behaviour. For that reason they are sometimes called *non-criminogenic needs*. They include: vaguely defined emotional or personal problems; individual self-esteem; physical activity seen as an end in itself; increasing cohesiveness among anti-social peers; showing respect for offenders' anti-social thinking (Dowden & Andrews, 1999b). Dwelling on these targets in an intervention programme is associated with sizeable average increases in recidivism (Andrews, 2001).

The evidence in support of substance abuse treatment and drug abstinence programmes as a means of reducing recidivism among young offenders is surprisingly weak, given the well-established association between the two types of problem. In two meta-analyses, the effects obtained were only mildly positive and not significantly different from zero (Dowden & Andrews, 1999b; Lipsey & Wilson, 1998).

Principal Trends

There are sizeable differences in effect sizes related to the age range of the target population of offenders. Cleland et al. (1997) analysed age trends in effect sizes across a set of 659 studies with a cumulative sample size of 157 038. All the effect sizes obtained were significantly different from zero. The average mean effect size for offender samples below 15 years of age was 0.09; for those aged 15–18, 0.04; and for adults, 0.05. When values for "appropriate treatment" were computed, the corresponding mean effect sizes for the three age groups were 0.16, 0.11 and 0.17 respectively.

Given the multiplicity of factors known to contribute to criminal behaviour, there is virtual unanimity among researchers and reviewers concerning the need for interventions to comprise a number of ingredients and target a range of risk factors. This has led to the development of what are known as "multi-modal" programmes. This has also been called the "breadth principle" (Palmer, 1992).

Additionally, several sets of results indicate that on balance, community-based interventions have larger effect sizes than those delivered in institutions (e.g. Andrews et al., 1990; Lipsey & Wilson, 1998; Polizzi, MacKenzie & Hickman 1999; Redondo, Garrido & Sánchez-Meca, 1997). When similar programmes were compared in their relative effects in institutional or community settings, the latter out-performed the former in terms of reduced recidivism in the ratio of approximately 1.75/1, though in other reviews the differential was somewhat lower than this at 1.33/1. This is an important point, as analysis of crime statistics suggests that there is no differential outcome between custodial and community *sentences* as such (McGuire, 2002). However, differences in effectiveness do emerge when structured programmes are provided in these settings.

However, there are important interaction effects to be noted in this respect. Poorly designed, inappropriate forms of interventions emerge as ineffective regardless of the criminal justice setting in which they are delivered. Better designed services are of maximum benefit when provided in a non-custodial setting. Further, even well-designed intervention programmes may have nil and possibly even negative effects if the quality of delivery is poor. This highlights the importance of the relationship between programme and organizational dimensions as defined by Bernfeld, Blase and Fixsen (1990). There are no known treatment or training materials that will achieve their goals in the absence of trained, committed and adequately resourced staff.

There is fairly strong support for the relationship between level of risk of future offending (assessed using predictive tools of several sorts) and intensity of services, though this has not emerged consistently from all reviews (Antonowicz & Ross, 1994). But in the main, larger effect sizes are usually obtained from work with more persistent offenders (Andrews et al., 1990). That may seem counter-intuitive given an expectation that those groups may be more resistant to change. Intervention programmes for more serious young offenders generally need to be of longer total duration, probably not less than 26 weeks on average, though not necessarily requiring a higher level of weekly contact (Lipsey, 1995).

A further frequently obtained finding is that effect sizes for acquisitive crimes (theft, burglary, robbery) have generally been lower than those obtained for personal (violent and sexual) crimes (e.g. Redondo, Sánchez-Meca & Garrido, 1999). While some approaches are promising, much more research is needed regarding this issue (McGuire, 2001a).

Most studies support the idea that intervention is more likely to be effective if it focuses on certain areas that have been shown to be *risk factors* for criminal activity. The evidence base for the potential usefulness of a risk factors approach is very wide and includes large-scale studies adopting a longitudinal approach to the development of delinquency, alongside group comparison studies of non-offender and persistent offender populations (Andrews & Bonta, 1998; Farrington, 1996; McGuire, 2000b; Rutter, Giller & Hagell, 1998). Such research highlights a range of psychosocial and individual factors that include the following: poor parental supervision or low attachment to families; experiencing difficulties in relation to school and employment prospects; having a network of associates involved in delinquency; manifestation of anti-social attitudes; distorted or biased patterns of information processing; possession or exercise of limited coping, problem-solving and social skills; low levels of self-control or a propensity towards impulsiveness. These factors can be described as *criminogenic* as they are theoretically and empirically associated with offending behaviour. In marked contrast to the findings for non-criminogenic needs described above, targeting them in intervention services is associated with substantial reductions in recidivism (Andrews, 2001).

Comparative Effectiveness of Interventions

Utilising meta-analysis, it has also been possible to examine the *variability* in the effect sizes observed when different types of intervention are evaluated separately. In many respects this variability, which can be found within each of the reviews, is of greater interest than the overall average effect. Its presence has enabled some researchers to conclude that effect sizes can be maximized by combining a number of elements in offender programmes (Andrews, 1995, 2001; Gendreau, 1996a, b; Hollin, 1999). Effective interventions are thought to possess certain common features which Andrews and his colleagues (1990) called "principles of human service".

When this framework was initially proposed, it was developed in three stages. First, a theoretical model of risk factors for offending behaviour was generated on the basis of criminological and psychological literature. Second, using the model heuristically, a set of hypotheses was formulated regarding key aspects of interventions most likely to contribute to reducing recidivism. Third, an empirical review was conducted in which 154 outcome studies were classified into four groups according to the extent to which they possessed those elements. These groups were designated *appropriate service, unspecified service, inappropriate service,* and *criminal sanctions* respectively. Outcome effects were found to differ systematically in the order predicted by the model. These findings were seminal in demonstrating that it was possible to identify with some confidence a cluster of factors that could be shown to lead to the much sought-after outcome of reduced recidivism. Those features might also be harnessed synergistically to construct what Wexler (1998) has called "likely to succeed" interventions.

The steadily developing research background has enabled Andrews (1995, 2001) to delineate a set of 18 "principles of human service" representing, in essence, a design for an evidence-based criminal justice service. A summary of the main elements of this is presented in Table 1.2. The list shown in this Table is not an exclusive set of those features associated with better outcomes. It is possible that additional methods or approaches, not yet fully researched, could prove equally, if not more, beneficial. It would be wise to keep in mind the reservation that such a set of principles cannot absolutely assure us that there will be a successful outcome. There are still numerous variables operating in the occurrence of criminal offences, not to mention within agencies delivering services, which are not fully understood. Nevertheless, the knowledge base now available represents a considerable advance on the position obtaining even a few years ago.

Effective Interventions

Based on the literature to date, the most effective programmes are probably those which yield the highest effect sizes with the highest degree of consistency across different studies. For adult offenders, the methods that emerge as most reliably effective entail the use of structured cognitive-behavioural programmes focused on risk factors for criminal recidivism (McGuire, 2000a). Variants of this approach have been well validated primarily for individuals with patterns of violent, sexual, and substance-related offending (Hollin, 2001b; Motiuk & Serin, 2001).

For serious or persistent young offenders, interventions in the most consistently effective category have been shown to have an average impact in reducing recidivism by 40% in community settings and 30% in custodial settings (Lipsey & Wilson, 1998). Programmes in this category for the most part employ the following types of methods: interpersonal skills training; behavioural interventions such as modelling, graduated practice and role-playing; cognitive skills training; mentoring linked to individual counselling with close

Table 1.2 Principles of effective interventions to reduce recidivism (adapted from Andrews, 2001)

1. Base intervention efforts on a psychological theory of criminal behaviour.	11. Assess specific responsivity and strengths using specially developed approaches.
2. Within this, adopt a personality and social learning perspective which has provided an extensive evidence based on risk factors for criminal behaviour.	12. Develop coordinated strategies of monitoring continuity of services and care, including relapse prevention elements.
3. Introduce human service strategies; avoid strategies based on retribution, restorative justice or deterrence.	13. Identify and clarify areas in which staff may exercise personal discretion in the application of principles.
4. Make use of community-based services where possible, in natural settings such as family; where custodial settings are required for other reasons they should be as community-oriented as possible.	14. Develop and make available a service plan or set of policies and guidelines regarding the application of these principles.
5. Assess risk levels and allocate individuals to different levels of service accordingly.	15. Establish procedures for monitoring programme and treatment integrity and for responding to departures from it; specify the elements within this, including staff selection, training, supervision and recording of information on all aspects of service delivery.
6. Assess dynamic risks/criminogenic needs and target interventions towards their remediation.	16. Staff: focus attention on detailed development of staff skills, including abilities in developing relationships, motivating others, structuring programmes and sessions.
7. Multi-modal approaches: focus on a range of criminogenic needs in recognition of the multiple factors associated with offending.	17. Management: ensure managers have foregoing staff competencies and in addition, extensive knowledge of background principles and the ability to coordinate processes of programme and site accreditation.
8. Use the best validated methods for assessment of risk and need factors.	18. The most effective agencies will locate programmatic interventions within broader social arrangements, giving attention to variations in local contexts and client groups and adapting services accordingly.
9. General responsivity: attempt to match services to the learning styles, motivations and aptitudes of participants within high quality interpersonal relationships.	
10. Specific responsivity: adapt intervention strategies to accommodate difference and diversity (age, gender, ethnicity/race, language) among participants and recognition of their strengths.	

matching of young people and mentors on key background variables; structured individual counselling within a reality therapy or problem-solving framework; and teaching family homes which involve specially trained staff acting in a parental role (Dowden & Andrews, 1999b; Lipsey & Wilson, 1998).

At an operational level, all the forms of intervention in the foregoing list can be described in detail and a systematic rationale provided for their use. Although this variable is not examined directly in outcome research, there appears to be a strong relationship between the clarity of objectives, theoretical base and methods employed within a programme and its overall effects. These are features of what has been called *programme integrity*: for this to be present, it should be possible first to provide a coherent account of the programme itself (Bernfeld, 2001; Hollin, 1995).

In work with young offenders, there is also support for a range of activities loosely described as *multiple services* or service brokerage, though their effect sizes are not as high or consistently found as for those just mentioned. In these programmes, project managers assemble an array of different types of intervention or access to community services designed according to the individual needs of young people. This might include a wide range of opportunities including academic, employment, behavioural, therapeutic, mentoring or other ingredients (Lipsey & Wilson, 1998). Positive effects have been obtained from studies evaluating the usefulness of structured foster care with high risk young offenders (Chamberlain & Reid, 1998).

Some studies have found *mentoring* to be a valuable and effective form of intervention. This finding, however, is not always easy to interpret, for two reasons. First, as a process, mentoring is occasionally the main aspect of intervention but far more often it is combined with some other ingredient, including participation in structured programmes. Second, the term "mentoring" may be applied to a diverse range of activities and roles on the part of the mentor (Thornton et al., 2000).

Most of the programmes that achieve consistent high effect sizes are also described as exemplifying the principle of responsivity. This is conceptualized in two ways. *General responsivity* refers to the use of active, engaging, and participatory programme ingredients, usually entailing the use of behaviour change or skills development methods. There is likely to be a mixture of methods within programme sessions that will serve to maintain the interest of participants. *Specific responsivity* refers to the provision of programmes in a flexible manner that will address variations between participants in age or level of maturity, learning styles, cultural background or other factors (Gendreau & Andrews, 1990; Andrews, 2001).

Contextual Factors

The above set of interventions can be described as having an individual focus. In other words, their primary objective is to address aspects of offenders related to the difficulties they may have in respect of attitudes, peer influences, behavioural or cognitive skills, or attainment in terms of education or employment.[5] An important supplementary finding concerns the extensiveness of interventions and the degree of involvement of services across a range of contexts of an individual's life, most importantly that of the family. Broadly speaking, the more areas of a person's life on which it is possible to have an influence, even if only an indirect one, the greater the likelihood of securing and maintaining change.

In work with young offenders, effect sizes have been shown to be larger when a "significant other" person in the young person's life works alongside him or her and also attends individual programmes of the types cited above. This may be a close relative with whom they have a positive relationship, or a mentor who is also familiar with the nature of the programme (Goldstein et al., 1994).

Effect sizes as high as 60% have been obtained from functional or behavioural family therapy, family empowerment and allied therapeutic approaches which involve working with young offenders and their families. For the most part, such programmes have been provided with young people at the higher range of offence seriousness. Some of these programmes also have reported lengthy follow-ups (Dembo et al., 2000; Gordon, Graves & Arbuthnot, 1995; and see Gordon, Chapter 7 of the present book).

Effective programmes involving young offenders and their families usually entail a specific focus on selected aspects of the family's functioning. Notably, they address areas such as parental supervision, training in negotiation and conflict resolution skills, and affectional bonds (Dowden & Andrews, 1999b). Such programmes do not revolve around the provision of general family support. Approaches that involve diffuse, poorly defined work with families have been associated with increased recidivism (Dowden & Andrews, 1999b).

When elements of programme-based intervention reach out yet further into other spheres of young offenders' activity, the strongest effect sizes to date have been obtained. This emerges from evaluative studies of Multi-Systemic Therapy (MST), in which work is done with the young person, his or her family and, in addition, school staff (Borduin et al., 1995; Henggeler et al., 1998). Obviously, programmes of this type are comparatively resource intensive.

Econometric Analysis of Offender Programmes

The question of what resources are required to deliver effective interventions in criminal justice settings is not a central theme of this chapter. However, it is worth noting that recent studies indicate that intervention programmes with offenders are also relatively cost-effective. One review of seven studies of tertiary intervention found benefit–cost ratios ranging from 1.13/1 to 7.14/1 (Welsh & Farrington, 2000, 2001a). Another wider-ranging review has adduced evidence of significant cost-efficiency in evidence-based correctional programmes, as compared with negative economic returns for punitive sanctions (Brown, 2001). Previous studies of the latter had already suggested that initial short-term savings from reduced incarceration rates were reversed by further expenses incurred later as a result of technical violations (Gendreau & Goggin, 1996; Gendreau et al., 1993).

IMPACT OF RESEARCH FINDINGS

The meta-analytic studies have been the subject of extensive discussion in the criminal justice field. Many policy-makers have been impressed by the fact that it is possible to identify with some confidence those features of treatment interventions that contribute to higher levels of effectiveness. The publication of several edited collections of reviews has helped to reinforce that message (Bernfeld, Farrington & Leschied, 2001; Harland, 1996; McGuire, 1995; Ross, Antanowicz & Dhaliwal, 1995). A review commissioned by the US National Institute of Justice examined these types of interventions alongside other approaches to crime prevention (Sherman et al., 1997). In the United Kingdom, Home Office researchers considered the role the findings could play in practical policies for offender services (Goldblatt & Lewis, 1998; Vennard, Sugg & Hedderman, 1997).

Much of the recent interest in these research findings, and the investment in strategies that flow from them, has centred on the use of structured intervention *programmes*. At its simplest, a programme can be defined as a structured sequence of opportunities for learning and change (McGuire, 2001b). This involves some advance planning and preparation. It also means that the product of such preparatory work can be made explicit to others and that some aspects of practice can be standardized. This in turn offers opportunities for dissemination of good practice and accountability of services to all those who have a legitimate interest in how they are designed, delivered, managed and financed.

Implementation

Several experts have commented that the question of how programmes are implemented has been relatively neglected in research (Gendreau, Goggin & Smith, 1999, 2001; Harris & Smith, 1996; Leschied, Bernfeld & Farrington, 2001). Programmes in themselves are potential vehicles of change, but their impact is substantially influenced by the manner and setting in which they are delivered. It is therefore crucial that attention is paid to aspects of this in any attempt to provide effective services (Goldstein & Glick 2001; Leschied, Bernfeld & Farrington, 2001; Lösel, 2001). The factors which may influence programme delivery include the extent to which the objectives and contents of a programme are understood and endorsed by the management and staff of a criminal justice agency, by their level of training and ability to deliver it, and by their resource capacity and its relationship to other aspects of their work (Gendreau, Goggin & Smith, 1999; and see Chapter 14 of the present volume).

Effective implementation is also influenced by issues such as the targeting of a programme towards appropriate user groups and the installation and usage of procedures for assessment and selection. This is particularly applicable in community settings (Gendreau, Goggin & Paparozzi, 1996; Lipsey & Wilson, 1998). In institutional settings, longer-established programmes that are well integrated in the institutional regime yield higher effect sizes than those not so firmly emplaced (Lipsey & Wilson, 1998). Behavioural management systems can play a valuable role in support of implementation in these contexts, provided they are themselves located within an institution-wide framework of practice and policy (Hollin, Epps & Kendrick, 1995).

In community settings, given the experience of high attrition rates, programmes with larger effect sizes entail additional mechanisms for improving attendance by young people. This has included such strategies as inducements to attend by offering participation linked to other benefits (Goldstein et al., 1994); provision of transport and arrangements for ensuring young people arrive at a programme site (Henggeler et al., 1998); or delivery of programmes at locations where they will be accessible to participants (Edwards et al., 2001).

It has generally been found that the extent of monitoring of a programme to ensure integrity of delivery is correlated with higher effect sizes. This is another aspect of programme integrity, mentioned earlier. Where procedures are in place to ensure that a programme is delivered as planned—adhering to the proposed theoretical model and using the designated methods well—effect sizes tend to be higher. This finding emerges from several meta-analyses (Lipsey, 1995) and has also been confirmed by recent research from the prison service in relation to cognitive skills programmes (Friendship et al., 2001).

Programme Personnel

Some official reports and documents have proposed guidelines for the nature of staff training. Emphasis is given to key aspects of interpersonal and communication skills and the ability to develop relationships with others. While this is rarely addressed in a direct fashion in outcome research in the offender field, evidence from adjoining fields such as mental health indicates that it is a pivotal issue. The development of a "working alliance" has been shown to be important in work with young offenders (Florsheim et al., 2000). Lipsey and Wilson's (1998) review of institutional treatment of young offenders found that higher effect sizes were associated with the provision of programmes by mental health professionals rather than by their criminal justice counterparts. This may be because the role of the latter in this respect is compromised by their responsibilities for security matters. Alternatively, it may be a product of the probable higher level of training of mental health staff in therapeutic or relationship-building skills.

Reviewing the training needs of staff delivering high-quality interventions for young people with histories of violent offending, Thornton et al. (2000) have proposed that it is possible to identify a minimal set of requirements. With only slight modifications, the list they suggest is plausible for most types of intervention work with offenders. To be effective, staff need skills in communication, team building and in the methods of delivery involved in specific intervention programmes. It is also crucial that they understand, and are able to apply, methods of risk–needs assessment (Bonta, 2001; Bonta et al., 2001). Provision of these skills requires that there be a staff-training manual and opportunities for both skills practice and ongoing skills maintenance training and review.

Research Findings, Policy and Practice

In 1998 the British government announced a major policy initiative—the *Crime Reduction Programme*—under which resources were made available for a series of innovations in criminal justice services. This signalled the introduction, on a significant and hitherto unparalleled scale, of evidence-based practice in work with offenders. It drew extensively on the findings of the meta-analytic reviews concerning tertiary prevention. To conclude this chapter, I will briefly illustrate the impact research has had by describing some aspects of this initiative. Part of the work is focused on the design and systematic delivery of structured programmes. Some are adapted versions of methods originally developed in Canada or the United States. Others have been prepared by independent experts or by practitioners themselves, sometimes with the advice of external consultants.

If programmes are to be accepted as suitable for use in criminal justice settings, they have to be scrutinized and validated by an independent group appointed within the Home Office, the *Joint Prison–Probation Accreditation Panel* (Home Office Probation Unit, 1999). The panel has devised and published a set of accreditation criteria that are used for the selection of appropriate interventions (for an overview see McGuire, 2001c). Before programmes can be approved under this procedure, a set of manuals and other documents has to be prepared. They include a *Theory Manual*, which outlines the rationale or model on which the programme is based and its research background. There should also be a *Programme Manual*, presenting session contents and with clear instructions on how the methods should be applied. This is usually supported by supplementary materials such as work sheets, information notes or other relevant documents. It should be accompanied by a *Staff Training Manual*, which describes how staff should be trained to run the sessions of the programme.

Several programmes have passed through this process, although others are still in development. The final product could be described as a national portfolio of offending behaviour programmes. Some are "generic" and include scope for working on multiple types of offence, as the focus is on dynamic risk factors that may contribute to different criminal acts. Programmes of cognitive skills training have been developed for use either in group formats (*Reasoning & Rehabilitation, Enhanced Thinking Skills, ThinkFirst*) or individually (*One-to-One*). Those attending may have committed a variety of offences, with no single type dominant. Other programmes are "offence specific" and are designed for individuals with a pattern dominated by one type of offence. Thus there are specialized programmes focused on violence (*Aggression Replacement Training, Focus on Violence*), sexual offending (*Sex Offenders Treatment Programme*), domestic violence (*Duluth*), substance abuse (*Addressing Substance-Related Offending*), and alcohol-impaired driving (*Drink-Impaired Drivers*). General cognitive skills programmes and those designed for work with sex offenders are available in separate versions for use in prison and probation settings respectively.

A central component of these initiatives from the outset was an emphasis on the importance of ongoing monitoring, research and evaluation with regard to all the programmes earmarked for development. It is seen as central that the work carried out focuses on both external and internal aspects of programmes. Programmes are expected to meet national standards and must be evaluated on that basis, but each is also a response to local demands, tailored to local circumstances with specific objectives. These aspects should also be evaluated. The most thorough approaches to evaluation follow such an integrative strategy and can been conceptualized as the application of a *program logic* model (McGuire, 2001d).

Recent Results

The development and dissemination of practical programmes of the kind just exemplified has been predicated on the basis of findings from large-scale, systematic reviews of the research literature. In recent years positive outcomes have been reported from a number of practical programmes focused on a variety of offences. They have included projects for car crime (Wilkinson, 1997); sex offender treatment programmes in probation settings (Beech et al., 2001); and interventions for domestic violence (Dobash et al., 1996).

While the process of implementing programmes for delivery on a national scale is still in its developmental stages, preliminary results have been encouraging. Initial analyses suggest that reductions in recidivism have been obtained following participation in prison-based cognitive skills programmes (Friendship et al., 2001), and community-based use of *Aggression Replacement Training* (McGuire & Clark, 2001). At the time of writing, evaluation of a wide spectrum of community-based *Pathfinder* programmes delivered within the probation services is still ongoing (Hollin et al., 2002). Results are also awaited from evaluation of programmes of several types provided in the youth justice services.

GAPS AND FURTHER INITIATIVES

The cumulative research effort that the meta-analyses listed earlier represent has significantly increased our knowledge in the field of work with offenders and led to a recognition that some interventions can be successful. Yet many key questions remain unanswered. The following are among the most important of them and are recommended as an agenda for future research, potentially forming part of a continuing progress towards evidence-based practice in tertiary crime prevention (Welsh & Farrington, 2001b).

As mentioned previously, although the number of primary studies conducted in this field is fairly large, when the total sample is sub-divided by different variables potentially relevant to outcome, the number remaining in some "cells" can be disappointingly low (Lösel, 2001). A first gap identified by many reviewers therefore is the need for more and better-conducted research on certain kinds of intervention, including replication studies of those interventions that in previous research have produced the most positive effects. At the same time, room must be left for exploratory studies of innovative approaches and new departures.

There is a requirement for more careful study of the kinds of variations that might need to be made in programmes to accommodate diversity among participants. This needs to take account of variations in age, gender, ethnicity or other cultural differences. It also needs to focus on the adaptation of materials for people with literacy problems, communication problems, or learning disabilities.

Little is known about the degree of appropriateness of programmes delivered on either a group or individual basis respectively. Research outcomes suggest the largest effect sizes are obtained when programmes are matched closely to individual needs and designed accordingly. This does not preclude the possibility that an individual may attend a group programme as an element in a larger "package" of activities. However, to date there is no firm basis for providing advice to agencies concerning a choice between one-to-one or group programmes, other than on exclusion principles informed by their own experience.

With reference to the distinction between generic and specific offence-focused programmes depicted earlier, research is needed that will clearly delineate which of these approaches may be the preferable option. Systematic research is also required on the likely impact of programmes that are undertaken partly in institutional and partly in community settings.

NOTES

1. This is distinct from the use of punishment primarily on the basis of retribution, which is not concerned with its instrumental effects.
2. Interestingly, while this policy is thought to be working where class sizes are reduced from just over 30 to the region of 25–26, the analyses of Glass and his colleagues show that meaningful differences only begin to be obtained when class sizes start to fall below 20.
3. Effect sizes are calculated and reported in a number of different ways. However, three types of statistics tend to predominate in the reviews published in this field (Rosenthal, 1994; Wilson, 2001). The most frequently used are correlation coefficients, usually Pearson's r or phi (ϕ), depicting the strength of the relationship between the independent variable (membership of treatment or control samples) and the dependent variable (outcome in terms of success or failure with regard to recidivism). A second widely used statistic is the standardized mean difference (Cohen's d) which is a measure of the extent of change in the means of experimental and control groups, expressed as a function of the pooled sample variance. Some recent reviews have used the odds ratio which expresses the odds of one of two dichotomous outcomes (e.g. recidivism) for the experimental (intervention) group relative to the comparison group.
4. The reviews listed in Table 1.1 are all concerned with "tertiary-level" intervention, i.e. studies of work with individuals arrested for or convicted of criminal acts, and in which the focus is on recidivism as an outcome variable. Petrosino (2000) has compiled an annotated listing of meta-analyses in criminology and allied disciplines, including others addressing primary and secondary prevention, and which focus on a wider range of outcome variables such as drug use, school vandalism, and sexual abuse.
5. Doing so does not mean that programmes do not also take into account important factors in an individual's environment which are associated with his or her difficulties, and play a part in contributing to offending behaviour (or potentially to its reduction). For example, interventions that entail problem-solving training often focus on difficulties posed by the situations in which offenders live. Programme activities often emphasize the importance of finding solutions that are most likely to work given certain situational constraints, while in other circumstances they may generate courses of action that involve changing the situations themselves.

REFERENCES

Alexander, M. A. (1999) Sexual offender treatment efficacy revisited. *Sexual Abuse: Journal of Research and Treatment, 11*, 101–116.

Andrews, D. A. (1995) The psychology of criminal conduct and effective treatment. In J. McGuire (Ed.) *What Works: Reducing Re-offending: Guidelines from Research and Practice.* Chichester: John Wiley & Sons.

Andrews, D. A. (2001) Principles of effective correctional programs. In L. L. Motiuk and R. C. Serin (Eds.) *Compendium 2000 on Effective Correctional Programming.* Ottawa: Correctional Service Canada.

Andrews, D. A. & Bonta, J. (1998) *The Psychology of Criminal Conduct* (2nd edition). Cincinnati, OH: Anderson.

Andrews, D. A., Zinger, I., Hoge, R. D., Bonta, J., Gendreau, P. & Cullen, F. T. (1990) Does correctional treatment work? A clinically relevant and psychologically informed meta-analysis. *Criminology, 28,* 369–404.

Antonowicz, D. & Ross, R. R. (1994) Essential components of successful rehabilitation programs for offenders. *International Journal of Offender Therapy and Comparative Criminology, 38,* 97–104.

Axelrod, S. & Apsche, J. (Eds.) (1983) *The Effects of Punishment on Human Behavior.* New York, NY: Academic Press.

Baron, S. W. & Kennedy, L. W. (1998) Deterrence and homeless male street youths. *Canadian Journal of Criminology, 40,* 27–60.

Beech, A. R., Erikson, M., Friendship, C. & Ditchfield, J. (2001) *A six-year follow-up of men going through probation-based sex offender treatment programmes.* Research Findings No. 144. London: Home Office Research, Development and Statistics Directorate.

Bernfeld, G. A. (2001) The struggle for treatment integrity in a "dis-integrated" service delivery system. In G. A. Bernfeld, D. P. Farrington & A. W. Leschied (Eds.) *Offender Rehabilitation in Practice: Implementing and Evaluating Effective Programs.* Chichester: John Wiley & Sons.

Bernfeld, G. A., Blase, K. A. & Fixsen, D. L. (1990) Towards a unified perspective on human service delivery systems: Application of the teaching-family model. In R. J. McMahon & R. DeV. Peters (Eds.) *Behavioral Disorders of Adolescence.* New York, NY: Plenum Press.

Bernfeld, G. A. Farrington D. P. & Leschied A. W. (Eds.) (2001) *Offender Rehabilitation in Practice: Implementing and Evaluating Effective Programs.* Chichester: John Wiley & Sons.

Bonta, J. (2001) Offender assessment: general issues and considerations. In L. L. Motiuk and R. C. Serin (Eds.) *Compendium 2000 on Effective Correctional Programming.* Ottawa: Correctional Service Canada.

Bonta, J., Bogue, B., Crowley, M. & Motiuk, L. (2001) Implementing offender classification systems: lessons learned. In G. A. Bernfeld, D. P. Farrington & A. W. Leschied (Eds.) *Offender Rehabilitation in Practice: Implementing and Evaluating Effective Programs.* Chichester: John Wiley & Sons.

Borack, J. I. (1998) An estimate of the impact of drug testing on the deterrence of drug use. *Military Psychology, 10,* 17–25.

Borduin, C. M., Mann, B. J., Cone, L. T. & Hengeller, S. W. (1995) Multi-systemic treatment of serious juvenile offenders: Long-term prevention of criminality and violence. *Journal of Consulting and Clinical Psychology, 63,* 569–578.

Brown, S. L. (2001) Cost-effective correctional treatment. In L. L. Motiuk and R. C. Serin (Eds.) *Compendium 2000 on Effective Correctional Programming.* Ottawa: Correctional Service Canada.

Byrne, J. M., Lurigio, A. J. & Petersilia, J. (Eds.) (1992) *Smart Sentencing: The Emergence of Intermediate Sanctions.* Newbury Park, CA: Sage Publications.

Carroll, J. & Weaver, F. (1986) Shoplifters' perceptions of crime opportunities: A process-tracing study. In D. B. Cornish & R. V. Clarke (Eds.) *The Reasoning Criminal: Rational Choice Perspectives on Offending.* New York, NY: Springer-Verlag.

Chamberlain, P. & Reid, J. B. (1998) Comparison of two community alternatives to incarceration for chronic juvenile offenders. *Journal of Consulting and Clinical Psychology, 66,* 624–633.

Chambless, D. L. & Hollon, S. D. (1998) Defining empirically supported therapies. *Journal of Consulting and Clinical Psychology, 66,* 7–18.

Cheatwood, D. (1993) Capital punishment and the deterrence of violent crime in comparable counties. *Criminal Justice Review, 18,* 165–181.

Cleland, C. M., Pearson, F. S., Lipton, D. S. & Yee, D. (1997) *Does age make a difference? A meta-analytic approach to reductions in criminal offending for juveniles and adults.* Paper presented at the Annual Meeting of the American Society of Criminology, San Diego, California.

Cook, T. D. & Campbell, D. T. (1979) *Quasi-Experimentation: Design and Analysis Issues for Field Settings.* Boston, MA: Houghton Mifflin.

Dembo, R., Ramírez-Garnica, G., Rollie, M. W. & Schmeidler, J. (2000) Impact of a family empowerment intervention on youth recidivism. *Journal of Offender Rehabilitation*, 30, 59–98.

Department of Health (2001) *Treatment Choice in Psychological Therapies and Counselling: Evidence Based Clinical Practice Guideline.* Available to download from the Department of Health Website: *http://www.doh.gov.uk/mentalhealth/treatmentguideline/index.htm*

Dobash, R., Dobash, R. E., Cavanagh, K. & Lewis, R. (1996) *Re-education programmes for violent men – an evaluation.* Research Findings No. 46. London: Home Office Research and Statistics Directorate.

Dobson, K. S. & Craig, K. D. (Eds.) (1998) *Empirically Supported Therapies: Best Practice in Professional Psychology.* Thousand Oaks, CA: Sage Publications.

Dowden, C. & Andrews, D. A. (1999a) What works for female offenders: A meta-analytic review. *Crime and Delinquency*, 45, 438–452.

Dowden, C. & Andrews, D. A. (1999b) What works in young offender treatment: A meta-analysis. *Forum on Corrections Research*, 11, 21–24.

Dowden, C. & Andrews, D. A. (2000) Effective correctional treatment and violent re-offending: A meta-analysis. *Canadian Journal of Criminology*, 449–467.

Edwards, D. L., Schoenwald, S. K., Henggeler, S. W. & Strother, K. B. (2001) A multi-level perspective on the implementation of multisystemic therapy (MST): Attempting dissemination with fidelity. In G. A. Bernfeld, D. P. Farrington & A. W. Leschied (Eds.) *Offender Rehabilitation in Practice: Implementing and Evaluating Effective Programs.* Chichester: John Wiley & Sons.

Farrell, D. M. (1985) The justification of general deterrence. *Philosophical Review*, XCIV, 367–394.

Farrington, D. P. (1996) The explanation and prevention of youthful offending. In J. D. Hawkins (Ed.) *Delinquency and Crime: Current Theories.* Cambridge: Cambridge University Press.

Farrington, D. P. & Petrosino, A. (2001) The Campbell Collaboration Crime and Justice Group. *Annals of the American Academy of Political and Social Science*, 578, 35–49.

Fitzmaurice, C. & Pease, K. (1986) *The Psychology of Judicial Sentencing.* Manchester: Manchester University Press.

Florsheim, P., Shotorban, S., Guest-Warnick, G., Barratt, T. & Hwang, W.-S. (2000) Role of the working alliance in the treatment of delinquent boys in community-based programs. *Journal of Clinical Child Psychology*, 29, 94–107.

Friendship, C., Blud, L., Erikson, M., Travers, R. & Thornton, D. (2001) *Cognitive-behavioural Treatment for Imprisoned Offenders: An Evaluation of HM Prison Service's Cognitive Skills Programme.* Offending Behaviour Programmes Unit, HM Prison Service.

Gallagher, C. A., Wilson, D. B., Hirschfield, P., Coggeshall, M. B. & MacKenzie, D. L. (1999) A quantitative review of the effects of sexual offender treatment on sexual re-offending. *Corrections Management Quarterly*, 3, 19–29.

Garland, D. (1990) *Punishment and Modern Society: A Study in Social Theory.* Oxford: Clarendon Press.

Garrett, C. G. (1985) Effects of residential treatment on adjudicated delinquents: A meta-analysis. *Journal of Research in Crime and Delinquency*, 22, 287–308.

Gendreau, P. (1996a) The principles of effective intervention with offenders. In A. T. Harland (Ed.) *Choosing Correctional Options That Work: Defining the Demand and Evaluating the Supply.* Thousand Oaks, CA: Sage Publications.

Gendreau, P. (1996b) Offender rehabilitation: What we know and what needs to be done. *Criminal Justice and Behavior*, 23, 144–161.

Gendreau, P. & Andrews, D. A. (1990) Tertiary prevention: What the meta-analyses of the offender treatment literature tell us about "what works". *Canadian Journal of Criminology*, 32, 173–184.

Gendreau, P. & Goggin, C. (1996) Principles of effective correctional programming. *Forum on Corrections Research*, 8, 38–41.

Gendreau, P., Goggin, C. & Cullen, F. T. (1999) *The Effects of Prison Sentences on Recidivism.* Report to the Corrections Research and Development and Aboriginal Policy Branch. Ottawa: Solicitor General of Canada.

Gendreau, P., Goggin, C., Cullen, F. T. & Andrews, D. A. (2001) The effects of community sanctions and incarceration on recidivism. In L. L. Motiuk & R. C. Serin (Eds.) *Compendium 2000 on Effective Correctional Programming*. Ottawa: Correctional Service Canada.

Gendreau, P., Goggin, C. & Paparozzi, M. (1996) Principles of effective assessment for community corrections. *Federal Probation, 60*, 64–70.

Gendreau, P., Goggin, C. & Smith, P. (1999) The forgotten issue in effective correctional treatment: Program implementation. *International Journal of Offender Therapy and Comparative Criminology, 43*, 180–187.

Gendreau, P., Goggin, C. & Smith, P. (2001) Implementation guidelines for correctional programs in the "real world". In G. A. Bernfeld, D. P. Farrington & A. W. Leschied (Eds.) *Offender Rehabilitation in Practice: Implementing and Evaluating Effective Programs*. Chichester: John Wiley & Sons.

Gendreau, P., Paparozzi, M., Little, T. & Goddard, M. (1993) Does "Punishing Smarter" work? An assessment of the new generation of alternative sanctions in probation. *Forum on Corrections Research, 5*, 31–34.

Gendreau, P. & Ross, R. R. (1987) Revivification of rehabilitation: evidence from the 1980s. *Justice Quarterly, 4*, 349–407.

Gensheimer, L. K., Mayer, J. P., Gottschalk, R. & Davidson, W. S. (1986) Diverting youth from the juvenile justice system: A meta-analysis of intervention efficacy. In S. A. Apter & A. P. Goldstein (Eds.) *Youth Violence: Programs and Prospects*. Elmsford, NJ: Pergamon Press.

Gibbs, J. P. (1986) Deterrence theory and research. In G. B. Melton (Ed.) *The Law as a Behavioral Instrument: Nebraska Symposium on Motivation 1985*. Lincoln and London: University of Nebraska Press.

Glass, G. V. (1976) Primary, secondary, and meta-analysis of research. *Educational Researcher, 5*, 3–8.

Glass, G. V., McGaw, B. & Smith, M. L. (1981) *Meta-analysis in Social Research*. Newbury Park, CA: Sage Publications.

Goldiamond, I. (1974) Toward a constructional approach to social problems: Ethical and constitutional issues raised by applied behavior analysis. *Behaviorism, 2*, 1–84.

Goldblatt, P. & Lewis, C. (1998) *Reducing Offending: An Assessment of Research Evidence on Ways of Dealing with Offending Behaviour*. Home Office Research Study No.187. London: Home Office.

Goldstein, A. P. & Glick, B. (2001) Aggression Replacement Training: Application and evaluation management. In G. A. Bernfeld, D. P. Farrington & A. W. Leschied (Eds.) *Offender Rehabilitation in Practice: Implementing and Evaluating Effective Programs*. Chichester: John Wiley & Sons.

Goldstein, A. P., Glick, B., Carthan, W. & Blancero, D. A. (1994) *The Prosocial Gang: Implementing Aggression Replacement Training*. Thousand Oaks, CA: Sage.

Gordon, D.A., Graves, K. & Arbuthnot, J. (1995) The effect of functional family therapy for delinquents on adult criminal behavior. *Criminal Justice and Behavior, 22*, 60–73.

Gottschalk, R., Davidson, W. S., Gensheimer, L. K. & Mayer, J. P. (1987a) Community-based interventions. In H. C. Quay (Ed.) *Handbook of Juvenile Delinquency*. New York, NY: John Wiley & Sons.

Gottschalk, R., Davidson, W. S., Mayer, J. & Gensheimer, L. K. (1987b) Behavioral approaches with juvenile offenders: A meta-analysis of long-term treatment efficacy. In E. K. Morris & C. J. Braukmann (Eds.) *Behavioural Approaches to Crime and Delinquency*. New York, NY: Plenum Press.

Greenwood, P., Rydell, C. P., Abrahamse, A. F., Caulkins, J. P., Chiesa, J., Model, K. E. & Klein, S. P. (1996) Estimated costs and benefits of California's new mandatory-sentencing law. In D. Shichor & D. K. Sechrest (Eds.) *Three Strikes and You're Out: Vengeance as Public Policy*. Thousand Oaks, CA: Sage Publications.

Hall, G. C. N. (1995) Sexual offender recidivism revisited: A meta-analysis of recent treatment studies. *Journal of Consulting and Clinical Psychology, 63*, 802–809.

Harland, A. T. (Ed.) (1996) *Choosing Correctional Options That Work: Defining the Demand and Evaluating the Supply*. Thousand Oaks, CA: Sage Publications.

Harris, P. & Smith, S. (1996) Developing community corrections: An implementation perspective. In A. T. Harland (Ed.) *Choosing Correctional Options That Work: Defining the Demand and Evaluating the Supply*. Thousand Oaks, CA: Sage Publications.

Henggeler, S. W., Schoenwald, S. K., Borduin, C. M., Rowland, M. D. & Cunningham, P. B. (1998) *Multisystemic Treatment of Antisocial Behavior in Children and Adolescents*. New York, NY: Guilford Press.

Henstridge, J., Homel, R. & Mackay, P. (1997) *The Long-term Effects of Random Breath Testing in Four Australian States: A Time Series Analysis*. Canberra: Federal Office of Road Safety.

Hollin, C. R. (1995) The meaning and implications of programme integrity. In J. McGuire (Ed.) *What Works: Reducing Re-offending: Guidelines from Research and Practice*. Chichester: John Wiley & Sons.

Hollin, C. R. (1999) Treatment programmes for offenders: Meta-analysis, 'what works', and beyond. *International Journal of Law and Psychiatry*, 22, 361–371.

Hollin, C. R. (2001a) To treat or not to treat? An historical perspective. In C. R. Hollin (Ed.) *Handbook of Offender Assessment and Treatment*. Chichester: John Wiley & Sons.

Hollin, C. R. (Ed.) (2001b) *Handbook of Offender Assessment and Treatment*. Chichester: John Wiley & Sons.

Hollin, C. R., Epps, K. J. & Kendrick, D. J. (1995) *Managing Behavioural Treatment: Policy and Practice with Delinquent Adolescents*. London: Routledge.

Hollin, C. R., McGuire, J., Palmer, E., Bilby, C., Hatcher, R. & Holmes, A. (2002) *Introducing Pathfinder Programmes into the Probation Service: An interim report*. Home Office Research Study 247. London: Home Office Research, Development and Statistics Directorate.

Home Office (1993) *Digest 2: Information on the Criminal Justice System in England and Wales*. London: Home Office Research and Statistics Department.

Home Office Probation Unit (1999) *What Works Initiative: Crime Reduction Programme. Joint Prison and Probation Accreditation Criteria*. London: Home Office.

Honderich, T. (1976) *Punishment: The Supposed Justifications*. Harmondsworth: Penguin Books.

Hood, R. (1996) *The Death Penalty: A World-Wide Perspective* (2nd edition). Oxford: Oxford University Press.

Izzo, R. L. & Ross, R. R. (1990) Meta-analysis of rehabilitation programmes for juvenile delinquents. *Criminal Justice and Behavior*, 17, 134–142.

Kershaw, C., Goodman, J. & White, S. (1999) *Reconviction of Offenders Sentenced or Released from Prison in 1995*. Research Findings No.101. London: Home Office Research and Statistics Department.

Klemke, L. W. (1982) Reassessment of Cameron's apprehension-termination of shoplifting finding. *California Sociologist*, 5, 88–95.

Lambert, M. J. & Bergin, A. E. (1994) The effectiveness of psychotherapy. In A. E. Bergin & S. L. Garfield (Eds.) *Handbook of Psychotherapy and Behavior Change*. New York, NY: John Wiley & Sons.

Leschied, A. W., Bernfeld, G. & Farrington, D. P. (2001) Implementation issues. In G. A. Bernfeld, D. P. Farrington & A. W. Leschied (Eds.) *Offender Rehabilitation in Practice: Implementing and Evaluating Effective Programs*. Chichester: John Wiley & Sons.

Light, R., Nee, C. & Ingham, H. (1993) *Car Theft: The Offender's Perspective*. Home Office Research Study No. 130. London: HMSO.

Lipsey, M. W. (1992) Juvenile Delinquency treatment: A meta-analytic inquiry into the variability of effects. In T. Cook, D. Cooper, H. Corday, H. Hartman, L. Hedges, R. Light, T. Louis & F. Mosteller (Eds.) *Meta-analysis for Explanation: A Casebook*. New York, NY: Russell Sage Foundation.

Lipsey, M. W. (1995) What do we learn from 400 studies on the effectiveness of treatment with juvenile delinquents? In J. McGuire (Ed.) *What Works: Reducing Re-offending: Guidelines from Research and Practice*. Chichester: John Wiley & Sons.

Lipsey, M. W. (1999) Can rehabilitative programs reduce the recidivism of juvenile offenders? An inquiry into the effectiveness of practical programs. *Virginia Journal of Social Policy and the Law*, 6, 611–641.

Lipsey, M. W., Chapman, G. L. & Landenberger, N. A. (2001) Cognitive-behavioral programs for offenders. *Annals of the American Academy of Political and Social Science*, 578, 144–157.

Lipsey, M. W. & Wilson, D. B. (1993) The efficacy of psychological, educational, and behavioral treatment: Confirmation from meta-analysis. *American Psychologist*, 48, 1181–1209.

Lipsey, M. W. & Wilson, D. B. (1998) Effective intervention for serious juvenile offenders: A synthesis of research. In R. Loeber & D. P. Farrington (Eds.) *Serious and Violent Juvenile Offenders: Risk Factors and Successful Interventions.* Thousand Oaks, CA: Sage Publications.

Lipton, D. S., Pearson, F. S., Cleland, C. & Lee, D. (1997) *Synthesizing correctional treatment outcomes: Preliminary CDATE findings.* Paper presented at the 5th Annual National Institute of Justice Conference on Research and Evaluation in Criminal Justice, Washington, July.

Lloyd, C., Mair, G. & Hough, M. (1994) *Explaining Reconviction Rates: A Critical Analysis.* Home Office Research Study No.136. London: HMSO.

Lösel, F. (1995) The efficacy of correctional treatment: A review and synthesis of meta-evaluations. In J. McGuire (Ed.) *What Works: Reducing Re-offending: Guidelines from Research and Practice.* Chichester: John Wiley & Sons.

Lösel, F. (2001) Evaluating the effectiveness of correctional programs: Bridging the gap between research and practice. In G. A. Bernfeld, D. P. Farrington & A. W. Leschied (Eds.) *Offender Rehabilitation in Practice: Implementing and Evaluating Effective Programs.* Chichester: John Wiley & Sons.

Lösel, F. & Köferl, P. (1989) Evaluation research on correctional treatment in West Germany: A meta-analysis. In H. Wegener, F. Lösel & J. Haisch (Eds.) *Criminal Behaviour and the Justice System: Psychological Perspectives.* New York, NY: Springer-Verlag.

MacKenzie, D. L. (1997) Criminal justice and crime prevention. In L. W. Sherman, D. Gottfredson, D. L. MacKenzie, J. Eck, P. Reuter & S. Bushway (Eds.) *Preventing Crime: What Works, What Doesn't, What's Promising.* Washington, DC: Office of Justice Programs.

MacKenzie, D. L. & Souryal, C. (1994) *Multisite Evaluation of Shock Incarceration.* Washington, DC: National Institute of Justice.

MacKenzie, D. L., Wilson, D. B. & Kider, S. B. (2001) Effects of correctional boot camps on offending. *Annals of the American Academy of Political and Social Science*, 578, 126–143.

Mayer, J. P., Gensheimer, L. K., Davidson, W. S. & Gottschalk, R. (1986) Social learning treatment within juvenile justice: A meta-analysis of impact in the natural environment. In S. A. Apter & A. P. Goldstein (Eds.) *Youth Violence: Programs and Prospects.* Elmsford, NJ: Pergamon Press.

Mayhew, P. & White, P. (1997) *The 1996 International Crime Victimisation Survey.* Research Findings No. 57. London: Home Office Research and Statistics Directorate.

McGuire, J. (Ed.) (1995) *What Works: Reducing Re-offending: Guidelines from Research and Practice.* Chichester: John Wiley & Sons.

McGuire, J. (2000a) *Cognitive-Behavioural Methods: An Introduction to Theory and Research.* London: Home Office.

McGuire, J. (2000b) Explanations of offence behaviour. In J. McGuire, T. Mason & A. O'Kane (Eds.) *Behaviour, Crime and Legal Processes: A Guidebook for Practitioners.* Chichester: John Wiley & Sons.

McGuire, J. (2001a) Property offences. In C. R. Hollin (Ed.) *Handbook of Offender Assessment and Treatment.* Chichester: John Wiley & Sons.

McGuire, J. (2001b) Defining correctional programs. In L. L. Motiuk & R. C. Serin (Eds.) *Compendium 2000 on Effective Correctional Programming.* Ottawa: Correctional Service Canada.

McGuire, J. (2001c) What works in correctional intervention? Evidence and practical implications. In G. A. Bernfeld, D. P. Farrington & A. W. Leschied (Eds.) *Offender Rehabilitation in Practice: Implementing and Evaluating Effective Programs.* Chichester: John Wiley & Sons.

McGuire, J. (2001d) Development of a program logic model to assist evaluation. In L. L. Motiuk & R. C. Serin (Eds.) *Compendium 2000 on Effective Correctional Programming.* Ottawa: Correctional Service Canada.

McGuire, J. (2002) Criminal sanctions versus psychologically-based interventions with offenders: A comparative empirical analysis. *Psychology, Crime and Law*, 8, 183–208.

McGuire, J. & Clark, D. (2001) *A national dissemination programme.* Paper presented at the first conference of the European Centre for Aggression Replacement Training. Convention Center, Malmö, Sweden.

Moffitt, T. E. (1983) The learning theory model of punishment: Implications for delinquency deterrence. *Criminal Justice and Behavior*, *10*, 131–158.

Morrison, S. & O'Donnell, I. (1994) *Armed Robbery: A Study in London*. Oxford: Centre for Criminological Research.

Motiuk, L. L. and Serin, R. C. (Eds.) (2001) *Compendium 2000 on Effective Correctional Programming*. Ottawa: Correctional Service Canada.

Nathan, P. E. & Gorman, J. M. (Eds.) (1998) *A Guide to Treatments That Work*. New York, NY: Oxford University Press.

Newman, G., Bouloukos, A. C. & Cohen, D. (Eds.) (2001) *World Factbook of Criminal Justice Systems*. Washington, DC: Department of Justice. Available from web-site: *http://www.ojp.usdoj.gov/bjs/pub/ascii/wfbcjhon.txt*

Palmer, T. (1992) *The Re-emergence of Correctional Intervention*. Newbury Park, CA: Sage Publications.

Pearson, F. S., Lipton, D. S. & Cleland, C. M. (1997) *Rehabilitative programs in adult corrections: CDATE meta-analyses*. Paper presented at the Annual Meeting of the American Society of Criminology, San Diego.

Persons, J. B. (1991) Psychotherapy outcome studies do not accurately represent current models of psychotherapy: A proposed remedy. *American Psychologist*, *46*, 99–106.

Persons, J. B. & Silbersatz, G. (1998) Are the results of randomised controlled trials useful to psychotherapists? *Journal of Consulting and Clinical Psychology*, *66*, 126–135.

Petersilia, J. & Turner, S. (1993) Intensive probation and parole. *Crime and Justice*, *17*, 281–335.

Petrosino, A. (2000) Crime, drugs and alcohol. In *Evidence from Systematic Reviews of Research Relevant to Implementing the Wider Public Health Agenda*. University of York: NHS Centre for Reviews and Dissemination. Available from website: *http://www.york.ac.uk/inst/crd/wph.htm*

Petrosino, A., J., Turpin-Petrosino, C. & Finckenhauer, J. O. (2000) Well-meaning programs can have harmful effects! Lessons from experiments of programs such as Scared Straight. *Crime and Delinquency*, *46*, 354–379.

Polizzi, D. M., MacKenzie, D. L. & Hickman, L. J. (1999) What works in adult sex offender treatment? A review of prison- and non-prison-based treatment programs. *International Journal of Offender Therapy and Comparative Criminology*, *43*, 357–374.

Redondo, S., Garrido, V. & Sánchez-Meca, J. (1997) What works in correctional rehabilitation in Europe: A meta-analytical review. In S. Redondo, V. Garrido, J. Pérez & R. Barberet (Eds.) *Advances in Psychology and Law: International Contributions*. Berlin: Walter de Gruyter.

Redondo, S., Sánchez-Meca, J. & Garrido, V. (1999) The influence of treatment programmes on the recidivism of juvenile and adult offenders: An European meta-analytic review. *Psychology, Crime and Law*, *5*, 251–278.

Roberts, A. R. & Camasso, M. J. (1991) The effect of juvenile offender treatment programs on recidivism: a meta-analysis of 46 studies. *Notre Dame Journal of Law, Ethics and Public Policy*, *5*, 421–441.

Robson, C. (1993) *Real World Research: A Resource for Social Scientists and Practitioner-Researchers*. Oxford: Blackwell.

Rosenthal, R. (1994) Parametric measures of effect size. In H. Cooper & L. V. Hedges (Eds.) *Handbook of Research Synthesis*. New York, NY: Russell Sage Foundation.

Ross, R. R., Antonowicz, D. H. & Dhaliwal, G. K. (1995) *Going Straight: Effective Delinquency Prevention and Offender Rehabilitation*. Ottawa: Air Training and Publications.

Roth, A. & Fonagy, P. (1996) *What Works for Whom? A Critical Review of Psychotherapy Research*. New York, NY: Guilford Press.

Rutter, M., Giller, H. & Hagell, A. (1998) *Antisocial Behavior by Young People*. Cambridge: Cambridge University Press.

Sherman, L. W. (1988) Randomized experiments in criminal sanctions. In H. S. Bloom, D. S. Cordray & R. J. Light (Eds.) *Lessons from Selected Program and Policy Areas*. New Directions for Program Evaluation, No. 37. San Francisco, CA: Jossey-Bass.

Sherman, L. W., Gottfredson, D., McKenzie, D., Eck, J., Reuter, P. & Bushway, S. (1997) *Preventing Crime: What Works, What Doesn't, What's Promising*. Washington, DC: Office of Justice Programs.

Shichor, D. & Sechrest, D. K. (Eds.) (1996) *Three Strikes and You're Out: Vengeance as Public Policy*. Thousand Oaks, CA: Sage Publications.

Simon, L. M. J. (1998) Does criminal offender treatment work? *Applied and Preventive Psychology*, 7, 137–159.

Stack, S. (1993) Execution publicity and homicide in Georgia. *American Journal of Criminal Justice*, 18, 25–39.

Stafford, M. C. & Warr, M. (1993) A reconceptualisation of general and specific deterrence. *Journal of Research on Crime and Delinquency*, 30, 123–135.

Thornton, D., Curran, L., Grayson, D. & Holloway, V. (1984) *Tougher Regimes in Detention Centres: Report of an Evaluation by the Young Offender Psychology Unit*. London: HMSO.

Thornton, T. N., Craft, C. A., Dahlberg, L. L., Lynch, B. S. & Baer, K. (2000) *Best Practices of Youth Violence Prevention: A Sourcebook for Community Action*. Atlanta, GA: National Center for Injury Prevention and Control.

Vennard, J., Sugg, D. & Hedderman, C. (1997) *Changing Offenders' Attitudes and Behaviour: what works?* Home Office Research Study No.171. London: HMSO.

Von Hirsch, A., Bottoms, A. E., Burneu, E. & Wikström, P. O. (1999) *Criminal Deterrence and Sentencing Severity: An Analysis of Recent Research*. Oxford: Hart.

Walker, N. (1991) *Why Punish? Theories of Punishment Reassessed*. Oxford: Oxford University Press.

Weisburd, D., Sherman, L. W. & Petrosino, A. J. (1990) *Registry of randomized criminal justice experiments in sanctions*. Unpublished report, Rutgers University, University of Maryland and Crime Control Institute.

Wells-Parker, E., Bangert-Drowns, R., McMillen, R. & Williams, M. (1995) Final results from a meta-analysis of remedial interventions with drink/drive offenders. *Addiction*, 90, 907–926.

Welsh, B. C. & Farrington, D. P. (2000) Correctional intervention programs and cost benefit analysis. *Criminal Justice and Behavior*, 27, 115–133.

Welsh, B. C. & Farrington, D. P. (2001a) Evaluating the economic efficiency of correctional intervention programs. In G. A. Bernfeld, D. P. Farrington & A. W. Leschied (Eds.) *Offender Rehabilitation in Practice: Implementing and Evaluating Effective Programs*. Chichester: John Wiley & Sons.

Welsh, B. C. & Farrington, D. P. (2001b) Toward an evidence-based approach to preventing crime. *Annals of the American Academy of Political and Social Science*, 578, 158–173.

Wexler, D. B. (1998) How the law can use *What Works*: A therapeutic jurisprudence look at recent research on rehabilitation. *Behavioral Sciences and the Law*, 15, 368–369.

Whitehead, J. T. & Lab, S. P. (1989) A meta-analysis of juvenile correctional treatment. *Journal of Research in Crime and Delinquency*, 26, 276–295.

Wilkinson, J. (1997) The impact of Ilderton motor project on motor vehicle crime and offending. *British Journal of Criminology*, 37, 568–581.

Wilson, D. B. (2001) Meta-analytic methods for criminology. *Annals of the American Academy of Political and Social Science*, 578, 71–89.

Wilson, D. B., Gallagher, C. A. & MacKenzie, D. L. (2000) A meta-analysis of corrections-based education, vocation and work programs for adult offenders. *Journal of Research in Crime and Delinquency*, 37, 568–581.

Wilson, S. J. & Lipsey, M. W. (2000) Wilderness challenge programs for delinquent youth: A meta-analysis of outcome evaluations. *Evaluation and Program Planning*, 23, 1–12.

Zamble, E. & Quinsey, V. (1997) *The Criminal Recidivism Process*. New York, NY: Cambridge University Press.

Zimring, F. E. & Hawkins, G. (1994) The growth of imprisonment in California. *British Journal of Criminology*, 34 (Special Issue), 83–96.

Zimring, F. E. & Hawkins, G. (1995) *Incapacitation: Penal Confinement and the Restraint of Crime*. New York, NY: Oxford University Press.

Chapter 2

THE EFFECTS OF THERAPEUTIC COMMUNITIES AND MILIEU THERAPY ON RECIDIVISM

Meta-analytic Findings from the Correctional Drug Abuse Treatment Effectiveness (CDATE) Study

DOUGLAS S. LIPTON[1]; FRANK S. PEARSON[2]; CHARLES M. CLELAND[2]; AND DORLINE YEE[2]

[1] Lipton Consulting, 8 Appletree Lane, East Brunswick, NJ 08816, USA
[2] National Development and Research Institutes, New York, USA

This chapter[*] reports the results of a meta-analysis on the effectiveness of programmes providing therapeutic community (TC) and milieu therapy (MT) treatment in correctional settings (such as prisons and jails) in reducing recidivism. It is part of a comprehensive detailed review and meta-analysis of the evaluation research on the effectiveness of criminal justice-based rehabilitation programmes for offenders in any form of custody. The overall meta-analysis is of primary research reports collected as part of the Correctional Drug Abuse Treatment Effectiveness (CDATE) project, funded for four years by the National Institute on Drug Abuse (NIDA). Over 1500 evaluation research studies—both published and unpublished—conducted since 1968 on the effectiveness of treatment programmes for offenders, adult and juvenile, drug abusing and non-drug abusing, have been collected. Over ten thousand purported evaluation documents completed between 1 January 1968 and 31 December 1996 from all countries were screened, assembled, and/or annotated, and all studies meeting inclusion criteria became part of the meta-analyses. Different levels of confidence in the results based on each study's methodology were used to make distinctions in outcomes. Hypotheses were generated regarding the impact of the various treatments on several outcome measures,

[*] This project was supported under grant number R01 DA08607 from the National Institute on Drug Abuse at the National Institutes of Health, US Department of Health and Human Services. Points of view in this document are those of the authors and do not necessarily reflect the official position of any US Government agency.

Offender Rehabilitation and Treatment: Effective Programmes and Policies to Reduce Re-offending. Edited by James McGuire.
© John Wiley & Sons, Ltd.

particularly drug abuse and recidivism. The effectiveness of each of the modalities of treatment has been examined in the light of a variety of moderator variables hypothesized to have an impact on effect sizes, such as nature of clientele, staff, setting, degree of isolation, duration of treatment, completeness of implementation and continuity of treatment.

THE CONTEXT

The current re-emphasis on drug abuse treatment in prisons and jails appears to be anchored in the need to do something about the large numbers of drug abusers in custody. This is complemented with recent research findings that drug abuse treatment is effective (Hubbard et al., 1989; Gerstein & Harwood, 1992; Simpson & Knight, 1998). Large-scale, NIDA-funded field outcome studies of drug abuse treatment, such as the Drug Abuse Reporting Project (DARP), the Treatment Outcome Prospective Study (TOPS) and the Drug Abuse Treatment Outcome Study (DATOS)—essentially three replications with large numbers of participants in each—have demonstrated substantial consistency in rates of treatment success for community-based treatments such as outpatient group counselling scheduled several times per week and residential therapeutic community treatment, despite relatively high attrition experienced by persons in each kind of treatment. A fourth national study—the National Treatment Improvement Evaluation Study (NTIES), funded by the Substance Abuse and Mental Health Services Administration—also found similar results.

The treatment outcomes among those persons in these studies under criminal justice supervision have however, only rarely been disaggregated from the national findings. Collins et al. (1983), for example, in their analysis of the TOPS data, showed that criminal justice clients in outpatient programmes had better retention rates than clients who were not legally required to attend treatment, and had similar rates of success. They found that, as with non-CJ clients, the effectiveness of drug abuse treatment is specifically related to the length of time an individual remains in treatment. It should also be noted that these four large-scale studies compare individuals' behaviours before and after treatment and use no comparison population. Hence, their outcome data regarding criminal justice clients are not included in the CDATE analysis. It should be noted that Anglin et al. (1998) have recently assembled the literature on coercion and echo Collins' findings, viz. "... (T)he weight of evidence clearly supports the use of legal coercion in its various forms as an effective means for enhancing treatment retention and post-treatment outcomes for many substance-using offenders."

It is axiomatic that drug abuse is both a chronic and a relapsing disorder once a person is addicted. Hence, full recovery from drug abuse is difficult to achieve once a person has become dependent for a protracted period. The chronicity and relapsing aspects of drug abuse often make the effectiveness of drug abuse treatment difficult for many to understand. Viewed from a traditional health perspective, treatment should be followed by "cure" and no drug abuse. Viewed from the perspective of the legislator and the lay public, treatment that reduces or eliminates substance abuse should also reduce or eliminate criminal behaviour.

Within corrections, these goals are compatible but are not frequently implemented coherently. There is also the opinion that drug abuse treatment is futile in the long run in spite of the favourable research results noted earlier—especially favourable for serious drug users when combined with criminal justice sanctions (Leukefeld & Tims, 1988; Lipton, 1995; Simpson & Knight, 1998). This opinion underlies some of the hesitation to start programmes. Most correctional administrators are realists, not idealists. Many may seek to use drug abuse treatment programming to achieve salutary change, but many still use treatment to keep inmates actively engaged.

The expansion of drug use and associated crime in US cities—crack cocaine in the 1980s and methamphetamine in the 1990s as well as a recent resurgence of heroin—has crammed the correctional facilities and absorbed community supervision and treatment facility resources as never before. Fully 80% of incarcerated men and women, about 1.4 million inmates, are seriously involved with substance abuse, and about three out of four of these persons regularly used substances in the month prior to entry to prison or jail. In 1996 substance-abusing inmates cost American taxpayers $30.4 billion just to build prisons and jails to house them (Belenko et al., 1998). It is thus no surprise that there is increased interest in applying alternative means for dealing with offenders other than "warehousing" them. Along with this interest is the recognition that this expanding drug abuser population presents an opportunity to implement drug abuse treatments that are documented with research data as consistently effective.

Experience related to treating drug abusers in prisons and jails is largely from the United States over the last two decades and has been closely related to the rapid expansion of drug use and its associated crime. Such "epidemics", e.g. crack cocaine, have strained both correctional facilities and community treatment settings. The current drug abuse situation provides criminal justice practitioners with a window of opportunity to establish specific drug abuse treatment interventions that are research documented as consistently effective and supported by practice. However, their awareness of drug abuse treatment evaluations results based on research in prisons and jails, and the comparative success of treatment approaches, is influenced to a considerable degree by three decades of scepticism (Wilkinson, 1998).

PRIOR STUDIES

It has been more than a quarter of a century since the 231 programme evaluations surveyed in *The Effectiveness of Correctional Treatment: A Survey of Treatment Evaluation Studies* (hereafter the ECT) were completed. This book, by Douglas S. Lipton, Robert Martinson and Judith Wilks (published in 1975), systematically annotated research studies that were produced between 1945 and 1967. The aim was to bring the weight of scientific knowledge about the effectiveness of rehabilitation to bear on State legislation. It evaluated several types of correctional-based rehabilitation programmes and assessed the relative effects of these treatments on recidivism, institutional adjustment, educational achievement, drug and alcohol re-addiction, and other outcomes. A year before this book was published, however,

Robert Martinson, *on his own*, published an article, in *The Public Interest* entitled, "What Works?—Questions and Answers About Prison Reform". His central conclusion was that "...with few and isolated exceptions, the rehabilitative efforts that have been reported so far have no appreciable effect on recidivism" (1974, p. 25). The book length scholarly assessment, the ECT, concluded, however, that "the field of corrections has not as yet found satisfactory ways to reduce recidivism by significant amounts" (Lipton, Martinson & Wilks, 1975, p. 627). Authors of earlier reviews of evaluation studies of rehabilitation programmes had come to essentially the same conclusion (Kirby, 1954; Bailey, 1966; Logan, 1972). Since that time, some careful meta-analyses have been conducted.

It is at least 30 years now since the studies reviewed in the ECT were completed. The CDATE project was funded by NIDA to update the ECT in the light of the reawakening, during the last decade, to the rehabilitative potential within the criminal justice system. A growing body of evaluation studies has come under careful scrutiny. Several authors have concluded that certain rehabilitation programmes effectively reduce recidivism (viz. Palmer, 1975, 1986; Geismar & Wood, 1985, Garrett, 1985; Greenwood & Zimring, 1985; Ross & Fabiano, 1985; Mayer et al., 1986; Gendreau & Ross, 1987; Van Voorhis, 1987; Visher, 1987; Wexler, Falkin & Lipton, 1988, 1990; Basta & Davidson, 1988; Currie, 1989; Cullen & Gendreau, 1989; Lipsey, 1989, 1991; Lipton, 1990; Andrews et al., 1990; Izzo & Ross, 1990; Wexler, 1994; Antonowicz & Ross, 1994; McGuire, 1995).

A current view held by many is that "The effectiveness of correctional treatment is dependent upon what is delivered to whom in particular settings"—a view asserted by Andrews and co-workers (1983, 1990), Cullen and Gendreau (1989), Gendreau and Ross (1979, 1981, 1987), Antonowicz and Ross (1994), and echoed by many others. Critics of rehabilitation are not in short supply, however, as Walker (1989, p. 231) asserts: "It is wishful thinking to believe that additional research is going to uncover a magic key that has somehow been overlooked for 150 years." Greenberg (1977), Brody (1976) and Rosenbaum (1988) echo this point. Lab and Whitehead, reporting on the correctional treatment of juveniles, stated that, "In general, at least half of the studies reported negative or no impact on recidivism and many of the positive findings were based on dubious subjective evaluations" (1988, p. 60). In the following year Whitehead and Lab reported a meta-analysis[1]* of correctional treatment of juveniles, saying, "The results show that interventions have little positive impact on recidivism and many appear to exacerbate the problem" (1989, p. 276). Whitehead and Lab (1989) conclude that the "nothing works" belief with respect to recidivism for juvenile treatment is unfortunately still viable, although they are careful to deny their alliance with the "*nothing works*" ideologues and assert limited optimism (Lab & Whitehead, 1990). Collectively, the views of the others who have critically reviewed segments of the adult and juvenile correctional rehabilitation evaluation studies since the ECT survey are less pessimistic than theirs.

Twenty-eight meta-analyses and cross-study analyses of correctional treatment evaluation studies have been conducted: Andrews et al., 1990; Anglin & Hser, 1990;

---

* Notes are presented at the end of the chapter

Bonta, Law & Hanson, 1998; Farrington, 1983; Garrett, 1985; Gendreau, Little & Goggin, 1996; Gensheimer et al., 1986; Gerber & Fritsh, 1993; Gottschalk et al., 1987a, 1987b; Izzo & Ross, 1990; Lipsey, 1992; Lösel, Koferl & Weber, 1987; Lösel & Koferl, 1989; Lösel, 1993; McGuire & Priestley, 1993; Mayer et al., 1986; Redondo, Garrido & Sánchez-Meca, 1996; Roberts & Camasso 1991; Ross, Antonowicz & Dhaliwal, 1995; Sherman et al., 1997; Tobler, 1986; Tolan & Guerra, 1994; Sherman, 1988; Weisburd, Sherman & Petrosino, 1990; Wells-Parker et al., 1994; Wells-Parker & Bangert-Drowns, 1990; Whitehead & Lab, 1989.

Two meta-analyses—Andrews et al. (1990) and Lipsey (1992)—are particularly noteworthy because they are widely cited. In 1990, Andrews, Zinger, Hoge, Bonta, Gendreau and Cullen published a meta-analytical study taking issue with Lab and Whitehead. In the introductory material, they argue that "what works" in correctional treatment is *appropriate* correctional service. Appropriate correctional service reflects three principles: "(1) delivery of service to higher risk cases, (2) targeting of criminogenic needs, and (3) use of styles and modes of treatment (e.g. cognitive and behavioural) that are matched with client need and learning styles" (Andrews et al., 1990, p. 369). By "criminogenic needs", Andrews and his colleagues mean dynamic risk factors reflected in intermediate targets of intervention. The most promising intermediate targets include (p. 375): changing antisocial attitudes, feelings, and peer associations; promoting identification with anti-criminal role models; increasing self-control and self-management skills; replacing the skills of lying, stealing, and aggression with other, more pro-social, skills; and reducing chemical dependencies. Appropriate styles and modes of treatment, "typically, but not exclusively, involve the use of behavioural and social learning principles of interpersonal influence, skill enhancement, and cognitive change". Generally *inappropriate* interventions would include: unstructured, non-directive, peer-oriented group counselling (e.g. guided group interaction) and traditional psychodynamic and non-directive client-centred therapies.

Lipsey (1992) conducted a meta-analysis of research reports on interventions aimed at reducing, preventing, or remedying juvenile delinquency or antisocial behaviour problems similar to delinquency in the United States, and in Australia, Britain and Canada. Out of 443 studies, 64.3% reported favourable effects of treatment, compared to 29.6% reporting unfavourable effects.[2] There were 397 studies reporting enough information to calculate an effect size and the unweighted (but n-adjusted) mean effect size using Cohen's d was +0.172. (By CDATE calculations, this effect size is roughly equivalent to a Pearson correlation coefficient or phi coefficient of +0.09.) Lipsey went on to analyse the effect size distributions using more rigorous techniques, such as inverse variance weighting, tests for homogeneity and cluster analysis. In a stepwise regression analysis he found that the clusters of predictor variables reflecting the methodological aspects of the studies (such as sample size, the initial equivalence of the E and C groups, etc.) accounted for over 20% of the variability in the effect size distribution. He also found that studies in which the researcher was influential in the treatment setting tended to be associated with larger effect sizes. (This variable showed an 11% R^2 change.) Treatment dosage accounted for a 3% R^2 change in that studies of treatments with more meaningful contact and treatments of longer treatment tended to have larger effect sizes. Treatment philosophy showed a 2% R^2 change in which studies with a more sociological, and less psychological, orientation tended to have larger effect sizes. Finally, there was a 2% R^2 change in that treatments of higher risk juveniles tended to show larger effect sizes than treatments of lower risk juveniles.

In the light of so many reviews of effectiveness studies, one might ask "Why another?". In May 1990 Leukefeld and Tims identified areas of agreement as to why this work must continue: "A historical review of past programmatic efforts using meta-analytic procedures should be initiated to add clarity about the impact of correctional *drug abuse* treatment programs" and "A standardized correctional drug abuse treatment typology should be developed which incorporates uniform definitions of treatment and system components (i.e. assessment, education, intervention, treatment, and continuity of care)", are just two of the cited reasons. Moreover, important changes in treatment technology have occurred, particularly in the last ten years, that merit re-evaluating the evaluation research. Other important reasons are: most of the meta-analyses noted above focused on a limited population, i.e. juveniles; none focused on drug abusers as a treatment sub-population; none is comprehensive, i.e. all examined only a limited number of studies, all of which were chosen from the published literature; and, for the most part, the literature chosen for examination was from English-speaking countries.

Further, there is a growing awareness that effective rehabilitation programmes must be developed to reduce the high recidivism rates that are a major factor in serious crime and the prime cause of prison overcrowding. A clear understanding of which programmes produce effective rehabilitation outcomes for particular offenders, and which obstacles interfere with the successful implementation of programmes, is much needed. Knowledge accumulated from research since the studies surveyed in the ECT were completed has shown that some treatment methods are effective at reducing recidivism among certain groups. There have also been attempts to identify the programmatic factors responsible for successful outcomes (see Hamm & Schrink, 1989; Lipton, 1989; Andrews et al., 1990; Antonowicz & Ross, 1994).

In this chapter we present the results of two categories of intervention—therapeutic communities and milieu therapy—on the outcome variable—recidivism. While there is overlap across these two categories, there is sufficient distinction between them to warrant a separation for meta-analytical purposes.

THERAPEUTIC COMMUNITIES AND MILIEU THERAPY

A typical therapeutic community (TC) is a community-based residence with a few professional staff, but primarily recovered addicts serving as staff. Residents are asked to spend about 9 to 18 months in residence, but the dropout or attrition rate is quite high—usually 60–80% are gone within the first three months (Baekeland & Lundwall, 1975; De Leon, 1991). A core characteristic of most TCs is the use of work as an organizing therapeutic activity. This means residents are involved in all aspects of the community's operations including administration, maintenance and food preparation. Drug abuse is seen as a disorder of the whole person, so the treatment problem to be addressed is the person, not the drug. In this perspective, drug abuse is seen as a symptom, not the essence, of the disorder and the pattern of drug use is less important than the accompanying psychological and behavioural disorders.

Drug abuse is seen as a symptom of immaturity, thus the abuser is seen as unable to postpone gratification, unable to tolerate frustration, and has difficulty maintaining stable, healthy relationships. Beside immaturity, most abusers have conduct or behaviour problems and low self-esteem. These characteristics are targets for the behaviour change techniques used by the TC staff and senior residents. Recovery is considered to involve the development of a personal identity and global change in lifestyle, including the conduct, attitudes and values consonant with "Right Living", and is a lifelong continuing process. Right Living develops from committing oneself to the values of the therapeutic community, including *positive social* values such as the work ethic, social productivity and communal responsibility, and *positive personal* values such as honesty, self-reliance and responsibility to oneself and significant others. The goals of treatment are congruent with these values, viz.: abstinence from drug use, termination of illicit behaviours, gainful legal employment/or college matriculation, and maintenance of positive stable social relationships (De Leon, 1995).

TCs are hierarchically organized and stratified. Staff and resident roles are aligned in a clear chain of command. New residents are assigned to work teams with the lowest status, but can move up strata as they demonstrate increased competency and emotional growth. Thus, they have an incentive to earn better work positions, associated rights and privileges, and living accommodations.

For success in the TC one must accept the notion of "acting as if", which requires new residents to suspend judgement and *make believe* that they accept the basic TC values and rules conduct. The TC resident then continues to "act as if" until the community values and attitudes become internalized. Maturity develops as roles and responsibilities are taken on and increase. The stratified character of the TC facilitates the working through of authority problems and helps residents to accept appropriate authority as they move out to assume responsible positions within the society. The distinguishing feature of the TC, in contrast with other treatment approaches, is the "purposive use of the *community* as the primary method for facilitating social and psychological change in individuals" (De Leon, 1995) as it blends confrontation and support to help residents to undergo the arduous changes that are necessary. This perception of the *community* is constantly emphasized.

The programme uses groups and meetings to provide "positive persuasion" to change behaviour, and confrontation by peer groups whenever values or rules are breached. On the other hand, peers also provide supportive feedback such as reinforcement, affirmation, instruction and suggestions for changing behaviour and attitudes, and assist the residents during group meetings as they recall painful memories from childhood and adolescence. It should be noted that the TC regimen of today often provides additional services such as family treatment and educational, vocational, medical and mental health services, and that staffing is augmented by increasing proportions of professionals from the mental health, medical and education fields (De Leon, 1994).

There are several distinctions between therapeutic communities operating in prisons and therapeutic communities based in the community as described above.

1. In prisons, a TC is much more constrained by rules and policies, particularly those relating to security.
2. As a corollary, the range of programmatic autonomy, clinical creativity and independence of action is wider in standard community-based TCs (CBTC) than in modified prison-based and correctional TCs (PBTC). For example, operating in a prison environment prohibits the PBTC from sending its residents into the public community as they approach re-entry and their progress warrants such action.
3. Likewise, PBTCs usually have fewer recovering persons acting as staff compared with CBTCs; thus, there are usually relatively fewer role models consisting of recovering ex-addict ex-offenders with whom the inmates may identify, and from whom they may draw encouragement. The proportion of role model staff, however, differs rather markedly programme to programme.
4. In PBTCs, mixed gender resident groups are rarely found, unlike in community-based TCs. This difference denies each gender the opportunity to learn how to develop positive working and social relationships with the other, but at the same time prevents the formation of inimical sexual relationships.
5. In CBTCs, work plays a major organizing role in the development of responsibility. In PBTCs a number of work functions are performed by work crews in prison industry, and not by programme participants (e.g. cooking, landscaping, painting and maintenance). This places limits on growth in personal development, opportunities for status improvement, learning about leadership and learning the responsibilities of being an employee. It also creates demands on staff to develop surrogate tasks.
6. In a CBTC, breaking a rule—such as the theft of another resident's personal property—is regarded as a constructive opportunity to teach the offender the consequences of his or her act. In PBTCs, the security staff may require a rule break to be reported for adjudication and possible criminal action. Hence, in prison, this kind of event is likely to be seen negatively and bring punishment (albeit there is learning from consequences). In the community-based facility, however, it is more likely to be seen as an opportunity for personal and *community* growth.
7. In this same regard, the PBTC staff are compelled to report the offence, and failure to do so would negatively affect the programme's reputation in the facility and could bring the force of the institutional administration down on the programme. In the CBTC, the offence would be brought to the resident group. Residents would participate together with staff in an encounter or a group meeting where the incident would be discussed and appropriate consequences be assigned, such as loss of job status.
8. Another distinction is the restricted range of rewards and incentives that a PBTC can use compared with a CBTC. The absence of a variety of housing, work and clothing options in prison inhibits the number and variety of positive sanctions that can be used as incentives and rewards for positive growth during treatment.
9. Prison-based TCs have lower dropout rates, averaging around 50% within a year, compared to 70–90% in CBTCs.

Milieu therapy (MT) also involves the use of the *community* in the human change process. MT differs from the TC in the following ways: MT typically is more permissive, less structured, democratic rather than hierarchically organized, uses less confrontational methods and rather than promoting recovering ex-addicts or ex-offenders employs more professionally trained staff and especially trained correction officers. The group techniques used in MT overlap to a degree, but the TC involves more role-rehearsal, i.e. "acting as if", and more direct confrontation for rule breaches and failure to progress, while the MT more frequently emphasizes the use of traditional group counselling and psychotherapy, i.e. psychodrama, as well as individual psychotherapeutic methods. Further, their perspectives on human change differ in that the TC typically proceeds to create change by re-socializing the residents from "infancy" to "adulthood" as it were, and focuses on "content", while the MT utilizes the "community" to support the process of introspective self-examination, moral suasion and developing accountability towards authority and the collective group, and focuses more on group interpersonal processes. In our investigation we included programmes coded as Holistic Milieu Therapy (HMT) and Other Milieu Therapy (OMT) in this category.

HYPOTHESIS INVESTIGATION

For CDATE analyses of these two modalities (as with all the modalities) a three-phase approach was used. In Phase I, we tested all hypotheses regarding these two modalities that had been formulated prior to analyses of our data. Many of these were straightforward: research hypotheses that each specific type of programme would have a successful impact on recidivism. After seeing the results of Phase I, some new hypotheses (generally refinements of Phase I hypotheses but introducing predicted moderator variables) were formulated and tested as Phase II hypotheses. After seeing the results from our Phase II test, all subsequent analyses were considered to be exploratory data analysis rather than rigorous hypothesis testing, and these were labelled Phase III analyses.

THE HYPOTHESES

Phase I: A. Conditional upon a clientele of at least 18 years of age, and conditional upon isolation from the general population of offenders, therapeutic community or milieu therapy interventions are more effective than comparison group interventions (generally reported as "treatment as usual") at reducing recidivism.
1. Standard, modified and correctional therapeutic community interventions are more effective than comparison group interventions at reducing recidivism.
2. Social therapy interventions are more effective than comparison group interventions at reducing recidivism.

Phase II
1. A greater total dosage of treatment (e.g. measured in months of treatment in the programme), such as that experienced by programmes at the 75th percentile of dosage, is associated with a more successful effect on the outcome variable than that observed in programmes with a much lower total dosage of treatment, such as that at the 25th percentile of dosage.

Methods

The Research Design: Meta-analysis

Glass, McGaw and Smith (1981, p. 21) distinguish *primary analysis* (the original re-search study's statistical analysis of data), *secondary analysis* (a subsequent study's re-analysis of the data from the original study, usually with better statistical tech-niques or asking new questions of the original data), and *meta-analysis* (the statistical analysis of the summary findings of several independent research studies—a few investigators using these methods prefer the term "quantitative research synthe-sis" to "meta-analysis"). Although meta-analysis can integrate the findings of as few as two studies, it is an especially valuable method to use when there are many studies of essentially the same phenomenon, such as evaluating the effectiveness of a treatment programme. Some persons hold the misconception that meta-analysis combines fundamentally different kinds of studies ("apples and oranges") and/or mixes the poor quality studies with those of good quality. Rather, meta-analysis can (and should) be used in ways to eliminate irrelevant studies from the analysis beforehand and/or compensate in the analysis for important differences (using weights or "moderator variables") to take into account differences in the nature or quality of the individual studies. Discussions of meta-analysis and its place in science relative to narrative reviews of research literature can be found in many publications, i.e. DuMouchel (1994), Glass, McGaw and Smith (1981), Hunter and Schmidt (1990), Light and Pillemer (1984), Mullen (1989) and Rosenthal (1991). In meta-analysis,[3] the following tasks are undertaken:

- A research problem is formulated (e.g. Does intervention X have an appreciable positive effect on outcome variable Y?).
- An effort is made to search for and collect all the potentially relevant primary research studies.
- Fair, relevant criteria are applied to maximize the inclusion of relevant primary research studies and to minimize the inclusion of studies which are not truly relevant to the research problem formulated.
- One or more research hypotheses are formulated regarding each treatment modality (e.g. intervention X will have a significant positive effect on outcome variable Y).
- An effect size is computed for each comparison in the collection of primary research.
- Statistical methods are used to describe the distribution of effect sizes and make statistical inferences (e.g. whether the effects are significantly greater than zero).
- Statistical methods are used to ascertain the degree to which the relation between the independent and outcome variable depends on the values of another variable (e.g. strength of treatment, dosage, age of subjects), which is termed a *moderator variable*.

Searching for Primary Research Studies

Five search methods were used in searching for primary research studies: the first consisted of searching more than 24 electronic computerized bibliographic databases. The second consisted of screening bibliographies listed in books, articles, reports and dissertations. As the project compiled documents, the reference list at the end of *each* of the reports was canvassed for additional titles, e.g. all the citations listed in previous meta-analyses on correctional treatment and related topics were reviewed. These identified bibliographic citations of possible relevance to CDATE, and each of these was reviewed to identify other bibliographic citations, and so on. The third method involved a classic hand search of all issues of major journals. Within the CDATE inclusion time frame (1968–1996), hand searches were conducted on all issues of journals with potential relevant content, e.g. all criminological and correctional journals.

The fourth method involved examining the books and monographs available at several large libraries, chiefly the Lloyd Sealy Library of the John Jay College of Criminal Justice, the City University of New York, and the Criminal Justice/NCCD Collection at the Newhouse Center for Law and Justice at Rutgers University School of Criminal Justice Library in New Jersey. These library collections yielded many reports that did not exist elsewhere. For example, the Lloyd Sealy library has a particular collection with numerous unique evaluation studies of correctional treatment that Robert Martinson compiled in connection with a research project, but was not completed at the time of his death. These research reports are held in a locked "Special Collections" room at the College. All reports in that collection that met CDATE inclusion criteria were photocopied. In addition, the Principal Investigator's large personal collection of reports that were not included in the ECT was also screened.

The fifth search method, requesting documents from authors and organizations, included soliciting the leading researchers in the field. The existence of the CDATE project was publicized at all major criminological meetings in the United States and Europe, and requests for research reports were published in several major English-language journals. Announcements describing the project and requesting research documents were circulated in all major criminal justice newsletters. CDATE was also publicized and documents requested through "Usernet newsgroups" and mailing lists on the Internet. To discover research reports not written in English, colleagues were contacted in 14 non-English-speaking countries (including, for example, Korea, Thailand and Japan).

On the positive side, reports on 294 non-US studies have been coded in the CDATE project, including 97 from Canada, 64 from Great Britain, 31 from Germany, 22 from Spain and 19 from the Scandinavian countries, as well as scattered studies from other countries. Reports in German (and Dutch) were screened, coded and annotated by Rudolf Egg and his assistants in Germany; reports in the Nordic languages by Eckart Kühlhorn and Erik Grevholm in Sweden; and Spanish (and Italian and French) studies by Santiago Redondo, Vicente Garrido, Julio Sánchez-Meca and Fulgencio Marin-Martinez in Spain. CDATE also employed several foreign-language-speaking staff members who translated documents received from Latin America and Europe.

Relying on published studies alone would produce only a partial assessment of the current state of knowledge. Evaluation studies are not published for a variety of reasons: evaluators are often not encouraged to publish studies of unsuccessful programmes; and final reports—usually large, complex, equivocal and sensitive—do not lend themselves to distribution or translation to journal article form. In trying to locate specific unpublished research reports, numerous archival sources, government agencies and quasi-government organizations were contacted. Unfortunately, such efforts to obtain unpublished documents were occasionally unsuccessful. For example, through Internet connections to university and government libraries, we learnt of several unpublished research documents, but this information came too late for us to solicit copies of them. Thus, in the time span of this project, we obtained only about 92% of the unpublished evaluation research reports that were identified. Virtually all of those published in journals and books, however, were obtained. Nevertheless, through the intercession of numerous authors who were solicited, many valuable and unpublished research reports were added to the CDATE database. Hence, the results from journal articles and books may be compared with the results reported in dissertations and in unpublished research reports.

Criteria for Inclusion and Exclusion

CDATE *included* a study if:

- it used behavioural/social science research methods, *and*
- it examined the effect or impact of any credible treatment, rehabilitation or intervention programme, *and*
- its subjects were either adult or juvenile offenders in criminal justice custody (whether in a residential correctional facility or on probation or parole), *and*
- it used any credible outcome measures (including, but not restricted to, effects on drug use and recidivism), *and*
- it was either published or unpublished, *and*
- it was produced between 1 January 1968 and 31 December 1996.

CDATE, while comprehensive and detailed with respect to evaluation studies of correctional intervention, *excluded* studies for several specific reasons. A study was excluded if:

- it was incomplete at the time of the report (e.g. only a pilot study, with treatment or research methods not yet settled upon);
- it did not report outcome analyses comparing the treatment group with a control group or comparison group or (the weakest design included) with pre-test values of the treatment group;
- it did not state the size of group(s), i.e. no N stated;
- it did not report sampling procedures;
- it did not provide a sufficient description of intervention method or treatment, making it impossible to code;
- it only described the programme, and provided no outcome data;
- it only subjectively evaluated the programme, or only provided clinical speculation of outcomes or anecdotal data—i.e. no objective data were reported;
- it contained outcome measures that were too vague or invalid to be informative, e.g. "good social adjustment" or "got better", with no clear definition);
- it contained findings that were inextricably confounded by external factors;
- it was not in the 1968–1996 time frame (chosen because the earlier ECT study had covered 1945–67).[4]

A study was also excluded if it was NOT a *correctional* treatment programme. Only studies of treatment that were under the jurisdiction or ultimate control of the criminal justice system or the juvenile justice system were included. This includes the systems of police processing, courts, corrections, probation and parole. Studies of treatment of addicts, alcoholics, psychologically disturbed individuals and problem youth in schools, etc. were included only if they reported *separate* figures for persons in their sample who were under the jurisdiction of the criminal justice system or juvenile justice system while in the programme.

Measurement of Variables

For this treatment "nest",[5] CDATE coders identified programmes where persons in a residential setting attended scheduled meetings for group therapy while participating in a holistic "community" experience, carrying out roles oriented towards drug-free "right living" designed to further rehabilitation, and earned status or privileges by long-term good behaviour in therapy, work, recreation and other areas. Within this overall "nest" of TC/MT treatments, the specific types of programmes coded were:

- Standard TC (e.g. Synanon, Phoenix House, Daytop Village)
- Modified TC—i.e. prison-based (or work-release based), ex-offender led (e.g. Stay'n Out, Key-Crest, Amity at Donovan)
- Correctional TC—i.e. mainly correctional staff comprise programme staff (e.g. Cornerstone, Abraxas)
- Social therapy—i.e. the German system of residential milieu therapy which includes an eclectic mix of individual and group psychotherapeutic sessions, social skills training and, generally, educational and/or vocational training
- Other TC/MT treatments (e.g. New York's Correctional Substance Abuse Treatment (ASAT) and CASAT programmes; Great Britain's TC at HM Prison Grendon).

In the analyses presented here, programmes were considered to be of the relevant treatment type if that treatment was rated by CDATE coders as showing a significant difference between the experimental (E) and comparison (C) groups.

The dependent (outcome) variable—recidivism—in these studies consisted mainly of rearrest and/or reincarceration. In most cases the CDATE researchers had no choice but to accept the recidivism outcome variable stipulated in the study being annotated in whatever form it took. Very few studies included more than one recidivism outcome variable. Still the most practical definition of recidivism for correctional evaluation work is one based on arrest. When findings were adequately reported for both rearrest and reincarceration recidivism measures, the measure used in the CDATE meta-analysis was arrest. Arrest is procedurally and temporally closer to the crime event than is reincarceration[6] (Maltz, 1984, pp. 138ff).

CDATE coders had a 155-page codebook providing hundreds of variables to record relevant aspects of the primary research study available in all the report(s) on the primary research. For example, some of the variables included the research design used, other treatment components used, in addition to the main approach, the length of treatment in the programme, outcome measure(s) used, follow-up period in the community, analyses and statistics reported, and (for both the experimental group and the comparison group) subjects' characteristics, environment of the programme and staff characteristics).

Quality Control, Reliability and Validity

An estimate of coding reliability was generated on the basis of a selected subset of all available CDATE studies. In the standard coding procedure followed for all studies, documents were assigned to one individual coder for a full coding. Once a full, initial coding was produced, documents for a given study proceeded to a "quality controller" who reviewed the initial codings and documents. If necessary, changes were made to the initial codings by the quality controller, and reasons for the changes were discussed with the original coder. Importantly, only the final quality controlled codings for each study were included as observations in the CDATE dataset.

The studies selected for reliability analysis were quality controlled by the Project Director and the Senior Research Associate. For the reliability assessment, both of these quality controllers had the study documents and initial codings available to them, but each remained unaware of codings made by the other. The analysis of intercoder reliability was based on 30 pairwise comparisons for each variable coded. Once again, the rationale for estimating the intercoder reliability between the project's two quality controllers was based on the fact that the final database used for meta-analyses only included records that had undergone a thorough check by the quality controllers.

In the reliability assessment, in order to deal with the contingent nature of meta-analytic coding decisions identified by Yeaton and Wortman (1993), raters were provided with a minimal amount of verbal information directing them to the appropriate comparison and outcome. A subset of 30 comparisons was randomly selected for an assessment of intercoder reliability. Three types of reliability estimates are presented for key variables in the meta-analysis. For all variables, percentage of agreement between coders is reported. For categorical variables that produced a symmetric cross-tabulation, Cohen's *kappa* coefficient is reported. *Kappa* is an index of agreement which reflects "the best possible improvement over chance that is actually obtained by the raters" (Orwin, 1994, p. 148). For continuous, ordinal and dichotomous variables, *Pearson, Spearman,* or *phi* coefficients are reported.

Results of the reliability assessment are presented in Table 2.1. The percentage agreement for the variables presented ranged from 67 to 100. Percentage of exact agreement on calculated effect sizes was 83%, but also note that the *Pearson* coefficient estimate of effect size reliability, $r = 0.99$, indicates very high intercoder reliability on calculated effect sizes. Also, coders agreed on the specific type of outcome in 87% of the 30 comparisons. Reliability for other variables was also generally

Table 2.1 Reliability estimates

Variable	CDATE variable name	Percent agreement	Kappa	Pearson/ Spearman
Variables used to compute effect size				
Measure of central tendency	MCFU1A01	90.00	–	–
– Value for E	CFU1AE01	93.33	–	0.80
– Value for E	CFU1AC01	96.67	–	0.87
Measure of dispersion	MEAVRA01	86.67	0.72	–
– Value for E	VFU1AE01	96.67	1.00	1.00
– Value for E	VFU1AC01	96.67	1.00	1.00
Direction of E vs. C difference	DDFU1A01	93.33	0.86	–
Type of Stat. test	STAT1A01	90.00	–	–
– Value reported	TRFU1A01	90.00	–	0.99
Degrees of freedom	DFFU1A01	76.67	–	0.74
N of E group	NFU1A101	90.00	–	0.99
N of C group	NFU1A201	90.00	–	0.92
Exact probability	PRFU1A01	90.00	–	–
1 or 2 tailed test	TLFU1A01	93.33	–	–
Signif. level	SGFU1A01	83.33	0.76	0.64
Measure of Association	MRPT1A01	96.67	1.00	1.00
– Value reported	MRFU1A01	90.00	–	1.00
Treatment variables				
Most important treatment:				
– General Tx "nest"	EYCN101	87.00	–	–
– Specific, exact Tx code	EYCN101	70.00	–	–
Avg. length of Tx	ET1ALT01	86.67	–	0.99
– unit of time for that	ET1AUT01	86.67	–	–
Quality of study				
Rating of method	Res. Qual.	53.33	–	0.62
Published (or not)	PUBLIC	*	*	*

* A computed variable (using the bibliographic citation database) generated from the type of citation for the primary document used to code the study.

adequate. Moderate reliability coefficients were observed for location of treatment, assignment of subjects to conditions and percentage of African Americans in the sample. Very high reliability was observed for the date of publication, the age category of the sample, the length of treatment in days and the total sample size. The agreement on the general type of correctional treatment/intervention (the 20 "treatment nests") was 87%.

High reliability was found for the length of treatment in days and the total sample size. The percentage agreement on the *exact* type of treatment coded as the most important specific type of correctional treatment/intervention (e.g. both agreeing on standard TC) was 70%. The reliability for the rating of the overall quality of research methods used in the study was adequate: the agreement was 53.33% and the Pearson coefficient *r* was 0.62.

The publication status variable, published, was not produced by individual coders but was a computed variable. The bibliographic citation database we used,

ProCite™, uses different "workforms" for different types of citations (e.g. books, articles, dissertation, conference papers, reports). A computer program was written to identify workforms designating books, journal articles and chapters in books, and to count the studies containing at least one of these as having a 'published report'. The remaining studies—i.e. those only with workforms designating unpublished dissertations, conference papers and reports—were identified as "unpublished".

Effect size computations were made on the basis of information available in primary research reports. Two potential problems in a meta-analysis are the miscalculation of effect sizes and the lack of information in a primary research document required to compute effect sizes. The first problem was handled by starting with equations for computing Pearson's r from information such as cross-tabulations, chi-square values, F-statistics, t-statistics, etc. (Rosenthal, 1991), then entering the equations in a computer program to compute effect sizes automatically from the best and most reliable information available in a primary document. The program, developed using SPSS 6.0.1 for Windows, underwent several tests and refinements. When effect sizes could not be calculated, this was because the reports from the primary research study did not present the requisite statistics to permit calculation of an effect size.

To avoid confusion in interpretation, the following convention was used. An effect size with a positive sign indicates that the treatment group outcome was more desirable than the control or comparison group outcome (e.g. lower percentages of offenders rearrested in the treatment group compared with the "treatment-as-usual" group, but higher percentages of offenders successfully completing their terms of parole). Conversely, an effect size with a negative sign indicates that the treatment group outcome was less desirable than the control or comparison group outcome.

Methods of Statistical Analysis

Independence of Comparisons in these Analyses

The vast majority of the studies in this body of research literature, report only independent comparisons in which a particular experimental group is analytically compared with just one comparison group. This is fortunate because there are important statistical problems to grapple with when one experimental group is analytically compared with more than one comparison group in a study, or when one comparison group is compared with more than one experimental group. For example, if a study used two experimental groups, E1 and E2, and two comparison groups, C1 and C2, and reported analytical comparisons among all combinations, E1 vs. C1, E1 vs. C2, E2 vs. C1, and E2 vs. C2, the four comparisons are *not* really independent of one another. In the analyses reported in this chapter we selected only a subset composed of independent comparisons, say for example, E1 vs. C1 and E2 vs. C2. When we refer to independent comparisons in this chapter, this is what we mean. In making such selections we tried to pick the fairest, most pertinent comparison group relative to each particular experimental group. We also concentrated on comparisons that the treatment group would naturally be expected to surpass—that is, groups receiving only treatment as usual or treatment thought to be irrelevant to the outcome variable under focus.[7]

Effect Size Estimates

The two most common measures of the size of the effect that an intervention has are Pearson's correlation coefficient r (including its variations such as the phi coefficient) and Hedges' g. Fortunately, there are formulas that allow transformation from one metric to the other. We use r as the effect size, in part because it is widely known and thus easily interpretable. To deal with departures from normality, however, meta-analysts prefer to carry out certain statistical operations on the Fisher's Z_r transformation. Following that advice, r is first transformed to Z_r before performing the statistical computations; after obtaining the results, the transformation is reversed to display the results in terms of r itself (Rosenthal, 1994).

Using a Random-Effects Model

The primary method used in the CDATE meta-analyses was random-effects, inverse-variance weighted multiple regression. Because effect size estimates were expected to be more reliable if they were based on larger primary research samples (Hedges & Olkin, 1983, 1985), studies were weighted according to the number of subjects used to test a given hypothesis. According to Raudenbush (1994, p. 302), in any research synthesis "a long list of *possible* moderators of effect size can be enumerated, many of which cannot be ascertained by the most careful reading of each study's report". This is an accurate characterization of research on correctional-based interventions/treatments. A random-effects analysis of effect sizes assumes that there are at least two important sources of effect size variance—sampling error and "estimation variance"—and the random-effects model assumes variation in *true* effect sizes; that is, a distribution of effect sizes. This source of variance in the random-effects model is variously referred to as "population variance", "the variance component", or "between-studies variance". Once an estimate of the variance component, the between-studies variance, is derived by the random-effects model, this source of variance is literally added to the variance due to sampling error ('the within studies variance'). A random-effects model "permits generalization to other studies from the same population from which the retrieved studies were sampled" (Rosenthal, 1995, p. 187).

A second consideration is the statistical significance and size of the variance components. When between-studies variance components are large and statistically significant (in other words, when the studies are heterogeneous rather than homogeneous) and when explanatory moderators cannot be identified, the random-effects analysis is preferable.[8] Because of these considerations, CDATE's primary approach to the meta-analyses was random-effects, inverse-variance weighted multiple regression (Bryk & Raudenbush, 1992, pp. 155–174), using HLM software (Bryk,

Raudenbush & Congdon, 1996), generally supplemented with graphical displays and occasionally with exploratory data analysis techniques.

FINDINGS

In the broad area of therapeutic community and milieu treatment, 42 studies met our criteria and yielded an effect size for the recidivism outcome. Before conducting the analyses, we decided to restrict the hypothesis tests to comparisons in which an experimental programme was compared with a no treatment or treatment-as-usual group. This would avoid the confusion created by comparing one good experimental treatment against another yielding a zero effect size which would mistakenly give the impression that neither had an effect when they might actually both have positive effects of about equal magnitude. Thus, a few of the studies of TC/MT were not included since they did not have a "no treatment" or "treatment-as-usual" group, but only included alternative treatments as comparison groups. Also, a number of TC/MT programme "evaluations" were excluded because the only available comparison group consisted of treatment failures (i.e. dropouts). *In our judgement, studies that compare only the "successes" in the experimental programme, with only "failures" in the comparison group, have such serious problems of selection bias that the overall quality of the research methods is too poor to merit inclusion in the analyses.*

A summary of the studies reviewed for possible inclusion in the meta-analyses is presented in Appendix 1 and the studies themselves are listed in Appendix 2. As *background* for the subsequent meta-analyses, Figure 2.1 shows a correlation

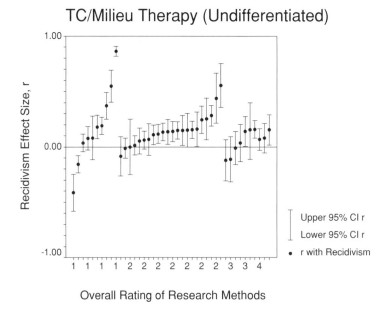

Figure 2.1   Therapeutic Community/Milieu Therapy, undifferentiated ($k = 42$)

Table 2.2 Therapeutic Community/Milieu Therapy (adults only)

No. of studies, k	35
Total N, Windsorized	10881
Weighted mean of r	0.141
Upper 95% CI of r	0.217
Lower 95% CI of r	0.064
1-Tailed probability	0.0004
Homogeneity indicators	0
Method rating beta	−0.114
Verification level	1

coefficient, r, effect size with recidivism as the outcome variable for all 42 studies of TC/MT (undifferentiated by specific treatment type). Each r is plotted in the middle of a vertical bar representing the 95% confidence interval for that r. The studies are sorted by the overall rating of the quality of the research methods used in the study (1 = poor, 2 = fair, 3 = good, 4 = excellent) and, within that rating, by the favourableness of the outcome. Notice that only three studies (those on the far right of the graph) were rated as having *excellent* research methods.

Following our *a priori* expectations, only programmes for adults were included in the Phase I hypothesis tests. Of 42 potential studies, seven that were not programmes for adults were excluded, leaving 35 studies for the Phase I hypothesis tests. The studies of juveniles were later examined in the Phase III exploratory data analysis. Our hypothesis in respect of the first set of analyses is presented below.

Phase I: A. *Conditional upon a clientele of at least 18 years of age, and conditional upon isolation from the general population of offenders, therapeutic community or milieu therapy interventions are more effective than comparison group interventions at reducing recidivism.*

A "ballot box" tabulation shows that 86% of the 35 studies found positive effects associated with TC/MT treatment. Table 2.2 shows an r effect size with recidivism as the outcome variable for all 35 studies of TC/MT (undifferentiated by specific treatment type) which met our Phase I testing criteria. Here again, each r is plotted; each can be found in the middle of a vertical bar representing the 95% confidence interval for that r, and the studies are sorted by the overall rating of the research methods used in the study and, within that rating, by the propitiousness of the outcome.

Key statistical findings from the meta-analyses were as follows. As stated, our primary effect size estimator is the Pearson correlation coefficient, r. However, to compensate for complications which arise as the population value of r gets further and further from zero, we used Fisher's Z transformation of r, that is Z_r (Rosenthal, 1991, pp. 21–22). The inverse-variance weighted mean Fisher's Z_r for these 35 studies was 0.142 which translates to a Pearson correlation coefficient of $r = 0.141$. A t-test was computed for the null hypothesis that the overall mean of the effect sizes is zero. For these studies, the null hypothesis can be rejected, $t(34) = 3.688$, $p < 0.001$. There is an indication of a research methods artifact, however, since the beta coefficient for the overall method rating was −0.114. Because the possible method artifact makes the results somewhat questionable, we assign to this hypothesis a verification rating of 1 indicating a grey area between $0 =$ disconfirmed and $2 =$ confirmed.

Phase I: A.1. *Standard, modified, and correctional therapeutic community interventions are more effective than comparison group interventions at reducing recidivism.*

For the 16 TC studies within this category, the null hypothesis can be rejected, $t(15) = 2.52$, $p = 0.012$. However, the beta coefficient for the overall method rating was -0.157. Because the possible method artifact makes these results questionable also, we assign a verification rating of 1 here as well.

One issue to address is whether the set of effect sizes is homogeneous (desirable for clear, simple interpretation) or heterogeneous (suggesting that different kinds of phenomena are intermixed in the set of observed effect sizes). There are three conventionally used indicators that we used to assess the homogeneity.

First, we examined the homogeneity of the effect sizes by decomposing the total variance into that part which is due to sampling error (the within-studies variance) and a second part due to variation in the true effect size parameters (the between-studies variance), designated tau^2 (tau-squared). A between-studies variance[9] approaching zero is an indicator of the homogeneity of the effect sizes. As the tau^2 departs from zero, the less homogeneous are the effect sizes, implying inconsistency or heterogeneity in the effect sizes. The estimated between-studies variance for therapeutic community programmes, tau^2, is 0.0873, not sufficiently close to zero to be considered homogeneous.

Second, when the percentage of the total variance attributable to sampling error is large (e.g., over 75%), the effect sizes may be considered homogeneous. For these TC and MT programmes, only 11.67% of the total variance was due to sampling error, indicating they are not homogeneous.

Third, the Q test for homogeneity for these studies was statistically significant, $Q(15) = 271.37$, $p < 0.001$, leading us to reject the hypothesis of homogeneity and infer that there is heterogeneity in this set of effect sizes. An inspection of the data suggested that one study (CDATE study ID 7121-3-1, a study of the Amity Incorporated Therapeutic Community), had an effect size which was strikingly different from the others.[10] Once this result is set aside, the remaining studies of TC treatment appear far more consistent in the graph, although still heterogeneous in terms of the available statistical measures of homogeneity (e.g. Q (15) $81.55 = p <$ 0.001). Results for these 15 TC studies are presented in Table 2.3 which provides summary statistics for the findings graphed in Figure 2.2.

The weighted effect size r for these 15 studies is reduced by the elimination of the extremely high Amity Incorporated study from 0.188 to 0.117. There is a conversion relationship, the Binomial Effect Size Display (BESD), which provides some indication of the practical importance of the effect size (Rosenthal, 1991, pp. 132–136). A BESD relates a Pearson correlation coefficient, r, to a percentage differential between the E and C group, using 50% as a mid-point anchor. For example, the weighted mean correlation of $r = 0.117$ can be thought of as the E group being 11.7 percentage points better (or more effective) than the C group, using 50% as a mid-point anchor. Thus, the BESD would be: 55.85%[11] successes in the E group versus 44.15% successes in C. (As a check, 55.85% $-44.14\% = 11.7\%$.)

Table 2.3   Therapeutic Community without Amity

No. of studies, k	15
Total N, Windsorized	6343
Weighted mean of r	0.117
Upper 95% CI of r	0.179
Lower 95% CI of r	0.054
1-Tailed probability	0.001
Homogeneity indicators	0
Method rating beta	0.043
Verification level	2

Introduced as a potential moderator variable, the quality of research methods used in these studies showed a positive correlation with the effect sizes ($r = 0.043$), although not statistically significant ($p = 0.188$), so there is no obvious research method artifact at work. If an E group had about 55.85% who were not rearrested and a fair comparison group had about 44.14% not rearrested, most policy-makers would consider that difference to be of practical significance.

When significant variation in effect sizes is observed, as in the case of TC and MT programmes, there are at least two strategies available for explaining or reducing that variation. One method categorizes the available studies a second time into coherent subcategories which are no longer heterogeneous. A second method employs multiple regression techniques to explain the variance in terms of moderators of effectiveness. Actually, the Phase I hypotheses used in this study already capture two subcategories thought to be important: Standard, modified, and correctional therapeutic community interventions on the one hand, and German Social Therapy

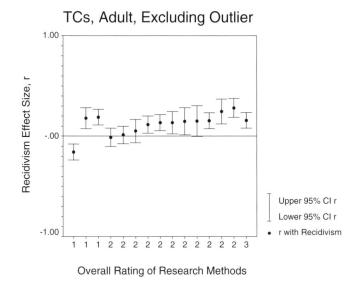

Figure 2.2   Therapeutic Communities ($k = 15$)

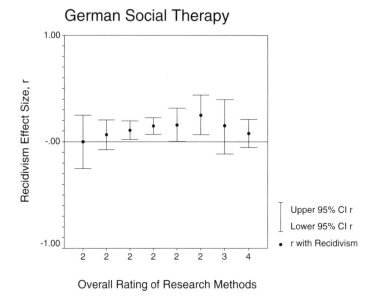

Figure 2.3   German Social Therapy ($k = 8$)

studies on the other. The I.A.1 hypothesis refers to German Social Therapy studies that were conducted in the social therapeutic institutions in Germany.

Phase I: A.2. *Social therapy interventions are more effective than comparison group interventions at reducing recidivism.*

Eight studies of what has been referred to as "social therapy", all conducted in the former Federal Republic of Germany, had a mean recidivism effect size of Fisher's $Z_r = 0.127$ ($r = 0.126$). The null hypothesis that the mean effect size for these programmes is zero can be rejected, $t(7) = 5.267$, $p < 0.001$. Also, the effects reported over these studies appear to be homogeneous, $Q(7) = 4.46$, $p = 0.500$. Essentially, all of the variance could be attributed to sampling error alone since the estimated variance component was effectively zero ($tau^2 = 0.00002$). However, six of the eight studies reporting on social therapy received a research method quality rating of 2 (denoting "fair, limited confidence"). Only one of the studies used methods we rated $4 =$ excellent ($r = 0.08$), and one study was rated $3 =$ good ($r = 0.15$). Findings from these studies are shown in Figure 2.3 with summary statistics in Table 2.4.

These German Social Therapy programmes underwent considerable change since their conception in the early 1970s. First, they changed from classical psychoanalysis to a heterogeneous mix of whatever works, including behaviour modification, cognitive-behavioural approaches, client-centred therapy, communication and systems therapy. Although psychotherapeutic methods continue today, they are no longer the centre-piece of treatment. Work in housing groups, social-educational measures (e.g. social training courses) as well as social surroundings (family and work) have gained in importance. Lösel and Egg (1997) refer to them

Table 2.4 German Social Therapy

No. of studies, k	8
Total N, Windsorized	1767
Weighted mean of r	0.126
Upper 95% CI of r	0.182
Lower 95% CI of r	0.070
1-Tailed probability	0.001
Homogeneity indicators	3
Method rating beta	*2*
Verification level	2

as "heterogeneous ... eclectic ... not always oriented toward the empirical knowledge [now available]". Second, their staffing changed from medical psychotherapists to a combination of psychologists, special educators and social workers. The therapists determine the specific programme according to their special competencies, knowledge and attitudes. "A uniform and systematic concept of the social-therapeutic institution does not exist" (Lösel & Egg, 1997). Third, their clientele focus changed from a planned emphasis on recidivists with serious personality disorders such as dangerous sexual offenders, young adult (especially crime prone) offenders and criminally non-responsible offenders to "quite heterogeneous" clientele in terms of both formal admission criteria (e.g. age, offence type, sentence remaining) as well as motivational and other personality criteria.

Lösel and Egg (1997) assert there is no common assessment scheme. Various schemes apply: DSM-IV, ICD-10, and differing assessments of antisocial personality. Also, there was wide scope among institutions regarding admission and rejection of prisoners and dropouts. Fourth, their management orientation changed from medical physician management (to ensure dominance of therapeutic orientation in decision-making) to psychologists, special educators or lawyers (the latter predominate in normal prisons). Social-therapeutic prisons, however, do have more social scientists in senior management positions.

The original concepts of social therapy in the German penal system emphasized that they must be independent institutions separated from the rest of the penal system. In this way they could guarantee that restrictive regulations would not hinder treatment. Prison law also permits the development of social-therapeutic departments in normal prisons. In recent times, this option has been chosen more often, and this change makes possible testing special therapeutic approaches or the treatment of special offender groups without having to set up totally new institutions. Hence it allows more flexibility and reduces problems of selection and dropout. "The social-therapeutic prison is one of those rare cases in Germany in which the plan was to base crime policy directly on empirical research" (Lösel & Egg, 1997). Unfortunately this was never quite realized. It should also be noted that there are only 832 inmates in ST prisons in Germany out of a total prison population exceeding 20000 (Lösel & Egg, 1997).

Another CDATE hypothesis was framed in Phase II: *A greater total dosage of treatment (e.g. measured in days of treatment in the programme), such as that experienced by TC*

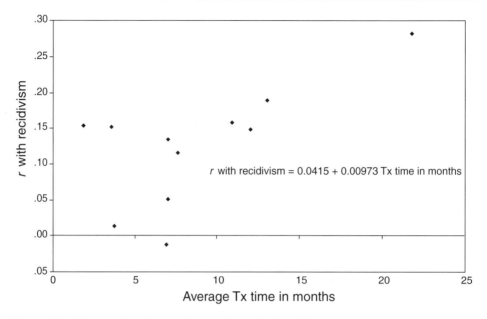

Figure 2.4 Therapeutic Community studies only ($k = 11$)

programmes at the 75th percentile of dosage, is associated with a more successful effect on the outcome variable than that observed in programmes with a much lower total dosage of treatment, such as that at the 25th percentile of dosage.

Using HLM software, random-effects, inverse-variance weighted multiple regression analyses were conducted to investigate the relationship between average time in treatment in TC programmes and the effect size, r, on recidivism. We continued to exclude the outlier Study 7121-3-, and four other studies did not report time in treatment information, leaving 11 studies on which to investigate this hypothesis. We found that additional months in treatment were indeed significantly related to recidivism effect sizes: beta $= 0.010335$, std. error $= 0.003886$, $t(9) = 2.660$, $p = 0.026$. Furthermore, the standardized regression coefficient for time in treatment remained virtually unchanged and still statistically significant when the overall rating of research methods was included as a covariate (beta $= 0.010299$, std. error $= 0.004159$, $t(8) = 2.476$, $p = 0.038$.

The guideline for the hypothesis of a treatment dosage difference from was from the 25th to the 75th percentile. This is approximately from 5 to 11 months for the 11 TC studies that reported the average time in treatment for the E subjects. Based on the simple unweighted linear regression equation in Figure 2.4 (i.e., r with recidivism $= 0.0415 + 0.00973 \times$ treatment time in months), the results show an increase from 5 months ($r = 0.09$) to 11 months ($r = 0.15$), an improvement in r of $+0.06$.[12]

Overall, it seems fair to say that there is a significant time in treatment effect upon the favourableness of recidivism outcomes.[13]

We now turn to our Phase III exploratory data analyses. The 11 studies in the residual set of "holistic milieu therapy and other TC/Milieu" did not reach the

Table 2.5   Holistic/other

No. of studies, k	11
Total N, Windsorized	2649
Weighted mean of r	0.088
Upper 95% CI of r	0.196
Lower 95% CI of r	−0.023
1-Tailed probability	0.053
Homogeneity indicators	0
Method rating beta	−0.066
Verification level	1

0.05 level of statistical significance, and the negative method rating beta of −0.066 suggests the possibility of at least a slight research method artifact. Findings are shown in Table 2.5.

As seen in Table 2.6 the studies of juveniles did not reach the 0.05 level of statistical significance. However, since there were only seven of these studies available, since the weighted mean r was appreciable (0.147), and since there was no evidence of research method artifact, we consider MT for juveniles well worth further research.

In addition to time in treatment, other potential moderator variables were also investigated to attempt to explain the variation in effect sizes. In the overall, undifferentiated TC/MT collection (42 studies), there is a negative correlation ($r = -0.185$) between *publication status* and successful recidivism outcome (i.e. published studies yield *lower* effect sizes), but not statistically significant ($p = 0.241$). This is contrary to our expectation that studies with statistically significant, larger "results" would be more likely to get published. Also, there is a negative correlation ($r = -0.191$) between the overall rating of the research methods used in the study and successful recidivism outcome (i.e. the studies employing stronger evaluation designs yield lower effect sizes), but it too is not statistically significant ($p = 0.226$). Although these patterns are not statistically significant at conventional alpha levels, the magnitude and sign of each of these moderator effects justify attention in future work.

Table 2.6   Therapeutic Community/Milieu Therapy (juveniles only)

No. of studies, k	7
Total N, Windsorized	1353
Weighted mean of r	0.147
Upper 95% CI of r	0.445
Lower 95% CI of r	−0.181
1-Tailed probability	0.158
Homogeneity indicators	0
Method rating beta	−0.01
Verification level	1

DISCUSSION

What were the main findings and how much confidence do we have in them? From this meta-analysis on the efficacy of therapeutic community (TC) and milieu therapy (MT) treatment of offenders in the criminal justice system, it can be concluded that these treatments are generally associated with moderate effect sizes for recidivism outcomes. The efficacy of standard, modified and correctional TC treatment is consistent and sizeable. Our meta-analyses indicated that these TC/MT programmes for adult offenders, taken overall as a quite heterogeneous collection (Hypothesis I: 1), *do* show significant positive effects at reducing recidivism, averaging $r = 0.141$, as do the apparently more homogeneous treatment subsets, therapeutic communities, $r = 0.117$ (Hypotheses I.1a and I.1b) and German Social Therapy $r = 0.126$ (Hypothesis I.2). All three hypotheses were specified in advance of our organizing and analysing the data. In particular, the evidence for the two refined hypotheses (just TCs and just Social Therapy) leads us to be confident that these treatments do in fact work consistently better than their "treatment as usual" comparison groups.

The smallest of the r values for these hypotheses is 0.117. This would be equivalent to 55.85% successes in the E group versus 44.15% successes in C. On the other hand, if an E group reliably had about 55.85% who were not rearrested and a fair treatment-as-usual comparison group had about 44.15% not rearrested, most policy-makers would consider that difference to be of practical significance, indicating that the treatment intervention was working somewhat better than the usual treatment. The eight studies of "German Social Therapy", all conducted at various prisons in the FRG, had a mean recidivism effect size of 0.13 (i.e. $r = 0.126$, $p < 0.001$). This translates for these eight studies to an equivalent difference of 56.50% successes among those receiving the "social therapy" treatment in comparison with 43.50% successes achieved by those in no-treatment control groups. From the standpoint of correctional-based treatments, this meta-analytic result is of practical interest for most policy-makers, and the effects reported over these studies appear quite homogeneous (despite the heterogeneity in the programmes themselves). The research method quality of six studies, however, was rated as 2, equal to only "fair, of limited confidence". The effect of the "good" study was r = 0.15, and that of the study using "excellent" methods was r = 0.08.

However, there are weaknesses to be noted in this body of research evidence. First, for the overall (and most heterogeneous) set of TC/MT programmes there does appear to be a pattern of the studies with better quality research methods showing lower effect sizes, although the correlation with the *Research Quality* variable did not reach the level of statistical significance for these 42 studies. Second, although the 16 TC-only studies had the most impressive average effect size ($r = 0.188$), when the outlier TC study which relied on poor-quality methods was removed, the average r fell to 0.117. On the other hand, with that outlier removed, the remaining 15 studies had a *positive* correlation ($r = 0.236$) with effect size, i.e. on the average, the *better quality studies showed more favourable effect sizes*. Third, because neither the combined set of TC/MT studies nor the set of TC-only studies satisfied statistical criteria of homogeneity, the confidence intervals may understate the amount of variability which should actually be expected to occur. It would be prudent to expect that the effects of new (but similar) treatment programmes would vary in effectiveness over a broader interval, with more than 5% doing poorer than the lower confidence limit presented here and more than 5% doing better than the upper confidence limits.

Another CDATE hypothesis framed in Phase II (after some of the analyses had begun) was supported: a greater number of months of treatment is associated with more successful outcomes. This finding remained virtually unchanged and was still statistically significant when the overall Quality Rating of research methods was included as a covariate, even in this small subset of studies ($k = 11$, df $= 8$). Based on the regression equation, the results show an increase in time in treatment from 5 months ($r = 0.09$) to 11 months ($r = 0.15$) yielding an improvement in effect size of $+0.06$. In other words, in BESD terms, the linear trend–fit to the data indicates approximately a 6% differential in recidivism success rates associated with increased time in treatment from 5 months to 11 months. However, as mentioned, one study with an average of over 21 months of treatment appears to be a particularly influential data point raising the regression slope coefficient. To gauge the sensitivity of these results, we re-analysed the data with this study recoded to the values of the study with the next longest time in treatment (13 months), but the results were approximately the same. Our assessment is that this hypothesis too has been supported by these data, but the effects are more variable and more modest than we expected.

The variability of effects is a reminder that there is heterogeneity remaining in these studies. We examined the three more specific subsets of treatment within this TC set. However, the modified TC set ($k = 10$) and the correctional TC set ($k = 5$) did not differ from each other in terms of recidivism patterns. (There is only one study using a standard TC.)

When outcomes of short-term TC programmes (such as in-jail studies that last about 90 days) are compared with outcomes of longer TC programmes lasting for more than six months, the differences are negligible. It must be noted, however, that this lack of difference is likely to be contingent on the continuation of TC treatment in the community following release from incarceration or detention, all other things (such as quality of care, integrity of treatment) being equal. In other words, length of treatment in a TC should be measured from onset in the penal institution, through the transition to community-based TC treatment, to discharge from the community-based TC. Thus, if an individual stays only three months in a PBTC, and 18 months in a CBTC following release, it may be equivalent *in effect* to a stay of nine months in the PBTC followed by 12 months in a CBTC. This line of research, that is, measuring the effects of systematic variations in TC setting, duration and sequence on outcomes still remains to be undertaken.

There is no question from a clinical standpoint that it takes considerable time to change people who have spent years in an active predatory drug-using lifestyle to become responsible, drug-free, honest and socially functional persons. Moreover, from a clinical standpoint, treatment in the prison-based therapeutic community works when it successfully creates a social and psychological environment conducive to bringing someone to recovery. The aims of TC treatment in this respect are to change the negative patterns of behaviour, thinking, and feeling to develop a responsible drug-free lifestyle. Stable recovery requires successfully integrating conduct, emotions, skills, attitudes and values. Thus, enduring change in lifestyle and a positive personal–social identity requires a holistic approach focusing on lifestyle rather than drug abuse, criminality or any one problem alone, and this takes time—clinical observation says in total about two years on the average. The process of human change during tenure in a prison-based TC, followed by continuing treatment in a community-based programme, may be seen as a passage through stages of incremental learning wherein change at each stage facilitates change at the next, each in turn reflecting movement towards recovery.

CONCLUSION

Challenged by the sweeping generalization that "no correctional interventions are truly effective", and profiting from work done in other meta-analyses over the past 30 years, the CDATE project has been engaged in compiling and reviewing evaluation research on many forms of correctional interventions. Based on the most comprehensive meta-analytic database in the domain of therapeutic communities and milieu therapy for adult offenders, our conclusion is that, on the average, therapeutic communities and milieu therapy *do significantly reduce recidivism.*

Recovery, however, depends on positive and negative pressures to change, and remaining in treatment requires continued motivation to change. As De Leon (1995, p. 1610) puts it,

> Treatment is not provided but made available to the individual in the TC environment, in its staff and peers, the daily regime of work, groups, meetings, seminars, and recreation. The effectiveness of these elements is dependent, however, upon the individual who must fully engage in the treatment regime. Self-help recovery means that the individual makes the main contribution to the change process . . . each individual in the process contributes to change in others, [with all elements] mediated by peers through confrontation and sharing in groups, by example as role models, and as supportive, encouraging friends in daily interactions.

Recovery in the social learning model used by contemporary TCs involves altering offenders' negative behavioural patterns, attitudes and dysfunctional roles that were learned in interaction with a dysfunctional family and with delinquent and criminal peers. Thus, recovery depends on learning by doing and participating as a community member in a variety of socially responsible roles. This change is acquired by acting these roles, and through training to avoid anger or other triggering emotions. Changes in lifestyle and identity are gradually learned through participating in various roles in the community, supported by the other community members similarly engaged in the learning process and a trained, experienced and highly supportive staff of recovered ex-substance-abusing offenders, and professionals. It is clear from the research that the process only begins in the prison and, to be genuinely and lastingly effective, it must continue in the community. Although the history of therapeutic communities in prison is relatively short, there are now explicit theoretical underpinnings for guiding the development of this modality, but an insufficient number of well-trained recovering persons to staff them.

Addiction treatment is a critical component of the US war on drugs, and the incarceration of persons found guilty of various crimes who are also chronic substance abusers presents a propitious opportunity for treatment. It is propitious because these persons would be unlikely to seek treatment on their own, are extremely likely to continue their drug use and criminality after release without treatment and there are now cost-effective technologies to effectively treat them while in custody. This judgement comes with guarded optimism regarding the system's generalized ability to effectively treat persons normally deemed by conventional wisdom to be "very high risk" (namely, chronic heroin and cocaine users with extensive predatory criminal histories). Competent evaluations of intervention efforts in several states and in countries with diverse populations show levels of success that are remarkably consistent. Substantial reductions in recidivism after treatment—reductions of sufficient size likely to yield a tangible improvement in the quality of life—emerge from studies from these diverse settings. Still, this evidence needs further replication and dissemination to convince the sceptical public, legislatures and policy-makers that high rate addict-felons can be effectively and cost-efficiently helped.

What should policy-makers and practitioners take from these findings? One thing they should *not* do is assume that one kind of TC/MT intervention is as good as another and choose any programme in the area to use as their model: *some* of the programmes in our database showed just about zero effects. Another thing they should *not* do is assume that the programme reporting the highest effect size in our database is the one to use as a model for their own programme. First, some of the studies used poorer quality research methods, so large effect sizes in those studies should be taken with several "grains of salt". Second, the meta-analytic approach focuses on the idea that there generally are many *random factors* operating, so even among studies with better research methods, the programme showing the largest effect size in this collection of studies may not necessarily be the best when the programme models are replicated over and over again in many different sites. Policy-makers and practitioners should try to learn from all of the programmes that had correlation effect sizes above 0.05 in this database. With this information they can adapt the common programme elements from those good programmes that best fit their own programming needs.

Gender and race were not introduced as moderator variables in this meta-analysis because the included studies were not designed to investigate possible effects of gender or race on programme effectiveness. Few of the reports on the evaluations of these TC/MT programmes disaggregated recidivism results by gender or by race.[14] More primary research in this area is obviously needed. More generally, we are beginning to learn "what works" in TC/MT interventions. More primary research studies are required, however, to get at the specific programme elements which are needed, how to improve those elements, how those elements should be integrated and what types of clients profit best from what programmes.

NOTES

1. Meta-analysis is a statistical method for integrating the results of multiple studies (the number of studies which can be included in a meta-analysis is unlimited). Properly used, meta-analysis avoids the subjective biases typically found in conventional narrative reviews of research literature, and it also avoids the statistical errors involved in simply pooling data from different studies (DuMouchel, 1994).

2. This is sometimes termed a "ballot box" analysis.
3. Some good general sources in this field of statistics are Cooper and Hedges (1994), Hedges and Olkin (1985), Hunter and Schmidt (1990), Rosenthal (1991).
4. Some apparent exceptions to this time criterion were made for studies that produced interim findings in the 1968–96 time frame that were annotated, but produced a final report or publication in 1997. The latter were then included.
5. We have established the following treatment categories or "nests". *Full physical custody*, e.g. imprisonment, boot camp. *Partial physical custody*, e.g. work release, halfway house. *Economic Sanctions*, e.g. fines, restitution. *Community supervision*, e.g. electronic monitoring, intensive supervision. *Drug/alcohol treatment methods*, e.g. relapse prevention, substance abuse counselling, methadone maintenance, other chemotherapy. *Therapeutic community* (TC), e.g. standard TC (e.g. Phoenix House, Daytop Village); modified TC (e.g. Stay'n Out, KEY-Crest); correctional TC (e.g. Cornerstone). Milieu therapy, e.g. Grendon TC; German Social Therapy. *Educational methods*, e.g. Literacy training, College courses. *Vocational skills development methods*, e.g. Specific vocational skills (e.g. auto repair course), job seeking. *Standard behaviour modification/social learning*, e.g. aversive conditioning, training in anger management. *Other skills training*, e.g. cognitive skills, problem-solving, moral–ethical training. *Variant techniques in behaviour modification*, e.g. biofeedback training, transcendental meditation. *Scheduled individual psychotherapy*, e.g. psychoanalytic therapy, transactional analysis, reality therapy. *Scheduled group counselling*, e.g. group psychotherapy, T-groups, family therapy, guided group interaction. *Case management and casework*, e.g. Social work models. *Document-focused therapy*, e.g. bibliotherapy. *Experiential challenge programming*, e.g. Outward Bound, ROPES course. *Incentive programmes*, e.g. contingency contracting, token economy. *Alternative medical approaches*, e.g. acupuncture, plastic surgery, chemical castration. *Self-help group efforts*, e.g. Alcoholics Anonymous, other 12-Step programmes.
6. Criminologists generally conclude that in the aggregate, rearrest is the most reliably reported measure of recidivism. Although some individuals are innocent of the crime charged, using only reconviction or reincarceration would understate the true recidivism rates because, of those who reoffend, not all are arrested, prosecuted, go to trial or become incarcerated. On the average, in a one year follow up study for each of those who are reincarcerated, 2.11 are rearrested and 1.24 are reconvicted. In a two year follow up, for each of those who are reincarcerated, 1.66 are rearrested and 1.17 are reconvicted. In a three year follow up, for each of those who are reincarcerated, 1.51 are rearrested and 1.13 are reconvicted (Beck & Shipley, 1989, p. 2).
7. A related point is that we use only designed comparisons (if adequate information is reported for the designed comparison) rather than moving to after-the-fact comparisons of other categories, such as disaggregating into high risk vs. low risk subgroups, *if that contrast was not part of the study design*. We think the main approach should be to analyse in conformity with the research design. The exceptions were generally cases where the information on a designed comparison would not yield an effect size, but disaggregated findings would yield an effect size (results broken down by age, sex or race, for example). In such cases we did turn to after-the-fact comparisons.
8. However, DuMouchel (1994) has pointed out that failing to reject the hypothesis of effect size homogeneity is not the same thing as proving that homogeneity is present (p. 4). Therefore, even in cases where the Q test for effect size heterogeneity is not statistically significant, a random-effects model is still defensible, particularly when the power of the Q test is small.
9. Instead of using the term *between-studies variance* some authors use the term the *population variance* or simply the *variance component*.
10. This very large effect size was based on an evaluation design that was qualitatively different from the designs used in the remaining studies. The Amity Incorporated programme was evaluated by means of a one-group pre-test/post-test design (i.e. the offenders recidivism after treatment was compared with levels of recidivism before treatment began).
11. We are using multiple digits in these numbers not as an indication of measurement accuracy, but just to illustrate the BESD calculation.

12. The results using inverse-variance weighted regression estimates are almost identical.
13. Note that one study (ID 716701), reporting an average of over 21 months of treatment, appeared to be a particularly influential data point that might be raising the regression slope coefficient inordinately. To assess the relationship with this study treated as no more influential than the others, the study was re-coded to the next highest time in treatment (about 13 months). The unweighted regression coefficient did not change very much: r with recidivism $= 0.0394 + 0.01098 \times$ treatment time in months.
14. Two exceptions in this set of studies are Study IDs 2116 and 4405, which did disaggregate by gender.

REFERENCES

Andrews, D. A. (1983) The assessment of outcome in correctional samples. In M. L. Lambert, E. R. Christensen & S. S. DeJulio (Eds.) *The Measurement of Psychotherapy Outcome in Research and Evaluation*. New York, NY: Wiley.

Andrews, D. A., Zinger, I., Hoge, R. D., Bonta, J., Gendreau, P. & Cullen, F. T. (1990) Does correctional treatment work? A clinically relevant and psychologically informed meta-analysis, *Criminology, 28* (3), 369–404.

Anglin, M. D. & Hser, Y. (1990) Treatment of drug abuse. In M. Tonry & J. Q. Wilson (Eds.) *Drugs and Crime* (pp. 393–460). Chicago, IL: University of Chicago Press.

Anglin, M. D., Farabee, D. & Prendergast, M. (1998) *The Role of Coercion in Offender Drug Treatment*. A Report to the Physician Leadership on National Drug Policy, 30 September 1998.

Antonowicz, D. H. & Ross, R. R. (1994) Essential components of successful rehabilitation programs for offenders. *International Journal of Offender Therapy and Comparative Criminology, 38*, 97–104.

Baekeland, F. & Lundwall, L. (1975) Dropping out of treatment: A critical review. *Psychological Bulletin, 82* (5), 738–783.

Bailey, W. C. (1966) Correctional outcome: An evaluation of 100 reports. *Journal of Criminal Law, Criminology and Police Sciences, 57* (2), 153–160.

Basta, J. M. & Davidson, W. S. (1988) Treatment of juvenile offenders: Study outcomes since 1980. *Behavioral Sciences and the Law, 6*, 355–384.

Beck, A. J. & Shipley, B. E. (1989) *Recidivism of Prisoners Released in 1983*. Bureau of Justice Statistics. Special Report. Washington, DC: US Department of Justice, April 1989 (rev. 2/19/97).

Belenko, S., Foster, S., Kurzweil, B., Liu, H., Peugh, J. & Usdansky, M. (1998) *Behind Bars: Substance Abuse and America's Prison Population*. New York, NY: The National Center on Addiction and Substance Abuse at Columbia University.

Bonta, J., Law, M. & Hanson, K. (1998) The prediction of criminal and violent recidivism among mentally disordered offenders: A meta-analysis. *Psychological Bulletin, 123* (2), 123–142.

Box, S. & Hale, C. (1985) Unemployment, imprisonment and prison overcrowding. *Contemporary Crises, 9*, 209–228.

Brody, S. R. (1976) *The Effectiveness of Sentencing: A Review of the Literature*. Home Office Research Report No.35. London: Her Majesty's Stationery Office.

Brown, B. S. (1992) Program models. In C. G. Leukefeld & F. M. Tims (Eds.) *Drug Abuse Treatment in Prisons and Jails* (pp. 31–37). Washington, DC: US Government Printing Office.

Bryk, A. S. & Raudenbush, S. W. (1992) *Hierarchical Linear Models: Applications and Data Analysis Methods*. Newbury Park, CA: Sage Publications, Inc.

Bryk, A. S., Raudenbush, S. W. & Congdon, R. T. Jr. (1996) *Hierarchical Linear and Nonlinear Modeling with HLM/2L and HLM/3L Programs*. Lincolnwood, IL: Scientific Software International.

Campbell, D. T. & Stanley, J. C. (1963) *Experimental and Quasi-experimental Designs for Research*. Boston, MA: Houghton Mifflin.

Collins, J. J. & Allison, M. A. (1983) Legal coercion and retention in drug abuse treatment, *Hospital and Community Psychiatry, 34* (12), 1145–1149.

Cooper, H. & Hedges, L. V. (Eds.) (1994) *The Handbook of Research Synthesis*. New York, NY: Russell Sage Foundation.

Cullen, F. & Gendreau, P. (1989) The effectiveness of correctional rehabilitation. In L. Goodstein & D. L. MacKenzie (Eds.) *The American Prison: Issues in Research Policy*. New York, NY: Plenum.

Currie, E. (1989) Confronting crime: Looking toward the 21st century. *Justice Quarterly, 6*, 5–23.

De Leon, G. (1994) Therapeutic communities. In M. Galanter & H. Kleber (Eds.) *The American Psychiatric Press Textbook of Substance Abuse Treatment*. Chicago, IL: American Psychiatric Press.

De Leon, G. (1995) Therapeutic communities for addictions: A theoretical framework. *International Journal of the Addictions, 30*, 1603–1645.

De Leon, G. (1991) Retention in drug free therapeutic communities. In R. W. Pickens, C. G. Leukefeld & C. R. Schuster (Eds.) *Improving Drug Abuse Treatment*, NIDA Research Monograph No. 106, DHHS Publication No. (ADM) 91–1754. Washington, DC: US Government Printing Office.

DeLone, M. (1990) *Labor market marginality and imprisonment: An assessment of empirical evidence*. Presented at 1990 annual meetings of the American Society of Criminology.

Dickover, R., Maynard, V. & Painter, J.(1971) *The Employer of the Vocational Trainee*. California Department of Corrections. Report No. 40, 89–100.

Duguid, S. (1981) Rehabilitation through education: A Canadian model. *Journal of Offender Counseling, Services and Rehabilitation. 6* (1/2), 53–67.

DuMouchel, W. (1994) *Hierarchical Bayes Linear Models for Meta-analysis*. Research Triangle Park, NC: National Institute of Statistical Sciences.

Farrington, D. P. (1983) Randomized experiments on crime and justice. In N. Morris & M. Tonry (Eds.) *Crime and Justice: A Review of Research* (Vol. 7, pp. 257–308). Chicago, IL: University of Chicago Press.

Field, G. (1989) A study of the effects of intensive treatment on reducing the criminal recidivism of addicted offenders. *Federal Probation, 53* (10), 51–56.

Garrett, C. J. (1985) Effects of residential treatment of adjudicated delinquents. A meta-analysis. *Journal of Research in Crime and Delinquency, 22*, 287–308.

Geismar, L. L. & Wood, K. M. (1985) *Family and Delinquency: Resocializing the Young Offender*. New York, NY: Human Sciences Press.

Gendreau, P., Little, T. & Goggin, C. (1996) A meta-analysis of the predictors of adult offender recidivism: What works! *Criminology, 34* (4), 575–608.

Gendreau, P. & Ross, R. R. (1979) Effective correctional treatment: Bibliography for cynics.*Crime and Delinquency, 25* (4), 463–489.

Gendreau, P. & Ross, R. R. (1981) Correctional potency: Treatment and deterrence on trial. In R. Roesch & R. Corrado (Eds.) *Evaluation Research and Policy in Criminal Justice*. Beverly Hills, CA: Sage Publications, Inc.

Gendreau, P. & Ross, R. R. (1984) Correctional treatment. Some recommendations for successful intervention. *Juvenile and Family Court Journal, 34* (Winter), 31–39.

Gendreau, P. & Ross, R. R. (1987) Revivification of rehabilitation: Evidence from the 1980s. *Justice Quarterly, 4* (3), 349–407.

Gensheimer, L. K., Mayer, J. P., Gottschalk, R. & Davidson, W.S. II (1986) Diverting youth from the juvenile justice system: A meta-analysis of intervention efficacy. In S. J. Apter & A. P. Goldstein (Eds.) *Youth Violence*. New York, NY: Pergamon Press.

Gerber, J. & Fritsh, E. J. (1993) *Prison Education and Offender Behavior: A Review of the Scientific Literature*. TX: Sam Houston State University.

Gerstein, D. R. & Harwood, H. (Eds.) (1992) *Treating Drug Problems* (Vol. 2, pp. 89–132). National Academy of Sciences, Institute of Medicine. Washington, DC: National Academy Press.

Glass, G. V., McGaw, B. & Smith, M. L. (1981) *Meta-analysis in Social Research*. Beverly Hills, CA: Sage.

Gottshalk, R., Davidson, W. S. II, Mayer, J. & Gensheimer, L. K. (1987a) Behavioral approaches with juvenile offenders: A meta-analysis of long-term treatment efficacy. In E. K. Morris & C. J. Braukmann (Eds.) *Behavioral Approaches to Crime and Delinquency: A Handbook of Application, Research and Concepts* (pp. 399–422). New York, NY: Plenum Press.

Gottschalk, R., Davidson, W. S. II, Gensheimer, L. K. & Mayer, J. P. (1987b) Community-based Interventions. In H. C. Quay (Ed.) *Handbook of Juvenile Delinquency.* New York, NY: Wiley & Sons.

Greenberg, P. F. (1977) The correctional effects of corrections: A survey of evaluations. In D. F. Greenberg (Ed.) *Corrections and Punishment* (pp. 111–148). Beverly Hills, CA: Sage.

Greenwood, P. W. & Zimring, F. E. (1985) *One More Chance: The Pursuit of Promising Intervention Strategies for Chronic Juvenile Offenders.* Santa Monica, CA: Rand.

Hamm, M. S. & Schrink, J. L. (1989) The conditions of effective implementation: A guide to accomplishing rehabilitative objectives in corrections. *Criminal Justice and Behavior, 16* (2), 166–182.

Hedges, L.V. & Olkin, I. (1983) Regression models in research synthesis. *American Statistician, 37,* 137–140.

Hedges, L. V. and Olkin, I. (1985) *Statistical Methods for Meta-analysis.* Boston, MA: Academic Press.

Hubbard, R. L., Marsden, M. E., Rachel, J. V., Cavanaugh, E. R. & Ginzburg, H. M. (1989) *Drug Abuse Treatment: A National Study of Effectiveness.* Chapel Hill, NC: University of North Carolina Press.

Hunter, J. E. & Schmidt, F. L. (1990) *Methods of Meta-analysis: Correcting Error and Bias Research Findings.* Newbury Park, CA: Sage Publications, Inc.

Izzo, R. L. & Ross, R. R. (1990) Meta-analysis of rehabilitation programs for juvenile delinquents. *Criminal Justice and Behavior, 17,* 134–142.

Kirby, B. C. (1954) Measuring effects of treatment of criminals and delinquents. *Sociology and Social Research, 38,* 368–374.

Lab, S. P. & Whitehead, J. T. (1988) An analysis of juvenile correctional treatment. *Crime and Delinquency, 34,* 60–83.

Lab, S. P. & Whitehead, J. T. (1990) From "nothing works" to "the appropriate works": The latest stop on the search for the secular grail. *Criminology, 28* (3), 405–418.

Leukefeld, C. G. & Tims, F. M. (1988) *Compulsory Treatment of Drug Abuse: Research and Clinical Practice.* National Institute on Drug Abuse Research Monograph 86. Washington, DC: US Government Printing Office.

Leukefeld, C. G. & Tims, F. M. (1990) Areas of Agreement. NIDA Technical Review Meeting, May 1990. *Drug Abuse Treatment in Prisons and Jails,* Draft Report, 6/90.

Light, R. J. & Pillemer, D. B. (1984) *Summing up: The Science of Reviewing Research.* Cambridge, MA: Harvard University Press.

Lipsey, M. W. (1989) *The efficacy of intervention for juvenile delinquency: Results from 400 studies.* Paper presented at the 41st annual meeting of the American Society of Criminology, Reno, Nevada.

Lipsey, M. W. (1991) Juvenile delinquency treatment: A meta-analytic inquiry into the variability of effects. *Meta-analysis for Explanation: A Casebook.* New York, NY: Russell Sage Foundation.

Lipsey, M. W. (1992) Juvenile delinquency treatment: A meta-analytic inquiry into the variability of effects. In T. D. Cook, H. Cooper, D. S. Cordray, H. Hartmann, L. V. Hedges, R. J. Light, T. A. Louis & F. Mosteller (Eds.) *Meta-analysis for Explanation: A Casebook* (pp. 83–127). New York, NY: Russell Sage.

Lipton, D. S. (1989) *The prevention of recidivism: A manifesto regarding the role of rehabilitation for drug-abusing offenders.* Presented at the 1989 annual meeting of the Academy of Criminal Justice Sciences.

Lipton, D. S. (1990) *Principles of successful correctional intervention.* Presented at the BJA (Bureau of Justice Assistance) State Justice Institute Regional Seminar: Drugs and the Judicial Response, Washington, DC, 26–27 January.

Lipton, D. S., Martinson, R. & Wilks, J. (1975) *The Effectiveness of Correctional Treatment.* New York, NY: Praeger Publishers.

Lipton, D. S. (1995) *The Effectiveness of Treatment for Drug Abusers under Criminal Justice Supervision* (NIJ Research Report). Washington, DC: US Department of Justice.

Logan, C. H. (1972) Evaluation research in crime and delinquency: A reappraisal. *Journal of Criminal Law, Criminology and Police Science, 63* (3), 378–387.

Lösel, F., Koferl, P. & Weber, F. (1987) *Meta-evaluation of Social Therapy*. Stuttgart: Ferdinand Enke Verlag.

Lösel, F. & Koferl, P. (1989) Evaluation research on correctional treatment in West Germany: A meta-analysis. In H. Wegener, F. Lösel & J. Haisch (Eds.) *Criminal Behavior and the Justice System: Psychological Perspectives*. New York, NY: Springer.

Lösel, F. (1993) The effectiveness of treatment in institutional and community settings. *Criminal Behaviour and Mental Health 3* (4), 416–437.

Lösel, F. and Egg, R. (1997) Social Therapeutic Institutions in Germany: Description and Evaluation. In E. Cullen, L. Jones & R. Woodward (Eds.) *Therapeutic Communities for Offenders* (pp 181–203). Chichester: John Wiley & Sons Ltd.

McGuire, J. & Priestley, P. (1993) *Offending Behavior: Skills and Stratagems for Going Straight*. London: Batsford.

McGuire, J. (Ed.) (1995) *What Works: Reducing re–offending*. Chichester: Wiley

Maltz, M. D. (1984) *Recidivism*. Orlando, FL: Academic Press, Inc.

Martin, S. E., Sechrest, L. B. & Redner, R. (Eds.) (1981) *New Directions in the Rehabilitation of Criminal Offenders*. Washington, DC: National Academy Press.

Martinson, R. (1974) What works? Questions and answers about prison reform. *The Public Interest, 35*, 22–45.

Martinson, R. (1979) New findings, new views: A note of caution regarding sentencing reform. *Hofstra Law Review 7*, 243–258.

Mayer, J. P., Gensheimer, L. K., Davidson, W. S. & Gottschalk, R. (1986) Social learning treatment within juvenile justice: A meta-analysis of impact in the natural environment. In S. J. Apter & A. Goldstein (Eds.) *Youth Violence: Programs and Prospects*. Elmsford, NY: Pergamon Press.

Mullen, B. (1989) *Advanced BASIC Meta-analysis*. Hillsdale, NJ: Lawrence Erlbaum Associates.

Murray, D. W. (1992) Drug abuse treatment programs in the Federal Bureau of Prisons: Initiatives for the 90's. In C. G. Leukefeld & F. M. Tims (Eds.) *Drug Abuse Treatment in Prisons and Jails*. NIDA Research Monograph No. 118 (pp. 62–83). Washington DC: US Government Printing Office.

Orwin, R. G. (1994) Evaluating coding decisions. In H. Cooper & L. V. Hedges (Eds.) *The Handbook of Research Synthesis*. New York, NY: Russell Sage Foundation.

Palmer,T. (1974) The youth authority's community project. *Federal Probation,* March, 9–14.

Palmer, T. (1975) Martinson revisited. *Journal of Research in Crime and Delinquency 12*, 133–152.

Palmer, T. (1986) The effectiveness issue today: An overview. In K. C. Haas & G. P. Alpert (Eds.) *The Dilemmas of Punishment*. Prospect Heights, IL: Waveland.

Peters, R. & May, B. (1992) Drug treatment services in jails. In C. G. Leukefeld & F. M. Tims (Eds.) *Drug Abuse Treatment in Prisons and Jails* (pp. 38–50). Washington, DC: US Government Printing Office.

Pillemer, D. & Light, R. (1980) Synthesizing outcomes: How to use research evidence from many studies. *Harvard Educational Review, 50*, 176–195.

Prendergast, M. L., Hser, Y. I., Chen, J. & Hsieh, J. (1992) *Drug treatment need among offender populations*. Presented at the 1992 Annual Meeting of the American Society of Criminology, New Orleans LA, 4–7 November.

Raudenbush, S. W. (1994) Random effects models. In H. Cooper & L. V. Hedges (Eds.) *The Handbook of Research Synthesis* (pp. 301–321). New York, NY: Russell Sage Foundation.

Redondo, S., Garrido, V. & Sanchez-Meca, J. (1996) *Is the treatment of offenders effective in Europe? The results of a meta-analysis*. Presented at the 1996 Annual Meeting of the American Society of Criminology, Chicago, IL, 20–23 November.

Reuter, P. (1992) *Hawks Ascendant: The Punitive Trend of American Drug Policy*. Santa Monica, CA: Rand.

Roberts, A. R. & Camasso, M. J. (1991) The effect of juvenile offender treatment programs on recidivism: A meta-analysis of 46 studies. *Notre Dame Journal of Law, Ethics and Public Policy, 5*, 421–441.

Rosenbaum, D. P. (1988) Community crime prevention: A review and synthesis of the literature. *Justice Quarterly, 5* (3), 323–395.

Rosenthal, R. (1991) *Meta-analytic Procedures for Research.* Newbury Park, CA: Sage Publications, Inc.

Rosenthal, R. (1994) Parametric measures of effect size. In H. Cooper & L. V. Hedges (Eds.) *The Handbook of Research Synthesis.* New York, NY: Russell Sage Foundation.

Rosenthal, R. (1995) Writing meta-analytic reviews. *Psychological Bulletin 118,* 183–192.

Ross, R., Antonowicz, D. & Dhaliwal, G. (1995) Going *Straight: Effective Delinquency Prevention and Offender Rehabilitation.* Ottawa: Air Training & Pub.

Ross, R. R. & Fabiano, E. (1985) *A Time to Think: A Cognitive Model of Delinquency Prevention and Offender Rehabilitation.* Johnson City, TE: Institute of Social Sciences and Arts.

Sherman, L. W. (1988) Randomized experiments in criminal sanctions. In H. S. Bloom, D. S. Cordray & R. J. Light (Eds.) *Lessons from Selected Program and Policy Areas* (pp. 85–98). San Francisco, CA: Jossey-Bass.

Sherman, L., Gottfredson, D., MacKenzie, D., Eck, J., Reuter, P. & Bushway, S. (1997) *Preventing Crime: What Works, What Doesn't, What's Promising.* Report to Congress by the University of Maryland, Department of Criminology and Criminal Justice, for the National Institute of Justice.

Simpson, D. D. & Knight, K. (1998) *Correctional Treatment in Community Settings.* Report to the Physician Leadership on National Drug Policy on Addiction & Health Care in the Criminal Justice System, 12 October 1998.

Spector, P. E. (1981) *Research Designs.* Beverly Hills, CA: Sage.

Tims, F. M. & Ludford, J. P. (1984)*Drug Abuse Treatment Evaluation: Strategies, Progress and Prospects.* National Institute on Drug Abuse Research Monograph 51. DHHS No. (ADM) 84–1349, Washington, D.C: US Government Printing Office.

Tobler, N. (1986) Meta-analysis of 143 adolescent drug prevention programs: Quantitative outcome results of program participants compared to a control or comparison group. *Journal of Drug Issues, 16* (4), 537–565.

Tolan, P. & Guerra, N. (1994) *Effectiveness of violence prevention and treatment programs.* Paper presented at the 1994 Annual Meeting of the American Society of Criminology, Miami, Florida.

Van Voorhis, P. (1987) Correctional effectiveness: The high cost of ignoring success. *Federal Probation, 51* (March), 56–62.

Visher, C. A. (1987) Incapacitation and crime control: Does a "lock-em up" strategy reduce crime? *Justice Quarterly, 4,* 513–544.

Walker, S. (1989) *Sense and Nonsense About Crime: A Policy Guide.* Pacific Grove, CA: Brooks/Cole.

Weisburd, D., Sherman, L. & Petrosino, A. J. (1990) *Registry of Randomized Criminal Justice Experiments in Sanctions.* Rutgers University School of Criminal Justice, 15 Washington Street, Newark, NJ.

Wells-Parker, E., Bangert-Drowns, R., McMillen, R. & Williams, M. (1994) *A Meta-analysis of Remedial Interventions with DUI Offenders.* Social Science Research Center, Mississippi State University, 103 Research Park, PO Box 5287, Mississippi State, MS.

Wells-Parker, E. & Bangert-Drowns, R. (1990) Meta-analysis of research on DUI remedial interventions. *Alcohol, Drugs and Driving, 6* (3–4), 147–160.

Wexler, H. K., Falkin, G. P. & Lipton, D. S. (1990) Outcome evaluation of a prison therapeutic community for substance abuse treatment. *Criminal Justice and Behavior, 17* (1) 71–92.

Wexler, H. K., Falkin, G. P. & Lipton, D. S. (1988) *A Model Prison Rehabilitation Program: an Evaluation of the "Stay'n Out" Therapeutic Community.* Final Report to the National Institute on Drug Abuse. New York, NY: Narcotic and Drug Research, Inc.

Whitehead, J. T. & Lab, S. P. (1989) A meta-analysis of juvenile correctional treatment. *Journal of Research in Crime and Delinquency, 26,* 276–295.

Wilkinson, R. A. (1998) Plenary Address by the President of the American Correctional Association at the 1998 Winter Conference, Phoenix, AZ.

Yeaton, W. H. & P. M. Wortman (1993) On the reliability of meta-analytic reviews: The role of inter-coder agreement. *Evaluation Review 17,* 292–309.

	STDYID	J	ANL	Res. Qual	Published	Time	Modality code	Recidivism ES	No. of Subj.	Odds Ratio
Adult										
1	4455	0	1	1	0	–	2520	-0.16	726	0.42
2	7135	0	1	1	0	–	2590	0.04	5603	14.54
3	2456	0	1	1	1	–	2590	0.08	100	1.50
4	2188	0	1	1	1	–	2530	0.18	323	2.06
5	6414	0	1	1	1	13.00	2520	0.19	674	2.75
6	4397	0	1	1	0	–	2590	0.37	193	5.10
7	7121	3	1	1	0	4.00	2520	0.86	122	–
8	2424	1	1	2	1	–	2590	-0.08	122	0.70
9	4405	2	1	2	0	–	2530	-0.01	453	0.93
10	9007	0	8	2	1	–	2550	0.00	62	1.00
11	4405	3	1	2	0	–	2530	0.01	503	1.05
12	9009	0	1	2	1	–	2550	0.03	57	1.13
13	2116	2	1	2	1	–	2520	0.05	285	1.47
14	4415	0	1	2	1	–	2590	0.06	836	1.41
15	9012	0	1	2	1	–	2550	0.07	192	1.36
16	9006	0	1	2	1	–	2550	0.11	483	1.84
17	4405	1	1	2	0	–	2530	0.12	524	1.80
18	2116	1	1	2	1	–	2520	0.13	594	1.88
19	7078	0	1	2	1	12.00	2530	0.13	297	2.46
20	6131	0	1	2	1	6.00	2590	0.14	439	–
21	9013	0	1	2	1	–	2550	0.15	126	–
22	9005	0	1	2	1	–	2550	0.15	1014	2.46
23	8338	0	1	2	0	12.00	2520	0.15	206	1.95
24	4464	1	1	2	0	3.00	2520	0.15	159	1.93
25	7036	0	1	2	0	1.84	2520	0.15	647	–
26	9007	0	1	2	1	–	2550	0.16	150	2.01
27	2486	0	1	2	1	6.00	2520	0.24	223	3.73
28	9003	0	1	2	1	–	2550	0.25	97	3.31
29	7167	0	1	2	0	–	2510	0.28	376	3.54
30	7467	0	1	2	1	–	2590	0.44	50	6.07
31	2206	0	1	3	1	5.92	2590	-0.12	110	0.57
32	7001	1	1	3	1	–	2590	-0.11	92	0.52
33	3047	0	1	3	1	–	2590	0.03	137	1.18

34	7001	2	1	3	1	–	2590	0.14	206	1.73
35	4454	0	1	3	1	–	2520	0.16	715	1.92
N	35	35	35	35	35	9	35	35	35	31
Mean	5839.71	0.49	1.20	1.94	0.69	7.0843	2550.00	0.1296	482.74	2.3975
Median	6414.00	0.00	1.00	2.00	1.00	6.0000	2550.00	0.1348	223.00	1.8392
Min	2116	0	1	1	0	1.84	2510	−0.16	50	0.42
Max	9013	3	8	3	1	13.00	2590	0.86	5603	14.54
Std Dev.	2501.70	0.89	1.18	0.59	0.47	4.1941	29.80	0.1797	926.29	2.5883
Juveniles										
1	7540	0	1	1	0	–	2540	−0.41	96	0.18
2	8251	0	1	1	1	–	2540	0.08	340	1.46
3	6540	0	1	1	0	–	2540	0.55	92	–
4	6539	0	1	2	0	–	2540	0.56	48	–
5	14	0	1	3	1	–	2510	−0.01	173	0.96
6	1592	0	1	4	0	7.00	2590	0.07	404	1.45
7	1637	0	1	4	0	–	2590	0.15	200	2.91
N	7	7	7	7	7	1	7	7	7	5
Mean	4587.57	0.00	1.00	2.29	0.29	7.0000	2550.00	0.1397	193.29	1.3914
Median	6539.00	–	1.00	2.00	0.00	7.0000	2540.00	7.658E−02	173.00	1.4460
Min.	8251	0	1	1	0	7.00	2510	−0.41	48	0.18
Max.	8251	1	4	4	1	7.00	2590	0.56	404	2.91
Std Dev.	3375.26	0.00	0.00	1.38	0.49	–	29.44	0.3362	133.67	0.9963
Total — Total N	42	42	42	42	42	10	42	42	42	36
Mean	5631.02	0.40	1.17	2.00	0.62	7.0759	2550.00	0.1313	434.50	2.2577
Median	6476.50	0.00	1.00	2.00	1.00	6.0000	2545.00	0.1346	206.00	1.7655
Min	14	0	1	1	0	1.84	2510	−0.41	48	0.18
Max	9013	3	8	4	1	13.00	2590	0.86	5603	14.54
Std Dev.	2660.87	0.83	1.08	0.77	0.49	3.9543	29.38	0.2082	852.09	2.4454

Notes: Res. Qual. is the rating by the coders of the overall quality of the research methods used in the study (where 1 = poor, low level of confidence; 2 = fair, limited confidence; 3 = very good, moderate level of confidence; 4 = excellent, highest level of confidence).
Published: 1 = published in a book or article, 0 = not so published.
Time [Tx (Treatment)] is presented in months. An entry "N" designates "Information not recorded in the research report(s)".
EYCN101 is the specific type of TC/MT programme.
Recidivism: r is the Pearson correlation coefficient effect size of the treatment with recidivism.
N is the number of subjects (persons) in the E group plus the C group of the study. In the Phase I hypothesis tests, the number of participants was Windsorized at 600.
The corresponding variable names in the CDATE data base are EYCN1 = Specific Treatment; ET1ALT = Length of Treatment; OVRRAT = Rating of Methods; Public = Published.
[The published variable data are missing in the E group plus the C group in the CDATE data base. Public = Published.]
Odds Ratio designates the odds of a successful outcome in the E group relative to the odds of a successful outcome in the C group. An entry "N" designates "Cannot be computed from information in the research report(s)".

APPENDIX 2: 37 DOCUMENTS REPORTING THE 42 INDEPENDENT COMPARISONS INCLUDED IN THE META-ANALYSES

Allen-Hagen, B. & Anderson, L. B. (1975) *Youth Crime Control Project: A Final Report on an Experimental Alternative to Incarceration of Young Adult Offenders*. Washington, DC: Department of Corrections. **Study ID: 1592**.

Angliker, C. C. J., Cormier, B. M., Boulanger, P. & Malamud, B. (1973) A therapeutic community for persistent offenders: an evaluation and follow-up study on the first fifty cases. *Canadian Psychiatric Association Journal, 18*, 289–295. **Study ID: 2456.**

Auerbach, A. W. (1977) *The role of the therapeutic community street prison in the rehabilitation of youthful offenders*. Doctoral Dissertation, George Washington University. **Study ID: 1637.**

Clarke, R. V. G. & Cornish, D. B. (1978) The effectiveness of residential treatment for delinquents, in Hersov, L. A., Berger, M. & Shaffer, D. (Eds.) *Aggression and Anti-Social Behaviour in Childhood and Adolescence*. Oxford: Pergamon Press. **Study ID: 14**.

Dünkel, F. & Geng, B. (1993) Zur rückfälligkeit von karrieretätern nach unterschiedlichen strafvollugs- und entlassungsformen, in Kaiser, G. & Kury, H. (Eds.) *Kriminologie Forschung in den 90er Jarhen* pp. 193–257). Freiburg: Max-Planck-Institut für ausländisches und internationales Strafrecht. **Study ID: 9006.**

Dünkel, F. (1979) Sozialtherapeutische behandlung und rückfälligkeit in Berlin-Tegel. *Monatsschrift für Kriminologie und Strafrechtsreform, 62*, 322–337. **Study ID: 9005.**

Egg, R. (1990) Sozial-therapeutische maβnahmen und rückfälligkeit in einem längerfristigen vergleich. *Monatsschrift für Kriminologie und Strafrechtsreform, 73*, 358–368. **Study ID: 9003.**

Eisenberg, M. & Fabelo, T. (1996) Evaluation of the Texas correctional substance abuse treatment initiative: The impact of policy research. *Crime and Delinquency, 42*, 296–308. **Study ID: 6414.**

Field, G. (1985) The Cornerstone program: A client outcome study. *Federal Probation, 49*, 50–55. **Study ID: 2188**.

Field, G. (1996) *Evaluation of the Powder River and Turning Point Alcohol and Drug Treatment Programs*. Salem, OR: Department of Corrections. **Study ID: 4405**.

Fischer, M. & Geiger, B. (1996) Resocializing young offenders in the kibbutz. *International Journal of Offender Therapy and Comparative Criminology, 40*, 44–53. **Study ID: 7467**.

Glider, P., Mullen, R., Herbst, D., Davis, C. & Fleishman, B. (1995) *Substance Abuse Treatment in a Jail Setting: A Therapeutic Community Model*. Tucson, AZ: Amity Incorporated. **Study ID: 7121**.

Gunn, J., Robertson, G., Dell, S. & Way, C. (1978) *Psychiatric Aspects of Imprisonment*. London: Academic Press. **Study ID: 2424**.

Hanson, R. K., Steffy, R. A. & Gauthier, R. (1993) Long-term recidivism of child molesters. *Journal of Consulting and Clinical Psychology, 61*, 646–652. **Study ID: 3047.**

Hynes, C. J. & Powers, S. A. (1995) *Drug Treatment Alternative-to-Prison of the Kings County District Attorney:* Fifth Annual Report of Operations. Brooklyn, NY: Office of the District Attorney. **Study ID: 7167**.

Inciardi, J. A., Martin, S. S., Butzin, C. A., Hooper, R. M. & Harrison, L. D. (1997) An effective model of prison-based treatment for drug-involved offenders. *Journal of Drug Issues, 27*, 261–278. **Study ID: 2486.**

Knight, K., Simpson, D. D., Chatham, L. R., Camacho, L. M. & Cloud, M. (1995) *Prison-Based Treatment Assessment (PTA):* Final Report on 6-Month Follow-Up Study. Fort Worth, TX: Institute of Behavioral Research. **Study ID: 7078.**

Lamb, H. R. & Goertzel, V. (1974) Ellsworth house: a community alternative to jail. *American Journal of Psychiatry, 131*, 64–68. **Study ID: 2206.**

Lowe, L. (1991) *A Process Evaluation of the R. J. Donovan Correctional Facility Amity Righturn Substance Abuse Program*. Sacramento, CA: Department of Corrections. **Study ID: 8338.**

Marshall, P. (1997) *A Reconviction Study of HMP Grendon Therapeutic Community*. Research Findings Report No. 53. London, UK: Information and Research Group. **Study ID: 4415.**

McGlothlin, W. H., Anglin, M. D. & Wilson, B. D. (1977) *An Evaluation of the California Civil Addict Program*. Washington, DC: US Department of Health, Education, and Welfare. **Study ID: 6131.**

McCord, W. & Sanchez, J. (1983) The treatment of deviant children: A twenty-five year follow-up study. *Crime and Delinquency, 29*, 238–253. **Study ID: 8251.**

Moore, C. B. (1977) *Ego strength and behavior: A study of a residential treatment program for delinquent girls*. Doctoral Dissertation. Los Angeles: California School of Professional Psychology. **Study ID: 6540**.

New York State Department of Correctional Services. (1993) *Veterans' Program Follow-Up*. Albany, NY: Department of Correctional Services. **Study ID: 7135.**

Ortmann, R. (1995) Zum resozialisierungseffekt der sozialtherapie anhand einer experimentellen längsschnittstudie zu justizvollzugsanstalten des landes Nordrhein-Westfalen. In Müller-Dietz, H. & Walter, M. (Eds.) *Strafvollzug in den 90er Jahren—Perspektiven und Herausforderungen* (pp. 86–114). Pfaffenweiler: Centaurus-Verlagsgesellschaft. **Study ID: 9013**.

Osterman, E.-L. (1980) *Ego strength and delinquent behavior*. Doctoral Dissertation. Los Angeles: California School of Professional Psychology. **Study ID: 6539**.

Pease, S. E. & Love, C. T. (1996) *Evaluation of a prison-based therapeutic community for female substance abusers: Return to custody one year following release*. Presented at the *Annual Meeting of the American Society of Criminology*, Chicago, November 1996. **Study ID: 4397.**

Rasch, W. & Kühl, K.-P. (1978) Psychologische befunde und rückfälligkeit nach aufenthalt in der sozialtherapeutischen modellanstalt düren. *Bewährungshilfe—Fachzeitschrift für Bewährungs-, Gerichts- und Straffälligenhilfe, 25*, 44–57. **Study ID: 9009.**

Rehn, G. & Jürgensen, P. (1983) Rückfall nach sozialtherapie: wiederholung einer im jahr 1979 vorgelegten untersuchung. In Kerner, H.-J., Kury, H. & Sessar, K. (Eds.) *Deutsche Forschungen zur Kriminalitätsentstehung und Kriminalitätskontrolle* (Vol. 3, pp. 1910–1948). Köln: C. Heymanns. **Study ID: 9007**.

Rehn, G. (1979) Rückfall nach sozialtherapie: vergleichende untersuchung aus drei Hamburger justizvollzugsanstalten. *Monatsschrift für Kriminologie und Strafrechtsreform, 62*, 357–364. **Study ID: 9012**.

Rice, M. E., Harris, G. T. & Cormier, C. A. (1992) An evaluation of a maximum security therapeutic community for psychopaths and other mentally disordered offenders. *Law and Human Behavior, 16*, 399–412. **Study ID: 7001.**

Siegal, H. A., Wang, J. Falck, R. S., Rahman, A. M. & Carlson, R. G. (1997) *An Evaluation of Ohio's Prison-Based Therapeutic Community Treatment Programs for Substance Abusers*. Dayton, OH: Wright State University, School of Medicine. **Study ID: 4455.**

Taxman, F. S. & SPINNER, D. L. (1994) *Recidivism Reduction: The Jail Addiction Services (JAS) Demonstration Project in Montgomery County, Maryland*. College Park, MD: University of Maryland. **Study ID: 7036**.

Tunis, S., Austin, J., Morris, M., Hardyman, P. & Bolyard, M. (1996) *Evaluation of Drug Treatment in Local Corrections*. NCJ 159313. Washington, DC: National Institute of Justice. **Study ID: 4464.**

Tupker, H. E. & Prescott, M. (1970) *Two Types of Treatment Programs at the Iowa Training School for Boys: A Comparative Study of Resident Characteristics and Treatment Outcome*. No. RR1. Eldora, IA: Iowa Training School for Boys. **Study ID: 7540.**

Wexler, H. K., De Leon, G., Thomas, G., Kressel, D. & Peters, J. (1999) The Amity prison TC evaluation: reincarceration outcomes. *Criminal Justice and Behavior, 26* (2), 147–167. **Study ID: 4454.**

Wexler, H. K., Falkin, G. P., Lipton, D. S., Rosenblum, A. B. & Goodloe, L. (1988) *A Model Prison Rehabilitation Program: An Evaluation of the "Stay'n Out" Therapeutic Community*. New York, NY: Narcotic and Drug Research, Inc. **Study ID: 2116.**

Chapter 3

THE EFFECTIVENESS OF COGNITIVE-BEHAVIOURAL TREATMENT METHODS ON OFFENDER RECIDIVISM

Meta-analytic Outcomes from the CDATE Project

Douglas S. Lipton[1]; Frank S. Pearson[2]; Charles M. Cleland[2]; and Dorline Yee[2]

[1]*Lipton Consulting, 8 Appletree Lane, East Brunswick, NJ 08816, USA*
[2]*National Development and Research Institutes, New York, USA*

This chapter* reports the results of a major meta-analysis on the effectiveness of programmes providing cognitive-behavioural approaches in correctional settings (such as prisons and jails) in reducing recidivism. It is part of a comprehensive detailed review and meta-analysis of the evaluation research on the effectiveness of criminal justice-based rehabilitation programmes for offenders in any form of custody. The overall meta-analysis is of primary research reports collected as part of the Correctional Drug Abuse Treatment Effectiveness (CDATE) project, a project funded for four years by the National Institute on Drug Abuse. The general nature of this project and a number of key methodological considerations have been described in some detail in Chapter 2.

As outlined in that chapter, the expansion of illicit drug use and associated crime has brought numerous abusers of illicit drugs into correctional facilities with many others under community supervision; and the combined pressures have stretched treatment facility resources as never before. Fully 80% of incarcerated men and women, about 1.4 million inmates, are seriously involved with substance abuse, with approximately two out of every three persons arrested testing positive for some type of illegal drug (usually cocaine). These rates were highly stable during the 1990s (NIJ, Alcohol and Drug Abuse Monitoring Programme, 1998). Among

* This research described in this chapter was supported under grant number RO I DA08607 from the National Institute on Drug Abuse at the National Institutes of Health, US Department of Health and Human Services. Points of view in this document are those of the authors and do not necessarily reflect the official position of any government agency.

Offender Rehabilitation and Treatment: Effective Programmes and Policies to Reduce Re-offending. Edited by James McGuire.
© John Wiley & Sons, Ltd.

probationers, about seven out of ten have at some stage used illegal drugs, and about half of these had used in the month before their last offence (Bonczar, 1998).

It is thus no surprise that there is increased interest in applying alternatives to warehousing for reducing the re-offending behaviour of offenders. In 1995, however, only 17% of probationers (Bonczar, 1998) and 12% of prison inmates (Gilliard & Beck, 1998) received any form of treatment for their substance use. Hence, during the 1990s there has been an increased legislative and congressional focus on this expanding drug abuser population. This has led the legislatures in some states, and the US congress to enact legislation recognizing that placing drug offenders in custody presents an opportunity to apply effective drug abuse treatment to a generally unmotivated population that would, for the most part, otherwise remain untreated.

THE COGNITIVE AND BEHAVIOURAL APPROACHES

The CDATE study examined research studies evaluating the effects of programmes within 20 distinct treatment intervention categories. In this chapter we present the results of one of these categories of intervention, cognitive-behavioural approaches, on the outcome variable, recidivism. At the time of publication of *The Effectiveness of Correctional Treatment* (Lipton, Martinson & Wilks, 1975), this approach was only beginning to be clearly articulated. Methods subsumed under this general heading have emerged with positive results from a number of previous meta-analyses and other research reviews (Andrews et al., 1990a; Garrett, 1985; Gendreau, 1996; Gendreau & Ross, 1979, 1981, 1984, 1987; Gottschalk et al., 1987a, 1987b; Lipsey, 1992; Lipsey & Wilson, 1998; Lösel, 1993, 1995; Mayer et al., 1986; McGuire, 1995a; Redondo, Garrido & Sánchez-Meca, 1996; Roberts & Camasso, 1991; Sherman et al., 1997; and see Hollin, 2001).

As an approach to addressing recidivistic behaviour, "cognitive-behavioural" modification is based on social learning theory. It assumes that offenders are shaped by their environment and have failed to acquire certain cognitive skills or have learned inappropriate ways of behaving. Their thinking may be impulsive and egocentric and their attitudes, values and beliefs may support antisocial behaviour. Advocates of this approach believe that, by drawing on a range of well-established cognitive and behavioural techniques, offenders can be helped to face up to the consequences of their actions, to understand their motives, and to develop new ways of controlling their behaviour (Husband & Platt, 1993; McGuire, 2000). Cognitive-behavioural approaches are frequently used as part of a wider programme of work that includes problem-solving training, social skills training, and pro-social modelling with positive reinforcement of non-criminal behaviour or attitudes. Exponents argue that cognitive-behavioural programmes are increasingly being seen as offering the best chance of success in reducing recidivism since they address such a broad range of needs and problems.

While there is overlap across the cognitive and behavioural categories, there is sufficient distinction among them to warrant separation for meta-analytical purposes. McGuire (2000) has drawn a continuum between behavioural and cognitive methods that is informative to this discussion.

One end of McGuire's continuum of behavioural to cognitive methods (McGuire, 2000) consists of a group of techniques labelled "behaviourally-oriented" or radical behaviourism. These are based on a stimulus–response learning conceptualization of behaviour through classical and operant conditioning, and elaborated behaviour patterns through complex schedules of reinforcement. Such *behaviour modification* (BM) techniques involve *shaping* — the progressive alteration of responses by making changes in contingencies of reinforcement, i.e. the consequences for an organism of a response it has made. Stated another way, this technique attempts to secure change by altering external reinforcement contingencies. The range of these behavioural modification techniques include: positive and negative reinforcement; extinction, satiation, fading, punishment, response-cost, over-correction, time out, differential reinforcement, backward chaining, successive approximation, behavioural assignment, behavioural or contingency contracting. Two themes persist: eliminative approaches (for unwanted behaviours) and constructional approaches (for building new replacement behaviours).

Behaviour therapy (BT) is based on conditioned learning, and the removal or reduction of maladaptive habits and responses that have been acquired (learned). BT uses behavioural modification techniques, but also involves "work on the conditioned connections which have been established between external stimuli and internal emotional states [usually interpreted as disturbance in physiological arousal level, viz. anxiety, anger, depression, distress]". The range of these behaviour therapies is wide. They include relaxation training, systematic desensitization, exposure training, response prevention, flooding, covert sensitization, thought stopping, assertion training.

Social skills (SS) training almost constitutes a kind of therapy. It is not a therapeutic approach, but a combination of behaviour therapy approaches focused on one problem, i.e. lack of skills for dealing with social encounters. The latter manifests as social withdrawal and isolation on the one hand, to inappropriate and maladaptive social behaviour on the other. Most SS training programmes contain similar elements: instruction, modelling, role-play practice, behavioural rehearsal, imaginal rehearsal, feedback, and coaching. More complex therapeutic tactics, such as guided group discussion, interaction skills training—including negotiation and persuasion, assertion training and assertiveness training—are also taught. There is a large amount of evidence demonstrating the effectiveness of these methods for the increase or alteration of social interactive behaviours for many client groups, including offenders. However, "the results do not generalize to other even closely adjacent social situations or behaviour response-classes" (McGuire, 1996). One effect of this has been the incorporation of cognitive methods such as self-instruction and problem-solving skills with Social Skills to increase the range of applicability and size of effect.

Self-instructional (SI) training (Meichenbaum, 1977) involves work with clients to internalize self-statements to avoid or minimize the use of unwanted words, statements, feelings or behaviours; and to promote selected behaviours using coping self-statements. SI methods are variously used to control pain, increase confidence, improve performance, avoid bizarre speech, and to deal with obsessive-compulsive rituals, as well as anger, stress and anxiety. Anger Control Training and Stress Inoculation Training (Novaco, 1975) are examples of SI training. Thought

Stopping (McGuire, 2000) at the simplest level and Cognitive Restructuring (Bush 1995; Bush, Glick & Taymans, 1997) at the more complex level are also examples of SI training.

Self-efficacy and social support (SESS) is an intervention that emphasizes achieving self-directed change by not only giving reasons for altering risky behaviours, but also the behavioural means, resources and social supports to do so. In order to achieve success, however, a strong self-belief in one's efficacy to exercise personal control is necessary (Bandura, 1977, 1986, 1989). Personal efficacy is concerned with self-beliefs that people can exert control over their own motivation, thought processes, emotional states, and patterns of behaviour. This affects what they choose to do, how much effort they can mobilize, how long they persevere, whether they engage in self-destructive, debilitating or encouraging thought patterns, and the amount of stress, anxiety, or depression they experience in taxing situations. When people lack self-efficacy, they do not manage situations effectively even though they may know what to do and possess the requisite skills—their self-doubts override knowledge and self-protective behaviour. Little evidence supports its use with serious offender populations. A related therapeutic approach for addictive behaviour is known as *Motivational Interviewing* (Miller & Rollnick, 1992) which grew out of a technique for attempting to increase motivation to change among alcohol-dependent persons (Miller, 1983).

Problem-solving (PS) training is a form of therapy based on the finding that individuals who have many problems, and who act out or become ill as a result, often lack a repertoire of problem-solving skills for dealing with difficulties as they arise in everyday life (D'Zurilla & Goldfried, 1971). Platt and colleagues (1973, 1974) and later Spivack, Platt and Shure (1976)—see also Platt, Perry and Metzger. (1980)— elaborated the *Interpersonal Cognitive Problem-Solving* skills as follows: problem awareness, problem recognition, distinguishing facts from opinions, generating alternative solutions, means–end reasoning, consequential thinking, perspective taking, and social cause-and-effect thinking. They developed techniques and training exercises to impart the required skills for each of these in correctional and drug abuser treatment fields, as well as in school, health and mental health areas.

Multimodal Approaches

Drawing from this and other work, Ross and Fabiano (1985) incorporated these and other ingredients to create a programme of cognitive training for persistent offenders who were found in several Canadian studies to lack these skills as compared to non-offenders. Ross, Fabiano and Ewles' (1988) *Reasoning and Rehabilitation* (R&R) programme includes these components: problem-solving, self-control, self-monitoring of emotions, critical reasoning, empathy building (or perspective shifting), moral reasoning, and abstracting vs. concretizing. R&R also includes new interpersonal skills (how to negotiate rather than confront; how to persuade rather than manipulate; how to express complaints, how to make requests, how to ask for help), and anger control training. R&R appears to be a research-based carefully articulated and sequenced cognitive skills [or "cog skills"] training package of 36 sessions [plus booster sessions to sustain effects] specifically designed to be responsive to offenders' learning styles, literacy and interests (Porporino, 1998).

Rational-emotive therapy (RET), an approach developed by Ellis (1962), holds that a wide range of personal difficulties and disorders are caused by sets of negative, dysfunctional and/or maladaptive statements that individuals make to themselves concerning events in their lives (a widely held position in all cognitive therapies). However, Ellis holds that these in turn are a product of more deeply held, and often completely irrational, beliefs which distressed individuals rarely examine or question. The aim of RET is to unearth these distorted perceptions of events and disproportionate emotional reactions and modify them: to replace them with more rational and realistic sets of values and expectations. The RET technique uses Socratic discourse and direct questioning. Clients are asked to justify statements they have made by providing evidence for their statements under repeated and pointed questioning, and to demonstrate to the therapist why they hold the views they express. There is sound evidence of the effectiveness of this approach (Lyons & Woods, 1991). However, it has limited scope with offenders and its use requires special training in the forms of Socratic dialogue that therapists must use. The Socratic method is used as part of the ETS "cog skills" programme in the British Prison Service with some success (Lipton et al., 1998; Friendship et al., 2002).

Cognitive therapy (CT) is at the other end of the continuum (Beck et al., 1979). CT is probably the most widely used of the cognitive-behavioural therapies, particularly for the treatment of depression in conjunction with medication, but is little used with offenders. As in other cognitive approaches, techniques involve the identification and modification of dysfunctional thoughts [often automatic thinking in response to external events or internal stimuli] that are elicited from clients in interviews and from self-observational diaries. *Cognitive therapy* techniques are used to alter and replace cognitive errors that Beck et al. identified. Some of the errors include: focusing on the negative; expecting the worst; drawing inappropriate conclusions; all-or-nothing thinking, i.e. seeing no middle ground regarding people, events or outcomes; inappropriate personalizing of references; self-deprecating comparisons; there's always someone to blame; unrealistic expectations; inability to separate feelings about reality from reality; pain and sacrifice will be rewarded. One variant of this approach is *Re-attribution Therapy* to help individuals to develop less self-damaging patterns in the attributions they make about the causes of events, to their own actions and others.

OVERVIEW OF STUDIES OF COGNITIVE-BEHAVIOURAL WORK WITH JUVENILE AND ADULT OFFENDERS

Individual studies have produced conflicting results about which forms of behavioural and cognitive-behavioural work are most effective with juveniles and young offenders. Hollin (1990, 1993, 1996) and McGuire (1996) reviewed a wide range of studies and concluded that interventions based solely on social skills training (e.g. Klein, Alexander & Parsons, 1977) have had limited success while those based solely on individual behaviour therapy have sometimes been successful but are unpopular with young offenders. Approaches which combine behavioural techniques with social learning and cognition, including teaching young offenders self-control, appear to be the most promising in reducing recidivism. For example, Feindler and Ecton (1986) developed a programme for young offenders which successfully taught them how to control anger, while McDougall et al. (1987) reported significant anger reductions among inmates in young offenders' institutions who had undergone an anger management programme combining cognitive procedures, specifically self-instruction and self-statements to use in situations of anger, with role-playing to improve behavioural responses and an educational module to help offenders to understand their anger. The sample size in the McDougall study was small ($n = 18$) and the measurement of effectiveness was limited to a comparison between treatment and controls in the use of staff reports three months after completion of the programme. Lochman (1992), moreover, assessed a similar programme in a school and found that, although self-esteem and social problem-solving skills were increased, there was no long-term impact on recidivism.

A study by Borduin et al. (1995) examined the long-term effectiveness of "multisystemic therapy" (MST), an approach which directly addresses personal (including cognitive) and social (family, peer group and school) factors that are believed to be associated with adolescent antisocial behaviour. A sample of 176 families with a juvenile offender (aged 12–17) were randomly assigned to MST and conventional individual therapy (IT). All of the offenders had records of serious criminal involvement. Following therapy, the two groups were compared on a number of measures related to the goals of improving individual adjustment and family relations and reducing involvement in criminal activity. The MST group showed significant improvements on all outcome measures, and the control group reported no such improvements. At the end of the four-year follow-up, the overall arrest rate for MST completers (22%) was less than one-third the rate for the individual therapy group (71%). Those who dropped out of MST were at higher risk of arrest (47%) than those who completed but were still at lower risk than those who underwent individual therapy. MST was also associated with significantly fewer serious crimes among those who were arrested. Bourduin et al. consider that the success of MST with high-risk young offenders may be due to its recognition of the multiple determinants of antisocial behaviour and its explicit focus on ameliorating behavioural problems within the context of problematic family relations.

Turning to the findings from meta-analyses of programmes which have been undertaken with juveniles and young offenders, Lösel (1993, 1995) has estimated an overall effect size of 0.10 for all the meta-analyses he considered, which means that recidivism for treatment groups was 10% less than for the control groups. Programmes that yielded the best results were "cognitive-behavioural, skills orientated and multimodal".

Similarly, Palmer (1994) found that approaches classified as behavioural were among the most successful with juveniles (i.e. had the largest average effect sizes or reductions in recidivism when comparing experimental and control groups). Programmes that used cognitive-behavioural, or combinations of cognitive and life skills approaches, also showed success—though often under other labels such as "social skills training"—as did those simply classified as multimodal. Palmer reports that the least effective approaches are those which employ confrontation, group counselling/therapy (unless carefully focused), and individual counselling/therapy.

Lipsey's review of published and unpublished research concerning 443 programmes for juvenile offenders has been influential because it is one of the most systematic and rigorous to date (Lipsey 1989, 1992, 1995; Palmer, 1994). Lipsey's sample included offenders in the 12–21 age range, although most were aged 18. For 285 (64%) of the programmes recidivism was lower for the treatment groups. Even more important was the finding that in 131 (30%) studies treatment programmes actually increased delinquency. These were punishment or deterrence-based interventions, such as shock incarceration and boot camps, which provided little by way of education, training or therapy. Having controlled for factors such as the different measures used by each study to judge recidivism (e.g. arrest, conviction, etc.) and the type of research design (randomized or non-randomized treatment and control groups), Lipsey concluded that programmes that were multimodal and had a more concrete, behavioural or "skills-oriented" character, had the greatest impact both within and outside the juvenile justice system with effect sizes of 0.20–0.32 (equivalent to a 10–16% reduction in recidivism against untreated controls). Lipsey did not attempt to disentangle the ingredients of successful multimodal packages and cautioned that the "inherent fuzziness of these coded categories" makes futile any discussion of whether particular forms of intervention are universally superior to others (Lipsey, 1995). Like Palmer, however, Lipsey found that concrete, structured approaches focused directly on overt behaviour were more successful than were traditional counselling and casework techniques.

An earlier meta-analysis by Whitehead and Lab (1989) is notable for the fact that the authors reached more pessimistic conclusions about the success of rehabilitative work with juveniles than in subsequent meta-analyses. On the basis of an analysis of 50 programmes for juvenile offenders Whitehead and Lab found that only 24–32% of programmes were successful in terms of achieving significant reductions in recidivism. They concluded that no single type of intervention "displayed overwhelmingly positive results on recidivism". It should be noted, however, that of the 50 studies in their meta-analyses, 30 involved juvenile diversion, which may not have included any form of intervention intended to address offending behaviour. Previous studies have indicated that diversionary approaches, which tend not to be used with relatively serious offenders, produce smaller effect sizes than other forms of intervention, perhaps because the offenders are judged to be fairly good risks in the first place.

This finding is generally considered to be a consequence of the researchers' use of very strict criteria for success that would require large reductions in recidivism, not simply a statistically significant difference between experimental and control groups. The equivalent effect sizes were larger than those noted in other meta-analyses (Palmer, 1994; Lösel, 1995; Farrington, 1996). When Andrews and colleagues (1990a) re-analysed 45 of the 50 studies considered by Whitehead and Lab and included a further 35 studies (a third of which covered programmes for adult offenders), their conclusions agreed more with those reached by Lösel, Lipsey and others. The authors speculate that effect sizes may have risen throughout the 1980s precisely because of the increasing use of cognitive methods within behavioural programmes.

Drawing on the findings of previous studies, Andrews et al. differentiated between "appropriate" and "inappropriate" services. Appropriate services were defined as those which delivered more intensive treatment to higher risk offenders; targeted the criminogenic needs associated with offending; and used cognitive or behavioural approaches. Inappropriate services were those which delivered treatment to low-risk offenders, or failed to match the teaching styles of staff to offenders' learning styles; or used group approaches with no specific aims (Palmer, 1994). For appropriate programmes, recidivism rates were on average 53% lower than for inappropriate services. Andrews et al., like Lipsey, also reported increased recidivism rates where the intervention was intended to punish or deter rather than rehabilitate through appropriate service.

Although Whitehead and Lab were critical of Andrews et al.'s analysis and conclusions regarding appropriate correctional approaches (Lab & Whitehead, 1990), Andrews et al. (1990b) reasserted in a rejoinder that their empirical findings were robust and reliable. They conceded, however, that Whitehead and Lab were correct in noting the need for further research to support the theory that the connection between treatment and recidivism is mediated by change in criminogenic factors. In other words, there is a need for more research " . . . on the links among treatment, intermediate change and recidivism".

Izzo and Ross's (1990) analysis of 46 juvenile offender studies conducted during the period 1970–1985 also indicated that programmes which incorporate a cognitive component were more than twice as effective as those which did not, again, using effect size as a measure of the difference between experimental and control groups. Izzo and Ross described individual cognitive programmes as using one or more of the following: problem-solving; negotiation skills training; interpersonal skills training; rational–emotive therapy; role-playing and modelling; or cognitive-behavioural modification. Effective programmes targeted offenders' cognitions, self-evaluations, expectations and values, and also behaviour as well as vocational or interpersonal skills. A review carried out by Antonowicz and Ross (1994) was confined to studies of adults and juveniles that (a) were published between 1970 and 1991, (b) utilized experimental or quasi-experimental designs and (c) included a community-based follow-up (including reconviction rates).

Their focus on well-designed and controlled studies meant that only 44 published reports fitted their qualifying criteria. Chi-squared tests were used to find the differences in recidivism between treatment and control groups. Successful programmes were characterized by a sound conceptual model; a focus upon criminogenic needs; responsiveness to offenders' learning styles (using role play and modelling); and the use of cognitive skills training. Programmes containing these elements comprised 75% (15/20) of successful programmes compared to 38% (9/24) of those that were unsuccessful. Programmes based on deterrence or psychodynamic methods lacked success in demonstrating a statistically significant improvement in recidivism when compared with the control groups. Behaviourally oriented programmes that did not include a cognitive component were also unsuccessful. Antonowicz and Ross differentiated between cognitive therapy or cognitive-behavioural modification (designed to modify what an offender thinks) and cognitive skills training (designed to teach an offender how to think). They concluded from the studies examined that cognitive skills training should precede attempts to modify what they think. While Antonowicz and Ross could not say which particular cognitive skills methods were most successful, they did show that the following were more prevalent in successful than in unsuccessful programmes: training in social perspective taking; training in self-control; interpersonal problem-solving; and values enhancement (a form of moral education).

A cognitive skills-based programme that has been used in a variety of different settings in Canada, Mexico and Europe is known as the Reasoning and Rehabilitation (R&R) programme and was developed by Robert Ross and his colleagues, Elizabeth Fabiano and Frank Porporino (Ross, Fabiano & Ross, 1989). This is an intensive cognitive skills programme for high-risk offenders, based on a long-term research project that included a review of the literature published over the previous 40 years. The review was not strictly a meta-analysis as the 44 studies were not combined to produce an overall treatment effect or to discover key characteristics. The research indicated that effective programmes included an intervention technique that could influence cognitive deficits, whereas ineffective programmes did not. This suggested to the researchers that cognitive skills training is a key element in any successful programme. The programme is multimodal in that it is designed to modify many aspects of offenders' thinking, including egocentricity, impulsiveness and failure to understand the views and feelings of others.

More details can be found in the handbook *Reasoning and Rehabilitation* (Ross, Fabiano & Ross, 1989). In 1988 the R&R programme, which consists of 80 hours of intensive training delivered to groups of four to six offenders by five specially trained probation officers, was first piloted in Ontario, Canada. Offenders were randomly assigned to a control group of regular probationers ($n = 23$); to a group of regular probationers given additional life skills training ($n = 17$); and to the Reasoning and Rehabilitation group ($n = 22$). The average age of the offenders was 24. All members of the sample had similar levels of risk (calculated through use of the Level of Supervision Inventory or LSI), although the R&R group had slightly more previous convictions. The nine-month reconviction results were very impressive as only 18% of the R&R group were reconvicted compared to 69% of regular probationers and 47% of the life skills group. Although the results are favourable, the sample sizes for each group were small and the follow-up period (nine months) was short. Nonetheless, the programme has been widely adopted in the United States, Canada and Europe. In the Correctional Services of Canada (CSC), which includes 47 prisons and community residencies across Canada, the core curriculum for R&R has been adopted (Ross, Antonowicz & Dhaliwal, 1995; Ross & Ross, 1995). By late 1993, programmes based on *Reasoning and Rehabilitation* had been developed by 13 probation departments in the United Kingdom. In most probation departments only anecdotal evaluation data has been collected via client feedback (McGuire, 1995b). However, the programme implemented in 1991 by the Mid-Glamorgan Probation Service entitled "STOP"—*Straight Thinking On Probation*—has been evaluated. STOP comprises 35 intensive sessions based on the R&R programme. To date, over 150 offenders have received STOP orders from courts (Raynor & Vanstone, 1996; Knott, 1995) and their performance on the project has been subjected to independent evaluation. The research design consisted of comparing the patterns of reconviction for a group of offenders attending

STOP with that of comparison groups subject to: standard probation; probation orders with day centre requirements; community service orders; immediate custody of up to 12 months; and suspended sentences. For each group predicted risk of reconviction scores were also calculated. These scores enabled Raynor and Vanstone (1994, 1996, 2001) to assess how each group fared in comparison to their expected reconviction scores. After 12 months, the reconviction rate for those who completed the STOP programme was better than predicted (35% compared to 42% predicted). This pattern was not evident for the comparison groups. For example, 49% of the custodial group were reconvicted compared to a predicted rate of 42%. However, the results were not sustained in the second year when 63% of STOP completers were reconvicted (against a predicted rate of 61%) (Raynor & Vanstone, 1996). Raynor and Vanstone also noted that after 12 months only 5 (8%) of the 59 STOP completers has been reconvicted of a serious offence (violent/sexual offences or burglary) compared to 34 (21%) of those given custody and 19 (18%) of those sentenced to STOP but who did not complete the programme. Again, these differences were not sustained in the second year: after 24 months the percentages reconvicted for serious offences for the STOP full sample, custody and STOP completers were 27%, 25% and 22%, respectively. However, the STOP completers were still more likely to avoid prison when reconvicted, which Raynor and Vanstone believe may reflect a lesser degree of seriousness than simple offence codes indicate. Raynor and Vanstone consider that better results, both in terms of longer term outcome and completions, could be achieved by more appropriate offender selection, by offering support and follow-up to offenders who complete the programme and by applying the *Reasoning and Rehabilitation* model outside the actual group sessions.

A recent British study of five probation-run group programmes for adult offenders investigated their short-term effectiveness in achieving their stated aims and attempted to identify the links between process characteristics, e.g. integrity, coherent aims, etc., and eventual outcome, as measured by pre- and post-treatment assessment (McGuire et al., 1995). The five programmes considered were: a seven-week programme for drunk-driving offenders; a structured activity programme for traffic offenders; a day centre activity programme of the type used by many probation services; a cognitive skills training package based on the 'Reasoning and Rehabilitation' programme; and a group for women offenders. The drunk-driving programme, the cognitive skills programme and the programme for women offenders all used cognitive-behavioural methods to some degree. The study's short time scale did not permit examination of reconviction rates following completion of the programme, but a number of psychological measures were used including a range of pre/post-treatment psychological tests, and a self-esteem scale. There were other tests specific to each programme (e.g. alcohol knowledge tests, driving behaviour, etc.). The cognitive skills programme was assessed via six additional tests which measured alternative thinking, impulsiveness and locus of control (the degree to which offenders perceive events to be out of their control). Comparison groups were selected among offenders who had been recommended for placement on the programmes, but who received other sentences (mostly to custody or community service). The results of this programme were mixed. Only the drunk-driving programme achieved statistically significant pre- and post-test differences on the various tests, while no significant differences were detected in the comparison group. Other programmes, including the course on cognitive training, showed promising but non-significant results. The authors believe that the failure to demonstrate a statistically significant improvement could be a function of the small number of offenders (a total of 65 offenders across the five programmes) and the dearth of standardized tests for evaluating these types of intervention. In addition, some of the programmes lacked one or more of the features described above which meta-analysts have identified as distinguishing the more successful offender programmes. Whereas the drunk-driving programme incorporated all the success factors, the cognitive-training programme lacked specific targeting and programme integrity (or at least these requirements were not evident in the questionnaire responses). The women offenders group used cognitive-behavioural methods and had a directive style of working but lacked programme integrity, had no clear aims or specific treatment targets, and was not highly structured. The day centre programme had a directive approach but lacked any of the other success criteria. Despite the inconclusive findings from this study, the researchers consider that they lend support to the conclusions of large-scale meta-analyses regarding the combination of ingredients which yield the most promising results with high-risk, or relatively high-risk, offenders.

To summarize this subsection, the available research on juvenile and adult offender programmes points to a broad consensus as to the types of approach which achieve the greatest impact on offending behaviour (expressed in terms of experimental studies achieving lower recidivism rates than controls). Those which combine cognitive-behavioural techniques with the other success factors identified in the meta-analysis (targeting, structured approaches, programme integrity) appear to offer the best chance of reducing rates of recidivism. Although the findings are limited with regard to adult offenders, the message with regard to cognitive-behavioural approaches is consistent with that reported in the more numerous studies of young offenders. The reviews by Lipsey (1992) and Andrews et al. (1990a) also indicate that, while some forms of intervention are associated with fairly large reductions in recidivism, those based on the use of punitive measures actually appear to increase the chances of reoffending. As Lipsey (1995) concludes, however, only general and broad brush advice on effective interventions is possible on the basis of meta-analyses which aggregate over a wide range of studies. All interventions must be developed and delivered in accordance with the particular needs and circumstances of the offender. This is consistent with Palmer's (1994) observation that "which particular combinations of experimental programme features have commonly yielded positive results with large portions of their populations— and which have not—has seldom been systematically explored and is largely unknown". Moreover, in order to make progress in determining which particular forms of cognitive-behavioural training and combinations seem promising, Palmer stresses that researchers and others need first to develop and agree on definitions for the various components of any given combination.

Briefly, although the simple labels typically allocated to programmes do not permit careful eliciting of the components associated with reduced recidivism, Lipsey and others find sufficient evidence in the pattern of results to permit some broad inferences. The consistently strong effect of multimodal combinations reported in several meta-analyses does suggest that there may be an advantage, having assessed an offender's criminogenic needs, in seeking to address them within a single, integrated programme.

VIOLENT OFFENDERS

There is a growing body of research evidence which links aggressive and violent behaviour with early family experiences, in particular poor child rearing and parenting, harsh and authoritarian discipline. Cohort studies, such as that undertaken by Farrington (1996), indicate that the roots of aggression and violence, like other forms of antisocial behaviour, are learned, and that the family plays a key role in determining whether early patterns of aggressive behaviour become established. While not denying the importance of early environmental and socialization factors, in order to improve the effectiveness of interventions with those whose aggressive behaviour has become established, psychologists have also sought a fuller understanding of the cognitive processes which underlie and trigger this form of behaviour.

One of the most prolific researchers in the area of violent offending has been Novaco (1975, 1978). Novaco describes anger as being caused by a physiological arousal which is then labelled by an individual, the labelling being dependent on how the individual perceives his or her social or environmental situation. Hence, "it is suggested that cognitive restructuring of a violent person's perception of social events, and their relationships with others, can help in reducing aggressive behaviour and hostility" (Browne & Howells, 1996). Where cognitive techniques are used with violent offenders these typically follow Novaco's approach (Blackburn, 1993). This combines the use of cognitive self-control with relaxation techniques and an educational element to help offenders understand their behaviour. Novaco found that the self-control element combined with relaxation had a greater impact on anger than relaxation alone. Later research by Schlicter (1978; Schlicter & Horan, 1981) confirmed that a combination of relaxation training with self-instructional methods of anger control and "coping skills" had a greater impact on aggressive adolescents than basic group counselling. Feindler and Ecton (1986) also obtained promising results with aggressive adolescents when using cognitive-behavioural techniques in a programme of anger-control and social skills training.

Glick and Goldstein (1987) reviewed and evaluated many of these techniques in developing their Aggression Replacement Training (ART) for young violent offenders, which has been adapted for use with violent young adults. The combination of anger-control training techniques (based in part on Novaco's work) with social skills training, problem-solving and moral education has been found to improve self-control and there is some evidence of a reduction in recidivism (e.g. Leeman, Gibbs & Fuller, 1993). However, whether programmes such as ART can significantly reduce the rate of violent offending is uncertain. One study found that the beneficial effect failed to reach statistical significance once allowance was made for differences in levels of supervision received by the treatment and control group following the programme (Glick et al., 1989).

The influence of the family upon adolescent antisocial and aggressive behaviour has led some psychologists to involve the family in therapy through the use of cognitive skills training and problem-solving methods. In the study reported by Borduin et al. (1995) on the effectiveness of "multisystemic treatment" (which addressed behaviour problems in the context of family, peer group and school), offenders aged 12–17 were randomly assigned to multisystemic treatment (MST) or individual therapy. Outcome measures included arrests for violent crimes (rape, attempted rape, aggravated assault, etc.) during a four-year follow-up. The youths who participated in MST, many of whom had previously committed offences of violence, were significantly less likely to be arrested for further violent crimes than were youths who received individual therapy. The researchers concluded from this finding that interventions with violent young offenders are likely to be more effective if they are comprehensive, address behavioural problems within the context of problematic family relations, and are delivered in the family's home or at a community location.

Some evidence that cognitive-behavioural work with violent adult offenders can reduce re-offending has emerged from a recent evaluation funded by the Scottish Office and Home Office of two re-education programmes for perpetrators of domestic violence (Dobash et al., 1996). Both programmes adopted a cognitive-behavioural approach and consisted of weekly group sessions over a six- to seven-month period. The aim was to increase the offenders' insight into their violent behaviour and to model new ways of thinking and acting through the use of a range of behavioural and cognitive techniques. These included: teaching cognitive techniques for recognizing the sequence of events and the emotions associated with the onset of violence; use of continuous forms of self-assessment and monitoring as a means of reinforcing group work; practising new behaviour through role play; and didactic methods to enhance offenders' understanding of the nature of violent behaviour towards women.

In order to assess the effectiveness of these two programmes the study followed up two groups of men who participated in the programmes (a total of 41 men) and compared them with a group of 71 men who received other court sentences. Recidivism by the experimental and comparison groups was assessed by interviewing women partners 3 and 12 months after the completion of the programme, thus significantly reducing the effect of undetected offending inherent in most reconviction studies. The research could not control for the effects of selection either by Sheriffs or by programme staff and although there was no statistical difference between the programme and control groups in terms of the men's use of violence, there were a few differences between them in their ages, employment status and background of parental violence. Bearing in mind that the sample was quite small and may have been subject to some selection bias, the results are viewed by the researchers as encouraging. Only 33% of those who participated in the programme had committed a violent act against their partners after 12 months, compared to 75% among the comparison population. Women whose partners did undergo treatment also noted reductions in the coercive and controlling behaviour known to be associated with domestic violence, such as threats, shouting and restrictions on the women's social life.

On the basis of an examination of the use of behavioural and cognitive techniques with violent offenders, Blackburn (1993) concluded that training in anger management has indeed been shown to reduce aggression, at least in the short term, and its usefulness in maintaining order in institutions has been established. However, evidence of long-term success is inconclusive, particularly for the more persistent violent offenders who may require more intensive interventions. Hence Blackburn's observation in relation to violent offenders that "issues such as offender heterogeneity, effective treatment components and treatment intensity have yet to be addressed" (Blackburn, 1993, p. 382).

METHOD

Hypothesis Investigation

As with the evaluation of therapeutic communities and milieu therapy presented in Chapter 2, in examining behavioural and cognitive-behavioural interventions a three-phase approach was adopted. In Phase I, we tested all hypotheses that had been formulated prior to analyses of our data. These were straightforward: research hypotheses that each specific type of programme would have a successful impact on recidivism. After seeing the results of Phase I, some new hypotheses (generally refinements of Phase I hypotheses but introducing predicted moderator variables) were formulated and tested as Phase II hypotheses, Then after seeing the results from our Phase II tests, all subsequent analyses were considered to be exploratory data analysis rather than rigorous hypothesis testing, and these analyses were labelled Phase III analyses.

The Phase I Hypotheses

I.   Behavioural—cognitive/behavioural programmes (a broad category encompassing programmes ranging from token economy programmes up to cognitive-behavioural programmes) are more effective than comparison group interventions at reducing recidivism.

I.1 Behavioural reinforcement and incentive programmes[1*] are more effective than comparison group interventions at reducing recidivism.

I.2 Cognitive-behavioural programmes[2] are more effective than comparison group interventions at reducing recidivism.

Locating Primary Research Studies

As in other segments of CDATE, five search methods were used in searching for primary research studies. These entailed: searching more than 24 electronic computerized bibliographic databases; screening bibliographies listed in books, articles, reports and dissertations; a classic hand search of all issues of major journals with potential relevant content; examining the books and monographs available at several large libraries, yielding many reports which did not exist elsewhere; and finally, requesting documents from authors and organizations. Again we acknowledge colleagues from a number of countries for the help they provided in making available data contained in studies in languages other than English. Reports in German and Dutch were screened, coded, and annotated by Rudolf Egg and his assistants in Germany, others in the Nordic languages by Eckart Kühlhorn and Erik Grevholm in Sweden, and other studies in Spanish, Italian and French by Santiago Redondo, Vicente Garrido, Julio Sánchez-Meca and Fulgencio Marín-Martínez in Spain.

Where meta-analytic reviews rely on published studies alone they will, of course, produce only a partial assessment of the current state of knowledge. In CDATE,

---

* Notes are presented at the end of the chapter.

considerable effort was expended in trying to locate specific unpublished research reports, by searching numerous archival sources, and contacting government agencies and quasi-government organizations. As previously noted, such efforts to obtain unpublished documents were unsuccessful all too often. In the time span of this project, approximately 92% of the unpublished evaluation research reports that were identified were obtained. Virtually all of the published ones, however, were obtained. Nevertheless, through the intercession of numerous authors who were solicited, many valuable unpublished, and previously unknown, research reports were added to the CDATE database. Cumulatively, the CDATE collection of studies amounted to more than 10 000 documents, approximately 40% (39.3%) of which had not been previously published. Hence, one objective has been to compare the results from journal articles and books with those reported in dissertations and in unpublished research reports. Unfortunately, the entire collection of documents used in the CDATE study was stored in the World Trade Center in New York City. When these towers were destroyed on 11 September 2001, the collection was irretrievably lost.

Measurement of Variables

CDATE criteria for inclusion and exclusion of studies were described previously in Chapter 2. Within the overall "nest" of cognitive-behavioural programmes, the specific types of programmes coded were:

- Social skills development training. (Developing skills in communication, giving and receiving positive and negative feedback, assertiveness, conflict resolution, etc.)
- Problem-solving skills training (e.g. D'Zurrilla & Goldfried, 1971).
- Ross et al.'s programme materials on Cognitive Skills and "Reasoning and Rehabilitation" (e.g. Ross, Fabiano & Ewles, 1988).
- Thinking Errors approach.
- Social learning focused. These approaches include as variables: cognitions, verbalizations, and social modelling to explain (and to change) behaviour patterns.
- Cognitive behavioural. These approaches teach self-reinforcement, self-instruction, self-rehearsal, role-taking, self-control, and problem solving.
- Self-control training.
- Training in anger management or aggression management.
- Contingency contracting. An explicit contract with the client to deliver specific rewards (and possibly punishments) for specific named behaviours.
- Token economy.
- Relapse prevention programmes. These emphasize preparing the offender to deal with cravings, peer pressure, etc., to prevent relapse to the illicit behaviour (e.g. Marlatt & Gordon, 1985).

In the analyses presented here, programmes were considered to be of the relevant treatment type if that treatment was rated by CDATE coders as the most important treatment difference between the experimental (E) and the control (C) groups.

Table 3.1   Inter-rater reliability for variables coded in the meta-analysis

	Percentage agreement	Kappa	Pearson/Spearman
Decade of publication	100	1.00	1.00
Age category	100	1.00	1.00
Assignment to conditions	90	0.79	0.79
Location of treatment	90	0.80	0.80
% African American	80		0.88
Actual Tx program length	87		0.99
Total sample size	90		0.99
Treatment appropriateness	67	0.52	0.74
Sanction	93	0.71	0.71
Inappropriate	80	0.38	0.38
Unspecified	77	0.32	0.34
Appropriate	83	0.67	0.68
Behavioural intervention	100	1.00	1.00
Well-targeted	77	0.53	0.53
Outcome characteristics			
Outcome type	87		0.97
Computed effect size	83		0.99

In parallel with the outcome criteria used in studies outlined in Chapter 2, the dependent (outcome) variable, recidivism, in these studies consisted mainly of rearrest and/or reincarceration. In most cases the CDATE research team had no choice but to accept the recidivism outcome variable stipulated in the study being annotated in whatever form it took, and very few studies included more than one recidivism outcome variable.

Quality Control, Reliability and Validity

The present analysis was conducted along lines similar to those discussed in Chapter 2 (Hedges & Olkin, 1985; Hunter & Schmidt, 1990; Rosenthal, 1991; Yeaton & Wortman, 1993). Procedures for ensuring quality control and evaluating reliability of coding categories were discussed in some depth in that chapter, and results of some key reliability calculations were presented in Table 2.1. Additional reliability calculations were made in respect of variables associated with research reports on behavioural and cognitive-behavioural programmes, and these are presented in Table 3.1. Similarly, other methods of statistical analysis, most importantly effect size estimates, were computed using procedures identical to those employed in other subgroupings of studies within CDATE. The logic of hypothesis testing was founded on a similar basic model as previously described.

RESULTS

The presentation of findings begins with a "broad-brush" approach. It includes every form of treatment which has been categorized as "behavioural" or "cognitive

Table 3.2 Behavioural or cognitive behavioural frequency programmes

Social skills development training	14
Problem-solving skills training	1
Cognitive skills training	7
Thinking errors approach	2
Other social skills training	2
Aversive conditioning focused	1
Social learning focused	3
Cognitive behavioural	10
Self-control training	1
Training in anger management	1
Other standard behaviour modification	5
Contingency contracting	13
Token economy	6
Relapse prevention model	3
Total	69

behavioural". Thus, Table 3.2 shows the specific categories used for the most important treatment component in the programme under study, and includes such behavioural approaches as behaviour modification, contingency contracting, and token economies, and such cognitive-behavioural approaches as social skills development training, problem-solving skills training, and cognitive skills training.

As background for the meta-analyses, Figure 3.1 shows a correlation coefficient (r) effect size with recidivism as the outcome variable for all 69 studies (undifferentiated by specific treatment type). Each r is plotted in the middle of

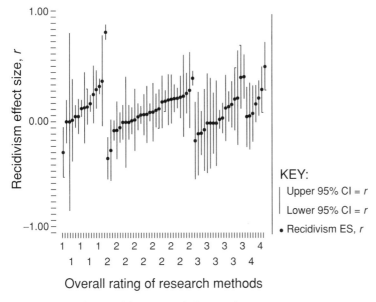

KEY:

Upper 95% CI = r

Lower 95% CI = r

• Recidivism ES, r

Figure 3.1 Behavioral/cognitive behavioral.

Table 3.3 Recidivism by 68 behavioural or cognitive-behavioural programmes

Verified?	Yes			
No. of studies (k)	68			
Total N, Windsorized	10 428			
Weighted mean of r	0.118			
One-tailed probability	0.0000003			
Homogeneity	0			
Method rating beta	0.012			
Method rating	k studies	Mean r	Median r	Std. Dev.
Excellent	7	0.207	0.177	0.165
Good	17	0.119	0.046	0.209
Fair	29	0.091	0.092	0.173
Poor	15	0.110	0.123	0.164
Total	68	0.114	0.092	0.179

a vertical bar representing the 95% confidence interval for that r. The studies are sorted by the overall rating of the research methods used in the study (1 = poor, barely acceptable, very low confidence; 2 = fair, a low level of confidence; 3 = good, a mid-level of confidence; 4 = excellent, a high level of confidence) from left to right on the graph and, within that rating, by the favourableness of the outcome. Notice that only seven studies (those on the far right of the graph) were rated as having excellent research methods. The study with the largest effect size ($r = +0.81$) appears to be an outlier which does not seem to "belong" with this collection of studies. Examination showed that this was a study with especially weak methods: it did not have a separate set of participants to serve as a comparison group, so, for the experimental group only, it used arrest rates before and after the programme. We exclude this study (Study ID = 2266) from all subsequent analyses.

The test of this broad, overall nest is presented in Table 3.3.

We considered a hypothesis to be verified when the inverse-variance-weighted mean effect size, r, was greater than or equal to 0.05 (with no clear evidence of research method artifact) and the t-test resulted in a one-tailed probability less than 0.05. If r was less than 0.05 we considered the hypothesis to be disconfirmed. There is a conversion relationship, the Binomial Effect Size Display (BESD), which provides some indication of the practical importance of the effect size (Rosenthal, 1991, pp. 132–136). A BESD relates a Pearson correlation coefficient, r, to a percentage differential between the E and C group, using 50% as a mid-point anchor. For example, a correlation of $r = 0.05$ can be thought of as the E group being 5 percentage points better than the C group, using 50% as a mid-point anchor. Thus, the BESD would be: 52.5% successes in the E group versus 47.5% successes in C. We set this as our minimal criterion of practical significance. This test excludes the outlying study (CDATE ID 2266).

In our assessments there was also a possibility for results to fall in a borderline "grey area". One reason for this designation could be that, although the r was greater than or equal to 0.05, the t-test did not result in a one-tailed probability less than 0.05. Another reason could be that there are indications of a research method artifact in which the poorer quality studies show a substantial effect while the better quality studies do not show any substantial effect. The broad nest did not show any clear method artifact: the beta coefficient for the rating of the quality of research methods is essentially zero, and the (unweighted) mean r values meet our criterion in each level of the method rating variable.

The number of studies (here, $k = 68$) refers to the number of independent comparisons (one experimental group, E, relative to one comparison group, C). The total N refers to the number of individual subjects (persons) in the Experimental (E) plus Comparison (C) groups of each study, Windsorized at 600. The summary table also includes the mean inverse-variance-weighted Pearson correlation coefficients r, and the null-hypothesis exact probability associated with the t-test used.

There are three conventionally used indicators of homogeneity: (1) at least 75% of the observed variance is accounted for by sampling error, (2) the 'Q' chi-square test is not significant, and (3) the amount of residual variance is less than 25% of the estimated population effect size. The entry for homogeneity in the summary tables designates how many of these three criteria indicate homogeneity. As expected, the general nest of behavioural and cognitive-behavioural studies was not homogeneous; none of the three criteria indicated homogeneity.[3]

The "Methods Rating beta" entry in the table gives the inverse-variance-weighted hierarchical linear regression beta coefficient for the overall rating of research methods. The beta coefficient of +0.012 indicates that the effect sizes show a very slight (negligible) positive linear relationship with the quality of research methods used. That there is no research method artifact can also be seen in the section immediately below the methods rating beta, in which the unweighted correlation effect sizes are shown within each of the research method rating categories.

BEHAVIOUR MODIFICATION

The behaviour modification approach is now, of course, well known. This approach emphasizes conditional positive reinforcement to change behaviour patterns. A token economy is a reinforcement system in which offenders/inmates who perform specific behaviours satisfactorily (such as, cleaning their living area, helping other inmates, etc.) are rewarded with tokens which can later be exchanged for privileges (more time to watch television) or desired goods (snacks from the canteen). In a contingency contracting system the offender signs a contract with the person supervising him or her in which punishment and rewards are contingent upon specific behaviours. It can include punishments for certain specified behaviours (e.g. a stricter curfew for a positive urine test) and rewards for certain other specific named behaviours (e.g. good time credits for satisfactory work performance).

The summary table for the subnest of treatments comprising behavioural programmes, including contingency contracting, token economy programmes, and other standard behaviour modification programmes is presented in Table 3.4.

Although the result was not quite statistically significant at the 0.05 level, the inverse-variance-weighted mean r of 0.066 does exceed our (rather lenient) 0.05 criterion.[4] The corresponding BESD is 53.3% success in the E groups and 46.7% success in the C groups. The research method rating moderator variable showed a slight positive linear relationship with the effect sizes (beta = +0.042), indicating that the better quality studies found slightly larger effect sizes, on the average. In

Table 3.4   Behavioural reinforcement incentive programmes and recidivism

Verified?	Borderline			
No. of studies (k)	23			
Total N, Windsorized	1935			
Weighted mean of r	0.066			
One-tailed probability	0.0686			
Homogeneity	0			
Method rating beta	0.042			
Method rating	k studies	Mean r	Median r	Std. Dev.
Excellent	4	0.171	0.159	0.117
Good	3	0.181	0.000	0.366
Fair	11	0.048	0.074	0.201
Poor	5	−0.017	0.000	0.154
Total	23	0.073	0.060	0.206

the detail method rating panel in the lower section of the same table the studies rated as excellent and good have unweighted mean r values of 0.17 and 0.18. There are two weaknesses, however, that should be pointed out. First, post hoc exploration of the cases revealed that of the three of the four excellent entries are actually three independent comparisons from one overarching study.[5] Second, the median unweighted r in the good category is 0.00. Therefore, adopting our cautious and conservative stance we are unwilling to state that the effectiveness of behavioural reinforcement/incentives programmes has been confirmed or that it has been disconfirmed, but rather we characterize it as being on the borderline of verified effectiveness.

As summarized in Table 3.5, our meta-analyses showed the other subnest (i.e. cognitive- behavioural treatments) to be effective in reducing recidivism. For the 44 studies the weighted mean r was 0.144. The corresponding BESD is 57.2%

Table 3.5   Cognitive-behavioural programmes and recidivism

Verified?	Yes			
No. of studies (k)	44			
Total N, Windsorized	8435			
Weighted Mean of r	0.144			
One-tailed probability	0.0000002			
Homogeneity	0			
Method rating beta	0.003			
Method rating	k studies	Mean r	Median r	Std. Dev.
Excellent	3	0.254	0.177	0.234
Good	14	0.106	0.091	0.179
Fair	17	0.129	0.093	0.149
Poor	10	0.173	0.150	0.133
Total	44	0.140	0.127	0.161

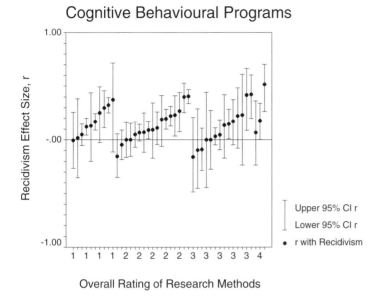

Figure 3.2   Cognitive Behavioural.

successes in the experimental group versus 42.8% successes in the comparison group. The correlation coefficients are above 0.05 in both the good and excellent research method rating categories. Figure 3.2 shows a correlation coefficient, r, effect size with recidivism as the outcome variable for all 44 studies (undifferentiated by specific treatment type).

However, as the summary table showed, these 44 studies are not statistically homogeneous, suggesting that some moderator variable or variables might further partition the studies into those with relatively stronger effect sizes and those with weaker effect sizes.

After reviewing the results of the above three Phase I hypothesis tests, the following post hoc, exploratory analyses were conducted. Within the subnet of behavioural and incentives treatments, there were five or more studies in each of the three specific types of treatment (i.e. contingency contracting, token economies, and other standard behaviour modification), but none of these specific behavioural treatments could be verified (post hoc) as effective in reducing recidivism.

Within the cognitive-behavioural subnet, only three specific types of treatment included more than three studies: social skills development training, cognitive skills training (also known as Reasoning and Rehabilitation), and studies specifically coded as cognitive behavioural. As shown in Table 3.6, based on 14 primary research studies, social skills development programmes do meet our criteria as verified effective in reducing recidivism. The inverse-variance-weighted mean r of 0.17 corresponds to a BESD of 58.5% success in the experimental group and 41.5% in the comparison group.

There are only seven research studies dealing with the cognitive skills programmes developed by Ross and his colleagues (also known as *Reasoning and Rehabilitation* programmes), but they still meet our criteria of verified effectiveness.

Table 3.6 Social skills development programmes and recidivism

Verified?	Yes			
No. of studies (k)	14			
Total N, Windsorized	1924			
Weighted mean of r	0.170			
One-tailed probability	0.0036			
Homogeneity	0			
Method rating beta	−0.011			
Method rating	k studies	Mean r	Median r	Std. Dev.
Excellent	1	0.068	0.068	–
Good	7	0.157	0.136	0.206
Fair	4	0.130	0.081	0.194
Poor	2	0.272	0.272	0.144
Total	14	0.160	0.114	0.181

The weighted mean r is 0.147, which corresponds to a BESD of 57.4% successes in the E group and 42.7% successes in the C group.

Lastly, there were 10 primary research studies of other programmes CDATE researchers coded as specifically cognitive behavioural.[6] They, too, are verified effective, as shown in Table 3.8. The weighted mean r of 0.114 corresponds to 55.7% successes in E and 44.3% successes in C. This collection of studies does meet one of the three conventionally used indicators of homogeneity: more than 75% of the observed variance is accounted for by sampling error.

DISCUSSION

Before analysing these studies, we expected both the behavioural reinforcement/incentives programmes and the cognitive-behavioural programmes to be

Table 3.7 Cognitive skills (R&R) and recidivism

Verified?	Yes			
No. of studies (k)	7			
Total N, Windsorized	1112			
Weighted mean of r	0.147			
One-tailed probability	0.033			
Homogeneity	0			
Method rating beta	0.054			
Method rating	k studies	Mean r	Median r	Std. Dev.
Excellent	1	0.517	0.517	–
Good	3	0.145	0.171	0.102
Fair	2	0.119	0.119	0.099
Poor	1	0.016	0.016	–
Total	7	0.172	0.171	0.174

Table 3.8   Other cognitive-behavioural programmes and recidivism

Verified?	Yes			
No. of studies (k)	10			
Total N, Windsorized	2125			
Weighted mean of r	0.114			
One-tailed probability	0.003847			
Homogeneity	1			
Method rating beta	−0.006			
Method rating	k studies	Mean r	Median r	Std. Dev.
Excellent	0	–	–	–
Good	1	−0.160	−0.160	–
Fair	7	0.132	0.110	0.111
Poor	2	0.150	0.150	0.142
Total	10	0.106	0.101	0.139

verified effective. Based on the meta-analyses, we think that the behavioural re-inforcement/incentives programmes (i.e. standard behaviour modification pro-grammes, token economies, and contingency contracting programmes) should at this time still be viewed as neither confirmed nor disconfirmed.

Some might find this surprising since the behavioural reinforcement approach has been shown in many good laboratory studies to control subhuman and human behaviour patterns. In retrospect, we think that programmes which focus on contin-gencies of reinforcement (in accordance with known principles of operant condi-tioning) will be verified effective in reducing undesirable behaviours. However, if the necessary contingencies of reinforcement are not in effect after the programme, the clients are likely to resume committing those undesirable behaviours. Several of the studies mentioned this behavioural reality:

1322–2-1 "(T)he question remains whether concentrated training in specific be-haviours can be transferred to the wide variety of situations that confront children after discharge" (p. 15).

17-0-1 "The immediate efficacy of its behaviour-modification techniques is veri-fied. However, follow-up results . . . indicate the failure of the programme to produce desirable social outcomes for discharged youth" (p. 296).

54-0-1 "Post-treatment persistence of appropriate social behaviour does not fol-low naturally from effective control over institutional behaviour. The meaningfulness of the predictive value of institutional adaptation is questionable" (p. 171).

131-0-1 "The results showed difference during treatment favouring the Teaching-Family programmes on rate of alleged criminal offenses. . . . In the post-treatment year, none of the differences between the groups was significant on any of the outcome measures" (p. 11).

The three independent comparisons from Study ID $= 41$ all used experimental methods we rated as Excellent. All three treatments consisted of setting up behavioural contracts for juvenile offenders and engaging in advocacy on behalf of those youth. In two of the conditions undergraduates were trained in the techniques and implemented them. These two treatment conditions showed the highest effect sizes ($r = 0.23$ and 0.31). The third treatment condition involved teaching the juvenile's family to do behavioural contracting with, and advocacy for, the juvenile ($r = 0.06$). The only other contingency contracting study using excellent research methods used, as its treatment, setting up behavioural contracts between the youth and teachers and between the youth and parents ($r = 0.09$). In our opinion, volunteers from outside the client's family, peer group, and school (or job) environments are unlikely to stay involved with the client for very long. Our opinion is that behavioural reinforcement programmes will be verified effective if and only if they can develop and maintain strong contingencies of reinforcement in the natural environment of the clients, for example, maintained by parents (or spouses) and teachers (or employers).

A different focus—one that cognitive-behavioural programmes tend to adopt—is to use behavioural learning techniques to change the general adaptive behaviours of the clients, that is, to have the clients return to their natural environment with new repertoires of skills so that they can obtain reinforcement in socially acceptable ways instead of illegal ways. The meta-analyses reported here show that cognitive-behavioural programmes can reduce recidivism rates by a significant amount. The cognitive skills (*Reasoning and Rehabilitation*) programme is a good example. We use the words *can* work rather than *do* work to reflect two problems. First, some programme directors who refer to their programmes as "cognitive-behavioural" may not use the elements that were used in the cognitive-behavioural models discussed in the studies cited here. Second, even when the models intended are the same as those discussed here, some programmes (for a variety of reasons) are unable to implement the cognitive-behavioural model in their particular correctional programme adequately.

Reducing recidivism has been notoriously difficult. It is a relief to know that some correctional programmes can indeed work to reduce recidivism by significant amounts. The programming challenge now is to help promote the "technology transfer" so the effective programme models diffuse throughout the correctional community and become well implemented. The research challenge is to expand and develop the existing body of research evidence, so the effective elements of the behavioural/cognitive-behavioural models can be specified, then used to improve the programme models still further.

TREATING DRUG OFFENDERS WITH COGNITIVE-BEHAVIOURAL APPROACHES

There is some evidence that treatment programmes (such as methadone maintenance, therapeutic communities, and milieu therapy) located within the criminal justice system can reduce illegal drug use and drug-related crime (Gerstein &

Harwood 1992; Simpson & Knight, 1998; Lipton 1995; Hough, 1996; McMurran, 1996). Questions remain, however, concerning which approaches work best for different types of offenders. The reviews of the research literature by Hough (1996), Anglin, Farabee and Prendergast (1998) and Satel (2000) suggest that: (1) legally coerced treatment accepted as a condition of the court can be as effective as treatment entered into "voluntarily"; (2) drug testing can help to identify illegal drug use and sustain compliance with treatment conditions; and, (3) drug testing should form an integral part of treatment, rather than be used simply as a form of surveillance.

To be successful such treatment must also ensure that users with serious drug/alcohol problems enter treatment quickly; stay in treatment for as long as necessary (from a minimum of three months to a maximum of 18 months); and are treated in a positive and supportive environment. Hough's literature review also highlights the importance of developing effective linkages between the criminal justice system and treatment services. Experience in the United States confirm that methods need to be pro-active and sufficiently financed, with in-court drug workers having direct access to offenders (Belenko, 1999). Merely providing information about community-based drug programmes results in low programme admission. Tentative conclusions concerning the cost-effectiveness of referral methods are that successful, resulting in contact with treatment agencies, can pay for itself through reductions in medical costs, social security benefits and drug-related crimes. A preliminary evaluation by HMPS researchers of a drug treatment programme introduced at a British prison (HMP Downview) in 1992 produced promising results in terms of abstinence from drug and alcohol use in the short term, and a favourable change in attitudes towards families and criminal behaviour were reported by those who remained in treatment.

Austin reported a 1997 NCCD random-assignment evaluation study of the effectiveness with substance-abusing offenders of the R&R cognitive skills programme ($n = 70$) compared with a multiphase drug treatment programme involving urinalyses, psycho-social assessment, drug counselling, and treatment planning. Despite some loss of integrity due to inconsistent implementation, the R&R participants were less likely to be arrested during follow-up (25%) than those receiving the drug treatment programme (32%). Whether the R&R programme would have been enhanced if the drug treatment elements in this instance were combined with it is unknown. However, the State of Colorado (Johnson & Hunter, 1995) experimentally compared three interventions: regular probation, a specialized drug programme, and R&R cognitive skills programme *combined* with the specialized drug programme. Twenty-five percent of the probationers in the latter condition had their probation revoked during the follow-up period, as compared with 29% of those in the drug programme alone, and with almost 42% of the regular probationers. An examination of the effects of these three interventions upon the most severely drug/alcohol involved probationers revealed even greater positive gains for those in the condition in which R&R was combined with specialized drug treatment: 18% of the probationers in R&R combined with drug treatment were revoked vs. 43% revoked among those receiving specialized drug treatment alone vs. 60% revoked among those randomly assigned to regular probation.

Drug Use Relapse Findings

Ten programmes with a behavioural or cognitive-behavioural treatment emphasis measured substance abuse relapse as an outcome. When compared with correctional treatment as usual, this set of studies did have a statistically significant weighted mean effect size ($r = +0.08$) indicating reduced substance abuse relapse overall (see Table 3.9 and Figure 3.3). This corresponds to a BESD of 54% success in the E group versus 46% in the C group. The single study given an excellent rating for research methods (the "Jackson Public Drunkenness" study) had a very large reduction in substance abuse ($r = 0.488$). Even if there were hidden problems in that particular study (such methodological problems might very well be unknown to the authors of the study as well), the three studies with a "good" rating of methods still had a substantial effect size ($r = 0.092$).

RESEARCH IMPLICATIONS

Implications for future primary research with cognitive-behavioural methods with offender populations appear to lie in three areas: clinical platform, methodology, and clientele.

With respect to clinical platform, the sequencing and integration of cognitive-behavioural elements into programmes need to be evaluated. There is some question as to the utility of delivering cognitive-behavioural methods early in the prison sentence if achieving maximum reductions in re-offending is the primary goal unless booster programmes are administered to programme graduates shortly before their release and again about six months after release. Being reintegrated into

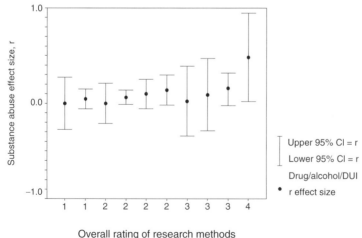

Figure 3.3 Effects (r) of behavioural and cognitive-behavioural treatments on substance abuse relapse.

Table 3.9 Behavioural and cognitive-behavioural programmes and substance abuse

Verified?	Yes			
No. of studies (k)	10			
Total N, Windsorized	1633			
Weighted mean of r	0.080			
One-tailed probability	0.006			
Homogeneity	3			
Method rating beta	0.00			
Method rating	k studies	Mean r	Median r	Std. Dev.
Excellent	1	0.488	0.488	–
Good	3	0.092	0.092	0.069
Fair	4	0.078	0.084	0.061
Poor	2	0.025	0.025	0.352
Total	10	0.114	0.092	0.179

the general prison population for a long sentence following cognitive-behavioural treatment will vitiate the programme's effects for most offenders unless booster sessions are held and the programme graduates can continue to associate with other graduates. The time during the programme when particular cognitive-behavioural elements are introduced, such as problem-solving skills training, *vis-à-vis* anger management elements for example, may also affect the degree to which they are effective in reducing the likelihood of specific kinds of re-offending.

The mix of elements appears to be quite different in programmes labelling themselves as cognitive-behavioural methods. Thus there is a need to examine systematically the effects of adding non-cognitive-behavioural elements, such as drug/alcohol treatment, as well as other programmatic dimensions and cognitive skills elements. With respect to clientele, there are two issues of concern: gender and age. CDATE researchers have found only 49 independent comparisons of evaluations of women-only programmes or programmes that provide separate data on women in all of the approximately 6000 studies examined. However, because these 49 are distributed sparsely across treatment modalities, there are only *three* treatment areas (cognitive behavioural, miscellaneous drug treatment counselling, and family treatment) where at least *four* studies are to be included in a meta-analysis. Obviously, more primary research is needed that permits evaluations of outcomes for women.

Similarly, with respect to age, the research on cognitive-behavioural approaches to juvenile offenders shows promise, but needs considerably more research investigation in order to effectively inform policy and programme implementation. It is worthy of note, however, that CDATE findings with juveniles reveal that counselling programmes oriented to family treatment were confirmed as successful in reducing recidivism ($r = +0.122$), and that experiential challenge programmes also appear to be, on the average, effective in reducing recidivism ($r = +0.146$). Mentoring, as a correctional intervention with juveniles, has one of the highest effect sizes in reducing recidivism. The CDATE researchers have found its weighted mean correlation coefficient effect size is 0.274, and it has only been implemented with juveniles.

CONCLUSION

It is the general conclusion of the CDATE research that successful treatment approaches include those focusing on behavioural or cognitive-behavioural treatment methods. In the overall grouping or nest of 68 studies, the weighted r is +0.128. For ease of interpretation this may be viewed as a percentage difference between experimental and control subjects in favour of those receiving treatment. From a social science evaluation research perspective this size difference from a large grouping of studies is very unusual. It is also noteworthy that an examination of this distribution of studies apparently reveals that positive outcomes of similar size occurs with studies of varying research quality indicating to this research team its robustness as a general outcome. Broadly speaking, the trends obtained here are congruent with those obtained in other meta-analytic reviews of offender treatment, including those of Andrews et al. (1990a,b), Lipsey (1992), and Lipsey and Wilson (1998); and also with those concerning the use of cognitive-behavioural approaches in mental health and related fields (Nathan & Gorman, 1998).

We also found that reinforcement and incentives programmes, a subset of the nest of 68 studies noted above, were also on average generally successful in reducing recidivism ($r = +0.093$). However, the single grouping of these 68 studies revealing the largest positive outcomes were the cognitive and social learning approaches that were shown to be effective with an $r = +0.144$. Included in this group were social skills training programmes and cognitive skills training programmes. An examination of the subset of research findings from evaluations of programmes utilizing *solely* problem-solving approaches, however, do not meet our success criteria.

When one examines the social and public health aim of reducing relapse to drugs among offenders, however, we have 67 independent comparisons with drug use relapse as the outcome variable. These are spread out over many diverse treatment nests, preventing comprehensible meta-analyses except in a few instances. Because of the relative paucity of good primary research studies, CDATE findings here fall mainly in the promising, but still largely unverified, treatment approaches. Nonetheless, the *cognitive-behavioural programmes* have the *highest* mean effect size on drug use relapse of the various treatment modalities in the CDATE database with a mean r of +0.287. This corresponds to a BESD of 64% success in the E group versus 36% in the C group. However, this is based on only four studies, and there does appear to be some level of research artifact bias present in this collection of studies.

From an overall perspective in dealing with offenders who are serious drug abusers it would appear that a logical, cost-effective, and convenient point of intervention is while they are in custody. Most would not enter drug use treatment voluntarily while free in their communities, or, if they have, they have done so several times for periods too short to have much effect. Without treatment, most will relapse to drug use within six weeks after release from custody and return to crime. These behaviours are part of a lifestyle that is both highly destructive and resistant to change (Walters, 1992). It has been shown in this current CDATE research, as well as in recent studies finished after the CDATE cut-off, that a substantial proportion of even hard-core offenders can be helped to change while in custody (Lipton, 2001). Thus, criminal justice custody is a point of opportunity to apply proven treatment measures such as cognitive-behavioural approaches (and therapeutic communities) in order to accomplish what the public desires and all elements in the political spectrum desire.

Our current research shows that therapeutic communities (see Chapter 2) as well as cognitive-behavioural methods are effective with serious drug abusers across diverse locales and populations, and even that high-rate offenders, each of whom commits many robberies and burglaries and drug offences a year, can be helped dramatically. It is clear that the greater the investment in rehabilitating the most severely substance-dependent offenders, the greater the probable impact. In addition to keeping returning inmates drug free and out of prison, these programmes are quite cost-effective. In the studies conducted in the United States, taxes paid in by recovered offenders, and savings in crime-related and drug-use associated costs cover the funds needed for treatment in less than three years; a focus of attention on such evidence is long overdue (van Voorhis, 1987). While it appears to be a sound investment, prison drug abuse treatment, despite some signs of light, is still currently limited in terms of the numbers of offenders in need of treatment who are given this opportunity.

NOTES

1. This category included contingency contracting and token economy programmes, but excluded aversive conditioning programmes.
2. Here cognitive-behavioural programmes are broadly defined to encompass a variety of approaches including social learning approaches. Such non-cognitive-behavioural programmes as token economies are excluded, however.
3. See Note 8, Chapter 2.
4. If we had not excluded the outlier (Study ID 2266), the weighted mean r would have been $+0.121$, and the exact probability of the significance test would have been 0.037.
5. That is with Study ID $= 41$.
6. Of course, cognitive skills programmes are cognitive-behavioural, too. These clearly identified programmes were given a separate code as cognitive skills, rather than put in with the other cognitive-behavioural programmes (which would have made that aggregated group more heterogeneous).

REFERENCES

Andrews, D. A., Zinger, I., Hoge, R. D, Bonta, J., Gendreau, P. & Cullen, F. T. (1990a) Does correctional treatment work? A clinically relevant and psychologically informed meta-analysis. *Criminology, 28*, 369–404.

Andrews, D. A., Zinger, I., Hoge, R. D., Bonta. J., Gendreau, P. & Cullen, F. T. (1990b) A Human Science Approach or more punishment and pessimism: A rejoinder to Lab and Whitehead. *Criminology, 28*, 419–429.

Anglin, M. D., Farabee, D. & Prendergast, M. (1998) *The Role of Coercion in Offender Drug Treatment*. A Report to the Physician Leadership on National Drug Policy, 30 September 1998.

Antonowicz, D. & Ross, R. R. (1994) Essential components of successful rehabilitation programs for offenders. *International Journal of Offender Therapy and Comparative Criminology, 38*, 97–104.

Austin, J. (1997) *Evaluation of the drug aftercare program and the reasoning and rehabilitation program in California probation*. Unpublished manuscript. Washington, DC: National Council on Crime and Delinquency.

Bandura, A. (1977) Self-efficacy: Towards a unifying theory of behavior change. *Psychological Review, 84*, 191–215.

Bandura, A. (1986) *Social Foundations of Thought and Action: A Social Cognitive Theory.* Englewood Cliffs, NJ: Prentice-Hall.

Bandura, A. (1989) Self-regulation of motivation and actions through internal standards and goal systems. In L. A. Pervin (Ed.) *Goal Concepts in Personality and Social Psychology* (pp. 19–85). Hillsdale, NJ: Erlbaum.

Beck, A. T., Rush, A. J., Shaw, B. F. & Emery, G. (1979) *Cognitive Therapy of Depression.* New York: Guilford Press.

Belenko, S. R. (1999) Research on drug courts: A critical review 1999 update. *National Drug Court Institute Review, 2* (2), 1–58.

Blackburn, R. (1993) *The Psychology of Criminal Conduct: Theory, Research and Practice.* Chichester: Wiley.

Bonczar, T. P. (1998) *Characteristics of Adults on Probation, 1996.* Bureau of Justice Statistics. Special Report. Washington DC: US Department of Justice.

Borduin, C. M., Mann, B. J., Cone, L. T., Henggeler, S. W., Fucci, B. R., Blaske., D. M. & Williams, R. A. (1995) Multisystemic treatment of serious juvenile offenders: Long-term prevention of criminality and violence. *Journal of Consulting and Clinical Psychology, 63* (4), 569–578.

Browne, K. & Howells, K. (1996) Violent offenders. In C. R. Hollin (Ed.) *Working with Offenders: Psychological Practice in Offender Rehabilitation.* Chichester: Wiley.

Bush, J. (1995) *Cognitive Self Change: A Program Manual.* Burlington, VT: Vermont Department of Corrections.

Bush, J., Glick, B. & Taymans, J. (1997) *Thinking for a Change: Integrated Cognitive Behavior Change Program.* Boulder, CO: National Institute of Corrections.

Dobash, R., Dobash, R., Cavanagh, K. & Lewis, J. (1996) *Research Evaluation of Programmes for Violent Men.* Edinburgh: Scottish Office.

D'Zurilla, T. J. & Goldfried, M. R. (1971) Problem solving and behavior modification. *Journal of Abnormal Psychology, 78*, 107–126.

Ellis, A. (1962) *Reason and Emotion in Psychotherapy.* New York, NY: Lyle Stuart.

Farrington, D. (1996) Criminological psychology: Individual and family factors in the explanation and prevention of offending. In C. R. Hollin (Ed.) *Working with Offenders: Psychological Practice in Offender Rehabilitation.* Chichester: Wiley.

Feindler, E. L. & Ecton, R. B. (1986) *Adolescent Anger Control: Cognitive-Behavioral Techniques.* New York NY: Pergamon.

Friendship, C., Blud, L., Erikson, M. & Travers, R. (2002) *An evaluation of cognitive behavioural treatment for prisoners.* Findings 161. London: Home Office Research, Development and Statistics Directorate.

Garrett, C. J. (1985) Effects of residential treatment of adjudicated delinquents. A meta-analysis. *Journal of Research in Crime and Delinquency, 22*, 287–308.

Gendreau, P. (1996) The principles of effective intervention with offenders. In A. T. Harland (Ed.) *Choosing Correctional Options that Work* (pp. 117–130). Thousand Oaks, CA: Sage.

Gendreau, P. & Ross, R. R. (1979) Effective correctional treatment: Bibliotherapy for cynics. *Crime and Delinquency, 25*, 463–489.

Gendreau, P. & Ross, R. R. (1981) Correctional potency: treatment and deterrence on trial. In R. Roesch & R. Corrado (Eds.) *Evaluation Research and Policy in Criminal Justice.* Beverly Hills, CA: Sage.

Gendreau, P. & Ross, R. R. (1984) Correctional treatment. Some recommendations for successful intervention. *Juvenile and Family Court Journal, 34* (Winter), 31–39.

Gendreau, P. & Ross, R. R. (1987) Revivification of rehabilitation: Evidence from the 1980s. *Justice Quarterly, 4* (3), 349–407.

Gerstein, D. R. & Harwood, H. (Eds.) (1992) *Treating Drug Problems* (Vol. 2, pp. 89–132). National Academy of Sciences, Institute of Medicine. Washington, DC: National Academy Press.

Gilliard, D. K. & Beck A. J. (1998) *Prison and Jail Inmates at Midyear 1997.* Bureau of Justice Statistics Bulletin. Washington DC: US Dept. of Justice.

Glick, B. & Goldstein, A. P. (1987) *Aggression Replacement Training*. Champaign, IL: Research Press.

Glick, B., Goldstein, A., Irwin, M. J., Pask-McCartney, C. & Rubama, I. (1989) *Reducing Delinquency:Interventions in the Community*. New York, NY: Pergamon.

Gottshalk, R., Davidson, W. S. II, Mayer, J. & Gensheimer, L. K. (1987a) Behavioral approaches with juvenile offenders: A meta-analysis of long-term treatment efficacy. In E. K. Morris & C. J. Braukmann (Eds.) *Behavioral Approaches to Crime and Delinquency: A Handbook of Application, Research and Concepts* (pp. 399–422). New York, NY: Plenum.

Gottschalk, R., Davidson, W. S. II, Gensheimer, L. K. & Mayer, J. P. (1987b) Community-based Interventions. In H. C. Quay (Ed.) *Handbook of Juvenile Delinquency*. New York, NY: Wiley.

Hedges, L. V. & Olkin, I. (1985) *Statistical Methods for Meta-analysis*. Boston: Academic Press.

Hollin, C. R. (1990) *Cognitive-Behavioural Interventions with Young Offenders*. New York, NY: Pergamon.

Hollin, C. R. (1993) Advances in the psychological treatment of delinquent behaviour. *Criminal Behaviour and Mental Health, 3*, 142–157.

Hollin, C. R. (1996) Young offenders. In C. R. Hollin (Ed.) *Working with Offenders: Psychological Practice in Offender Rehabilitation*. Chichester: Wiley.

Hollin, C. (Ed.) (2001) *Handbook of Offender Assessment and Treatment*. Chichester: Wiley.

Hough, M. (1996) *Drugs Misuse and the Criminal Justice System: A Review of the Literature*. Drugs Prevention Initiative, Paper 15. London: Home Office.

Hunter, J. E. & Schmidt, F. L. (1990) *Methods of Meta-analysis: Correcting Error and Bias in Research Findings*. Newbury Park, CA: Sage.

Husband, S. D. & Platt, J. J. (1993) The cognitive skills component in substance abuse treatment in correctional settings: A brief review. *Journal of Drug Issues, 23*, 31–45.

Izzo, R.J. & Ross, R. R. (1990) Meta-analysis of rehabilitation programs for juvenile delinquents. *Criminal Justice and Behavior, 17*, 144–167.

Johnson, G. & Hunter, R. M. (1995) Evaluation of the specialized drug offender program. In R. D. Ross & D. R. Ross (Eds.) *Thinking Straight: The Reasoning and Rehabilitation Program for Delinquency Prevention and Offender Rehabilitation*. Ottawa: Air Training and Publications.

Klein, N. C., Alexander, J. F. & Parsons, B. V. (1977) Impact of family systems intervention on recidivism and sibling delinquency: A model of primary prevention and program evaluation. *Journal of Consulting and Clinical Psychology, 51*, 655–660.

Knott, C. (1995) The STOP Programme: Reasoning and rehabilitation in a British setting. In J. McGuire (Ed.)*What Works: Reducing Re-offending*. Chichester: Wiley.

Lab, S. P. & Whitehead, J. T. (1988) An analysis of juvenile correctional treatment. *Crime and Delinquency, 34*, 60–83.

Lab, S. P. & Whitehead, J. T. (1990) From "nothing works" to "the appropriate works": The latest stop on the search for the secular grail. *Criminology, 28* (3), 405–418.

Leeman, L. W., Gibbs, J. C. & Fuller, D. (1993) Evaluation of a multi-component group treatment program for juvenile delinquents. *Aggressive Behavior, 19*, 281–292.

Lipsey, M. W. (1989) *The efficacy of intervention for juvenile delinquency: Results from 400 studies*. Paper presented at the 41st annual meeting of the American Society of Criminology, Reno, Nevada.

Lipsey, M. W. (1992) Juvenile delinquency treatment: A meta-analytic inquiry into the variability of effects. In T. D. Cook, H. Cooper, D. S. Cordray, H. Hartmann, L. V. Hedges, R. J. Light, T. A. Louis & F. Mosteller (Eds.) *Meta-analysis for Explanation: A Casebook* (pp. 83–127). New York, NY: Sage.

Lipsey, M. W. (1995) What do we learn from 400 research studies on the effectiveness of treatment with juvenile delinquents? In: J. McGuire (Ed.) *What Works: Reducing Re-offending*. Chichester: Wiley.

Lipsey, M. & Wilson, D. (1998) Effective intervention for serious juvenile offenders: A synthesis of research. In R. Loeber & D. P. Farrington (Eds.), *Serious and Violent Juvenile Offenders: Risk Factors and Successful Interventions* (pp. 83–127). New York, NY: Sage.

Lipton, D. S. (1990) *Principles of successful correctional intervention*. Presented at the BJA— Bureau of Justice Assistance-State Justice Institute Regional Seminar: Drugs and the Judicial Response, Washington, DC, 26–27 January.

Lipton, D. S. (1995) *The Effectiveness of Treatment for Drug Abusers under Criminal Justice Supervision.* National Institute of Justice Research Report. Washington, DC: US Department of Justice.

Lipton, D. (2001) Therapeutic community treatment programming in corrections. In C. R. Hollin (Ed.) *Handbook of Offender Assessment and Treatment* (pp. 155–177). Chichester: Wiley.

Lipton, D. S., Martinson, R. & Wilks, J. (1975) *The Effectiveness of Correctional Treatment.* New York, NY: Praeger.

Lipton, D. S., Pearson, F. S., Cleland, C. & Yee, D. (1998) *How do cognitive skills training programs for offenders compare with other modalities: A meta-analytic perspective.* Presented at the Stop and Think Conference, Her Majesty's Prison Service, York, UK.

Lochman, J.E. (1992) Cognitive-behavioral intervention with aggressive boys: Three-year follow-up and preventive effects. *Journal of Consulting and Clinical Psychology, 60,* 426–432.

Lösel, F. (1993) The effectiveness of treatment in institutional and community settings. *Criminal Behaviour and Mental Health, 3* (4), 416–437.

Lösel, F. (1995) The efficacy of correctional treatment: A review and synthesis of meta-evaluations. In J. McGuire (Ed.) *What Works: Reducing Re-offending.* Chichester: Wiley.

Lösel, F. & Köferl, P. (1989) Evaluation research on correctional treatment in West Germany: A meta-analysis. In H. Wegener, F. Lösel & J. Haisch (Eds.) *Criminal Behavior and the Justice System: Psychological Perspectives.* New York, NY: Springer.

Lyons, L. C. & Woods, P. J. (1991) The efficacy of rational-emotive therapy: A quantitative review of the outcome research. *Clinical Psychology Review, 11,* 357–369.

Marlatt, G. A. & Gordon, J. R. (1985) *Relapse Prevention: Maintenance Strategies in the Treatment of Addictive Behaviors.* New York, NY: Guilford.

Mayer, J. P., Gensheimer, L. K., Davidson, W. S. & Gottschalk, R. (1986) Social learning treatment within juvenile justice: A meta-analysis of impact in the natural environment. In S. J. Apter & A. Goldstein (Eds.) *Youth Violence: Programs and Prospects.* Elmsford, NY: Pergamon Press.

McDougall, C., Barnett, R. Ashurst, B. & Willis, B. (1987) Cognitive control of anger. In B. McGurk, D. Thornton & M. Williams (Eds.) *Applying Psychology to Imprisonment: Theories and Practice.* London: HMSO.

McGuire, J. (Ed.) (1995a) *What Works: Reducing Re-offending.* Chichester: Wiley.

McGuire, J. (1995b) Community-based reasoning and rehabilitation programmes in the UK. In R. D. Ross & D. R. Ross (Eds.) *Thinking Straight: The Reasoning and Rehabilitation Program for Delinquency Prevention and Offender Rehabilitation.* Ottawa: Air Training and Publications.

McGuire, J. (1996) Community-based interventions In C. R. Hollin (Ed.) *Working with Offenders: Psychological Practice in Offender Rehabilitation.* Chichester: Wiley.

McGuire, J. (2000) *Cognitive-behavioural Approaches: An Introduction to Theory and Research.* London: Home Office.

McGuire, J. Broomfield, D., Robinson C. & Rowson, B. (1995) Short-term impact of probation programs: An evaluative study. *International Journal of Offender Therapy and Comparative Criminology, 39,* 23–42.

McMurran, M. (1996) Alcohol, drugs and criminal behaviour. In C. R. Hollin (Ed.) *Working with Offenders: Psychological Practice in Offender Rehabilitation.* Chichester: Wiley.

Meichenbaum, D. A. (1977) *Cognitive-Behavior Modification: An Integrative Approach.* New York, NY: Plenum.

Miller, W. R. (1983) Motivational interviewing with problem drinkers. *Behavioural Psychotherapy, 11,* 147–172.

Miller, W. R. & Rollnick, S. (1992) *Motivational Interviewing: Preparing People to Change Addictive Behavior.* New York, NY: Guilford.

Nathan, P. E. & Gorman, J. M. (Eds.) (1998) *A Guide to Treatments that Work.* New York, NY: Oxford University Press.

Novaco, R. W. (1975) *Anger Control: The Development and Evaluation of an Experimental Treatment.* Lexington, KY: D.C. Heath & Co.

Novaco, R. W. (1978) Anger and coping with stress. In J. P. Foreyt & D. P. Rathjen (Eds.) *Cognitive Behavior Therapy*. New York, NY: Plenum.

Palmer, T. (1994) *A Profile of Correctional Effectiveness and New Directions for Research*. Albany, NY: State University of New York.

Platt, J. J., Perry, G. M. & Metzger, D. S. (1980) An evaluation of heroin addiction treatment program within a correctional environment. In R. R. Ross & P. Gendreau (Eds.) *Effective Correctional Treatment*. Toronto: Butterworths.

Platt, J. J., Scura, W. C. & Hannon, J. R. (1973) Problem-solving thinking of youthful incarcerated heroin addicts. *Journal of Community Psychology, 1*, 278–281.

Platt, J. J., Spivack, G. & Swift, M. (1974) *Interpersonal Problem-solving Group Therapy*. Research and Evaluation Report #31. Philadelphia, PA: Hahnemann Medical College.

Porporino, F. (1998) Personal Communication, 4/16/1998.

Raynor, P. & Vanstone, M. (1994) *Straight Thinking on Probation*. Third Interim Report. Bridgend: Mid-Glamorgan Probation Service.

Raynor, P. & Vanstone, M. (1996) Reasoning and rehabilitation in Britain: The results of the Straight Thinking on Probation (STOP) program. *International Journal of Offender Therapy and Comparative Criminology, 40* (4), 272–284.

Raynor, P. & Vanstone, M. (2001) "Straight Thinking on Probation": evidence-based practice and the culture of curiosity. In C. R. Hollin (Ed.) *Handbook of Offender Assessment and Treatment*. Chichester: Wiley.

Redondo, S., Garrido, V. & Sánchez-Meca, J. (1996) *Is the treatment of offenders effective in Europe? The results of a meta-analysis*. Presented at the 1996 Annual Meeting of the American Society of Criminology, Chicago, IL, 20–23 November.

Roberts, A. R. & Camasso, M. J. (1991) The effect of juvenile offender treatment programs on recidivism: A meta-analysis of 46 studies. *Notre Dame Journal of Law, Ethics and Public Policy, 5*, 421–441.

Rosenthal, R. (1991) *Meta-analytic Procedures for Research*. Newbury Park, CA: Sage.

Ross, R. R., Antonowicz, D. & Dhaliwal, G. (Eds.) (1995) *Going Straight: Effective Delinquency Prevention and Offender Rehabilitation*. Ottawa: Air Training & Publications.

Ross, R. R. & Fabiano, E. (1985) *A Time to Think: A Cognitive Model of Delinquency Prevention and Offender Rehabilitation*. Johnson City, TN: Institute of Social Sciences and Arts.

Ross, R. R., Fabiano, E. A. & Ewles, C.D. (1988) Reasoning and rehabilitation. *International Journal of Offender Therapy and Comparative Criminology, 32*, 29–35.

Ross, R. R., Fabiano, E. A. & Ross, B. (1989) *Reasoning and Rehabilitation: A Handbook for Teaching Cognitive Skills*. Ottawa: The Cognitive Centre.

Ross, R. D. & Ross, D.R. (Eds.) (1995) *Thinking Straight: The Reasoning and Rehabilitation Program for Delinquency Prevention and Offender Rehabilitation*. Ottawa: Air Training and Publications.

Satel, S. (2000) Drug treatment: The case for coercion. *National Drug Court Institute Review, 3* (1), 1–56.

Schlicter, K. J. (1978) *An application of stress inoculation in the development of anger management skills in institutionalised juvenile delinquents*. Dissertation Abstracts International.

Schlicter, K. J. & Horan, J. J. (1981) Effects of stress inoculation on the anger and aggression management skills of institutionalized juvenile delinquents. *Cognitive Therapy and Research, 5*, 359–365.

Sherman, L. W., Gottfredson, D., MacKenzie, D., Eck, J., Reuter, P. & Bushway, S. (1997) *Preventing Crime: What Works, What Doesn't, What's Promising*. Report to Congress by the Department of Criminology and Criminal Justice, University of Maryland, for the National Institute of Justice.

Simpson, D. D. & Knight, K. (1998) *Correctional Treatment in Community Settings*. Report to the Physician Leadership on National Drug Policy on Addiction & Health Care in the Criminal Justice System, October 12, 1998.

Spivack, G., Platt, J. J. & Shure, M. B. (1976) *The Problem-solving Approach to Adjustment*. San Francisco, CA: Jossey-Bass.

Van Voorhis, P. (1987) Correctional effectiveness: The high cost of ignoring success. *Federal Probation, 51* (March), 56–62.

Walters, G. D. (1992) Drug-seeking behavior: Disease or lifestyle. *Professional Psychology: Research and Practice, 23* (2), 139–145.

Whitehead, J. T. & Lab, S. P. (1989) A meta-analysis of juvenile correctional treatment. *Journal of Research in Crime and Delinquency, 26,* 276–295.

Yeaton, W. H. & Wortman, P. M. (1993) On the reliability of meta-analytic reviews: The role of inter-coder agreement. *Evaluation Review, 17,* 292–309.

APPENDIX 1: COGNITIVE-BEHAVIOURAL TREATMENTS AND SUBSTANCE ABUSE RELAPSE

Ashkanazi, G. S. (1990) *Outcome Evaluation of a Relapse Prevention and Drug Education Program with Federal Inmates.* Doctoral Dissertation, Florida State University.

Cook, D. S. (1990) *The Effects of an Experimental Intervention on Juvenile Female Recidivism and Drug Relapse.* Doctoral Dissertation, University of Washington.

Donovan, D. M., Salzberg, P.M., Chaney, E. F., Queisser, H. R. & Marlatt, G. A. (1990) Prevention Skills for Alcohol-Involved Drivers. *Alcohol, Drugs, and Driving, 6,* 169–188.

Greenwood, P. W. & Turner, S. (1993) Evaluation of the Paint Creek Youth Center: A Residential Program for Serious Delinquents. *Criminology, 31,* 263–279.

Johnson, G. & Hunter, R. M. (1992) *Evaluation of the Specialized Drug Offender Program.* Boulder, CO: Center for Action Research, University of Colorado.

Miller, P. M. (1975) A Behavioral Intervention Program for Chronic Drunkenness Offenders. *Archives of General Psychiatry, 32,* 915–918.

Vigdal, G. L., Stadler, D. W., Goodrick, D. D. & Sutton, D. J. (1980) Skills Training in a Program for Problem-Drinking Offenders: A One-Year Follow-Up Evaluation. *Journal of Offender Counseling, Services and Rehabilitation, 5,* 61–73.

Wexler, H. K., Magura, S., Beardsley, M. M. & Josepher, H. (1991) *Project ARRIVE: AIDS Risk Reduction Among IV Drug Users on Parole. Final Evaluation Report.* New York, NY: Narcotic and Drug Research, Inc.

Winkler, W., Jacobshagen, W. & Nickel, W.-R. (1988) *Wirksamkeit von Kursen für wiederholt alkoholauffällige Kraffahrer.* Unfallund Sicherheitsforschung Staffenverkehr, Heft 64.

Chapter 4

CRIME TREATMENT IN EUROPE: A REVIEW OF OUTCOME STUDIES

SANTIAGO REDONDO,[1] JULIO SÁNCHEZ-MECA[2] AND VICENTE GARRIDO[3]

[1] Faculty of Psychology, University of Barcelona, Spain
[2] Faculty of Psychology, University of Murcia, Spain
[3] Faculty of Psychology and Education, University of Valencia, Spain

PHILOSOPHICAL AND LEGAL ASPECTS OF REHABILITATION

All penal systems have as their main purpose, explicit or implicit, the punishment of those who break the law. To achieve this aim different penalties are used. By and large, the most frequently used are fines and the most severe, sentences of imprisonment. The latter is also the most traditional or long-standing measure. Other approaches, directed towards compensating the victim or the community for the damage caused by crime, are of much more recent origin.

One of the implicit aims of most penalties is to "correct" or change the offender's behaviour: in the case of high-risk, repetitive offenders, to help them avoid relapse into crime. This reformative aspiration emerged in nineteenth-century penal thought and nowadays it is sometimes known in criminology as the "rehabilitative ideal".

Across the board, it is hoped that all penalties applied to an offender (reprimand, fine, community work, probation, prison and parole) will be effective, and that they will dissuade the individual from committing new offences. However, in practice, the recidivism rates for crime in general, after many of the above-mentioned penalties have been imposed, are high. On average, about 50% of all convicted criminals re-offend.

The growing pessimism regarding the rehabilitative ability of the penal system has led, in the last few decades, to the development and application of other strategies—not strictly penal ones—for the prevention of crime and treatment of offenders. A century of scientific criminology has shown that criminal behaviour

Offender Rehabilitation and Treatment: Effective Programmes and Policies to Reduce Re-offending. Edited by James McGuire.
© John Wiley & Sons, Ltd.

depends not only on volitional elements and rational decisions that could be suppressed through the threat of penalties, but also on other factors. These other factors can be social: ineffective child-rearing, school failure, unemployment, drug-trafficking, strains between social groups, criminal subcultures; or they may be individual factors: low educational level, aggressive tendencies, lack of occupational skills, drug addiction, frustration, beliefs and criminal values, egocentrism, impulsiveness and the lack of a social perspective. By developing a model of tertiary crime prevention that incorporates these factors, it becomes possible to devise strategies directly designed to neutralise the roots of delinquency and criminal behaviour. These strategies are collectively known as "treatment" or "intervention" programmes. In theory, they can be conducted either in the community or in closed institutions.

At present, the "ideal of rehabilitation", in the context of the penal system, is achieved by applying educational strategies and giving social support. The aims of this are to address problems theoretically linked to an individual's illicit conduct (i.e. criminogenic needs). Some of the methods used for this purpose consist of: literacy and other basic skills training, developing negotiation skills as an alternative to violent behaviour, treatment of substance abuse, improving tolerance to frustration, developing pro-social values and attitudes, or learning to control impulsiveness. Associated interventions encompass a wide and heterogeneous range of possibilities.

International organisations such as the United Nations and the Council of Europe have issued principles, procedures and recommendations for different nations in the field of offender treatment, so that they may serve as the basis for laws and practices in this matter. They include principles regarding treatment in prison. For example, the Council of Europe has issued the following recommendations (Recommendation NR (87) 3):

- The principal objectives of treatment are to safeguard prisoners' health and dignity, as well as to develop their sense of responsibility and to provide them with those competencies that will help them to return to society, not to offend again and to provide for their own needs.
- It is an important goal, also, to reduce the stigma that follows from the experience of detention.

With this aim, the Council Recommendation proposes that all possible means be used to provide individualised treatment for convicted prisoners. This should include the use of the following strategies:

- The development of a specific occupational activity.
- The application of information and management systems that improve the relationships between staff and prisoners, in order to make prison regimes and treatments more effective.
- The establishment of open prison regimes.
- The design of treatment programmes that take account of individual differences.
- The establishment of specific systems to promote prisoners' cooperation and participation in their treatment process.

- The establishment of educational and recreational programmes and promoting the use of prison libraries.
- The use of progressive and conditional release systems, with community-based services cooperating in this task.

To date, not all European countries have included these recommendations in their own legislative frameworks. The penitentiary laws of Belgium, Germany, Italy, Netherlands, Spain and Sweden explicitly link the application of prison sentences and the provision of treatment services. By contrast, the French and the English/Welsh prison laws do not explicitly mention the ideal of the rehabi litation.

Many factors influence the extent to which different states are prepared to act on these recommendations. For example, the application of treatment programmes depends on the type of criminological philosophy prevailing in any given country. Specifically, it is important that crime prevention and the rehabilitation of offenders are considered—in the academic arena and by politicians and the public—as having a contribution to make to the struggle against criminality. A second factor is the level of development reached by the social-science disciplines devoted to designing, applying and evaluating intervention programmes focused on delinquency and crime. These disciplines include psychology, criminology, education and social work. The maturity and level of establishment that these sciences, and their respective professional memberships, may have achieved in the correctional field will be especially relevant for the development of rehabilitation programmes. The assistance given by such practitioners in prisons, juvenile institutions and other facilities for offenders, does not guarantee the development of correctional programmes, but does make it more probable. Finally, to facilitate the evaluation and diffusion of applied treatment programmes, it is usually necessary that at least some of the professionals in charge of the programmes have a proper methodological training and motivation to pursue rehabilitation as an objective.

The regrettable fact is that despite lengthy debates concerning rehabilitation held over the last few years, in some countries very few changes have occurred. Governments and penal systems throughout the world invariably respond to offenders through punishment, especially the use of imprisonment; but only very few states have established educational and treatment facilities for offenders. Furthermore, only some of those penal systems within which educational measures are statutorily available actually deliver them. Even where this happens, the number of offenders included in them is very small, sometimes for practical reasons: lack of resources or training; organisational disinterestedness; lack of motivation on the part of the potential participants, and so on.

RECIDIVISM AND TREATMENT PROGRAMMES

Reducing recidivism is not an easy aim that can be achieved exclusively through deterrence. Often, preparing offenders to avoid committing new crimes entails restoring an endless number of positive social ties that have been broken: to improve their family situation, education, job opportunities, social skills and self-control; or to reduce the use of alcohol or other drugs. Furthermore, social action is necessary to offer offenders new social and economic opportunities: social relationships and alternatives to crime; stable employment; access to housing; and other social services.

During recent years various types of treatment programmes have been developed. Some of them have offered educational facilities, others vocational training; some have treated drug addiction, others have trained hygiene habits or communication skills. Often perhaps, excessive confidence has been placed in these methods, and it has been hoped that they would categorically eliminate criminal recidivism. However, after participation some offenders still commit new offences. Then, the conclusion sometimes drawn—as simplistic and disproportionate as was the initial excessive expectation—is that since these treatment initiatives has been not fully effective, they must be completely useless. From such a perspective, the ideal of rehabilitation has apparently failed.

Placing this on a more realistic perspective, however, it would be completely unreasonable to hope that the limited changes in partial aspects of an offender's life that are promoted through intervention programmes will always produce a final interruption of their criminal careers. It would be more sensible to expect that if treatment programmes are applied, *some* offenders will change sufficiently to avoid breaking the law again. This prudent expectation is confirmed by correctional research. Some programmes (mainly cognitive-behavioural or family oriented), when applied appropriately, moderately reduce the recidivism rates of treated groups of offenders. On average, this level of reduction has a magnitude between 10% and 15%.

Compare the expectations of "treatment success" with what is expected of students graduating from university and seeking employment. The outcome of this is influenced by innumerable factors. Some of them are distant, such as the education that the individual has received in his/her family and at school and relationships with friends. Personality characteristics, social skills, friendliness, motivation and other factors also play a part. University education linked to vocational skills is superimposed on these factors and cumulatively they combine to influence the individual's overall competence. Yet cumulatively, none of this guarantees that someone will secure a good job. The latter depends also on external factors, such as supply and demand in the occupational sector of interest (connected in turn with a wide spectrum of factors, such as the state of the domestic economy). Situational factors, such as the degree of the access that the individual has to the information about the job market and the competition among candidates interested in the same job, also affect the outcome. Even though a proportion of graduates do not obtain employment consistent with university training, that does not imply that university education has completely failed in a country and should therefore be abolished. University training is a requirement for some jobs, but it is not a guarantee. In a similar way then, the application of programmes for offenders does not ensure their social reintegration. That depends on very heterogeneous factors, both personal and social.

The foregoing discussion is designed to provide a context of social and philosophical issues that arise when considering what is possible and feasible in attempting to act upon the "rehabilitative ideal". Treatment programmes can play an important, but not exclusive, part in recidivism reduction and we should be realistic about their outcomes. In what follows, we will review European research on offender treatment, before focusing on a new meta-analytic study of the impact of treatment on recidivism that we have recently carried out.

CRIMINOLOGICAL MODELS AND TREATMENT STRATEGIES IN EUROPE

In criminology, different theoretical conceptions on criminal behaviour co-exist, and from them different applications for offender treatment are derived. In Europe, according to our own reviews on this field, the principal theoretical models used as a rationale for treatment are the following (Redondo, 1994; Redondo, Garrido & Sánchez-Meca, 1997; Redondo, Sánchez-Meca & Garrido, 1999; Garrido, Stangeland & Redondo, 1999):

Theoretical Conceptions

Emotional Distress and Non-behavioural Psychological Therapies

The belief that offenders experience a series of deep emotional distresses and that criminal conduct is an external statement or symptom of these distresses has a long tradition in corrections. According to this conception, treatment of offenders would have to be directed towards their underlying psychological problems. As a result of the success obtained in psychological therapy, criminal behaviour would be reduced, or even disappear. In this model, a heterogeneous set of techniques is included: those founded on the psychodynamic model, on a medical or pathological model of crime, or on client-centred counselling.

Educational Attainments and Compensatory Intervention

Many adjudicated offenders did not complete their secondary or high school education and consequently may have a large educational or skills deficit. The conclusion drawn from this is that if we want to help this group of offenders, one main task is to increase their educational level through intensive schooling programmes. These programmes consist of basic skills training, or other school-like learning, focused on literacy, numeracy or similar remedial activities. In programmes of this type, basic education is given more emphasis than the training of practical skills.

The Learning of Criminal Behaviour and Behavioural Intervention

Learning theories (such as social learning or differential association models) consider that criminal conduct, like any other complex human behaviour, is learned. The objective of behavioural programmes is to employ learning mechanisms to reverse the learning process, so that participants can learn to inhibit criminal conduct and can put new, socially acceptable, behaviour into practice. Two paradigmatic applications of these models are token economy programmes and contingency management programmes. The former are have been particularly widely used in corrections (Morris & Braukmann, 1987). To apply such programmes effectively, all the staff of an institution must be involved and led by a group of specialists who are in charge of the design, supervision and evaluation of the programme (Redondo, 1993).

Social Interaction Skills and Cognitive-Behavioural Intervention

This approach is based on the cognitive-behavioural model, which emphasizes the need to teach offenders abilities that will facilitate interaction with others in family, job, or other social contexts. Perhaps the most comprehensive cognitive-behavioural programme is that which follows the model of "Reasoning and Rehabilitation" (Ross & Fabiano, 1985; see also McGuire & Priestley, 1989). It involves initial assessment of the offenders' deficits in cognitive and interaction skills. Following this, for those identified as requiring the programme, treatment is applied in a group setting for a series of weekly sessions.

The strategies within the programme itself are the following: *interpersonal cognitive problem-solving, social skills*, for successful interaction in social encounters; *emotional control* of explosive anger; *critical reasoning*, to teach participants to think in a more reflective and critical way about their own and other people's behaviour; *values enhancement*, to develop empathy and role taking; *negotiation abilities*, in which negotiation is taught as an alternative strategy to confrontation and violence; and *creative thinking*, to enable the individual to develop alternative ideas instead of the more habitual anti-social solutions that many offenders tend to use. Currently, cognitive-behavioural programmes are the most widely used in work on most types of offence behaviour (see Ross & Ross, 1995).

Deterrence Theory and the Hardening of Prison Regime

Toughening a prisoner's life conditions can scarcely be considered a therapeutic technique. However, during the last years in some countries there has been a trend towards designing stricter regimes with tough, military-style discipline. Prisoners, young and adult, are offered a choice between serving their sentences entirely in a standard prison or serving a reduced sentence in these "special" institutions.

Use of these methods is based on the classical doctrine of deterrence. According to this, the application of penal sanctions to offenders will remove or reduce their future criminal tendencies. The stricter and more severe the punishment, the greater will be its deterrence effects. The basic elements of this model therefore are: (1) rigid daily discipline and supervision; (2) fixed activities including work (not always of a useful character), gymnastics, parades and, sometimes, group sessions; and (3) application of an inflexible sanctions system. The pioneer country in this "new" operation is the United States of America. Fortunately, this restrictive direction has not been fully imitated in any European countries.

Healthy Institutional Environments and Therapeutic Communities

Therapeutic communities try to encompass all of a prisoner's daily life in an institution. Relationships between imprisoned people and institutional staff are defined similarly to those of patient/nurses in a therapeutic context. The main theoretical assumption is that healthy and participatory environments in custodial institutions will bring about greater psychological balance in prisoners and will reduce their anti-social behaviour, both during the individual's stay in the custodial institution and afterwards. In therapeutic communities, the kind of rigid controls and sanction systems that are common in closed institutions are suppressed. Thus, the control of prisoners' behaviour depends on the community, composed of prisoners and staff. Periodic community assemblies are held to discuss the daily problems that arise. The correct operation of a therapeutic community requires all staff to participate and to have appropriate training. This treatment modality has been very widely used with drug addiction as well as in units for violent offenders serving long-term sentences.

Avoiding Labelling Through Diversion Programmes

Labelling theory states that one of the factors that maintains criminal conduct is the subject's sense of stigmatisation through criminal justice processing. This (especially if it has involved imprisonment) will produce negative effects on the person's sense of identity and be likely to promote persistence in a criminal career. To avoid it, action should be taken to divert young offenders from the justice system, and especially from institutionalisation. This can be accomplished through alternative programmes such as mediation and reparation, or sometimes though social work intervention and supervision in the community.

THE EFFECTIVENESS OF EUROPEAN CORRECTIONAL PROGRAMMES

During the last few decades, extensive research has been conducted on the practical effectiveness of different strategies applied to groups of offenders (Lösel, 2001; McGuire, 2001). More than 20 meta-analyses have been carried out on the effectiveness of correctional treatment (e.g. Andrews et al., 1990; Dowden & Andrews, 1999, 2000; Gallagher et al., 1999; Garrett, 1985; Lipsey, 1999a, 1999b; Polizzi, McKenzie & Hickman, 1999; Wilson, Gallagher & McKenzie, 2000; Wilson & Lipsey, 2000). While most of these reviews were based on research conducted in North America, several have focused on European studies. One of them was the Lösel, Koferl and Weber (1987) meta-analysis on the effectiveness of socio-therapeutic prisons in West Germany, which used recidivism as one of its outcome measures. The other two were conducted by Redondo, Garrido and Sánchez-Meca (1997; see also Redondo, 1994) and Redondo, Sánchez-Meca and Garrido (1999), both of which related to treatment programmes applied in different European countries.

The Review of German Programmes of Lösel, Köferl and Weber

In 1987, Lösel, Köferl and Weber published the first European meta-analysis on treatment programmes (see Lösel, Köferl & Weber, 1987; Lösel & Köferl, 1989). It evaluated, from different studies published in the Federal Republic of Germany between 1977 and 1985, socio-therapeutic programmes applied in 16 German prisons.

The so-called socio-therapeutic prisons did not have a unitary conception of treatment. Their broad concept of social therapy included different elements such as the following: changes in the prisoners' life conditions, group processes, organisational factors, training in everyday skills, contact between prisoners and the community, external jobs, furloughs and programmes to prepare for release from prison.

Outcome studies were divided into two groups, according to the measure used as the success criterion: recidivism or personality features. Recidivism has been evaluated by means of different criteria, using follow-up periods from 3 to 5 years. Personality constructs have been evaluated through questionnaires, attitude scales and self-reports.

As is usual in meta-analysis Lösel and his collaborators coded the prison, participant, treatment, research design features, and the results as separate variables in the studies. Where necessary, they asked the original authors for complementary information in order to improve data validity and reliability.

The *effect size* indexes of personality variables were calculated by Cohen's d coefficient, and recidivism (in dichotomous terms) by means of Freedman's r_m coefficient. With the objective of evaluating the success of treatment regimes, they obtained five graduated estimations of *effect sizes*, from a conservative one to an optimistic one.

In all recidivism analyses reported, the effects found were positive (meaning there was a reduction of recidivism), with one exception. The studies that used personality outcomes exhibited some problems of manipulation.

According to the results obtained in the different estimations of success, the effects were generally moderate but consistent (ranging between $r_m = 0.309$ and 0.000). The average *effect size* of the five evaluative models ranged between 0.075 and 0.136, and that of separate studies, belonging to all kind of models, between 0.017 and 0.255. The confidence interval of 95% was between 0.077 and 0.181 for the most optimistic effect estimation, and between 0.038 and 0.112 for the most conservative. The most frequently obtained effect was $r_m = 0.110$.

Unfortunately, the small number of studies analysed and the deficiencies of information limited the possibilities for analysing relationships between the *effect sizes* and independent variables within treatment, participants, or context.

The main conclusion obtained by Lösel and his colleagues, related to the effectiveness of the socio-therapeutic prison regimes, was that the desired effect—non recidivism—could be anticipated for 10% more inmates in socio-therapeutic prisons than for those incarcerated in normal prisons.

Previous Meta-analyses of Redondo, Sánchez-Meca and Garrido

Recently, Redondo, Sánchez-Meca and Garrido (Redondo, Garrido & Sánchez-Meca, 1997; Redondo, Sánchez-Meca & Garrido, 1999) have published two meta-analyses on treatment programmes applied in European countries.

Treatment Effectiveness on Different Variables

The first meta-analysis by Redondo, Garrido and Sánchez-Meca (1997) analysed the effectiveness of 57 treatment programmes developed in six different countries (five European countries—Germany, Netherlands, Spain, Sweden and the United Kingdom—and Israel).

In coding the meta-analytic variables, the features of four kinds of antecedent factors (treatment, participants, context of intervention and methodology) were analysed. These features were related to six outcome measures (treatment implementation level, institutional adjustment, psychological adjustment, educational adjustment, vocational adjustment, interaction skills adjustment and recidivism).

Eight categories of theoretical models were established, underpinning the treatments used (similar to those described earlier):

1. Non-behavioural therapy, such as individual or group psychotherapy (a category to which 9 studies were assigned).
2. Educational–informational interventions, such as school or delivery of educational material (6 studies).
3. Behavioural therapy, exclusively founded on classical or operant conditioning models as in the case of token economies or environmental outlines based on contingencies (11 studies).
4. Cognitive-behavioural therapy, such as social skills training or psycho-social competence programmes (19 studies).
5. Classical penal theory based on retribution, such as models of "shock incarceration" or increasing levels of institutional control (1 study).
6. Therapeutic community where prisoner–staff relationships were conceived as similar to patient–nurse relationships, or with decreasing levels of institutional control (5 studies).
7. Diversion programmes or community treatment (5 studies).
8. Others, for instance psychiatric institutions (1 study).

A standardised mean difference (d) was used in order to calculate the effect size (ES) of each programme. For the studies comparing two groups (experimental–control), d was defined as the difference between the means of both groups divided by the within-group standard deviation; for one group pre-test/post-test studies d was the difference between the means of the pre-test and post-test divided by the within-group standard deviation. When a programme was effective, d had a positive value, and a negative value in the contrary case. Finally, all d indexes were transformed (using the procedure of Rosenthal, 1991) into Pearson's correlation coefficients (r), permitting a direct interpretation in terms of percentages of experimental and comparison sample recidivating.[1*]

The main characteristics of the European programmes were as follows. The *intervention magnitude*, defined as the total number of treatment hours per offender, had a low intensity (median = 22.5 hours). The *total sample* included 7728

---

*Notes are presented at the end of the chapter.

participants: the vast majority was male with a median age of 19 years, sentenced for property offences. Of this sample, 4284 were in treatment groups and 3444 in control groups. The median duration of programmes was 2.5 months, with 3.75 treatment hours per week. Behavioural and cognitive-behavioural models of treatment were the most frequently employed. Programmes were more often delivered in juvenile prisons, adult prisons and in the community. The median length of the follow-up periods was 12 months, while the mean was 19.7 months. The most commonly employed design was quasi-experimental.

The following were the most important results of this evaluation:

- The vast majority of programmes—50 (87%) from the 57 analysed—obtained positive effects.
- The average Pearson correlation coefficient was $r = 0.15$ ($d = 0.3039$, statistically significant with $p < 0.0001$). This means that treated groups surpassed controls by 15 points.
- In terms of crime typology, the greatest effectiveness was obtained with offenders against persons ($r = 0.419$), and the least with sexual offenders ($r = 0.085$).
- The greatest effectiveness was achieved in juvenile centres ($r = 0.257$) and in juvenile prisons ($r = 0.193$), and the smallest in adult prisons ($r = 0.119$).
- Behavioural ($r = 0.279$) and cognitive-behavioural programmes ($r = 0.273$) produced the greatest levels of effectiveness, and retribution programmes ($r = 0.039$) the least.
- Concerning recidivism, the mean ES had a value of $r = 0.12$ ($p < 0.001$). Cognitive-behavioural ($r = 0.265$) and behavioural programmes ($r = 0.232$) produced a reduction of recidivism rates that was double the mean for the programmes as a whole.

Treatment Effectiveness on Recidivism

In a second study, Redondo, Sánchez-Meca and Garrido (1999) analysed the specific influence of 32 European treatment programmes (applied during the 1980s) on recidivism. As we have said previously, recidivism is a final product of the failure of different social agents, such as family, school, employment, and public safety measures, in the task of community integration. From a criminological perspective, recidivism is necessarily the "bottom line" criterion when evaluating treatment effectiveness.

The same process as outlined above was used to code the studies. Standardised mean difference (d) was the effect size index selected to summarise the results of each empirical study. Meta-analytical procedures developed by Hedges (1994) and Hedges and Olkin (1985) were applied, weighting each effect size by its inverse-variance.

Recidivism was defined broadly, as any measure of new delinquent or criminal behaviour: contacts with the police, arrests, parole and probation revocation, vandalism, self-reported offences, new sentences, return to juvenile institutions or prisons, and so on.

The effectiveness of the European treatment programmes on recidivism was of $d = 0.242$ (95% confidence interval: 0.196 and 0.287). This corresponds to an average correlation coefficient of $r = 0.120$. That means that recidivism was reduced by 12% in treated groups. This result is very similar to the value of recidivism reduction obtained in other meta-analyses.

The effectiveness of European programmes in reducing recidivism rates was characterised by the following factors:

- Behavioural and cognitive-behavioural programmes were the most effective.
- Treatments were more successful with juvenile offenders. However, the reason for this greater efficacy with juveniles was probably due to the fact that they were treated with the most successful techniques (behavioural and cognitive-behavioural).
- As in our previous meta-analysis concerning crime typology, the greatest effectiveness was achieved with violent offenders (not sex offenders), which seems to confirm the *risk principle* (Andrews et al., 1990). This principle holds that larger effects can be expected from programmes applied to high-risk offenders, who usually receive the most intensive and highest quality correctional services.

A NEW META-ANALYSIS ON THE EFFECTIVENESS OF EUROPEAN TREATMENT PROGRAMMES ON RECIDIVISM REDUCTION (1980–1998)

Purpose of the Meta-analysis

Both the meta-analysis conducted by Redondo, Sánchez-Meca and Garrido (1999) and the one now presented in this chapter, were exclusively focused on evaluation studies that used some kind of recidivism measure. However, there are several differences between them. First, the previous meta-analysis covered the years 1980 to 1991, whereas the present one covers 1980 to 1998. Second, the prior meta-analysis included different research designs, mixing one-group pre-test/post-test design with two-group designs. The current meta-analysis, in order to achieve more homogeneity among the studies, was restricted to studies with two or more groups, one of which was the control group. Third, the previous meta-analysis included different measures of recidivism, such as prevalence indexes (i.e. dichotomous measures, such as recidivism versus no recidivism) and incidence indexes (i.e. the average number of offences committed by the sample of offenders). In this new analysis, only dichotomous measures of re-offending were included, again in order to achieve more homogeneity. Fourth, because of the homogeneity produced by the studies' methodological characteristics, it was possible in the present meta-analysis to apply more adequate effect size indexes, such as the odds ratio, in preference to the *phi* coefficient and the standardised mean difference. In spite of the popularity of the latter measures, they cannot be considered the most advisable indexes to summarise dichotomous data (Haddock, Rindskopf & Shadish, 1998). Finally, our prior meta-analysis on recidivism did not distinguish between different methods of operationalising recidivism, whereas in the current study, three recidivism definitions were adopted, as explained below.

Our present research focuses on testing the effectiveness of correctional programmes implemented in Europe to reduce recidivism, with the following main objectives: (a) to determine the global effectiveness of correctional treatment compared to control groups; (b) to explain the variability in effect sizes by detecting the characteristics that moderate the results in the empirical studies, such as treatment type, the type of offenders, the age of offenders and so on; and (c) to compare the effectiveness of European programmes with those obtained in previous American meta-analyses.

Method

Literature Search

The target population of studies was defined by selection criteria, and to be retained a study had to: (a) include offenders under the control of the criminal justice system (young or adult offenders); (b) use a treatment strategy for some time; (c) apply a controlled group design; (d) include some dichotomous measure of recidivism; and (e) have been implemented in Europe. The search covered the period 1980 to 1998. Several information sources were used to identify the literature. First, computer databases such as *Criminal Justice Periodical Index, Pascal*, and *PsycLIT* were consulted. Second, a manual search of 55 (mostly European) specialised journals was carried out. Third, letters requesting studies on the topic were sent to 118 key researchers and 82 European institutions linked to the field. Finally, all references cited in the selected studies were also reviewed. The literature search enabled us to select a total of 23 research papers that produced 26 studies meeting the inclusion criteria. The total sample in these studies was of 5764 subjects, 2570 belonging to the treatment groups and the remaining 3194 assigned to the control groups.

Coding Moderator Variables

The characteristics of the studies that might moderate the results were classified in five clusters: treatment, subject, setting, methodological and extrinsic variables (Lipsey, 1994; Sánchez-Meca, 1997). The *treatment* cluster included: (a) the theoretical treatment model (non-behavioural psychological treatments, educational/informational programmes, behavioural therapy, cognitive-behavioural therapy, deterrence theory, therapeutic community, diversion programmes and other), (b) the length of the programme (in months), and (c) the intensity of the programme (in hours per person per week). The cluster of *subject* variables was composed of: (a) the age of the members of the sample (adolescents, juveniles, mixed and adults), (b) the most common offence type in the sample (property, people, sex, drug traffic, alcohol and mixed), and (c) the sample gender (percent male). The cluster of *setting* variables included: (a) the setting in which the programme was applied (juvenile reform centre, juvenile prison, adult prison, in the community and other), (b) the regime of the participants (closed, semi-open, open and other), and (c) the country. Regarding the variables related to the *methodology*, the following were included: (a) the procedure for assignment of subjects to the groups (random versus non-random), (b) the attrition rate of treated group, and (c) the follow-up period (in months). Finally, the following *extrinsic variables* were included: (a) the year in which the paper was published, and (b) the literature source (published versus unpublished).

Recidivism Measures

The literature on correctional treatment evaluation shows the great diversity of definitions that researchers have applied to recidivism as an outcome. The most commonly used measure of recidivism is based on a dichotomous record (recidivist versus non-recidivist) of each individual's behaviour during a given follow-up period after his or her release, regardless of the number of offences committed. Thus, the proportion of the sample re-offending size constitutes a *prevalence index* of sample recidivism, as compared to *incidence indexes* which consists of dividing the number of offences by the sample size. We focused on prevalence rates of recidivism because they are the most commonly used.

Another problem in homogenising the definition of recidivism is the great diversity of terms used in empirical studies (Lipsey, 1992). It is easy to find very different definitions of recidivism, such as "new police contacts", "new arrests or detentions", "new sentences", "commission of new offences", "imprisonment", "revocation of probation" and so on. Following a previous study (Sánchez-Meca, Marín-Martínez & Redondo, 1996), we proposed three prevalence rates of recidivism, two of them based on official records of the juvenile criminal justice services or the police, and the third based on informal data. The two official indices of recidivism were the "General recidivism rate" and the "Serious recidivism rate". The former is a broad definition of re-offending and includes any terms related to the commission of new offences, new sentences, rearrests, reconvictions, new police contacts, or new confinement. On the other hand, "serious recidivism" refers only to the commission of new offences that give rise to the loss of freedom (return to prison or revocation of probation). Thus, "serious recidivism" will be dominated by the gravest offences, whereas "general recidivism" represents less serious offences. The third index employed is "Self-reported recidivism", which is obtained by means of interviews or questionnaires applied to the offenders. Although used less frequently, self-reported recidivism can complement the other two official indexes, especially when the offences are not serious (e.g. driving under the influence of alcohol, vandalism).

Effect Size Indexes

The result of each empirical study included in our meta-analysis can be summarised as a 2×2 contingency table, group membership being one of the variables (treated versus control groups) and the dichotomous measure of recidivism being the other variable (recidivism versus non-recidivism). The *phi* coefficient and the standardised mean difference (*d*) have been the effect size indexes usually applied in meta-analysis to measure the effectiveness of correctional treatment. However, recent research has shown that *phi* and *d* indexes applied to a set of 2×2 tables underestimate the true effect size (Fleiss, 1994; Haddock, Rindskopf & Shadish, 1998; Sánchez-Meca, Redondo & Marín-Martínez, 1998). Instead, other indexes, such as the "odds ratio", have been recommended that more accurately estimate the population effect size. The "odds ratio" can be translated to *d* and *r* indexes, enabling its comparison with the results of other related meta-analyses (Hasselblad & Hedges, 1995). Therefore, in this meta-analysis the odds ratio was the effect size index used, but our results are presented as correlation coefficients (*r*) in order to compare the results with those of other meta-analyses.

Statistical Analysis

The statistical model used in our meta-analysis is based on the approach proposed by Hedges and Olkin (1985) adapted to the integration of a set of 2×2 tables. It consists of weighting the effect size of each study by the inverse of its variance, in order to give more weight to the studies with the larger sample sizes. Thus, the following statistical analyses were applied: (a) a weighted mean of the *r* index, (b) a 95% confidence interval around the mean, and (c) a homogeneity test of the set of indexes around the mean. Finally, (d) if the effect sizes showed more heterogeneity around the mean than expected from sampling error, then a search for moderator variables was carried out.

Results

Descriptive Characteristics of the Studies

Most of the studies (61.5%) included samples of adult offenders with an average age of 25.5 years, with most samples consisting of males. The offence types in the samples were: mixed offences (28%), alcohol-related offences (24%), property offences (20%), sex offences (12%), drug-traffic offences (12%), and person offences (4%).

The theoretical treatment models found in the studies were: non-behavioural psychological therapies (26.9%), educational programmes (19.2%), diversion programmes (19.2%), cognitive-behavioural programmes (15.4%) and therapeutic community programmes (15.4%). The programmes presented a median duration of 4.5 months with 4 hours of treatment per week.

The programmes were most frequently applied in the community (50%) and in adult prisons (20.8%). Among the latter, the samples of offenders usually received the programmes in open regimes (39.1%) and in closed regimes (30.4%). The most frequently represented country was the UK (11 studies, 42.3%) followed by Germany (5 studies, 19.2%), Sweden (5 studies, 19.2%), Netherlands (4 studies, 15.4%) and Israel (1 study, 3.9%).

Only two studies (7.7%) randomly assigned the subjects to the groups and the average attrition rate in treated groups was 36.8%. Follow-up periods ranged from 6 to 120 months and had a median of 24 months. Most of the studies were published in journals or books (22 studies, 84.6%). Finally, more than the half of the studies were published between 1988 and 1991 (14 studies, 53.9%).

The Average Effect Size

Table 4.1 shows the summary statistics of the correlation coefficients (r) obtained for each recidivism measure (general, serious and self-reported recidivism). The 23 studies that presented data about general recidivism achieved a mean effect size of $r_+ = 0.21$; this magnitude is statistically significant ($z = 15.22$, $p < 0.001$). Therefore, in general, the groups of treated offenders showed a lower re-offending rate than the control groups. In particular, applying the Binomial Effect Size Display (BESD) of Rosenthal (1991) the treated groups had a recidivism rate of 39.5% as compared to 60.5% of the control groups—that is, a differential recidivism rate of 21%.

The measure of serious recidivism was reported in only eight studies, presenting a mean effect size of $r_+ = 0.22$, also in favour of the treated groups and statistically significant ($z = 6.63$, $p < 0.001$). This result implies a 22% differential rate of re-offending or, applying the BESD, a recidivism rate of 39% in treated groups, as opposed to a rate of 61% in control groups. Thus, the general effectiveness of programmes in terms of serious recidivism was very similar to that for general recidivism. Regarding self-reported re-offending, it was possible to report this type of measure only in three studies, achieving an average effect size of $r_+ = 0.31$ and being statistically significant in favour of the treated groups ($z = 9.32$, $p < 0.001$). The three studies applied programmes to reduce the recidivism of offences related to vandalism (Kruissink, 1989) and drunk driving (Bovens, 1987; Van Dalen, 1989).

Owing to the scarcity of studies that included measures of serious and self-reported recidivism, these results cannot be accepted in any general sense. However, the results obtained with respect to general recidivism can be compared to those of other meta-analyses already carried out on the effectiveness of correctional treatment. It is worth noting that the average effect size achieved in our meta-analysis was clearly higher than that obtained in previous reviews. The present mean value of $r_+ = 0.21$ can be compared to effect sizes of $r_+ = 0.12$ (Lösel & Koferl, 1989; Redondo, Sánchez-Meca & Garrido, 1999; Whitehead & Lab,

Table 4.1 Summary statistics of correlation coefficients for each recidivism measure

	Recidivism		
Statistics	General	Serious	Self-reported
No. of studies	23	8	3
No. of treated subjects	2102	375	468
No. of control subjects	2813	413	381
Proport. of positive ES's	18/23 = 0.78	8/8 = 1.0	3/3 = 1.0
Minimum	−0.55	0.06	0.14
Maximum	0.75	0.66	0.71
Weighted mean	0.21	0.22	0.31
95% Confidence Interval	0.20/0.22	0.16/0.28	0.25/0.37
Significance test, z	15.22*	6.63*	9.32*
Homogeneity test, Q_T	146.53*	39.97*	78.32*

*$p < 0.05$.

1989), $r_+ = 0.16$ (Pearson et al., 1995), $r_+ = 0.10$ (Andrews et al., 1990), $r_+ = 0.065$ (Garrett, 1985) or $r_+ = 0.05$ (Lipsey, 1992).

The reason for these differences is the procedure for estimating the effect size from the 2×2 contingency tables. The *phi* and *d* indexes usually applied in previous meta-analyses are negatively biased estimates of the true effect size (Haddock et al., 1998); in fact, the average *phi* coefficient obtained in our meta-analysis was $phi_+ = 0.12$, very similar to that of previous meta-analyses. By contrast, the correlation coefficient calculated through the odds ratio provides a more accurate estimate of the true programme effect size. This evidence casts doubt on the apparently low efficacy of programmes exhibited in previous meta-analyses. As a consequence, our results offer a less pessimistic picture of the global effectiveness of correctional treatment. Use of the odds ratio as an effect size index in meta-analyses of 2×2 tables should be more frequently considered in future review work.

Searching for Moderator Variables

The three indexes of re-offending showed a very high heterogeneity in effect sizes (Table 4.1)—even in the case of serious and self-reported recidivism—in spite of the low number of studies (serious recidivism: $Q_T[7] = 39.97$, $p < 0.001$; self-reported recidivism: $Q_T[2] = 78.32$, $p < 0.001$). Thus, attempts were made to find moderator variables that could explain such heterogeneity. Because general recidivism was the most commonly reported index in the studies reviewed ($k = 23$) and with the highest variability ($Q_T[22] = 146.53$, $p < 0.001$), the search for moderator variables focused on this index.

Tables 4.2 and 4.3 present the results of the analyses of variance and regression, all of them weighting by the inverse of the variance of each effect size, applied to different moderator variables. One of the more important characteristics of the studies was the theoretical model of the programmes applied. Our results (Table 4.2) show that the theoretical model is statistically related to the effectiveness ($Q_B[5] = 30.98$, $p < 0.001$), with 21.1% of explained variance. Although all of the theoretical models exhibited a statistically significant effectiveness, the largest effect sizes were achieved with educational programmes ($r_+ = 0.49$) and cognitive-behavioural therapy ($r_+ = 0.30$), with therapeutic community ($r_+ = 0.13$) and diversion programmes ($r_+ = 0.14$) the least effective. The duration and intensity of the programmes did not seem to be related to effectiveness (Table 4.3).

Programme setting was related to effect size ($Q_B[3] = 17.94$, $p < 0.001$), with 12.8% of explained variance (Table 4.2). With the exception of programmes implemented in juvenile prisons ($r_+ = 0.05$) the remaining settings showed statistically significant effect sizes, with community being the setting in which the programmes demonstrated the largest effect sizes ($r_+ = 0.26$), together with "other settings" ($r_+ = 0.28$) such as psychiatric centres. On the other hand, the regime of the participants in the programmes was also related to effectiveness ($Q_B[3] = 28.67$, $p < 0.001$), with 19.8% of explained variance (Table 4.2). The best results were obtained when the offenders received the treatments in open regimes ($r_+ = 0.28$).

With the exception of the only study from Israel (Cohen et al., 1991), the different countries represented in the meta-analysis showed statistically significant effect

Table 4.2 Results of the analyses of variance for the qualitative variables on general recidivism

Cluster/moderator variables	k_j	r_+	Q_B	R^2
I. TREATMENT CLUSTER				
• *Theoretical model* ($k = 23$)			30.98*	0.211
Nonbehavioural psychological therapies	7	0.24*		
Educational programmes	3	0.49*		
Cognitive-behavioural therapy	4	0.30*		
Therapeutic community	4	0.13*		
Diversion programmes	4	0.14*		
Other	1	0.25*		
II. SUBJECT CLUSTER				
• *Sample age* ($k = 23$)			13.86*	0.095
Adolescents (<16)	2	0.35*		
Juveniles (16–21)	6	0.16*		
Mixed	1	0.14*		
Adults (>21)	14	0.24*		
• *Main offence type* ($k = 22$)			15.95*	0.112
Property offences	5	0.23*		
People offences	1	0.25*		
Sex offences	3	0.30*		
Drug traffic offences	3	0.12*		
Alcohol related offences	4	0.25*		
Mixed	6	0.24*		
III. SETTING CLUSTER				
• *Programme setting* ($k = 21$)			17.94*	0.128
Juvenile prison	4	0.05		
Adult prison	4	0.18*		
In the community	10	0.26*		
Other	3	0.28*		
• *Regime of participants* ($k = 23$)			28.67*	0.198
Closed	6	0.18*		
Semi-open	1	−0.18		
Open	8	0.28*		
Other	6	0.26*		
• *Country* ($k = 23$)			13.43*	0.092
Germany	5	0.23*		
Great Britain	11	0.24*		
Israel	1	0.05		
Netherlands	2	0.35*		
Sweden	4	0.18*		
IV. METHOD CLUSTER				
• *Random assignment* ($k = 23$)			0.98	0.007
Random	2	0.10		
Nonrandom	21	0.21*		
V. EXTRINSIC CLUSTER				
• *Publication source* ($k = 23$)			5.29*	0.036
Published	20	0.23*		
Unpublished	3	0.16*		

*$p < 0.05$. k_j = No. of studies. Q_B = Between groups significance test. R^2 = Proportion of explained variance.

Table 4.3 Results of the weighted simple regression analyses for the quantitative variables on general recidivism

Cluster/moderator variable	k	B_j	Q_R	R^2
I. TREATMENT CLUSTER				
Programme duration (months)	15	0.004	2.049	0.022
Programme intensity (hours week)	12	−0.001	0.624	0.011
II. SUBJECT CLUSTER				
Sample gender (% of men)	20	−0.001	0.516	0.004
III. METHOD CLUSTER				
Attrition (% in treated group)	17	−0.001	0.503	0.005
Follow-up (months)	22	−0.002	8.994*	0.061
IV. EXTRINSIC CLUSTER				
Publication year	23	−0.001	0.047	0.000

*$p < 0.05$. k = Number of studies. B_j = Unstandardised regression coefficient. Q_R = Significance test of the regression coefficient. R^2 = Proportion of explained variance.

sizes. The two studies from Netherlands exhibited the largest mean effect size ($r_+ = 0.35$), followed by the UK ($r_+ = 0.24$), Germany ($r_+ = 0.23$) and Sweden ($r_+ = 0.18$). The differences between the countries were statistically significant ($Q_B[4] = 13.43$, $p < 0.01$).

With respect to the characteristics of the offenders, our results showed differential effectiveness as a function of the type of offences committed ($Q_B[5] = 15.95$, $p < 0.01$), with 11.2% of explained variance. Although all the mean effect sizes were statistically significant, the largest effect size was achieved with sex offences ($r_+ = 0.30$) and the lowest for drug-trafficking-related offences ($r_+ = 0.12$). On the other hand, the age of the offenders was also related to effect size ($Q_B[3] = 13.86$, $p < 0.01$), with 9.5% of explained variance. The largest effect sizes were obtained with adolescents ($r_+ = 0.35$), although all the age categories achieved significant positive results.

Methodological variables, such as the attrition in the treated group and assignment type of the subjects to the groups, did not reach statistical significance (Tables 4.2 and 4.3). Nonetheless, it is worth noting that the two studies that applied random assignment to the groups did not show a significant effect size ($r_+ = 0.10$), as opposed to the studies with non-random assignment ($r_+ = 0.21$). As expected, the follow-up period was negatively related to effect size ($Q_B[1] = 8.99$, $p < 0.05$), with 6.1% of explained variance; that is, as the follow-up period increases, the effectiveness decreases (Table 4.3). Finally, the three unpublished studies showed a lower mean effect size ($r_+ = 0.16$) than the published ones ($r_+ = 0.23$), the difference reaching statistical significance ($Q_B[1] = 5.29$, $p < 0.05$); but in both cases the mean effect sizes exhibited a significant positive direction.

AN AGENDA FOR THE FUTURE

Rehabilitation, it seems, works. However, some issues that have arisen from treatment effectiveness research remain as important challenges for the future. In the remainder of this chapter, we would like to propose some key areas requiring further investigation.

Improving the Effectiveness of Treatment Practitioners

Lipsey and Wilson (1993) conducted the most extensive meta-analyses of the effectiveness of psychological interventions. These analyses show at least modest positive effect sizes for interventions of almost all types for almost all problems. In fact, psychological treatments are generally helpful as opposed to harmful or ineffective. The other issue is *to describe how the effect is produced*, because at this level of analysis the type of treatment administered appears to be irrelevant. These findings are compatible with the repeated finding that the level of practitioner training and experience is unrelated to treatment effectiveness (see Quinsey et al., 1998).

However, a more detailed analysis indicates that particular approaches to intervention yield much larger treatment effect sizes. In the area of child and adolescent psychotherapy, behavioural treatments have been shown to produce larger treatment effect sizes than non-behavioural treatment (Weisz et al., 1995). Further, in relationship to correctional treatment, research clearly points out that behavioural and cognitive-behavioural treatments directed towards relevant problems (criminological needs) of moderately high-risk offenders have been shown to reduce criminal recidivism more than other treatment approaches (Andrews et al., 1990; McGuire, 1992).

These examples of particularly effective treatments share common elements, the most important of which for our argument is that the treatment methods be sufficiently well-specified so that they can be taught to intelligent lay people.

> The general conclusion seems to be that clinical intuition, experience and training at least as traditionally conceived are not helpful in either prediction or treatment delivery. Although discouraging, this conclusion is not nihilistic. Training, in the sense of knowing the empirical literature and relevant scientific and statistical techniques, must improve the selection of appropriate treatments, treatment programme planning, and evaluation. (Quinsey et al., 1998, p. 72)

On Dissemination and Adoption of Innovative Psychosocial Interventions

Why does correctional evaluation have so little impact on the policy field? Backer, Liberman and Kuchnel (1986) studied the dissemination and adoption of innovative psychosocial interventions. After reviewing the literature, they concluded the reason was that clinicians read little of this literature because it is written primarily for researchers as opposed to practitioners. Professional meetings and workshops similarly have limited effectiveness because they are primarily didactic and do not involve the active-directive training known to be more effective with adult learners. Gendreau et al. (Chapter 14 of the present volume) discuss other factors influencing the slow take-up of research findings.

Backer, Liberman and Kuchnel (1986) documented the characteristics of three successful programme dissemination efforts. The common characteristics of these efforts were: personal contact between developers and potential adopters; external consultation on the adoption process; organised support for the innovation; consistent advocacy by agency staff; adaptability of the innovation to new circumstances; credible evidence of the innovation's effectiveness; and complete descriptions of how to conduct the treatment. However, it is clear that a great gap remains between what research has shown to be possible or effective and what happens in practice. "This paradoxical situation arguably ought to be a central issue in criminal justice policy. Yet, in the face of recurrent widespread concern over crime, there are continuing difficulties in including the issue of effective intervention on the public policy agenda" (McGuire, 1996, pp. 85–86).

Offenders with Mental Disorders

Although most insanity acquittees are sent to secure hospitals and most convicted persons are sent to prison, the differences between secure hospitals and prisons are often slight. Although the presumption is that insanity acquittees require treatment for their mental disorder, sometimes no effective treatments are available. In addition, when treatments are available, many patients refuse them. Moreover, even when effective treatments are known and patients are willing to participate, programmes are sometimes not available (Quinsey et al., 1998).

Some data suggest that there is considerable overlap between the offender populations of criminal justice systems and the mentally disordered populations of ordinary psychiatric hospitals. After studying prison and mental hospital populations in several Europeans countries, Penrose (1939) noted a strong negative correlation between them. He proposed "Penrose's Law": as the size of the prison population goes up, the size of the mental hospital population goes down proportionately, and vice versa. In North America, evidence for this hydraulic model has been mixed (Teplin, 1991).

Thus, mentally disordered offenders overlap heavily with both offender and mentally disordered populations. Mentally disordered offenders, like other offenders, have committed a wide range of offences, from fraud, shoplifting or vagrancy to multiple murder. The disorders from which they suffer also cover a broad range, including all those listed on axes I and II of the DSM-IV (APA, 1994), although not all would be sufficient in themselves to earn them the label "mentally disordered offender". "Little is known about effective intervention for mentally disordered offenders specifically, and almost nothing about how different demographic and status variables moderate any intervention effects" (Quinsey et al., 1998, p. 79).

Rice et al. (1990) examined the long-term recidivism rates of a large group ($n = 280$) of insanity acquittees and compared them with of a group of convicted men ($n = 238$). Overall, the predictors of violent recidivism in this study were consistent with those that have been found to predict re-offending in other studies of criminal recidivism. They included arrest at an early age, criminal history, alcohol abuse, aggression, impulsiveness, school maladjustment, parental separation, parental crime, employment, marital status, a diagnosis of personality disorder and score of the Level of Supervision Inventory (LSI). In addition, the pattern of results revealed remarkable similarity between the two groups in the ways recidivism was related to each study variable. These findings are important because they lend strong support to the argument that the same variables that predict criminal recidivism among offenders in general, also predict criminal recidivism among mentally disordered offenders (Bonta, Law & Hanson, 1998). Since the antisocial behaviour of mentally disordered offenders is related to the same factors associated with crime in non-mentally disordered offenders, basing the release of insanity acquittees solely on psychopathological symptoms and recovery would be a serious mistake. The results of the studies carried out by Rice et al. (1990) suggest that treatment programmes for mentally disordered offenders must include programmes designed to attend to their "criminogenic needs" such as substance abuse, antisocial attitudes and values, and criminal associates. The evaluation of correctional programmes focused on these targets has produced the most promising results (Andrews, Bonta & Hoge, 1990).

Psychopathy

Offenders classifiable as being "psychopathic" occupy many beds in both criminal justice and forensic mental health facilities. Wong (1984) found that as many as 30% of Canadian federal prisoners could be categorised as psychopaths; the percentage increasing with institutional security level. The treatability of psychopaths has long concerned criminologists and mental health experts. Early reports indicated positive effects of psychotherapy (Corsini, 1958; Thorne, 1959), but other researchers have critically evaluated the evidence and have argued that treatment for adult psychopaths is ineffective (e.g. McCord, 1982; Woody et al., 1985). We will not discuss the issue extensively here; however, it is interesting to underscore that new developments are coming, albeit slowly.

> Some relatively consistent patterns of results appear: small to medium efficacy can be demonstrated for cognitive-behavioural programmes, multi-modal treatment, structured therapeutic community programmes and social therapy for serious and personality-disordered offenders. (Lösel, 1998, p. 330)

Clearly the need to improve the quality of research noted in the general offender literature is even more markedly felt in the case of psychopaths. In particular, empirically based criminological need assessments are yet to be conducted, because assessment is driven mainly by clinical practice, theory and speculation (Polaschek & Reynolds, 2001).

So, we need to work hard. As McMurran (2001, p. 476) wrote:

> Researchers and clinicians working in the field of personality disordered offenders . . . are searching for answers to the fundamental question: "What works best with whom under which conditions?" There will never be a simple, one-line answer to this important and socially relevant question.

Sex Offenders

The results of our meta-analysis are positive in relation to the treatment of sex offenders, but the small number of studies analysed (3) is not sufficient for the drawing of firm conclusions. This is an area in which findings to date have been somewhat mixed. In a meta-analysis by Hanson and Bussière (1998), focused primarily on prediction of sexual re-offending, treatment did not appear to reduce sexual recidivism. In another meta-analysis, this time involving treatment studies, Hall (1995) found that hormonal and cognitive-behavioural approaches produced medium effect sizes (whereas behaviourally oriented intervention failed to reach significance). Overall, the meta-analysis yielded a small effect size for treatment of sex offenders. However the effect size closely approximated zero in the case of studies that used a matching or randomised design (Rice & Harris, 1997).

Whereas some specialists in this field have remained pessimistic regarding treatment outcomes with sex offenders, others have drawn more positive conclusions. Quinsey, Khana and Malcom (1998, pp. 642–643) concluded that "we are much better at measuring risk than we are at modifying it . . . much stronger treatment effects will have to be shown than those demonstrated in the present study or heretofore in the literature". By contrast, Marshall, Anderson and Fernandez (1999) have been critical of this dismissal of treatment efforts and have adduced findings of a more positive nature. More research is required in order to resolve these disputes. (See Mann & Beech, Chapter 10 of the present volume, for a review of recent work in this field.)

Alongside this, there is a considerable need for research on adolescent sexual offenders (Hudson & Ward, 2001). Optimism concerning the amount of change that is possible among adolescents in general has to be yet supported in the case of sex offenders, due to the important gaps in the knowledge of the sexual criminal career development. Anyway, it is a priority to realise that continuing with treatment is the only way we will develop better techniques and, consequently, be able to save money and the pain of innocent people (Marshall, 2001).

Supervision in the Community

The literature on the effects of supervision among offenders in general, suggests that although intensive supervision programmes run the risk of "widening the net" by including low-risk offenders, supervision that is limited to offenders of moderate to high risk and that includes rehabilitation components, can reduce the risk of recidivism (Gendreau, Cullen & Bonta, 1994). Such supervision might include the use of technology, such as electronic monitoring and drug testing. However, no data are available on the effectiveness of such measures for sex offenders or sexually violent predators in particular (Quinsey et al., 1998).

One obvious factor that should be considered is the effectiveness of supervision upon early release. The early literature on the effectiveness of parole contains few studies and is methodologically weak (Nietzel & Himelein, 1987). Gottfredson, Mitchell-Herzfeld and Flanagan (1982) concluded that supervision had but small effects on recidivism. In the light of recent reviews, it is possible to conclude that an important cause of these early results was the inadequate knowledge of the specific antecedents of recidivism; that is, of the dynamic (changing) conditions of the offender or identifiable environmental events that cause recidivism. Today this knowledge has improved, and rehabilitative efforts in community corrections are able to address specific events (criminological needs) related to recidivism.

The results of a study by Gendreau (1999) stress this point. He assessed the effectiveness of "intermediate sanctions", a form of sentencing which includes intensive supervision and other intrusive-punitive measures such as boot camps, "scared straight" and so on, as compared with regular probation and parole. The database encompassed a total ample in the region of 50 000. The results indicated no effect at all on recidivism. However, there was an important moderate variable: the inclusion of "treatment" in the programme:

> Those few intermediate sanctions that made an attempt at providing some treatment, although it was not their primary goal (but they provided more treatment than did the regular probation control group) reduced recidivism by 10%. The ones that did not include treatment, increased recidivism by the same amount... More important, when those programmes that followed the "principles of effective intervention" (e.g. programmes that target criminogenic needs, higher risk cases and are cognitive-behaviourally oriented) were examined, the average effect size was a 29% reduction in recidivism. There were, regrettably, just 45 such instances in the literature. (Gendreau, 1999, p. 18)

Public Support for Rehabilitative Policies

Opponents to rehabilitation often say that the public do not support rehabilitative policies. Gendreau (1999) mentions that there is still strong support for rehabilitative practices, even in traditionally conservative areas of United States. Considering that Europe has a long history in advocating progressive measures of penal reform, the following conclusions derived from Gendreau regarding the USA could apply even more to most European countries. First, opinion polls have presented a misleading picture of public crime by assessing only surface views; public opinion is quite complex, and favours a balanced approach to crime. High-risk offenders are thought to merit punishment, yet it is also important to rehabilitate most offenders. Second, community treatment is considered worth while if constructive tasks are provided. Third, rehabilitation for juveniles is advocated as well as early intervention, even favouring the use of taxes for these programmes rather than building more prisons.

Understanding and Overcoming Offender Resistance to Change

The possible reasons for offender resistance are profuse (Elliot & Walters, 1991). Perhaps the main reason is the fact that incarcerated offenders frequently see nothing wrong with their offences, have no desire for change, and seriously question the motives and intentions of those offering treatment. A related matter is the absence of tangible rewards and incentives for changing behaviour. Another important obstacle is offender resistance in its various forms (denials and rationalisations), which enables the individual to avoid facing the self-defeating and socially destructive nature of his or her acts. Finally, it is likely that some offenders re-enact long-standing patterns of interpersonal manipulation and coercion with practitioners, which eventually serve to impede the rehabilitation process.

In the same way, failure to complete treatment successfully is a serious problem facing juvenile residential treatment providers. Non-completers do not appear to be as successful later in life as those who complete residential treatment, and they also appear to be more psychologically maladjusted, as evidenced by elevated profiles on a variety of personality measures (Kraemer, Salisbury & Spielman, 1998). Despite the importance of research for successful intervention in this area, few studies identify pre-treatment factors associated with non-completion.

CONCLUSIONS

This chapter has dealt with three areas of main relevance for the present situation in offender rehabilitation. First, we have discussed which expectations about treatment seem reasonable in a criminal policy agenda. It is now time to put effectiveness in the place where it belongs: that of helping some offenders desist from criminal behaviour, through supporting innovation in correctional services.

Second, we have updated a previous review of offender rehabilitation in Europe. Our results support the efficacy of correctional treatment, offering estimates of effectiveness even higher than those of previous meta-analyses. Positive effects have been reached for the three recidivism measures—general, serious, and self-reported re-offending—though the results should be interpreted cautiously because of the low number of studies that recorded serious and self-reported recidivism. The heterogeneity of effect sizes can be explained by the influence of such factors as the theoretical model of treatment, the programme setting, the regime of the offenders, or the type of offences committed. The best results are obtained when programmes are implemented in the community and the treatment model is educational or based on cognitive-behavioural methods. Finally, we recommend using the odds ratio in meta-analysis as the more suitable effect size index when the results of each empirical study are given in a 2×2 table (Fleiss, 1994; Haddock, Rindskopf & Shadish, 1998; Sánchez-Meca, Redondo & Marín-Martínez, 1998).

Finally, the results of European studies, as well as those from North America, help to develop some lines of inquiry for future research. Sexual and psychopathic offenders and offenders with learning disabilities deserve closer scrutiny in terms of programme effectiveness. Community-based services, public support for rehabilitative policies, and the inclusion of these innovations in the political agenda, are other important points on which to work.

NOTE

1. The reader has to take into account that the Pearson correlation coefficient, r, coincides with the *phi* coefficient when it is applied in a 2×2 contingency table.

REFERENCES

(References preceded by an asterisk were included in the meta-analysis)

Andrews, D. A., Bonta, J. & Hoge, R. D. (1990) Classification for effective rehabilitation: Rediscovering psychology. *Criminal Justice and Behavior, 17*, 19.

Andrews, D. A., Zinger, I., Hoge, R. D., Bonta, J., Gendreau, P. & Cullen, F. T. (1990) Does correctional treatment work? A clinically relevant and psychologically informed meta-analysis. *Criminology, 28*, 369–404.

American Psychiatric Association (1994) *Diagnostic and statistical manual of mental disorder* (4th ed.) (DSM-IV). Washington, D. C.: Author.

Backer, T. E., Liberman, R. P. & Kuchnel, T. G. (1986) Dissemination and adoption of innovative psychosocial interventions. *Journal of Consulting and Clinical Psychology, 54*, 111–118.

*Belfrage, H. (1991) The crime preventive effect of psychiatric treatment on mentally disordered offenders in Sweden. *International Journal of Law and Psychiatry, 14*, 237–243.

*Berggren, O. & Svärd, H. (1990) *The Österaker project: A further follow-up of the drug misuser treatment programme at Österaker prison.* Kriminalvarden, Forsknings gruppen, Research paper No. 1.

*Bishop, N., Osborne, A. S. & Pettersson, T. (1987) *The Drug Free Programme at the Hinseberg Prison for Women.* National Prison and Probation Administration (Report 1987: 4).

Bonta, J., Law, M. & Hanson, K. (1998) The prediction of criminal and violent recidivism among mentally disordered offenders: A meta-analysis. *Psychological Bulletin, 122*, 123–142.

*Bovens, R. (1987) The alcohol programme: An educational programme for drunken drivers in prison. In M. J. M. Brand-Koolen (Ed.) *Studies on the Dutch Prison System* (pp. 151–157). Kugler.

*Brownlee, I. D. (1995) Intensive probation with young adult offenders. *British Journal of Criminology, 35*, 599–612.

*Cohen, B.-Z., Eden, R. & Lazar, A. (1991) The efficacy of probation versus imprisonment in reducing recidivism of serious offenders in Israel. *Journal of Criminal Justice, 19*, 263–270.

*Collins, S. A. & Tate, D. H. (1988) Alcohol related offenders and a voluntary organisation in a Scottish community. *The Howard Journal, 27*, 44–57.

*Cook, D. A. G., Fox, C. A., Weaver, C. M. & Rooth, F. G. (1991) The Berkeley group: Ten years' experience of a group for non-violent sex offenders. *British Journal of Psychiatry, 158*, 238–243.

*Cooke, D. J. (1991) Psychological treatment as an alternative to prosecution: A form of primary diversion. *The Howard Journal, 30*, 53–65.

Corsini, R. (1958) Psychodrama with a psychopath. *Group Psychotherapy, 11*, 33–39.

*Deering, J., Thurston, R. & Vanstone, M. (1996) Individual supervision and reconviction: An experimental programme in Pontyprid. *Probation Journal, 43*, 70–76.

Dowden, C. & Andrews, D. A. (1999) What works for female offenders: A meta-analytic review. *Crime and Delinquency, 45*, 438–452.

Dowden, C. & Andrews, D. A. (2000) Effective correctional treatment and violent re-offending: A meta-analysis. *Canadian Journal of Criminology*, October, 449–467.

*Dünkel, F. (1982) Selection and recidivism after different models of imprisonment in West Berlin. Edited by the Criminological Research Unit: *Research in Criminal Justice* (pp. 452–470). Freiburg: Max-Planck-Institute for Foreign and International Penal Law.

Elliot, W. N. & Walters, G. D. (1991) Coping with offender resistance to psychoeducational presentations on the criminal lifestyle. *Journal of Correctional Education, 42*, 172–177.

Fleiss, J. L. (1994) Measures of effect size for categorical data. In H. Cooper & L. V. Hedges (Eds.) *The Handbook of Research Synthesis* (pp. 245–260). New York: Sage.

Gallagher, C. A., Wilson, D. B., Hirschfield, P., Coggeshall, M. B. & McKenzie, D. L. (1999) A quantitative review of the effects of sexual offender treatment on sexual re-offending. *Corrections Management Quarterly, 3*, 19–29.

Garrido, V., Stangeland, P. & Redondo, S. (1999) *Principios de Criminología [Principles of Criminology]*. Valencia: Tirant lo Blanch.

Garrett, P. (1985) Effects of residential treatment of adjudicated delinquents: A meta-analysis. *Journal of Research in Crime and Delinquency, 22*, 287–308.

Gendreau, P. (1999) Rational policies for reforming offenders. *The ICCA Journal of Community Corrections, 9*, 16–20.

Gendreau, P., Cullen, F. T. & Bonta, J. (1994) Intensive rehabilitation supervision: The next generation in community corrections. *Federal Probation, 58*, 72–78.

Gottfredson, M. R., Mitchell-Herzfeld, S. D. & Flanagan, T. J. (1982) Another look at the effectiveness of parole supervision. *Journal of Research in Crime and Delinquency, 19*, 277–298.

Haddock, C. K., Rindskopf, D. & Shadish, W. R. (1998) Using odds ratios as effect sizes for meta-analysis of dichotomous data: A primer on methods and issues. *Psychological Methods, 3*, 339–353.

Hall, G. C. N. (1995) Sexual offender recidivism revisited: A meta-analysis of recent treatment studies. *Journal of Consulting and Clinical Psychology, 63*, 802–809.

Hanson, R. K. & Bussière, M. T. (1998) Predicting relapse: A meta-analysis of sexual offender recidivism studies. *Journal of Consulting and Clinical Psychology, 66(2)*, 348–362.

Hasselblad, V. & Hedges, L. V. (1995) Meta-analysis of screening and diagnostic tests. *Psychological Bulletin, 117*, 167–178.

Hedges, L. V. (1994) Fixed effects models. In H. Cooper & L. V. Hedges (Eds.), *The handbook of research synthesis* (pp. 285–299). New York: Sage.

Hedges, L. V. & Olkin, I. (1985) *Statistical Methods for Meta-analysis*. Orlando, FL: Academic Press.

Hudson, S. M. & Ward, T. (2001) Adolescent sexual offenders: assessment and treatment. In C. V. Hollin (Ed.) *Handbook of Offender Assessment and Treatment* (pp. 363–378). Chichester: Wiley.

Kraemer, B. D., Salisbury, S. B. & Spielman, C. R. (1998) Pretreatment variables associated with treatment failure in a residential juvenile sex-offender programme. *Criminal Justice and Behavior, 25*, 190–202.

*Kruissink, M. (1989) *Diversion of vandals in the Netherlands ("Halt-Projects"): Preliminary results of an evaluation study*. Paper presented at the VII Journées Internationales de Criminologie Juvenile, Noordujijkerhout (Pays-Bas).

*Kury, H. (1989) Treatment of young remand prisoners: Problems and results of a research project. In H. Wegener, F. Lösel & J. Haisch (Eds.) *Criminal Behavior and the Justice System* (pp. 356–381). New York: Springer-Verlag.

Lipsey, M. W. (1992) Juvenile delinquency treatment: A meta-analytic inquiry into the variability of effects. In T. D. Cook, H. Cooper, D. S. Cordray, H. Hartmann, L. V. Hedges, R. J. Light, T. A. Louis & F. Mosteller (Eds.) *Meta-analysis for Explanation: A Casebook* (pp. 83–127). New York: Sage.

Lipsey, M. W. (1994) Identifying potentially interesting variables and analysis opportunities. In H. Cooper & L. V. Hedges (Eds.) *The Handbook of Research Synthesis* (pp. 111–123). New York: Sage.

Lipsey, M. W. (1999a) Can intervention rehabilitate serious delinquents? *Annals of the American Academy of Political and Social Science, 564*, 142–166.

Lipsey, M. W. (1999b) Can rehabilitative programmes reduce the recidivism of juvenile offenders? *Virginia Journal of Social Policy and the Law, 6*, 611–641.

Lipsey, M. W. & Wilson, D. B. (1993) The efficacy of psychological, educational, and behavioral treatment: Confirmation from meta-analysis. *American Psychologist, 48*, 1181–1209.

Lösel, F. (1998) Treatment and management of psychopaths (pp. 303–354). In D. J. Cooke, A. E. Forth, & R. D. Hare (Eds.) *Psychopathy: Theory, Research and Implications for Society*. Dordrecht: Kluwer.

Lösel, F. (2001) Evaluating the effectiveness of correctional programmes: Bridging the gap between research and practice. In G. A. Bernfeld, D. P. Farrington & A. W. Leschied (Eds.) *Offender Rehabilitation in Practice: Implementing and Evaluating Effective Programmes* (pp. 67–92). Chichester: Wiley.

Lösel, F. & Koferl, P. (1989) Evaluation research on correctional treatment in West Germany: A meta-analysis. In H. Wegener, F. Lösel, & J. Haisch (Eds.) *Criminal Behavior and the Justice System: Psychological Perspectives* (pp. 334–355). New York: Springer-Verlag.

Lösel, F., Koferl, P. & Weber, F. (1987) *Meta-Evaluation der Sozialtherapie*. Stuttgart: Enke.

Marshall, W. L. (2001) Adult sexual offenders against women. In C.V. Hollin (Ed.) *Handbook of Offender Assessment and Treatment* (pp. 333–348). Chichester: Wiley.

Marshall, W. L., Anderson, D. & Fernandez, Y. (1999) *Cognitive Behavioural Treatment of Sexual Offenders*. Chichester: Wiley.

McCord, M. W. (1982) *The Psychotherapy and Milieu Therapy*. New York: Academic Press.

McGuire, J. (1992) Enfocaments psicològics per a la reducció de la conducta delictuosa: Investigació recent i implicacions pràctiques. [Psychological strategies for reduction of offending behaviour: Recent research and practical implications.] *Papers d'Estudis i Formació, 10*, 67–77.

McGuire, J. (1996) Community based interventions. In C. R. Hollin (Ed.) *Working with Offenders* (pp. 63–93). Chichester: Wiley & Sons.

McGuire, J. (2001) What works in correctional intervention? Evidence and practical implications. In G. A. Bernfeld, D. P. Farrington & A. W. Leschied (Eds.) *Offender Rehabilitation in Practice: Implementing and Evaluating Effective Programmes* (pp. 25–43). Chichester: Wiley.

McGuire, J. & Priestley, Ph. (1989) *Offending Behaviour: Skills and Stratagems for Going Straight*. London: BT Batsford Ltd.

McMurran, M. (2001) Offender with personality disorders. In C. V. Hollin (Ed.) *Handbook of Offender Assessment and Treatment* (pp. 467–480). Chichester: Wiley.

*McMurran, M. & Boyle, M. (1990) Evaluation of a self-help manual for young offenders who drink: A pilot study. *British Journal of Clinical Psychology, 29*, 117–119.

*Müller-Isberner, J. R. (1996) Forensic psychiatric aftercare following hospital order treatment. *International Journal of Law and Psychiatry, 19*, 81–86.

Nietzel, M. T. & Himelein, M. J. (1987) Probation and parole. In E. K. Morris & C. J. Braukmann (Eds.) *Behavioral Approaches to Crime and Delinquency: Application, Research and Theory* (pp. 109–133). New York: Plenum Press.

Pearson, F. S., Lipton, D. S., Cleland, C. M. & O'Kane, J. B. (November, 1995) *Meta-analysis on the effectiveness of correctional treatment: Another approach and extension of the time frame to 1994: A progress report*. Paper presented at the Annual Meeting of the American Society of Criminology, Boston, Massachusetts.

Penrose, L. (1939) Mental disease and crime: Outline of a comparative study of European statistics. *British Journal of Medical Psychology, 18*, 1–15.

*Pettersson, T., Sundin-Osborne, A. & Bishop, N. (1986) *Results of the Drug Misuser Treatment Programme at the Österaker Prison*. National Prison and Probation Administration (Report 1986: 2).

Polascheck, D. L. & Reynolds, N. (2001) Assessment and treatment: violent offenders. In C. V. Hollin (Ed.) *Handbook of Offender Assessment and Treatment* (pp. 415–432). Chichester: Wiley.

Polizzi, D. M., McKenzie, D. L. & Hickman, L. J. (1999) What works in adult sex offender treatment? A review of prison and non-prison based treatment programmes. *International Journal of Offender Therapy and Comparative Criminology, 43*, 357–374.

*Proctor, E. (1994) Sex offender programmes: Do they work? *Probation Journal, 41*, 31–32.

Quinsey, V. L., Coleman, G., Jones, B. & Altrows, I. (1997) Proximal antecedents of eloping and re-offending among mentally disordered offenders. *Journal of Interpersonal Violence, 12*, 794–813.

Quinsey, V. L., Harris, G. T., Rice, M. E. & Cormier, C. A. (1998) *Violent Offenders. Appraising and Managing Risk*. Washington: American Psychological Association.

Quinsey, V. L., Khana, A. & Malcom, P. B. (1998) A retrospective evaluation of the regional treatment centre sex offender treatment programme. *Journal of Interpersonal Violence, 13*, 621–644.

Redondo, S. (1993) *Evaluar e intervenir en las prisiones. [Evaluating and Intervening at the Prisons]*. Barcelona: Promociones y Publicaciones Universitarias.

Redondo, S. (1994) *El tratamiento de la delincuencia en Europa: Un estudio meta-analítico. [The treatment of offenders in Europe: A meta-analysis.]* Unpublished Doctoral Thesis, University of Barcelona (Spain).

Redondo, S., Garrido, V. & Sánchez-Meca, J. (1997) What works in correctional rehabilitation in Europe: A meta-analytic review. In S. Redondo, V. Garrido, J. Pérez & R. Barberet (Eds.) *Advances in Psychology and Law: International Contributions* (pp. 499–523). Berlin: De Gruyter.

Redondo, S., Sánchez-Meca, J. & Garrido, V. (1999) The influence of treatment programmes on the recidivism of juvenile and adult offenders: An European meta-analytic review. *Psychology, Crime, and Law, 5*, 251–278.

Rice, M. E. & Harris, G. T. (1997) Cross validation and extension of the Violence Risk Appraisal Guide for child molesters and rapists. *Law & Human Behavior, 21*, 231–242.

Rice, M. E., Harris, G. T., Lang, C. & Bell, V. (1990) Recidivism among male insanity acquittees. *Journal of Psychiatry and Law, 18*, 379–403.

*Robertson, M. & Gunn, J. (1987) A ten-year follow-up of men discharged from Grendon prison. *British Journal of Psychiatry, 151*, 674–678.

Ross, R. & Fabiano, E. A. (1985) *Time to Think: A Cognitive Model of Delinquency Prevention and Offender Rehabilitation.* Johnson City, TN: Institute of Social Sciences and Arts.

Ross, R. & Ross, R. (1995) *Thinking Straight.* Ottawa: Air Training & Publications.

Rosenthal, R. (1991) *Meta-analytic Procedures for Social Research* (rev. edn.). Newbury Park, CA: Sage.

*Rosner, A. (1988) Evaluation of a drinking-driver rehabilitation programme for first offenders. In G. Kaiser & I. Geissler (Eds.) *Crime and Criminal Justice* (pp. 319–336). Freiburg: Eigenverlag Max-Planck-Institute.

Sánchez-Meca, J. (1997) Methodological issues in the meta-evaluation of correctional treatment. In S. Redondo, V. Garrido, J. Pérez & R. Barberet (Eds.) *Advances in Psychology and Law: International Contributions* (pp. 486–498). Berlin: De Gruyter.

Sánchez-Meca, J., Marín-Martínez, F. Redondo, S. (1996) Reincidencia: Evaluación internacional. [Recidivism: An international assessment.] In J. Funes, E. Luque, A. Ruiz & J. Sánchez-Meca (Eds.) *Reincidència: En la justícia de menors/Avaluació internacional [Recidivism: In Juvenile Justice/International Assessment]* (pp. 93–200). Barcelona: Generalitat de Catalunya.

Sánchez-Meca, J., Redondo, S. Marín-Martínez, F. (November, 1998) *A reanalysis of the work of Whitehead and Lab (1989): A meta-analysis of juvenile correctional treatment.* Paper presented at the Annual Meeting of the American Society of Criminology, Washington, DC.

*Scholte, E. M. & Smit, M. (1987) Early social assistance for juveniles at risk. *International Journal of Offender Therapy and Comparative Criminology*, 209–218.

Shadish, W. R. & Haddock, C. K. (1994) Methods for combining effect size estimates. In H. Cooper & L. V. Hedges (Eds.) *The Handbook of Research Synthesis* (pp. 261–281). New York: Sage.

*Slot, N. W. Bartels, A. A. J. (1983) Outpatient social skills training for youth in trouble theoretical background, practice, and outcome. In W. Everaerd, C. B. Hindley, A. Bot & J. J. van der Werf ten Bosch (Eds.) *Development in Adolescence: Psychological, Social and Biological Aspects* (vol. 10, pp. 176–191). Martinus Nijhoff.

Teplin, L. A. (1991) The criminalization hypothesis: Mith, misnomer, or management strategy. In S. A. Shah & B. D. Sales (Eds.) *Law and Mental Health: Major Developments and Research Needs* (pp. 149–183). Rockville, MD: National Institute of Mental Health.

Thorne, F. C. (1959) The etiology of sociopathic reactions. *American Journal of Psychotherapy, 13*, 310–330.

*Van Dalen, W. E. (1989) Education: A successful instrument for reducing drunken driving in the Netherlands. In R. B. Waahlberg (Ed.) *Prevention and Control/Realities and Aspirations* (vol. IV, pp. 714–722). Oslo: NDPADP.

Weisz, J. R., Weiss, B., Han, S. S., Granger, D. A. & Mortin, T. (1995) Effects of psychotherapy with children and adolescents revisited: A meta-analysis of treatment outcome studies. *Psychological Bulletin, 117*, 450–468.

Whitehead, J. T. & Lab, S. P. (1989) A meta-analysis of juvenile correctional treatment. *Journal of Research in Crime and Delinquency, 26*, 276–295.

Wilson, D. B., Gallagher, C. A. & McKenzie, D. L. (2000) A meta-analysis of corrections-based education, vocation, and work programmes for adult offenders. *Journal of Research in Crime and Delinquency, 37*, 347–368.

Wilson, S. J. & Lipsey, M. W. (2000) Wilderness challenge programmes for delinquent youth: A meta-analysis of outcome evaluations. *Evaluation and Programme Planning, 23*, 1–12.

*Wilkinson, J. (1997) The impact of Ilderton motor project on motor vehicle crime offending. *British Journal of Criminology, 37*, 568–581.

Wong, S. (1984) *The criminal and institutional behaviors of psychopaths (Programs Branch User Report)*. Ottawa, Canada: Ministry of the Solicitor General of Canada.

Woody, G. E., McLellan, A. T., Robersky, L. & O'Brien, C. P. (1985) Sociopathy and psychotherapy outcome. *Archives of General Psychiatry, 42*, 1081–1086.

Chapter 5

DEVELOPMENTAL PREVENTION PROGRAMMES: EFFECTIVENESS AND BENEFIT–COST ANALYSIS

DAVID P. FARRINGTON[1] AND BRANDON C. WELSH[2]

[1]*Institute of Criminology, University of Cambridge, UK*
[2]*Dept. of Criminal Justice, University of Massachusetts at Lowell, USA*

The major methods of reducing crime can be classified as developmental, community, situational or criminal justice prevention (Tonry & Farrington, 1995). Developmental prevention refers to interventions designed to prevent the development of criminal potential in individuals, especially those targeting risk and protective factors discovered in studies of human development (Farrington, 1994; Tremblay & Craig, 1995; Wasserman & Miller, 1998). This is sometimes termed "criminality prevention" in the United Kingdom (Graham & Bennett, 1995), and Utting has very usefully reviewed British developmental prevention initiatives (Utting, Bright & Henricson, 1993; Utting, 1995, 1996). Community prevention refers to interventions designed to change the social conditions and institutions (e.g. families, peers, social norms, clubs, organizations) that influence offending in residential communities (Rosenbaum, 1988; Hope, 1995). Situational prevention refers to interventions designed to prevent the occurrence of crimes by reducing opportunities and increasing the risk and difficulty of offending (Clarke, 1995, 1997). Criminal justice prevention refers to traditional deterrent, incapacitative and rehabilitative strategies operated by law enforcement and criminal justice system agencies (Blumstein, Cohen & Nagin, 1978; Sechrest, White & Brown, 1979; von Hirsch et al., 1999).

This chapter has two main aims. The first is to review evaluations of the effectiveness of developmental prevention in reducing offending and antisocial behaviour, and the second is to review economic analyses of the monetary benefits and costs of developmental prevention programmes.

Offender Rehabilitation and Treatment: Effective Programmes and Policies to Reduce Re-offending. Edited by James McGuire.
© John Wiley & Sons, Ltd.

EVALUATING DEVELOPMENTAL PREVENTION

The most convincing method of evaluating developmental or other intervention programmes is the randomized experiment (Farrington, 1983), which is often referred to as the "gold standard" of evaluation designs. The key feature of randomized experiments is that the experimental and control groups are equated before the experimental intervention on all possible extraneous variables. Hence, any subsequent differences between them must be attributable in some way to the intervention.

The randomized experiment, however, is only the most convincing method of evaluation if a sufficiently large number of units can be randomly assigned to ensure that the programme group is equivalent to the control group on all possible extraneous variables (within the limits of statistical fluctuation). As a rule of thumb, at least 50 units in each category are needed (Farrington, 1997). This number is relatively easy to achieve with individuals—the focus of the present review—but very difficult to achieve with larger units such as areas or schools. For larger units, the best and most feasible design usually involves before-and-after measures in experimental and control areas, together with statistical control of extraneous variables (see Painter & Farrington, 1997, 2001). Non-randomized experiments and before–after designs without a control group are less convincing methods of evaluating crime reduction programmes.

Apart from randomized experiments, assessing the methodological quality of research designs, and thus determining internal validity or the level of confidence which can be attributed to the observed effects, is somewhat more difficult. This chapter largely overcomes this problem by focusing only on the highest quality evaluations of developmental prevention programmes. An extremely valuable tool for assessing the methodological quality of the full range of research designs of intervention studies is the "scientific methods scale" developed by Sherman and his colleagues (1997) of the University of Maryland. This is as follows, with level 1 being the lowest and level 5 the highest:

1. Correlational evidence: low offending correlates with the programme at a single point in time.
2. Non-equivalent control group or one-group before-after design: (a) programme group compared with non-equivalent control group; or (b) programme group measured before and after intervention (with no control group).
3. Equivalent control group design: programme group compared with comparable control group, including before–after and experimental-control comparisons.
4. Control of extraneous variables: programme group compared with control group, with control of extraneous influences on the outcome (e.g. by matching, prediction scores, or statistical controls).
5. Randomized experiment: units assigned at random to programme and control groups.

This methodological rating scale assesses overall internal validity of evaluations; external validity, or the generalizability of internally valid results (Sherman et al., 1998, p. 3), was not addressed as part of the scientific methods score, although it was taken into account in assessing what did or did not work. We used the scientific methods score to assess the methodological adequacy of the few non-randomized studies included here (e.g. Hawkins et al., 1999). Only programmes with a scientific methods score of at least 3 are reviewed in this chapter.

It is important to note that Sherman et al. (1997) did not take account of differences between individual and area/school studies. As noted above, it is very difficult to assign areas or schools at random to experimental and control conditions and analyse them as such; that is, without creating the problem of mixed units of analysis. Mixed units of analysis occur when the unit of analysis differs from the unit of assignment; for example, if areas or schools are assigned and individuals are analysed. Therefore, it could be argued that the "gold standard" for area/school evaluation designs should be level 4. Also, for randomized (individual) studies where there are design problems (e.g. because of substantial loss of cases) or design changes (e.g. because of the addition of a quasi-experimental control group; see Hawkins et al., 1999), it may be appropriate to downgrade the initial scientific methods score.

EVALUATION OF SPECIFIC PROGRAMMES

In this chapter, developmental prevention programmes are divided into 10 categories: home visiting, day care, preschool, skills training, parent training, school, anti-bullying, mentoring, community and multi-systemic therapy. Because many interventions were multi-modal, it was not easy to assign studies unambiguously to one of these categories. Our aim in each of these categories is to describe one programme in detail (often because it was the subject of a benefit–cost analysis that is discussed later). In general, evaluations are chosen because they are published, because they include an outcome measure of offending or antisocial behaviour, because the evaluation design was of high quality methodologically, and because the initial sample size was at least 100 or so persons (see also Farrington, 1999; Farrington & Welsh, 1999).

Home-Visiting Programmes

Teenage mothers can be helped, child abuse can be reduced, and problems in pregnancy and infancy can be alleviated by intensive home-visiting programmes. In Elmira (New York State), Olds et al. (1986) randomly allocated 400 mothers either to receive home visits from nurses during pregnancy, or to receive visits both during pregnancy and during the first two years of life, or to a control group who received no visits. Each visit lasted about one and a quarter hours, and the mothers were visited on average every two weeks. The home visitors gave advice about prenatal and postnatal care of the child, about infant development, and about the importance of proper nutrition and avoiding smoking and drinking during pregnancy.

The results of this experiment showed that home visits during pregnancy led to teenage mothers having heavier babies. Also, women who had previously smoked decreased their smoking and had fewer pre-term deliveries. In addition, the postnatal home visits caused a decrease in recorded child physical abuse and neglect during the first two years of life, especially by poor unmarried teenage mothers; 4% of visited mothers versus 19% of non-visited mothers of this type were guilty of child abuse or neglect. This last result is important because of the common observation that being physically abused or neglected as a child predicts later violent offending (Widom, 1989).

Unusually, this experiment had a 15-year follow-up, and the main focus in the follow-up was on lower class unmarried mothers. Among these mothers, those who received prenatal and postnatal home visits had fewer arrests than those who received prenatal visits or no visits (Olds et al., 1997). Also, children of these mothers who received prenatal and/or postnatal home visits had less than half as many arrests as children of mothers who received no visits (Olds et al., 1998). This study and other similar evaluations (Larson, 1980; Kitzman et al., 1997) show that intensive home visiting can help poor unmarried mothers and reduce later delinquency by their children.

Day Care Programmes

One of the very few prevention experiments beginning in pregnancy and collecting outcome data on delinquency was the Syracuse (New York State) Family Development Research Programme of Lally (1988). The researchers began with a sample of pregnant women (mostly poor African American single mothers) and gave them weekly help with child-rearing, health, nutrition and other problems. In addition, their children received free full-time day care, designed to develop their intellectual abilities, up to age 5. This was not a randomized experiment, but a matched control group was chosen when the children were aged 3. The experimental children had significantly higher intelligence than the controls at age 3 but were not significantly different at age 5. Ten years later, 119 experimental and control children were followed up to about age 15. Significantly fewer of the experimental children (2% as opposed to 17%) had been referred to the juvenile court for delinquency offences, and the experimental girls showed better school attendance and school performance.

Desirable results were also obtained in a day care intervention in Houston by Johnson and Walker (1987) but not by McCarton et al. (1997) in the large-scale Infant Health and Development Program. This programme, implemented in eight sites across the United States, had encouraging results at age 3; however, the experimental and control children were not significantly different in behaviour problems at age 8.

Preschool Programmes

One of the most successful delinquency prevention programmes has been the Perry preschool project carried out in Ypsilanti (Michigan) by Schweinhart and Weikart (1980). This was essentially a "Head Start" programme targeted on disadvantaged African American children, who were allocated (approximately at random) to experimental and control groups. The experimental children attended a daily preschool programme, backed up by weekly home visits (to involve the mother in the programme), usually lasting two years (covering ages 3–4). The aim of the "plan-do-review" programme was to provide intellectual stimulation, to increase thinking and reasoning abilities, and to increase later school achievement.

About 120 children in the two groups were followed up to age 15, using teacher ratings, parent and youth interviews, and school records. As demonstrated in several other Head Start projects, the experimental group showed gains in intelligence that were rather short-lived. However, they were significantly better in elementary school motivation, school achievement at age 14, teacher ratings of classroom behaviour at 6 to 9, self-reports of classroom behaviour at 15 and self-reports of offending at 15. Furthermore, a later follow-up of this sample (Berrueta-Clement et al., 1984) showed that, at age 19, the experimental group was more likely to be employed, more likely to have graduated from high school, more likely to have received college or vocational training, and less likely to have been arrested.

By age 27, the experimental group had accumulated only half as many arrests on average as the controls (Schweinhart, Barnes & Weikart, 1993). Also, they had significantly higher earnings and were more likely to be home-owners. More of the experimental women were married, and fewer of their children were born out of wedlock. Hence, this preschool intellectual enrichment programme led to decreases in school failure, to decreases in offending, and to decreases in other undesirable outcomes. Desirable results were also obtained in other preschool evaluations (Pagani et al., 1998; Webster-Stratton, 1998).

Skills Training

Perhaps the best-known method of skills training was developed by Ross and Ross (1995). This programme aimed to teach offenders to stop and think before acting, to consider the consequences of their behaviour, to conceptualize alternative ways of solving interpersonal problems, and to consider the impact of their behaviour on other people, especially their victims. It included social skills training, lateral thinking (to teach creative problem-solving), critical thinking (to teach logical reasoning), values education (to teach values and concern for others), assertiveness training (to teach non-aggressive, socially appropriate ways to obtain desired outcomes), negotiation skills training, interpersonal cognitive problem-solving (to teach thinking skills for solving interpersonal problems), social perspective training (to teach how to recognize and understand other people's feelings), role-playing and modelling (demonstration and practise of effective and acceptable interpersonal behaviour).

Ross carried out his own "Reasoning and Rehabilitation" programme in Ottawa, and found (in a randomized experiment) that it led to a large decrease in reoffending for a small sample of adult offenders in a short 9-month follow-up period. His training was carried out by probation officers, but he believed that it could be carried out by parents or teachers. His programme has been implemented widely in several different countries, including the United Kingdom.

As an example, a similar programme, entitled "Straight Thinking on Probation" was implemented in Glamorgan by Raynor and Vanstone (2001). Offenders who received the skills training programme were compared with similar offenders who received custodial sentences. After one year, offenders who completed the programme had a lower re-conviction rate than control offenders (35% as opposed to 49%), although both had the same predicted re-conviction rate of 42%. However, the benefits of the programme had worn off at the two-year follow-up point, when re-conviction rates of experimentals (63%) and controls (65%) were similar to each other and to predicted rates. Nevertheless, it seems likely that the experimental offenders committed fewer crimes than the controls during the two-year follow-up period.

Skills training was used as part of a multi-modal programme by Tremblay et al. (1995) in Montreal. They identified about 250 disruptive (aggressive/hyperactive) boys at age 6 for a prevention experiment. Between ages 7 and 9, the experimental group received training to foster social skills and self-control. Coaching, peer modelling, role-playing and reinforcement contingencies were used in small group sessions on such topics as "how to help", "what to do when you are angry" and "how to react to teasing". Also, their parents were trained using the parent management training techniques developed by Patterson (1982).

This prevention programme was quite successful. By age 12, the experimental boys committed less burglary and theft, were less likely to get drunk, and were less likely to be involved in fights than the controls. Also, the experimental boys had higher school achievement. At every age from 10 to 15, the experimental boys had lower self-reported delinquency scores than the control boys. Interestingly, the differences in antisocial behaviour between experimental and control boys increased as the follow-up progressed.

For this chapter, the most relevant skills training experiment is the evaluation of the United States Job Corps by Long, Mallar and Thornton (1981), because it included a benefit–cost analysis. The main aim of the Job Corps was to improve the employability of participants by offering vocational and educational skills training and health care. Long, Mallar and Thornton (1981) matched Job Corps participants who had been out of the programme for an average of 18 months with non-participating youth of similar age (about 18) and socio-economic status (usually low). The sample as a whole included approximately 5100 youths.

Job Corps participants showed increased job productivity (as measured by employment during and after the programme) and reduced criminal activity. In the 18-month follow-up period, participants were one-third less likely to be arrested. Also, they earned more than non-participants and were less likely to be dependent on welfare benefits. A more recent evaluation of Job Corps (Schochet, Burghardt & Glazerman, 2000), which has yet to be subjected to a benefit–cost analysis, found that, at 30 months follow-up, the experimentals compared to the controls had lower arrest rates, were more likely to be employed and had higher earnings, and had higher educational attainment.

Parent Training

Perhaps the best-known method of parent training was developed by Patterson (1982) in Oregon. Parents were trained to notice what a child is doing, monitor behaviour over long periods, clearly state house rules, make rewards and punishments contingent on the child's behaviour, and negotiate disagreements so that conflicts and crises did not escalate. His treatment was shown to be effective in reducing child stealing and antisocial behaviour over short periods in small-scale studies (Dishion, Patterson & Kavanagh, 1992; Patterson, Chamberlain & Reid, 1982; Patterson, Reid & Dishion, 1992).

Webster-Stratton and Hammond (1997) evaluated the effectiveness of parent training and child skills training with 97 Seattle children (average age 5.7) referred to a clinic because of conduct problems. The children and their parents were randomly allocated to receive either (a) parent training, (b) child skills training, (c) both parent and child training, or (d) to a control group. The skills training aimed to foster prosocial behaviour and interpersonal skills using video modelling, while the parent training involved weekly meetings between parents and therapists for 22–24 weeks.

Parent reports and home observations showed that children in all three experimental conditions had fewer behaviour problems than control children, both in an immediate and in a one-year follow-up. There was little difference between the three experimental conditions, although the combined parent and child training condition produced the most significant improvements in child behaviour at the one-year follow-up. Similar desirable results were obtained in other evaluations of parent training (Kazdin, Siegel & Bass, 1992; Scott et al., 2001; Strayhorn & Weidman, 1991; Webster-Stratton, Kolpacoff & Hollinsworth, 1988).

School Programmes

An important school-based prevention experiment (the Seattle Social Development Project) was carried out by Hawkins and colleagues (1991, 1992). This combined parent training, teacher training and skills training. About 500 first-grade children (aged 6) in 21 classes in eight schools were randomly assigned to be in experimental or control classes. The children in the experimental classes received special treatment at home and school which was designed to increase their attachment to their parents and their bonding to the school, on the assumption that offending was inhibited by the strength of social bonds. They were also trained in interpersonal cognitive problem-solving, based on the work of Spivack, Platt and Shure (1976). In addition, their parents were trained to notice and reinforce socially desirable behaviour in a programme called "Catch them being good". Their teachers were trained in classroom management, for example to provide clear instructions and expectations to children, to reward children for participation in desired behaviour, and to teach children prosocial (socially desirable) methods of solving problems.

In an evaluation of this programme 18 months later, when the children were in different classes, Hawkins, von Cleve and Catalano (1991) found that the boys who received the experimental programme were significantly less aggressive than the control boys, according to teacher ratings. This difference was particularly marked for White boys rather than African American boys. The experimental girls were not significantly less aggressive, but they were less self-destructive, anxious and depressed. Later analyses included not only the original first-grade children but also children added to the study in the fifth and sixth grades, some of whom received the experimental intervention at this time. Hawkins et al. (1992) found that, in the fifth grade (age 11), the experimental children were less likely to have initiated delinquency and substance use (according to self-reports).

O'Donnell et al. (1995) focused on children in low income families and reported that, in the sixth grade (age 12), experimental boys were less likely to have initiated delinquency, while experimental girls were less likely to have initiated drug use. In the latest follow-up of 643 children studied at age 10, Hawkins et al. (1999) found that, at age 18, the full intervention group (receiving the intervention from grades 1–6) admitted less violence, less alcohol abuse and fewer sexual partners than the late intervention group (grades 5–6 only) or the controls. Other school-based prevention experiments have also been successful in reducing antisocial behaviour, including the important experiment carried out by Kolvin et al. (1981) in Newcastle-upon-Tyne.

Anti-Bullying Programmes

Several school-based programmes have been designed to decrease bullying. The most famous of these was implemented by Olweus (1993, 1994) in Norway. It aimed to increase awareness and knowledge of teachers, parents and children about bullying and to dispel myths about it. A 30-page booklet was distributed to all schools in Norway describing what was known about bullying and recommending what steps schools and teachers could take to reduce it. Also, a 25-minute video about bullying was made available to schools. Simultaneously, the schools distributed to all parents a four-page folder containing information and advice about bullying. In addition, anonymous self-report questionnaires about bullying were completed by all children.

The programme was evaluated in Bergen. Each of the 42 participating schools received feedback information from the questionnaire, about the prevalence of bullies and victims, in a specially arranged school conference day. Also, teachers were encouraged to develop explicit rules about bullying (e.g. do not bully, tell someone when bullying happens, bullying will not be tolerated, try to help victims, try to include children who are being left out) and to discuss bullying in class, using the video and role-playing exercises. Also, teachers were encouraged to improve monitoring and supervision of children, especially in the playground. The programme was successful in reducing the prevalence of bullying by half.

A similar programme was implemented in 23 Sheffield schools by Smith and Sharp (1994). The core programme involved establishing a "whole-school" anti-bullying policy, raising awareness of bullying and clearly defining roles and responsibilities of teachers and students, so that everyone knew what bullying was and what they should do about it. In addition, there were optional interventions tailored to particular schools: curriculum work (e.g. reading books, watching videos), direct work with students (e.g. assertiveness training for those who were bullied) and playground work (e.g. training lunch-time supervisors). This programme was successful in reducing bullying by 15% in primary schools, but it had relatively small effects in secondary schools; bullying was reduced by only 5%.

Mentoring

The most relevant mentoring project for this chapter is the Quantum Opportunities Programme, which was implemented in five sites across the United States. It aimed to improve the life course opportunities of disadvantaged, at-risk youth during the high school years (Hahn, 1994, 1999). The programme lasted four years and included peer tutoring for educational development and staff assistance with life skills, career-planning and community service. Participants received cash incentives to stay in the programme, and staff received cash incentives for keeping youth in the programme.

Fifty youth aged about 14 were randomly assigned to experimental or control conditions in each site, making an initial sample size of 250. The programme was successful. Experimental youth were more likely to graduate from high school (63% versus 42%) and less likely to be arrested (17% versus 58%). During the 6-month follow-up period, experimental youth were more likely to have volunteered as a mentor or tutor themselves (28% versus 8%) and less likely to have claimed welfare benefits. Other experiments using adult mentors have produced mixed results (Baker, Pollack & Kohn, 1995; O'Donnell, Lydgate & Fo, 1979).

Community Programmes

Jones and Offord (1989) implemented a skills training programme ('Participate and Learn Skills') in an experimental public housing complex in Ottawa and compared it with a control complex. The programme centred on non-school skills, both athletic (e.g. swimming and ice hockey) and non-athletic (e.g. guitar and ballet). The aim of developing skills was to increase self-esteem, to encourage children to use time constructively and to provide desirable role models. Participation rates were high; about three-quarters of age-eligible children in the experimental complex took at least one course in the first year.

The study employed an experimental-control design with before–after measures to assess the effects of the community-based intervention. The programme was successful. During its 32 months, the monthly average number of juveniles charged by the police was 80% less at the experimental site compared to the control site. During the 16-month follow-up period, the delinquency rate was about 50% less at the experimental site.

More recently, the large-scale Children At Risk (CAR) programme targeted high risk youths (average age 12.4) in poor neighbourhoods of five cities across the United States (Harrell, Cavanagh & Sridharan, 1999). Eligible youths were identified in schools and randomly assigned to experimental or control groups. The programme was a comprehensive community-based prevention strategy targeting risk factors for delinquency, including case management and family counselling, family skills training, tutoring, mentoring, afterschool activities, and community policing. The programme was different in each neighbourhood.

The initial results were disappointing (see Harrell et al. 1997), but a one-year follow-up showed that (according to self-reports) experimental youths were less likely to have committed violent crimes and used or sold drugs. The process evaluation showed that the greatest change was in peer risk factors. Experimental youths associated less often with delinquent peers, felt less peer pressure to engage in delinquency, and had more positive peer support. In contrast, there were few changes in individual, family, or community risk factors, possibly linked to the low participation of parents in parent training and of youths in mentoring and tutoring. The implementation problems of the programme were related to the serious and multiple needs and problems of the families.

Multi-Systemic Therapy

Multi-systemic therapy (MST) is a multiple component treatment programme conducted in families, schools and communities (Henggeler et al., 1998). The particular type of treatment is chosen according to the particular needs of the youth; therefore, the nature of the treatment is different for each person. The treatment may include individual, family, peer, school and community interventions, including parent training and skills training.

Henggeler and colleagues (1992, 1993) evaluated MST for serious juvenile offenders. MST was compared with the usual Department of Youth Services treatment, involving out-of-home placement in the majority of cases. In a randomized experiment with 84 offenders, MST was followed by fewer arrests, lower self-reported delinquency and less peer-oriented aggression. Borduin et al. (1995) also showed that MST was more effective in decreasing arrests and antisocial behaviour than was individual therapy.

The results were somewhat less favourable in a real world implementation of MST using therapists recruited and trained in each site. Previous experiments (reviewed above) had been implemented and closely monitored by MST experts. Henggeler et al. (1997) randomly allocated 155 chronic and violent juvenile offenders either to MST or to the usual services (which in this case mainly involved probation and restitution). MST led to a decrease in arrests, self-reported delinquency and antisocial behaviour, but only when treatment fidelity was high. They concluded that, in real world applications, therapist adherence to MST principles was a crucial factor.

BENEFIT–COST ANALYSIS

In practical terms, a benefit–cost analysis or any other type of economic analysis is an extension of an outcome evaluation, and is only as defensible as the evaluation upon which it is based. Weimer and Friedman (1979, p. 264) recommended that benefit–cost analyses should only be carried out for programmes which have been evaluated with an experimental or strong quasi-experimental design.

Economic analysis is a tool which allows choices to be made between alternative uses of resources or alternative distributions of services (Knapp, 1997, p. 11). Our interest was in assessing the economic benefits and costs of developmental prevention programmes. Of the two main techniques of economic analysis—benefit–cost and cost-effectiveness analysis—only benefit–cost analysis enables an assessment of both costs and benefits. A cost-effectiveness analysis is an incomplete benefit–cost analysis, because no attempt is made in it to estimate the monetary value of programme effects produced (benefits), only resources used (costs). A cost–effectiveness analysis can demonstrate, for example, the number of crimes prevented per £1000 spent on a programme. Another way to think about how benefit–cost and cost-effectiveness analysis differ is that "cost-effectiveness analysis may help one decide among competing program models, but it cannot show that the total effect was worth the cost of the program" (Weinrott, Jones & Howard, 1982, p. 179), unlike benefit–cost analysis.

A benefit–cost analysis is a step-by-step process which follows a standard set of procedures. There are six main steps: (a) define the scope of the analysis; (b) obtain estimates of programme effects; (c) estimate the monetary value of costs and benefits; (d) calculate present value and assess profitability; (e) describe the distribution of costs and benefits (an assessment of who gains and who loses, e.g. programme participant, government/taxpayer, crime victim); and (f) conduct sensitivity analyses (Barnett, 1993, pp. 143–148). It is beyond the scope of this chapter to discuss each step, but interested readers should consult the excellent use of this methodology for early childhood intervention programmes by Barnett (1993, 1996) and Barnett and Escobar (1987, 1990).

An economic analysis, whether it be a benefit–cost or cost-effectiveness analysis, is concerned principally with efficiency: achieving maximum outcomes from minimum inputs. We have used the benefit–cost ratio to measure the economic efficiency of programmes rather than net value (benefits minus costs) for two principal reasons: (a) the benefit–cost ratio provides a single measurement of the benefit of a programme which is derived from a one-monetary-unit (e.g. one British pound) investment of expenditure, and (b) for all comparisons, the benefit–cost ratio controls for the particular time period of each programme (e.g. a benefit–cost ratio of a programme which used 1992 US dollars can reasonably be compared with the benefit–cost ratio of a programme which used 1976 British pounds). Importantly, however, an economic evaluation says nothing about fairness or equity in the distribution of services available (e.g. Are those persons most in need of services receiving them?).

One important feature of benefit–cost analysis is the perspective taken in measuring programme costs and benefits. The government/taxpayer and "society" (government/taxpayer, crime victim, and programme participant) are the two most common perspectives used in economic analysis. The decision about which perspective to take has important implications for evaluating the programme, particularly if it is being funded by public money. That is, if conclusions are to be drawn about the monetary benefits or costs of a programme to the public, the benefits or costs must be those which the public will either receive or incur. In reporting on the benefit–cost findings of the reviewed studies, we have used, as far as possible, the perspective of the government/taxpayer and crime victim.

BENEFITS AND COSTS OF SPECIFIC PROGRAMMES

Benefit–cost research on developmental prevention, and crime prevention programmes in general, has become an increasingly important element of an evidence-based approach to preventing crime. The Home Office's Crime Reduction Programme, which involves spending £250 million over three years to "reduce crime through investing in evidence and effectiveness" (Home Office, 1999, p. 2), places a strong emphasis on benefit–cost research. The principal aim of the Home Office research is to help answer empirically such important questions as: For which programmes do benefits outweigh costs? To which parties (e.g. government/taxpayer, crime victim) do savings accrue? How long does it take for developmental, situational, and other crime prevention programmes to pay back costs?

In many ways, the interest in benefit–cost analysis (and economic analysis research in general) on preventing delinquency and crime can be seen as an outgrowth of the focus on "what works" in this area. Efficiency, performance measures and targeting resources (among other terms) have become the common currency of discussions about crime prevention. However, little is known about the monetary costs and benefits of crime prevention programmes (Welsh & Farrington, 2000, 2001). There is a similar lack of knowledge in other areas of intervention, such as child and adolescent mental health (Knapp, 1997) and substance abuse (Bukoski & Evans, 1998; Plotnick, 1994; Rajkumar & French, 1997).

Of all the longitudinal-experimental, developmental prevention programmes discussed in this chapter, only five (Hahn, 1999; Jones & Offord, 1989; Long, Mallar & Thornton, 1981; Olds et al., 1997; Schweinhart, Barnes & Weikart, 1993) carried out a benefit–cost analysis which allowed for an assessment of economic efficiency. Some of these and other developmental prevention programmes have been the subject of (retrospective) benefit–cost analyses by independent researchers. Karoly and her colleagues (1998; see also Greenwood et al., 2001) at the US-based RAND Corporation reanalysed the costs and benefits of the Perry preschool (Schweinhart, Barnes & Weikart, 1993) and Elmira home-visiting (Olds et al., 1997) programmes. Aos and his colleagues (1998, 1999, 2001) at the Washington State Institute for Public Policy applied their benefit–cost model to the developmental prevention programmes by Hahn (1999), Hawkins et al. (1999), Lally, Mangione and Honig (1988), Olds et al. (1997), and Schweinhart, Barnes and Weikart (1993).

From our previous research on the monetary costs and benefits of developmental prevention programmes (Welsh, 2001, 2002; Welsh & Farrington, 2000, 2001), we identified one other benefit–cost study (Lipsey, 1984), but this has not been reviewed here because a weak evaluation design—one group (no control group) before and after—was used to evaluate programme effects on crime and there was no follow-up of programme effects after the intervention ended. As already stated, we reviewed only programmes with a high-quality evaluation design (at least 3 on the Maryland scientific methods scale).

Elmira Home-Visiting Programme

A benefit–cost analysis of the Elmira nurse home-visiting programme (Olds et al., 1993), two years after the programme ended or when the children were 4 years of age, found that, for the higher risk mothers, programme benefits slightly outweighed costs, for a benefit–cost ratio of 1.06. For the whole sample (higher and lower risk mothers), programme costs exceeded benefits, resulting in an undesirable benefit–cost ratio of 0.51.

The average cost per family of the two-year programme was US$3133 for the higher risk sample. Only operating costs were estimated, as the intervention did not require any capital expenditure. Three types of operating costs were included: (a) direct costs of nurse home-visiting services (e.g. nurse salaries, transportation); (b) costs of community services (e.g. Special Supplemental Food Program for Women, Infants, and Children); and (c) costs of the taxi service for prenatal and child visits to physicians. Costs of child sensory and developmental screening were not included in the estimate of programme costs, because the treatment and control groups received this service at the same level.

Of government savings to the higher risk sample (US$3313 per family) at age 4, the largest portion (56%) was attributed to reductions in Aid For Dependent Children (AFDC) payments. Reductions in Food Stamps accounted for 26% of the savings; Medicaid, 11%; and increases in tax revenue, 5%. Fewer cases of child abuse and neglect among the treatment compared to the control group accounted for only 3% of the government savings (to Child Protective Services).

A later benefit–cost analysis of the Elmira programme by Karoly et al. (1998) at the most recent assessment of 13 years post-intervention, which measured programme effects on children's delinquency and mothers' life course development, found a more favourable benefit–cost ratio of 4.06 for the higher risk sample and an unfavourable ratio of 0.62 for the lower risk sample. Again, the analysis by Karoly and colleagues was limited to savings to government—in the form of reduced criminal justice, health care and social service usage costs and increased income taxes. Aos et al. (2001) also performed a benefit–cost analysis of the Elmira programme, focusing on the higher risk sample at 13 years post-intervention. Criminal justice system and crime victim benefits were found to cover programme costs, for a benefit–cost ratio of 1.54. The difference between the benefit–cost ratios of Karoly et al. and Aos et al. is largely attributable to the former including non-crime benefits, which made up the majority of the benefits in this project.

Perry Preschool Project

A benefit–cost analysis of the Perry Preschool project (Barnett, 1993), when the sample was 27 years of age, found that for every dollar spent on the project over 7 dollars was saved to taxpayers and crime victims, for a benefit–cost ratio of 7.16. Total costs of the programme were estimated at US$12 356 per programme group participant. These were made up of basic operating costs (e.g. instruction, administration, overhead) and capital costs (e.g. rental of classrooms). Total programme benefits were estimated at US$88 433 per programme group participant.

Savings from reduced crime (to the criminal justice system and victims of crime) accounted for the majority (80%) of the benefits. The other benefits produced by the programme included higher educational output and reduced schooling costs, increased revenue generated from taxes on increased earnings, and reduced social service usage costs.

Participants' arrest and incarceration histories were used to estimate savings to the main components of the criminal justice system (police, prosecutors, court, probation, and prison). Savings to crime victims were estimated in a two-step process. First, participants' arrest histories were linked with national data on the ratio of arrests to crimes committed, which provided an estimate, by age, of the numbers and types of crimes committed by programme group participants. Second, these crime estimates were then combined with previously developed estimates of crime-specific costs to victims (Cohen, 1988), which produced estimates of costs to victims of crimes committed by programme group participants at each age (Barnett, 1993, p. 160). Costs to crime victims included tangible or out-of-pocket monetary losses (e.g. lost property and wages, medical expenses) and intangible costs of reduced quality of life, pain, and suffering. (For a discussion of these victims costs, see Cohen, 1998, 2001.)

Two earlier benefit–cost analyses of the Perry project, when subjects were aged 15 and 19, also showed that the programme was a sound investment of taxpayer money. At age 15, a benefit–cost ratio of 2.48 was reported (Schweinhart & Weikart, 1980; Weber, Foster & Weikart, 1978) and at age 19 a benefit–cost ratio of 3.00 was reported (Berrueta-Clement et al., 1984).

Karoly et al.'s (1998) reanalysis of the costs and benefits of Perry, when subjects were age 27, found that the programme produced a desirable benefit–cost ratio; however, the ratio of 2.09 was substantially less than that of 7.16 calculated by Barnett (1993), because Karoly et al. (1998) examined benefits from the perspective of the government only—savings to crime victims, which accounted for the majority of the benefits in the benefit–cost analysis by Barnett (1993), were not included. Aos et al.'s (2001) benefit–cost analysis at the age 27 follow-up found that criminal justice system and crime victim benefits covered programme costs, for a benefit–cost ratio of 1.50. It is important to note that crime victim costs here were limited to tangible costs (e.g. property loss), and excluded intangible costs to victims. Non-crime benefits were also excluded.

Job Corps Programme

The comprehensive benefit–cost analysis of the Job Corps programme (Long, Mallar & Thornton, 1981) showed that it was a sound investment of public resources. Programme costs and benefits per participant were estimated at US$5070 and US$7343, respectively, resulting in a benefit–cost ratio of 1.45.

Programme costs included budgeted operating expenditures and unbudgeted costs. Benefits were measured from two frames of reference: immediate programme effects on reduced consumption of public services (e.g. welfare, criminal justice system) by participants while in the programme, and post-programme effects on participants' long-term employability. Reduced criminal activity per programme participant, as measured by reduced criminal justice costs, personal injury, property damage, and value of stolen property, accounted for 29% of the total benefits. Only programme participant output from employment surpassed the benefits of reduced criminal activity (at 63% of total benefits).

Quantum Opportunities Programme

A benefit–cost analysis of the Quantum Opportunities programme (Hahn, 1994) revealed substantial benefits for both the participants and taxpayers. Dividing benefits per programme participant (US$39 037) by costs per programme participant (US$10 600) produced a desirable benefit–cost ratio of 3.68. However, present value was not calculated, meaning that costs and benefits were neither adjusted for inflation nor discounted. One of the limitations of not calculating present value is that benefits are overestimated slightly. The reason for this is that the calculation of present value reduces future benefits relative to present costs.

Monetary benefits were limited to gains in education and fewer children. Excluded were potential benefits from reduced criminal activity, reduced dependence on public assistance, and services provided to the community (other areas in which the experimentals fared better than the controls). Concerning the educational benefits, it was assumed that those who were enrolled in two- and four-year postsecondary degree programmes would complete the programmes. Benefits from fewer children were derived from reduced costs for health and welfare services for teenage mothers. No other information was provided on how benefits were calculated, which seriously limits the confidence that can be placed in the benefit–cost findings.

In their benefit–cost analysis of the Quantum Opportunities programme, Aos et al. (2001) found that it was poor economic value purely for preventing crime; an undesirable benefit–cost ratio of 0.13 was produced. So, for each dollar spent on the programme, only 13 cents was saved to crime victims and government in the form of reduced criminal justice costs. However, as already pointed out, the programme had other benefits.

Participate and Learn Skills Programme

A benefit–cost analysis of the skill development programme for children and youth in a public housing project in Ottawa, Canada (Jones & Offord, 1989), produced a desirable benefit–cost ratio of 2.55. Programme costs (operational and research) and immediate benefits for the intervention and follow-up periods were measured. The calculation of monetary benefits included only those areas where significant differences were observed between the experimental and control complexes: fewer police charges against juveniles, reduced private security reports, and reduced calls for fire department service. Altogether, benefits were estimated for four publicly funded agencies: police, housing authority, community centre, and fire department.

Over the course of the 48 months (intervention and follow-up periods), programme costs totalled C$258 694 and benefits were estimated at C$659 058. The city housing authority reaped the largest share of the benefits (84%). These benefits were caused by the reduced demand for private security services in the experimental housing complex relative to the control complex. The next largest portion of the total benefits from the programme were realized by the city fire department (13%). Monetary benefits accruing to the youth liaison section of the city police were relatively small (2%).

Other Benefit–Cost Analyses

Aos et al. (2001) applied their benefit–cost model to two developmental prevention programmes (the Seattle Social Development Project of Hawkins et al., 1999; and the Syracuse Family Development programme of Lally, Mangione and Honig, 1988) that had not previously been the subject of benefit–cost analyses. Again limiting the measurement of benefits to those which potentially accrued only to the criminal justice system and crime victims (tangible benefits only), Aos et al. found that the Seattle project produced a desirable benefit–cost ratio of 1.79, while the Syracuse programme produced an undesirable benefit–cost ratio of 0.34.

For the Seattle project, there was just about an equal split in the contribution of criminal justice system and crime victim benefits to the project's overall economic worth: 0.90 and 0.89, respectively. For the Syracuse programme, savings from re-duced crime failed to pay back programme costs, hence resulting in an undesirable benefit–cost ratio. Costs per participant were a very high US$45 092 and benefits per participant were only US$15 487. However, as previously pointed out, non-crime benefits need to be taken into account in a comprehensive benefit–cost analysis.

Comparative Economic Efficiency

These individual benefit–cost analyses provide a useful, albeit limited (due to the small number of studies), assessment of the economic efficiency of developmental prevention as an overall strategy to reduce delinquency and crime. What is perhaps more useful, and a more important issue facing policy-makers today, is a compara-tive understanding of economic efficiency. Specifically: (a) compared to other devel-opmental prevention programmes, which one provides the best economic return and (b) compared to other types of prevention strategies (e.g. correctional interven-tion, situational crime prevention) which one provides the best economic return?

The small number of studies, not to mention the different outcomes valued and the varied methodological features of the benefit–cost analyses, limit our ability to say which of the developmental prevention programmes represents the best invest-ment for the public. However, from the five benefit–cost analyses performed by Aos et al. (2001), some conclusions can be drawn. This is possible because comparable measures of crime and costs to the criminal justice system and crime victims, as well as identical methods of benefit–cost analysis (e.g. present value was calculated), were used.

The Seattle project of Hawkins et al. (1999), with a benefit–cost ratio of 1.79, was the most economically efficient of the five programmes. The Elmira programme was second with a benefit–cost ratio of 1.54, followed closely by the Perry pro-gramme with a ratio of 1.50. The other two programmes produced undesirable benefit–cost ratios: Syracuse (0.34) and Quantum Opportunities (0.13). Based on this "bottom line" ratio based on crime benefits alone (there are many important non-economic criteria on which developmental prevention programmes should be judged), a criminal justice policy-maker, faced with the decision of having to fund one developmental crime prevention programme, might choose to implement the Seattle project.

The best-known study comparing the economic efficiency of developmental prevention to other types of crime prevention strategies is RAND's *Diverting Children from a Life of Crime* (Greenwood et al., 1996). This compared the cost-effectiveness of four intervention programmes (home visiting/day care, parent training, graduation incentives, and supervising delinquents) with California's "three strikes" law. Their home-visiting/day care programme was based on the Elmira and Perry programmes, parent training was based on Patterson (1982), their graduation incentives programme was based on the Quantum Opportunities Programme, and their supervision programme included skills training.

A mathematical model of "criminal populations in prison and on the street, as affected by criminal career initiation, arrest and sentencing, release, and desistance from criminal activity" was used to compute each programme's impact on crime and criminal justice system costs (Greenwood et al., 1996, p.17). General and offender population datasets for the State of California were used to derive estimates. The study found that the developmental prevention programmes of parent training and graduation incentives were the most cost-effective of the five programmes. The number of serious crimes prevented per US$1 million was estimated at: 258 for graduation incentives, 157 for parent training, 72 for delinquent supervision, 11 for home-visiting/day care, and 60 for the three strikes law. (These were crimes prevented in a birth cohort, not per year.)

Similarly, Donohue and Siegelman investigated "whether the social resources that will be expended a decade or more from now on incarcerating today's youngsters could instead generate roughly comparable levels of crime *prevention* if they were spent today on the most promising social programs" (1998, p. 31, emphasis in original). On the basis of a 50% increase in the US prison population over a 15-year period, assumed from the level in December 1993 and trends at the time, it was estimated that this policy would cost between US$5.6 and US$8 billion (in 1993 dollars) and result in a 5–15% reduction in crime. From the selected early developmental prevention programmes (Perry Preschool and Syracuse), it was found that comparable reductions in crime could be achieved if they were allocated the upper bound amount that would have been spent on prisons.

CONCLUSIONS

It is clear that many types of developmental prevention programmes are effective in reducing offending and antisocial behaviour. Less is known about the benefits and costs of these programmes, but clearly in some cases the monetary benefits outweighed the monetary costs.

In order to advance knowledge about the effectiveness and economic efficiency of developmental crime prevention, we make the following recommendations.

First, greater use of experimental research designs, particularly randomized experiments, is needed. For programmes based on larger units such as communities or schools, experimental-control designs with before and after measures are most appropriate and feasible. As a benefit–cost analysis is only as convincing as the evaluation upon which it is based, the stronger the research design of the outcome evaluation, the more confidence which can be placed in the findings of the benefit–cost analysis.

Second, research is needed to identify the active ingredients of successful (and promising) developmental prevention programmes. Most programmes are multimodal, making it difficult to isolate the independent effects of different components. Future experiments are needed which attempt to disentangle the effects of different elements of the most successful programmes, such as the home-visiting programme of Olds et al. (1998) and the teacher/skills training programme of Hawkins et al. (1999).

Third, policy-makers and researchers should play a greater role in ensuring that developmental prevention programmes include, as part of the original research design, provision for an economic analysis, preferably a benefit–cost analysis. Prospective economic analyses have many advantages over retrospective ones. Fourth, researchers must ensure that benefit–cost analyses are not only methodologically rigorous, but also comprehensive; all resources used (costs) and all relevant programme effects (benefits) need to be valued.

Fifth, there is a need for a standard list of costs and benefits which should be measured in all benefit–cost analyses. This is an important issue which we have identified previously (Welsh, 2001, 2002; Welsh & Farrington, 2000). Key decisions need to be made about the inclusion of certain types of costs and benefits, particularly the intangible costs to crime victims of pain, suffering, and reduced quality of life. Key outcome variables which should be measured in all developmental prevention programmes include crime and delinquency, antisocial behaviour, substance abuse, education, employment, health, and family factors. A standard list of costs and benefits would greatly facilitate comparisons of the benefit–cost findings of developmental and other types of crime prevention programmes.

Sixth, funding bodies must be prepared to finance high-quality outcome and economic evaluation research. Government agencies with responsibility for the prevention of crime, health, education and employment problems should commit a percentage of their research budgets to support outcome and benefit–cost evaluations of new and existing developmental prevention programmes. Also, government agencies, foundations, private sector organizations, and other groups which fund crime prevention schemes need to make future funding conditional upon a built-in evaluation component which includes an assessment of monetary costs and benefits.

The Home Office, through its Crime Reduction Programme, has already initiated a number of these recommendations about economic evaluation research of crime prevention programmes (see Dhiri & Brand, 1999; Brand & Price, 2000; Dhiri et al., 2001). Other Western countries such as Canada, the United States, and Australia, also are developing the research technologies to assess monetary costs and benefits of crime prevention programmes (Welsh, Farrington & Sherman, 2001).

In a book devoted to the effectiveness of offender rehabilitation and treatment, this chapter is not intended to detract from the voluminous and high-quality evidence which shows that many types of offender treatments work and others show a great deal of promise in reducing re-offending in the community. Instead, this chapter highlights the importance of a complementary approach of effective offender treatment programmes combined with effective developmental crime prevention programmes. The slogan "never too early, never too late" (Loeber & Farrington, 1998) perhaps best captures this important union.

REFERENCES

Aos, S., Barnoski, R. & Lieb, R. (1998) Preventive programs for young offenders effective and cost-effective. *Overcrowded Times, 9* (2), 1, 7–11.

Aos, S., Phipps, P., Barnoski, R. & Lieb, R. (1999) *The Comparative Costs and Benefits of Programs to Reduce Crime: A Review of National Research Findings with Implications for Washington State,* version 3.0. Olympia, Washington: Washington State Institute for Public Policy.

Aos, S., Phipps, P., Barnoski, R. & Lieb, R. (2001) The comparative costs and benefits of programs to reduce crime: A review of research findings with implications for Washington State. In B. C. Welsh, D. P. Farrington & L. W. Sherman (Eds.) *Costs and Benefits of Preventing Crime* (pp. 149–175). Boulder, Colorado: Westview Press.

Baker, K., Pollack, M. & Kohn, I. (1995) Violence prevention through informal socialization: An evaluation of the South Baltimore Youth Center. *Studies on Crime and Crime Prevention, 4,* 61–85.

Barnett, W. S. (1993) Cost–benefit analysis. In L. J. Schweinhart, H. V. Barnes & D. P. Weikart, *Significant Benefits: The High/Scope Perry Preschool Study Through Age 27* (pp. 142–173). Ypsilanti, Michigan: High/Scope Press.

Barnett, W. S. (1996) *Lives in the Balance: Age-27 Benefit–cost Analysis of the High/Scope Perry Preschool Program.* Ypsilanti, Michigan: High/Scope Press.

Barnett, W. S. & Escobar, C. M. (1987) The economics of early educational intervention: A review. *Review of Educational Research, 57,* 387–414.

Barnett, W. S. & Escobar, C. M. (1990) Economic costs and benefits of early intervention. In S. J. Meisels & J. P. Shonkoff (Eds.) *Handbook of Early Childhood Intervention* (pp. 560–582). Cambridge: Cambridge University Press.

Berrueta-Clement, J. R., Schweinhart, L. J., Barnett, W. S., Epstein, A. S. & Weikart, D. P. (1984) *Changed Lives: The Effects of the Perry Preschool Program on Youths Through Age 19.* Ypsilanti, Michigan: High/Scope Press.

Blumstein, A., Cohen, J. & Nagin, D. (Eds.) (1978) *Deterrence and Incapacitation.* Washington, DC: National Academy Press.

Borduin, C. M., Mann, B. J., Cone, L. T., Henggeler, S. W., Fucci, B. R., Blaske, D. M. & Williams, R. A. (1995) Multisystemic treatment of serious juvenile offenders: Long-term prevention of criminality and violence. *Journal of Consulting and Clinical Psychology, 63,* 569–587.

Brand, S. & Price, R. (2000) *The Economic and Social Costs of Crime.* Research Study 217. London: Home Office Research, Development and Statistics Directorate.

Bukoski, W. J. & Evans, R. I. (Eds.) (1998) *Cost–Benefit/Cost-Effectiveness Research of Drug Abuse Prevention: Implications for Programming and Policy.* (NIDA Research Monograph 176.) Washington, DC: National Institute on Drug Abuse.

Clarke, R. V. (1995) Situational crime prevention. In M. Tonry & D. P. Farrington (Eds.) *Building a Safer Society: Strategic Approaches to Crime Prevention* (pp. 91–150). Chicago: University of Chicago Press.

Clarke, R. V. (1997) Introduction. In R. V. Clarke (Ed.) *Situational Crime Prevention: Successful Case Studies* (2nd edn., pp. 1–43). Guilderland, New York: Harrow & Heston.

Cohen, M. A. (1988) Pain, suffering, and jury awards: A study of the cost of crime to victims. *Law and Society Review, 22,* 537–555.

Cohen, M. A. (1998) The monetary value of saving a high-risk youth. *Journal of Quantitative Criminology, 14,* 5–33.

Cohen, M. A. (2001) The crime victim's perspective in cost-benefit analysis: The importance of monetizing tangible and intangible crime costs. In B. C. Welsh, D. P. Farrington & L. W. Sherman (Eds.) *Costs and Benefits of Preventing Crime* (pp. 23–50). Boulder, Colorado: Westview Press.

Dhiri, S. & Brand, S. (1999) *Analysis of Costs and Benefits: Guidance for Evaluators.* Guidance Note 1. London: Home Office Research, Development and Statistics Directorate.

Dhiri, S., Goldblatt, P., Brand, S. & Price R. (2001) Evaluation of the United Kingdom's 'Crime Reduction Programme': Analysis of costs and benefits. In B. C. Welsh, D. P. Farrington & L. W. Sherman (Eds.) *Costs and Benefits of Preventing Crime* (pp. 179–201). Boulder, Colorado: Westview Press.

Dishion, T. J., Patterson, G. R. & Kavanagh, K. A. (1992) An experimental test of the coercion model: Linking theory, measurement and intervention. In J. McCord & R. E. Tremblay (Eds.) *Preventing Antisocial Behavior: Interventions from Birth through Adolescence* (pp. 253–282). New York: Guilford.

Donohue, J. J. & Siegelman, P. (1998) Allocating resources among prisons and social programs in the battle against crime. *Journal of Legal Studies, 27,* 1–43.

Farrington, D. P. (1983) Randomized experiments on crime and justice. In M. Tonry & N. Morris (Eds.) *Crime and Justice* (Vol. 4, pp. 257–308). Chicago: University of Chicago Press.

Farrington, D. P. (1994) Early developmental prevention of juvenile delinquency. *Criminal Behaviour and Mental Health, 4,* 209–227.

Farrington, D. P. (1997) Evaluating a community crime prevention program. *Evaluation, 3,* 157–173.

Farrington, D. P. (1999) Risk-focussed crime prevention through families, peers, schools and communities. In D. Curran & W. McCarney (Eds.) *Psychological Perspectives on Serious Criminal Risk* (pp. 1–24). Leicester: British Psychological Society.

Farrington, D. P. & Welsh, B. C. (1999) Delinquency prevention using family-based interventions. *Children and Society, 13,* 287–303.

Graham, J. & Bennett, T. (1995) *Crime Prevention Strategies in Europe and North America.* Monsey, New York: Criminal Justice Press.

Greenwood, P. W., Karoly, L. A., Everingham, S. S., Houbé, J., Kilburn, M. R., Rydell, C. P., Sanders, M. & Chiesa, J. (2001) Estimating the costs and benefits of early childhood interventions: Nurse home visits and the Perry preschool. In B. C. Welsh, D. P. Farrington & L. W. Sherman (Eds.) *Costs and Benefits of Preventing Crime* (pp. 123–148). Boulder, Colorado: Westview Press.

Greenwood, P. W., Model, K.E., Rydell, C. P. & Chiesa, J. (1996) *Diverting Children from a Life of Crime: Measuring Costs and Benefits.* Santa Monica, California: RAND.

Hahn, A. (1994) *Evaluation of the Quantum Opportunities Program (QOP): Did the Program Work?* Waltham, Massachusetts: Brandeis University.

Hahn, A. (1999) Extending the time of learning. In D. J. Besharov (Ed.) *America's Disconnected Youth: Toward a Preventive Strategy* (pp. 233–265). Washington, DC: Child Welfare League of America Press.

Harrell, A. V., Cavanagh, S. E., Harmon, M. A., Koper, C. S. & Sridharan, S. (1997) *Impact of the Children At Risk Program: Comprehensive Final Report,* Vol. 1. Washington, DC: The Urban Institute.

Harrell, A. V., Cavanagh, S. E. & Sridharan, S. (1999) Evaluation of the Children At Risk Program: Results 1 year after the end of the program. *Research in Brief* (November). Washington, DC: National Institute of Justice, US Department of Justice.

Hawkins, J. D., Catalano, R. F., Kosterman, R., Abbott, R. & Hill, K. G. (1999) Preventing adolescent health-risk behaviors by strengthening protection during childhood. *Archives of Pediatrics and Adolescent Medicine, 153,* 226–234.

Hawkins, J. D., Catalano, R. F., Morrison, D. M., O'Donnell, J., Abbott, R. D. & Day, L. E. (1992) The Seattle social development project: Effects of the first four years on protective factors and problem behaviors. In J. McCord & R. E. Tremblay (Eds.) *Preventing Antisocial Behavior: Interventions from Birth Through Adolescence* (pp. 139–161). New York: Guilford.

Hawkins, J. D., von Cleve, E. & Catalano, R. F. (1991) Reducing early childhood aggression: Results of a primary prevention program. *Journal of the American Academy of Child and Adolescent Psychiatry, 30*, 208–217.

Henggeler, S. W., Melton, G. B., Brondino, M. J. & Schere, D. G. (1997) Multisystemic therapy with violent and chronic juvenile offenders and their families: The role of treatment fidelity in successful dissemination. *Journal of Consulting and Clinical Psychology, 65*, 821–833.

Henggeler, S. W., Melton, G. B. & Smith, L. A. (1992) Family preservation using multisystemic therapy: An effective alternative to incarcerating serious juvenile offenders. *Journal of Consulting and Clinical Psychology, 60*, 953–961.

Henggeler, S. W., Melton, G. B., Smith, L. A., Schoenwald, S. K. & Hanley, J. H. (1993) Family preservation using multisystemic treatment: Long-term follow-up to a clinical trial with serious juvenile offenders. *Journal of Child and Family Studies, 2*, 283–293.

Henggeler, S. W., Schoenwald, S. K., Borduin, C. M., Rowland, M. D. & Cunningham, P. B. (1998) *Multisystemic Treatment of Antisocial Behavior in Children and Adolescents.* New York: Guilford.

von Hirsch, A., Bottoms, A. E., Burney, E. & Wikström, P.-O. H. (1999) *Criminal Deterrence and Sentence Severity: An Analysis of Recent Research.* Oxford: Hart.

Home Office (1999) *Reducing Crime and Tackling its Causes: A Briefing Note on the Crime Reduction Programme.* London: Home Office Communication Directorate.

Hope, T. (1995) Community crime prevention. In M. Tonry & D. P. Farrington (Eds.) *Building a Safer Society: Strategic Approaches to Crime Prevention* (pp. 21–89). Chicago: University of Chicago Press.

Johnson, D. L. & Walker, T. (1987) Primary prevention of behavior problems in Mexican-American children. *American Journal of Community Psychology, 15*, 375–385.

Jones, M. B. & Offord, D. R. (1989) Reduction of antisocial behaviour in poor children by nonschool skill-development. *Journal of Child Psychology and Psychiatry, 30*, 737–750.

Karoly, L. A., Greenwood, P. W., Everingham, S. S., Houbé, J., Kilburn, M. R., Rydell, C. P., Sanders, M. & Chiesa, J. (1998) *Investing in Our Children: What We Know and Don't Know about the Costs and Benefits of Early Childhood Interventions.* Santa Monica, California: RAND.

Kazdin, A. E., Siegel, T. C. & Bass, D. (1992) Cognitive problem-solving skills training and parent management training in the treatment of antisocial behavior in children. *Journal of Consulting and Clinical Psychology, 60*, 733–747.

Kitzman, H., Olds, D. L., Henderson, C. R., Hanks, C., Cole, R., Tatelbaum, R., McConnochie, K. M., Sidora, K., Luckey, D. W., Shaver, D., Engelhardt, K., James, D. & Barnard, K. (1997) Effect of prenatal and infancy home visitation by nurses on pregnancy outcomes, childhood injuries, and repeated childbearing: A randomized controlled trial. *Journal of the American Medical Association, 278*, 644–652.

Knapp, M. (1997) Economic evaluations and interventions for children and adolescents with mental health problems. *Journal of Child Psychology and Psychiatry, 38*, 3–25.

Kolvin, I., Garside, R. F., Nicol, A. R., MacMillan, A., Wolstenholme, F. & Leitch, I. M. (1981) *Help Starts Here: The Maladjusted Child in the Ordinary School.* London: Tavistock.

Lally, J. R., Mangione, P. L. & Honig, A. S. (1988) The Syracuse University Family Development Research Program: Long-range impact of an early intervention with low-income children and their families. In D. R. Powell (Ed.) *Parent Education as Early Childhood Intervention: Emerging Directions in Theory, Research and Practice* (pp. 79–104). Norwood, New Jersey: Ablex.

Larson, C. P. (1980) Efficacy of prenatal and postpartum home visits on child health and development. *Pediatrics, 66*, 191–197.

Lipsey, M. W. (1984) Is delinquency prevention a cost-effective strategy? A California perspective. *Journal of Research in Crime and Delinquency, 21*, 279–302.

Loeber, R. & Farrington, D. P. (1998) Never too early, never too late: Risk factors and successful interventions for serious and violent juvenile offenders. *Studies on Crime and Crime Prevention, 7*, 7–30.

Long, D. A., Mallar, C. D. & Thornton, C. V. D. (1981) Evaluating the benefits and costs of the Job Corps. *Journal of Policy Analysis and Management, 1*, 55–76.

McCarton, C. M., Brooks-Gunn, J., Wallace, I. F., Bauer, C. R., Bennett, F. C., Bernbaum, J. C., Broyles, R. S., Casey, P. H., McCormick, M. C., Scott, D. T., Tyson, J., Tonascia, J. & Meinert, C. L. (1997) Results at age 8 years of early intervention for low-birth-weight premature infants: The Infant Health and Development Program. *Journal of the American Medical Association, 277*, 126–132.

O'Donnell, C. R., Lydgate, T. & Fo, W. S. O. (1979) The buddy system: Review and follow-up. *Child Behavior Therapy, 1*, 161–169.

O'Donnell, J., Hawkins, J. D., Catalano, R. F., Abbott, R. D. & Day, L. E. (1995) Preventing school failure, drug use, and delinquency among low-income children: Long-term intervention in elementary schools. *American Journal of Orthopsychiatry, 65*, 87–100.

Olds, D. L., Eckenrode, J., Henderson, C. R., Kitzman, H., Powers, J., Cole, R., Sidora, K., Morris, P., Pettitt, L. M. & Luckey, D. (1997) Long-term effects of home visitation on maternal life course and child abuse and neglect: Fifteen-year follow-up of a randomized trial. *Journal of the American Medical Association, 278*, 637–643.

Olds, D. L., Henderson, C. R, Chamberlin, R. & Tatelbaum, R. (1986) Preventing child abuse and neglect: A randomized trial of nurse home visitation. *Pediatrics, 78*, 65–78.

Olds, D. L., Henderson, C. R., Cole, R., Eckenrode, J., Kitzman, H., Luckey, D., Pettitt, L., Sidora, K., Morris, P. & Powers, J. (1998) Long-term effects of nurse home visitation on children's criminal and antisocial behavior: 15-year follow-up of a randomized controlled trial. *Journal of the American Medical Association, 280*, 1238–1244.

Olds, D. L., Henderson, C. R., Phelps, C., Kitzman, H. & Hanks, C. (1993) Effects of prenatal and infancy nurse home visitation on government spending. *Medical Care, 31*, 155–174.

Olweus, D. (1993) *Bullying at School*. Oxford: Blackwell.

Olweus, D. (1994). Bullying at school: Basic facts and effects of a school based intervention programme. *Journal of Child Psychology and Psychiatry, 35*, 1171–1190.

Pagani, L., Tremblay, R. E., Vitaro, F. & Parent, S. (1998) Does preschool help prevent delinquency in boys with a history of perinatal complications? *Criminology, 36*, 245–267.

Painter, K. A. & Farrington, D. P. (1997) The crime reducing effect of improved street lighting: The Dudley project. In R. V. Clarke (Ed.) *Situational Crime Prevention: Successful Case Studies* (2nd edn., pp. 209–226). Guilderland, New York: Harrow & Heston.

Painter, K. A. & Farrington, D. P. (2001) Evaluating situational crime prevention using a young people's survey. *British Journal of Criminology, 41*, 266–284.

Patterson, G. R. (1982) *Coercive Family Process*. Eugene, Oregon: Castalia.

Patterson, G. R., Chamberlain, P. & Reid, J. B. (1982) A comparative evaluation of a parent training program. *Behavior Therapy, 13*, 638–650.

Patterson, G. R., Reid, J. B. & Dishion, T. J. (1992) *Antisocial Boys*. Eugene, Oregon: Castalia.

Plotnick, R. D. (1994) Applying benefit–cost analysis to substance use prevention programs. *International Journal of the Addictions, 29*, 339–359.

Rajkumar, A. S. & French, M. T. (1997) Drug abuse, crime costs, and the economic benefits of treatment. *Journal of Quantitative Criminology, 13*, 291–323.

Raynor, P. & Vanstone, M. (2001) "Straight thinking on Probation": Evidence-based practice and the culture of curiosity. In G. Bernfeld, D. P. Farrington & A. W. Leschied (Eds.) *Offender Rehabilitation in Practice: Implementing and Evaluating Effective Programmes*. Chichester: Wiley. (pp. 189–203).

Rosenbaum, D. P. (1988) Community crime prevention: A review and synthesis of the literature. *Justice Quarterly, 5*, 323–395.

Ross, R. R. & Ross, R. D. (Eds.) (1995) *Thinking Straight: The Reasoning and Rehabilitation Programme for Delinquency Prevention and Offender Rehabilitation*. Ottawa, Canada: Air Training and Publications.

Schochet, P. Z., Burghardt, J. & Glazerman, S. (2000) *National Job Corps Study: The Short-Term Impacts of Job Corps on Participants' Employment and Related Outcomes*. Princeton, New Jersey: Mathematica Policy Research, Inc.

Schweinhart, L. J., Barnes, H. V. & Weikart, D. P. (1993) *Significant Benefits: The High/Scope Perry Preschool Study Through Age 27*. Ypsilanti, Michigan: High/Scope Press.

Schweinhart, L. J. & Weikart, D. P. (1980) *Young Children Grow Up: The Effects of the Perry Preschool Program on Youths Through Age 15*. Ypsilanti, Michigan: High/Scope Press.

Scott, S., Spender, Q., Doolan, M., Jacobs B. & Aspland, H. (2001) Multicentre controlled trial of parenting groups for childhood antisocial behaviour in clinical practice. *British Medical Journal*, 323, 194–196.

Sechrest, L., White, S. O. & Brown E. D. (1979, Eds.) *The Rehabilitation of Criminal Offenders: Problems and Prospects*. Washington, DC: National Academy of Sciences.

Sherman, L. W., Gottfredson, D. C., MacKenzie, D. L., Eck, J. E., Reuter, P. & Bushway, S. D. (1997) *Preventing Crime: What Works, What Doesn't, What's Promising*. Washington, DC: US National Institute of Justice.

Sherman, L. W., Gottfredson, D. C., MacKenzie, D. L., Eck, J. E., Reuter, P. & Bushway, S. D. (1998) Preventing crime: What works, what doesn't, what's promising. *Research in Brief* (July). Washington, DC: US National Institute of Justice.

Smith, P. K. & Sharp, S. (1994) *School Bullying*. London: Routledge.

Spivack, G., Platt, J. J. & Shure, M. B. (1976) *The Problem Solving Approach to Adjustment*. San Francisco: Jossey-Bass.

Strayhorn, J. M. & Weidman, C. S. (1991) Follow-up one year after parent–child interaction training: Effects on behavior of preschool children. *Journal of the American Academy of Child and Adolescent Psychiatry, 30*, 138–143.

Tonry, M. & Farrington, D. P. (1995) Strategic approaches to crime prevention. In M. Tonry & D. P. Farrington (Eds.) *Building a Safer Society: Strategic Approaches to Crime Prevention* (pp. 1–20). Chicago: University of Chicago Press.

Tremblay, R. E. & Craig, W. M. (1995) Developmental crime prevention. In M. Tonry & D. P. Farrington (Eds.) *Building a Safer Society: Strategic Approaches to Crime Prevention* (pp. 151–236). Chicago: University of Chicago Press.

Tremblay, R. E., Pagani-Kurtz, L., Mâsse, L. C., Vitaro, F. & Pihl, R. O. (1995) A bimodal preventive intervention for disruptive kindergarten boys: Its impact through mid-adolescence. *Journal of Consulting and Clinical Psychology, 63*, 560–568.

Utting, D. (1995) *Family and Parenthood: Supporting Families, Preventing Breakdown*. York: Joseph Rowntree Foundation.

Utting, D. (1996) *Reducing Criminality among Young People: A Sample of Relevant Programmes in the United Kingdom*. London: Home Office.

Utting, D., Bright, J. & Henricson, C. (1993) *Crime and the Family: Improving Child-Rearing and Preventing Delinquency*. London: Family Policy Studies Centre.

Wasserman, G. A. & Miller, L. S. (1998) The prevention of serious and violent juvenile offending. In R. Loeber & D. P. Farrington (Eds.) *Serious and Violent Juvenile Offenders: Risk Factors and Successful Interventions* (pp. 197–247). Thousand Oaks, California: Sage.

Weber, C. U., Foster, P. W. & Weikart, D. P. (1978) *An Economic Analysis of the Ypsilanti Perry Preschool Project*. Ypsilanti, Michigan: High/Scope Press.

Webster-Stratton, C. (1998) Preventing conduct problems in Head Start children: Strengthening parenting competencies. *Journal of Consulting and Clinical Psychology, 66*, 715–730.

Webster-Stratton, C. & Hammond, M. (1997) Treating children with early-onset conduct problems: A comparison of child and parent training interventions. *Journal of Consulting and Clinical Psychology, 65*, 93–109.

Webster-Stratton, C., Kolpacoff, M. & Hollinsworth, T. (1988) Self-administered videotape therapy for families with conduct-problem children: Comparison with two cost-effective treatments and a control group. *Journal of Consulting and Clinical Psychology, 56*, 558–566.

Weimer, D. L. & Friedman, L. S. (1979) Efficiency considerations in criminal rehabilitation research: Costs and consequences. In L. Sechrest, S. O. White & E. D. Brown (Eds.) *The Rehabilitation of Criminal Offenders: Problems and Prospects* (pp. 251–272). Washington, DC: National Academy of Sciences.

Weinrott, M. R., Jones, R. R. & Howard, J. R. (1982) Cost-effectiveness of teaching family programs for delinquents: Results of a national evaluation. *Evaluation Review, 6*, 173–201.

Welsh, B. C. (2001) Economic costs and benefits of early developmental prevention. In R. Loeber & D. P. Farrington (Eds.) *Child Delinquents: Development, Intervention and Service Needs* (pp. 339–355). Thousand Oaks, California: Sage.

Welsh, B. C. (2002) Economic costs and benefits of primary prevention of delinquency and later offending: A review of the research. In D. P. Farrington & J. W. Coid (Eds.) *Early Prevention of Adult Antisocial Behaviour*. Cambridge: Cambridge University Press (in press).

Welsh, B. C. & Farrington, D. P. (2000) Monetary costs and benefits of crime prevention programs. In M. Tonry (Ed.) *Crime and Justice* (Vol. 27, pp. 305–361). Chicago: University of Chicago Press.

Welsh, B. C. & Farrington, D. P. (2001) A review of research on the monetary value of preventing crime. In B. C. Welsh, D. P. Farrington & L. W. Sherman (Eds.) *Costs and Benefits of Preventing Crime* (pp. 87–122). Boulder, Colorado: Westview Press.

Welsh, B. C., Farrington, D. P. & Sherman, L. W. (2001, Eds.) *Costs and Benefits of Preventing Crime*. Boulder, Colorado: Westview Press.

Widom, C. S. (1989) The cycle of violence. *Science, 244*, 160–166.

PART II

SPECIFIC INTERVENTIONS, MODELS AND OUTCOMES

Chapter 6

LOW-LEVEL AGGRESSION: DEFINITION, ESCALATION, INTERVENTION

THE LATE ARNOLD P. GOLDSTEIN

Center for Research on Aggression, Syracuse University, New York, USA

Whether via direct or vicarious experiences, it is now generally well established that aggression is primarily a learned behaviour (Bandura, 1973; Baron & Richardson, 1994; Huesmann, 1988). A distinction is usually made, however, between learning a behaviour (i.e. acquisition) and actually carrying it out (i.e. performance). Once one knows how to share, confront, cooperate, ignore, or aggress, then whether or not one chooses to do so is largely a matter of rewards or punishments for such behaviour in the past, and one's appraisal of how likely the behaviour will be rewarded or reinforced if used now. The core purpose of this chapter revolves around the key consequence of reinforced performance on the continued, and especially escalated, use of the behaviour rewarded. If a young student curses or swears at a teacher, and by that act believes he has grown in stature in the eyes of his classmates, continued cursing becomes all the more probable. If a late adolescent deals with jealousy by smacking his girlfriend when he sees her talking to another boy, her subsequent obedience to his wishes makes further smacking more likely when, in his view, she has transgressed in other ways. So, too, for the adult who bullies at the workplace, the daughter or son who abuses or neglects an aged parent, the husband or wife who scream at each other, and the parent who disciplines with harsh spankings. Unfortunately, it is not only the continued use of cursing, smacking, bullying, abuse, neglect, or screaming that is made more likely by their perceived success, it is also their escalation to progressively higher levels of more serious and more injurious forms of aggression.

This chapter is very much about escalation. My central belief—a belief increasingly finding at least initial empirical support—is that we, as a society, have far too often ignored the very manifestations of low-level aggression which, when rewarded, grow (often rapidly) into those several forms of often intractable high-level aggression which are currently receiving a great deal of society's attention. Thus, our schools, our media, our politicians, and our social and behavioural

Offender Rehabilitation and Treatment: Effective Programmes and Policies to Reduce Re-offending. Edited by James McGuire.
© John Wiley & Sons, Ltd.

scientists focus broadly and in depth on murder, rape, assault, gangs, guns, and other forms and correlates of serious aggression, but largely ignore their aggressive precursors—such as cursing, threats, insults, incivilities, vandalism, bullying, and harassment. "Catch it low to prevent it high" is an intervention prescription that I and others have increasingly begun to apply, evaluate, and promote, and I shall pursue it consistently throughout this chapter.

DEFINITIONS OF LOW-LEVEL AGGRESSION

In the research and applied literature on aggression, "aggression" is commonly defined as intentional physical or psychological injury to another person. On the face of it, then, providing a companion definition for low-level aggression may appear simple to accomplish. Perhaps it should be defined as intentional physical or psychological injury which is only mildly injurious to another person, or moderately so. Indeed, as we shall see, consensus of a sort can be reached among researchers at least as to what constitutes "mild" or "moderate" injury. Yet serious definitional questions immediately arise. Whose perspective—the perpetrator's, the target's, third-party observer's—should be called upon to provide such seriousness or severity ratings or rankings. Shall we take the perpetrator's view and define it along a scale of expressive intensity, or the target victim's, and seek a measure of injuriousness or harm done? If we opt for a harm-based definition, how shall injury or harm to the target be measured, and when, and again by whom? And what of frequency or repetitiveness? Is a steady diet of cutting insults from peers higher level aggression than occasional hard smacks to the face? Though I believe that, ultimately, low-level aggression must be defined subjectively, by its target and is incident-specific, a number of definitional approximations are appropriate.

Across-Incidents Chronology

The tracing of aggression pathways is one contributing approach to the task of defining low-level aggression because, generally, less harmful (target's perspective) or less intense (perpetrator's perspective) aggressive behaviours precede its more harmful and/or intense expression. (Such a sequence, although typical, is by no means invariant. One can imagine, for example, incidents in which a perpetrator first shoots a target person, and only *then* curses him or her.)

Loeber et al. (1993) have identified three common developmental pathways from "less serious manifestations" to "more serious manifestations" followed by a large percentage of the boys they studied as they progressed from disruptiveness to delinquency.

The *Authority Conflict* pathway is the earliest age-wise. It begins with stubborn behaviour; proceeds to defiance such as refusal and disobedience; and is followed by authority avoidance, as concretized by truancy and running away from home. The *Covert* pathway starts with frequent lying, shoplifting, and other "minor covert behaviours", moves on to property damage as incurred by vandalism or firesetting, and culminates in moderate to serious covert delinquency, such as fraud or burglary. The *Overt* pathway commences with minor overt behaviours such as annoying others or bullying, proceeds to individual or gang physical fighting and reaches its extreme severity in assault, rape or other violent behaviour.

Other pathway models have been offered to depict common routes of escalation from minor to serious levels of aggression or delinquency (Elliott, 1994; Farrington, 1991; LeBlanc, 1996; Moffitt, 1993; Nagin, Farrington & Moffit, 1995). According to these models the timing (age of onset) of aggressive acts, their variety, their rate of escalation and their chronicity are each proposed to relate to their eventual level of seriousness.

Within-Incidents Chronology

Low-level aggression may be further concretized, again by examining the sequencing of behaviour, but in this instance within the temporal confines of single aggressive incidents. To start such an effort by noting incident beginnings, Table 6.1 lists, in order of frequency, opening moves made by perpetrators toward targets in violent incidents occurring in school settings (National Institute of Justice, 1997).

Consistent with our urging of a "catch it low" strategy, these authors propose:

> Reducing the occurrence of opening moves appears to be the most promising approach to preventing escalation to violence . . . One of the most frequent opening moves is offensive touching. The design of school-based violence prevention programmes could include policies and practices that strongly discourage this type of behavior, however minor some of its expressions may appear. The study findings reveal many instances in which these opening moves escalate to fierce combats, suggesting that efforts to reduce this behavior will reduce serious violent incidents. (pp. 5, 7)

When such policies and practices are not in place, or do exist but fail, aggressive opening moves are often followed by an escalating sequence some have termed "character contests". These are retaliatory progressions of verbal and

Table 6.1 Opening moves in violent incidents among students

Unprovoked offensive touching: throws, pushes, grabs, shoves, slaps, kicks, or hits
Possessions: interferes with something owned or being used
Request to do something
Backbiting: someone says something bad about another person to someone else and
    this gets back to the person
Play: verbal teasing (playful "put downs") or rough physical play
Insults: not meant to be playful
Crimes
Accusations of wrongdoing
Defence of others
Challenges: physical or non-verbal gestures
Threats of physical harm
Advances to boyfriend or girlfriend of actor
Told authority figure about bad behaviour of actor
Other actions perceived as offensive

---

eventually physical attempts to harm, to save face and, ultimately to defeat one's antagonist.

Felson (1978) has studied such character contests in his work on aggression as impression management. He comments:

> ...an insult...places the target into an unfavorable situational identity by making the person appear weak, incompetent and cowardly. A successful counterattack is one effective way of nullifying the imputed negative identity by showing one's strength, competence, and courage...Given the sacredness and vulnerability of the self, the ambiguous line between disagreement and disparagement, and the tendency for perceived attack to result in counterattack, small arguments readily escalate through a reciprocal process into aggressive encounters. (pp. 207, 211)

Though Athens (1985) has challenged the pervasiveness of character contests, other researchers have described this very same process of the escalation of aggression as resulting from disinhibition (Goldstein, Davis & Herman, 1975), amplification (Berkowitz, Lepinski & Angulo, 1969), positive feedback (Marsh, Rosser & Harré, 1978), interaction sequencing (Raush, 1965), affronts (Tuppen & Gaitan, 1989), and posturing (Grossman, 1995).

Ratings and Rankings

In an investigation of the criteria employed when making judgements about the seriousness of antisocial behaviour, Forgas, Brown and Menyhart (1980) also found probability of occurrence to be a significant influence upon such ratings, along with the perceived justifiability of the act and the degree to which the act was sanctioned or not by those in authority.

Alternatively, judgement of the seriousness level of an aggressive act may be based jointly on its wrongfulness and harmfulness. Thomas and Bilchik (1985, p. 440) observe:

> Felonies are more serious than misdemeanors, and misdemeanors more serious than infractions. Among sins, the mortal variety is more serious than the venial. At first glance, the meaning of the phrase seriousness of violations may seem quite straightforward. However, studies suggest that people's judgments of seriousness can be based either on an act's moral impropriety (wrongfulness) or on the extent of harm it causes (harmfulness). And for some people, seriousness can involve some combination of wrongfulness and harmfulness.

In a seriousness rating study conducted by O'Connell and Whelan (1996), raters were asked to judge the seriousness of an array of offences, and apparently, as Thomas and Bilchik (1985) assert, did so based on a joint reflection of harmfulness and wrongfulness.

Five clusters of ratings emerged. The lowest in seriousness, the authors note, were crimes held by some to be "victimless", namely dealing in soft drugs and consensual under-age sex. The next cluster, consisting of dole fraud and fraud on business do have a victim but "it is either diffuse or is an impersonal institution,

Table 6.2   School house incident categories

1. Horseplay	6. Bullying	10. Out-of-control behaviour
2. Rules violation	7. Sexual harassment	11. Fights
3. Disruptiveness	8. Physical threats	12. Attacks on teachers
4. Refusal	9. Vandalism	13. Group aggression
5. Cursing		

so that the impact on any particular individual is diluted" (p. 308). In the third cluster, (corrupt police, fraud on public), the researchers note, the victim is a more concentrated, less diffuse group of people harmed by the offence. The final two clusters (burglary, mugging, assault on police; and murder, respectively) show increasing levels of individualized violation and personal harmfulness.

In judging seriousness, the authors conclude:

> ...our interpretation would suggest that people think mainly of degree of bad-
> ness of the offending conduct and of the offender who commits it, but also,
> to a lesser extent, try to estimate the impact on the victim when considering
> seriousness of an offence. (p. 309)

Goldstein and colleagues (1995) took a complementary approach to defining aggression levels. Their national survey of American teachers yielded a pool of 1000 descriptions of in-school aggressive incidents along with the details of how each incident was resolved. Via what may best be described as an intuitive cluster analysis, these investigators grouped the 1000 incident reports into 13 categories arrayed from low-level, through moderate-level, to high-level aggression, as depicted in Table 6.2.

Consistent with their core approach to aggression control and reduction, Goldstein et al. (1995, pp. 19–20) stated:

> ...any act of aggression can escalate quickly into a serious situation. In fact,
> it is only possible to judge the level of severity of an aggressive incident in
> the specific context in which it occurs. What we can say, however, is that poor
> management of aggression at the lower levels facilitates high level expression.
> Conversely, the teacher skilled at maintaining compliance or thwarting student
> disruptiveness is, we believe, considerably less likely to be faced with vandal-
> istic, out-of-control, or armed students. "Catch it low, to prevent it high" is a
> productive intervention strategy.

What then is low-level aggression? We have examined a number of diverse operational definitions in aggression seriousness research conducted both across and within incidents, and employing either rating or ranking methodologies. Although one can pull from this body of research a general consensus regarding which particular behaviours are deemed to be "low level", it must be quickly acknowledged that judgements about the level of intensity of an aggressive act must retain very much in the eyes of its target. Different people will experience the same aggressive act quite differently. For example, Sparks, Genn and Dodd (1977) found that given acts of aggression are perceived to be more serious with increasing age of the rater. Victims of aggressive behaviour rate such actions as more serious than do the perpetrators of the behaviour. Walker (1978) reported that men rate violent offences more seriously than women do, and persons of higher social class also perceive violent offences as significantly more serious than do raters from lower social class backgrounds. The reverse social class finding emerged in work by Sparks, Genn and Dodd (1977) for property offences. Consistent ethnic differences in aggression seriousness ratings have also been reported (Lubel, Wolf & Krausz, 1991; Rossi et al., 1974). Rose and Prell (1955) found that women tended to rate child-beaters, bigamists, forgers and drunk drivers as significantly more serious than did men. Levi and Jones (1985) report that while ordinary citizens and police officers share similar rankings of crime seriousness, the citizens gave most offences higher absolute ratings than did the police. Finally, and perhaps not surprisingly, prison inmates who have committed certain crimes rate those crimes as less serious than do either inmates who have not perpetrated the particular offences being rated or prison staff.

Though there exists some research reporting no effect of age, sex, or income on crime seriousness ratings (Cullen, Clark & Polanzi, 1982), the thrust of the studies just reviewed is of considerable individual variation in such ratings. Thus, what constitutes low-level aggression in any given incident must in the final analysis be defined via the subjective experience of the person to whom it is directed.

THE ESCALATION OF LOW-LEVEL AGGRESSION: RESEARCH FINDINGS

Insults, threats, teasing, and even many forms of bullying, harassment and verbal abuse are often merely unpleasant, annoying or aversive—and not seriously injurious. In the present chapter we are less concerned with these several incarnations of low-level aggression in their own right, but focus upon them because of their not infrequent high-level aggressive sequelae. In the previous sections we described pathway models and aggressive incident chronologies which asserted that such escalation was a common phenomenon. In the present section, we wish to provide research which supports this assertion.

Laboratory Research

An initial series of investigations conducted by Goldstein and colleagues consistently found what these researchers termed a "trials effect" (Goldstein, Davis & Herman, 1975; Goldstein et al., 1981). As several others have also reported, studies using the Buss (1961) aggression machine find that both experimental and control participants regularly increase the level of shock they believe they are administering to another person, in both intensity and duration, as the study's trials proceed. Examining alternative explanations for this consistent escalation result, their findings yielded evidence in support of a process of disinhibition. As the researchers state, "... once punishment is administered, it becomes increasingly easy to administer more intense punishment, regardless of the behavior of the learner [target]"

(Goldstein, Davis & Herman, 1975, p. 167). Others have suggested that pain cues from the victim may be able to break into this process and halt the escalation by the aggressor, although, in some circumstances, such feedback has served as reinforcement for pain infliction and caused it to continue to escalate, not diminish (Suedfeld, 1990; Zimbardo, 1969).

Taylor, Shuntich and Greenberg (1979) had their research participants engage in a short series of aggressive interactions in the form of competitive encounters in which, as above, progressively greater shock intensities were seemingly administered. The researchers then examined each participant's behaviour in a subsequent session, one in which the other party did not behave in a provocative manner. In this session too, however, participants continued to behave in a highly aggressive manner—a finding explained by the researchers both as a trials or practice effect, as well as a response to anticipated counter-aggression in the face of one's own, aggressive provocation.

In addition to disinhibition with practice and anticipated retaliation, a third explanation for the escalation of aggression rests on the concept of de-individuation. A construct first introduced by Festinger, Pepitone and Newcombe (1952), de-individuation is the circumstance in which individuals, usually in groups, experience diminished self-awareness and self-regulation, lessened inner restraint, and heightened freedom to engage in aggressive or other deviant behaviours. Examples of de-individuation can be found in mob behaviour, in group bullying, in gang violence, and in the thug-like behaviour of fans at football or other athletic events. It is a process engendered by high levels of emotional arousal, by diffusion of personal responsibility, by the anonymity of single persons in collectives, and a process whose expression in aggressive behaviour is further facilitated by modelling and contagion influences. Jaffe and Yinon (1979) and Jaffe, Shapir and Yinon (1981) studied this phenomenon in a laboratory context, and indeed found consistent outcomes when comparing individual versus group-administered aggression, as measured by the pace and intensity of (apparent) shock administered. On both escalation criteria, persons in groups significantly exceeded individuals acting alone, thus strongly suggesting support for the role of de-individuation in the escalation of (especially, group) aggression.

Whether and why escalation occurs is largely a function of the appraisals and behaviour of the parties involved, but it is also a function of the physical and social context in which the character contest takes place. I have examined aggression and its growth as a 'person-environment duet' elsewhere, in an exploration of the ecology of aggression (Goldstein, 1994). Its likelihood of escalation, to be sure, is influenced by qualities of the persons involved—their impulsiveness (Halperin et al., 1995), their level of self-esteem (Kernis, Granneman & Barclay, 1989), cognitive biases (Dodge & Frame, 1982), temperamental difficulties (Kingston & Prior, 1995), school and family bonding (O'Donnell, Hawkins & Abbott, 1995), values (McCarthy, 1994), dominance needs (Weisfeld, 1994), and more. However, as a duet, these several person qualities take on their escalation potency as they interact with the qualities of the setting in which the event is based. Some of these qualities are physical. Aggression and its escalation in schools is more likely on the playground, in the (boys') bathrooms, in the cafeteria, and in the hallways between classes than in the classroom or other venues (Goldstein & Conoley, 1997). In the home, the bedroom is the deadliest room, the kitchen next most dangerous, followed by the living room and other sites; with the safest room in the house being the bathroom (Gelles, 1972). Stores are most vulnerable to becoming violent crime sites when they are (1) close to major transportation routes, (2) on streets with small amounts of vehicular traffic, (3) next to vacant ground, and (4) in areas with few other stores or commercial activity (Duffalo, 1976). Alcohol intoxication, a person quality, certainly has been shown to prime character contests and their escalated aggressive responding (Pernanen, 1991), but the degree to which such escalation takes place has also been demonstrated to be a result of qualities of the bar or other drinking establishment itself (Felson, Baccaglini & Gmelch, 1986; Leather & Lawrence, 1995). Neighbourhoods, too, matter a great deal in determining whether or not aggression is likely, and its escalation frequent. Later in this chapter I shall note the relevance of a series of neighbourhood incivilities, since it is in this domain that the spirit of "catch it low" largely began (Goldstein, 1994).

The social environment plays an equally significant role in the escalation process. The group de-individuation example has been discussed above. Audience effects have been shown to matter a great deal, especially in the context of character contests (Borden, 1975; Cratty, 1981). Perhaps most important, however, regarding the social ecology component of the person–environment duet is the behaviour of the target person. Floyd (1985, p. 9) is correct in asserting that "... victimization needs to be understood in terms of the reciprocal behaviors in a relationship between an aggressor and a victim". With regard to bullying, for example, it is the behaviour of *both* the bully and the whipping boy which may make the bullying, if not begin, continue and at times escalate. Here, as with rape, assault, murder or other victims, one must be especially careful not to *blame* the target for his or her own victimization when nonetheless, one seeks to identify the target's contribution to the aggressive incident. Laboratory study of the aggression escalation process is modest in amount, interesting in result, and pregnant in potential. I strongly encourage its continuance and expansion.

Delinquency Research

Research tracing delinquent youths' progression along the three pathways noted earlier and posited by Loeber et al. (1993) shows that although there are diverse exceptions—crossing pathways, starting in the middle of a pathway, progress on two pathways simultaneously, concomitantly perpetrating both more and less serious crimes within one pathway—a great many youths do indeed follow at least one of the pathways quite as described. Loeber, Keenan and Zhang (1997) and Loeber and Stouthamer-Loeber (1998) importantly observe that the model's fit is best when a distinction is made between youths whose antisocial behaviour is a transient event (i.e. "experimenters") and those for whom aggression and criminal behaviour continue over an extended period of time (i.e. "persisters"). It is these latter youths whom these investigators, as well as Elliott (1994), have shown most clearly follow the pathway sequences proposed. Loeber and Stouthamer-Loeber (1998, p. 105) observe:

In summary, the prediction of serious outcomes such as violence can best be conceptualized according to a model in which steps toward violence are specified. That is, few individuals begin a full-blown violent career. Instead, they 'ease' into it through minor offences, and the earlier these begin, the more likely the individual will eventually show more examples of violent behavior.

Related escalation outcomes have been reported by a number of investigators (Mitchell & Rosa, 1981; Viemero, 1996) and, in each investigation, childhood aggression emerged as an antecedent of later frequency of often considerably more severe adolescent and adult criminal offending. LeBlanc (1996, pp. 11–12), based upon his own findings, describes this sequence well:

> ... we find that there are five stages in the development of offending and that they form a sequence. They are, in order, emergence, exploration, explosion, conflagration, and out-burst. At first, usually between age 8 and 10, the delinquent activities are homogeneous and benign, almost always expressed in the form of petty larceny; this is the stage of emergence. This period is followed, generally between ages 10 and 12, by a diversification and escalation of the offences, essentially comprising shoplifting and vandalism; this stage is one of exploration. Later, at about age 13, there is a substantial increase in the variety and seriousness of the crimes; and four new types of crime develop—common theft, public disorder, burglary, and personal theft; this is the stage of explosion. ... Around age 15, variety and seriousness increase further as four more types of crime are added—drug trafficking, motor vehicle theft, armed robbery, and personal attack; this is the stage of conflagration. [There is] also a fifth stage which occurs only during adulthood; it is a progress toward more sophisticated or more violent forms of criminal behavior; it is called outburst.

Tracking a large sample of youth from their adolescent years into adulthood, Stattin and Magnusson (1989) found that compared to youngsters who were low or average on aggression, high-aggressive youth were, as adults, (a) involved in more serious crimes, (b) involved in more frequent crimes, and (c) particularly more likely to engage in confrontive and destructive offences.

Focusing on school-based predictors, Hamalainen and Pulkkinen (1996) found adult serious crime at age 27 to be accurately forecast by age 8 as aggressive (verbal and physical) and norm-breaking (disobedience, truancy) behaviour. Many investigators have shown that aggression is a remarkably stable behaviour over the life span. It is clear, however, that for a great many of its perpetrators, it is its very presence in their lives which shows stability. The intensity or seriousness of such behaviour is far from stable and, in contrast, often shows substantial and predictable escalation of intensity.

Incivility Research

The escalation of aggression and kindred behaviours has also been well demonstrated in field studies that focus on the consequences of physical and social incivilities. Further, beginning evidence has emerged in this arena in clear support of a "catch it low" intervention strategy. Physical incivilities are concrete ecological features which serve as both reflections of and impetus for neighbourhood disuse, disdain, decay and deterioration. They include trash and litter; graffiti; abandoned or burned-out stores, houses and automobiles; dirt; vacant ground; broken windows and streetlights; ill-kept buildings; vandalism of diverse sorts; and similar expressions of a cycle of decline. Physical incivilities are accompanied by social incivilities, in an often dramatic display of person–environment reciprocal influence. Such social incivilities may include increased presence of aggressive gangs, drug users, prostitutes, "skid row" alcoholics, and bench or street sleepers; increased presence of drug purveyors; increased crime by offenders and increased fear of crime by neighbourhood residents; and increased harassment, chronic loitering, gambling and drinking.

Does the level of incivility relate to, and perhaps actually help to cause, the level of neighbourhood crime? Taylor and Gottfredson (1986) reported a correlation of 0.63 between incivilities and crime rates. Skogan's (1990) investigation in this domain gathered information regarding incivilities and their consequences from an average of 325 people in each of 40 different neighbourhoods in the United States. In his appropriately titled report, *Disorder and Decline*, he found strong evidence that perceived crime, fear of crime, and actual level of crime victimization were each a function of neighbourhood physical and social incivility.

Others have observed similar aggression-escalating consequences of disorder and incivility in school settings. Wilson and Petersilia (1995), for example, describe graffiti on school walls, debris in corridors, students coming to school late, wandering the halls as the foundation upon which more serious violence rests.

> [Low level] disorder invites youngsters to test further and further the limits of acceptable behavior. One connection between the inability of school authorities to maintain order and an increasing rate of violence is that, among students with little faith in the usefulness of the education they are supposed to be getting, challenging rules is part of the fun. When they succeed in littering or writing on walls, they feel encouraged to challenge other, more sacred rules, like the prohibition against assaulting fellow students and even teachers. (p. 149)

Incivility does relate to crime and violence, and it is likely to do so in a cause-and-effect manner. A major step forward in both planning and evaluating a citywide "catch it low to prevent it high" incivility intervention programme was reported by Kelling and Coles. In their aptly titled book, *Fixing Broken Windows*, Kelling and Coles (1996, pp. 242–243) comment:

> In their field study, enhanced police attention to an array of low level infractions or quality of life crimes—panhandling, subway fare beating, graffiti, loitering—decreased not only these behaviors, but also an extended series of more serious crimes. . . .
>
> Four elements of the Broken Windows strategy explain its impact on crime reduction. First, dealing with disorder and low-level offenders both informs police about, and puts them into contact with, those who have also committed index crimes, including the hard-core "6 percent" of youthful offenders. Second, the high visibility of police actions and the concentration of police in areas characterized by high levels of disorder protect "good kids", while sending a message to "wannabes" and those guilty of committing marginal crimes that their actions will no longer be tolerated. Third, citizens themselves begin to assert control over public spaces by upholding neighbourhood standards for behavior,

and ultimately move onto center stage in the ongoing processes of maintaining order and preventing crime. Finally, as problems of disorder and crime become the responsibility not merely of the police but of the entire community, including agencies and institutions outside but linked to it, all mobilize to address them in an integrated fashion. Through this broadly based effort, a vast array of resources can be marshaled, and through problem solving, targetted at specific crime problems.

Implications and Applications

What are the policy implications of such findings? In American schools today, for example, there is growing use of a zero-tolerance intervention stance. "You bring a weapon to school. No questions asked. You are expelled for a year. No appeal considered." We need, I believe, an equally rigorous, zero tolerance approach to low-level infractions. Sanctions or punishments, when such behaviours occur, need not be severe but they do need to be perceived by their recipients as unpleasant, and be administered in a consistent manner. "Ann, we are going out to the playground. I'm sorry but you know the rules of this class. Because you said those curse words you have to stay here this period and work on these exercises. You'll be staying in Mr. Green's room. Hope you can join us tomorrow."

I have long believed that one of the most important socializing lessons which parents or teachers can impart to their children is that both compliance and non-compliance with rule demands have consequences. Follow the rules of life—be it in the home, the classroom, the street or elsewhere—and positive consequences are likely to follow. Violate those rules, and the consequences will almost certainly be negative. When they are not, when contrariwise low-level infractions are rewarded, the escalation process is launched. It is thus in the spirit of and towards the goal of "catch it low to prevent it high" that I list in Table 6.3 what I view as the major pool of low level aggressive behaviours in need of such consistent consequating (Goldstein, 1999). I then turn to two illustrative descriptions of the type of comprehensive intervention effort which might profitably constitute such consequating and, indeed, prevent or minimize both the inappropriate behaviours themselves as well as their escalation.

Table 6.3   Forms of low-level aggression

Verbal maltreatment	*Criminal maltreatment*
Verbal Abuse	Vandalism
Teasing	Shoplifting
Cursing	Sabotage
Gossip	Animal cruelty
Ostracism	Stalking
Reducing verbal maltreatment	Road rage
Physical maltreatment	*Minimal maltreatment*
Bullying	Rough-and-tumble play
Sexual harassment	Hazing
	Baiting
	Booing
	Tantrums

BULLYING

Definitions and Escalation

Bullying is harm-intending behaviour of a verbal and/or physical character which is typically both unprovoked and repeated. Olweus (1993) has employed a definitional distinction between direct and indirect bullying. The former are face-to-face confrontations, open physical attacks by bully on victim, and the use in such contexts of threats and intimidating gestures. Indirect bullying is exemplified by social exclusion and isolation, scapegoating, the spreading of rumours and similar behaviours more akin to the verbal maltreatments listed in Table 6.3.

Bullying has received relatively little attention in the United States (Hoover & Hazier, 1991). Its early recognition and research examination occurred primarily in Scandinavian countries (Olweus, 1993) and in Great Britain (Elliott, 1997a, b; Smith & Sharp, 1994). In spite of its substantial frequency of occurrence, it is often the school's best kept secret. Teachers and administrators may be preoccupied with acts reflecting higher levels of aggression, or they may simply ignore it because most victims, as we shall see, elect not to call it to their attention. When it does occur, it is more likely on the playground or in the school corridors between classes, rather than in the classroom—and seldom therefore, disrupts the class. Further, even when its reality is acknowledged, its pursuit may still be ignored given the belief of many school personnel (and parents) that bullying is a "natural" part of growing up and perhaps even a positive contributor to the toughening up purported to be so useful in a competitive society. Thus, school staff may be unaware that bullying is taking place or, if aware, may choose to ignore it. Others, too, may be blind or mute to its occurrence. The bully won't tell; why should he or she volunteer to get into trouble? The victim won't tell for fear of bringing on further and perhaps more severe episodes of the very behaviour he or she wishes to avoid. Other students, more often than not, elect not to speak up out of concern for becoming targets themselves and out of reluctance to break the far-too-frequent code of silence that prevails among students regarding such matters. The victim's parents are also likely to be unaware that bullying is taking place. They may wonder why their child comes home during the school day to use the bathroom, or how his clothing gets torn, or why she seems so hungry at supper time; unaware that the school bathroom was too scary, the clothing was ripped by a bully, or that her lunch money was extorted earlier. Thus, bullying in American schools is little studied, little spoken about and, therefore, infrequently thwarted.

In consequence, as with all other forms of low-level aggression similarly ignored, its incidence continues and grows in frequency, and its sequelae emerge and escalate in intensity. Greenbaum, Turner and Stephens (1989) report that adults who had been childhood bullies are five times more likely to have a serious criminal record by age 30 than are childhood non-bullies. In a longitudinal study conducted by Olweus (1991), 60% of the boys who were identified as bullies in grades 6 through 9 had, by age 24, at least one criminal conviction, and 40% of them had three or more arrests. Such was true only 10% of boys who earlier were neither bullies nor victims. Eron et al. (1987) found that youths who bullied at age 8 had a 1 in 4 chance of having a criminal record by age 30, as compared to the 1 in 20 chance most children have. It is not only early adult arrest record that illustrates the escalation-potential of physical maltreatment via bullying. So, too, for school dropout, spouse abuse, drug dealing and vandalism (Eron et al., 1987). Bullying escalation findings stand in direct confirmation of the earlier cited literature concerning developmental pathways begun with low-level aggression.

Intervention

Beginning with the pioneering school bullying programme developed by Olweus (1993), and progressing through the similarly comprehensive interventions offered by Elliott (1995), Garrity and colleagues (1994), Pepler and colleagues (1994), Roland (1994), and Stephenson and Smith (1995), it has become clear that the optimal intervention strategy for dealing effectively with bullying by and of students is a whole school approach. All acts of aggression derive from a multiplicity of causes and, thus, will yield best when broached by an equally complex and comprehensive intervention programme. Whatever its components, it must be offered with integrity (i.e. true to plan), intensity, prescriptiveness and in consultation with its recipients. Here, drawing upon and merging the several such comprehensive programmes enumerated above, I provide a menu or pool of useful anti-bullying, school-based procedures, and urge the school-located reader to select and sequence whichever of the means appear to fit one's own institutional climate, readiness and resources. Following Olweus (1993), but expanding substantially on his specific offerings, I group programme intervention components at the school, class and individual levels. To flesh out the contents of components selected from this pool of alternatives, I especially recommend the training manuals *Bully-Proofing Your School* (Garrity et al., 1994) and *Bullying at School* (Olweus, 1993).

School Level Interventions

- School-wide survey to determine amount, frequency and locus of bullying.
- Discussion of bullying (nature, sources, signs, prevention) at PTA/PTO meetings.
- Discussion of bullying (nature, sources, signs, prevention) at whole school and by-grade assemblies.
- Increased quantity and quality of student surveillance and supervision.
- Establishment of school anti-bullying policy concretized by mission statement distributed to all staff, students and parents.
- Creation of a school-wide "telling" climate legitimizing informing about bullying, concretized by a phone hotline, an anonymous mail drop, or other means.
- Regular staff meetings to exchange bullying-relevant information and monitor intervention effectiveness.
- Development and dissemination of anti-bullying rules via posters, memos and other means.
- Restructuring of high bullying school locations.
- Separate break time for younger and older students.

Class Level Interventions

- Discussions of bullying (nature, sources, signs, prevention) at class meetings.
- Regular role plays of bullying response measures.

- Announcement of use of non-violent sanctions in response to bullying behaviour.
- Training of students as helpful bystanders/informers when bullying occurs.
- Formation of victim support groups.
- Increased use of cooperative learning for curriculum delivery.
- Use of student run "bully courts" to adjudicate incidents.
- Avoidance of use of bullying behaviour by teachers.
- Monitoring of student understanding of and compliance with school-wide, anti-bullying policy and rules.
- Contracting with students for compliance with anti-bullying rules.
- Use of stories, art and activities to communicate and reinforce anti-bullying policy and rules.
- Announcement and use of positive consequences for bully rule following behaviour.

Individual Level Intervention

For bullies:

> Social skills training
> Sanctions for bullying behaviour
> Employ as a cross-age tutor
> Individual counselling
> Anger control training
> Empathy training

For victims:

> Assertiveness training
> Martial arts training
> Social skills training
> Change of class or school
> Encourage association with new peers
> Individual counselling

Whole school, anti-bullying programmes employing variable combinations of these several school, class and individual level components have been systematically evaluated by a number of investigators in widely dispersed locations and have consistently yielded substantial, bullying reduction outcomes (Arora, 1994; Olweus, 1993; Pepler et al., 1994; Roland, 1994; Smith & Sharp, 1994). Whole school intervention programming is a comprehensive strategy that is well deserving of implementation.

VANDALISM

Vandalism has been defined as:

> The willful or malicious destruction, injury, disfigurement or defacement of property without the consent of the owner or person having custody or control

by cutting, tearing, breaking, marking, painting, drawing, covering with filth, or any such means as may be specified by local law. (Federal Bureau of Investigation, 1993, p. 217)

School and other vandalism is an expensive fact of life in many countries. Comprehensive monetary costs estimates of vandalism have been put forth; these collectively illustrate that the expense of vandalism, like its incidence, is both absolutely high and increasing. In the approximately 84 000 schools in the United States, for example, monetary vandalism cost estimates over the past 25 years show a near-linear upward trend, peaking in recent years at $600 million (Stoner, Shinn & Walker, 1991).

Arson, a particularly dangerous form of vandalism, perhaps deserves special comment. Whereas window breaking is the most frequent single act of aggression towards property in schools, arson is clearly the most costly, typically accounting for approximately 40% of total vandalism costs annually.

The costs of vandalism are not only monetary but social, as described by Vestermark and Blauvelt (1978, p. 138) regarding its expensive impact in school settings:

> By limiting criteria of vandalism's impact to only monetary costs, we overlook those incidents that have low monetary cost but, nevertheless, tremendous impact upon the school. The impact of a seventy-nine cent can of spray paint, used to paint racial epithets on a hallway wall, far exceeds the monetary cost of removing the paint. A racial confrontation could result, which might force the closing of the school for an indefinite period. How does one calculate that type of expense: confrontation and subsequent closing of a school?

Intervention Strategies: Changing the Ecology of the School

An ecological perspective on vandalism control and reduction has appeared and reappeared under a variety of rubrics: "utilitarian prevention" (Cohen, 1973), "de-opportunizing design" (Wiesenthal, 1990), "architectural determinism" (Zweig & Ducey, 1978), "crime prevention through environmental design" (Wood, 1991), "situational crime prevention" (Clarke, 1992), and "environmental criminology" (Brantingham & Brantingham, 1991). Unlike the person-oriented strategies, all of which in a variety of ways seek to reduce the potential or actual vandal's motivation to perpetrate such behaviour, the environment-oriented strategies seek to alter the physical setting, context or situation in which vandalism might occur, so that the potential or actual vandal's opportunity to perpetrate such behaviour is reduced. This ecological strategy, of altering the physical or social environment to prevent or reduce the occurrence of vandalism, has been an especially popular choice, particularly in a society as technologically oriented as the United States. Thus, venues as diverse as school districts, mass transit systems, museums, shopping malls, national and state parks, and many others have time and again opted for target-hardening, access-controlling, offender-deflecting, entry exit-screening, surveillance-increasing, inducement-removing, and similar environment-altering intervention strategies as their first, and often only, means of defence against vandalism. I have enumerated and catalogued the several dozen concrete intervention tactics which follow from strategies of this sort (Goldstein, 1996).

Yet, paradoxically, very little other than anecdotal, impressionistic, or testimonial evidence exists for the actual vandalism control effectiveness of these widely used strategies. Furthermore, the very scope of their implementation—in their most extreme form, the "Bastille response" (Ward, 1973) or the "crime-proof fortress" (Zweig & Ducey, 1978)—has in some settings had a very negative impact on the very mission for which the setting was created in the first place. For example, "More and more high schools are becoming mechanical systems ruled by constraints on timing, location, and behavior. The similarity between schools and jails is becoming ever more pronounced" (Csikszentmihalyi & Larsen, 1978, p. 25).

Not only may the setting's mission be compromised, but as a sort of paradoxical self-fulfilling prophecy, the environmental alterations put in place to reduce vandalism may be experienced by a vandal-to-be as an inviting, potentially enjoyment-providing challenge to his or her vandalistic skills, and thus may actually serve to increase such behaviour (Wise, 1982; Zweig & Ducey, 1978). The fence around the school, the graffiti-resistant wall surface, the theft-proof parking meter, the slash-proof bus seat, toughened glass, the aisle store camera—each is a possible opportunity-reducing deterrent and, as such, each is also a challenging invitation to vandalism.

Thus, the "down side" of reliance on alterations to the physical environment as the means of vandalism control and reduction is not inconsiderable. Yet an important "up side" also exists. First, without concurring with a position as extreme as Weinmayr's (1969) assertion that "ninety percent of what is labeled vandalism can be prevented through design" (p. 286), one may still accept and act on the belief that venue changes can be significant components of effective person–environment interventions. First, design innovations may be relevant to de-opportunizing vandalism in more than one way. Wiesenthal (1990), for example, observes that "property damage can be avoided by design elements that do more than resist attack; design can be used to subtly steer the user away from destruction or defacement" (p. 289). Wise (1982) suggests that design may be employed to channel attention away from potentially damaging activities, to reduce the effects of natural processes (e.g. erosion, weathering) that vandals may augment, and to eliminate or reduce the type of environmental feedback that may serve to reinforce vandalistic behaviour. Levy-Leboyer (1984) augments the case for design-as-intervention by noting that some locations are more prone to vandalism than others—a view also put forth by Christensen et al. (1996) in their call for a predictive framework for identifying various degrees of site vulnerability. Public sites, newer sites, sites previously vandalized, those previously damaged by something other than vandalism, those located in "low-status" institutions, and the venues providing inadequate service are all common targets—and thus desirable sites for environmental alteration. Those taking a deterministic view believe that individuals choose to engage in vandalistic behaviour in response to characteristics not only of their physical environment, but also of their social environment. This is purported to be the case on both micro and macro levels. At the micro, immediate, level the central socio-ecological intervention concept is perceived and actual surveillance. Vandalism, it is held, is less likely to occur if the potential perpetrator believes he or she will be observed and perhaps apprehended. Thus, for example, Blauvelt (1980, p. 49) urges making the school "occupied", and claims:

> The key to controlling vandalism is to make the school a place that in some sense is continuously occupied by some form of human or mechanical presence, which will deter or respond to the vandal. The heart of any effective approach to controlling vandalism will be establishing that sense of "presence" which defines the building as no longer being an inert target.

Added bus conductors, real and dummy TV cameras in stores, Neighbourhood Watch programmes, improved neighbourhood lighting, and increased number of store employees are all examples of opportunity-reducing, surveillance-increasing socio-ecological interventions.

Intervention Strategies: Changing the Vandal

In contrast to intervention efforts directed towards the actual or potential vandal's physical or social environment, the intervention target may be the vandal himself or herself. Cohen (1974) suggests three such person-oriented strategies:

1. *Education*. Here the effort is made to increase the potential vandal's awareness of the costs and other consequences of vandalistic behaviour. These interventions assume that once this awareness is increased, the person will consider the possible consequences and choose to refrain from perpetrating vandalism.
2. *Deterrence and retribution*. These strategies rely on threat, punishment, or forcing those committing vandalistic acts to make restitution. Punishment strategies are especially widely employed. Ward (1973, p. 256) comments:
   > The most frequent public reaction to vandalism is "Hit them hard": all that is needed is better detection by the police and stiffer sentences by the court. The general tendency is to support heavier fines, custodial sentences. . . Other, extra-legal sanctions include banning offenders from swimming baths, sports fields, youth clubs or play centers. Some local authorities have suggested the evicting of tenants whose children are responsible for vandalism.
3. *Deflection*. These strategies "attempt to understand and redirect the motivational causes of vandalism into non-damaging means of expression" (Cohen, 1974, p. 54). They include allowing controlled destruction, providing substitute targets, or furnishing alternative outlets for energetic activity.

Koch (1975) describes a parallel array of person-oriented strategies, employing either coercive controls, the indoctrination of information, legal regulations, or the substitution of functional equivalents.

To repeat an earlier-mentioned distinction, environment-focused interventions target opportunity reduction; person-oriented efforts seek to alter motivation. Although punishment, as noted above, appears to be an especially frequently used person-oriented strategy (Heller & White, 1975; Stoner, Shinn & Walker, 1991), there is evidence that heavy reliance on it may often actually result in an increase, not a decrease, in the frequency of vandalism (Greenberg, 1969; Scrimger & Elder, 1981). These same investigators, as well as others, report a substantial decrease in vandalism as punitiveness decreases and such interventions as increased use of teacher approval for desirable student behaviours are used more frequently (Mayer & Butterworth, 1979; Mayer et al., 1987).

One further point regarding vandal-oriented intervention strategies concerns the desirability of a prescriptive response plan. Ideally, who the vandals are (Griffiths & Shapland, 1979) and the level their vandalistic behaviours have reached (Hauber, 1989) will, in part, determine the nature of the intervention implemented. Griffiths and Shapland (1979) correctly assert that the vandal's motives and the very meaning of the act itself change with age and context, and that strategies need to vary accordingly:

> The preventive measures that need to be taken to make any given environment vandal-proof may be different according to the nature of the vandal...As an example, of this, look at how a window in a deserted house may be broken. This may have been done by kids getting in to play; by older children as a game of skill; by adolescents or adults in order to remove the remaining furniture or fittings; by someone with a grudge against the person or previous landlord; by a pressure group to advertise the dereliction of empty property; or by [a vagrant] to gain attention or to [get in to spend] the night. (pp. 17–18)

Intervention Strategies: Person–Environment

Every act of vandalism would appear to spring from both person and environment sources—a dualism that must similarly characterize efforts at its prevention and remediation. The separate person-oriented and environment-oriented vandalism intervention strategies I have now explored will optimally be implemented in diverse, prescriptively appropriate combinations. Casserly, Bass and Garrett (1980), Cohen (1973), Geason and Wilson (1990), Kulka (1978), Vestermark and Blauvelt (1978) and Wilson (1979) are among the several vandalism theorists and researchers also championing multi-level, multi-modal, person–environment intervention strategies. Several practitioners have already put in place such joint strategies, and at least impressionistically report having done so to good advantage (Hendrick & Murfin, 1974; Jamieson, 1987; Levy-Leboyer, 1984; Mason, 1979; Panko, 1978; Scrimger & Elder, 1981; Stover, 1990; Weeks, 1976; White & Fallis, 1980). Vandalism, like all instances of aggression, is a complexly determined behaviour. Every act of vandalism derives from several causes, and therefore is best combated with equally complex interventions.

Below, I draw upon the large pool of vandalism interventions that I have presented elsewhere (Goldstein, 1996) in order to illustratively reorganize samples of these interventions into just such multi-level, multi-channel configuration. In the absence of efficacy evaluations, no particular interventions or intervention configurations can be singled out for recommended use at this time. However, I believe that this emphasis on the selection and implementation of meaningful intervention combinations is likely to prove a major step towards truly effective vandalism prevention, control and reduction.

Table 6.4 presents a level-by-mode intervention schema targeted to the reduction of vandalism in school contexts. My intent here is to urge both practitioners and evaluators of vandalism prevention/reduction efforts to make sure that

Table 6.4 A multi-level, multi-channel schema for the reduction of school vandalism

Level of Intervention	Mode of Intervention				
	Psychological	Educational	Administrative	Legal	Physical
Community	"Youth vacation vigil" programme	Arson education	"Adopt-a-school" programmes	Monetary fines	Citizen, police, or parent patrols
School	Conflict negotiation programmes	Year-round education	Schools within-a-school	Code of rights and responsibilities	Lighting, painting, paving programmes
Teacher	School-home collaboration	Multicultural sensitivity training	Reduced teacher-student ratio	Property marking with school ID	Distribution of staff offices throughout school
Students	Interpersonal skills training	Vandalism awareness walks	School detention, suspension	Restitution, vandalism accounts	Graffiti boards, mural walls

interventions at all levels and through all channels are included in their packages of interventions.

Other factorial schemas seeking to reflect in their particulars the desirable complexity of vandalism intervention programming have been offered by Harootunian (1986) and by Zweir and Vaughn (1984). They, too, accurately reflect in their comprehensive intervention response the complexity of causation underlying the vandalistic act.

Low-level aggression has for too long been ignored by practitioner and researcher alike. Approaches to defining what behaviours constitute low-level aggression of necessity yield to idiographic definitions obtained from its targets. Such behaviour is of interest in its own right, but assumes its major significance via its demonstrated tendency to escalate as its rewards become apparent. We have enumerated its several forms, and illustrated by means of a lengthier consideration of bullying and vandalism what we recommend as an effective comprehensive intervention strategy.

REFERENCES

Arora, C. M. J. (1994) Is there any point in trying to reduce bullying in secondary schools? *Educational Psychology in Practice, 10*, 155–162.

Athens, L. (1985) Character contests and violent criminal conduct: A critique. *The Sociological Quarterly, 26*, 419–431.

Bandura, A. (1973) *Aggression: A Social Learning Analysis*. Englewood Cliffs, NJ: Prentice-Hall.

Baron, R. A. & Richardson, D. R. (1994) *Human Aggression*. New York, NY: Plenum.

Berkowitz, L., Lepinski, J. P. & Angulo, E. J. (1969) Awareness of own anger level and subsequent aggression. *Journal of Personality and Social Psychology, 11*, 293–300.

Blauvelt, P. D. (1980) School security doesn't have to break the bank. *Independent School, 40*, 47–50.

Borden, R. J. (1975) Witnessed aggression: Influence of an observer's sex and values on aggressive responding. *Journal of Personality and Social Psychology, 31*, 567–573.

Brantingham, P. J. & Brantingham, P. L. (1991) *Environmental Criminology*. Newbury Park, CA: Sage.

Buss, A. H. (1961) *The Psychology of Aggression*. New York, NY: Wiley.

Casserly, M. D., Bass, S. A. & Garrett, J. R. (1980). *School vandalism: Strategies for Prevention*. Lexington, MA: Lexington Books.

Christensen, H. H., Johnson, D. R. & Brookes, M. (1988) *Vandalism: Research, Prevention, and Social Policy*. Portland, OR: US Department of Agriculture Forest Service.

Christensen, H. H., Mabery, K., McAllister, M. E. & McCormick, D. P. (1996) Cultural resource protection: A predictive framework for identifying site vulnerability, protection priorities, and effective protection strategies. In A. P. Goldstein (Ed.) *The Psychology of Vandalism*. New York, NY: Plenum Press.

Clarke, R. V. (Ed.) (1992) *Situational Crime Prevention: Successful Case Studies*. New York, NY: Harrow & Heston.

Cohen, S. (1973) Campaigning against vandalism. In C. Ward (Ed.) *Vandalism*. London: Architectural Press.

Cohen, S. (1974) Breaking out, smashing up and the social context of aspiration. *Working Papers in Cultural Studies, 5*, 37–63.

Cratty, B. J. (1981) *Social Psychology in Athletics*. Englewood Cliffs, NJ: Prentice-Hall.

Csikszentmihalyi, M. & Larsen, R. (1978) *Intrinsic Rewards in School Crime*. Hackensack, NJ: National Council on Crime and Delinquency.

Cullen, F. T., Clark, G. A. & Polanzi, C. (1982) The seriousness of crime revisited. *Criminology, 2*, 83–102.

Dodge, K. A. & Frame, C. L. (1982) Social cognitive biases and deficits in aggressive boys. *Child Development, 53*, 620–635.

Duffalo, D. C. (1976) Convenience stores, armed robbery and physical environmental features. *American Behavioral Scientist, 20*, 227–246.

Elliott, D. S. (1994) Serious violent offenders: Onset, developmental course, and termination. *Criminology, 32*, 1–21.

Elliott, M. (1995) A whole-school approach to bullying. In M. Elliott (Ed.) *Bullying: A Practical Guide to Coping for Schools*. London: Pitman Publishing.

Elliott, M. (1997a) Bullies and victims. In M. Elliott (Ed.) *Bullying: A Practical Guide to Coping for Schools*. London: Pitman Publishing.

Elliott, M. (1997b) Bullying and the under fives. In M. Elliott (Ed.) *Bullying: A Practical Guide to Coping for Schools*. London: Pitman Publishing.

Elliott, M. & Kilpatrick, J. (1994) *How to Stop Bullying: A Kidscape Training Guide*. London: Kidscape.

Eron, L. D., Huesmann, R., Dubow, E., Romanoff, R. & Yarmel, P. W. (1987) Aggression and its correlates over 22 years. In D. H. Crowell, I. M. Evans & C. P. O'Connell (Eds.) *Childhood Aggression and Violence*. New York, NY: Plenum.

Farrington, D. P. (1991). Childhood aggression and adult violence: Early precursors and later-life outcomes. In D. J. Pepler & K. H. Rubin (Eds.) *The Development and Treatment of Childhood Aggression*. Hillsdale, NJ: Erlbaum.

Federal Bureau of Investigation (1993) *Crime in the United States*. Washington, DC: US Government Printing Office.

Felson, R. B. (1978) Aggression as impression management. *Social Psychology, 41*, 205–213.

Felson, R. B., Baccaglini, W. & Gmelch, G. (1986) Barroom brawls: Aggression and violence in Irish and American bars. In A. Campbell & J. J. Gibbs (Eds.) *Violent Transactions: The Limits of Personality*. Oxford: Blackwell.

Festinger, L., Pepitone, A. & Newcombe, T. (1952) Some consequences of deindividuation in a group. *Journal of Abnormal and Social Psychology, 47*, 382–389.

Floyd, N. M. (1985) "Pick on somebody your own size": Controlling victimization. *The Pointer, 29*, 9–17.

Forgas, J. P., Brown, L. B. & Menyhart, J. (1980). Dimensions of aggression: The perception of aggressive episodes. *British Journal of Social and Clinical Psychology, 19*, 215–227.

Garrity, C., Jens, K., Porter, W., Sager, N. & Short-Camilli, C. (1994) *Bully-proofing Your School*. Longmont, CO: Sopris West.

Geason, S. & Wilson, P. R. (1990) *Preventing Graffiti and Vandalism*. Canberra, Australia: Australian Institute of Criminology.

Gelles, R. J. (1972) "It takes two": The roles of victim and offender. In R. J. Gelles (Ed.) *The Violent Home: A Study of Physical Aggression between Husbands and Wives*. Thousand Oaks, CA: Sage.

Goldstein, A. P. (1994) *The Ecology of Aggression*. New York, NY: Plenum Publishing Co.

Goldstein, A. P. (1996) *Violence in America*. Palo Alto, CA: Davies-Black.

Goldstein, A. P. (1999) *Low Level Aggression: First Steps on the Ladder to Violence*. Champaign, IL: Research Press.

Goldstein, A. P. & Conoley, J. C. (1997) *School Violence Intervention: A Practical Handbook*. New York, NY: Guilford.

Goldstein, A. P., Palumbo, J., Striepling, S. H. & Voutsinas, A. (1995) *Break It Up: A Teacher's Guide to Managing Student Aggression*. Champaign, IL: Research Press.

Goldstein, J. H., Davis, R. W. & Herman, D. (1975) Escalation of aggression: Experimental studies. *Journal of Personality and Social Psychology, 31*,162–170.

Goldstein, J. H., Davis, R. W., Kernis, M. & Cohn, E. S. (1981) Retarding the escalation of aggression. *Social Behaviors and Personality, 9*, 65–70.

Greenbaum, S., Turner, B. & Stephens, R. D. (1989) *Set straight on bullies*. Malibu, CA: National School Safety Center.

Greenberg, B. (1969) *School Vandalism: A National Dilemma*. Menlo Park, CA: Stanford Research Institute.

Griffiths, R. & Shapland, J. M. (1979) The vandal's perspective: Meanings and motives. In P. Rural (Ed.), *Designing against Vandalism*. New York, NY: Van Nostrand Reinhold.

Grossman, C. D. (1995) *On Killing*. Boston, MA: Little, Brown.

Halperin, J. M., Newcorn, J. H., Matier, K., Bedi, S., Hall, S. & Sherma, V. (1995) Impulsivity and the initiation of fights in children with disruptive behavior disorders. *Journal of Child Psychology and Psychiatry, 36*, 1199–1211.

Hamalainen, M. & Pulkkinen, L. (1996) Problem behavior as a precursor of male criminality. *Development and Psychopathology, 8*, 443–455.

Harootunian, B. (1986) School violence and vandalism. In S. J. Apter & A. P. Goldstein (Eds.) *Youth Violence: Programs and Prospects*. New York, NY: Pergamon Press.

Hauber, A. R. (1989) The social psychology of driving behaviour and the traffic environment: Research on aggressive behavior in traffic. *International Review of Applied Psychology, 29*, 461–474.

Heller, M. C. & White, M. A. (1975) Rates of teacher verbal approval and disapproval to higher and lower ability classes. *Journal of Educational Psychology, 67*, 796–800.

Hendrick, C. & Murfin, M. (1974) Project library ripoff: A study of periodical mutilation in a university library. *College and Research Libraries, 35*, 402–411.

Hoover, J. & Hazler, R. J. (1991) Bullies and victims. *Elementary School Guidance and Counseling, 25*, 212–219.

Huesmann, L. R. (1988) An information processing model for the development of aggression. *Aggressive Behavior, 14*, 1324.

Jaffe, Y., Shapir, N. & Yinon, Y. (1981) Aggression and its escalation. *Journal of Cross-Cultural Psychology, 12*, 21–36.

Jaffe, Y. & Yinon, Y. (1979) Retaliatory aggression in individuals and groups. *European Journal of Social Psychology, 9*, 177–186.

Jamieson, B. (1987) Public telephone vandalism. In D. Challinger (Ed.) *Preventing Property Crime*. Canberra, Australia: Australian Institute of Criminology.

Kelling, G. L. & Coles, C. M. (1996) *Fixing Broken Windows*. New York, NY: Free Press.

Kernis, M. H., Grannemann, B. D. & Barclay, L. C. (1989) Stability and level of self-esteem as predictors of anger arousal and hostility. *Journal of Personality and Social Psychology, 56*, 1013–1022.

Kingston, L. & Prior, M. (1995) The development of patterns of stable, transient, and school-age onset aggressive behavior in young children. *Journal of the American Academy of Child and Adolescent Psychiatry, 34*, 348–358.

Koch, E. L. (1975) School vandalism and strategies of social control. *Urban Education, 10*, 54–72.

Kulka, R. A. (1978) School crime as a function of person-environment fit. *Theoretical Perspectives on School Crime, 1*, 17–24.

Leather, P. & Lawrence, C. (1995) Perceiving pub violence: The symbolic influence of social and environmental factors. *British Journal of Social Psychology, 34*, 395–407.

LeBlanc, M. (1996) Changing patterns in the perpetration of offences over time: Trajectories from early adolescence to the early 30s. *Studies on Crime and Crime Prevention, 5*, 151–165.

Levi, M. & Jones, S. (1985) Public and police perception of crime seriousness in England and Wales. *British Journal of Criminology, 25*, 234–250.

Levy-Leboyer, C. (Ed.) (1984) *Vandalism: Behavior and Motivations*. North Holland: Amsterdam.

Loeber, R., Keenan, K. & Zhang, Q. (1997) Boys' experimentation and persistence in developmental pathways toward serious delinquency. *Journal of Childd and Family Studies, 6*, 321–357.

Loeber, R. & Stouthamer-Loeber, M. S. (1998) Development of juvenile aggression and violence: Some common misconceptions and controversies. *American Psychologist, 53*, 242–259.

Loeber, R., Wung, P., Keenan, K., Giroux, B., Stouthamer-Loeber, M., Van Kammen, W. B. & Maughan. B. (1993) Developmental pathways in disruptive child behavior. *Development and Psychopathology, 5*, 103–133.

Lubel, S., Wolf, Y. & Krausz, E. (1991) Judgment of aggressiveness among Jews of Middle-Eastern/North-African (Sephardic) and European (Ashkenazi) descent. *Megamot, 33*, 232–251.

Marsh, P., Rosser, E. & Harré, R. (1978) *The Rules of Disorder*. London: Routledge.

Mason, D. L. (1979) *Fine Art of Art Security—Protecting Public and Private Collections against Theft, Fire, and Vandalism*. New York, NY: Van Nostrand Reinhold.

Mayer, G. R. & Butterworth, T. W. (1979) A preventive approach to school violence and vandalism: An experimental study. *Personnel and Guidance Journal, 57*, 436–441.

Mayer, G. R., Nafpaktitis, M., Butterworth, T. & Hollingsworth, P. (1987) A search for the elusive setting events of school vandalism: A correlational study. *Education and Treatment of Children, 10*, 259–270.

McCarthy, B. (1994) Warrior values: A socio-historical survey. In J. Archer (Ed.) *Male Violence*. London: Routledge.

Mitchell, S. & Rosa, P. (1981) Boyhood behavior problems as precursors of criminality: A fifteen-year follow-up study. *Journal of Child Psychology and Psychiatry, 22*, 19–33.

Moffitt, T. E. (1993) Adolescence-limited and lifecourse-persistent antisocial behavior: A developmental taxonomy. *Psychological Review, 100*, 674–701.

Nagin, D. S., Farrington, D. P. & Moffitt, T. E. (1995) Life-course trajectories of different types of offenders. *Criminology, 33*, 111–139.

National Institute of Justice (October 1997) *Research in Brief*. Washington, DC: Author.

O'Connell, M. & Whelan, A. (1996) Taking wrongs seriously. *British Journal of Criminology, 36*, 299–318.

O'Donnell, J., Hawkins, J. D. & Abbott, R. D. (1995) Predicting serious delinquency and substance abuse among aggressive boys. *Journal of Consulting and Clinical Psychology, 63*, 529–537.

Olweus, D. (1991) Bully/victim problems among school children: Basic facts and effects of a school based intervention program. In D. Pepler & K. H. Rubin (Eds.) *The Development and Treatment of Childhood Aggression*. Hillsdale, NJ: Erlbaum.

Olweus, D. (1993) *Bullying at School: What we Know and what we Can Do*. Oxford: Blackwell.

Panko, W. L. (1978) *Taxonomy of school vandalism*. Doctoral dissertation. Pittsburgh, PA: University of Pittsburgh.

Pepler, D. J., Craig, W. M., Ziegler, S. & Charach, A. (1994) An evaluation of an anti-bullying intervention in Toronto schools. *Canadian Journal of Community Mental Health, 13*, 95–110.

Pernanen, K. (1991) *Alcohol in Human Violence*. New York, NY: Guilford.

Raush, H. L. (1965) Interaction sequences. *Journal of Personality and Social Psychology, 2*, 487–499.

Roff, J. D. & Wirt, R. D. (1984) Childhood aggression and social adjustments as antecedents of delinquency. *Journal of Abnormal Child Psychology, 12*, 111–126.

Roland, E. (1994) A system oriented strategy against bullying. In E. Roland & E. Munthe (Eds.) *Bullying: An International Perspective*. London: Fulton.

Rose, A. M. & Prell, A. E. (1955) Does the punishment fit the crime? A study in social valuation. *American Journal of Sociology, 61*, 247–259.

Rossi, P. H., Waite, E., Bose, C. E. & Berk, R. E. (1974) The seriousness of crimes: Normative Structure and individual differences. *American Sociological Review, 39*, 224–237.

Scrimger, G. C. & Elder, R. (1981) *Alternative to Vandalism—"Cooperation or Wreakreation"*. Sacramento, CA: California Office of the Attorney General School Safety Center.

Skogan, W. G. (1990) *Disorder and Decline*. Berkeley, CA: University of California Press.

Smith, P. K. & Sharp, S. (1994) *School Bullying: Insights and Perspectives*. London: Routledge.

Sparks, R., Genn, H. & Dodd, D. (1977) *Surveying Victims*. London: Wiley.

Stattin, H. & Magnusson, D. (1989) The role of early aggressive behavior in the frequency, seriousness, and types of later crimes. *Journal of Consulting and Clinical Psychology, 57*, 710–718.

Stephenson, P. & Smith, D. (1995) Why some schools don't have bullies. In M. Elliott (Ed.) *Bullying: A Practical Guide to Coping for Schools*. London: Pitman Publishing.

Stoner, G., Shinn, M. R. & Walker, H. M. (Eds.) (1991) *Intervention for Achievement and Behavior Problems*. Silver Spring, MD: National Association of School Psychologists.

Stover, D. (1990) How to be safe and secure against school vandalism. *The Executive Educator*, November, 20–30.

Suedfeld, P. (1990) *Psychology and Torture*. New York, NY: Hemisphere Publishing.

Taylor, R. B. & Gottfredson, S. (1986) Environmental design, crime, and prevention: An examination of community dynamics. In A. J. Reiss & M. Tonry (Eds.) *Communities and Crime*. Chicago, IL: University of Chicago Press.

Taylor, S. P., Shuntich, R. J. & Greenberg, A. (1979) The effects of repeated aggressive encounters on subsequent aggressive behavior. *The Journal of Social Psychology, 107*, 199–208.

Thomas, C. W. & Bilchik, S. (1985) Prosecuting juveniles in criminal courts: A legal and empirical analysis. *Journal of Criminal Law and Criminology, 76*, 439–479.

Tuppen, C. J. S. & Gaitan, A. (1989) Constructing accounts of aggressive episodes. *Social Behavior, 4*, 127–143.

Vestermark, S. D. & Blauvelt, P. D. (1978) *Controlling Crime in the School: A Complete Security Handbook for Administrators*. West Nyack, NY: Parker Publishing Co.

Viemero, V. (1996) Factors in childhood that predict later criminal behavior. *Aggressive Behavior, 22*, 87–97.

Walker, M. A. (1978) Measuring the seriousness of crimes. *British Journal of Criminology, 18*, 348–364.

Ward, C. (1973) *Vandalism*. New York, NY: Van Nostrand.

Weeks, S. (1976) Security against vandalism: It takes facts, feelings and facilities. *American School and University, 48*, 36–46.

Weinmayr, V. M. (1969) Vandalism by design: A critique. *Landscape Architecture, 59*, 286.

Weisfeld, G. (1994) Aggression and dominance in the social world of boys. In J. Archer (Ed.) *Male Violence*. London: Routledge.

White, J. & Fallis, A. (1980) *Vandalism Prevention Programs used in Ontario Schools*. Toronto, Canada: Ontario Ministry of Education.

Wiesenthal, D. L. (1990) Psychological aspects of vandalism. In P. J. D. Drenth, J. A. Sergeant & R. J. Takens (Eds.) *European Perspectives in Psychology* (Vol. 3). New York, NY: Wiley.

Wilson, J. Q. & Petersilia, J. (1995) *Crime*. San Francisco, CA: Institute for Contemporary Studies Press.

Wilson, S. (1979) Observations on the nature of vandalism. In P. Bural (Ed.) *Designing against Vandalism*. New York, NY: Van Nostrand Reinhold.

Wise, J. (1982) A gentle deterrent to vandalism. *Psychology Today*, September, 28–31.

Wood, D. (1991) In defense of indefensible space. In P. J. Brantingham & P. L. Brantingham (Eds.) *Environmental Criminology*. Prospect Heights, IL: Waveland Press.

Zimbardo, P. G. (1969) The human choice: Individuation, reason and order versus deindividuation, impulse and chaos. In W. J. Arnold & D. Levine (Eds.) *Nebraska Symposium on Motivation*. Nebraska: University of Nebraska Press.

Zweig, A. & Ducey, M. H. (1978) *A paradigmatic field: A review of research on school vandalism*. Hackensack, NJ: National Council on Crime and Delinquency.

Zweir, G. & Vaughn, G. M. (1984) Three ideological orientations in school vandalism research. *Review of Educational Research, 54*, 263–292.

Chapter 7

INTERVENING WITH FAMILIES OF TROUBLED YOUTH: FUNCTIONAL FAMILY THERAPY AND PARENTING WISELY

DONALD A. GORDON

Dept. of Psychology, Ohio University, Ohio, USA

OVERVIEW

Both the need for and availability of empirically validated interventions for families in crisis and at risk has never been greater. The great majority of service providers to these children and families are not using effective methods, while the number of effective interventions has substantially increased in the past half decade. This conundrum, although deeply frustrating, inspires creative solutions and drives governmental funding to bridge the gap between research and practice. The past decade has seen a consensus among behavioural scientists that parent and family interventions should at least be included (if not the sole focus) when children exhibit behavioural or adjustment problems. Carr (2000) presents a recent review of all of the interventions for children and adolescents based upon studies with comparison groups and pre- and post-treatment measures. Included are treatments for child abuse, enuresis and encopresis, attention deficit disorder, oppositional defiant disorder, adolescent conduct disorder, depression, anxiety disorders, drug abuse, and anorexia and bulimia. The most effective treatments for these disorders usually involved the parents or family, who were included as principal components of effective treatment in all.

Among the most effective treatments for adolescent behaviour problems in general, and conduct problems in particular, is family therapy (Carr, 2000; Gordon & Arbuthnot, 1987). Those models with the greatest empirical support are *Multisystemic Therapy* and *Functional Family Therapy* (FFT). Currently, these approaches are enjoying strong governmental support for dissemination. In this chapter, I will describe the FFT model based upon the experiences of my students trained to use this model with young offenders over a 20-year period. I will also describe the

Offender Rehabilitation and Treatment: Effective Programmes and Policies to Reduce Re-offending. Edited by James McGuire.
© John Wiley & Sons, Ltd.

development of a parent training programme on CD-ROM to both augment the FFT approach and to reach greater numbers of families who could or would not receive FFT or did not need FFT. I also present the research on both programmes, and the important issues relating to their dissemination.

FAMILY-RELATED RISK FACTORS

The view that the family is the cause of criminality has surged and faded and now resurged in the history of the study of criminal behaviour. It is now accepted as a well-established principle that the roots of adult criminal behaviour can be traced to hostility and aggression in childhood, which, along with other antecedents of criminal behaviour, are socialized in and controlled by the family (Lorion, Tolan & Wahler, 1987). Travis Hirschi, in his extensive study of the causes of delinquency, found that the number of children's self-reported delinquent acts was powerfully influenced by their attachment to their parents, communication with the father, and supervision by the mother. Social class and the influence of peer groups, long thought to be predictors of delinquency, pale in comparison to family factors. A variety of thorough investigations has supported these findings, which point to discipline, problem-solving, monitoring, and support as central to parenting skills, the absence of which is related to delinquency (McCord, 1982; Snyder & Patterson, 1987; Farrington, 1995).

The most compelling demonstration of the causative role of the family in delinquent behaviour comes from the efforts to change family (particularly parent) behaviour. Most of the studies (Gordon, Jurkovic & Arbuthnot, 1998; Tolan et al., 1986) showed reductions in delinquent behaviour such as re-arrests, recidivism, and truancy following family therapy. In Tolan et al.'s (1986) review, all the studies that included measures of family functioning, and the few that also included recidivism, reported some improvement. However, weaknesses in experimental design limit the strength of a conclusion that family therapy leads to improved family functioning and reduced delinquency. The many studies of FFT and Multisystemic Therapy attest to this causal role.

Adolescent substance abuse is also associated with delinquency and behaviour problems, and the risk factors for substance abuse are very similar to risk factors for delinquency. Low parental involvement with children (St. Pierre & Kaltreider, 1997), poor family communication (Glynn & Haenlein, 1988; Kumpfer & DeMarsh, 1986), and low family cohesion/attachment (Kumpfer & DeMarsh, 1986; McKay et al., 1991; Malkus, 1994) are related to adolescent substance use. McKay et al. (1991) found a direct relationship between levels of family dysfunction and levels of adolescent substance abuse.[1]

Regarding peer group influences, Brown and colleagues (1993) pointed out that parents have an indirect influence. Parent behaviours impact upon adolescent characteristics, which predict the type of peer group with which a child will associate. If the parent–child relationship is poor (little communication, high conflict, and little support), the child is more likely to become involved with deviant peers and, consequently, become involved in drug and alcohol use or delinquency (Brown et al., 1993; Patterson, 1982; Patterson, Dishion & Bank, 1984).

In our work with families of delinquents over the past 20 years, we have observed those characteristics that are well established in the literature. Discipline is ineffective, being either erratic and overly harsh, or permissive. High levels of parent–child conflict, and the blaming and anger that accompany this conflict, and low levels of parental supervision and monitoring communicate parental disinterest and distrust of the child. When children learn coercive social interaction patterns from their parents, they often transfer these to their peer group and are rejected by normal peers, as Patterson's (1982) research has demonstrated. When high conflict is associated with low family cohesion and parental affection and support for the child, the child's susceptibility to deviant peer group influence grows.

DESCRIPTION OF FFT

FFT combines social learning, cognitive-behavioural, interpersonal theory, and family systems theories. It was developed in the 1970s primarily for a behaviourally disturbed adolescent population whose parents were unable to control their acting-out behaviour. The adolescent's behaviour was viewed in the context of the interpersonal needs of various family members, as well as the teenager's own developmental needs. The developers paid attention to family members' thoughts of each other's behaviour, and determined via observation and interview the meaning that recurrent interaction sequences held for each family member, and the needs these sequences met. Methods of changing these sequences are, first, cognitive-behavioural, accomplished by therapists' relabelling patterns to change their meaning, followed by didactic instruction, modelling, role-play, and feedback to teach new skills. Many of the behaviour change methods arose from the parent training methods developed by G. R. Patterson and others, reviewed by Serketich and Dumas (1996). The primary contributions of the FFT approach were the evaluation of family interaction patterns from a family systems perspective, the conceptualization of repetitive sequences from an interpersonal need for distance or closeness position, and the standardization of methods for conceptualizing and dealing with family members' resistance to change.

Description of the Functional Family Therapy Approach

The initial structure of the FFT model delineated five phases (introduction/credibility, assessment, therapy, education, and generalization). In the past few years, since the *Blueprints for Violence Prevention* were developed to disseminate effective programmes (Alexander et al., 2000), these five phases were reduced to three: engagement/motivation, behaviour change, and generalization. In the initial sessions, therapists focus on building alliances with family members and reducing negativity and hopelessness. Listening and eliciting family members' goals substitutes for giving advice, as therapists lay the groundwork for a motivational context for change. Assessment in the recent version of FFT continues throughout each of the phases. It consists of the evaluation, by observation and interview, of family behaviour patterns, cognitions and feelings, and the reinforcers maintaining those patterns. Repetitive relational styles for each dyad are assessed as meeting basic interpersonal needs for contact or connectedness, distance or autonomy, or something in between (midpointing). Assessing these interpersonal functions is critically important to understanding which behaviours will be more resistant to change, as interpersonal functions are seen as relatively enduring. In our implementation of the FFT model, within the first and second sessions, the therapists interviewed members in detail about problem behaviours. We attempted to take a snapshot of daily family life by focusing in detail on the major transition points each day: getting up and preparation for school, arrival of children after school, dinner arrangements, after dinner activities, and bedtime routines. Among the delinquent populations we have served, the most common problem behaviours that parents identified were: curfew violations in about two-thirds of the families; frequent non-compliance with parental requests in over three-quarters of the families; and daily parent–child conflict in all of the families. When two parents were in attendance, parental inconsistency in providing consequences was present in virtually all of the families. Serious marital discord was present in less than half of the intact families. The therapists also gathered information on problem behaviours from school personnel, county caseworkers and court personnel. Just before and after the first session, the therapists met with their supervisor to decide on the initial focus of therapy.

The therapy phase (now called the engagement/motivation phase) was designed to alter attitudes, expectations, cognitive sets, labels, emotional reactions and perceptions of relationships between family members in such a way as to reduce blaming and to portray each member as an unwitting victim of a poor learning history. Therapists substituted benign motives for the more malevolent motives that family members assigned to each other's behaviours. *Reframing* is a powerful technique used to change the meaning of an interaction or a behaviour. Its value lies in its ability to confuse family members initially, then have them see each other in a more compassionate light. Therapists must not only be able to empathize with family members' frustrations and anger and hurt, but also be able to get them to see a different meaning behind the frustrating behaviour. Novice therapists have more difficulty learning to reframe problematic interactions than most other skills, so this skill has been emphasized in training. Appendix B lists common problem behaviours and 'reframes' that apply, and Alexander lists a number of reframes in his *Blueprint* (Alexander et al., 2000, p. 30).

Consistent with a systems framework, the family was viewed as a dysfunctional unit. Thus, the goal of treatment was to resolve problematic interactions among family members, recognizing that more than a dyad was involved in the problems. This goal was attained through focusing attention away from the juvenile as 'the problem', and towards other family relationships and the contributions of the 'non-combatants' before and after disruptive episodes (Alexander & Parsons, 1982).

The education or behaviour change phase was designed either to teach family members skills they lacked or to prompt them to make more frequent use of the skills they had. This phase is similar to parent-training procedures used by Patterson's group. Thus, the education phase consisted of teaching communication and problem-solving skills, providing technical aids to assist in reinforcing functional behaviour, and instituting interpersonal family tasks. Among the communication skills taught to the families via modelling and prompting were active listening, source responsibility, 'I' messages, directness and feedback. The technical aids, designed to provide concrete ways of reinforcing the new functional family interaction patterns, included contingent reinforcement, contingency contracting, time-out, charts and graphs, and note and message centres. Considerable emphasis was placed on these parenting techniques; particularly contingency contracting, since most parents showed substantial skill deficits in these areas. Later sessions were devoted largely to ensuring that family members were generalizing newly developed problem-solving and communication skills across varied situations. Handouts with instructions for using the various methods, along with homework exercises, were usually given to the families. Interpersonal tasks, such as asking a mother to set up a homework routine with her child, were designed to provide families with the opportunity to practise communication skills, reinforce positive interaction patterns, engage in conflict management, and spend enjoyable time together. In two-parent families, parents were prompted to verbally support each other's use of new skills with their children, particularly applying immediate consequences for changes in deviant child behaviour. Interparental support of skill practice has been shown to increase the persistence of treatment gains.

Because a majority of the adolescents lived in families where there was no father, one therapeutic goal was either to establish (especially when the child was a boy) the child's contact with the father, to increase the frequency of contact, or to establish a supportive relationship with an adult male in the community (relative, neighbour, church member). When the mother had a boyfriend who was responsible and interested in the children, positive contact between that boyfriend and the delinquent (especially the male) was monitored and encouraged.

The final phase, generalization, focuses on the generalization of the skills the family has learned to a variety of naturally occurring situations, with the therapist assigning homework requiring progressively more independence. The frequency of sessions declines; and the last two or three sessions are often scheduled for every 2–3 weeks. Therapists support the maintenance of change, and warn the family that occasional setbacks are to be expected, but that they should rely on the new skills they learned rather than regress towards earlier (ineffective) methods. Therapists often take on the role of case manager to access community support for the family, such as school consultation to increase support for the delinquent, financial support, job placement services, and advocating for the family with the juvenile court. Court advocacy usually involves recommending against out-of-home placement, unless that is clearly indicated on the basis of the therapist's knowledge of the family. We routinely schedule booster sessions with the family two to three months after termination.

Case Example

The following is a case example of functional family therapy that is fairly typical of our population of low income families with a delinquent (reprinted from Gordon, 1995):

Larry is a 16-year-old referred for family therapy by the juvenile court following his third theft, as well as gang fights after school, as an alternative to institutional placement. Mr. G, Larry's stepfather, is physically disabled and stays home where he does household chores. Mrs. G works in a paper plant. They also have a daughter, Heather, 14 years old. Two therapists, recently trained in the FFT model, meet with most of the family weekly in the family's home.

Over three sessions, their assessment of the family reveals that communication is defensive with much blaming and little listening. Members believe the worst of each other's motives and small problems don't get resolved, often escalating into severe conflict after which one person leaves the house. Larry is frequently criticized by both parents, often for his temper. He seeks distance from his mother but wants contact with his father. Both parents want distance from Larry. They often pick at him until he loses his temper and leaves to be with his delinquent friends. Heather is her father's favorite, and reliably gets both parents' attention by tattling on Larry. Her poor compliance with chores and homework is not noticed by Mr. G and is only sporadically targeted for criticism by Mrs. G Mr. G loosely monitors the children while Mrs. G is at work, and does not carry out Mrs. G's restrictive policies with either child. The children have no input into rules or consequences, and the parents complain of irresponsible academic, peer, and sibling behaviour.

During the therapy phase, covering much of the next five sessions (as well as part of the first three sessions), the family's resistance to each other and to the therapists is lessened through reframing and pointing out strengths. (Supervisor requirements were greatest during this phase to provide ideas for handling resistance and to support the therapists.) The therapists explained how each family member unwittingly got locked into defensive patterns, and how the parents' lack of support for compliance and appropriate behaviours was a result of their own parents' teaching. Larry's motives for acting-out with his friends, seen by his parents as lack of respect for them, was portrayed as seeking the approval from peers that he was missing at home, and as wanting his parents to be proud of his independence and ability to make decisions that weren't disastrous. Mr. G's distancing of Mrs. G was relabelled as respecting her need for privacy after a tiring day at work. Heather's tattling on Larry was relabelled as her desire for her parents' approval and to get Larry's attention. Mr. G's not carrying out his wife's restrictive policies with the children was relabelled as not wanting to hurt his relationship with the children. The presence of family conflict was repeatedly tied to poor communication skills and the lack of a specific conflict resolution plan rather than ascribing them to negative personality traits and motives of family members.

The education phase, covering most of the next four sessions, included teaching and prompting the parents to use reinforcement (verbal, granting privileges) for the children's compliance. Larry was also taught stress reduction techniques such as taking a walk outside when he noticed that he was getting angry, telling himself that he was strong enough to withstand provocation by immature peers, and taking several deep breaths while telling himself that he could keep his "cool". Heather agreed to report only on Larry's improved behaviour (thereby allowing her to continue to get parental attention). Mr. G relayed these messages to Larry via notes placed on his bedroom door, allowing him to maintain his distance from Larry. Family members practised active listening and 'I' messages during therapy sessions and also with weekly homework assignments (which they completed about 50% of the time). The therapists structured a problem-solving format for the family to follow and led them through several rehearsals. The family worked out a contract on their own between sessions, which were spaced out to twice per month in preparation for termination. In their contract, Larry agreed to report to Mr. G when he was going to be late coming home from school (or be grounded the next day) and Mr. G agreed to refrain from criticizing Larry when he brought his friends home. Improved homework and chore compliance led to Larry's being allowed to have friends stay overnight, which increased the supervision he received from his parents. With the decrease in conflict, Mrs. G and Mr. G spent more time discussing improvements and started some family activities, such as trips to a local skating rink and renting movies selected by all. Two follow-up therapy sessions four weeks and three months after termination revealed minimal conflict and confidence that the family could resolve future problems on their own.

Adaptations of the FFT Model

In the early 1980s, I adapted the FFT model for low-income high-risk families of delinquents, as evidenced from the example above. The graduate students in my family therapy course sequence began seeing families of court-referred delinquents in their homes, and we collected data on these families and those in a probation-only control group. These studies, explained in more detail in the next section, demonstrated substantial reductions in recidivism for the delinquents receiving FFT (Gordon et al., 1988; Gordon, Graves & Arbuthnot, 1995; Gordon, 1995). These findings were similar to, or more striking than, Alexander's results (Alexander & Parsons, 1973; Alexander et al., 1976), in spite of the fact that we worked with families who were of a lower income group than Alexander's samples and who also were non-Mormon. While following the model as outlined in Alexander and Parson's (1982) treatment manual on FFT, I increased emphasis during several of the five phases of intervention on a behavioural approach. During the assessment phase, I stressed a behavioural assessment of daily interactions of family members which appeared, from a social learning perspective, to promote or maintain problem child behaviour. Detailed interviewing of family members followed the style of Peter Falk in the television programme *Columbo*. In the Therapy or Motivational phase, I emphasized not only reframing motives and problematic family interactions, but using a salesperson's approach to motivate the family to try new skills when interacting. In this approach, the therapists point out the costs that family members (primarily the parent(s)) are paying for using their current methods (coercion, stonewalling, ignoring, shaming). Such costs may include chronic stress, exhaustion, depression, self-medicating through substance abuse, alienation and disengagement, and many parents realize that their methods are not "good enough" and accept the need for change. The therapists try to raise the family's awareness of these hidden costs, and specify the advantages of learning "new" methods, and showing how the new methods will help them to reach their goals more efficiently, even though the initial investment of time and energy seems high. During the educational or behaviour change phase, therapists give very specific instruction in teaching communication skills, problem-solving, and contingency management. This instruction is a combination of didactic instruction, demonstration, role-playing and coaching. An empowerment approach is used to motivate the family to make the changes for themselves, using skill practice and psycho-educational aids. These aids seem to be powerful to help the families to learn and implement the new skills, and include handouts, videotapes, and, in the past five years, use of the Parenting Wisely CD-ROM. Homework assignments are regularly given. During the generalization phase, as in the FFT model, therapists focus on motivating the family to implement the new skills for a greater variety of situations, and provide technical assistance to do so. Booster sessions are added to improve generalization and provide additional support to the family.

RESEARCH

Alexander et al. (2000) report the effects of FFT on recidivism in 14 studies (three of which are ours). About half of the studies involved random assignment to control or "treatment as usual" groups. Recidivism rates for FFT treatment varied from one-sixth to two-thirds of the comparison groups, with a variety of risk levels and multicultural backgrounds of offenders. The average reduction in recidivism or out-of-home placements was 34.6%. Follow-up periods ranged from one to five years.

I will summarize the evaluations we conducted in Ohio. The first evaluation, reported elsewhere (Gordon et al., 1988; Gordon, Graves & Arbuthnot, 1995) was a home-based programme of family therapy conducted in a rural southeastern (Appalachian) Ohio county. The court selected 27 delinquents for the treatment who were likely to recidivate, and/or be placed out of the home. Most of the delinquents were 14–16 years old and had committed status offences (57%), misdemeanors (30%) and felonies (13%). The participants in the comparison group were 27 delinquents with fewer offences but a similar breakdown of types of offences. Both groups were similar in family income (very low), divorced/intact status, and types of schools attended. After a 2–2.5 year follow-up period, recidivism (court adjudications) for the treatment group was 11% versus 67% for the controls. These delinquents were followed for another 32 months into adulthood, with the family therapy group showing a 9% recidivism rate for criminal offences versus 41% for the probation-only group (Gordon, Graves & Arbuthnot, 1995).

The second evaluation was conducted on a court-run programme using paraprofessionals hired by the court to do home-based functional family therapy. The setting was a suburban county outside Columbus, Ohio, having a mixture of social classes and a variety of social services. The 40 juveniles referred to the treatment programme were the most serious, chronic offenders in the county. They were referred for family therapy after release from a state institution for juvenile offenders. Most had had three or four prior institutional commitments. The treatment group averaged seven offences prior to treatment; they had started offending at age 13, and were 17 to 18 years old at the time of referral. There was no comparison group, other than statistics, as the judge referred all delinquents upon institutional release.

After an average of 18 months following the end of treatment, 30% of the 40 delinquents receiving treatment had a new offence (status, misdemeanor, or felony), while 10% required another institutional commitment. As no comparison group at similar high risk for re-offending from the county could be obtained, a statistical group was constructed, based upon risk for recidivating (age at first offence, number and type of offences, age at referral). Such a group would be expected to have a 60–75% recidivism rate, and a recommitment rate of 50–60% (Gordon, 1995).

The third evaluation was conducted on a programme of aftercare treatment similar to the second evaluation. In five counties of southeastern Ohio (Appalachia), delinquents were referred to the home-based functional family therapy programme (delivered by graduate students at Ohio University) after release from state institutions for juvenile offenders. The five counties were very similar in demographics to that described in the first evaluation (rural, low-income families, high unemployment, poor social services). The 27 referred delinquents came from lower to lower middle income families where the biological father was rarely in the home. They had an average of two prior institutional commitments, four prior juvenile offences, and were 16 to 17 years old. The comparison group was matched for risk for re-offending, age, and social class. The 25 comparison delinquents received standard probation services, with many being referred to mental health centres. After an average of 16 months following the start of treatment, the recidivism rate for the treatment group was 33% being recommitted to a state institution for delinquents.

The comparison group had a recommitment rate of 64%, which is the rate expected given their risk for re-offending (Gordon, 1995).

DISSEMINATION

Since 1998, the US Government has funded several investigators to identify the most effective interventions that reduce violence, delinquency and substance abuse. Two of these, Delbert Elliott at the University of Colorado and Karol Kumpfer at the University of Utah, identified FFT as among the most effective. Elliott's *Blueprints for Violence Prevention*, mentioned earlier, have been widely requested by communities seeking federal funding to implement those identified, evidence-based interventions. Similarly, Kumpfer's *Strengthening America's Families* project identified and promoted family-focused programmes for treatment and prevention of substance abuse. The result has been a growing demand for training in FFT. Another family therapy intervention, *Multisystemic Therapy* (MST) was identified by both Elliott and Kumpfer and has enjoyed explosive growth. The challenges of widely disseminating these complex interventions to communities distant from the programme developers are daunting. The FFT and MST groups are paying careful attention to details of community preparation, training, supervision, treatment integrity, monitoring process and outcome, and ongoing technical support.

My experience with training practitioners in community settings to deliver FFT in a consistent fashion faithful to the model was humbling compared to training graduate students. In the course of training graduate students, I relied on teaching the model over a 6–10 week period (12–20 hours), close supervision of therapy sessions through having therapists complete checklists of activities for each family session, listening to audiotapes of the sessions, and group discussions of each family weekly (20–30 minutes per family). The caseloads were very small, with students carrying one to three families at a time. Part of the reason for our impressive outcomes for recidivism is probably the more intensive nature of the supervision, as well as the use of graduate students in clinical psychology. These students are an elite group selected from a large pool of graduate school applicants. They are very personable, diligent, intellectually curious, and quite intelligent. They are also aware that they know little about working with families and subsequently are eager to learn. For all these reasons, it was not difficult to maintain treatment integrity.

When I trained experienced professionals in FFT, I ran into obstacles similar to those Barton noted in his replication of FFT (Alexander et al., 2000). The behavioural specificity required in FFT was opposed by psychodynamic and humanistic therapists, and by eclectic therapists unwilling to put in the organized, disciplined work required in behavioural approaches. Many were not knowledgeable about behaviour change methods to be taught to parents, and resisted learning these without insistence from the supervisor. Cognitive-behavioural therapists were quite comfortable with the model, but many therapists objected to the accountability required (filling out session checklists, making regular supervision meetings, measuring outcomes). Another challenge for therapists was accepting the FFT model's view that it was the therapist's responsibility to engage difficult families. These therapists are used to blaming the families rather than their methods when there is a failure to engage.

These challenges are not unique to implementing FFT. Resistance to change is as endemic to governments, agencies and therapists, as it is to parents. Introducing innovations, regardless of how logical and cost effective they may be (as are family interventions), meets with resistance. Many policy-makers and administrators lack information about effective practices, and agencies often have limited abilities to plan and implement new programmes, as well as limited start-up funds. The operational changes required of agencies to train, monitor, evaluate, motivate and maintain changes for practitioners are wrenching (Mendel, 2000).

Bickman and Noser (1999) express concern about therapists' likelihood of following a defined treatment protocol if ongoing close supervision and consequences are not in place. We need to implement continuous quality improvement systems to give service providers feedback about their procedures and outcomes. Supervisors must have effective consequences at their disposal to motivate practitioners to adhere to the treatment protocols. Implementing these procedures has been a very difficult challenge because service providers resist attempts to limit their autonomy, and are not accustomed to receiving feedback on their effectiveness. As Chambless (1999) notes in her discussion of the problems with disseminating empirically validated treatments, practitioners are hampered by time, distance and money in getting supervised training. However, the recent availability of state and federal funds is helping agencies to afford the training and supervision. Another challenge is recruiting and retaining providers with personal attributes and skills to benefit from training. When the practitioners do not have strong science-based academic training, they are more sceptical of empirically validated interventions when certain procedures conflict with their usual practices, their clinical experience, and personal beliefs. Paul Gendreau, a prominent Canadian psychologist who, along with Don Andrews, helped to start the movement towards evidence-based treatment, warns about the "common sense revolution" (Gendreau, 2001). This revolution is manifested by the disregard for empirically validated treatments—an anti-empirical bias of those with personal experience with the topic (crime, family relations, problem child behaviour). If a certain treatment practice makes common sense to these practitioners, administrators and policy-makers, they feel that there is no need to look for evidence to support such treatments or to evaluate them. The tragedy of this attitude is shown by the widespread use of individual counselling or therapy for troubled children and adolescents with behaviour problems, in spite of research reviews and large-scale well-designed studies showing that such community interventions do not lead to positive outcomes for children (Weiss, Catron, Harris & Phung, 1999; Bickman & Noser, 1999).

Another hindrance to the dissemination of effective treatments is the poor marketing and packaging of these programmes, which compete against the well-financed and expert marketing of ineffective or unevaluated programmes. Most of the programme developers who have conducted thorough research are academics with little knowledge of marketing, and their universities either discourage or do not provide the finance or incentives for them to take the time to learn such ventures (Gordon, 2000). Many developers do not want to limit their research activities in order to focus on dissemination.

When the target population is young offenders, most practitioners and juvenile courts have an individual responsibility orientation which focuses rehabilitative and punitive efforts primarily if not exclusively on the delinquent. It is easier for courts to mandate the delinquent to treatment, and it is easier for service providers to focus on one person than on a family, school, or community. When the treatment occurs outside the community, as in regional institutional settings, it is often impossible to meaningfully include other important social systems. The problem of informing providers and courts about effective family interventions is compounded when politicians call for tougher sanctions for the delinquent as the principal method of reducing juvenile crime.

Both the MST and FFT research groups are addressing the challenges of improving compliance with implementation standards in innovative ways. After extensive training in FFT, therapists must complete checklists after each session that guide them as to the appropriate activities for the session and provide the supervisor with evidence of adherence to the model. These checklists are often supplemented with audio or videotapes, and weekly telephone conferences between a team of FFT-trained therapists with a supervisor at FFT headquarters.

Resistant Families

Families of young offenders, substance-abusing and behaviour problem adolescents, are often in a low income group, poorly educated, with a history of unpleasant experiences with schools and public service agencies. Parents of these teenagers may have disengaged from active involvement with them due to a history of feeling defeated and ineffective (Spoth & Redmond, 1995). These parents are in the pre-contemplation stage of change, as they do not see a need for parenting interventions. Other parents do not have the resources to attend multiple session family interventions or parent education classes (reliable transportation, funds to pay for or public transportation, child care providers, or a flexible schedule to mesh with the therapist's schedule). For other high-risk families, parents will avoid mental health clinics or therapists because of their fear of the stigma such services have among low-income areas. Attendance and retention in family therapy is enhanced when the treatments are delivered in the homes using a flexible approach that works with whoever is present at each session. We have had success among such high-risk families with a very pragmatic and practical application of the FFT model, and with the much briefer *Parenting Wisely* programme.

PARENTING WISELY

Several years ago we developed a family-centred intervention which is not dependent upon social service personnel for its delivery, is inexpensive, and can be replicated and sustained in communities without training for service providers. In addition it minimizes the barriers to low-income families of cost, accessibility and social stigma. The intervention is a self-administered CD-ROM, *Parenting Wisely* (PW), which teaches parents and their children and teenagers important skills, the

Table 7.1 Comparison of therapy and interactive CD-ROM

Therapy	Interactive CD-ROM
1. Verbal descriptions of parenting	Detailed verbal and visual examples of parenting
2. Judgement by therapist	No judgement by computer
3. Client defensiveness main obstacle to progress	Minimal client defensiveness
4. Client discloses parenting errors	Client recognizes parenting errors by actors
5. Feedback on parenting errors infrequent and indirect	Client actively seeks feedback on parenting errors performed by actors in programme
6. Client rarely asks for repetition of unclear advice	Client can repeat any part of programme any time
7. Often pace selected by therapist	Pace always selected by client
8. Infrequent reinforcement of good parenting practices	Frequent reinforcement of good parenting practices
9. Focus on therapist–client relationship	Exclusive focus on teaching good parenting
10. Majority of therapy time and cost devoted to resistance	Little of programme time devoted to resistance
11. Difficult to improve therapist skills	Relatively easy to improve programme content

lack of which has been implicated in the causation of delinquency and substance abuse (communication, support, supervision and discipline). The programme's development was based on two premises, which are well supported in the literature. One premise is that interactive videodisk programmes increase knowledge and performance more efficiently than do standard methods of instruction, and produce mean effect sizes of 0.53 (Fletcher, 1990; McNeil & Nelson, 1991; Niemiec & Walberg, 1987). The other is that videotaped modelling of parenting skills is as effective in producing improvements in child behaviour as are parent education discussion groups and parent training with a therapist (Webster-Stratton, Hollinsworth & Kolpacoff, 1989; Webster-Stratton, Kolpacoff & Hollinsworth, 1998). Some comparisons between face-to-face therapy and interactive CD-ROM are noted in Table 7.1.

The programme requires and invites interaction by presenting nine live-action scenarios of common parent–child problems followed by three possible solutions for each one, along with explanations of why each solution is or is not the most effective. Problems include homework, sibling conflict, defiance, chore avoidance, disrespectful talk, and associating with undesirable peers. After the problems are played, the parent has an opportunity to choose one of three solutions that is most similar to the way they would handle that particular situation. A video clip of that solution is then played on the screen. Following the presentation of the solution, a series of question and answer screens deliver a critique of the solution they just viewed, providing feedback to the parent on positive and negative consequences of dealing with the problem in that particular manner. If the solution that the parent chose is not the best possible choice, the computer will instruct the parent to choose another. After the correct solution is chosen, an on-screen quiz is provided to give the parent an opportunity to see how well he or she learned the techniques taught in the programme thus far. In the context of normal family interactions, effective parent-ing skills are demonstrated, such as active listening, "I" messages, contracting, su-pervision, assertive discipline, contracting and contingency management. Parents and children can use the programme together, prompting helpful discussions. The programme uses a family systems, cognitive-behavioural and social-learning ap-proach. The FFT model was influential in the design of the programme. For instance, the interrelationships among family members leading to different outcomes for children were emphasized, as well as attempts to discourage scapegoating or tri-angulating. Developmental changes in children's need for contact and distance is also part of the instruction, and parental needs for those two functions are acknowl-edged. The PW programme also teaches parents and young people the connection between making malevolent attributions and conflict, or benign attributions and cooperation. Each family/parent using the programme receives a workbook con-taining the text of the programme, and skill-building exercises for the skills taught in the programme. The use of these exercises provides skill practice that facilitates implementation of the skills.

The goals and outcomes of the PW programme are increased knowledge of good parenting skills and principles, improved parenting practices, improvements in child problem behaviour, and improved family interactions. Another goal is high parental satisfaction, and improved confidence that parents can deal with child problem behaviour using the skills taught in the programme. Also we sought to increase the number of parents who would use PW from among those who refuse to attend parent education classes or family interventions.

Controlled research demonstrates high parental satisfaction, increased access of high-risk families to parenting interventions, improvements in knowledge and use of skills, improvements in family relations, and large improvements in child prob-lem behaviour. For difficult children and adolescents, behaviour improved by more than 50% (Lagges & Gordon, 1999; Kacir & Gordon, 1999; Gordon & Kacir, 1998). Because of this research evidence, which is summarized in Table 7.2, the PW programme was rated Model Program and Exemplary II by the Center for Sub-stance Abuse Prevention (CSAP) and the Office of Juvenile Justice and Delinquency Prevention, respectively.

In a study using participants referred from outpatient clinics and a residential treatment centre for juvenile delinquents, Segal et al. (in press) found significant de-creases in the number and intensity of child problem behaviours. Parents also re-ported an increased use of effective parenting skills and showed greater knowledge of parenting skills taught in the programme. They also reported very high satisfac-tion with the programme and high confidence that they could use the parenting skills taught to improve their children's behaviour.

Using randomly assigned control and treatment groups, Kacir and Gordon (1999) investigated the effectiveness of the PW programme with parents of adolescents recruited through local public schools. At a one-month follow-up, parents in the treatment group demonstrated significantly greater knowledge of parenting skills than did parents in the control group. At one- and four-month follow-ups, parents in the treatment group also reported greater decreases, from 14 to 6, than control subjects in the number and intensity of child problem behaviours on the Eyberg Child Behaviour Inventory (ECBI: Eyberg & Ross, 1978; Eyberg & Robinson, 1983).

Table 7.2 Comparison of studies of Parenting Wisely

Study	Participants (n)	Site	Design	Follow-up period	Child problem behaviour PW effect size (Cohen's d)
Segal et al. (in press)	Parents of 11–18 year olds (42)	Community mental health and juvenile detention	RA* to two treatment groups	1 month	0.78[†], 1.27[‡]
Lagges & Gordon (1999)	Teenage parents of infants and toddlers (62)	School	RA to treatment and control	2 months	0.67[§]
Kacir & Gordon (1999)	Parents of problem adolescents (38)	University	RA to treatment and control	2, 4 months	1.2[†]
Gordon & Kacir (1998)	Parents of delinquents	Community and university	Treatment and matched control	1, 3, 6 months	0.59[†], 0.76[‡]
Woodruff & Gordon (1999)	Parents of 9–13 year olds	Home	RA to two treatment groups	2, 6 months	0.37[†]

* RA: Random Assignment
[†] Eyberg Child Behaviour Inventory
[‡] Parents Daily Report
[§] Parental response to hypothetical problem behaviour

Most young people in the treatment group showed clinically elevated scores on the ECBI prior to their mothers using the programme. Four months after programme use, 50% of the teens were classified as recovered on the ECBI (scoring in the normal range). The average effect size for all measures was 0.46, similar to those in Segal et al. (in press).

While prior research focused on individual administration of the programme to parents of adolescents, Lagges and Gordon (1999) investigated the effectiveness of using the PW programme with teenage parents. Their children were infants and toddlers. Compared to control subjects, teenage parents in the treatment group demonstrated greater increases in their knowledge of adaptive parenting skills at a one-month follow-up. Parents in the treatment group were also more likely than control subjects to endorse the effectiveness of adaptive parenting practices over coercive practices at follow-up. This study demonstrates the flexibility of the PW programme, and its potential for use in a variety of contexts.

Gordon and Kacir (1998) examined the effectiveness of the PW programme when used with court-referred low-income parents of juvenile delinquents. These parents were often resistant to treatment, unmotivated and had repeatedly demonstrated poor parenting practices in the past. Nevertheless, these parents also showed improvement, in comparison to a no-treatment control group, on both the Eyberg Child Behaviour Inventory Total Problems Scale (Eyberg & Ross, 1978) and on a parenting knowledge test. These improvements were demonstrated at three and six months post-treatment. Additionally, the children of parents who used the PW programme showed decreases in negative behaviours, as reported on the Parent Daily Report (Chamberlain & Reid, 1987) collected one week, one month, three months and six months following treatment. Effect sizes ranged from 0.49 to 0.76, indicating a robust treatment effect. Tests of clinical significance showed that 82% of children in the treatment group showed reliable change, with 71% being classified as recovered (scoring in the normal range) on the Eyberg Child Behaviour Inventory. No children in the control group recovered.

A recent study of PW as a family intervention has found that family functioning, as measured by the Family Assessment Device (Miller et al., 1985), improved after parents and children used the programme (Woodruff, Gordon & Lobo, 2000). High-risk, disadvantaged families with a fourth- to sixth-grade student were randomly assigned to receive in their homes either the PW programme (on a laptop computer) or parent education booklets covering similar content. The PW group showed larger effect sizes for reductions in child problem behaviour (on the Eyberg Child Behaviour Inventory) and improvements in family functioning.

When the PW programme was implemented with at-risk families through urban schools, the programme reduced family violence (Rolland-Stanar, Gordon & Carlston, 2001). Spousal conflict showed a significant reduction, as well as conflict and aggression between parents and children (via child report). General violence scores, as well as verbal aggression and severe violence sub-scores, all improved. Children reported that their hyperactive behaviours declined, relative to an untreated control group.

In all the studies conducted on PW, parents who used the programme reported overall satisfaction and found the teaching format easy to follow. They also found the scenarios realistic, the problems depicted to be relevant to their families, and the parenting skills taught reasonable solutions to those problems. The parents felt confident they could apply the skills in their families. These findings may help explain why parents were willing to spend two to three hours in one sitting using the programme, and why improvements in child behaviour were evident as soon as a week after parents used the programme.

The size of the treatment effect is highly unusual, given the very brief duration of the treatment. Although effect sizes for other studies using interactive video were also moderately large (McNeil & Nelson, 1991; Niemiec & Walberg, 1987), high-risk families have not, until now, been exposed to this technology, nor has CD-ROM or interactive video been applied to parenting and family living skills. These large treatment effects are probably due to a combination of at least three factors: videotaped modelling of excellent and highly relevant content, a very high level of required user interaction, and the privacy, self-paced, and non-judgemental format of a computer (Gordon, 2000).

DISSEMINATION OF PARENTING WISELY

The PW programme is being used in over 200 locations in the USA and in dozens of communities in England, Ireland and Australia. It has enjoyed a fairly rapid dissemination, due to a number of factors. The method is packaged as a stand-alone programme requiring no training of practitioners. The time and expense that agencies must devote if they want to ensure and maintain treatment integrity is not an issue, since Parenting Wisely is a computer CD-ROM programme. Its brevity and non-threatening nature increases its access to families, particularly high-risk families. It also lends itself to evaluation since most families complete outcome measures when they first use the programme, and most families complete the programme in a short period of time. The programme includes a range of good pre-test and post-test measures, with simple instructions on how to conduct programme evaluation. The effectiveness of the programme has contributed to its popularity. Publicity from CSAP and the Centers for Application of Prevention Technology has stimulated interest. A more detailed analysis of factors contributing to successful implementation of the programme, following a survey of sites implementing PW, has just been completed (Gordon & Stanar, in press).

In order to market the programme, I formed a company through Ohio University's business incubation centre. This centre exists to assist faculty members in taking their inventions to market and to create jobs for the area. The company, Family Works Inc., developed a professional look for the programme, integrated new research findings into upgrades of the programme, and conducted marketing activities to make the programme known to service providers who deal with at-risk children and families. Elsewhere, I discuss the advantages and disadvantages to programme developers in forming companies to market their programmes (Gordon, 2000). While we must be careful not to let the business aspects of these companies influence our focus on continuously evaluating and enhancing effectiveness, the dissemination of these programmes leads to independent evaluations. We know of at least a dozen independent evaluations of the PW programme currently underway.

INTEGRATION OF FFT WITH PARENTING WISELY

The idea of using these two programmes in tandem as a routine practice came after anecdotal feedback from several families of offenders who had used PW either before or after receiving FFT. These families reported that they had a much clearer understanding of the skills we were attempting to train during the educational phase of FFT once they used the PW programme. For those who used PW first, the parents were less resistant to discussing their parenting practices and practising the skills needed to improve.

When FFT is implemented first with a family, an appropriate time to introduce PW is during the education or behaviour change phase. The skill training the therapists do during the sessions will be reinforced by the PW programme, as well as giving the family a different format for learning (more interactive, private, multimedia presentations—video, audio, text, graphics). Therapists can spend less time with skill training, and can work more on motivating and prompting parents to practise skills between therapy sessions. It may be a better use of therapists' time and skills to focus on other matters while letting the technology handle much of the skill training. Similarly, therapists can use videos, audiotapes and instructional handouts to teach parenting skills during this phase.

We have also used PW as a follow-up or booster treatment a month or two after terminating sessions with a family. Most families are very receptive to recommendations of their therapist at that point. We have found PW to be useful as a recruitment method for families for FFT. In our programme targeting the highest risk families whose young offenders have had several institutional placements, most parents refuse to participate in family therapy. More than half of these treatment refusers will allow someone to bring a laptop computer into their home and will use the PW programme with their adolescent. Of those who do, some of them subsequently agree to participate in FFT. One effect of the PW programme is to convince parents that their parenting techniques are related to their child's misbehaviour, and that they can improve such behaviour by changing their methods. The programme gives them some confidence that they will be able to do this. However, given the severe problems they face with their children, some parents then are open to receiving more help.

Continuum of Services

Some agencies have developed a continuum of parenting/family interventions to serve families with varying needs and abilities to engage in treatment. For those families with children with mild to moderate behaviour problems, or for those who are unwilling or unable to commit to more than one or two appointments, the PW programme is used without other services. Most families are advised to use the PW programme several times to absorb more information in the programme. Other families receive PW, then participate in ongoing parent education groups. Highly dysfunctional families, when motivated, receive PW and family therapy.

Recently I developed a curriculum/treatment manual for four sessions of family intervention (Appendix A). This very brief programme is based on my adaptation of the FFT model and is intended for use in the following three circumstances:

(1) families who use PW and either do not need more than several consultations with a therapist to resolve most of their problems; (2) families who will not engage for more than several sessions; (3) where a shortage of family therapists cannot meet the demand for full-length family therapy. This model is more psycho-educational than psychotherapeutic, and focuses on empowering families to use the skills they were exposed to in the PW programme and its workbook. Rather than telling families how to resolve problems, the therapists prompt parental recall of programme scenes and skills that might resolve current problems. Therapists motivate parents to practise and implement the skills presented in the PW programme and, in this way, the families' dependence on the therapist as a problem-solver and crisis interventionist is minimized. During some of the sessions, parents are encouraged to apply the skills they have learned to a greater variety of challenging child behaviour problems (substance abuse, theft, aggression and violence, self-harm, hygiene problems).

This four-session family consultation model is being implemented and tested in locations in Ireland, England and the USA. Evaluations will determine any additive effect of these consultations upon changes produced by the PW programme alone.

Where do we Go from Here?

The challenges to disseminate these effective parent and family intervention are plentiful. We cannot rely upon recent evaluations to show that these approaches are more effective and cost-effective than traditional approaches, or for the rational acceptance of this information to continue. Educating legislatures and policy-makers about the need to fund and maintain these training programmes adequately is paramount. Accountability at the local level of implementation must be established to avoid practitioners rejecting the training or drifting away from the manualized treatment models.

The families who can benefit from these interventions must be recruited and engaged more effectively. Early exposure to parenting training will increase later acceptance, so parents should be enticed to receive such training when their children are very young, preferably before they enter school. If we can set the expectation that receiving this training is expected of all parents throughout the child's development, the stigma attached to parenting help will diminish. As more programmes are disseminated, we will be better able to offer a continuum of effective services that are matched to the families' needs.

APPENDIX A: MANUAL FOR INDIVIDUAL CONSULTATION WITH FAMILIES WHO HAVE USED PARENTING WISELY

Objectives and Philosophy:

The purpose of this manual is to teach family intervention skills to service providers to effectively extend the skill training of Parenting Wisely (PW) and address other risk factors in only four sessions with family (mother and at least one child).

This very brief family intervention model presents basic effective components of family therapy and parent training, and should be accompanied by the use of psycho-educational aids such as pamphlets, videos, handouts and homework assignments from the PW workbook. *The purpose of these four sessions is to empower family members to transfer the skills learned from the PW programme to all parenting challenges.* As the PW model relies upon psycho-education rather than a client–therapist relationship, the consultant's main role will be motivating parents to use these psycho-educational resources rather than relying on the consultant for emotional and functional support.

Prior to working with families, service providers must have used the PW programme and be familiar with its operation and content, as well as having read the PW parent workbook carefully. This is necessary since prompting parents to recall specific parts of the PW programme and refer to the workbook is a central feature of the family consultations. In addition, rapport is improved when the providers disclose their experiences with the programme and implementation of the skills with their own children.

Practitioners or service providers come from a variety of backgrounds. This manual focuses on teaching very basic skills for working with families. With increasing experience, practitioners will make use of the more advanced material in this workbook. Each of the four sessions of consultation with the families is outlined as to the basic tasks to be accomplished. As trainees gain experience and effectiveness, they will react more dynamically to the families' needs. They will be able to change the order of material covered in the four sessions and supplement the basic tasks as needed, with additional interventions (such as guidance for dealing with depression or marital conflict).

This model of family interventions is briefer than others, and different in focus. Since families (at least the primary parent) will have *used* the PW programme prior to these four sessions, most will be more able to focus on the objectives of these sessions instead of requiring many sessions of rapport-building and preparations to begin discussions of parenting issues. The objectives of these four sessions is to encourage practice of the PW skills, to help parents to use the skills learned from PW in different situations, and to increase the number of PW skills they use in their daily lives. Thus, we are trying to get parents (and other family members) to transfer, extend and generalize what they learned or started to learn in the PW programme. In time these skills should become second nature and will be integrated into the day-to-day behaviour of the family.

BASIC STEPS

Session 1

A. *Build rapport and trust:* Various methods of building trust may be intuitive to many trainees. These include pleasant discussions of issues the trainee and parent or child have in common, such as the trainees being parents themselves to objects in the family's home the trainee can relate to. These pleasantries should not take more than a few minutes (10–15) before getting down to the objectives of the first session. Length of the session should be between 45 and 90 minutes, depending upon your availability and the family's ability to maintain their attention.

B. *Objectives:* Establish family goals, review effects of PW use on family relations, help parents recall their use of skills, and promote recall of skills demonstrated in PW programme applicable to current concerns about child behaviour.

1. Establish family goals. Parents will buy into taking your advice on using better parenting skills if they understand how this advice connects to goals they have agreed to.

Common goals most parents will agree to are: increased respect among family members, decreased conflict, increased cooperation, increased support, increased maturity and trust. For instance, if the mother resists practising Active Listening (by not doing workbook exercises or role plays with you), you need to tell her how using this skill with her children will increase the respect she wants from them. If parents deny any problems with their children and cannot endorse any of the goals mentioned above, they will agree with the goal of keeping the court off their backs (i.e. by not giving them any more Parenting Orders).

2. Review effects of PW programme. Ask family members what changes they noticed after using the PW programme. Get them to be specific. If they cannot verbalize changes, review the different skill areas and ask them specifically (communication, discipline, compliance with parental requests, problem-solving, using charts, etc.). Be very supportive of changes and look for opportunities to empower family members. If they report increased problems, empathize with their frustrations, then get more information which will allow you to remind them of specific scenarios in the PW programme that would be most relevant to solving the current problems.

3. Discuss the parents' most pressing current concern regarding the children's behaviour. If the offender is not a concern, focus on other children's behaviour as skills the parent uses with these problems can be applied later to the offender. The reason for focusing on the most current concerns is to engage the parents as soon as possible. When several behaviour problems of the children are mentioned, focus on those that are most frequent and susceptible to improvement following the use of good parenting skills. For example, if the parent mentions sibling arguments, occasional stealing from stores, substance abuse, and getting to school late in the mornings, focus on the sibling arguments and getting to school late. It is important that parents experience initial success when they try new parenting skills, so problems that are likely to be more responsive to better discipline, communication, contracting, etc., should be chosen.

4. Look for opportunities to relabel or reframe negative motives that parents and children attribute to each other. [*See Appendix B for common relabels you can use for different kinds of parental and child behaviour.*]

5. Before the end of the first session, choose a parenting skill most relevant to solving one or more of the problems you discovered in step 3. Assign as homework the workbook exercises for that skill. Mention that you will go over the homework with them on the next session. It is better if they do the homework on their own rather than have you go through it with them (which may be necessary if they are having trouble or are unmotivated to do the homework). In this way they can take more credit for the improvement and be empowered to solve problems on their own after you stop working with them.

6. As part of normal procedures, the parents will need to use the PW programme a second time, preferably with another family member who has not used the programme. During the first and subsequent sessions, be prepared to recommend this second use. The rationale for a second use is that all families are recommended to do this as the information in the programme cannot be absorbed totally after only one use. Generally, allow 2–4 weeks to elapse before the PW programme is repeated.

Session 2

1. Build rapport for several minutes before beginning to go through the content.
2. Review homework. Use your judgement about how firmly to deal with any failure to do the homework. Inquire about application of the skills practised in homework to family life, being very supportive of any attempts to implement these skills.
3. Review family goals identified in the first session. The purpose of this review is to remind the family they have goals that can be met with the use of the skills in the programme (and you will often need to show them the link between their goals and specific skills). At any point in the four sessions you meet with resistance to working on developing skills, discuss the link between their goals and the skills. It is important that the family not feel you are trying to get them to do something which is not in their acknowledged interests.

4. Inquire about child behaviour problems since the last session. [Be careful that while you empathize you do not get sidetracked for too long. Many of these single parents are hungry for social contact, as they are often isolated and depressed. The social support you provide, while important, will have only short-term benefits. Try to steer the single parent to ongoing sources of social support, such as developing friendships with other single parents, contacting relatives, becoming active in a church or community organization, or seeking counselling (and/or medication) for depression.] Prompt parents to think about the parenting skills from PW that may help resolve the recent behaviour problems. You may need to take a longer view and suggest improving communication rather than only implementing assertive discipline or contracting. Ultimately, the relationship between parent and child can be improved and deepened through the positive attention that accompanies good communication skills.

5. Continue to look for opportunities to recall specific scenarios from the programme that are relevant to current parental concerns. You can help them generalize the problem areas and skills from the programme to different problems they are experiencing with their children. [See Appendix C, Problems Not Covered in PW and Applicable Skills.] Your goal is to promote the learning of core parenting skills which are applicable to most parenting challenges they will face. You should avoid being too direct with advice-giving such that you are solving their problems for them.

6. Assign homework from the workbook that seems to be most relevant to the areas the parents are most motivated to address.

7. If parents used the programme a second time since the first session, review their reactions and what they learned from the second use.

Session 3

1. Review homework, and focus on family members' (particularly parents') implementation of the skills. Suggest new opportunities to implement the skills practised during homework. If family members are struggling with communication (active listening, "I" statements) skills or problem-solving, use the suggestions and exercises in the Therapist Manual for Communication and Problem Solving Skills to provide additional practice.

2. Repeat steps 4 and 5 from Session 2. That is, enquire about child behaviour problems since the last session. Then ask parents about which parenting skills might help. As in step 5, help the parent generalize these skills to problems not covered in PW.

3. Again, as in the earlier sessions, be alert for chances to recommend the family use PW again. They may be more motivated to consider doing this by the third or fourth session than they were in the first or second session. For convenience, you could lend them the PW video series to view at home.

4. If parents have younger children or less mature teens, and if they have not learned how to use point systems and charts, you should motivate them to begin using this skill. Review the workbook exercises with them, or give this as a homework assignment. This is a powerful tool that most parents can learn and succeed with quickly. For parents of teens and pre-teens, contracting is a skill they need to learn. Prompt parents to think about situations where contracting would be helpful, then go over the steps in contracting/problem-solving.

5. If the parents are practising and understanding the parenting skills, discuss the basic processes present in the core parenting skills. For instance, point out the sequence of listening, making "I" statements, and problem-solving, contracting, or using point systems and charts. Discuss with the more highly functioning parents how this increases mutual respect and promotes responsibility among all family members.

6. Assign homework from the workbook exercises. If you have not done so, assign the contracting exercises for review in the next (last) session.

Session 4

1. Review homework, and recommend continued practice of the skills that are most difficult for the family to use. Reassure them that the awkwardness they experience is normal and will gradually diminish the more they use the skills.

2. Repeat steps 4 and 5 from Session 2. That is, enquire about child behaviour problems since the last session. Then ask parents about which parenting skills might help. As in step 5, help the parent generalize these skills to problems not covered in PW.
3. If you have not discussed school issues, and if they are relevant, discuss the following:
    (a) Importance of increasing child's self-confidence for school work, reduce criticism
    (b) Developing good homework habits: set up a predictable routine, using a collaborative rather than authoritarian approach
    (c) Parental monitoring, limit setting (preferably by contracting)
    (d) Using point systems to motivate
    (e) Communicating with teachers:
        (1) need for parental advocacy
        (2) effective strategies for discussions with teachers
        (3) promoting continuity between home and school—notes, phone, in person
        (4) supporting teachers and encouraging their involvement with the child.
4. Repeat step 5 from Session 3, on core parenting skills and basic processes underlying them, if there is time and if the parents seem able to understand.
5. Assign homework. Focus on the skills most needed for continued improvement.

If contracting or family problem-solving has not been learned, assign this as homework.

6. Reviewing the family's accomplishments, giving their effort and use of new skills credit for positive changes. This is the essence of empowerment. Avoid taking credit yourself, but be aware of the crucial role you played.

APPENDIX B: PROBLEM BEHAVIOURS TO BE REFRAMED

Child Behaviours to be Reframed to Parents

sibling conflicts: seeking attention, kids are bored, or jealous
curfew violations: wanting to be with friends, parents are upset because they are worried
not doing homework: too difficult, child lacks confidence, low on priorities, embarrassed to ask for help, peers pressure child not to do homework
child talks back to parent: need for independence, child showing they can think on their own, practicing their debating skills, may be imitating an argumentative parent
child curses parent: does not know how to put their feelings into words, wants some space or privacy, seeks attention, imitation of others in the family who curse, immature impulse control
child avoids being at home: feels more comfortable with peers, trying to reduce family conflict
child hits parents: poor impulse control, does not know how to put feelings into words, afraid
child hangs out with peers parents don't like: wants to make own decisions, seeking approval from others

Parent Behaviours to be Reframed to Children

parent nags children to be more responsible: wants them to succeed later, may have unrealistic expectations for children's maturity or age, wants children to feel sense of pride *parent is uninvolved with children:* parent needs space, is under pressure, parent does not know how to be involved without being controlling (did not learn how from own parents), respects children's privacy

parent yells at children: parent is tired or frustrated, parent cares too much, takes their job to give guidance and teach maturity too seriously, has learned that yelling works to get things done

parent hits children: does not know other methods, believes children need spanking, parent is frustrated and does not know how to put feelings into words, learned this from his/her parents and never questioned it

marital conflict: parents unaware it is upsetting to children and not paying attention

parent is overly controlling: parent tries too hard to make sure child is safe or behaves properly, learned this from his/her parents, parent is too attached to child, cares too much, parent has hard time trusting

parent calls child names: temper control problems, hopes to shock child into behaving well, learned to do this growing up

APPENDIX C: PROBLEMS NOT COVERED IN PW PROGRAMME AND APPLICABLE SKILLS

General theme: apply previously learned skills to new problems, emphasizing listening. Apply only enough discipline to solve problem

1.   Verbal and Physical Aggression (Anger Control Problems)

- *Child threatens parent with force or assault:* Defuse situation (i.e. by leaving or asking child to take a time out), meet and make "I" statement, state you want to hear what the child was feeling and thinking that led to the threat, using active listening. Call family together at convenient time to problem solve about ideas to prevent such threats, make agreement to try a particular method and re-evaluate later. Specify what kinds of verbal aggression are permitted and which are not. When problem-solving, first define the problem specifically, then brainstorm possible solutions, evaluating the suggestions, reaching consensus, then writing down agreement.
- Problem-Solving
  Regulates family communication
  Involves all family members—teens buy into process when they have a say
  Control of conflict, accountability established
  Expectations become specified, consequences are established
  A process of mutual respect is established
  Problem-Solving Steps
  1. Problem definition—specificity, actively listen, solicit each perspective
  2. Brainstorming—everyone adds at least one possible solution, suspend evaluation
  3. Evaluation—pros and cons for each; which will "fly"
  4. Consensus—combination of solutions all can live with
  5. Establish consequences and write down
  6. Identify a regular family meeting time to review the agreement
- *child hits parent:* Parent makes "I" statement and using assertive discipline states a consequence immediately. Later, parent states expectation that force is not permissible, and encourages child to participate in discussion of future consequences for hitting. Discuss alternative forms of expressing anger and relieving stress.

2.   Theft

- *Parent discovers child has stolen property (shoplifting) in community:* Parent asks child why the theft occurred, using active listening to determine underlying motivations, then states own feelings about stealing with "I" statement. Family problem-solving discussion should follow, with focus on consequences the family thinks will be most effective, as well as alternative methods for child getting needs met. Restitution should be emphasized.

- *Parent discovers child has stolen property from someone in the family:* If first time, parent uses "I" statement and then assertive discipline (stating consequence for the current theft and consequences for future thefts). If recurring problem, parent calls family meeting and states expectations regarding privacy and security of each family members' belongings. Parent solicits others' thoughts on this issue. Proceed to problem-solving, first defining the problem specifically, then brainstorming possible solutions, evaluating the suggestions, reaching consensus, then writing down agreement.

3.   Substance Abuse

- *Child returns home and is drunk:* Using an "I" statement, parent tells child of his/her concern and wish to discuss the situation when the child is sober. If a first offence, discuss the circumstances leading to the inebriation and other decisions the child could have made. Active listening enables parent to learn of peer pressure, stress, curiosity, etc., as reasons for getting drunk. Discuss parental expectations about substance use. Explore alternatives to getting into unsafe situations (i.e. driving under the influence) and reach agreement (contract, if necessary). If a repetitive problem, use problem-solving strategy leading to a formal agreement (contract) spelling out consequences for success and failure. Be very specific.

4.   Curfew Violations

- *Child returns home an hour later than permitted:* Parent begins by using "I" statement, then re-flects response by child, usually a reason for the delay. Rephrase "I" statement if necessary. Give child choice of discussing consequence for curfew violation now or at a specific time within the next day. Ask child to recollect the consequence. If consequences for curfew violation had not been specified in advance, problem-solve around the issue of current and future consequences. Involve other family members when appropriate in the problem definition, brainstorming, and evaluation of solution phases.

5.   Self-harm

- *Child lacerates part of body, or hits head on hard object:* Parent asks child to desist if caught in the act, or restrains child if necessary. Parent states worry with "I" statement, invites child to talk about feelings, reflecting whatever child says with active listening, especially underlying feelings. Involve other family members if appropriate in subsequent family discussion. Use problem-solving format, stressing supervision, safety and alternate methods of child expressing feelings. Develop method for increasing support for appropriate child behaviour to increase child's feelings of self-efficacy. Consider point systems or contracts for child earning increased freedom from close supervision.

6.   Poor hygiene

- *Child goes for days without bathing or brushing teeth:* Parent tells child he/she would like to sit down and discuss ways to encourage child to show better hygiene, and gives child choice of times to do this. Parent begins with "I" statements, then listens actively to child's point of view. Parent presents his/her reasons for improved hygiene. Problem-solve, inviting child to make suggestions about improvements and decide issue of reminders from parent. Be specific. Consider using contingency management, point systems for younger children. Let child monitor progress, with regular supportive feedback from parent when improvement occurs.

Contingency Management
—Systematizes objectives and feedback
—Specifies goals and consequences
—Breaks down goals into component parts
—Tracks performance

—Increases parental monitoring
—Reduces conflict

Principles of Contingency Management
—Goals consistent with abilities
—Frequency or duration
—Reward menu varied
—Child input
—Establish trade-in times
—Regular review at family meetings.

REFERENCES

Alexander, J. F., Barton, C., Schiavo, R. S. & Parsons, B. V. (1976) Systems behavioral intervention with families of delinquents: Therapist characteristics, family behavior, and outcome. *Journal of Consulting and Clinical Psychology, 44*, 656–664.

Alexander, J. F. & Parsons, B. V. (1973) Short-term behavioral intervention with delinquent families: Impact on family process and recidivism. *Journal of Abnormal Psychology, 81*, 218–225.

Alexander, J. F. & Parsons, B. V. (1982) *Functional Family Therapy.* Monterey, CA: Brooks/Cole.

Alexander, J. F., Pugh, C., Parsons, B. & Sexton, T. (2000) Book three: Functional Family Therapy. In D. S. Elliott (Ed.) *Blueprints for Violence Prevention.* Golden, CO: Venture Publishing.

Bickman, L. & Noser, K. (1999) Meeting the challenges in the delivery of child and adolescent mental health services in the next millennium: The continuous quality improvement approach. *Applied and Preventive Psychology, 8*, 247–256.

Brown, B. B., Mounts, N., Lamborn, S. D. & Steinberg, L. (1993) *Preventing Childhood Disorders, Substance Abuse, and Delinquency* (pp. 215–240). Thousand Oaks, CA: Sage Publications.

Carr, A. (Ed.) (2000) *What Works for Children and Adolescents: A Critical Review of Psychological Interventions with Children, Adolescents, and Their Families.* London: Routledge.

Chamberlain, P. & Reid, J. B. (1987) Parent observation and report of child symptoms. *Behavioral Assessment, 9*, 97–109.

Chambless, D. L. (1999) Empirically validated treatments—what now? *Applied and Preventive Psychology, 8*, 281–284.

Eyberg, S. M. & Robinson, E. A. (1983) Conduct problem behavior: Standardization of a behavioral rating scale with adolescents. *Journal of Clinical Child Psychology, 12*, 347–354.

Eyberg, S. M. & Ross, A. W. (1978) Assessment of child behavior problems: The validation of a new inventory. *Journal of Clinical Psychology, 16*, 113–116.

Farrington, D. P. (1995) The twelfth Jack Tizard memorial lecture: The development of offending and antisocial behaviour from childhood: Key findings from the Cambridge study in delinquent development. *Journal of Child Psychology and Psychiatry and Allied Disciplines, 360*, 929–964.

Fletcher, J. D. (1990) *Effectiveness and Cost of Interactive Videodisc Instruction in Defense Training and Education* (Report No. P-2372. Institute for Defense Analysis.

Gendreau, P., Goggin, C., Cullen, F. T. & Paparozzi, M. (2002) The common sense revolution and correctional policy. In J. McGuire (Ed.), *Offender Rehabilitation and Treatment: Effective Programmes and Policies to Reduce Re-offending* (pp. 359–386). Chichester: John Wiley & Sons.

Glynn, T. J. & Haenlein, M. (1988) Family theory and research on adolescent drug use: A review. *Journal of Chemical Dependency and Treatment, 1* (2), 39–56.

Gordon, D. A. (1995) Functional Family Therapy. In R. R. Ross, D. Antonowicz & G. Dhaliwal (Eds.) *Going Straight: Effective Delinquency Prevention and Offender Rehabilitation* (pp. 163–178). Ottawa, Ontario: Air Training and Publications.

Gordon, D. A. (2000) Parent training via CD-ROM: Using technology to disseminate effective prevention practices. *Journal of Primary Prevention, 21* (2), 227–251.

Gordon, D. A. (2001) *Factors predictive of successful implementation of a parent training program.* Unpublished manuscript, Ohio University.

Gordon, D. A. & Arbuthnot, J. (1987) Individual, group, and family interventions. In H. C. Quay (Ed.), *Handbook of Juvenile Delinquency* (pp. 290–324). New York, NY: John Wiley & Sons.

Gordon, D. A. & Stanar, C. R. (in press) Lessons learned from the dissemination of Parenting Wisely, a parent training CD-ROM. *Cognitive Behavior and Practice.*

Gordon, D. A. & Kacir, C. (1998) Interactive videodisc training for court mandated parents. Unpublished manuscript, Ohio University.

Gordon, D. A., Jurkovic, G. & Arbuthnot, J. (1998) Treatment of the juvenile offender. In R. Wettstein (Ed.) *Treatment of Offenders with Mental Disorders* (pp. 365–428). New York, NY: Guilford Press.

Gordon, D. A., Arbuthnot, J., Gustafson, K. & McGreen, P. (1988) Home-based behavioral-systems family therapy with disadvantaged delinquents. *American Journal of Family Therapy, 16,* 243–255.

Gordon, D. A., Graves, K. & Arbuthnot, J. (1995) The effect of functional family therapy for delinquents on adult criminal behaviour. *Criminal Justice and Behavior, 22,* 60–73.

Kacir, C. & Gordon , D. A. (1999) Parenting Adolescents Wisely: The effectiveness of an interactive videodisk parent training programme in appalachia. *Child and Family Behavior Therapy, 21* (4), 1–22.

Kumpfer, K. L. & DeMarsh, J. (1986) Family environmental and genetic influences on children's future chemical dependency. *Journal of Children in a Contemporary Society, 18* (1–2), 49–91.

Lagges, A. & Gordon, D. A. (1999) Use of an interactive laserdisc parent training program with teenage parents. *Child and Family Behaviour Therapy, 21,* 19–37.

Lorion, R. P., Tolan, P. H. & Wahler, R. G. (1987) Prevention. In H. C. Quay (Ed.) *Handbook of Juvenile Delinquency* (pp. 383–416). New York, NY: Wiley.

Malkus, B. M. (1994) Family dynamic and structural correlates of adolescent substance abuse: A comparison of families of non-substance abusers and substance abusers. *Journal of Child and Adolescent Substance Abuse, 3* (4), 39–52.

McCord, W. M. (1982) *The Psychopath and Milieu Therapy.* New York, NY: Academic Press.

McKay, J. R., Murphy, R. T., Rivinus, T. R. & Maisto, S. A. (1991) Family dysfunction and alcohol and drug use in adolescent psychiatric inpatients. *Journal of the American Academy of Child and Adolescent Psychiatry, 30* (6), 967–972.

McNeil, B. J. & Nelson, K. R. (1991) Meta-analysis of interactive video instruction: A 10 year review of achievement effects. *Journal of Computer-Based Instruction, 18* (1), 1–6.

Mendel, R. A. (2000) *Less Hype, More Help: Reducing Juvenile Crime, What Works—and What Doesn't.* Washington, DC: American Youth Policy Forum.

Miller, I. W., Epstein, N. B., Bishop, D. S. & Keitner, G. I. (1985) The McMaster Family Assessment Device: Reliability and validity. *Journal of Marital and Family Therapy, 11,* 345–356.

Niemiec, R. & Walberg, H. J. (1987) Comparative effects of computer-assisted instruction: A synthesis of reviews. *Journal of Educational Computing Research, 3* (1), 19–37.

Patterson, G. R. (1982) *Coercive Family Process.* Eugene, OR: Castalia.

Patterson, G. R., Dishion, T. J. & Bank, L. (1984) Family interaction: A process model of deviancy training. *Aggressive Behavior, 10,* 253–267.

Rolland-Stanar, C., Gordon, D. A. & Carlston, D. (2001) *A school-based parent training intervention to reduce family violence.* Unpublished manuscript, Ohio University.

Segal, D., Chen, P. Y., Gordon, D. A., Kacir, C. & Gylys, J. (in press) Development and evaluation of a parenting intervention program: Integration of scientific and practical approaches. *International Journal of Human–Computer Interaction.*

Serketich, W. J. & Dumas, J. E. (1996) The effectiveness of behavioral parent training to modify antisocial behaviour in children: A meta-analysis. *Behaviour Therapy, 27,* 171–186.

Snyder, J. & Patterson, G. R. (1987) Family interaction and delinquent behaviour. In H. C. Quay (Ed.) *Handbook of Juvenile Delinquency.* New York, NY: Wiley.

Spoth, R. & Redmond, C. (1995) Parent motivation to enroll in parenting skills programs: A model of family context and health belief predictors. *Journal of Family Psychology, 9,* 294–310.

St. Pierre, T. L. & Kaltreider, D. L. (1997) Strategies for involving parents of high-risk youth in drug prevention: A three-year longitudinal study in Boys and Girls Clubs. *Journal of Community Psychology, 25,* 473–485.

Tolan, P. H., Cromwell, R. E. & Basswell, M. (1986) The application of family therapy to juvenile delinquency: A critical review of the literature. *Family Process, 15,* 619–650.

Webster-Stratton, C., Hollinsworth, T. & Kolpacoff, M. (1989) The long-term effectiveness and clinical significance of three cost-effective training programs for families with conduct-problem children. *Journal of Consulting and Clinical Psychology, 57,* 550–553.

Webster-Stratton, C., Kolpacoff, M. & Hollinsworth, T. (1988) Self-administered videotape therapy for families with conduct-problem children: Comparison with two cost-effective treatments and a control group. *Journal of Consulting and Clinical Psychology, 56,* 558–566.

Weiss, B., Catron, T., Harris, V. & Phung, T. (1999) The effectiveness of traditional child psychotherapy. *Journal of Consulting and Clinical Psychology, 67,* 82–85.

Woodruff, C., Gordon, D. A. & Lobo, T. R. (2000) *Reaching high risk families through home-based parent training: A comparison of interactive CD-ROM and self-help parenting programs.* Unpublished manuscript, Ohio University.

Chapter 8

ALCOHOL, AGGRESSION AND VIOLENCE

Mary McMurran

School of Psychology, Cardiff University, Cardiff, UK

In Western societies, there is ample evidence from both criminal statistics and scientific research of a strong relationship between alcohol intoxication and aggressive and violent behaviour (Graham et al., 1998; Murdoch, Pihl & Ross, 1990). It is also true, however, that a great deal of drinking is done by a large number of people without aggression or violence resulting. Any intoxicated individual will show changes in behaviour by comparison with his or her sober state, such as becoming maudlin, giggly, or indiscreet, but by no means all drunks are violent. Even those who can be aggressive or violent under the influence of alcohol are not so on every drinking occasion. What, then, causes some people on some occasions to resort to alcohol-related aggression or violence? To come to a better understanding of alcohol-related violence, the aim in this chapter is to take a look at those risk factors implicated in the development of an increased likelihood of intoxicated violence, including developmental risk factors, the effects of alcohol itself, and the social settings in which aggression and violence occur. With this information available, attention will then be turned to what can be done to reduce the likelihood of alcohol-related violence.

DEVELOPMENTAL RISK FACTORS

Across the lifespan, what are the risk factors for aggression and violence, and where does drinking fit in? Farrington (1995), based on the analysis of data from his longitudinal study of males from the age of 8 years through to 32 years, concluded that the predictors of convictions for violence are highly similar to those which predict delinquency in general, namely antisocial childhood behaviour, hyperactivity–impulsivity–attention deficit, low intelligence and poor school attainment, family criminality, family poverty, and poor parental child-rearing practices. "The causes of aggression and violence", he suggests, are "essentially the same as the causes of persistent and extreme antisocial, delinquent, and criminal behaviour" and

Offender Rehabilitation and Treatment: Effective Programmes and Policies to Reduce Re-offending. Edited by James McGuire.
© John Wiley & Sons, Ltd.

aggression is just one element of a general antisocial tendency (Farrington, 1995, p. 17).

Substance use also shares this list of risk factors (Hawkins, Catalano & Miller, 1992) and, indeed, is one of those terms often used to define antisocial behaviour, especially when illicit or over-indulged. Longitudinal studies have shown that delinquency appears first, followed by drinking, indicating that drinking does not cause delinquency at least in the early stages of life (Elliott, Huizinga & Ageton, 1985). Indeed, delinquency and drinking, along with a number of other disapproved behaviours, are not uncommon in young people and these so-called problem behaviours emerge between the ages of 13 and 17 years (Graham & Bowling, 1995; Jessor & Jessor, 1977). While problem behaviours are essentially a part of growing up for many young people, there is a subgroup that shows troublesome behaviour and aggression at an early age and continues with crime and violence into adulthood (Farrington, 1996; Loeber, 1988, 1990). This same group is more likely to drink heavily, and heavy drinking at age 18 is predictive of the persistence of crime into adulthood (Farrington & Hawkins, 1991).

It is probable that reciprocal interactions over the lifespan between individual characteristics and the social environment (i.e. parents, school and peers) can serve to compound and exacerbate the likelihood of crime, heavy drinking and drug use, and alcohol-related crime (McMurran, 1996). It is instructive to investigate risk factors for aggression, violence and drinking as they unfold across the life-span.

Temperament and Traits

Research into the precursors of both serious antisocial behaviour and substance abuse in adulthood can be traced as far back as difficult temperament in early childhood, a "difficult temperament" being characterized by irregularities in eating and sleeping, inflexibility to changes in the environment, and frequent negative moods (Loeber, Stouthamer-Loeber & Green, 1991). What is labelled a "difficult temperament" in a very young child is, as the child grows older, likely to be evident through different behaviours and attract a different label. Aggression is evident in some children from a very early age and is remarkably stable over time. Although only about one-third of aggressive children end up becoming serious offenders, early aggression is nonetheless a strong predictor of later violence and other serious offending (Tolan & Gorman-Smith, 1998). That is, aggression is an early risk factor that needs an accumulation of other problems to end in serious adult criminality; aggression in itself is no guarantee of persistent or escalating problems (Hämäläinen and Pulkkinen, 1996). One robust finding is the relationship of early hyperactivity with later aggressive offending and later substance misuse (e.g. Klinteberg et al., 1993). The childhood psychiatric disorder of attention deficit/hyperactivity disorder (ADHD) places children at greater risk of both later aggressive offending and substance misuse, and the prediction of these later problems is increased where ADHD develops into conduct disorder (Maughan, 1993; Wilens & Biederman, 1993).

Aggression and hyperactivity are behaviours or constellations of behaviours that may be behavioural indicators of an underlying trait of impulsivity. Impulsivity has been construed as a disinhibited personal style that, if occurring in conjunction with certain risk factors, can lead to various problem behaviours. Impulsivity is associated with a range of personality disorders, particularly antisocial and border-line (Siever & Davis, 1991), and also substance use disorders (O'Boyle & Barratt, 1993). Indeed, these personality disorders and substance misuse commonly co-occur (Verheul, van den Brink & Hartgers, 1995), which hints at a possible common explanatory factor. Impulsivity may have a biological basis, and one prime suspect is serotonin, a neurotransmitter that inhibits behaviour. Low serotonergic function-ing is associated with a variety of impulse control problems, including aggression, violence and alcoholism (Moffitt et al., 1998).

Impulsivity may have two separate components: a behavioural component, based upon an imbalance of behavioural inhibition and activating systems; and a cognitive component, based upon deficits in executive cognitive functioning—i.e. the higher order cerebral activities such as attention, abstracting relevant informa-tion, reasoning, problem-solving, planning, and self-regulation (White et al., 1994). Serotonin deficits are associated with both behavioural disinhibition and impaired cognitive functioning (Pihl & Lemarquand, 1998). Some cognitive deficits may be a result of failure to learn thinking skills early in life, learning being impeded by behaviour control problems (McMurran, Blair & Egan, in press). Impaired exec-utive cognitive functioning is associated with aggressiveness, impulsive violent crime and with antisocial personality disorder (Giancola et al., 1996; Golden et al., 1996).

Male children who are hyperactive and aggressive, particularly where these problems flourish into conduct disorders in later childhood, are strong candidates for later serious violence, alcohol problems and personality disorder diagnoses. A longitudinal study of males from the ages of 13 to 26 showed that hyperactive boys (i.e. poor concentration and motor restlessness), by comparison with non-hyperactive boys, were eight times more likely to commit a violent offence and three times more likely to develop alcohol problems (Klinteberg et al., 1993). In the same study, it was observed that the co-occurrence of hyperactivity, alcohol prob-lems and violence in the same people occurred ten times more often than expected by chance. This suggests not only that these problems have shared roots, but also that alcohol use may exacerbate violence if a vulnerable person drinks. Later in this chapter, we will look at how alcohol might exert this effect.

Family Management

When hyperactivity develops into conduct problems in later childhood, this sub-stantially increases the likelihood of persistent problem behaviours (Maughan, 1993; Wilens & Biederman, 1993). Conduct problems are likely to develop through an interaction between the child and his or her carers. Reviews of risk factors for later delinquency and substance use point out that family management practices which increase risk are characterized by unclear expectations for behaviour, lax supervision, little in the way of rewards for positive behaviour, harsh punish-ment for unwanted behaviour, and inconsistency in the application of rewards and punishments (Farrington & Hawkins, 1991; Hawkins, Catalano & Miller, 1992).

Laboratory evidence suggests that hyperactive children are stressful for parents to deal with and some parents, notably those with a history of alcohol problems in the family, may drink to help them to cope (Pelham & Lang, 1993). Under the influence of alcohol, those family management practices predictive of delinquency and substance use emerge (Pelham & Lang, 1993), and in these circumstances the child is less likely to learn to behave appropriately.

Parents who drink heavily also present a model that excessive drinking is acceptable, and pro-substance use norms have been shown to predict both delinquency and substance use in a longitudinal study of aggressive boys (O'Donnell, Hawkins & Abbott, 1995). Furthermore, if the parents are aggressive or violent when intoxicated, the child may witness or experience aggression, increasing the likelihood that the child will become aggressive in adulthood (Milner & Dopke, 1997).

School Bonding and Academic Achievement

The child who misbehaves in school and is unable to concentrate on schoolwork is neither the most successful nor the most popular pupil. Being scolded by the teacher, being unpopular with pro-social peers, and failing to achieve academic success makes school an unpleasant experience which some children may escape through truancy. Low commitment to school has been shown to be strongly related to persistence in crime into early adulthood (Farrington & Hawkins, 1991; Le Blanc, 1994). Poor performance at school is predictive of poor job instability in adulthood, and this is a major risk factor for criminality in later life (Le Blanc, 1994).

Peer Associations

School failure is also posited to lead to association with substance using and delinquent peers (Sher & Trull, 1994), with young people selecting peer groups who are similar to themselves and being socialized into the norms of their peer group (Kandel, 1985). Truants gravitate towards other truants, and delinquency and substance use are the normative pastimes. In their longitudinal study of adolescents, Elliott, Huizinga and Ageton (1985) found that bonding with delinquent peers was strongly associated with both delinquency and drug use, in that order. In the early stages at least, drinking and drug use do not cause crime, but delinquency, drinking and drug use emerge as part of a cluster of commonly co-occurring problem behaviours.

Hostile Attributional Biases

In life so far, the difficult child may have experienced repeated chastisement from parents and teachers, as well as unpopularity with pro-social peers. The experience of harshness and unpopularity may lead to the acquisition of hostile attributional biases; that is, children see the world as antagonistic and unfriendly towards them.

Hostile attributional biases have been shown to correlate with anger and aggression in children and adolescents (Dodge et al., 1990; Slaby & Guerra, 1988).

Intoxication

Once drinking begins, its effects become evident. In a longitudinal study of New Zealand children from birth through to adolescence, Fergusson, Lynskey and Horwood (1996) found that males and females who misused alcohol were almost six times more likely to commit violent offences than those who did not misuse alcohol, and they were 12–13 times more likely to commit property offences. There appeared to be an overlap of risk factors associated with alcohol misuse and offending, in that these problems were more likely in those who were socially disadvantaged and exposed to high levels of family adversity. However, when they statistically adjusted for these confounding risk factors, a significant relationship between alcohol misuse and violent offending remained. Youngsters who misused alcohol were still three times more likely to commit violent offences, and in the adjusted analysis there was no significant relationship between alcohol misuse and property offending. The suggestion is that alcohol misuse and violent offending arise via a similar route—the antecedent risk factors are highly similar—but that there is also a direct cause and effect between alcohol misuse and violent offending. Alcohol consumption increases aggression.

In laboratory studies, alcohol does seem to have the general effect of making people aggressive. A typical procedure is to set up a situation where two people in different rooms are pitted against each other in a computerized reaction time competition—for instance, learning to press one of six cards when a particular light appears. The winner is instructed to administer an electric shock to the loser. Various aspects of the situation can be manipulated, for example alcohol consumption, the magnitude of the shock, and the supposed effect on the experimental subject's competitor, who is, of course, bogus. Overall, individuals who receive alcohol are more aggressive in laboratory tests compared to those who do not receive alcohol or those who are given a placebo (i.e. think they are drinking alcohol but are not) and the more people drink the more aggressively they respond (Chermack & Giancola, 1997). However, aggression in these laboratory tests is greater for those who are of an aggressive disposition in the first place (Chermack & Giancola, 1997).

Pihl and Hoaken (1997) describe four mechanisms by which drugs can have a physiological effect on an individual to increase the likelihood of violence: (1) altering the anxiety-threat system; (2) altering the psychomotor system; (3) altering the pain system; and (4) altering the cognitive control system. Anxiety protects against punishment by inhibiting behaviour in the presence of novel or threatening stimuli. Alcohol is an anxiolytic drug and by reducing anxiety it increases the likelihood of aggressive behaviour (Pihl & Peterson, 1993). Alcohol stimulates psychomotor activity, at least at lower doses, and this may be associated with aggression (Pihl & Hoaken, 1997). At high doses, alcohol is an analgesic. "Feeling no pain" is a common euphemism for drunkenness and one can imagine how violence seems less of a problem for a drunk. Alcohol also takes its effect by disrupting executive cognitive functioning. Intoxicated individuals tend to what has been called 'alcohol myopia'

(Josephs & Steele, 1990), in that they attend primarily to salient and proximal situational factors. Put another way, they attend to the immediate events around them, and are more affected by instigatory situational cues (e.g. an insult), less affected by distal inhibitory cues (e.g. the consequences of punching the insulting person), and less able to figure out alternatives to aggression. As we have seen, aggressiveness may be linked to impulsivity, and this is linked with cognitive deficits in attention, abstracting relevant information, reasoning, problem-solving, planning, and self-regulation. Alcohol further impairs cognitive functioning, increasing the risk of aggression in those who are anyway at risk.

Alcohol-related Outcome Expectancies

As they get older, young people venture into social settings to do their drinking, and violence is clearly more likely to happen where people are grouped together, particularly if others are also drunk and of an aggressive disposition. Impulsive, aggressive people are, arguably, more gregarious and so more likely to go out drinking. It has been shown, for example, that violent young offenders expect alcohol to help them to join in and have fun (McMurran, 1997). Thus, people who are high risk for aggression and violence are likely to be found together, drinking heavily.

Violence most commonly occurs in and around city centre licensed premises and entertainment venues, especially where young men gather and drink heavily on weekend nights (Hope, 1985; Lang et al., 1995; Ramsay, 1982). Indeed most untoward events after drinking occur in entertainment venues where young men gather and drink heavily (Lang et al., 1995). It is likely that the probability of aggression would be elevated in such venues, regardless of the occurrence of drinking (Lang & Sibrel, 1989), and, while this may be true, drinking is usually part of the picture and the co-occurrence of drinking and violence is an important consideration.

The effects of drinking are not only pharmacological; they are partly learned, through instruction, observation and experience. The effects one expects to experience from drinking are not only cognitive representations of past experience, but they also predict future behaviour (Goldman, 1994; Goldman, Brown & Christiansen, 1987). Some of these alcohol-related outcome expectancies can be criminogenic. The frequent co-occurrence of drinking and violence, observed and experienced, is likely to lead to the outcome expectancy that drinking alcohol will lead to aggression and violence, which then sets the scene for alcohol-related violence to occur. While the pharmacological effects of alcohol are probably more potent than expectancies, at high doses of alcohol consumption those who think alcohol makes them aggressive are more extremely aggressive (Chermack & Taylor, 1995).

Interactions

Not only is the assailant likely to be intoxicated, but so is the victim of violence (Lindqvist, 1991). This could be accounted for by the fact that violence is common in social drinking venues, where there is a high probability that the assailant and the victim are both intoxicated. It is also probable, however, that sober people are better able to ignore threats or prevent escalation of conflict, whereas drunks rise (or sink) to the challenge. As Graham et al. (1998) point out, "if alcohol increases the likelihood of aggression in one drinker, then theoretically, the effect should be multiplicative in a *group* of drinkers" (p. 669).

Lifestyle

Most people grow out of substance use and delinquency as they acquire respon-sibilities relating to work, accommodation, partners and children, but for some people heavy drinking and a criminal record may present obstacles to a conven-tional lifestyle, and crime and substance use become a way of life (Walters, 1998). Lifestyles of crime and substance use lead people into social contexts that breed further crime, make relationships difficult to sustain, and make job prospects dimin-ish, until eventually the person seems trapped in an antisocial lifestyle. Offenders rationalize their behaviour, developing and strengthening beliefs that crime is a reasonable way to live or that they are driven to crime by necessity, and these antisocial attitudes militate against change (Walters, 1998).

Summary of Risk Factors

In this chapter the development of aggression, drinking and intoxicated violence has been presented as a developmental risk factor approach, which is summarized in Figure 8.1. These risk factors include personality traits; troublesome behaviour in childhood that is allowed to flourish through poor family management; family models of drinking and aggression or violence; failure to settle at school and do

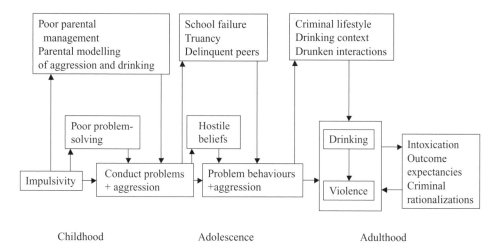

Figure 8.1 Developmental risk factors for alcohol-related violence.

well academically; association with delinquent peers, and the development of a criminal lifestyle which is rationalized by antisocial attitudes. The use of alcohol from the teenage years onwards is associated with early risk factors and predicts the continuity of crime and violence. Alcohol intoxication makes aggressive people violent in certain circumstances, and the repeated co-occurrence of drinking and violence increases the likelihood that drinking will precipitate violence in the future.

INTERVENTIONS

A developmental risk factor approach to intoxicated violence points towards a variety of different interventions depending upon the stage in the developmental pathway that is targeted and the factors associated with the problem. Prevention, harm minimization and individual treatment are all relevant at different times.

Prevention

It is important to prevent alcohol-related violence by addressing the broad context in which drinking occurs (Edwards and Members of the Alcohol and Public Policy Project, 1994; McMurran, 1994). National and local legislation controls the availability of alcohol, determining who may drink alcohol, where and when. Public safety is addressed through local licensing and bye-laws, for example, banning the sale of alcohol at sports grounds and prohibiting drinking in certain public places. Policing practices also contribute, for example, a weekend night-time police presence in city centres aims to reduce and limit drunken violence. Prevention efforts are also the concern of the licensed trade, through altering seating, noise levels and decor in pubs and clubs, using toughened glass, training bar staff to handle awkward customers, and by staggering closing times so that not all happy revellers are decanted onto the street at precisely the same time. In the UK, in association with relaxation of the licensing laws, the Government intends to take into account in granting licences crime prevention measures put in place by licensees, as well as increasing police powers to close disorderly houses (Home Office, 2001). While these changes to the drinking context are important in tackling alcohol-related violence, the aim within this chapter is to focus upon individuals who engage in alcohol-related violence.

Those risk factors relating to family and school indicate areas to target in programmes aimed at preventing the development of delinquency in general. Given that the early precursors of drinking and drug use, delinquency and violent crime are highly similar, it is not unreasonable to suppose that effective early programmes will, in the long run, reduce alcohol-related violence, even though not they are not specifically targeted at this. Supporting parents and helping them to manage their children effectively, family therapies, pre-school enrichment programmes and improving school affiliation are all important (Farrington, 1995; Kazdin, 1997; Mulvey, Arthur & Repucci, 1993). Prevention programmes are described in detail by Farrington and Welsh in chapter 5 of this book.

Harm Reduction

Most adolescents become involved in a range of so-called problem behaviours as part of growing up. Acts of delinquency are not uncommon among adolescents, and, unlike early-onset aggressive problems which are often persistent into adult-hood, these late-onset problem behaviours tend to be "adolescent-limited" (Moffitt, 1993). In similar vein, youngsters usually drink because it is the done thing among that age group, and a fair number will drink to excess during the adolescent years. Most people grow out of these problem behaviours, becoming less delinquent and drinking less. Change is attributable to factors associated with growing up: get-ting a job, forming intimate relationships, taking on domestic responsibilities, and socializing in more sober and sedate venues. Some people are at risk, however, of getting into trouble during the adolescent years, and it is important to help them to minimize harm so that settling down is not impeded by the acquisition of a criminal record.

Treatment

Interventions specifically addressing alcohol-related violence are underdeveloped. In their review of intoxicated aggression, Graham et al. (1998) conclude that "there is an immediate and long-term need for research on interventions that are success-ful in reducing the violent behaviour of particular individuals. Research is espe-cially needed on interventions that not only employ standard treatment techniques (e.g., anger management), but also use knowledge of the effects of alcohol and the process of aggression in treating violent individuals" (p. 670). In the absence of identified effective comprehensive interventions for intoxicated aggression, it is prudent to integrate what we know about violence and alcohol problems to pro-vide a working model from which an intervention to reduce intoxicated violence may be deduced.

For those working with offenders, criminal behaviour is the main target for change, and related issues such as alcohol use are, in criminological terms, rele-vant only insofar as they affect the behaviour of interest. Thus, we might justifiably place aggression and violence at the centre of our model for understanding in-toxicated violence. If we accept that drunken aggression and violence is typically emotionally driven, rather than instrumental, then Novaco's (1994) approach to anger management is relevant. Novaco (1994) conceptualizes anger as an emo-tional state that is a causal determinant of aggression. Anger is precipitated by an external event, which is appraised by the individual as threatening, leading to phys-iological arousal which is labelled anger, leading then to aggression and violence as the learned method of coping. A simplified version of this model is presented in the central part of Figure 8.2. We can add to this a number of factors that potentiate the likelihood of aggression, identified in the literature review given earlier. These are related to both criminality and drinking and include personality factors such as cognitive and behavioural impulsivity, alcohol-related risk factors such as intox-ication and criminogenic outcome expectancies, frequenting places that increase the likelihood of meeting with provocation, and learned aggression and violence

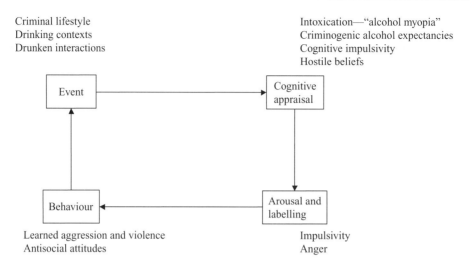

Criminal lifestyle
Drinking contexts
Drunken interactions

Intoxication—"alcohol myopia"
Criminogenic alcohol expectancies
Cognitive impulsivity
Hostile beliefs

Learned aggression and violence
Antisocial attitudes

Impulsivity
Anger

Figure 8.2   An augmented model of angry aggression.

as means of addressing interpersonal problems, bolstered by antisocial attitudes. These risk factors are presented in Figure 8.2.

This description of the process of angry aggression and violence, potentiated by personality characteristics, intoxication and other alcohol-related issues, contexts and learned interpersonal styles points to the components of a comprehensive intervention that might reasonably be expected to reduce the likelihood of intoxicated violence. These components are presented in Figure 8.3. Underpinning the intervention are two core components: anger management and problem-solving skills training. The latter, as will be explained more fully below, is intended to address

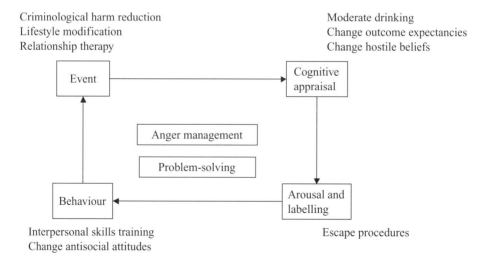

Criminological harm reduction
Lifestyle modification
Relationship therapy

Moderate drinking
Change outcome expectancies
Change hostile beliefs

Interpersonal skills training
Change antisocial attitudes

Escape procedures

Figure 8.3   Comprehensive therapy for alcohol-related aggression.

impulsivity in both cognitive and behavioural manifestations. Other components address crime, alcohol consumption, cognitions (beliefs, expectancies, attitudes), relationships, interpersonal skills and lifestyle.

Anger Management

A meta-analyis of the effectiveness of treatment for anger problems using methodologically sound treatment evaluation studies published between 1974 and 1994 found only 18 studies worthy of inclusion (Edmondson & Conger, 1996). However, effect sizes for all treatment types were medium to large, with relaxation, social skills training, cognitive-relaxation, and cognitive treatment all showing positive and sustained effects.

Novaco's (1975) anger management intervention incorporates all the effective components identified in the meta-analysis as efficacious, such as recognizing triggers for anger, arousal reduction techniques, cognitive restructuring aimed at changing the way events are appraised, teaching non-aggressive coping skills, and stress inoculation for preparing to deal with difficult situations. Novaco (1997) places emphasis on stress inoculation as a key component of his approach, and a review of anger interventions with offenders that have included stress inoculation indicate successful outcomes. Stress inoculation is the application of relaxation and coping skills, in imagination, role-play, and reality, to ever more provocative situations arranged in a hierarchy. There is evidence that Novaco's approach is effective with juvenile delinquents, adult offenders, and mentally disordered offenders (Novaco, 1997; Renwick et al., 1997).

Problem-Solving Skills Training

Problem-solving approaches teach people to "stop and think", and are relevant to the treatment of both behavioural and cognitive impulsivity. One approach is that of D'Zurilla and colleagues (D'Zurilla & Goldfried, 1971; D'Zurilla & Nezu, 1982), which teaches people to orient to bad feelings and treat these as a cue for rational problem-solving. The process includes defining the problem clearly, identifying a number of different potential solutions, weighing up the advantages and disadvantages of each solution, then selecting a potentially effective action plan. The process teaches people the art of executive cognitive functioning, such as attention to relevant information, abstract reasoning, and forward planning. A pilot study with mentally disordered offenders has indicated that problem-solving training leads to improvement on the Social Problem-Solving Inventory—Revised (D'Zurilla, Nezu & Maydeu-Olivares, 2000), although changes in behaviour have yet to be proved (McMurran et al., 1999).

Criminological Harm Reduction

While change is underway, it is important to help the client to identify simple procedures for avoiding violence. An understanding of the venues, company, and interactions that the client typically finds problematic is essential to setting rules for minimizing the likelihood of violence until more fundamental changes take effect. These rules, which should be elicited from the client, may include avoiding certain places and people. Avoidance may be complete, for the time being, or at specified times, such as weekend nights.

In recognition of the fact that some situations cannot be avoided altogether—for example, where there is a risk of violence towards the person one lives with—escape procedures may be important to negotiate. The potentially violent person should be taught to recognize anger arousal by identifying physical changes, for example stomach churning, temperature rising and muscles tensing. These should be taken as signs to leave the situation instantly, without further deliberation. Once away from the risky situation, the first task is to calm down by whatever method is preferred—a burst of vigorous exercise, deep breathing, or even a loud curse. Thereafter, consideration may be given to what should be done next. Escape procedures may be memorized using the following cues: Feel angry? Leave. Calm down. What now? In some cases, the angry person's partner is the first to recognize anger arousal, and a pair may negotiate a code word to be issued by the non-angry person at a time of risk, signalling the angry person to leave the situation. Alternatively, the potential victim may be instructed to leave for safety.

Moderating Drinking

A number of broad-based cognitive-behavioural programmes for treating substance misuse and offending have been published (e.g. McMurran & Hollin, 1993; Wanberg & Milkman, 1998). Included within these are components directly addressing alcohol consumption, most notably motivating people to change, behavioural self-control training, and relapse prevention.

Motivating people to change their drinking is a necessary preliminary to any action-based intervention. Unless a client has made a robust decision to reduce his or her alcohol consumption, teaching the skills for change will be pointless. Motivational interviewing, described by Miller and Rollnick (1991), is an interviewing strategy whereby a client's ambivalence about change can be tipped in favour of action. The technique is non-confrontational and aims to elicit from the client arguments in favour of change. A brief motivational enhancement therapy alone has been shown to have positive outcomes comparable with more intensive broad-based therapies, and is particularly effective with clients who are high in anger (Project MATCH Research Group, 1997).

Behavioural self-control training can be described as teaching the drinker to become a personal scientist by collecting and analysing information about his or her drinking, setting goals for change, altering triggers to drinking, changing the drinking behaviour *per se*, and changing the consequences of drinking. This intervention is successful for drinkers who are not dependent on alcohol and whose aim is moderation rather than abstinence, although many participants may actually end up abstaining from alcohol (Miller et al., 1992).

Through repeated association, certain cues become associated with drinking and can themselves come to elicit the desire to drink. Cues can be simple, for example the sight of a bottle, or complex, for example being in a social situation.

Exposure to drink-related cues without permitting drinking to follow (i.e. response prevention) can attenuate this conditioned desire to drink, although there is debate about whether this operates by conditioning processes or by increasing self-efficacy. Cue exposure and response prevention have been shown to reduce alcohol consumption in problem drinkers (Rohsenow et al., 1991).

Relapse prevention aims to help people to maintain change over time by recognizing and coping with situations which present a high risk of relapse to problem drinking, for example unpleasant emotions, experiencing cravings, or social pressure (Marlatt, 1996; Marlatt & Gordon, 1985). An individual profile of high-risk situations is drawn up and coping strategies are taught. Relapse prevention is a promising intervention for reducing the intensity of relapses, particularly for those who show deficits in coping skills (Carroll, 1996).

The approaches presented above can be applied to moderating alcohol consumption or achieving abstinence. Those who wish to aim for abstinence may, as an alternative, benefit from the self-help support that is provided by Alcoholics Anonymous or professionally led versions of this, known as 12-Step Programmes. Substance abusers with impulsive, sensation-seeking and sociopathic traits have been shown to benefit from 12-Steps followed by self-help affiliation (Morgenstern, Kahler & Epstein, 1998).

Changing Cognitions

Antisocial attitudes and hostile beliefs need to be identified and challenged. When using the term "challenge" with respect to changing attitudes and beliefs, this is not an invitation to confront, contradict and criticize the client. When dealing with antisocial and hostile clients, a confrontational approach is likely to disaffect the client and confirm his or her beliefs in a hostile world. Beck and Freeman (1990) describe changing antisocial attitudes as gradually moving people from a position of unqualified self-interest to one of qualified self-interest, where the person is persuaded to take others' feelings into account because there is personal gain in so doing. Identification of core unconditional beliefs, challenging their validity, and encouraging experimentation with alternative behaviours are the basic tenets of schema-focused therapy (Young, 1990), which has been shown to have positive outcome for clients with antisocial personality disorder (Davidson & Tyrer, 1996). This therapeutic approach may be useful in attenuating hostile beliefs.

In reducing alcohol-related violence, the outcome expectancy "alcohol makes me violent" needs to be attenuated. Expectancy challenge may take a number of different forms. Socratic challenge is one method whereby the therapist aims to elicit evidence—or lack of it—for a client's beliefs (Beck et al., 1993). Examples of the way a therapist might challenge the "alcohol makes me violent" expectancy are: Are you always violent after drinking? Tell me about the times when you have taken a drink and not been violent. What is it about those occasions that distinguish them from the times you are violent?

Expectancy challenge has also been conducted with the use of placebo drinks. Darkes and Goldman (1993) provided male college students with drinks, some containing alcohol and others not, without the students knowing who had actually consumed alcohol. The group then participated in a debate, and participants were asked to identify who had consumed alcohol and who had not, with many identification errors being made. Students who participated in the expectancy challenge subsequently reduced their drinking more than students in alcohol education or assessment only. Although this type of intervention may be difficult to arrange in some quarters, and while safety issues would be a major consideration in working with people that become aggressive or violent after drinking, expectancy challenge using placebo drinks is worth further thought.

Relationship Therapy

Drunken interactions can get out of hand and result in violence, and if both parties are drunk the situation is even riskier. As mentioned earlier, the victim of violence is often drunk as well as the perpetrator. Domestic violence is one important area for therapeutic change. Generally violent men, as described by the developmental pathway presented earlier in this chapter, form one sub-group of perpetrators of domestic violence, this sub-group being more severely violent and characterized by being themselves abused as children, having witnessed parental violence, and having high rates of substance abuse (La Taillade & Jacobson, 1997). The developmental antecedents of partner abuse are largely similar for women, although negative early family relationship experiences predict abuse more strongly for women (Magdol et al., 1998). Domestic violence treatments may address communication, conflict resolution and intimacy skills (Markman et al., 1993), as well as the alcohol consumption of one or both parties.

Interpersonal Skills Training

Most programmes aimed at reducing violence and problematic alcohol consumption contain interpersonal skills training components. These typically include communication, assertiveness, negotiation and resisting peer pressure (Browne and Howells, 1996; Monti et al., 1989). The aims of skills training are slightly different in treating violence and problem drinking. Where problematic drinking is concerned, the aim is to make people feel competent in social situations so that they do not resort to drinking as a means of providing courage, confidence or control. Using alcohol to cope with social anxiety is, perhaps, not a major issue with the gregarious, aggressive drunk that has been the focus in this chapter. With this group, violence reduction is the main aim, through minimizing the frustration caused by poor interpersonal communication skills, and providing a choice of positive alternatives to violence as a means of solving conflict. The procedures of social skills training are the same irrespective of the aim, namely instruction, modelling, rehearsal and feedback.

Lifestyle Modification

Walters (1998) argues for a whole lifestyle approach to changing lives of crime and drugs. In a lifestyle approach, the therapist encourages the client to change his or her involvements (i.e. routines, activities and relationships), commitments (i.e. goals, values and priorities), and identity (i.e. identification of and resocialization into a new lifestyle). Resocialization into conventional networks is a strong predictor of positive outcome in substance users and criminals (Meyers & Smith, 1995; Walters, 1998).

Special Needs Groups

The comprehensive intervention programme described above is relevant for alcohol-abusing offenders who may be deemed concurrently to show high levels of antisocial personality problems (Rounsaville et al., 1998). There are, however, other groups who may be violent when intoxicated and have special needs that require different interventions.

Multiple Drug Use

Many alcohol abusers are also illicit drug users, and there is evidence that multiple drug use is associated with higher levels of criminality, particularly violent crimes (Dowden & Brown, 1998; Hodgins & Lightfoot, 1988;). In the US, therapeutic communities are the treatment of choice for drug users. Therapeutic communities (TCs) are therapeutic social milieus aimed at addressing the problems people experience because they cannot relate to the society in which they live. The four central tenets of TCs are: (1) democratic decision-making, with diminution of the staff–patient divide; (2) communalism, in that there is shared responsibility for the practicalities of running the community; (3) reality confrontation, where residents' behaviours are challenged in respect of their appropriateness and impact on others; and (4) permissiveness, in that mistakes are tolerated as part of the learning process (Rapoport, 1960). Although TCs may not be effective as a treatment for non-specified personality problems in offenders (McMurran, Egan & Ahmadi, 1998; Rice, Harris & Cormier, 1992), there is evidence of success when TCs aim specifically to treat substance abuse problems (Wexler, 1997). Such concept-based TCs see drug abuse as a disorder of the person, of which the drug use is a symptom, and the aim is to enhance social and personal values, and so eliminate drug use and crime and encourage gainful employment and stable relationships (Lipton, 1998). The success of TC programmes in the US has been reviewed by Lipton (1998; and see chapter 2 of the present book), showing that, when comparing those completing TC programmes with no intervention controls, rates of rearrest and reincarceration were significantly reduced, as was drug use. Effects were particularly impressive when TC participants went on to receive aftercare focusing on reintegration into the community.

Mentally Ill Alcohol Abusers

A combination of schizophrenia and alcohol abuse increases the risk for violence. In a Finnish longitudinal study, men diagnosed as suffering from schizophrenia who abused alcohol were identified as 25 times more likely to commit violent crimes than healthy men, and those diagnosed with schizophrenia who were not alcohol abusers were less that four times more likely to commit a violent offence (Räsänen et al., 1998). An epidemiological study by Swanson (1994) indicated that those with dual diagnosis of mental illness and substance abuse were indeed most likely to be violent, but that the mental illness added only a little to the risk over and above the substance abuse. It may be that the potent factor where violence is concerned is the substance abuse and that, while mental illness adds to that risk, mental illness is not the causal factor. This position is certainly supported in a meta-analysis of predictors of risk in mentally disordered offenders (Bonta, Law & Hanson, 1998). Major predictors of risk were found to be the same for mentally disordered offenders as for non-mentally disordered offenders. Assumptions that psychopathology is the major cause of recidivism have meant that "normal" risk factors have received little attention in this group, and it is interesting to note that the role of alcohol use in violent recidivism has not been recorded in the studies contributing to the meta-analysis.

Mentally ill substance users are less likely to comply with treatment, are more likely to relapse, and show more pronounced difficulties in independent living (Edens, Peters & Hills, 1997). Integrating substance use programmes with psychiatric treatment and rehabilitation is considered optimal for this dually diagnosed group, although the evidence for the effectiveness of integrated treatment is weak (Ley et al., 2001). In their review of US dual diagnosis treatment programmes in prisons, Edens, Peters and Hills (1997) note that the core elements of these programmes are similar to those of general substance abuse programmes, but with the addition of a strong community atmosphere, medication, case management and basic life skills training. Preliminary results indicate that such programmes improve retention in treatment and reduce criminal recidivism.

People with Learning Disabilities who Abuse Alcohol

Novaco's anger management approach has been effective in reducing aggressive incidents with quite severely developmentally delayed adults (Rose, 1996). Recommendations for adaptations to Novaco's programme that are better suited to people with learning disabilities have been made, and include teaching people to identify emotions and enhancing communication skills (Black, Cullen & Novaco, 1997). Interventions aimed at helping people with learning disabilities to moderate their drinking have also been devised, altering the style of presentation rather than the content to suit people with different levels of ability (McMurran & Lismore, 1993).

CONCLUSION

Alcohol is a potent risk factor for violence, particularly in individuals who are aggressive without the aid of drinking. A comprehensive intervention to reduce intoxicated violence should take into account the multiplicity of factors that lead up to and unleash violence. Such an intervention will be applicable with prison populations, mentally disordered offenders, and offenders or potential offenders in the community. Treatment should form part of a broad strategy, including prevention efforts addressing the problem of intoxicated violence from a number of angles—cultural, social, familial and individual. Intoxicated violence is not a new phenomenon. We strive to develop our understanding of the development, maintenance, and treatability of this complex behaviour in an ever-changing social context. The work will never be done, but participating in this endeavour is useful and rewarding.

REFERENCES

Beck, A. T. & Freeman, A. (1990) *Cognitive Therapy of Personality Disorders*. New York: Guilford Press.

Beck, A. T., Wright, F. D., Newman, C. F. & Liese, B. S. (1993) *Cognitive Therapy of Substance Abuse*. New York: Guilford Press.

Black, L., Cullen, C. & Novaco, R. W. (1997) Anger assessment for people with mild learning disabilities in secure settings. In B. Stenfert-Kroese, D. Dagnan, & K. Loumidis (Eds.) *Cognitive Behaviour Therapy for People with Learning Disabilities*. London: Routledge.

Bonta, J., Law, M. & Hanson, K. (1998) The prediction of criminal and violent recidivism among mentally disordered offenders: A meta-analysis. *Psychological Bulletin*, 123, 123–142.

Browne, K. & Howells, K. (1996) Violent offenders. In C. R. Hollin (Ed.) *Working with Offenders*. Chichester: Wiley.

Carroll, K. M. (1996) Relapse prevention as a psychosocial treatment: A review of controlled clinical trials. *Experimental and Clinical Psychopharmacology*, 4, 46–54.

Chermack, S. T. & Giancola, P. R. (1997) The relation between alcohol and aggression: An integrated biopsychosocial conceptualization. *Clinical Psychology Review*, 17, 621–649.

Chermack, S. T. & Taylor, S. P. (1995) Alcohol and human physical aggression: Pharmacological versus expectancy effects. *Journal of Studies on Alcohol*, 56, 449–456.

Darkes, J. & Goldman, M. S. (1993) Expectancy challenge and drinking reduction. *Journal of Consulting and Clinical Psychology*, 61, 344–353.

Davidson, K. M. & Tyrer, P. (1996) Cognitive therapy for antisocial and borderline personality disorders: Single case study series. *British Journal of Clinical Psychology*, 35, 413–429.

Dodge, K. A., Price, J. M., Bachorowski, J. & Newman, J. P. (1990) Hostile attributional bias in severely aggressive adolescents. *Journal of Abnormal Psychology*, 99, 385–392.

Dowden, C. & Brown, S. L. (1998) Substance abuse. *Forum on Corrections Research*, 10, 28–31.

D'Zurilla, T. J. & Goldfried, M. R. (1971) Problem solving and behaviour modification. *Journal of Abnormal Psychology*, 78, 107–126.

D'Zurilla, T. J. & Nezu, A. M. (1982) Social problem solving in adults. In P. C. Kendall (Ed.) *Advances in Cognitive-Behavioral Research and Therapy*, Vol. 1. New York: Academic press.

D'Zurilla, T. J., Nezu, A. M. & Maydeu-Olivares, A. (2000) *Social Problem-Solving Inventory— Revised*. North Tonawanda, NY: Multi-Health Systems, Inc.

Edens, J. F., Peters, R. H. & Hills, H. A. (1997) Treating prison inmates with co-occurring disorders: An integrative review of existing programs. *Behavioral Sciences and the Law*, 15, 439–457.

Edmondson, C. B. & Conger, J. C. (1996) A review of treatment efficacy for anger problems: Conceptual, assessment, and methodological issues. *Clinical Psychology Review*, 16, 251–275.

Edwards, G. & Members of the Alcohol and Public Policy Project (1994) *Alcohol Policy and the Public Good*. Oxford: Oxford University Press.

Elliott, D. S., Huizinga, D. & Ageton, S. S. (1985) *Explaining Delinquency and Drug Use*. Newbury Park, CA: Sage.

Farrington, D. P. (1995) The development of offending and antisocial behaviour from childhood: Key findings from the Cambridge study in delinquent development. *Journal of Child Psychology and Psychiatry*, 36, 929–964.

Farrington, D. P. (1996) Individual, family and peer factors in the development of delinquency. In C. R. Hollin & K. Howells (Eds.) *Clinical Approaches to Working with Young Offenders*. Chichester: Wiley.

Farrington, D. P. & Hawkins, J. D. (1991) Predicting participation, early onset, and later persistence in officially recorded offending. *Criminal Behaviour and Mental Health, 1,* 1–33.

Fergusson, D. M., Lynskey, M. T. & Horwood, L. J. (1996). Alcohol misuse and juvenile offending in adolescence. *Addiction, 91,* 483–494.

Giancola, P. R., Martin, C. S., Tarter, R. E., Pelham, W. E. & Moss, H. B. (1996) Executive cognitive functioning and aggressive behaviour in preadolescent boys at high risk for substance abuse/dependence. *Journal of Studies on Alcohol, 57,* 352–359.

Golden, C. J., Jackson, M. L., Peterson-Rohne, A. & Gontkovsky, S.T. (1996) Neuropsychological correlates of violence and aggression: A review of the clinical literature. *Aggression and Violent Behaviour, 1,* 3–25.

Goldman, M. S. (1994) The alcohol expectancy concept: Applications to assessment, prevention, and treatment of alcohol abuse. *Applied and Preventive Psychology, 3,* 131–134.

Goldman, M. S., Brown, S. A. & Christiansen, B. A. (1987) Expectancy theory: Thinking about drinking. In H. T. Blane & K. E. Leonard (Eds.) *Psychological Theories of Drinking and Alcoholism.* New York: Guilford.

Graham,. J. & Bowling, B. (1995) *Young People and Crime.* Home Office Research Study, No. 145. London: Home Office.

Graham, K., Leonard, K. E., Room, R., Wild, T. C., Pihl, R. O., Bois, C. & Single, E. (1998) Current directions in research on understanding and preventing intoxicated aggression. *Addiction, 93,* 659–676.

Hämäläinen, M. & Pulkkinen, L. (1996) Problem behavior as a precursor of male criminality. *Development and Psychopathology, 8,* 443–455.

Hawkins, J. D., Catalano, R. F. & Miller, J. Y. (1992) Risk and protective factors for alcohol and other drug problems in adolescence and early adulthood: Implications for substance abuse prevention. *Psychological Bulletin, 112,* 64–105.

Hodgins, D. C. & Lightfoot, L. O. (1988) Types of male alcohol- and drug-abusing incarcerated offenders. *British Journal of Addiction, 83,* 1201–1213.

Home Office (2001) *Time for Reform: Proposals for the Modernisation of our Licensing Laws.* Cm 4696. Norwich: The Stationery Office.

Hope, T. (1985) Drinking and disorder in the inner city. In *Implementing Crime Prevention Measures.* Home Office Research Study, No. 86. London: HMSO.

Jessor, R. & Jessor, S. L. (1977) *Problem Behavior and Psychosocial Development: A Longitudinal Study of Youth.* New York: Academic Press.

Josephs, R. A. & Steele, C. M. (1990) The two faces of alcohol myopia: Attentional mediation of psychological stress. *Journal of Abnormal Psychology, 99,* 115–126.

Kandel, D. B. (1985) On processes of peer influence in adolescent drug use: A developmental perspective. *Advances in Alcohol and Substance Use, 4,* 139–163.

Kazdin, A. E. (1997) Psychosocial treatments for conduct disorder in children. *Journal of Child Psychology and Psychiatry, 38,* 161–178.

Klinteberg, B. A., Andersson, T., Magnusson, D. & Stattin, H. (1993) Hyperactive behavior in childhood as related to subsequent alcohol problems and violent offending: A longitudinal study of male subjects. *Personality and Individual Differences, 15,* 381–388.

Lang, A. E. & Sibrel, P. A. (1989) Psychological perspectives on alcohol consumption and interpersonal aggression. *Criminal Justice and Behavior, 16,* 299–324.

Lang, E. Stockwell, T., Rydon, P. & Lockwood, A. (1995) Drinking settings and problems of intoxication. *Addiction Research, 3,* 141–149.

La Taillade, J. J. & Jacobson, N. S. (1997) Domestic violence: Antisocial behavior in the family. In D. M. Stoff, J. Brieling & J. D. Maser (Eds.) *Handbook of Antisocial Behavior.* New York: Wiley.

Le Blanc, M. (1994) Family, school, delinquency, and criminality: The predictive power of an elaborated social control theory for males. *Criminal Behaviour and Mental Health, 4,* 101–117.

Ley, A., Jeffrey, D. P., McLaren, S. & Siegfried, N. (2001) Treatment programmes for people with both severe mental illness and substance misuse (Cochrane Review). *The Cochrane Library, Issue 2.* Oxford: Update Software.

Lindqvist, P. (1991) Homicides committed by abusers of alcohol and illicit drugs. *British Journal of Addiction*, 86, 321–326.

Lipton, D. S. (1998) Therapeutic community treatment programming in corrections. *Psychology, Crime and Law*, 4, 213–263.

Loeber, R. (1988) Natural histories of conduct problems, delinquency, and associated substance use. In B. B. Lahey & A. E. Kazdin (Eds.) *Advances in Clinical Child Psychology*, Vol. 11. New York: Plenum Press.

Loeber, R. (1990) Development and risk factors of juvenile antisocial behavior and delinquency. *Clinical Psychology Review*, 10, 1–41.

Loeber, R., Stouthamer-Loeber, M. & Green, S. M. (1991) Age at onset of problem behaviour in boys, and later disruptive and delinquent behaviours. *Criminal Behaviour and Mental Health*, 1, 229–246.

Magdol, L., Moffitt, T. E., Caspi, A. & Silva, P. A. (1998) Developmental antecedents of partner abuse: A prospective-longitudinal study. *Journal of Abnormal Psychology*, 107, 375–389.

Markman, H. J., Renick, M. J., Floyd, F. J., Stanley, S. M. & Clements, M. (1993) Preventing marital distress through communication and conflict management training: A 4- and 5- year follow-up. *Journal of Consulting and Clinical Psychology*, 61, 70–77.

Marlatt, G. A. & Gordon, J. R. (Eds.) (1985) *Relapse Prevention*. New York: Guilford.

Marlatt, G. A. (1996) Taxonomy of high-risk situations for alcohol relapse: Evolution of a cognitive-behavioral model. *Addiction*, 91 (Supplement), S37–S49.

Maughan, B. (1993) Childhood precursors of aggressive offending in personality disordered adults. In S. Hodgins (Ed.) *Mental Disorder and Crime*. Newbury Park, CA: Sage Publications.

McMurran, M. (1994) *The Psychology of Addiction*. London: Taylor & Francis.

McMurran, M. (1996) Substance use and delinquency. In C. R. Hollin and K. Howells (Eds.) *Clinical Approaches to Working with Young Offenders*. Chichester: Wiley.

McMurran, M. (1997) Outcome expectancies: An important link between substance use and crime? In S. Redondo, V. Garrido, J. Perez & R. Barbaret (Eds.) *Advances in Law and Psychology*. Berlin: de Gruyter.

McMurran, M., Blair, M. & Egan, V. (in press). An investigation of the correlations between aggression, impulsiveness, social problem-solving, and alcohol use. *Aggressive Behavior*.

McMurran, M., Egan, V. & Ahmadi, S. (1998) A retrospective evaluation of a therapeutic community for mentally disordered offenders. *Journal of Forensic Psychiatry*, 9, 103–113.

McMurran, M. & Hollin, C. R. (1993) *Young Offenders and Alcohol-Related Crime: A Practitioner's Guidebook*. Chichester: Wiley.

McMurran, M. & Lismore, K. (1993) Using videotapes in alcohol interventions for people with learning disabilities. *Mental Handicap*, 21, 29–31.

McMurran, M., Richardson, C., Egan, V. & Ahmadi, S. (1999). Social problem-solving in mentally disordered offenders: A brief report. *Criminal Behaviour and Mental Health*, 9, 315–322.

Meyers, R. J. & Smith, J. E. (1995) *Clinical Guide to Alcohol Treatment: The Community Reinforcement Approach*. New York: Guilford Press.

Miller, W. R., Leckman, A. L., Delaney, H. D. & Tinkcom, M. (1992) Long-term follow-up of behavioral self-control training. *Journal of Studies on Alcohol*, 53, 249–261.

Miller, W. R. & Rollnick, S. (1991) *Motivational Interviewing: Preparing People to Change*. New York: Guilford.

Milner, J. S. & Dopke, C. (1997) Child physical abuse: Review of offender characteristics. In D. A. Wolfe, R. J. McMahon & R. DeV. Peters (Eds.) *Child Abuse: New Directions in Prevention and Treatment Across the Lifespan*. Thousand Oaks, CA: Sage.

Moffitt, T. E. (1993) Adolescent-limited and life-course-persistent antisocial behavior: A developmental taxonomy. *Psychological Review*, 100, 674–701.

Moffitt, T. E., Brammer, G. L., Caspi, A., Fawcett, J. P., Raleigh, M., Yuwiler, A. & Silva, P. (1998) Whole blood serotonin relates to violence in an epidemiological study. *Biological Psychiatry*, 43, 446–457.

Monti, P. M., Abrams, D. B., Kadden, R. M. & Cooney, N. L. (1989) *Treating Alcohol Dependence*. London: Cassell.

Morgenstern, J., Kahler, C. W. & Epstein, E. (1998) Do treatment process factors mediate the relationship Type A–Type B and outcome in 12-Step oriented substance abuse treatment? *Addiction*, *93*, 1765–1776.

Mulvey, E. P., Arthur, M. W. & Repucci, N. D. (1993) The prevention and treatment of juvenile delinquency: A review of the research. *Clinical Psychology Review*, *13*, 133–167.

Murdoch, D., Pihl, R. O. & Ross, D. (1990) Alcohol and crimes of violence: Present issues. *International Journal of the Addictions*, *25*, 1065–1081.

Novaco, R. W. (1975) *Anger Control: The Development and Evaluation of an Experimental Treatment*. Lexington, MA: D.C. Heath.

Novaco, R. W. (1994) Anger as a risk factor for violence among the mentally disordered. In J. Monahan & H. J. Steadman (Eds.) *Violence and Mental Disorder: Developments in Risk Assessment*. Chicago: University of Chicago Press.

Novaco, R. W. (1997) Remediating anger and aggression with violent offenders. *Legal and Criminological Psychology*, *2*, 77–88.

O'Boyle, M. & Barratt, E. S. (1993) Impulsivity and DSM-III personality disorders. *Personality and Individual Differences*, *14*, 609–611.

O'Donnell, J., Hawkins, J. D. & Abbott, R. D. (1995) Predicting serious delinquency and substance use among aggressive boys. *Journal of Consulting and Clinical Psychology*, *63*, 529–537.

Pelham, W. E. & Lang, A. R. (1993) Parental alcohol consumption and deviant child behavior: Laboratory studies of reciprocal effects. *Clinical Psychology Review*, *13*, 763–784.

Pihl, R. O. & Hoaken, P. N. S. (1997) Clinical correlates and predictors of violence in patients with substance use disorders. *Psychiatric Annals*, *27*, 735–740.

Pihl, R. O. & Lemarquand, D. (1998) Serotonin and aggression and the alcohol-aggression relationship. *Alcohol and Alcoholism*, *33*, 55–65.

Pihl, R. O. & Peterson, J. B. (1993) Alcohol, serotonin, and aggression. *Alcohol Health and Research World*, *17*, 113–116.

Project MATCH Research Group (1997) Project MATCH secondary a priori hypotheses. *Addiction*, *92*, 1671–1698.

Ramsay, M. (1982) *City Centre Crime: The Scope for Situational Prevention*. Research and Planning Unit Paper, No. 10. London: Home Office.

Rapoport, R. (1960) *The Community as Doctor*. London: Tavistock.

Räsänen, P., Tiihonen, J., Isohanni, M., Rantakallio, P., Lehtonen, J. & Moring, J. (1998) Schizophrenia, alcohol abuse, and violent behavior: A 26-year follow-up study of an unselected birth cohort. *Schizophrenia Bulletin*, *24*, 437–441.

Renwick, S. J., Black, L., Ramm, M. & Novaco, R. W. (1997) Anger treatment with forensic hospital patients. *Legal and Criminological Psychology*, *2*, 103–116.

Rice, M. E., Harris, G. T. & Cormier, C. A. (1992) An evaluation of a maximum security therapeutic community therapeutic community for psychopaths and other mentally disordered offenders. *Law and Human Behavior*, *16*, 399–412.

Rohsenow, D. J., Niaura, R. S., Childress, A. R., Abrams, D. B. & Monti, P. M. (1991) Cue reactivity in addictive behaviors: Theoretical and treatment implications. *International Journal of the Addictions*, *25*, 957–993.

Rose, J. (1996) Anger management: A group treatment program for people with mental retardation. *Journal of Developmental and Physical Disabilities*, *8*, 133–149.

Rounsaville, B. J., Kranzler, H. R., Ball, S., Tennen, H., Poling, J. & Triffleman, E. (1998) Personality disorders in substance abusers: Relation to substance abuse. *Journal of Nervous and Mental Disease*, *186*, 87–95.

Sher, K. J. & Trull, T. J. (1994) Personality and disinhibitory psychopathology: Alcoholism and antisocial personality disorder. *Journal of Abnormal Psychology*, *103*, 92–102.

Siever, L. J. & Davis, K. L. (1991) A psychobiological perspective on the personality disorders. *American Journal of Psychiatry*, *48*, 1647–1658.

Slaby, R. G. & Guerra, N. G. (1988) Cognitive mediators of aggression in adolescent offenders: 1. Assessment. *Developmental Psychology*, *24*, 580–588.

Swanson, J. W. (1994) Mental disorder, substance abuse, and community violence: An epidemiological approach. In J. Monahan & H. J. Steadman (Eds.) *Violence and Mental Disorder: Developments in Risk Assessment.* Chicago: University of Chicago Press.

Tolan, P. H. & Gorman-Smith, D. (1998) Development of serious and violent offending careers. In R. Loeber and D. P. Farrington (Eds.) *Serious and Violent Juvenile Offenders.* Thousand Oaks, CA: Sage.

Verheul, R., van den Brink, W. & Hartgers, C. (1995) Prevalence of personality disorders among alcoholics and drug addicts: An overview. *European Addiction Research, 1,* 166–177.

Walters, G. D. (1998) *Changing Lives of Crime and Drugs.* Chichester: Wiley.

Wanberg, K. W. & Milkman, H. B. (1998) *Criminal Conduct and Substance Abuse Treatment.* Thousand Oaks, CA: Sage.

Wexler, H. K. (1997) The success of therapeutic communities for substance abusers in American prisons. In E. Cullen, L. Jones & R. Woodward (Eds.) *Therapeutic Communities for Offenders.* Chichester: Wiley.

White, J. L., Moffitt, T. E., Caspi, A., Bartusch, D. J., Needles, D. J. & Stouthamer-Loeber, M. (1994) Measuring impulsivity and examining its relationship to delinquency. *Journal of Abnormal Psychology, 103,* 192–205.

Wilens, T. E. & Biederman, J. (1993) Psychopathology in preadolescent children at high risk for substance abuse: A review of the literature. *Harvard Review of Psychiatry, 1,* 207–218.

Young, J. E. (1990) *Cognitive Therapy for Personality Disorders: A Schema-focussed Approach.* Sarasota, FL: Professional Resource Exchange.

Chapter 9

CHANGING BELIEFS OF SPOUSE ABUSERS

MARY NÔMME RUSSELL

School of Social Work, University of British Columbia, Vancouver, B.C., Canada

Spouse abuse, or more specifically abuse of women by their male partners, has been, and continues to be, a serious social problem. In Canada, for instance, a national survey revealed that 29% of women have experienced abuse at the hands of an intimate male, and in 45% of these cases, physical injury of the woman resulted (Statistics Canada, 1993). In addition, over 60% of women murdered in a given year were killed by their husbands or live-in partners (Canadian Centre for Justice Statistics, 1987). Similar surveys in the United States indicate that, during the course of a year, one in eight husbands were abusive towards their wives, resulting in 1.8 million women being abused. Three-quarters of women murdered were killed by a spouse (Straus & Gelles, 1990). For the United Kingdom, using British Crime Survey data, it has been estimated that in 1995 there were 6.6 million incidents of domestic physical assault, 2.9 million involving injury. Nearly a quarter of women (23%) aged 16 to 59 said they had been physically assaulted by a current or previous partner at some time (Mirrlees-Black, 1999).

The consequences of abuse on women subject to it and children observing it are considerable. Assault by men against their female partners has been found to be a major reason for hospital emergency department visits, as well as physician visits for a range of medical conditions. Mental health sequelae of abuse such as depression, anxiety, and Post-traumatic Stress Disorder are common and can persist for as long as three years following the abuse (Campbell & Soeken, 1999).

Children in abusive families also suffer pervasive negative effects. Spouse abuse is accompanied by child abuse in approximately 50% of cases (Saunders, 1994). Furthermore, children observing spousal abuse demonstrate higher levels of personality disorder, behaviour problems, and lower levels of social competence than children from non-abusive homes (Jouriles, Murphy & O'Leary, 1989; Wolfe et al., 1985). Adolescents from abusive families tend to demonstrate higher levels of abuse in their own dating relationships (Sugarman & Hotaling, 1989), and as adult men,

Offender Rehabilitation and Treatment: Effective Programmes and Policies to Reduce Re-offending. Edited by James McGuire.
© John Wiley & Sons, Ltd.

the abuse they observed as children is frequently reproduced in their own marital relationships (O'Leary, Malone & Tyree, 1994).

Economic costs of spouse abuse are considerable. A Canadian study estimated costs to be $4.2 billion a year, including $2.3 billion in social services and education costs, $872 million in criminal justice system costs, $576 million in employment loses, and $408 million in medical care (Greaves, Hankivsky & Kingston-Riechers, 1995).

In sum, individual, familial, and social costs of wife abuse are high. Prevention and remediation efforts aimed at individual abusers are therefore frequently prescribed, utilizing either the criminal and/or mental health systems. However, individual remediation must take into account the support for abuse of women provided by the social context.

SOCIAL CONTEXT OF WIFE ABUSE

The high prevalence of men's abusiveness towards female partners suggests that such behaviour is more than individual pathology or misdemeanor, but rather behaviour that has some level of social support. Studies of attitudes towards wife abuse as well as studies of attitudes towards women provide confirmation of this theory.

Attitudes Towards Wife Abuse

Population surveys have indicated a surprisingly high tolerance for abuse of women by their intimate partners, and support for the notion that abused women deserve such treatment. Greenblat's (1985) survey of college students found that only 12% disapproved of a husband ever slapping his wife. Instead, 44% approved of a husband beating his wife in self-defence or defence of a child. A further 23% approved of wife beating because of infidelity, drunkenness and insulting behaviour. Approval of wife abuse in specified circumstances has also been reported by Stark and McEvoy (1970) who found that between 16 and 26% of respondents agreed that in some circumstances it is appropriate for a husband to hit his wife.

In conjunction with this tolerance of abuse, surveys have indicated that there is an enduring belief that victims of abuse are at least partially responsible for their abuse. Ewing and Aubrey (1987) found that 38% of the general population attributed at least partial blame to the abused wife. Even among professionals, up to 10% agreed that such blame was warranted (Davis, 1984).

More positive attitudes towards violence have been found among men who are abusive than among those who are not. Both in dating and marital relationships, a more positive attitude by men towards violence in intimate situations has been related to a greater likelihood of inflicting such violence (Sugarman and Hotaling, 1989). Dating males who are abusive have candidly described their instrumental use of violence to reach desired goals, such as compliance by and subservience from their female partners. Abusive husbands, in contrast, are more likely to rely heavily on a set of "out of control" reasons such as alcohol, drugs, anger or stress (Dutton, 1986). Finally, in a study of almost 1000 men, the single strongest difference between abusive and non-abusive men was the former's tolerance of wife assault (Hanson et al., 1997).

Confirmation of the importance of the social context in promoting abusive behaviour has been provided by wives of abusive men. Smith (1991) found that abused women were more likely than wives of non-abusive husbands to report that their husbands' friends approved of violence against women and believed that men should be in control in the marital relationship. Similarly, Bowker (1983) concluded on the basis of abused women's reports that their husbands spent more time with male peers, and that this immersion in a sub-culture of violence reinforced the husbands' abusive behaviours.

Attitudes that support wife abuse in particular circumstances and among particular segments of the population are, therefore, not uncommon. Men who are exposed to such attitudes are likely to adopt beliefs that abuse is warranted in certain circumstances. This belief in the acceptability of abuse is frequently also linked with negative attitudes towards women.

Attitudes Towards Women

Negative attitudes towards women have been found to be commonplace among abusive men. Smith (1991) refers to the set of beliefs, values and ideas that support domination of women as "patriarchal ideology". This patriarchal ideology views men as inherently superior to women, domination of women as natural, and the use of violence to enforce this domination when necessary as acceptable. In a telephone survey of 604 Toronto women, Smith found that the male partners who adhered to an ideology of familial patriarchy were more likely to have been assaultive at some point in their relationship.

Dutton and Starzomski (1997) found that assaultive men subscribed to notions of Male Privilege to an extent that was not observed in non-assaultive men. Assaultive men endorsed items indicating their entitlement to treat their partner like an inferior, demand obedience from her, treat her as a servant and order her around, at a considerably higher level than non-assaultive men. Similarly, Harris and Bologh (1985) found that abusive men believed in their own moral superiority over their partners, and had an expectation of subservience and deference from them.

Greenblat (1985) found that respondents with traditional sex-role orientation were more likely to approve of wives being slapped or beaten by their husbands, and Rosenbaum and O'Leary (1981) found that men who had more conservative and patriarchal family attitudes were more likely to actually be abusive towards their partners.

The conjuncture between beliefs about abuse and beliefs about women was elucidated through in-depth interviews conducted by Dobash and Dobash (1998) in their Violent Men Study. A distinct difference was observed in men speaking about violence against women as opposed to violence against men, and between men and women in describing violence against women. Descriptions by men of violence between men, or descriptions by women of violence against women, tended to be rich in detail regarding the violent acts themselves. In contrast, violent men's descriptions of their violence towards women gave almost no detail but instead emphasized the outcome—the "winning" over or defeating of the women, putting her in her place, showing her who was boss. Affirmation of masculine identity in man-to-woman violence did not lie in the act of violence as it did in male-to-male violence. Instead masculinity was affirmed in the outcome of obtaining some desired end, inflicting punishment for some perceived wrongdoing or maintaining authority over the female partner. In effect, male violence against women was based on men's beliefs about the superiority inherent in masculinity, about the expectation of male dominance in male–female relationships, about men's entitlement to privilege and benefits provided by women, and about the acceptability of using violence to secure all of the foregoing.

The social context, therefore, provides support for beliefs that wife abuse is acceptable and that women are deserving of such abuse in certain circumstances. Furthermore, the social context reinforces beliefs of masculinity that involve domination over women coupled with expectations of women's subservience. In order to prevent wife abuse or to change wife abusers' behaviours, it is therefore necessary to challenge these socially supported beliefs.

SOCIAL RESPONSES TO WIFE ABUSE

Identification of spousal abuse as a social problem in need of remedy was brought to public awareness by the women's movement in the 1960s, and this awareness has been growing steadily since. Social remedies prescribed have included both criminal justice and social service interventions.

Dutton's (1988) review of the criminal justice response to wife assault concluded that while only one in six assaults was reported to police, the police nevertheless came into contact with family violence more than any other government agency. Even so, the probability of a husband-to-wife assault resulting in arrest was only 1.4% and the punishment rate was 0.5%. The main impediment to criminal justice intervention, according to Dutton, was the tendency of victims to view the assault in non-criminal terms.

Investigations of the effectiveness of criminal justice interventions have been mixed. Sherman and Berk's (1984) study demonstrating an effective reduction of wife assault from 80% to 19% following arrest, has not been consistently replicated. The argument has been made, however, that individual alternate approaches have not been shown to be superior to arrest (Berk, 1993). The preferred alternative for at least some types of abusers has been shown to be a combination of arrest and group therapy (Buzawa & Buzawa, 1993; Dutton, 1988).

Many types of group treatment programmes for abusive men, either as diversion programmes mandated by the courts or as voluntary treatment typically provided by community social service agencies, have been developed. Most treatment programmes have addressed beliefs about abuse by stating clearly that wife abuse is never acceptable. Many programmes require participants to sign agreements that they will refrain from abuse during the programme. Policies developed around disclosure of abuse occurring during the programme include revocation of probation for court-mandated participants and full group discussion with a view to preventing recurrence for voluntary participants. Programme content generally reinforces the statement of unacceptability of abuse by providing and rewarding alternate behavioural responses.

However, not all treatment programmes have addressed the more complex, patriarchal beliefs about women and family structure. Without challenging such beliefs, it can be argued, the likelihood of successful outcome is compromised.

BEHAVIOURAL TREATMENT PROGRAMMES

A wide range of group treatment approaches for abusive men has been developed (Feazell, Mayers & Deschner, 1984; Pirog-Good & Stets-Kealy, 1985) with the most common type of programme being one with a behavioural focus. These programmes have aimed at reducing physical violence through behavioural methods such as "time out", relaxation, behavioural monitoring, and assertiveness training (Roberts, 1984). The theoretical premise underlying these programmes has been that a "male deficit" in relational skills results in abusive behaviour. The remedy, therefore, has been the development and application of such skills. Some programmes have supplemented this behavioural focus by including a limited discussion of sex-role attitudes considered to be associated with violent behaviour (Dutton, 1988).

Empirical evaluations of behavioural programmes have been generally positive. Results have indicated that these programmes have been effective in reducing physical abuse levels of men who completed the programmes. Drop-out levels, however, tend to be substantial. Furthermore, these programmes have been less successful in long-term maintenance of non-violent behaviour and in decreasing other types of abuse (Saunders, 1989; Tolman & Bennett, 1990). In fact, some studies have indicated that behavioural programmes that result in decreased physical abuse may have little effect on or may even increase psychological abuse (Gondolf 1986; Tolman & Bhosley, 1991).

As an alternative to these behaviourally focused programmes, belief confrontation programmes (based on theory and practice) that address fundamental aspects of self and relationships, have been developed. Belief confrontation programmes aim to alter beliefs that sustain and support abusive relationships with the expectation that changing abusive to respectful beliefs would produce more comprehensive and sustained change.

Dobash et al. (1996) reported an evaluation of two "re-education" programmes in Scotland that combined elements of belief modification with some behaviourally focused work. The CHANGE Project and the Lothian Domestic Violence Probation Project were both based in criminal justice system settings and delivered by social work staff. Group activities focused on challenging attitudes to women and on accepting responsibility for actions, while men were also involved in self-monitoring "homework" and the use of "time-out" to divert them from acting violently. During a 12-month follow-up, 33% of the partners of men participating in the programmes reported a further violent act, while 75% of partners of men subject to other types of sanction did so. Further, only 7% of the programme participants committed five or more violent incidents, as contrasted with 37% in the comparison groups. Members of the former group were also reported to engage in significantly less coercive and controlling behaviour.

BELIEF CONFRONTATION PROGRAMMES

Belief systems theory provides the framework for a comprehensive and fundamental understanding of self and relationships. Belief systems theory posits that the organization of personality rests on the basis on individual beliefs that direct behaviour and influence affect and cognitions (Ball-Rokeach, Rokeach & Grube, 1984; Rokeach, 1979). Abusive behaviours, therefore, can be conceptualized as reflecting basic beliefs about the self and others in relationships. These beliefs both direct and support abusive behaviours as well as mediate the affective and cognitive processes that accompany abuse.

Belief system change is said to produce enduring and comprehensive alterations in attitudes and behaviours (Rokeach, 1985; Rokeach & Regan, 1980). Beliefs as individual expressions of basic values are considered to have a greater effect on behaviour than simple behavioural reward and punishment. Beliefs as basic elements of personality influence a range of behaviours and are influential in directing much of social interaction. Beliefs are complex entities that integrate emotional, cognitive and behavioural aspects. To change abusive behaviours, therefore, a method that confronts beliefs that support such behaviours is necessary.

CONFRONTING ABUSIVE BELIEFS PROGRAMME

Confronting Abusive Beliefs was developed on the basis of the Duluth programme, which was the first to articulate the notion of challenging abusive beliefs in treatment of abusive men (Pence & Paymar, 1993). Confronting Abusive Beliefs extended the Duluth model through a more comprehensive explication of beliefs, through a more extensive and deliberate use of group process (Yalom, 1975), and through a more defined utilization of a female co-therapist in groups (Russell, 1995).

Belief systems of abusive men had not previously been subject to systematic investigation. In developing the Confronting Abusive Beliefs programme, it became apparent that further investigation of belief systems of abusive men and the nature of desired belief change was necessary. A study of programme completers was therefore undertaken, with 17 men being interviewed. Analysis of transcripts of these interviews revealed that abusive beliefs could be characterized as falling into three categories: *Self as Central and Separate*, *Self as Superior*, and *Self as Deserving*. Following treatment there was evidence of movement towards contrasting respectful beliefs of *Self as Connected*, *Self as Equal*, and *Self as Mutually Engaged*. These parallel and contrasting belief systems are presented in Table 9.1.

The nature of these beliefs was evident in the statements of the men as they described their views about their relationships before and after completion of group treatment.

Table 9.1 Abusive and respectful relationship beliefs

Abusive beliefs	Respectful beliefs
Self as Central	Self as Connected
Self as Superior	Self as Equal
Self as Deserving	Self as Mutually Engaged

From Self as Separate to Self as Connected

The belief in the *Central and Separate Self* was characterized by an exclusive concern about the self, a disregard for consequence of one's actions on the partner and a dis-connectedness from the other. Statements that typified this belief included:

"I wasn't abusive, only angry and unhappy."
"The consequences of my anger . . . I guess I just put them out of my head".

In contrast, following programme completion, there was evidence of a belief in the *Self as Connected*. This was characterized by the man attending to the partner, striving to understand her thoughts and feelings, and being aware of the consequences of his actions on her. Statements demonstrating this belief included the following:

"Before, I would think to myself why the hell did she do that . . . All of a sudden, I started realizing why . . . because she was feeling put down, or she was afraid."

"I understand her more (now) . . . I listen to her more . . . I care more about her feelings and show her that I care."

The deterrent effect of connection on abusiveness was evident as men described the consequences of understanding and empathizing with their partners' experiences of abuse. The following statement provides such an example:

"When I think about how she really must have felt when I was doing those things, it almost makes me physically sick. I almost feel like throwing up it upsets me so much."

In summary, abusive behaviour was likely to occur when a man's beliefs led him to think primarily of himself alone and to be unaware or neglectful of the consequences of his actions on others. Respectful behaviour was likely to occur when a man's beliefs led him to connect with his partner, to be cognizant of her as a significant person, and to fully empathize with the effects of his behaviour on her.

From Self as Superior to Self as Equal

The belief in the *Superior Self*, highly evident prior to treatment, was characterized by assertions that, as a man, one is intrinsically superior to his partner, should therefore expect to dominate her, and she should accept this domination. Relationships were viewed as inherently hierarchical and men expressed the fear that if they failed to dominate, then domination by women, which needed to be avoided at all costs, would ensue. Threats to male domination, therefore, were viewed as insurrections that justified any means, including violence, to suppress them. Statements evidencing this belief included the following:

> "You know there has to be a boss. I would make the decisions; my word was the last word."

> "I had a siege mentality and somehow I figured that if I didn't act first then she would get me ... "

At programme completion, there was evidence of movement to a belief in the *Equal Self*, characterized by regarding the partner as equal, valuing her as a distinct and different individual, and regarding evidence of her, competence as a bonus rather than a threat. Statements evidencing this belief included the following:

> "I respect her knowledge and am willing to admit that."

> "I don't feel rejected now when her opinion is different."

> "It's too bad I didn't stop to listen (to her) five years ago or I might not have caused all these problems."

In summary, abuse was likely to occur when a man's belief in superiority did not permit his partner to differ and he viewed difference as a threat. When that belief changed to one of equality, individual differences were accepted as inevitable or even beneficial.

From Self as Deserving to Self as Mutually Engaged

The *Self as Deserving* belief, evidenced primarily as a pre-treatment belief, denoted the man as the exclusive recipient of care and nurturance within the relationship. There was no consideration of the partner's wants and needs. The expectation that partners would unquestioningly accede to this belief was evidenced in statements such as:

> "I thought that (my partner) should appreciate what I, the man, as king of his castle, did for her."

When these expectations were not fulfilled or when the partner's or the children's needs intruded, abusive behaviour was perceived as a justified reaction. The following statement exemplified this belief:

> "I felt that a kind of sanctuary had been taken away from me ... I resented that and it made me mad too."

At programme completion there had been some modification of this belief with movement towards a belief in a *Mutually Engaged Self*. A belief in a *Mutually Engaged Self* was characterized by an awareness that maintenance of the relationship was a shared responsibility, that giving and taking must occur freely and without constraint in both directions, and that engagement with the other had the potential for personal change and growth. Statements indicating such movement included the following:

"There's much more give and take and it's real giving, not demanded giving."

"We are both concerned about each other and what we have to do, whereas before we were going in opposite directions".

The movement from *Self as Deserving* to *Self as Mutually Engaged*, in summary, represented a change from demanded service to generous and reciprocal interaction.

This expanded understanding of the abusive belief system provided a basis for more direct and specific confrontation of men's beliefs. Also, the additional understanding of respectful relationship beliefs aided in understanding how these beliefs acted as a deterrent to abusiveness. The process of naming beliefs helped in bringing beliefs to awareness so that they could be analysed in terms of behavioural manifestations as well as evident consequences. The identification of respectful beliefs also provided a yardstick to determine to what extent men's behaviours corresponded with underlying respectful beliefs.

In sum, the further study of abusive and respectful relationship beliefs provided a way of conceptualizing belief change and describing the nature of the desired change in a way that was congruent with and spoke to the men's experience.

EXTENDED USE OF GROUP PROCESS

Therapeutic groups for men provide a unique experience for most men who typically have not had opportunities to openly and honestly explore their beliefs about intimate relationships. This kind of self-exploration and self-confrontation has typically not been fostered and therefore remains rare in male culture. Men who have had the benefit of groups for abusive men disclose that the group process and group support were the most important elements in their change process (Gondolf, 1986; Tolman, 1990).

Groups, as opposed to individual therapy, provide numerous sources of input and feedback. Men in groups frequently identify with experiences of other group members, learn from examples provided by others, and give advice to others. Edleson and Tolman (1992) found that abusive men derived particular benefits from efforts to help other group members. Not only did giving such help reinforce the man's own sense of competence, but it reinforced his own change process as he verbalized his new awareness.

Therapeutic groups have been considered particularly powerful mechanisms for belief change (Nicholas, 1984). In the Confronting Abusive Beliefs programme the group environment was structured to support and sustain belief change by creating a milieu wherein abusive beliefs were challenged and respectful beliefs were modelled and reinforced. Furthermore, the group environment encouraged breaking male taboos, such as admitting weakness, and challenged traditional beliefs associated with masculinity.

Fostering group cohesion was considered necessary in that cohesion aided both challenges to abusive beliefs and maintenance of respectful beliefs. Confrontation of beliefs has generally been found to increase as group cohesion increases (Yalom, 1975), and therefore promoting positive connections between the men was considered an important first step in the belief change process. This was achieved through promoting positive interactions, such as sharing experiences and providing mutual support, between the men both during and outside group meetings.

Challenging Questions

Questions that provoked the examination of beliefs were emphasized in the group process. Challenging questions had the purpose of eliciting underlying beliefs, bringing beliefs to awareness and confronting men with the consequences of beliefs. In particular, challenging questions aimed to emphasize the consequences of abusive relationship beliefs.

Jenkins (1990) noted that questioning men in groups is likely to avoid defensive reactions when the questions are presented as invitations to participation in self-exploration and discovery. Challenging questions, therefore, aimed to promote and reinforce a curiosity about the self and partner through the analysis of beliefs and their consequences. Examples of such questions included the following:

"What was it like for your partner to experience your abuse?"

"When you ignore what your partner is saying, what belief about her are you demonstrating?"

Challenging questions, furthermore were used to raise group awareness of the nature and consequences of beliefs. Group process to foster group cohesion was therefore promoted through the utilization of challenging questions posed to the group as a whole. Examples of such questions included:

"How could you, as men, show respect for your partners?"

"If you all believed that your partners were equal to you, how would your behaviour be different?"

Fostering group cohesion through the promotion of an active and involved group process, including the use of challenging questions, was, therefore, considered an important aspect of the Confronting Abusive Beliefs programme. Group interactions were considered to be essential supplements to specific interventions by the co-therapists.

FEMALE AND MALE THERAPY TEAM

A female and male co-therapy team was considered essential, given abusive men's beliefs in their own centrality, superiority and deservedness. While these beliefs were most strongly evident in relation to their female partners, they often were extended to women in general. The presence of a female therapist in the group frequently resulted in vivid demonstrations of these beliefs as men chose to either ignore or disparage the female therapist's interventions. Without the presence of a female therapist, these abusive beliefs might not have become as clearly evident. Furthermore, female therapists tended to be more attuned to abusive behaviours towards women, and thus were better placed to confront men with beliefs underlying their actions.

The benefits of a female co-therapist were noted by the men in the programme and included comments such as:

"There is something about a male culture that gets broken down when you have a female intruder (sic), you know, a certain aspect of keeping it between us guys."

"The female leader embodied for us a female presence that represented our partner. She was more credibly able to raise questions about how our behaviour affected our partner."

The presence of a female therapist, therefore, made it more difficult for men to dismiss or ignore the consequences of their actions on their partners and on women generally. Furthermore, her presence made it possible for men to engage in egalitarian interactions with a woman, receive reinforcement for these behaviours, and receive support for extending such interactions to their own intimate relationships.

Women's participation in men's groups that aim to increase men's responsibility for their own behaviour can be viewed as a paradox. It has been argued that men alone should take responsibility for their behaviour, and women should not feel responsible, yet again, for dealing with relationship issues. However, it is clear that abusive men's beliefs in centrality, superiority and deservedness can be maintained quite comfortably in many segments of present-day society unless a female perspective intrudes. Given the pervasiveness and dominance of male belief systems, it is unlikely that much change can be engendered without a female protest, on either an individual or a group basis.

CONFRONTING ABUSIVE BELIEFS
PROGRAMME STRUCTURE

The Confronting Abusive Beliefs programme consisted of 12 weekly group sessions of $2\frac{1}{2}$ hours' duration. All sessions—excluding the first and last, which were devoted to introduction and termination issues—had a similar structure. Each session aimed at providing a balance between individual self-disclosures, group interaction, and introduction of new concepts by therapists. The format for sessions included a check-in by each group member in turn, presentation of new concepts ideally in response to disclosed material during check-in, group discussion of material presented, and a check-out by each member in turn.

The checking-in and checking-out processes played an important role in ensuring participation by all members of the group. The check-in process also assisted in monitoring the beliefs and behaviours of each group member as they discussed the events of the past week. Group cohesion was fostered as men began to identify with each other's experiences during these processes. In monitoring beliefs implicit in men's statements, the therapists could choose to confront them during the check-in, note them as topics for further discussion, and/or use the examples in introducing basic programme concepts.

Basic programme concepts considered necessary for understanding and altering beliefs included definition of abuse and respect; definition of beliefs; self-monitoring to increase awareness of beliefs; abusive and respectful relationship beliefs; consequences of beliefs; beliefs and conflict management; beliefs and dependence/independence; and integration of respectful beliefs in a redefined belief system.

EVALUATION OF THE CONFRONTING ABUSIVE BELIEFS PROGRAMME

To determine the effectiveness of Confronting Abusive Beliefs group therapy, a comparative study of two contrasting approaches was developed. Anger Management treatment, based on a skill deficit theory of abuse, was contrasted with Confronting Abusive Beliefs, based on belief-systems theory. Both programmes were of 12 weeks' duration and men were randomly assigned from the intake list of a large, metropolitan family services agency. Both the Anger Management and Confronting Abusive Beliefs programmes were led by female–male therapist teams, each respectively trained in the group approach they were providing.

A total of 48 abusive men were recruited for the study, as were 28 female partners. The men and women were followed from pre-programme to one year later. Men's levels of physical and psychological abuse were reported by both the men and their partners at four points in the study: pre-therapy, post-therapy, three-month follow-up and one-year follow-up. Men's levels of depression, as self-reported by the men, were also monitored at all four intervals.

Results indicated that both group therapy programmes resulted in significant decreases in levels of physical and psychological abuse, as reported by the men and their partners, and in men's levels of depression, from before treatment to after treatment. These significant decreases were maintained through both follow-up intervals. At one-year follow-up, however, results were only obtained from 17 men and 9 partners. No significant differences between the two treatment programmes were observed.

The conclusion reached, therefore, was that for this particular group of men, belief confrontation therapy was as effective as anger management therapy. The lack of significant differences between the programmes may have resulted from the common message provided by all therapists that abuse of women was unacceptable and should be replaced by respect. Previous studies have indicated that successful treatment is associated with increased convergence between client and therapist beliefs (Beutler & Bergan, 1991). It may have been the case in the current instance that all therapists were conveying respectful relationship beliefs, and regardless of programme content, the conveyance of these beliefs was responsible for significant changes observed in all the men.

Given the particular constellation of men in the study—namely, men who were primarily only abusive towards their partners and voluntarily sought treatment—it may be that belief confrontation is an approach that works particularly well with this population. The effectiveness of this approach with other populations is yet to be determined.

TYPOLOGIES OF ABUSIVE MEN

A number of studies have been conducted in an effort to determine whether reliable and valid typologies of abusive men could be established that might increase effectiveness of therapy through participant-treatment matching. A review of such typologies reveals that the three descriptive dimension that have been used in constructing typologies include severity of marital violence, generality of the violence and psychopathology/personality disorder. Furthermore, these dimensions generally resulted in three subtypes of batterers: family only, dysphoric/borderline, and generally violent/antisocial (Holtzworth-Munroe & Stuart, 1994).

Inasmuch as belief-confrontation therapy specifically addresses beliefs held about women, and particularly the female partner, it could be expected that Confronting Abusive Beliefs would be most effective with family-only abusers. Neither the generally violent/antisocial nor the dysphoric/borderline abusers have typically been found to respond well to short-term interventions (Dutton et al., 1997). The family-only abuser, therefore, may be the subtype most amenable to belief confrontation approaches.

TREATMENT ATTRITION

Dropping-out of treatment has been a frequently noted problem with wife abuse programmes, whether attendance was voluntary or court-ordered (Hamby, 1998). Programmes have been found to vary markedly in rates of completion, with one survey of 30 programmes finding that half reported completion rates of 50% or less (Gondolf, 1990).

In terms of programme evaluation, therefore, success rates are likely to be inflated, given that men who find the treatment ineffectual or problematic are likely to terminate prematurely. In belief-confrontation programmes, for example, the process of self-examination of beliefs and of confrontation of abusive beliefs may result in premature termination if a man is unprepared for such a process. The results of the present evaluation, therefore, were limited to those men who were ready and prepared for belief examination. In the future, information provided to prospective participants about the nature of the group, particularly about the belief confrontation component, may be one way of further increasing the match between men who can benefit from the programme and those who are less likely to do so.

BELIEF CHANGE IN WIFE ABUSERS

Can men who have been abusing their wives effectively change their behaviour to become non-abusive and respectful without undergoing some examination and alteration of their beliefs? That was the question that spurred the development of a belief-confrontation model of wife abuse treatment. Present evidence suggests that development of non-abusive or respectful behaviour is accompanied by changes in beliefs. Anecdotal evidence suggests that behaviour change that is not accompanied by change in belief systems may result in only superficial change or reduction of physical abuse without amelioration of psychological abuse.

Will belief change that is fostered in group programmes for abusive men be supported in the larger social context? It is unlikely that individual change alone will change the sociocultural milieu that still provides support for abusive behaviours. Individual belief change must be coupled with belief change at a societal level if we are to achieve respectful relationships between men and women that will put an end to abuse.

REFERENCES

Ball-Rokeach, S. J., Rokeach, M. & Grube, J. (1984) *The Great American Values Test: Influencing Behaviour and Belief through Television.* New York, NY: Free Press.

Berk, R. A. (1993) What the scientific evidence shows: On the average, we can do no better than arrest. In R. J. Gelles & D. R. Loseke (Eds.) *Current Controversies on Family Violence* (pp. 323–336). Newbury Park, CA: Sage.

Beutler, L. E. & Bergan, J. (1991) Value change in counseling and psychotherapy. *Journal of Counseling Psychology, 38*, 16–24.

Bowker, L. H. (1983) *Beating Wife Beating.* Lexington, MA: Lexington Books.

Buzawa, E. S. & Buzawa, C. G. (1993) The scientific evidence is not conclusive: Arrest is no panacea. In R. J. Gelles & D. R. Loseke (Eds.) *Current Controversies on Family Violence* (pp. 337–356). Newbury Park, CA: Sage.

Campbell, J. C. & Soeken, K. (1999) Women's responses to battering over time: An analysis of change. *Journal of Interpersonal Violence, 14*, 21–40.

Canadian Centre for Justice Statistics (1987) *Homicide in Canada 1987: A Statistical Perspective.* Ottawa, ON: Ministry of Supply and Services.

Davis, L. V. (1984) Beliefs of service providers about abused women and abusing men. *Social Work, 29*, 243–250.

Dobash, R. E. & Dobash, R. P. (1998) Violent men and violent contexts. In R. E. Dobash & R. P. Dobash (Eds.) *Rethinking Violence against Women* (pp. 141–168). Thousand Oaks, CA: Sage.

Dobash, R. P., Dobash, R. E., Cavanagh, K. & Lewis, R. (1996) Re-education programmes for violent men: An evaluation. *Home Office Research and Statistics Directorate, Research Findings No. 46.* London: Home Office.

Dutton, D. G. (1985) An ecologically nested theory of male violence toward intimates. *International Journal of Women's Studies, 8*, 404–413.

Dutton, D. G. (1986) Wife assaulters' explanations for assault: The neutralization of self-punishment. *Canadian Journal of Behavioural Science, 18*, 381–390.

Dutton, D. G. (1988) *The Domestic Assault of Women: Psychological and Criminal Justice Perspectives.* Boston, MA: Allyn & Bacon.

Dutton, D. G., Bodnarchuk, M., Kropp, R., Hart, S. D. & Ogloff, J. P. (1997) Client personality disorders affecting wife assault post-treatment recidivism. *Violence and Victims, 12*, 37–50.

Dutton, D. G. & Starzomski, A. J. (1997) Personality predictors of the Minnesota Power and Control Wheel. *Journal of Interpersonal Violence, 12*, 70–82.

Edleson, J. F. & Tolman, R. M. (1992) *Intervention for Men who Batter.* Newbury Park, CA: Sage.

Ewing, C. P. & Aubrey, M. (1987) Battered woman and public opinion: Some realities about the myths. *Journal of Family Violence, 2*, 257–263.

Feazell, C. S., Mayers, R. S. & Deschner, J. (1984) Services for men who batter: Implications for programmes and policies. *Family Relations, 33*, 217–233.

Ganley, A. L. (1989) Integrating feminist and social learning analyses of aggression: Creating multiple models for intervention with men who batter. In P. L Caesar & L. K. Hamberger (Eds.) *Treating Men who Batter: Theory, Practice and Programmes* (pp. 196–235). New York, NY: Springer.

Gondolf, E. W. (1986) Evaluating programmes for men who batter. Problems and perspectives. *Journal of Family Violence, 3,* 95–108.

Gondolf, E. W. (1990) An exploratory survey of court-mandated batterer programmes. *Response to Victimization of Women and Children, 13,* 7–11.

Greaves, L., Hankivsky, O. & Kingston-Riechers, J. (1995) *Selected Estimates of the Costs of Violence against Women.* London, ON: University of Western Ontario Research Park.

Greenblat, C. S. (1985) "Don't hit your wife . . . unless . . . ". Preliminary findings on normative support for the use of physical force by husbands. *Victimology: An International Journal, 10,* 221–241.

Hamby, S. L. (1998). Partner violence: Prevention and intervention. In J. L. Jasinski & L. M. Williams (Eds.) *Partner Violence: A Comprehensive Review of 20 Years of Research* (pp. 210–258). Thousand Oaks, CA: Sage.

Hanson, R. K., Cadeky, O., Harris, A. & Lalonde, C. (1997) Correlates of battering among 997 men: Family history, adjustment, and attitudinal differences. *Violence and Victims, 12,* 191–208.

Harris, R. N. & Bologh, R. W. (1985) The dark side of love: Blue and white collar wife abuse. *Victimology: An International Journal, 10,* 242–252.

Holtzworth-Munroe, A. & Stuart, G. L. (1994) Typologies of male batterers: Three subtypes and the differences among them. *Psychological Bulletin, 116,* 476–497.

Jenkins, A. (1990) *Invitation to Responsibility: The Therapeutic Engagement of Men who are Violent and Abusive.* Adelaide, South Australia's Dulwich Centre.

Jouriles, E., Murphy, C.M. & O'Leary, K. D. (1989) Interspousal aggression, marital discord, and child problems. *Journal of Consulting and Clinical Psychology, 57,* 453–455.

Mirrlees-Black, C. (1999) *Domestic Violence: Findings from a New British Crime Survey Self-completion Questionnaire.* Home Office Research Study 191. London: Home Office.

Nicholas, M. (1984) *Change in the Context of Group Therapy.* New York: Brunner/Mazel.

Pence, E. & Paymar, M. (1993) *Education Groups for Men who Batter: The Duluth Model.* New York, NY: Springer.

Pirog-Good, M. & Stets-Kealy, J. (1985) Male batterers and battering prevention programmes: A national survey. *Response,* Summer, 8–12.

O'Leary, K. D., Malone, J. & Tyree, A. (1994) Physical aggression in early marriage: Pre-relationship and relationship effects. *Journal of Consulting and Clinical Psychology, 62,* 594–602.

Roberts, A. R. (1984) *Battered Women and their Families: Intervention Strategies and Treatment Programmes.* New York, NY: Springer.

Rokeach, M. (1979) *Understanding Human Values: Individual and Societal.* New York, NY: Free Press.

Rokeach, M. (1985) Inducing change and stability in belief systems and personality structures. *Journal of Social Issues, 41,* 153–171.

Rokeach, M. & Regan, J. F. (1980) The role of values in counseling situations. *Personnel and Guidance Journal, 58,* 576–583.

Rosenbaum, A. & O'Leary, K. D. (1981) Marital violence: Characteristics of abusive couples. *Journal of Consulting and Clinical Psychology, 49,* 63–76.

Russell, M. N. (1995) *Confronting Abusive Beliefs: Group Treatment for Abusive Men.* Thousand Oaks, CA: Sage.

Saunders, D. G. (1989) Cognitive-behavioural interventions with men who batter: Applications and outcomes. In P. L. Casear & L. K. Hamberger (Eds.) *Treatment of Men who Batter* (pp. 77–100). New York, NY: Springer.

Saunders, D. G. (1994) Child custody decisions in families experiencing woman abuse. *Social Work, 39,* 51–59.

Sherman, L. W. & Berk, R. A. (1984) The specific deterrent effects of arrest for domestic assault. *American Sociological Review, 49,* 261–272.

Sigler, R. T. (1989) *Domestic Violence in Context: An Assessment of Community Attitudes.* Lexington, MA: Lexington Books.

Smith, M. D. (1991) Male peer support of wife abuse: An exploratory study. *Journal of Interpersonal Violence*, 6, 512–519.

Stark, R. & McEvoy, J. M. (1970) Middle class violence. *Psychology Today*, 4, 56–65.

Statistics Canada (1993) *The Violence against Women Survey.* Ministry of Industry, Science and Technology, Ottawa, ON.

Straus, M. A. & Gelles, R. J. (1990) *Physical Violence in American Families.* New Brunswick, NJ: Transaction Books.

Sugarman, D. B. & Hotaling, G. T. (1989) Dating violence: Prevalence, context and risk markers. In A. Pirog-Good & J. E. Stets (Eds.) *Violence in Dating Relationships: Emerging Social Issues* (pp. 3–32). New York, NY: Praeger.

Tolman, R. M. (1990) *The impact of group process and outcome of groups for men who batter.* Paper presented at the European Congress on the Advancement of Behaviour Therapy, Paris.

Tolman, R. M. & Bennett, L. W. (1990) A review of quantitative research on men who batter. *Journal of Interpersonal Violence*, 5, 87–118.

Tolman, R. M. & Bhosley, G. (1991) The outcome of participation in a shelter-sponsored programme for men who batter. In K. K. Knudson & J. L. Miller (Eds.) *Abused and Battered: Social and Legal Responses to Family Violence.* New York, NY: Aldine de Gruyter.

Wolfe, D. A., Jaffe, P., Wilson, S. K. & Zak, L. (1985) Children of battered women. The relation of child behaviour to family violence and maternal stress. *Journal of Consulting and Clinical Psychology*, 53, 657–664.

Yalom, I. (1975) *The Theory and Practice of Group Psychotherapy.* New York, NY: Basic Books.

Chapter 10

RECENT DEVELOPMENTS IN THE ASSESSMENT AND TREATMENT OF SEXUAL OFFENDERS

ANTHONY BEECH[1] AND RUTH MANN[2]

[1] School of Psychology, University of Birmingham, UK
[2] Offending Behaviour Programmes Unit, HM Prison Service, London, UK

The treatment of sexual offenders first became a topic of importance in the psychological literature in the late 1960s. Initially, in the 1960s and 1970s, the treatment of choice was behavioural therapy, with a particular emphasis on changing deviant sexual arousal and developing social skills. Behavioural therapy such as aversion therapy—in various forms, including electrical aversion, noxious odours, and shame aversion—was a popular approach. In the late 1970s, most treatment programmes for sexual offenders targeted no more than deviant sexual arousal and developing "appropriate" social skills. The emphasis here was exclusively on heterosexual social skills as male homosexuality was still considered a form of sexual deviance at the time (Adams & Sturgis, 1977). Cognitive influences on behaviour therapy—emerging in mainstream psychological treatments in the mid-1970s—were probably first adopted into sexual offender treatment by Abel and colleagues (e. g. Abel, Blanchard & Becker, 1978; Abel, Becker & Cunningham-Rathner, 1984). Over the next ten years, cognitive restructuring and empathy training were introduced into sexual offender treatment programmes. A further notable influence on programme design was the adaptation of the relapse prevention approach, originally developed for substance misusers (Marlatt & Gordon, 1985), to the treatment of sexual abusers (Marques, 1982; Pithers et al., 1983). Since the mid-1980s, most treatment programmes for sexual offenders have incorporated such approaches into an integrated package, aiming to change sexual arousal, enhance social and empathy skills, restructure offence-supportive attitudes, and improve self-management through the inculcation of relapse prevention techniques (Fisher & Beech, 1999).

Offender Rehabilitation and Treatment: Effective Programmes and Policies to Reduce Re-offending. Edited by James McGuire.
© John Wiley & Sons, Ltd.

This chapter will examine recent developments in understanding and treating sexual offenders. In particular, we will review recent improvements in the theoretical understanding of sexual offending, new approaches to treating sexual offenders and the current position on treatment effectiveness.

THEORY DEVELOPMENT

Due to the fact that sex offenders are a heterogeneous group (Bickley & Beech, 2001) it would not be expected that a single model of sex offending would be sufficient to cover the range of different sex offenders. Indeed, general theories of criminal behaviour emphasise that offending is not caused by a single factor but rather is the culmination of multiple factors that influence the individual's personality and functioning (Andrews & Bonta, 1994). Theories of sexual offending have tended to focus in the past on explaining one aspect of the aetiology of sexual abuse rather than on the integration of different factors. Thus, there are separate descriptions of the development of deviant sexual preference (e. g. Laws & Marshall, 1990), biological influences (e. g. Hucker & Bain, 1990; Langevin, 1990) and the role of cultural and societal influence on sexual behaviour (e. g. Burt, 1980; Stermac, Segal & Gillis, 1990). Until the last decade there were few attempts to construct an integrated theory of sexual offending. Outlined below are the best-known attempts to develop a comprehensive approach.

Marshall and Barbaree (1990) were among the first to describe a comprehensive theory of sexual offending with their publication of an "An integrated theory of sexual offending". This theory is a mutifactorial theory in that it takes account of biological, societal, individual and situational causal factors. In brief, their theory proposed that, biologically, the sexual and aggressive drives are similar. Therefore, learning to separate and express these drives appropriately is a task of socialisation. Some boys, who are exposed to antisocial influences as a result of poor parenting in childhood and at the time of puberty, do not learn to separate these two drives. Such boys look to society for messages that support their wish to act out aggressive sexual urges—and in Western society at least, such messages are readily available in both pornography and the wider media (Baxter & Craft, 1993; Silbert & Pines, 1993). Finally, Marshall and Barbaree noted the importance of situational factors in sexual assault. They described several situational factors that would act as final disinhibitors, such as alcohol, anonymity, anger or stress. Adults predisposed to sexual offending, because of their biological, societal and individual influences, would be most likely to offend in these particular circumstances.

More recently Marshall (Marshall & Marshall, 2000) appears to place less emphasis on biological factors and more on societal, individual and situational causal factors in the aetiology of offending. Here Marshall and Marshall suggest that the origin of sexual offending behaviour lies in the poor quality of the relationship the perpetrator has had in his childhood with his primary caregivers. This may be due to a number of reasons, including sexual, emotional, physical abuse; rejection; lack of support; emotional coldness; disruptive experiences and so forth. Such poor attachment[1][*] with primary caregivers leaves the individual more open to suffer sexual abuse from others as a child, due to lack of care, vulnerability and emotional need. Marshall and Marshall proposed that such lack the self-confidence to initiate relationships with appropriate others. High levels of masturbation in adolescence, coupled with this lack of self-confidence, may lead these individuals to engage in sexual fantasies that incorporate elements of power and control and may become more deviant over time. Such fantasies and low levels of social competence lead to a "disposition to offend" and such a disposition may be acted upon if the right circumstances to offend occur, coupled with "disinhibiting factors" such as stress and alcohol.

Marshall and Barbaree's integrated theory was the first attempt to describe formally the multiple influences on sexual assault. The theory is consistent with research investigations into the backgrounds of sexual offenders, but has not been empirically tested as a whole. However, in the limitations of the theory, and in Marshall and Marshall's more recent description, the idea that there are different pathways to sexual abuse is not addressed, yet these approaches are better able to explain child abuse than other kinds of sexual offending, i.e. rape, exhibitionism (Ward & Siegert, in press). Furthermore, this theory does not clearly point to an intervention strategy for individual offenders.

A second integrated approach—the Quadripartite Model—was proposed by Hall and Hirschmann (1991). Here, four pathways to sexual abuse are described: *physiological sexual arousal* (e.g. deviant sexual preference), *cognitions* (thoughts) justifying sexual assault, *poor emotional control*, and *personality problems* (caused by developmental damage or neglect). Hall and Hirschmann note that all four components may contribute to any individual offence, but proposed that for any given offender one component was likely to be the primary pathway. This model overcomes some of the weaknesses of Marshall and Barbaree's integrated theory in that it specifies different pathways to abuse, and points more obviously to treatment strategies. However, it lacks some of the strengths of the integrated theory, in that it places less emphasis on biological, cultural and situational components of sexual offending.

Malamuth and his colleagues (e.g. Malamuth, Heavey & Linz, 1993) attempted to improve on Hall and Hirschmann's model by emphasising that factors linked to offending are confluent rather than independent. In their "Two-path Interaction Model", they proposed that two independent personality characteristics may produce sexual aggression if they converge. These characteristics are *sexual promiscuity* and *hostile masculinity*. The concept of hostile masculinity refers to "a controlling, adversarial male orientation towards females". The concept of sexual promiscuity involves an emphasis on sexual conquest as a source of self-esteem, impulsivity, and an attraction to impersonal sex and pornography. The model takes into account developmental experiences as well as adult personality characteristics, and can also be linked to societal factors such as cultural views of sex roles and sexual activity. The strength of Malamuth's model lies in its empirical basis in that it has

---

[*] Notes are presented at the end of the chapter.

been created and tested on the basis of empirical data. However, the model has only been tested on self-reported sexually aggressive college students, rather than convicted offenders. Furthermore, it is only offered as an explanation for sexual abuse against adult women and is not intended to explain child abuse.

Ward has recently published critiques of Hall and Hirschman's and Marshall and Barbaree's models[2] (Ward, in press-b, in press-c), and presented a theory of sexual assault which attempts to integrate the best parts of these theories into what they term "a comprehensive aetiological theory" (Ward & Siegert, in press). Here it is suggested that the four pathways described by Hall and Hirschmann (1991) are not separate pathways to sexual abuse, but are mechanisms of which all four can be represented in any offence. In this model the "personality problems" pathway of Hall and Hirschman has been redefined as "intimacy deficits". Ward and Siegert suggest that in any given offence it is likely that one mechanism is more strongly activated than the others. A fifth pathway involved activation of all four mechanisms equally strongly. In a particular advance on the other theories, Ward and Siegert propose that certain types of offender are likely to show different primary mechanisms. For instance, an individual who has strong paedophilic tendencies, according to this model, would be likely to follow the multiple mechanisms pathway. Hence such an individual would demonstrate sexual preference for children, belief systems supporting sex with children, lack of interest in intimacy with adults, and positive emotion in the context of offending.

While the theory of Ward and Siegert represents some advancement over the previous theories, it still has its limitations. First, it is only proposed as a theory of child molestation. Second, it is an untested theory, and until its utility and applicability have been empirically established, it cannot be regarded as superior to previous theories. However, testing of this model should be relatively straightforward, especially as the four mechanisms proposed relate directly to the following risk domains, which are, respectively, levels of: [deviant] sexual interests, distorted attitudes, socio-affective functioning, and self-management. These have recently been identified by dynamic risk assessment projects in Canada and the UK (Beech, 1998a, 1998b; Hanson & Harris, 2001; Thornton, 2002).

Each of the theories described above has strengths and each model has contributed significantly to our understanding of sexual assault. The models are not mutually exclusive theories and there is considerable overlap between them. However, some problems remain outstanding. Can one theory of sexual abuse explain both child molestation and sexual offending against adults? Is intervention with individual offenders sufficient to prevent further offending? Which factors—biological, developmental, psychological, cultural, situational—are most crucial to the commission of an offence? How can a theory of sexual offending be tested?

One of the reasons why we have devoted a section of this chapter to reviewing theories of sexual assault is because of our concern that many treatment programmes for sexual offenders are not based on any underlying theory/model of offending. It is our contention that a treatment programme that does not consider current theories and aetiology of offending may address irrelevant or ill-chosen treatment goals. As such, any programme without a core understanding of the aetiology and sexual offence process may not actually reduce the risk of further offending.

An example of such a programme is described by Pithers (1997), in which un-supervised therapists began to develop their own theories of sexual offending and related treatment needs. Therapists in the programme began to focus on encouraging offenders to "revivify emotions associated with their own abuse" (p. 38). We would argue that such a treatment goal would not have been created if an underlying theory of offending was clearly understood by all therapists. As a result of this new and irrelevant goal being established, therapists began behaving in ways which Pithers described as "denigrating to the client, rather than fostering change in beliefs and behaviour" (p. 36).

NEW DEVELOPMENTS IN RESEARCH AND TREATMENT

Cognitive Distortions

A common term in the sexual offender literature is "cognitive distortion" (Abel et al., 1989; Murphy, 1990). Reduction of cognitive distortions (i.e. thinking errors) has also been seen as one of the primary goals of cognitive-behavioural treatment (Beckett, 1994, 1998; Marshall, Anderson & Fernandez, 1999). The term originates from cognitive therapy where it was originally used to refer to "idiosyncratic thought content indicative of distorted or unrealistic conceptualisations" (Beck, 1963, p. 324). The first author to establish usage of the term with sexual offenders was Abel (Abel et al., 1989, p. 134) who defined cognitive distortions as referring to:

> An individual's internal processes, including the justifications, perceptions, and judgements used by the sex offender to rationalise his child molestation behaviour…[which] appear to allow the offender to justify his ongoing sexual abuse of children without the anxiety, guilt and loss of self esteem that would usually result from an individual committing behaviours contrary to the norms of society.

However, despite its common use in research and treatment it seems to us that, to date, there are several problems in definition, measurement and approaches to treatment of cognitive distortions.

In terms of definition

- Cognitive distortion is a term that has suffered from a variety of definitions and unclear or inconsistent usage. For example, in the Abel et al. definition, it is not clear whether the term means that offenders consciously employ excuses and justifications in order to reduce the level to which they are vilified by others; or whether cognitive distortions are unconscious processes adopted to protect the offender from shame and guilt (or both).
- It is unclear whether cognitive distortions, such as attitudes supporting sexual abuse, are part of the same process as justifications and excuses and at what stage in the offence process these factors are pertinent. Abel et al. (1989) and Murphy (1990) both emphasised that cognitive distortions play a *maintenance* function, not a causal function, in offending. By contrast Finkelhor (1984), in his descriptive

model of the sexual abuse process, describes "overcoming internal inhibitions" via the process of excuse-making as a step that takes place *before offending*. Research by Beckett et al. (1994) would suggest that there is some evidence that cognitive distortions are more than merely post-hoc rationalisations for offending. These authors found that child abusers with high levels of cognitive distortions about children's sexuality generally showed reductions in levels of denial and minimisation related to their offending (i.e. they were no longer justifying and minimising their offending after treatment) regardless of whether their levels of cognitive distortions had reduced after treatment.[3] Fisher and Beech (1998), in their model of treatment for sexual offenders, place a clear distinction between excuses and justifications, which they see as the first aspect of offender problems that need to be addressed in treatment, and cognitive distortions which they see (as per Finkelhor, 1984) as part of a set of deep-rooted pro-offending attitudes. However, there has been little other investigation into the relationship between excuses for particular offences and more enduring attitudes supporting sexual offending, with perhaps the exception of Gudjonsson and his colleagues (Gudjonsson, 1990; Blumenthal, Gudjonsson & Burns 1999). Gudjonsson (1990) found a highly significant correlation between external attributions for offending and offence-supportive attitudes in a group of 25 paedophiles. In their follow-up study, Blumenthal, Gudjonsson and Burns (1999) found a positive association between attitudes supportive of rape and external attributions for their own offence among rapists. However, in a second study (which used a different measure of offence supportive attitudes) there was no correlation between child abuse supportive beliefs and external attributions for child molesters.

In terms of measurement

- Research has so far failed to distinguish between cognitive structures (such as schemas), cognitive processes, and cognitive output (situation-specific thoughts or beliefs). In summing up the problem of measurement, Neidigh and Kropp (1992) note that, "Idiosyncratic rationalisations may represent the offender's automatic thoughts or self-talk [but] they are not necessarily representative of the offender's deeper beliefs or attitudes" (p. 211).
- Despite some thorough reviews describing these problems and spanning almost ten years (e.g. Segal & Stermac, 1990; Ward et al., 1997; Drieschener & Lange, 1999), most of the research into cognitive factors in sexual offending has not gone beyond attitude measurement. There are fundamental problems with the measurement of distorted attitudes by questionnaire, in that attitudinal scales designed for this purpose, such as the Abel and Becker Cognitive Distortions Scale (Abel et al., 1984) and the Bumby MOLEST scale (Bumby, 1996) are transparent if not brutally direct in their content. By their very nature they sensitise respondents to a set of attitudes that are so socially unacceptable as to be immediately denied (Horley & Quinsey, 1994). As these scales are scored on a continuum of 1–5, respondents tend to score in the upper range of the scale (representing strong disagreement with the items), indicating that socially desirable rather than genuine answers are given by the respondents (Swaffer et al., 1999). This

has raised the question of whether it is possible to construct an unbiased scale (Langevin, 1991).
- Although considerable research has focused on measuring attitudes of sexual offenders, the only consistent finding is that beliefs supporting child sexual abuse are more strongly held by child molesters than by other groups of offenders or non-offenders (e.g. Abel et al., 1989; Stermac & Segal, 1989; Bumby, 1996; Fisher, Beech & Browne, 1999).
- There have been no consistent findings to date of distorted attitudes related to rape among rapists as compared to non-offenders.

In terms of treatment
- With respect to psychological change and readjustment, in the general attribution theory literature, excuse making for misdemeanours (employing external, variable, specific attributions) is seen as an adaptive process which improves functioning and subsequent effort to change (e.g. Snyder & Higgins, 1988). Therefore this is thought to be worth encouraging. In the sex offender literature, on the other hand, excuses for offending are seen as unacceptable responses which need to be discouraged and replaced with internal, stable, global attributions of cause and responsibility-taking (e.g. McCaghy, 1968; Loza & Clements, 1991).
- In some studies, any causal statement offered by a sexual offender to explain his offending has been categorised as an excuse or justification (e.g. Scully & Marolla, 1984). The act of trying to find an explanation for an offence is therefore a potential minefield for the offender.

Despite these uncertainties, most treatment programmes for sexual offenders concentrate on cognitive restructuring of offence-supportive attitudes, and overcoming excuses and justifications for offending. For instance, in an influential clinical text describing "best practice" sex offender treatment in the 1980s, it was noted that the primary purpose of a sex offender group is "to identify and confront cognitive distortions, rationalisations and excuses for offending" (Salter, 1988, p. 114). More recently, Marshall, Anderson and Fernandez (1999), after describing the limitations of the current research as above, conclude that "We are persuaded that cognitive distortions of one kind or another need to be addressed in treatment" (p. 69). However, theories of the relationship between cognition and behaviour (e.g. the social cognition model, cognitive therapy theory) would indicate a certain danger in focusing solely on cognitive products, such as excuses or beliefs.

Ward (Ward & Keenan, 1999) has been one of the few to provide a rigorous definition of the nature of cognitive distortions. His central suggestion is that cognitive distortions arise from a set of core schema held by the offender. In effect, these underlying schema generate the cognitive distortions that are measured at the surface level (Ward et al., 1997). Ward then suggests that these schemas are in effect "implicit theories" that the offender has about the world. Such theories are similar to scientific explanations in that they are used to understand, predict and interpret interpersonal phenomena. Ward and Keenan (1999) identify five such implicit theories that can collectively account for the majority of the specific types of distortions found in child abusers.

- *Children as sexual beings.* Here an offender has an implicit theory or schema in which children are perceived as having the capacity to, and wanting to, engage in sexual activity and being able to consent to, and not be harmed by, any sexual contact with adults. Here also is the idea that the existence of sexual desires is "natural, benign and harmless". In addressing this, we would suggest that Ward has perhaps identified the core schema of extrafamilial child abusers.
- *Entitlement.* This form of implicit theory is characterised by a type of thinking in which the offender considers that he is superior to, and more important than, others. Therefore, he sees himself as being entitled to have sex when he wants from those who are less powerful/less important than himself. We would suggest that this is the kind of implicit theory that is more likely to be held by the type of incest offender who also physically abuses his children and commits domestic assaults against his partner.
- *Nature of harm.* The main aspect of this schema is an assumption that sexual activity does not cause harm and may in fact be beneficial. The offender will also tell himself that there are degrees of harm and that, provided the offender does not inflict any serious physical damage, then little harm is caused.
- *Dangerous world.* Here the content of the implicit theory is that the world is a dangerous place in which others are abusive and rejecting. Therefore, the offender will tell himself (a) that it is important to fight back and achieve control over others and (b) that children are less likely to be abusive and rejecting and hence are more likely to be able to give him what he needs (sex and affection).
- *Uncontrollable.* In this schema, according to Ward, the offender perceives the world as uncontrollable. This implicit theory may have its roots in the offender being abused as a child or being exposed to other traumatic events. The types of distortions that arise out of this implicit theory relate to offences that are beyond the offender's control.

Empirical evidence for Ward's idea—i.e. that there is a higher order structure of cognitive distortions—has been found by Thornton (personal communication, November 1993). In a factor analysis of Beckett's Children and Sex Scale (1987), Thornton identified factors that can be seen to map clearly onto three of Ward's implicit theories:

- *Children as sexually knowing*—a factor which has content that is similar to Ward's "Children as sexual beings" implicit theory;
- *Harmless sex*—a factor which appears to be very similar to Ward's "Nature of harm" implicit theory;
- *Emotional congruence*—a factor which appears to be similar to Ward's "dangerous world" implicit theory.[4]

Examples of cognitive distortions in child abusers described separately by Ward and by Beckett (1987), which they have both depicted as commonly occurring in

Table 10.1 Examples of commonly held cognitive distortions in abusers and their relationship to implicit theories/deviant schemas

---

Children as sexual beings/Children as sexually knowing
Children often initiate sex and know what they want (W)
Children enjoy sexual contact with adults (W)
Sex is good for children (W)
Children know a lot about sex (B)
Children can lead adults on (B)

Entitlement
People do what I tell them and that includes sex (W)
If I don't do it someone else will, so it might as well be me (W)
A person should have sex whenever it is needed (W)
I'm just providing sex education (W)

Nature of harm/Harmless sex
Sex between a child and an adult is not harmful (W)
Many children who are sexually assaulted do not experience any major problems (W)
There is nothing wrong with sexual contact between children and adults (B)
Most sexual contact between adults and children does not cause any harm (B)

Dangerous world/Emotional congruence with children
You can't trust adults (W)
Children can give adults more acceptance and love than other adults (W)
Children stop me feeling lonely (B)
I prefer to spend my time with children (B)

Uncontrollable
A lot of times sexual assaults are not planned they just happened (W)
I was high on drugs or alcohol at the time (W)
A lot of sexual assaults are not planned they just happen (W)
I did it because I was sexually abused as a child (W)

W—cognitive distortions reported by Ward et al. (1997)
B—cognitive distortions reported by Beckett (1987)

child abusers, are given in Table 10.1, with an indication of how these relate to both the Ward implicit theories and Thornton's factor analysis.

Schema-based Therapy

We would suggest that the failure to address, in treatment, underlying cognitive schemas or implicit theories leaves an offender as open to future processing errors as he ever was. Changing one previously held situation-specific cognitive distortion (e.g. "I was entitled to sex with her") does not automatically lead to changes in enduring underlying entitlement beliefs (e.g. "I am entitled to take what I want in life"). Consequently, the offender whose schemas are not altered in treatment may be at no less risk of producing offence-justifying beliefs in the future, even if his justifications for past offending have been successfully challenged.

We would suggest that the current state of the art in this aspect of sexual offender treatment should extend beyond confronting offenders about their excuses and justifications for offending. More sophisticated cognitive therapy techniques should be used to enable offenders to identify patterns of beliefs and attitudes and to overcome the dysfunctional self-talk associated with these schemas. The targets for this work should include offence-justifying attitudes, but should also involve dysfunctional views of self and others—structures which, if left unchanged, would continue to lead to distorted interpretations of ambiguous or threatening situations in the future.

The present second author and Jo Shingler have developed such a schema-based treatment programme for high-risk sexual offenders in the English and Welsh Prison Service. In this programme, which is offered to offenders following completion of a standard offence-focused treatment intervention, participants are encouraged to identify lifelong dysfunctional thinking patterns (schemas) which have, in part, contributed to their offending. Common themes have emerged from this work, such as entitlement, need for respect and control, vengefulness, and resentfulness of a victim stance (Mann & Shingler, 1999). Using cognitive therapy techniques, these schemas are examined and deconstructed, and group participants, in role-play exercises, practise managing such schema-related thinking using various techniques including "disputing" and "cognitive restructuring".

Relapse Prevention

As we have noted earlier, the past 20 years has seen the development of a comprehensive cognitive-behavioural approach to the treatment of sexual abusers. Incorporated into this model has been a strong emphasis on relapse prevention (RP: Pithers et al., 1983). The RP approach in essence requires offenders to identify potential "high-risk situations" and other possible threats to avoidance of re-offending. When these have been effectively identified, the appropriate self-management skill can be developed in treatment to prevent relapse (Beech & Fisher, 2000; Laws, 1999; Pithers et al., 1983).

However, concern has been expressed about the way that the RP description of further sexual offending has been so uncritically accepted in the literature (Laws, 1999; Laws, Hudson & Ward, 2000; Eccles & Marshall, 1999). There has been some criticism of both the original, generic, model of RP developed by Marlatt (1982), and the adapted version of the model proposed by Pithers et al. (1983) for use with sex offenders (e.g. Laws et al., 2000; Ward & Hudson, 1996). Specifically, Ward and Hudson argue that the original Pithers model contains only a single process of how sex offenders go on to commit further sexual offences. Specifically, the RP model, when applied to sexual offending, indicates that re-offending occurs largely because of skills deficits and emphasises negative moods and/or adverse life events as the major precursors of relapse. Ward and Hudson argue that by placing particular emphasis on poor coping strategies and negative emotional states as the major precursors to offending, the model fails to consider situations in which individuals consciously decide to engage in sexually abusive behaviour. Ward's theoretical leap forward from this (Ward et al., 1995), and one that has strong face validity in the light of clinical observation (see Eldridge, 1998), is that although some offences are associated with "self-regulatory failure", others involve careful and systematic planning, accompanied by positive emotional states in the perpetrator.[5]

Consequently, it has been suggested that an adequate model of the offence process needs to account for this diversity in pathways to offending, and to accommodate individuals whose firmly entrenched beliefs about the legitimacy of sexual contact with children lead them to experience positive emotions during the offence process (Bickley & Beech, 2002). Here, we can draw upon Ward and Hudson's (1998) framework in which such a multiple pathway model of the sexual offence process is proposed. This model incorporates concepts from self-regulation research and describes the ways in which offenders control and direct their own actions. What is also useful about this model is that it describes both the initial offence process and any pathways to relapse. This "self-regulation" model has been developed using a grounded theory approach based on 26 incarcerated child abusers' own accounts of their offences. Ward and Hudson suggest that, based on such accounts, it is possible to identify clear patterns in the behaviour of sexual offenders. They further claim that it is possible to classify offenders according to one of four different routes to offending. These groups are defined by the individual offender's goal towards deviant sex (approach or avoidant), and the selection of strategies designed to achieve the desired goal (active or passive). Table 10.2 briefly summarises each of the four pathways.[6]

Bickley and Beech (2002) have tested out this model with a group of 88 child abusers and found that it can be reliably employed in terms of classification, both in terms of the approach/avoidant and active/passive dimensions.

- Approach-goal abusers were found to have high levels of "globalised" cognitive distortions regarding children. This type of offender was generally found to have offended outside, or inside and outside, the family and to have offended against boys or against both sexes.
- Avoidant-goal offenders were found to be like "low deviance" men. They were generally found to be married or in a long-term relationship at the time of the offence, to have their own children, and to have offended against girls.

Table 10.2 Summary of the four pathways proposed by the self-regulation model[*]

Pathway	Self-regulatory style	Description
Avoidant-passive	Under-regulation	Desire to avoid sexual offending but lacking the coping skills to prevent it from happening
Avoidant-active	Mis-regulation	Direct attempt to control deviant thoughts and fantasies but use of ineffective or counterproductive strategies
Approach-automatic	Under-regulation	Over-learned sexual scripts for offending, impulsive and poorly planned behaviour
Approach-explicit	Effective-regulation	Desire to sexually offend and the use of careful planning to execute offences, harmful goals concerning sexual offending

[*]Table reported in Bickley and Beech (2002).

- Men who were classified as taking a passive pathway in terms of *offence operandi* were more likely to blame external circumstances for their offending, and were more likely—compared to active pathway offenders—to have a previous conviction for a sexual offence.

Thus, a thorough understanding of the specific deficits and behaviours exhibited by offenders following each of the four pathways may provide a more effective foundation for treatment, rather than assume that all men follow the same pathway when offending. It is probably too early to comment on the impact that this approach may have, but it can be seen as an advance on the view that all offenders follow the same path to relapse and a new offence.

Bickley and Beech (2002) suggest that by assessing the type of goal and the self-regulatory deficits an individual possesses, the clinician can tailor an appropriate treatment plan to suit the offender's need. For example, interventions for child abusers who have an approach goal should focus on their entrenched beliefs about the appropriateness of sexual contact with children, by developing awareness of the harm caused to victims. In contrast, Bickley and Beech suggest that avoidant goal offenders are likely to need less emphasis on the challenge of such distorted thinking, with more input on the development of appropriate strategies to deal with threats to their restraint goal (i.e. in high-risk situations).

Self-regulation deficiencies on the other hand, such as under-control or mis-regulation, highlight markedly different treatment needs. These include: work on impulse control; mood management; problem-solving and strategy selection; and coping with unexpected high-risk situations (Bickley & Beech, in press). The aim of targeting these areas should be to aid the offender in taking greater responsibility for his actions, developing appropriate coping responses (e.g. assertiveness), and increasing self-efficacy beliefs about dealing with possible high-risk situations.

Matching Offenders to Treatment

There are now well-established principles in treatment programmes for offenders. Although there is popular support for the idea of "the more treatment the better" (Beckett et al., 1994) treatment designers should also take into account the knowledge that not all offenders are equal in terms of risk. For example, men who abuse boys are more likely to recidivate than men who abuse girls. Men who abuse outside the family are more likely to recidivate than incest offenders. The greater the variety in the age and gender of victims, the higher the rate of recidivism (Abel et al., 1988).

Therefore in terms of identifying need for treatment, measuring an offender's risk level would appear to be a good starting point. A great deal of work has taken place in developing risk prediction instruments for sexual offenders including, for example, the *Sex Offence Risk Appraisal Guide* (Quinsey et al., 1998); *Static-99*[7] (Hanson & Thornton, 2000); or the *Sexual Violence Scale* (Boer et al., 1997). Although these instruments have some face validity as measures of the need for treatment and of the intensity of pre-treatment problems, outcome studies have rarely reported[8] offenders' response to treatment according to risk level based on such instruments.

One exception is the study by Friendship, Mann and Beech (submitted), which reported the relationship between risk level and re-conviction of sex offenders who have completed the core Sex Offender Treatment Programme (SOTP) currently run in 26 UK prisons. Here Friendship et al. found that high-risk men appeared more difficult to treat than low-risk men. Specifically, 26% (13 out of 50) of high-risk men (as rated on *Static-99*, Hanson & Thornton, 2000) who had been through the programme had been re-convicted for sexual, or violent, offences within two years of leaving prison compared to 2% (5 out of 263) of low-risk men.[9]

However, static risk prediction instruments, such as the *Static-99*, are still fairly crude measures of pre-treatment problems and do not take into account dynamic factors, factors which have previously identified as amenable to change (Fisher & Beech, 1998; Marshall, Anderson & Fernandez, 1999). Recently there has been a move in the UK to assess treatment need in much greater detail. To date this has been most fully developed in terms of psychological characteristics, and criminogenic needs or dynamic factors originally by Beech (1998a, 1998b) and expanded by Thornton (2002).

In terms of criminogenic needs, those areas most commonly targeted in cognitive-behavioural treatment are pro-offending attitudes (e.g. perceiving children as willing to actively engage in sex with adults, lack of insight into the effects of abuse, emotional fixation on children), and socio-affective deficits (e.g. under-assertiveness, low self-esteem and emotional loneliness). The approach taken by Beech (1998b) has involved the development of a classification system for child abusers according to their level of pre-treatment problems based on a battery of psychological measures. Here two main type of child abuser have been identified which have been termed "high deviancy" and "low deviancy" in terms of differences between groups on a number of psychological measures. It should be noted that the definition of deviancy here relates to how different the scores of these measures are from scores of the relevant measures from men who are not sex offenders.

High-deviancy men, according to this system, are defined as having a high level of treatment need as they have high levels of pre-treatment problems. For example, they have been found to have significantly higher levels of cognitive distortions than non-offender controls (Fisher, Beech & Browne, 1999). Fisher and colleagues also found that this group have significantly poorer empathy for victims of sexual abuse than non-offenders. Other significant differences between high-deviancy men, and non-offenders, indicated that they reported difficulty in forming intimate adult attachments, while perceiving that their emotional needs could be better met by interacting with children rather than adults. Members of this group were also found to be significantly more under-assertive and to have significantly lower levels of self-esteem than non-offenders.

Low-deviancy men, according to the same system, are defined as having a lower level of treatment need than high-deviancy men. Fisher and colleagues (1999) found that this group did not have generalised cognitive distortions about children. In addition, they did not show the high levels of emotional identification with children seen in high deviancy men. On the contrary, emotional identification with children in this group was found to be significantly lower than non-offender controls (Fisher, Beech & Browne, 1999). This result probably contributed in part to their denial about future risk to children. Fisher and colleagues found that this group again showed significantly higher levels of social inadequacy problems than non-offenders, but this was not as marked as that found in high-deviancy men. Low-deviancy men, like the other group, were found to have poor empathy for their victims.

Evidence for the usefulness of this categorisation is also found when comparing the offence histories of men in these two groups: high-deviancy men, compared to low-deviancy men, were found to have significantly more victims, were more likely to have a previous conviction for a sexual offence, were more likely to have committed offences outside the family, and were more likely to have committed offences against boys. Low-deviancy men, compared to high-deviancy men, were found significantly more likely to be incest offenders, i.e. to have committed offences against their daughters or stepdaughters.

An argument might be made here that the high-deviancy/low-deviancy distinction is simply a renaming of paedophilic/incest distinctions previously articulated in the literature, using alternative terminology such as: fixated versus regressed (Groth, 1978); preferential versus situational (Howells, 1981); or high and low fixation (Knight & Prentky, 1990). However, it should be noted that nearly a third of the men who would be identified as regressed or situational perpetrators in such classifications (and would by definition be treated as low risk) were found to be classified as high-deviancy in this system. This provides a more subtle indication of dynamic risks or criminogenic needs than that obtained by examination of offence histories alone (static risk prediction).

We have recently reported a study (Beech, Erikson & Friendship, 2001; Beech et al., 2002) in which the relationship to re-conviction level of both static and dynamic risk has been taken into consideration.[10] This study was a six-year follow-up of men who had undergone community-based treatment in the UK in the early 1990s. Table 10.3 shows re-conviction level by static risk level (lower, low–medium, medium–high and high risk levels on the basis of Static-99) and Deviancy (high/low).

Although this is small study, it can be seen from Table 10.3 that re-conviction was predicted by static and historical factors and by dynamic risks, both making independent contributions to the prediction of sexual recidivism.

The deviance distinction has had an influence in the development of treatment programmes in the UK both in probation and prison settings, due to the finding

Table 10.3   Re-conviction rates in Static-99 risk and deviance categories

	Total (Sample)	Static-99			
		High risk	Medium–high risk	Medium–low risk	Lower risk
High Deviance	7/23 (30%)	2/4 (50%)	4/9 (44%)	0/2 (0%)	1/8 (13%)
Low Deviance	1/30 (4%)	0/1 (0%)	0/4 (0%)	0/6 (0%)	1/19 (5%)
Total Sample	8/53 (15%)	2/5 (40%)	4/13 (31%)	0/8 (0%)	2/27 (7%)

Table 10.4 Coding rules for allocating individuals to longer or shorter treatment

- Rapists should be automatically allocated to longer treatment.
- Those scoring as *High Risk* or *Very High Risk* on Risk Matrix 2000 should be automatically allocated to longer treatment.
- Those scoring as *High Deviance* should be allocated to longer treatment.
- Those identified as *Low Deviance* but who are also identified as being in high levels of denial about their offending behaviour (as identified by a dissimulating profile on the *Multiphasic Sex Inventory* and/or exhibiting impression management or self-deception on the *Balanced Inventory of Desirable Responding*) should be considered for longer treatment.

that high-deviancy child abusers require twice as many hours of treatment as do low-deviancy child abusers in order for a "treatment effect" to be shown (Beech, Fisher & Beckett, 1999). Such a finding obviously has implications for treatment, as it is important not to waste resources by either providing offenders with more input than they probably need, or by delivering treatment with little or no impact because it is not sufficient for the offender's problems. With reference to the accredited programmes for sex offenders in probation services in England Wales, [11] the rules for allocation to longer (200 + hours) or shorter treatment (around 100 hours) are shown in Table 10.4.

It can be seen from Table 10.4 that those with the most severe problems, as indicated by high scores on the more recent measure of static risk (*Risk-Matrix 2000*, developed by Thornton et al., submitted), and/or rated as high deviance, and/or in high levels of denial about their offences,[12] will be allocated the longest version of treatment available at the present time.

Similarly, in the English and Welsh Prison Service it was found that an earlier shorter version of the Core Sex Offender Treatment Programme, which involved about 80 hours of treatment, worked equally well with low-deviancy/low-risk offenders as compared to the more recent version which is a 180-hour programme (Beech, Fisher & Beckett, 1999). It has also been found that even the 180-hour programme had negligible impact on the highest risk/highest deviant offenders (Beech, Fisher & Beckett, 1999; Friendship, Mann & Beech, submitted). As a result, a shorter rolling programme of treatment has been introduced for the low-risk/low-deviancy group in the Prison Service, with an additional extended treatment programme (of around 140 hours) added to the core treatment programme for high-risk/high-deviancy men. Treatment provision is now matched to levels of risk and deviance in the Prison Service according to the criteria set out in Table 10.5.

The dynamic risk or criminogenic need classification system is somewhat different from the psychometric classification developed by Beech (1998b) which is used in the probation service. Here Thornton's *Structured Risk Assessment* (SRA) procedure is used. This involves both a static risk assessment (Thornton et al., submitted) and the ideographic assessment of four domains of dynamic risk which he has identified as indices of treatment need (Thornton, 2002):

1. Deviant sexual interest
2. Pro-offending attitudes
3. Socio-affective problems
4. Self-management problems.

Table 10.5   Allocation to treatment by static and dynamic risk level in the English and Welsh Prison Service (approximate hours of treatment indicated in brackets)

Static risk level[†]□	Dynamic risk level[*]□		
	Low	Medium	High
Low	Rolling programme (c. 100 hours[‡])	Rolling programme (c. 100 hours)	Rolling or core (100–180 hours)
Medium	Rolling or core (100–180 hours)	Core programme (c. 180 hours)	Core (c. 180 hours)
High	Core + extended (c. 320 hours)	Core + extended (c. 320 hours)	Core + extended (c. 320 hours)
Very high	Core + extended (c. 320 hours)	Core + extended (c. 320 hours)	Core + extended (c. 320 hours)

[*]Static risk is meassured by RM2000 (Thornton, 2002)—an update of Static-99 (Hanson & Thornton, 2000) standardised on British data.
[†]Dynamic risk is measured by Structured Risk Assessment (Thornton, 2002).
[‡]This figure is dependent upon the successful completion of each "assignment" for each individual and therefore could be a lot longer if individuals do not reach necessary criteria straightaway.

Considerable overlap can be seen between the systems in that domains 2 and 3 are essentially the same as the deviancy domains reported by Beech (1998a, 1998b). However, the SRA system is more wide-ranging than a purely psychometric assessment of treatment need. Conversely, the SRA is a more complex procedure to complete and requires considerable historical and clinical information before the level of treatment need can be fully determined. Psychometric scores which relate to the SRA domains have yet to be established.

Treatment Style

Treatment style has been an important empirical issue in the general psychotherapy literature, but was not addressed in the sexual offender treatment field until the late 1990s. Sex offender therapists have instead based their approach on received clinical wisdom, which has rather emphasised the importance of confrontation. For instance, Salter (1988) wrote that "... the group must be confrontative. Language that minimises the offence should not be tolerated ... Offenders should not be allowed to say they 'had intercourse with'; instead they should be required to say 'I raped so and so with my finger and with my penis'" (p. 114). The message was therefore one of a rather punitive, rule-bound treatment ethos.

In contrast, in the general psychotherapy literature, three core conditions of therapeutic style are agreed to be crucial to successful therapy—genuineness, empathic understanding and warmth (Rogers, 1980)—and in groupwork specifically, group cohesion is agreed to be a necessary component of a successful group (e.g. Yalom, 1975).

Marshall et al. (in press) have recently published a full review of aspects of therapy style and process issues which should be considered in sexual offender treatment. In addition to the three core conditions already mentioned, they emphasise the importance of respect, support, confidence, emotional responsivity, self-disclosure, open-ended questioning, flexibility, use of positive reinforcement, and use of humour. Negative therapist features to be avoided include confrontation, low interest, and expression of anger or hostility. The effects of these different therapist behaviours have been extensively documented in general psychotherapy research. It is surprising, therefore, that there has been so little empirical research into the process aspects of sexual offender treatment.

Beech and Fordham (1997) studied group environment in sex offender treatment groups using the Group Environment Scale (Moos, 1986). The study examined 12 sex offender groups, eight of which took place in community settings and four in a long-term residential facility, all in the United Kingdom. They found a range of treatment climates across these groups, particularly in terms of cohesion, emotional expressiveness, independence, task orientation, anger/aggression and order/organisation. The most successful group in the study (defined in terms of clinical change of participants) rated highly on cohesion, leader support, independence and order/organisation, and had a low rating on leader control. The least successful group showed low ratings on cohesion, independence and leader support, and a high rating on leader control. Based on these data, Beech and Fordham (1997, p. 234) conclude that successful sex offender group leaders should "set a clear structure and set of rules for the group, they should not be aggressively confrontational, but be supportive and model effective interpersonal interactions ... Leaders should be aware that if the group experience is too confrontational, members' ability to benefit will be impaired."

In a follow-up study, Beech, Fisher and Beckett (1999) used the GES to study 12 groups run in HM Prison Service of England and Wales. These groups were all cognitive-behavioural in orientation and had a relapse prevention focus. In this study, Beech and co-workers defined the clinical success of each group in terms of abandonment of pro-offending attitudes. In examining the relationship between therapeutic climate and clinical success, they adjusted for group length, prior deviance levels and prior levels of denial. Again, a very clear effect for group climate was observed, with cohesion being identified as the most important attribute of the group for successful treatment effect.

Further research on treatment style, again using data from the HM Prison Service Sex Offender Treatment Programme (SOTP), was conducted by Fernandez (1999). In this study, videotapes of sex offender groups were studied and rating scales were developed to measure therapist techniques and therapist style. Ratings were then related to clinical change measured by pre- and post-treatment psychometric testing, and by in-session behaviours by the group members. The therapist techniques measured were centred around three core skills: encouraging active participation, non-confrontational challenge and use of open questions. Aspects of therapist style measured included warmth, empathy, genuineness, hostility, coldness and deception. Dependent variables in this study were in-session behaviours by clients, such as level of participation in the treatment sessions and verbalisations indicating that clients took responsibility for their offending behaviour. Psychometric measures of perspective-taking, acceptance of future risk, knowledge of coping strategies, and self-esteem were also examined. Fernandez found that taking responsibility by clients was linked to warm, empathic and genuine behaviours by therapists. Group participation increased when therapists actively encouraged participation, used open questions, and challenged in a non-confrontational way. Improvements in perspective-taking were related to encouragement by therapists to participate and sincerity on the part of therapists. Acceptance of future risk was related to non-confrontational challenge and warmth/empathy/genuineness. Lastly, improvements in coping skills were related to the use of open questions by therapists. There was no relationship between changes in self-esteem and therapist behaviour.

An unpublished HM Prison Service study (Thornton, Mann & Williams, 2000) has further confirmed the general trend of these findings. This study examined differences between 30 SOTP core programme men whose therapists had been consistently warm and supportive, and 15 men who had been exposed to hostile questioning from at least one therapist. Both types of therapeutic style resulted in drastic reductions of levels of denial and minimisation in group members and in levels of offence-justifying thinking (rape myths and child offence supportive beliefs). However, the consistently warm therapists also achieved reductions in less directly targeted areas such as entitlement thinking, distrust of women, subjective personal distress and impulsiveness. A small improvement in self-reported personal adequacy was also achieved by warm therapists but not by hostile therapists.

Our conclusion from this research review is that therapists working with sexual offenders should clearly communicate respect, liking and caring for such offenders in treatment. Questions asked within this style can be challenging in their content, but not punitive, assumptive or confrontational in delivery. Sex offender treatment should rely almost entirely on positive reinforcement as its main change agent. These sentiments are clearly in agreement with the recommended approach for rehabilitation of general (i.e. non-sexual) offenders (Andrews & Bonta, 1994).

ISSUES IN WORKING WITH SEXUAL OFFENDERS

In this section, we address some issues of programme design and management that are not solely to do with content or process of sexual offender treatment. Because there has been so little written about some of these areas, there is often little empirical work to draw on. Below, we describe some of the treatment practices in which we have been involved in the English and Welsh Prison Service, in the hope that such descriptions will lead to independent research and testing of the ideas forwarded.

Matching Programmes to Responsivity

The responsivity principle states that treatment programmes should be geared to offenders' abilities and learning styles. In the broadest sense, this is taken to mean that rehabilitation programmes in criminal justice settings should be based on cognitive-behavioural/social learning principles. It also means, arguably, that programmes should be designed specifically for offenders who have learning disabilities, offenders from different cultural backgrounds, and offenders with personality disorders.

A particular problem arises in the treatment of sexual offenders who are classified as psychopaths (i.e. who score highly on the *Hare Psychopathy Checklist—Revised*: Hare, 1991). Although research in this area is limited, there are two studies that indicate that standard cognitive-behavioural treatment programmes are unlikely to be beneficial for psychopaths and may indeed lead to raised risk (Seto & Barbaree, 1999; Clark, 2000). At the time of writing, different jurisdictions differ in their response to this information: some exclude high-scoring psychopaths from treatment; some limit their influence to one such personality per group; and some take no account of psychopathy scores. In our opinion, if such men are not to be excluded from treatment, the therapists charged with treating them must receive additional training and supervision. Furthermore, high-scoring individuals, who apparently benefit from a programme, should be evaluated with caution. Another option is to develop new programmes especially designed to address the kinds of deficits observed in those with high scores on psychopathy assessments. Such work is currently underway under the aegis of the recent UK initiatives concerning Dangerousness and Severe Personality Disorders (Home Office/Department of Health, 1999).

Engaging Offenders in Assessment and Treatment

In some ways, sexual offenders are quite different from general psychotherapy clients. Often, sexual offenders enter treatment because they are mandated to do so, not through free choice. Furthermore, whereas general psychotherapy clients are usually motivated to change due to being distressed by some psychological state, sexual offenders often enjoy their offending and are not motivated to change. In addition, the stigma and vilification experienced by sexual offenders from the rest of society is unparalleled, so that in treatment they may be extremely sensitive to indications of labelling, hostility or lack of empathy by therapists. If treatment providers fail to take these dynamics into account, the value of treatment may be lessened.

In trying to address these issues, the experiences of those working in the substance misuse field are extremely helpful. In this field also, many therapists in the past tended to focus on confrontation and neglect the emphasis on empathy. Motivational Interviewing (Miller & Rollnick, 1991)—an approach originally developed for use with alcohol and drug abusers—has since been applied to all kinds of psychological issues. There is little empirical evaluation of motivational interviewing—in the forensic field, one controlled evaluation of motivational interviewing with substance abusers incarcerated in Canada (Ginsburg, 2000) and one case study of a sexual offender (Mann & Rollnick, 1995). There is, however, enthusiastic use of this technique in many correctional settings (Mann, Ginsburg & Weekes, in press). Motivational interviewing is in essence an orientation towards therapeutic work as much as it is a set of techniques, and it encourages sex offender treatment providers to consider their approach to their clients as well as specifying some helpful ways in which motivation and engagement can be enhanced.

Another area where motivation and engagement could be considered more carefully is the arena of risk assessment. When risk assessment procedures are reported in the literature, they are implicitly described as procedures "done to an offender" rather than "done with him". There is a danger that this kind of approach places a barrier between the offender and those assessing him, so that he feels disengaged from any helping process that might follow. Given that risk assessment is such a rapidly developing science, and it is now generally thought that therapists should engage in risk assessment as well as treatment, it seems important to consider ways in which the offender could be engaged and motivated in this aspect of his care. For example, in the Correctional Service of Canada's national sex offender programme (Yates, Goguen & Nicholaichuk, 2000) the items in a dynamic risk assessment procedure are shared within the treatment group, and each group member discusses and decides which items apply to him. Alternatively, some clinicians are enthusiastically engaging in 'collaborative risk assessment' (Mann & Shingler, 2001). This process draws on the motivational interviewing literature and the cognitive therapy principle of collaboration, and emphasises the benefits to the offender of an accurate risk assessment. The language of risk assessment is changed to emphasise need rather than risk, and the object of the process is to agree treatment goals rather than to report on predicted level of risk. This chimes in with Ward's ideas (Ward & Stewart, submitted) that treatment should be about treating human need rather than entirely focusing on criminogenic need.

Another important aspect of motivation and engagement is to consider the phrasing of treatment goals. Most people make more effort in an activity if they believe the outcome will enhance their lives in some way. Satisfaction is even higher if the outcome seems fairly easily achievable, and results happen quite quickly. Within the social psychological literature, there is a substantial body of evidence concerned with the study of motivation and goals. One essential finding indicates that approach goals (goals that people strive towards) are more motivational than avoidance goals (activities from which people strive to refrain). This finding has some interesting applications to sexual offender treatment. For instance, relapse prevention by definition is seen to embody an avoidance goal—the avoidance of relapse. Mann (2000) has described in more detail what an approach-oriented programme would look like. For example, an approach-oriented programme would encourage offenders to specify their desired outcomes in approach terms, such as, "to live a satisfying life that respects the rights of others". This goal is incompatible with offending, but also sounds more attractive and inspiring to the offender than "live a life that avoids offending".

Therapist Selection, Training, Support and Supervision

There has been little written about the qualities that should be looked for in an effective sexual offender therapist. What is written is more in the form of opinion than based on research evidence. Marshall et al.'s review of therapist characteristics, referred to above, contained a list of desirable qualities such as warmth, empathic ability, emotional expressiveness and confidence. Mann (2001) listed four essential qualities for an effective therapist, based on experience of training and supervising sex offender treatment providers: positive attitudes towards sexual offenders, self-evaluating approach, an enquiring mind, and a warm interpersonal style.

Even less has been written about how therapists should be trained. In North America, most therapists working with sexual offenders are trained through psychology or social work traditions, and undertake general study and training followed by a treatment internship. In the United Kingdom, sexual offender therapists tend to be either psychologists, probation officers or prison officers. HM Prison Service provides residential training for staff working on the national Sex Offender Treatment Programme, and the Probation Service is planning to follow suit imminently. Both services have accepted that comprehensive introductory training is essential when introducing trainee therapists to a structured sex offender programme, even if the trainees have previous experience of working with sexual offenders. Potential tutors are assessed on a range of competencies, based on research findings reported by Sacre (1995). The range of competencies covers the following areas: understanding of cognitive-behavioural theory and concepts; application of cognitive-behavioural techniques; warmth and empathy; impartiality; clear use of language; flexibility of style; discussion leading and presentation skills; team working; agenda skills; skills for giving feedback; questioning skills; maintenance of boundaries; tenacity; professionalism; preparation; participation and open coping style; and openness to feedback. Having been selected on the basis of these competencies they must then successfully complete the national training course. Staff are also expected to attend additional update course units on specific topics.

The underlying rationale here is to ensure that all therapists adhere to the same style and work towards the same goals. In the Prison Service, the introductory training covers theories of offending, treatment style, major methods of change (Socratic questioning, pro-social modelling, positive reinforcement), and the goals of sex offender treatment. This course is followed by programme-specific training that introduces therapists to the goals and methods of the particular treatment programme they are to facilitate.

Maintaining Treatment Integrity

Programme drift (Hollin, 1995; Johnson, 1981) is the term for what happens when therapists drift away from the declared aims of an intervention programme. Programme non-compliance (Hollin, 1995) is the term for the situation when the practitioners start changing the programme, omitting some bits and adding new material, as they see fit. When these processes are unchecked, programme effectiveness diminishes. Pithers (1997) provides a cautionary tale about the results of programme drift and non-compliance.

Managers of treatment programmes should ensure that they incorporate both supervision and monitoring into the programme schedule, to guard against programme drift. Supervision also allows therapists to improve in confidence and competence and to resolve uncertainties, resulting in more sophisticated programme delivery. Monitoring, which may involve a supervisor or consultant attending a treatment session or watching a tape of a session is also essential for correctional programming especially when it is organised on a large scale. Monitoring should in particular focus on three areas: adherence to the treatment manual, therapist style, and use of therapeutic techniques (modelling, positive reinforcement and cognitive restructuring). As a result of monitoring, formative feedback can be provided to therapists, recognising skill that exists and directing therapists towards goals for improvement.

TREATMENT EFFECTIVENESS

Finally, we address the question of whether treatment works. As we have said earlier, cognitive-behavioural therapy is now the dominant approach used in North America (Marshall, Anderson & Fernandez, 1999) and in the UK (Beckett, 1998, Fisher, Grubin & Perkins, 1998) for the treatment of sexual offenders. Although there are some studies supporting the effectiveness of cognitive-behavioural therapy (Alexander, 1999; Nicholaichuk et al., 2000), other studies have found this approach has had little impact on recidivism rates (e.g. Marques, 1998). The variability across studies may be linked to inadequate methods for evaluating offenders and inadequate methods for measuring the impact of treatment. To take these points separately:

- Although many studies report the relationship between risk and re-conviction, few report the responsivity to treatment of those at different risk levels.
- In a number of re-conviction studies, there is an implicit assumption that all offenders who have been through treatment have actually benefited from treatment. This is an assumption that would hardly seem credible when any type of psychological therapy is considered, especially when treating those who may not actually want treatment but are entering a programme for other reasons, such as to improve chances of parole.

Therefore, failure to take into account that fact that sex offenders have different levels of treatment need and may not all totally respond to any type of treatment given, would seem to reduce the likelihood of demonstrating that treatment works. We would argue that it is necessary to work out who is responding to treatment in order both to demonstrate that the treatment is effective as well as identifying those with whom treatment does not work. A study reported by Friendship, Mann and Beech (submitted), is one of the few to have considered offenders with differing levels of problems (as measured by static risk level) who have been through treatment, and compared to those who have not. This study used as its outcome measure any re-conviction for a sexual or violent offence over a two-year period after release from prison. Table 10.6 shows the results.

It is clear from Table 10.6 that if just overall scores are considered the treatment does not look markedly effective as compared with no treatment (4.6%

Table 10.6 Two-year sexual and/or violent re-conviction rates for treatment and comparison groups by Static-99 risk category

Risk category	Treatment group (N = 647)	Comparison group (N = 1910)
Low	1.9% (5/263)	2.6% (24/969)
Medium–low	2.7% (6/225)	12.7% (83/655)
Medium–high	5.5% (6/109)	13.5% (31/229)
High	26.0% (13/50)	28.1% (16/57)
Total sample	4.6% (30/647)	8% (154/1910)

compared to 8%). However, when differing risk levels are considered it is clear that treatment is having a strong impact on the medium–low and medium–high risk levels in terms of reductions in re-conviction rates in the treated compared to untreated samples. Further, it can also be seen that, for the high-risk group, treatment is appearing at the present time to have little impact. As the men in this study mainly went through a short period of treatment, this supports the view that high-risk men need longer treatment. It should additionally be noted that it is difficult to use re-conviction as a measure in low-risk men, given that rates of re-conviction are typically very low even in the untreated group. Finally, this study did not take into account deviance levels. Any future studies should use measures of both static and dynamic risk levels to test the responsiveness to treatment of these groups, and should include a measure of psychological responsivity to treatment.

The Beech, Erikson and Friendship (2001) study (reported earlier in Table 10.3), which addressed the relationship between static and dynamic risks and their relationship to re-conviction over a six-year period, also included a method of measuring treatment responsivity and how this related to re-conviction. The method employed used psychometric analysis to measure whether treatment had produced significant decreases in pro-offending attitudes. The analysis was done on a case-by-case basis using a methodology called clinically significant change (for details see Beech, Fisher & Beckett, 1999). Basically this is a measure of whether changes on attitudinal scales are sufficient to reach a predefined minimum 'score' on the group of measures concerned. In general, it was the men who were judged as "not responding to treatment" who were more likely to be re-convicted with 23% (6 out of 26) being re-convicted for a sexual offence compared to 10% (2 out of 21) of the men judged as benefiting from treatment.

However, in this study it was found that it was difficult to disentangle treatment change from the pre-treatment level of problems. Treatment appeared to work better with low-deviancy men (0% re-convicted compared to 10% in the untreated group) than with high-deviancy men, where approximately one-third re-offended regardless of how they responded to treatment. This result perhaps suggests that the treatment for the high-deviancy offenders did not persist as well as for the low-deviancy offenders.

It is difficult to draw too many conclusions from relatively small-scale projects, but the results of this and the study by Friendship and co-workers suggest that there is evidence that those at differing levels of risk and criminogenic need respond differently to treatment. In the not-too-distant past, the short answer to treatment for high-risk/highly deviant men has been "the more treatment the better" (Beckett et al., 1994). The more complete answer has been implemented in the Prison Service with the addition of the schema-based programme described earlier (Mann & Shingler, 1999). This programme adds to a conventional offence-focused programme for highly deviant men by helping them to gain a deeper understanding of their patterns of thoughts, feelings, sexual arousal and behaviours, by recognising dysfunctional patterns in these areas and by learning ways of taking control of such patterns when they recur. In the future more may need to be done to tailor programmes carefully to human needs than to have an exclusive focus on criminogenic needs (Ward & Stewart, submitted).

CONCLUSIONS

In this chapter we have attempted to document the advances in our understanding of the treatment of sexual offenders since the mid-1990s, by exploring how new elements have become integrated into comprehensive programmes, and how some key issues and assumptions are being re-examined. Therefore, we have outlined what is currently seen to be the "state-of-the-art" in sexual offender treatment. However, sexual offender treatment, like Disney World, is a project that will never be finished. What we describe as best practice today is likely to be outdated and even derided in 20 or 30 years. We suggest that this constant search for better understanding and more effective practice is an attitude that all those working in the field of sexual abuse should seek to maintain.

NOTES

1. Attachment as a concept is a big issue in itself. For a review of attachment style in sex offenders see Ward, Hudson, Marshall and Siegert (1995).
2. Ward (in press-a) has also critically assessed an earlier model of sexual offending by Finkelhor (1984). Space precludes a discussion of this earlier theory.
3. As measured by the Children and Sex Questionnaire (Beckett, 1987).
4. A fourth factor termed *Socially skilled with children* was also identified in the Thornton analysis. This factor does not map immediately onto the Ward model.
5. Here we should note the Eldridge was probably the first to make the distinction clinically between those with "continuous" (associated with belief systems that legitimise their behaviours) or "inhibited cycles" (associated with regulatory failure).
6. It should be pointed out that the pathways approach has been worked out with child abusers. Polaschek et al. (2001) have described a model of pathways in rapists offence process, but this has not been empirically tested as yet.
7. Static–99 is not an acronym: it was devised in 1999 and is based on items from Karl Hanson's Rapid Risk Assessment for Sexual Offense Recidivism (RRASOR, Hanson, 1997) and Thornton's Structured Anchored Risk Assessment Judgement (SACJ, reported in Grubin, 1998).
8. Surely this is a glaring omission in that static risk gives the clinician/researcher/treatment provider, at the most a basic level, an indication of the offender's problems.
9. Further information from this outcome study is shown in Table 10.5.
10. Based on a methodology reported by Allam (2000).
11. These programmes having been set as part of the UK Government's "What Works" initiative.
12. This again being seen as block to successful treatment (Beech, Fisher & Beckett, 1999).

REFERENCES

Abel, G. G., Becker, J. V. & Cunningham-Rathner, J. (1984) Complications, consent and cognitions in sex between children and adults. *International Journal of Law and Psychiatry, 7*, 89–103.

Abel, G. G., Blanchard, G. T. & Becker, J. (1978) An integrated treatment program for rapists. In R. Rada (Ed.) *Clinical Aspects of the Rapist* (pp. 161–214). New York: Grune & Stratton.

Abel, G. G., Gore, D. K., Holland, C. L., Camp, N., Becker, J. V. & Rathner, J. (1989) The measurement of the cognitive distortions of child molesters. *Annals of Sex Research, 2*, 135–152.

Abel, G. G., Becker, J. V., Cunningham-Rathner, J., Mittelman, M. S. & Rouleau, J. L. (1988) Multiple paraphilic diagnoses among sex offenders. *Bulletin of the American Academy of Psychiatry and the Law, 16*, 153–168.

Adams, H. E. & Sturgis, E. T. (1977) Status of behavioral re-orientation techniques in the modification of homosexuality: A review. *Psychological Bulletin, 84*, 1171–1188.

Alexander, M. A. (1999) Sexual offender treatment efficacy revisited. *Sexual Abuse: A Journal of Research and Treatment, 11*, 101–116.

Allam, J. (2000) *Community-based treatment for child sex offenders: An evaluation.* Unpublished doctoral dissertation. University of Birmingham, Edgbaston, Birmingham, UK.

Andrews, D. A. & Bonta, J. (1994) *The Psychology of Criminal Conduct.* Cincinnati: Anderson.

Beck, A. T. (1963) Thinking and depression: I: Idiosyncratic content and cognitive distortions. *Archives of General Psychiatry, 9*, 324–333.

Beckett, R. C. (1987) *Children and Sex Scale.* Available from Richard Beckett, Room FF39, The Oxford Clinic, Littlemore Health Centre, Sanford Rd., Littlemore, Oxford

Beckett, R. C. (1994) Cognitive behavioural treatment for men who sexually assault children. In T. Morrison, M. Erooga & R. C. Beckett (Eds.) *Sexual Offending against Children* (pp. 80–101). London: Routledge.

Beckett, R. C. (1998). Community treatment in the UK. In W. L. Marshall, S. M. Hudson, T. Ward & Y. M. Fernandez (Eds.) *Sourcebook of Treatment Programs for Sexual Offenders* (pp. 133–152). New York: Plenum Press.

Beckett, R. C., Beech, A. R., Fisher, D. & Fordham, A. S. (1994). Community-based treatment for sex offenders: An evaluation of seven treatment programmes. *Home Office Occasional Report.* Available from Home Office Publications Unit, 50, Queen Anne's Gate, London, SW1 9AT, England.

Beech, A. R. (1998a) A psychometric typology of child abusers. *International Journal of Offender Therapy and Comparative Criminology, 42*, 319–339.

Beech, A. R. (1998b) Towards a psychometric typology for assessing pretreatment level of problems in child abusers. *Journal of Sexual Aggression, 3*, 24–38.

Beech, A. R., Erikson, M. & Friendship, C. (2001) A six-year follow-up of men going through representative probation based sex offender treatment programmes. *Home Office Research Findings, 144*, 1–4. http://www.homeoffice.gov.uk/rds/pdfs/r144.pdf

Beech, A. R., Erikson, M., Friendship, C. & Hanson, R. K. (2002). Static and dynamic predictors of reconviction. *Sexual Abuse: A Journal of Research and Treatment, 14*, 153–165.

Beech, A. R. & Fisher, D. D. (2000) Maintaining relapse prevention skills and strategies in treated child abusers. In D. R. Laws (Ed.) *Remaking Relapse Prevention* (pp. 455–465). London: Sage.

Beech, A. R., Fisher, D. & Beckett, R. C. (1999) An evaluation of the Prison Sex Offender Treatment Programme. *U.K. Home Office Occasional Report.* Available from Home Office Publications Unit, 50, Queen Anne's Gate, London, SW1 9AT. http://www.homeoffice.gov.uk/rds/pdfs/occ-step3.pdf

Beech, A. & Fordham, A. S. (1997) Therapeutic climate of sexual offender treatment programs. *Sexual Abuse: A Journal of Research and Treatment, 9*, 219–237.

Bickley, J. & Beech, A. R. (2001) Classifying child abusers: Its relevance to theory and clinical practice. *International Journal of Offender Therapy and Comparative Criminology, 45*, 51–69.

Bickley, J. & Beech, A. R. (2002) An empirical investigation of the Ward and Hudson self-regulation model of the sexual offence process with child abusers. *Journal of Interpersonal Violence, 17*, 371–393.

Bickley, J. & Beech, A. R. (in press). Identifying pathways in the offending process of child molesters: Implications for treatment of the Ward and Hudson model. *Sexual Abuse: A Journal of Research and Treatment.*

Blumenthal, S., Gudjonsson, G. & Burns, J. (1999) Cognitive distortions and blame attribution in sex offenders against adults and children. *Child Abuse and Neglect, 23*, 129–143.

Boer, D., Hart, S., Kropp, R. & Webster, C. D. (1997) *Manual for the Sexual Violence Risk-20.* The Mental Health, Law and Policy Institute and the Simon Fraser University, Vancouver, B.C.

Bumby, K. (1996) Assessing the cognitive distortions of child molesters and rapists. Development and validation of the RAPE and MOLEST scales. *Sexual Abuse: A Journal of Research and Treatment, 8,* 37–54.

Burt, M. R. (1980) Cultural myths and support for rape. *Journal of Personality and Social Psychology, 38,* 217–130.

Clark, D. (2000) The use of the Hare PCL-R to predict offending and institutional misconduct in the English Prison system. *Prison Research and Development Bulletin, 9,* 10–14.

Baxter, T. & Craft, N. (1993) There are better ways of taking care of Erent Easton Ellis than censoring him. In D. E. H. Russell (Ed.) *Making Violence Sexy: Feminist Views on Pornography* (pp. 245–253). Buckingham: Open University Press.

Drieschener, K. & Lange, A. (1999) A review of cognitive factors in the etiology of rape: Theories, empirical studies and implications. *Clinical Psychology Review, 19,* 57–77.

Eccles, A. & Marshall, W. L. (1999) Relapse prevention. In W. L. Marshall, D. Anderson & Y. M. Fernandez (Eds.) *Cognitive Behavioural Treatment of Sexual Offenders* (pp. 127–146). Chichester: Wiley.

Eldridge, H. (1998) *Therapist Guide for Maintaining Change: Relapse Prevention for Adult Male Perpetrators of Child Sexual Abuse.* London: Sage.

Fernandez, Y. M. (1999) *Reliable identification of therapist features.* Paper presented at the 18th Annual Conference for the Treatment of Sexual Abusers, Orlando, Florida.

Finkelhor, D. (1984) *Child Sexual Abuse: New Theory and Research.* New York: Free Press.

Fisher, D. D. & Beech, A. R. (1998) Reconstituting families after sexual abuse: The offender's perspective. *Child Abuse Review, 7,* 420–434.

Fisher, D. D. & Beech, A. R. (1999) Current practice in Britain with sexual offenders. *Journal of Interpersonal Violence, 14,* 233–249.

Fisher, D., Beech, A. R. & Browne, K. D. (1999) Comparison of sex offenders to non-offenders on selected psychological measures. *International Journal of Offender Therapy and Comparative Criminology, 43,* 473–491.

Fisher, D., Grubin, D. & Perkins, D. (1998) Working with sexual offenders psychiatric settings in England and Wales. In W. L. Marshall, Y. M. Fernandez, S. M. Hudson & T. Ward (Eds.) *Sourcebook of Treatment Programs for Sexual Offenders* (pp. 191–201). New York: Plenum Press.

Friendship, C., Mann, R. E. & Beech, A. (submitted). Evaluation of a national prison-based treatment programme for sexual offenders in England and Wales.

Gudjonsson, G. H. (1990) Cognitive distortions and blame attributions among paedophiles. *Sexual and Marital Therapy, 5,* 183–185.

Ginsburg, J. I. D. (2000) *Using motivational interviewing to enhance treatment readiness in offenders with symptoms of alcohol dependence.* Unpublished doctoral dissertation, Carleton University, Ottawa, Canada.

Groth, A. N. (1978) Patterns of sexual assault against children and adolescents. In A. W. Burgess, A. N. Groth, L. L. Holstrom & S. M. Groi (Eds.) *Sexual Assault of Children and Adolescents* (pp. 3–24). Boston: Heath.

Grubin, D. (1998) Sex offending against children: Understanding the risk. *Police Research Series, Paper 99.* Available from the Research and Statistics Directorate, Home Office, 50 Queen Anne's Gate, London, SW1H 9AT, England.

Hall, G. C. N. & Hirschmann, R. (1991) Toward a theory of sexual aggression: A quadripartite model. *Journal of Consulting and Clinical Psychology, 59,* 662–669.

Hanson, R. K. (1997). *The development of a brief actuarial risk scale for sexual offense recidivism.* User Report 1997–04. Ottawa: Department of the Solicitor General of Canada.

Hanson, R. K. (2001) *Sex Offender Need Assessment Rating (SONAR).* Available from: www.sgc.gc.ca/epub/corr/e200001a/e200001b/e200001b.htm

Hanson, R. K. & Harris, A. J. R. (2001) A structured approach to evaluating change among sexual offenders. *Sexual Abuse: A Journal of Research and Treatment, 13,* 105–122.

Hanson, R. K. & Thornton, D. (2000) Improving risk assessments for sex offenders: A comparison of three actuarial scales. *Law and Human Behaviour, 24,* 119–136.

Hare, R. D. (1991) *Manual for the Revised Psychopathy Checklist*. Toronto: Multi-Health Systems.

Hucker, S. J. & Bain, J. (1990) Androgenic hormones and sexual assault. In W. L. Marshall, H. E. Barbaree & D. R. Laws (Eds.) *Handbook of Sexual Assault: Issues, Theories and Treatment of the Offender* (pp. 209–229). New York: Plenum Press.

Hollin, C. (1995) The meaning and implications of "programme integrity". In J. McGuire (Ed.), *What Works: Reducing Reoffending*. Chichester: Wiley.

Home Office/Department of Health (1999) *Managing People with Severe Personality Disorder*. London: Department of Health.

Horley, J. & Quinsey, V. L. (1994) Assessing the cognitions of child molesters: Use of the semantic differential with incarcerated offenders. *The Journal of Sex Research, 31*, 171–178.

Howells, K. (1981) Adult sexual interest in children: Considerations relevant to theories of etiology. In M. Cook & K. Howells (Eds.) *Adult Sexual Interest in Children* (pp. 55–94). London: Academic Press.

Hucker, S. J. & Bain, J. (1990) Androgenic hormones and sexual assault. In W. L. Marshall, H. E. Barbaree & D. R. Laws (Eds.) *Handbook of Sexual Assault: Issues, Theories and Treatment of the Offender* (pp. 93–102). New York: Plenum Press.

Johnston, L. & Ward, T. (1996) Social cognition and sexual offending: A theoretical framework. *Sexual Abuse: A Journal of Research and Treatment, 8*, 55–80.

Johnson, V. S. (1981) Staff drift: A problem in treatment integrity. *Criminal Justice and Behaviour, 8*, 223–232.

Knight, R. A. & Prentky, R. A. (1990) Classifying sexual offenders: The development and corroboration of taxonomic models. In W. L. Marshall, D. R. Laws & H. E. Barbaree (Eds.) *Handbook of Sexual Assault: Issues, Theories and Treatment of the Offender* (pp. 23–53). New York: Plenum Press.

Langevin, R. (1990) Sexual anomalies and the brain. In W. L. Marshall, H. E. Barbaree & D. R. Laws (Eds.) *Handbook of Sexual Assault* (pp. 103–114). New York: Plenum Press.

Langevin, R. (1991) A note on the problem of response set in measuring cognitive distortions. *Annals of Sex Research*, 288–292.

Laws, D. R. (1999) Relapse prevention: The state of the art. *Journal of Interpersonal Violence, 14*, 285–302.

Laws, D. R., Hudson, S. M. & Ward, T. (2000) *Remaking Relapse Prevention with Sex Offenders: A Sourcebook*. Newbury Park, CA: Sage.

Laws D. R. & Marshall, W. L. (1990) A conditioning theory of the etiology and maintenance of deviant sexual preferences and behavior. In W. L. Marshall, H. E. Barbaree & D. R. Laws (Eds.) *Handbook of Sexual Assault: Issues, Theories and Treatment of the Offender* (pp. 209–230). New York: Plenum Press.

Loza,W. & Clements, P. (1991) Incarcerated alcoholics and rapists' attributions of blame for criminal acts. *Canadian Journal of Behavioural Science, 23*, 76–83.

McCaghy, C. H. (1968) Drinking and deviance disavowal: The case of child molesters. *Social Problems, 16*, 43–49.

McFall, R. M. (1990) The enhancement of social skills: An information processing analysis. In W. L. Marshall, H. E. Barbaree & D. R. Laws (Eds.) *Handbook of Sexual Assault: Issues, Theories and Treatment of the Offender* (pp. 311–330). New York: Plenum Press.

Malamuth, N. M., Heavey, C. L. & Linz, D. (1993) Predicting men's antisocial behaviour against women: The interaction model of sexual aggression. In G. C. N. Hall, R. Hirschmann, J. R. Graham & M. S. Zaragoza (Eds.) *Sexual Aggression: Issues in theEtiology, Assessment and Treatment* (pp. 63–97). Washington, DC: Taylor & Francis.

Mann, R. E. (2000) Managing resistance and rebellion in relapse prevention intervention. In D. R. Laws, S. M. Hudson & T. Ward (Eds.) *Remaking Relapse Prevention with Sex Offenders: A Sourcebook* (pp. 187–200). Thousand Oaks, CA: Sage.

Mann, R. E. (2001, April). *Implementing and managing sex offender treatment programmes*. Paper presented at the Conference of the International Association for Forensic Mental Health, Vancouver, BC, Canada.

Mann, R. E. & Rollnick, S. (1995) Motivational interviewing with a sex offender who believed he was innocent. *Behavior and Cognitive Psychotherapy*, 24, 127–134.

Mann, R. E. & Shingler, J. (1999) *Working with cognitive schemas*. Workshop presented at the National Organisation for the Treatment of Abusers (NOTA) Annual Conference, York, England.

Mann, R. E. & Shingler, J. (2001) *Collaborative Risk Assessment*. Workshop presented at the National Organisation for the Treatment of Abusers (NOTA) Annual Conference, Pontyprith, Wales.

Mann, R. E., Ginsburg, J. I. D. & Weekes, J. (in press). Motivational interviewing with offenders. In M. McMurran (Ed.) *Motivating Offenders to Change*. Chichester: Wiley.

Marlatt, G. A. (1982) Relapse prevention: A self-control program for the treatment of addictive behaviors. In R. B. Stuart (Ed.) *Adherence, Compliance, and Generalization in Behavioral Medicine*. New York: Brunner/Mazel.

Marlatt, G. A. & Gordon, J. R. (1985) *Relapse Prevention: Maintenance Strategies in the Treatment of Addictive Behaviours*. New York: Guilford Press.

Marques, J. K. (1982, March) *Relapse prevention: A self-control model for the treatment of sex offenders*. Paper presented at the 7th Annual Forensic Mental Health Conference, Asilomar, CA.

Marques, J. (1998) How to answer the question "Does sexual offender treatment work?". *Journal of Interpersonal Violence*, 14, 437–451.

Marshall, W. L., Anderson, D. & Fernandez, Y. M. (1999) *Cognitive Behavioural Treatment of Sexual Offenders*. Chichester: Wiley.

Marshall, W. L. & Barbaree, H. E. (1990) An integrated theory of sexual offending. In W. L. Marshall, H. E. Barbaree & D. R. Laws (Eds.) *Handbook of Sexual Assault: Issues, Theories and Treatment of the Offender* (pp. 363–388). New York: Plenum Press.

Marshall, W. L., Fernandez, Y. M., Serran, G. A., Mulloy, R., Thornton, D., Mann, R. E. & Anderson, D. (in press). Process variables in the treatment of sexual offenders: A review of the relevant literature. *Aggression and Violent Behaviour*.

Marshall, W. L. & Marshall, L. (2000) The origins of sexual offending. *Trauma, Violence and Abuse*, 1, 250–263.

Moos, R. H. (1986) *Group Environment Scale Manual*. Available from Consulting Psychologists Press Palo Alto, CA.

Miller, W. R. & Rollnick, S. (1991) *Motivational Interviewing: Preparing People to Change Addictive Behaviors*. New York: Guilford Press.

Murphy, W. D. (1990) Assessment and modification of cognitive distortions in sexual offenders. In W. L. Marshall, H. E. Barbaree & D. R. Laws (Eds.) *Handbook of Sexual Assault: Issues, Theories and Treatment of the Offender* (pp. 331–340). New York: Plenum Press.

Nicholaichuk, T., Gordon, A., Gu, D. & Wong, S. (2000) Outcome of an institutional sexual offender treatment program: A comparison between treated and matched untreated offenders. *Sexual Abuse: A Journal of Research and Treatment*, 12, 139–153.

Niedigh, L. & Krop, H. (1992) Cognitive distortions among child sexual offenders. *Journal of Sex Education and Therapy*, 18, 208–215.

Pithers, W. D. (1997) Maintaining treatment integrity with sexual abusers. *Criminal Justice and Behaviour*, 24, 34–51.

Pithers, W. D., Marques, J. K., Gibat, C. C. & Marlatt, G. A. (1983) Relapse prevention with sexual aggressors: A self-control model of treatment and maintenance of change. In J. C. Greer & I. R. Stuart (Eds.) *The Sexual Aggressor: Current Perspectives on Treatment* (pp. 214–239). New York: Van Nostrand Reinhold.

Polaschek, D. L. L., Hudson, S. M., Ward, T. & Siegert, R. (2001) A descriptive model of the offense chain in rapists. *Journal of Interpersonal Violence*, 16, 523–544.

Rice, M. E., Harris, G. T. & Courmier, C. (1992) Evaluation of a maximum security therapeutic community for psychopaths and other mentally disordered offenders. *Law and Human Behaviour*, 16, 399–412.

Rogers, C. R. (1980) *A Way of Being*. Boston: Houghton Mifflin.

Sacre, G. (1995) *Analysis of the role of tutor on the National SOTP: A competency based approach*. Unpublished M.Sc. thesis. Birkbeck College, University of London.

Salter, A. C. (1988) *Treating Child Sex Offenders and their Victims: A Practical Guide*. Newbury Park: Sage.

Scully, D. & Marolla, J. (1984) Convicted rapists' vocabulary of motive: Excuses and justifications. *Social Problems, 31*, 530–544.

Scully, D. & Marolla, J. (1985) Riding the bull at Gilley's: Convicted rapists describe the rewards of rape. *Social Problems, 32*, 251–163.

Segal, Z. V. & Stermac, L. E. (1984) A measure of rapists' attitudes towards women. *International Journal of Law and Psychiatry, 7*, 437–440.

Segal, Z. V. & Stermac, L. E. (1990) The Role of cognition in sexual assault. In W. L. Marshall, D. R. Laws & H. E. Barbaree (Eds.) *Handbook of Sexual Assault: Issues, Theories and Treatment of the Offender* (pp. 161–176). New York: Plenum Press.

Silbert, M. H. & Pines, A. M. (1993) Pornography and the sexual abuse of women. In D. E. H. Russell (Ed.) *Making Violence Sexy: Feminist Views on Pornography* (pp. 113–119). Buckingham: Open University Press.

Snyder, C. R. & Higgins, R. L. (1988) Excuses: Their effective role in the negotiation of reality. *Psychological Bulletin, 104*, 23–35.

Seto, M. & Barbaree, H. E. (1999) Psychopathy, treatment behavior and sex offender recidivism. *Journal of Interpersonal Violence, 14*, 1235–1248.

Stermac, L. E. & Segal, Z. V. (1989) Adult sexual contact with children: An examination of cognitive factors. *Behavioral Therapy, 20*, 573–584.

Stermac, L. E., Segal, Z. V. & Gillis, R. (1990) Social and cultural factors in sexual assault. In W. L. Marshall, H. E. Barbaree & D. R. Laws (Eds.) *Handbook of Sexual Assault: Issues, Theories and Treatment of the Offender* (pp. 143–160). New York: Plenum Press.

Swaffer, T., Hollin, C., Beech, A., Beckett, R. C. & Fisher, D. (1999) An exploration of child sexual abusers cognitive distortions with special reference to the role of anger. *Journal of Sexual Aggression, 4*, 31–44.

Thornton, D. (2002) Constructing and testing a framework for dynamic risk assessment. *Sexual Abuse: A Journal of Research and Treatment, 14*, 137–151.

Thornton, D., Friendship, C., Erikson, M., Mann, R. & Webster, S. (submitted). Cross-validation of a static instrument for predicting sexual recidivism.

Thornton, D., Mann, R. E. & Williams, F. M. S. (2000) *Therapeutic Style in Sex Offender Treatment*. Available from: Offending Behaviour Programmes Unit, HM Prison Service, Room 725, Abell House, John Islip St., London SW1P 4LH.

Ward, T. (in press-a) Finkelhor's precondition of child sexual abuse: A critique. *Psychology, Crime and Law*.

Ward, T. (in press-b) Marshall and Barbaree's integrated theory of child sexual abuse: A critique. *Psychology, Crime and Law*.

Ward, T. (in press-c) A critique of Hall and Hirschmann's quadripartite model of child sexual abuse. *Psychology, Crime and Law*.

Ward, T. & Hudson, S. M. (1996) Relapse prevention: A critical analysis. *Sexual Abuse: A Journal of Research and Treatment, 8*, 177–200.

Ward, T. & Hudson, S. M. (1998) A model of the relapse process in sexual offenders. *Journal of Interpersonal Violence, 13*, 700–725.

Ward, T., Hudson, S. M., Johnston, L. & Marshall, W. L. (1997) Cognitive distortions in sex offenders: An integrative review. *Clinical Psychology Review, 17*, 479–507.

Ward, T., Hudson, S., Marshall, W. & Siegert, R. (1995) Attachment style and intimacy deficits in sex offenders: A theoretical framework. *Sexual Abuse: A Journal of Research and Treatment, 7*, 317–335.

Ward, T. & Keenan, T. (1999) Child molesters' implicit theories. *Journal of Interpersonal Violence, 14*, 821–838.

Ward, T., Louden, K., Hudson, S. M. & Marshall, W. L. (1995) A descriptive model of the offence chain for child molesters. *Journal of Interpersonal Violence, 10*, 452–472.

Ward, T. & Siegert, R. J. (in press). Towards a comprehensive theory of child sexual abuse: A theory knitting perspective. *Psychology, Crime and Law*.

Ward, T. & Stewart, C. (submitted). Criminogenic needs or human needs? A theoretical critique.

Yalom, I. D. (1985) *The Theory and Practice of Group Psychotherapy* (3rd edition). New York: Basic Books.

Yates, P. M., Goguen, B. C. & Nicholaichuk, T. P. (2000) *National Sex Offender Treatment Volume II: Moderate Intensity Program*. Ottawa: Correctional Service of Canada.

Chapter 11

SERIOUS MENTAL DISORDER AND OFFENDING BEHAVIOURS

PAUL E. MULLEN

Dept. of Psychological Medicine, Monash University, Melbourne, Victoria, Australia

This chapter focuses specifically on the management of those who have serious mental disorders (such as schizophrenia) major affective disorders and delusional disorders, and who have committed criminal offences, or are believed to be at risk of such behaviour in the future. The ambit is intentionally narrow: although, in practice, the boundaries may on occasion be blurred between psychosis and the manifestations of distress and disturbance in the vulnerable and seriously personality disordered, it is nevertheless useful to consider those with ongoing severe mental illness separately.

If significant associations exist between having a serious mental disorder and the frequency of criminal activity; if those associations are mediated by modifiable variables; and if modifying those variables falls within the domain of mental health practice; then, and only then, may mental health practitioners be properly considered to have a role in the prevention, or at least the minimization, of offending behaviors in the seriously mentally disordered.

Static and essentially immutable risk factors (such as age, gender, prior history) are frequently employed to predict the probability of future offending. Static factors themselves are by definition not open to modification and tend to encourage risk management approaches which emphasize confinement or other forms of incapacitations. Dynamic risk factors (e.g. substance abuse, lack of social supports, active psychotic symptoms) in contrast can point the way to strategies which reduce the probability of offending at the same time as improving the health and functioning of the identified individual. The proper roles of health professionals are in the treatment or amelioration of disturbance and distress, not in directing agencies and processes of social control (even assuming such directions to have any social utility). Their role should be in identifying and managing those dynamic risk factors which are relevant to mental health interventions, not in offering evaluations to courts and tribunals which legitimize coercive and punitive disposals.

Offender Rehabilitation and Treatment: Effective Programmes and Policies to Reduce Re-offending. Edited by James McGuire.
© John Wiley & Sons, Ltd.

In the mental health fields risk assessment and risk management have replaced the evaluation of "dangerousness". The shift to a focus on risk assessment and management is not just a change in language. A risk factor is any state of affairs, or event, which has a significant association to a future occurrence that is of interest. It neither requires, nor assumes, a causal connection, being merely a statistical relationship. In theory, if not in practice, using the language of risk circumvents the social and moral implications of attributions such as dangerousness by adopting the mantle of the actuarial, the objective and the value free. Risk assessment, however, acquires efficacy through the move to risk management. Management, unlike assessment, requires either mechanisms to incapacitate those designated high risk, or identifying what potentially changeable factors mediate the statistical associations of risk. This returns risk management irredeemably to the realms of social and moral judgement because it necessitates choosing the outcomes that are to be pursued and the price that is to be paid, by whom and for what desired result.

This chapter will consider:

1. Whether associations have been established between serious mental disorders and offending behaviours.
2. Whether such associations are sufficiently robust to support practical risk assessment strategies.
3. What mediates between such risk factors and criminal behaviour.
4. What risk management strategies, aimed at disrupting the link between the existing vulnerabilities and subsequent criminality, would be effective and ethical.
5. How mental health practice and service delivery could be altered to give effect to such risk management strategies.

THE ASSOCIATIONS BETWEEN MENTAL DISORDERS AND OFFENDING BEHAVIOURS

Three broad strategies exist for investigating the possible association between mental disorder and offending by examining:

(a) Rates of offending in those suffering from major mentally disorder.
(b) Rates of mental disorder in offender populations.
(c) The association between offending and mental disorder established independently in community samples.

Each strategy depends on adequate methodologies for defining and ascertaining both mental disorder and offending behaviour in the target populations. They also require samples of sufficient size to provide adequate power for analysis and samples sufficiently representative to allow generalization. Though there are probably no studies that will fully satisfy the methodological pedant bent on discrediting what he does not wish to hear, there are now good enough studies in each of the three approaches delineated above. These "good enough" studies support the existence of an association between some mental disorders and some forms of offending. For the purpose of this paper only a brief overview of each research strategy with a focus on representative studies will be provided.

Rates of Offending in the Seriously Mentally Disordered

Studies have examined rates of violent and criminal behaviours in mentally disordered individuals prior to admission to hospital, while hospitalized, and following discharge in the community. Studies of large representative samples of the mentally disordered prior to the 1980s tended to demonstrate either no increase in criminal behaviours, or increases which were attributed to confounding influences such as socioeconomic status (for reviews see Monahan & Steadman, 1983; Mullen, 1984). More recent studies have painted the less reassuring picture of a clear association between at least some types of mental disorder and violent criminal behaviours (for reviews see Hodgins, 1992; Torrey, 1994; Monahan & Steadman, 1994; Mullen, 1997).

The MacArthur collaboration represents, in many ways, the most sophisticated examination to date of the relationship between having a mental disorder and violent and criminal behaviour (Steadman et al., 1998; Monahan et al., 2000). A sample of over 1000 people admitted to public psychiatric inpatient facilities in Pittsburgh, Kansas City and Worcester, Massachusetts, were extensively evaluated and followed up every 10 weeks for the year following discharge (72% completed at least three follow-up interviews). Information about their offending behaviour was derived from self-report, from a collateral informant nominated by the subject, and from clinical and official records. Overt acts of violence were ascertained to have occurred in 27.5% of participants with 22.4% revealed by the individual's self-report and official records contributing most of the additional information. Only 4.5% had an episode of violence recorded in any agency files. The nature of the identified acts of violence covered the spectrum from hitting to attacks with weapons (three subjects committed homicide) but excluded what were termed "other aggressive acts" which were primarily throwing things, pushing, shoving and slapping. Addition of these lesser forms of violence raised the percentage of perpetrators to 56%. Those with a major mental disorder, which included depression and dysthymia as well as schizophrenia and other psychotic disorders, were less likely to be overtly violent than those with other mental disorders which consisted primarily of personality or adjustment disorders (almost invariably complicated by substance abuse). Those with coexisting substance abuse were, perhaps not surprisingly, significantly more prone to violence than those not similarly burdened.

In such studies one of the greatest problems is establishing a control group of non-disordered individuals who share as many as possible of the experimental sample's characteristics and from whom directly comparable information can be obtained. The MacArthur group made a valiant attempt to accomplish this but by the most generous of estimations only 43% of control subjects approached completed a relevant assessment. On the basis of comparisons with this control group it was concluded that patients with major mental disorders, including schizophrenia but without substance abuse, were no more likely to be violent than "others in their neighbourhood without symptoms of substance abuse". Substance abuse was, however, significantly more common among patients (31% versus 17%), and among patients with substance abuse the prevalence of violence was significantly higher than others in their neighbourhood.

One strategy for investigating the putative relationship between having a history of mental disorder and committing offences, including those involving violence, is to trace the criminal records of cohorts of individuals who have been admitted to hospital or otherwise had contact with the mental health services (Lindqvist & Allebeck, 1990; Wessley, Castle & Douglas, 1994; Modestin & Ammann, 1996). In a recent Australian study, Mullen and colleagues (2000) traced the criminal histories of just over 1000 people with a diagnosis of schizophrenia who had been first admitted in 1975 or 1985. The patterns of offending in these individuals were compared with those for age, gender and residential area matched controls. The control group was established by drawing on an existing database of random community samples whose criminal records had been ascertained (using identical methods) prior to being placed on the list of potential jurors. The control data was stripped of all identifying information and supplied to the researchers only distinguished by year of birth and gender. Males with schizophrenia had significantly higher rates of offending for all categories of offending except sexual. Over 20% of males with schizophrenia had been convicted of a criminal offence with over 10% having a conviction for violence. This was significantly higher than for controls, of whom 8% had a recorded offence, with violent offences being recorded for less than 2%. As with the study of Steadman and colleagues (1998) a coexisting diagnosis of substance abuse was significantly associated with the chance of acquiring a conviction (49% vs. 8.6%) including convictions for violence (17% vs. 2%).

The Steadman et al. study (1998) identified in the whole spectrum of psychiatric inpatients a wide range of violent acts, the vast majority of which never came to any official notice let alone led to a criminal conviction. The study of Mullen et al. (2000) confined itself to the range of recorded criminal convictions in those with schizophrenia. Not surprisingly, absolute levels of engagement in violent and antisocial behaviours varied widely between the two studies but the association with coexisting substance abuse was almost identical.

Rates of Mental Disorder Among Offenders

There have been numerous studies of the rates of mental disorder among offender populations, usually focusing on prisoners. Some studies concentrate on particular offences, with homicide being the favourite because of its importance and the high clear up rates which provides a more 'representative sample' (Eronen, Tiihonen & Hakola, 1996).

A study of a representative sample of sentenced prisoners in England and Wales reported rates of schizophrenia for males of 1.5% and females 1.1% (expected 0.5%) (Gunn, Maden & Swinton, 1991). Teplin (1990), in an American study of 728 remandees, ascertained 6.4% to have severe mental disorders of whom nearly half had schizophrenia. This was over twice the rates ascertained in the general population with similar instruments. The pre-eminent study in this area remains that of Taylor and Gunn (1984) who employed the Present State Examination to establish the levels of psychopathology in 1241 remand prisoners. They reported that

9% of those convicted of non-fatal violence and 11% convicted of homicide had schizophrenia (expected rates 0.6%). It was the results of this study that were critical in altering the views of researchers and clinicians in the UK on the relationship between offending and mental disorders, particularly in those with schizophrenia.

Most studies on offender populations employ methodologies which evaluate the psychiatric status of subjects after their incarceration or on the basis of pre-trial assessments. Wallace et al. (1998), in contrast, used a register which recorded all contact with public mental health services in the State of Victoria in Australia to establish the prior psychiatric histories of 4156 individuals (3838 males) convicted in the higher courts of that state between 1993 and 1995. Over 25% of these offenders had had prior contact with the mental health services. Interestingly the largest group of such contacts (11.8%) were those who had had only brief contact with services, usually while in crisis, and had received either no formal diagnosis or that of situational stress. The next biggest group were those who had received a primary diagnosis of substance abuse (7%). Schizophrenia, affective psychosis, affective disorders and personality disorders in males were over-represented among offenders in general and violent offences (including homicide) in particular. In addition to the primary diagnosis, the psychiatric register recorded associated disorders including substance abuse. A recorded co-morbid substance diagnosis was strongly associated with offending. Those males who had been diagnosed with schizophrenia and had also received a diagnosis of coexisting substance abuse were over 12 times more likely to be convicted than a member of the general population (Odds Ratio 12.4 (95% CI 9.1–16.7) compared to less than 2 (95% CI 1.4–2.4) for those without a substance abuse diagnosis. This disparity between those with and without substance abuse was similarly marked for violence (Odds Ratio 2.4 versus Odds Ratio 18.8) and homicide offences (OR 7.1 versus OR 28.8).

Community Studies

Studies on representative community samples, which ascertain both offending and mental health status, are formidable undertakings. Swanson (1994) and Swanson et al. (1990) analysed data on over 10 000 subjects from the Epidemiological Catchment Area Study which set out to establish the mental health status of the American population. The measure of violent and offensive behaviour was the response to questions canvassing self-reports of assaultative behaviour. Violent acts were reported by 2.4% of the non-disordered population but in those with schizophrenia this rose to 12%, in major depression to 11%, and in substance abuse diagnosis to 25%. Again those with major mental disorders who also abused substances accounted for a disproportionate amount of such violence. The work of Swanson and colleagues was critical in encouraging a shift in the US in professional attitudes to violence among the seriously mentally ill. The view was largely abandoned of the mentally ill as unfairly stigmatized. This paradigm was replaced by a perhaps all too ready acknowledgement of the link between mental disorders and criminality, mitigated only by arguments that better treatment could break that connection. Risk assessment moved to an increasingly central position in the management of the mentally ill. Treatment became overtly geared to violence prevention and shifted away from the social and psychological to an even stronger emphasis on pharmacology and even back to compulsory treatment and containment (Torrey, 1994).

Hodgins and her collaborators (1992, 1996) have employed birth cohorts followed up over many years to investigate the relationship between having received psychiatric inpatient care and having acquired criminal convictions. These studies have established a strong association between serious mental illness and offending, including violent offending. In the most recent of such studies 358 180 individuals born in Denmark between 1944 and 1947 were followed up using national registers and recording hospitalizations for mental illness and arrest for criminal offences (Brennan, Mednick & Hodgins, 2000). The study supported "the hypothesis that major mental disorders are associated with an increased likelihood of arrest for violence" (p. 497). Even when demographic factors and co-morbid substance abuse were controlled for, individuals hospitalized for schizophrenia had significantly higher rates of arrest for violence than those never hospitalized. Interestingly, this paper also identified males with organic psychosis as dramatically over-represented among such offenders.

TARGETING RISK ASSESSMENT AND RISK MANAGEMENT STRATEGIES

A range of studies employing widely different approaches and adequate methodologies have established significant associations between a number of mental disorders and violent and offending behaviours. This does not of itself ensure the practicality of predicting the probability that any individual with such a disorder is more or less likely to behave in such a manner. Nor does it establish whether the association is causal, and if so, what mediates that association, let alone how such mediation could be inhibited or interrupted.

In theory a knowledge of what increases and what decreases the probability of offending behaviours in the mentally disorder could inform strategies which:

(a) target individuals with risk factors, indicating a high probability of offending to alter their individual management (e.g. assertive follow up of "high-risk" subjects);
(b) target populations of patients to reduce the overall level of designated risk factors operative (e.g. give priority to decreasing substance misuse in all patients) without any specific focus on those supposed at high risk.

The project of targeting high-risk individuals leads down the road of increasingly sophisticated risk assessment and the focus of treatment resources on those identified. This approach may bring in its wake an increasing emphasis on compulsion and containment. After all, if priority is given to individuals designated at high probability of acting violently, it is difficult to avoid the safety of others becoming the primary focus. This tends to shift the emphasis from what is best for the patient to what is best for the patient's potential victims. Obviously it is against the patients' interests that they act violently to others: having done so they risk both alienating potential supports and being prosecuted. Managing such risks is a legitimate clinical objective, but placing this risk at the centre of care planning, and potentially allowing it to become the over-riding priority, is quite another matter. Such an approach risks the none-too-subtle shift from a therapeutics centred on the patients' needs to management strategies serving the community's needs (and potentially pandering to their fears and prejudices).

The alternative approach employs the accumulating links between mental disorders and violent and criminal behaviours to alter clinical practice in general. It is likely that the total burden of offending among the seriously mentally disordered would be reduced more effectively by changed management practices for all patients than by an intensive and assertive therapeutics directed at the few. Just as reducing the whole population's alcohol consumption by a little has more health benefits than struggling to change the habits of gross abusers, so it is likely that broadly based and universal strategies for improving mental health care will be more efficacious than spending time seeking out for special attention those supposed to be at high risk.

This being said, there is a practical problem that such theoretical arguments tend to overlook. A disproportionate amount of the violent and otherwise socially disruptive behaviour among the mentally ill is perpetrated by a relatively small group of patients, all too easily recognizable without the benefit of instrumentalities or finely tuned clinical insights. These are frightened, angry, often threatening, non-compliant, usually substance-abusing, predominantly, but not exclusively, male and more likely to be under 40. This group is difficult to engage, is intimidating for staff and is disruptive to other patients. In practice they are more likely to be lost to treatment than energetically followed up. Bans forbidding them entry to the clinic or interdicting their readmission are at least as common as attempts to maintain contact and return to active treatment. Such patients not infrequently start off being recognized and treated as having schizophrenia or major affective disorders, but as their more challenging behaviours impact they either find themselves stripped of the legitimacy of an illness and relabelled "personality disorders" or their symptoms are reformulated as drug induced. The labels of personality disorder and/or substance abuse are then often judged to place the patient outside the mental health service's responsibilities. In short, the problem in some mental health services is not excessive attention to high-risk patients but inattention and rejection. It would be an error to attribute such failures to ignorance or indolence. The clinical skills and service provisions which best serve the vast majority of the mentally disordered are not necessarily those relevant to this difficult subgroup. It takes very particular skills, a specific commitment and pride in such work to work well with chronically angry, potentially intimidating people with mental disorders.

Optimally, therefore, risk management strategies should be directed both at populations and at individuals. Risk management should not focus exclusively on those who fall into groups designated as more probable to offend in the future, but equally the needs of such groups should not be totally ignored.

FROM ASSOCIATIONS TO RISK ASSESSMENTS

A recent review by Binder (1999) concluded not only that "some mentally ill persons are dangerous" (p. 197) but "mental health clinician's responsibility becomes that of evaluating which of the mentally ill are dangerous" (p. 197). In similar vein

Steadman (2000) looked forward in the near future to "a tool to advise clinicians making release decisions as to risk levels of violence as one factor in release and supervision decisions" (p. 270).

The assumption that effective risk assessments strategies are now not only available but should form part of normal clinical practice for mental health professionals has important implications. When tragedies occur, be they death or injury to the patient or inflicted by the patient, the question is now almost certain to be raised about whether adequate risk assessment procedures were in place to prevent, or minimize, such an untoward outcome. The question may be raised by administrators eager to place any blame that is going on the clinicians, by coroners seeking to apportion contribution to the death, by enquiries deciding who to pillory and, most egregious of all, by colleagues prepared to self-righteously point the finger of blame. The assumption of efficacy for risk assessment strategies has led to increasing demands on mental health professionals to contribute to the decisions of courts, tribunals and boards charged with the incarceration or release of offenders. There are now even individual professionals and organizations which offer risk assessment services to employers and various agencies to identify those who may present risks of violent, disruptive or sexually inappropriate behaviours in the workplace.

The credulity about the effectiveness of risk assessments is not, however, universal. Mossman (2000) in a careful analysis of the mathematics of risk assessment procedures argues that neither now, nor in the immediate future, will assessments of the risk of violence provide clinicians. or judicial decision-makers, "prediction instruments with much practical utility". Mossman (2000) demonstrates that even the most optimistic levels of sensitivity and specificity being claimed for the best established of actuarial instruments, such as the HCR-20 and the VRAG, cannot generate clinically useful long-term predictions. This is not because these instrumentalities are not "better" at long-term predictions than clinical judgement alone: within their own terms they are. The problems inherent to all existing approaches is the level of false positives and false negatives thrown up by such actuarial methods. Actuarial methods were developed by the insurance industry to categorize populations into groups of differing overall risk. The specific risks of any individual member of the designated population was not of interest. The sensitivity and specificity of actuarial approaches were adjusted in line with maintaining profitability and, on a good day, natural justice. The worse that happens in the insurance business is that profits are reduced or competitiveness impaired by suboptimal placement of the cut-off points. The clinical enterprise and the criminal justice system is, however, concerned totally with the individual. Further the implications of being a false positive can be devastating for the individual, and being a false negative devastating for the community. The error levels both positive and negative which can be allowed for when calculating insurance policies are totally unacceptable when faced with questions of freedom from incarceration or danger to the community. Further, in practice with clinical and judicial risk assessments we are often attempting to identify those at high risk for rare events (homicide and other serious assaults) which inevitably increases the false negative rates. To add to the problems is the expectation placed on clinicians that when it comes to the worst outcomes, suicide and homicide, there should be a zero risk. I wouldn't envy the clinician trying to explain to a homicide enquiry that a 10%, 5% or even 1% risk of violence was considered acceptable and that yes, uncommon though it was, homicide was one possible expression of such violence.

It could be argued that despite the practical difficulties the actuarial assessment are for longer term risk appraisal an improvement on unaided clinical judgement. The problem is however the expectations generated and encouraged by advocates of these approaches. Such unrealistic hopes lead clinicians to offer spurious certainties based on a science which in application degenerates to a scientism. Far from reducing the chances of blame the professional enthusiasm for risk assessment is generating expectations which will be disappointed and creating responsibilities which will return to haunt us. Norko (2000) expressed succinctly the problem with the much vaunted risk assessment instruments when he wrote, "such techniques are traps; they will always oversimplify the situation and lead to a false sense of security ... (and are) unlikely to ever assist clinicians in the real time decisions they are called upon to make on a daily basis" (p. 280).

Monahan and Steadman (1994) argued that predictions of future damaging behaviours involved considering, firstly the nature of the significant associations, secondly the level of foreseen harm, and finally the probability of such harm. In considering associations between mental health variables and future violent and offending behaviours the best established variables are certain diagnoses and the presence of substance abuse, with combinations of the two generating far and away the strongest associations. Attempts to link specific abnormalities of mental state or syndromes (see Link & Stueve, 1994; Taylor, 1998) have come under increasing question (see Appelbaum, Clark Robbins & Monahan 2000). Whether or not associations will be established with specific types of abnormal mental phenomena is not clear. What is clear is that in long-term prediction of violence risk mental health variables, with the possible exception of substance abuse, pale into insignificance when they are placed alongside traditional criminological variables like gender, age, past history of offending, and social class.

In predictions of future violent and criminal behaviours it is important to be clear about the nature of behaviours to be targeted. Wallace et al. (1998) were able to calculate, for the State of Victoria in Australia, the annual probability of being convicted of serious crimes of violence. The risk of a conviction (which for this study also included insanity and related findings) for serious violence for those who had been treated for a major mental disorder, such as schizophrenic or affective illnesses, was 0.5% for males and 0.05% for females. For personality disorders it was 2.5% for males and 0.4% for females, and for those with a primary diagnosis of substance abuse 1.1% for males and 0.4% for females. Unsurprisingly the probabilities for homicidal violence were an order of magnitude less (e.g. for males with schizophrenia 0.09% and females 0.01%). Most interpersonal violence goes, if not unnoticed certainly unrecorded in crime statistics. The more serious the violence the more likely is it to be both recorded and lead to conviction and in homicidal violence ascertainment and conviction rates in most Western Nations provide a reasonably comprehensive picture. Studies employing self-report have suggested that assaultive behaviours involving predominantly pushing, punching and kicking in the mentally disordered may be as high as 10% (Swanson et al., 1996). Thus if the harm we wish to predict is pushing, punching and kicking then we will require predictive algorithms capable of separating out the 10% at risk, but if it is killing which you wish to target then levels of discrimination several magnitudes more sensitive will be required. All too often we adopt approaches which target a very wide range of interpersonal aggression in the hope of capturing specifically those at risk of killing and maiming. Such an approach stigmatizes large numbers of people in the hope of capturing the few. It also assumes that in the mentally disordered the risk factors for homicidal violence are the same, or similar, to those for far more mundane forms of violence, which they may well not be.

Is then the predictive enterprise and the hopes for prevention which flow from it both misbegotten and doomed to failure? The answer depends on which you are attempting to predict, in whom, and for what purpose. Short to medium term, from days to weeks, predictions of risk in the mentally ill are both practical and have clinical utility. Actively psychotic young men, socially alienated, angry, abusing alcohol and drugs, making threats and refusing professional support and treatment are obviously at far higher risk of immediate violence than well-controlled, socially integrated compliant patients with similar mental disorders. Short-term predictions, though they depend in part on static risk factors, such as age and prior history, are strongly influenced by dynamic factors, which include current mental state, social situation, current provocations, and the chances of intoxication. Thus with assessments for short-term risk come the opportunities for effective risk management (see Mullen, 2000). Conversely long-term risk predictions, from months to years, depend largely on static predictors, such as prior history, abuse during childhood, and age, but may also include reified characteristics such as psychopathy where dynamic factors are frozen into static persistent traits. Long-term predictions are inevitably less accurate and lead not to changes in clinical management but inexorably to restriction, compulsion and the initiation, or extension, of incarceration.

The risk assessment literature can, in my opinion, assist short-term prediction and management. It can also inform public policy, not as to how to deal with individuals but on how to reduce the risks of violent and criminal behaviours in populations. In the seriously mentally disordered as in the population as a whole factors such as child abuse, school failure, unemployment and substance abuse have demonstrable associations with subsequent criminal offending. Each factor is open to primary and or secondary prevention strategies which can be targeted not at individuals but at populations. Specifically in the mental health field such factors as poor social supports, substance abuse and active symptoms are probably associated with increased criminality. Such dynamic factors are open both to modification by targeting individual patients for appropriate support and treatment and to modification by improving mental health services to the whole population of the seriously mentally disordered.

Ethical Limitations

Boundaries need to be drawn around when, where and for what purpose mental health professionals can ethically, and with professional propriety, engage in assessing the probability of an individual committing violent or criminal acts and in being involved in the management of any ascertained risks (Mullen, 1997, 2000). Mental health professionals should, in this author's opinion, only engage in risk assessment and risk management strategies when the following criteria are satisfied.

1. The predictions and management are motivated primarily by the intention to provide the patient with better treatment and care. Protection of the public should be the welcome by-product of improved clinical care, not the goal of such management. If crime prevention were to become the primary objective the care of the patient would become a means to an end—an end which is external, and potentially inimicable, to the patient's interests.
2. A reasonable body of empirical evidence exists to guide clinical decision-making.
3. Mental health variables are a prominent feature of the individual's clinical picture and are also of potential relevance to the probability of future criminal behaviours.
4. The risks are expressed in terms of probabilities (not attributions of dangerousness) with clear admissions of the fallibility and potential variability in the prediction.
5. Any prediction and subsequent management is formulated to take account of the implications for the patient. Mental health professionals should not be contributing to the inflicting of punishment or to processes which aim to reduce potential future offending primarily by some form of detention or incapacitation.
6. A reasonable degree of proportionality is maintained between the level of harm apprehended and the response evoked. In practice, we are very unlikely to be able to predict, in the long-term future, acts of murderous or seriously damaging violence based on mental health variables. At best we may be able to place individuals in high-risk categories for a wide range of violent and criminal behaviours which will predominantly be of the type which frighten and distress, not of the type which kill and maim. Pushing, punching, frightening and stealing are unacceptable behaviours and the increased possibility of their occurring in the future demands greater care and attention on the part of the clinician. But it would be hard to justify on the basis of such possibilities incarceration or other major curtailments of the patient's civil rights. Even, in my opinion, the imposition of compulsory treatment in the community would be difficult to justify simply on this basis.

Summary

There are well-established correlations between serious mental illnesses—such as schizophrenia and major affective disorders—and increased rates of violent and offending behaviours. The level of those associations are unlikely to ever support clinically useful predictive algorithms directed at identifying those likely to kill and maim, but may well inform individual clinical decisions about those at higher risk of a far broader range of minor acts of violence and offending. The increasing knowledge about the dynamic factors which mediate between serious mental disorders and offending behaviours open up opportunities for preventive strategies directed both at individual patients and at the delivery of mental health services to all those with serious mental disorders. All such mental health interventions, if they are to remain ethically justified, should be directed primarily at improving the care and treatment of the patient with public safety being a welcome, emergent, but always secondary, benefit.

FROM ASSESSMENT TO MANAGEMENT AND PREVENTION

Knowledge of the relationship between serious mental disorder and offending, and more importantly what mediates that association, can be employed to inform three broad approaches to minimizing offending.

1. The treatment and rehabilitation of those with serious mental disorder who have offended.
2. The management in the seriously mentally disordered of those aspects of their clinical picture associated with an increased risk of offending (that is, targeting those factors which are dynamic and therefore potentially changeable rather than targeting the high-risk individuals per se).
3. Improving mental health services overall in a manner calculated to reduce total offending among the seriously mentally ill.

Treatment and Rehabilitation of the Mentally Abnormal Offender

Forensic mental health services around the world have the dual mandate of treating the patient and containing the offender. (See the Special Issue of the *International Journal of Law and Psychiatry* (2000), 23, 429–663, which examines forensic services across a range of nations.) In most countries the days are over of indefinite, or even very lengthy, detention for all but a tiny minority of mentally abnormal offenders. The vast majority of those with serious mental disorders who have offended are in the community, or will return to the community. Increasing awareness of the presence in prison populations of seriously mentally disordered people has, at least in most jurisdictions, provoked either attempts at diversion from prison to mental health services or attempts to provide some semblance of treatment in prison and follow-up on release. The traditional criminal lunatic asylums, which provided long-term containment in institutions which were often prisons in all but name, are slowly disappearing (very slowly in the UK) to be replaced by secure hospital facilities which are far more closely allied to general mental health and community services.

Rehabilitation and community management is becoming the focus for forensic mental health services (Russo, 1994; Ladds, 1997; Heilbrun & Griffin, 1998). Forensic mental health services are assuming the traditional tasks of psychiatric rehabilitation in providing patients with the skills necessary to live in the community with the minimum necessary support, and at their highest possible level of function (Anthony, 1979; McCulloch & Bailey, 1993). The centre of forensic mental health service activity is shifting from the large, secure hospitals towards the community, with prisons and smaller local secure and medium secure units now providing the main institutional supports (Mullen & Lindqvist, 2000). Rehabilitation and community management attempt to manage mental disorder, maximize psychological and social functioning and in the forensic context to minimize the risks of offending (Derks, Blankstein & Hendrick, 1993; Mullen, 1993; Heilbrun & Griffin, 1993). Given that lengthy periods of incarceration occur for a significant minority of forensic patients in secure units and prisons, an emphasis is necessary on maintaining living skills and on ameliorating the apathy and despair created by long-term confinement. Treatment-resistant patients are over-represented among forensic patient populations and this, compounded by lengthy incarceration, can produce some of the most disabled of patients.

Ideally the living spaces in forensic inpatient units need to be designed to reflect the mental health and security needs of the patients (Mullen & Lindqvist, 2000). A sense of movement and progress needs to be built into the architecture, as well as reflected in the attitudes of staff. It is essential to provide a long-term care environment that approximates closely to the realities of community living. Work, education (essential to so many who have never realized their potential), and recreation ideally need to be pursued in different spaces from sleeping and the daily domestic round. As soon as possible, the patient needs to take responsibility for personal care in domains such as cooking, washing and housekeeping. To counteract the destructive influence of isolation from the community, a gradual introduction of activities outside of the institutional boundaries needs to be established as early as possible consistent with both the patient's clinical state and public safety (Linhorst, 1995; Maier, Morrow & Miller, 1989). The most successful rehabilitative efforts occur in the least restrictive environments (Andrews et al., 1990; Test, 1992).

The aim of rehabilitation is to facilitate living in the community. Sadly, however, most prisons and forensic hospitals tend to inculcate the habits and attitudes conducive to an easy life in the institution which serve the patient poorly when he or she does return to the community. As the return to the community approaches, supervised and unsupervised excursions into community settings need to increase (Lloyd & Guerra, 1988; Evans, Souma & Maier, 1989). The final move to the community should be gradual, not sudden and, ideally, the primary care givers should remain constant during this all important transition. The physical requirements for the move to the community, in terms of a place to live, and the economic wherewithal to sustain a basic existence, are one thing, but establishing viable social roles and social networks is quite another (Mullen & Lindqvist, 2000). All too often ex-prisoners and ex-patients rely for a social circle on professionals, ex-prisoners or other mentally disordered people, because these are the only groups they know after their years of institutionalization. If a transition is not made from the social worlds of prison and hospital to that of the community, the probabilities of relapse and recidivism are increased. Family, for some, offers an entry into the wider community but, for many, family ties were either destroyed by the nature of their crime or withered with the passing years. For still others those very family ties are connections to substance abuse and/or offending.

To the goals of community reintegration and effective clinical management must be added the goal of minimizing recidivism. Few will be impressed with a forensic mental health service which produces optimal mental health outcomes if there is a high rate of further serious offending. Programmes of conditional release, as well as assertive follow-up and outreach services provided by those skilled in the forensic area, offer appropriate service delivery models (Dvoskin & Steadman, 1994; Bigelow, Bloom & Williams, 1990; Muller-Isberner, 1996; Heilbrun & Griffin, 1998). Implicit in these approaches is the development and maintenance of a forensic community service operating in parallel with general mental health services. Sadly, such service models meet considerable resistance from administrators concerned with keeping levels of funding to an absolute minimum. It is also unwelcome to those interested in maintaining the hegemony of general psychiatry, and to those who believe that forensic services are, by their nature, excessively stigmatizing (Nedopil & Banzer, 1996).

Community forensic mental health services are likely to have to take responsibility for a mixture of ex-inpatients of the forensic inpatient services, ex-prisoners, as well as referrals from general mental health and community correctional (probation) services. Given the frequency with which mental health patients acquire criminal convictions at some time, it is clear that the coexistence of an offending history and a mental disorder cannot be sufficient to define a "forensic patient". In practice, those whose past offending creates the most anxiety, or who are most effective at frightening professionals, will form the clientele of forensic services. Those with mental disorders whose entry into mental healthcare settings is primarily via the criminal justice system often fare poorly when it comes to the provision of the necessary mental health services. The difficulties of integrating mental health and correctional services with totally different cultures and objectives is often compounded by squabbles over funding.

Rehabilitation and community care form the core of modern mental health services. Sadly, on occasion, they are little more than systems for maintaining a stable level of disability and a continuing social isolation. At best they are about reintegration, maximizing function and effective therapeutic engagement. Forensic mental health services are moving closer to the systems of care delivery which dominate the rest of psychiatry. Hopefully it will be to the positive features of community care that they will move. In bringing forensic services into the community, there is a danger that this may accentuate an already troubling trend to extend compulsion and coercion from the hospital into the homes of patients. Hopefully, however, such trends will extend care and treatment to seriously mentally ill people with histories of offending who currently often face outright rejection, or marginalization, in existing services. The mentally abnormal offenders, if not optimally managed, may return to offending at a terrible cost to themselves, to their future victims and to the bean counters' bottom lines.

Managing those with Risk Factors for Offending

The concept of dangerousness almost inevitably led to individual patients having attributed to them this quality of being a potential, but ever-present, threat to the safety of others. In moving to the language of risk, such stigmatization was not always avoided as individuals continued to be classified as "high-risk patients" as if this were some abiding characteristic. The problems of identifying those at "high risk" has already been considered at length. One solution to the problem of reifying risk is not to address the problem of the identified high-risk patient, but to focus on the factors believed to mediate that risk. This can be accomplished by addressing the risk factors as issues in all seriously mentally disordered individuals and/or by giving special attention to the management of these risk factors in particular patients. Thus, one strategy would be to initiate programmes to combat substance abuse, or improve medication compliance in all those for whom a service is responsible. Conversely, those known to have particular problems with substance abuse, or who have been non-compliant with treatment, would be specifically targeted for more intensive intervention. Broadly, programmes that attempt to reduce substance abuse and improve compliance in the whole patient group are likely to deliver greater overall benefits. However, as already noted, a case can also be made for targeting specific patients with high needs.

Central to this approach is a shift away from identifying and managing the individual patient at risk of future criminality to managing clinical issues relevant to offending. This can be approached in individual clinical work and in planning service delivery for groups of patients. The focus is on providing needed care and support, not on controlling future behaviour. Substance abuse needs to be addressed because it destabilizes and otherwise damages someone with a serious mental illness—not simply because it is associated with increased offending. Social isolation and dislocation are causes for concern, irrespective of their contributions to offending. Addressing active symptoms is a core task for mental health professionals and it is a bonus if this also reduces the risk of criminal behaviour.

CONCLUSION

In the last decade there has been, both in research and in clinical practice, an increasing focus on the associations between serious mental illness and offending behaviours. This preoccupation has tended all too often to be productive of ideologies and practices focusing on blame and the minimizing of risk (with priority usually given to the risks to the managers and political masters of the mental health services). The time may have come for: (a) greater scepticism about the promises of risk assessment technologies; (b) a return to a traditional concern with the care and treatment of patients; and (c) making a real contribution to community safety by servicing the patients' needs.

REFERENCES

Andrews, D. A., Zinger I., Hoge, R. D., Bonta, J., Gendreau, P. & Cullen, F. T. (1990) Does correctional treatment work? A clinically relevant and psychologically informed meta-analysis. *Criminology, 28*, 369–404.

Anthony, W. A. (1979) *Principles of Psychiatric Rehabilitation*. Baltimore, MD: University Park Press.

Appelbaum, P. S., Clark Robbins, P. & Monahan, J. (2000) Violence and delusions: Data from the MacArthur Violence Risk Assessment Study. *American Journal of Psychiatry, 157*, 566–572.

Bigelow, D. A., Bloom, J. D. & Williams, M. H. (1990) Costs of managing insanity acquittees under a psychiatric security review board system. *Hospital and Community Psychiatry, 41,* 613–614.

Binder, R. L. (1999) Are the mentally ill dangerous? *Journal of American Academy of Psychiatry and Law, 24,* 189–201.

Brennan, P. A., Mednick, S. A. & Hodgins, S. (2000) Major mental disorders and criminal violence in a Danish birth cohort. *Archives of General Psychiatry, 57* (5), 494–500.

Derks, F. C. H., Blankstein, J. H. & Hendrick, J. J. P. (1993) Treatment and security: The dual nature of forensic psychiatry. *International Journal of Law and Psychiatry, 16,* 217–240.

Dvoskin, J. A. & Steadman, H. J. (1994) Using intensive case management to reduce violence by mentally ill persons in the community. *Hospital and Community Psychiatry, 45,* 679–684.

Eronen, M., Tiihonen, J. & Hakola, P. (1996) Schizophrenia and homicidal behavior. *Schizophrenia Bulletin, 22,* 83–89.

Evans, B., Souma, A. & Maier, G. J. (1989) A vocational assessment and training program for individuals in an inpatient forensic mental health center. *Psychosocial Rehabilitation Journal, 13,* 61–69.

Gunn, J., Maden, T. & Swinton, M. (1991) *Mentally Disordered Prisoners.* London: HMSO.

Heilbrun, K. & Griffin, P. (1993) Community based forensic treatment of insanity acquittees. *International Journal of Law and Psychiatry, 16,* 133–150.

Heilbrun, K. & Griffin, P. A. (1998) Community based forensic treatment. In R. M. Wettstein (Ed.) *Treatment of Offenders with Mental Disorders* (pp. 168–210). New York: Guilford Press.

Hodgins, S. (1992) Mental disorder, intellectual deficiency and crime: Evidence from a birth cohort. *Archives of General Psychiatry, 49,* 476–483.

Hodgins, S., Mednick, S., Brennan, P., Schulsinger, F. & Engberg, M. (1996) Mental disorder and crime: Evidence from a Danish birth cohort. *Archives of General Psychiatry, 53,* 489–496.

Ladds, B. (1997) Forensic treatment and rehabilitation: The growing need for more services and more research. *International Journal of Mental Health, 25,* 3–10.

Lindqvist, P. & Allebeck, P. (1990) Schizophrenia and crime: A longitudinal follow-up of 644 schizophrenics in Stockholm. *British Journal of Psychiatry, 157,* 345–350.

Linhorst, D. M. (1995) Implementing psychosocial rehabilitation in long term inpatient psychiatric facilities. *Journal of Mental Health Administration, 22,* 58–67.

Link, B. G. & Stueve, A. (1994) Psychotic symptoms and the violent/illegal behaviour of mental patients compared to community controls. In J. Monahan & J. H. Steadman (Eds.) *Violence and Mental Disorder* (pp. 137–159). Chicago, IL: University of Chicago Press.

Lloyd, C. & Guerra, F. (1988) A vocational rehabilitation program in forensic psychiatry. *British Journal of Occupational Therapy, 51,* 123–126.

Maier, G. J., Morrow, B. R. & Miller, R. (1989) Security safeguards in community rehabilitation of forensic patients. *Hospital and Community Psychiatry, 40,* 529–531.

McCulloch, M. & Bailey, J. (1993) Issues in the management and rehabilitation of patients in maximum secure hospitals. *Journal of Forensic Psychiatry, 4,* 25–44.

Modestin, J. & Ammann, R. (1996) Mental disorder and criminality: Male schizophrenia. *Schizophrenia Bulletin, 22,* 69–82.

Monahan, J. & Steadman, H. (1983) Crime and mental illness: An epidemiological approach. In N. Morris & M. Tonry (Eds.) *Crime and Justice,* Vol. 4. Chicago IL: University of Chicago Press.

Monahan, J. & Steadman, H. (Eds.) (1994) *Violence and Mental Disorder: Developments in Risk Assessment.* Chicago, IL: University of Chicago Press.

Monahan, J., Steadman, H. J., Applebaum, P. S., Robbins, P. C., Mulvey, E. P., Silver, E., Roth, L. H. & Grisso, T. (2000) Developing a clinically useful actuarial tool for assessing violence risk. *British Journal of Psychiatry, 176,* 312–319.

Mossman, D. (2000) Commentary: Assessing the risk of violence—Are "accurate" predictions useful? *Journal of American Academy of Psychiatry and Law, 28,* 272–281.

Mullen, P. E. (1984) Mental disorder and dangerousness. *Australian and New Zealand Journal of Psychiatry, 18,* 8–19.

Mullen, P. E. (1993) Care and containment in forensic psychiatry. *Criminal Behaviour and Mental Health, 3,* 212–225.

Mullen, P. E. (1997) A reassessment of the link between mental disorder and violent behaviour, and its implications for clinical practices. *Australian and New Zealand Journal of
Psychiatry*, *31*, 3–11.

Mullen, P. E. (2000) Dangerousness, risk and the prediction of probability. In M. G. Gelder, J.
J. López-Ibor & N. C. Andreasen (Eds.) *New Oxford Textbook of Psychiatry*. Oxford: Oxford
University Press.

Mullen, P. E., Burgess, P., Wallace, C., Palmer, S. & Ruschena, D. (2000) Community care and
criminal offending in schizophrenia. *The Lancet*, *355*, 614–617.

Mullen, P. E. & Lindqvist, P. (2000) Treatment and care in forensic mental health. In M. G.
Gelder, J. J. López-Ibor & N. C. Andreasen (Eds.) *New Oxford Textbook of Psychiatry*. Oxford:
Oxford University Press.

Muller-Isberner, J. R. (1996) Forensic psychiatric aftercare following Hospital Order treatment. *International Journal of Law and Psychiatry*, *19*, 81–86.

Nedopil, N. & Banzer, K. (1996) Outpatient treatment of forensic patients in Germany:
Current structure and future development. *International Journal of Law and Psychiatry*,
19, 75–79.

Norko, M. A. (2000) Commentary: Dangerousness—a failed paradigm for clinical practice
and service delivery. *Journal of American Academy of Psychiatry and Law*, *28*, 282–289.

Russo, G. (1994) Follow up of 91 mentally ill criminals discharged from the maximum
security hospital in Barcelona P.G. *International Journal of Law and Psychiatry*, *17*, 279–301.

Steadman, H. J. (2000) From dangerousness to risk assessment of community violence.
Journal of American Academy of Psychiatry and Law, *28*, 265–271.

Steadman, H., Mulvey, E., Monahan, J., Clark Robbins, P. et al. (1998) Violence by people
discharged from acute psychiatric inpatient facilities and by others in the same neigh-
borhoods. *Archives of General Psychiatry*, *55*, 393–401.

Swanson, J. W. (1994) Mental disorder, substance abuse and community violence: An
epidemiological approach. In J. Monahan & J. H. Steadman (Eds.) *Violence and Mental
Disorder*. Chicago, IL: University of Chicago Press.

Swanson, J., Borum, R., Swartz, M. & Monahan, J. (1996) Psychotic symptoms and disorders
and the risk of violent behaviour in the community. *Criminal Behaviour and Mental Health*,
6, 309–229.

Swanson, J. W., Holzer, C., Ganja, V. & Jono, R. (1990) Violence and psychiatric disorder in
the community: Evidence from the epidemiologic catchment area surveys. *Hospital and
Community Psychiatry*, *41*, 761–770.

Taylor, P. J. (1998) When symptoms drive serious violence. *Social Psychiatry and Psychiatric
Epidemiology*, *33*, Supp. 1, 547–554.

Taylor, P. J. & Gunn, J. (1984) Violence and psychosis I: The risk of violence among psychotic
men. *British Medical Journal*, *288*, 1945–1949.

Teplin, L. (1990) The prevalence of severe mental disorder among male urban jail detainees:
Comparison with the epidemiologic catchment area program. *American Journal of Public
Health*, *80*, 663–669.

Test, M. A. (1992) Training in community living. In R. Liberman (Ed.) *Handbook of Psychiatric
Rehabilitation* (pp. 153–170). New York, NY: Macmillan.

Torrey, E. F. (1994) Violent behavior by individuals with serious mental illness. *Hospital and
Community Psychiatry*, *45*, 653–662.

Wallace, C., Mullen, P. E., Burgess, P., Palmer, S., Ruschena, D. & Browne, C. (1998) Serious
criminal offending and mental disorder: A case linkage study. *British Journal of Psychiatry*,
172, 477–484.

Wessley, S., Castle, D. & Douglas, A. (1994) The criminal careers of incident cases of
schizophrenia. *Psychological Medicine*, *24*, 483–502.

PART III

IMPLEMENTATION AND POLICY ISSUES

Chapter 12

RISK–NEEDS ASSESSMENT AND ALLOCATION TO OFFENDER PROGRAMMES

CLIVE R. HOLLIN

Centre for Applied Psychology, University of Leicester, UK

Two of the main axioms to emerge from the meta-analyses of the offender treatment literature, and now ingrained in the "What Works" agenda (McGuire, 1995), are encapsulated in the *risk principle* and the *needs principle*. As explained by Andrews and Bonta (1994), the risk principle states that effective work with offenders will match the intensity of service delivery with the degree of risk posed by the offender. Thus, offenders assessed as medium to high risk of recidivism should be selected for intensive delivery of treatment; low-risk offenders will therefore be suited to low-level, less intense interventions. It follows that for good matching of offenders with level of delivery, effective risk assessment is necessary. Andrews and Bonta (1994, p. 176) have also explained the *need principle*:

> Many offenders, especially high-risk offenders, have a variety of needs. They need places to live and work and/or they need to stop taking drugs. Some have poor self-esteem, chronic headaches or cavities in their teeth. These are all "needs". The need principle draws our attention to the distinction between *criminogenic* and *non-criminogenic* needs. Criminogenic needs are a subset of an offender's risk level. They are dynamic attributes of an offender that, when changed, are associated with changes in the probability of recidivism. Non-criminogenic needs are also dynamic and changeable, but these changes are not necessarily associated with the probability of recidivism.

As conceived by Andrews and Bonta, there is a close relationship between risk and need: *criminogenic* needs are in themselves risk factors for recidivism. It follows that an assessment of risk and needs is absolutely fundamental to effective work to reduce offending. Assessment of risk will inform selection of participants and the intensity of service delivery; assessment of needs will inform programme targeting and content. As criminogenic needs are, by definition, risk factors, the assessment

Offender Rehabilitation and Treatment: Effective Programmes and Policies to Reduce Re-offending. Edited by James McGuire.
© John Wiley & Sons, Ltd.

of risk with offenders can subsume assessment of need. In other words, identify the source of the risk and the area of need becomes apparent. The following section considers some of the conceptual issues in risk assessment before looking in detail at predicting offending.

ASSESSMENT OF RISK

To assess risk is to try to predict the future. There are many spheres of everyday life in which prediction of the future is crucial: for example, insurance companies predict the risk of car accidents, financiers predict their profits and losses, medics predict the risks to patients of surgery, and bookmakers give odds on horses winning races.

Any attempt at prediction demands attention to two elements of the predictive equation. The first of these elements is the definition of the *criterion* of concern: for example, insurers may be specifically concerned with the risk of car accidents, or the risk of critical illness, or the risk of burglary. The second element is the identification of the *predictors* (or risk factors) that are reliably associated with the specified criterion. Thus, the driver's age may be a predictor of the likelihood of being in a car accident; smoking may be a predictor of the likelihood of developing certain types of ill health; and post code might be an accurate predictor of the likelihood of being burgled. Once established, such predictors set the level of risk and hence the insurance premium: the greater the risk, the more intense your payments become!

Attempts at predicting risk can have various outcomes, each of which has very different implications for those involved.

OUTCOME IN RISK ASSESSMENT

In attempting to predict risk, assessors are faced with the classic decision outcome matrix, as shown in Figure 12.1.

The ideal set of predictors for a given criterion will produce high levels of *true positive* decisions, i.e. the presence of the predictors will correctly predict the outcome.

	Actual Yes	Actual No
Predict Yes	True positive ("Hit")	False positive ("Miss")
Predict No	False negative ("Miss")	True negative ("Hit")

Figure 12.1   Hits and misses in prediction

Similarly, good predictors will give high levels of *true negative* decisions: in this case it may be the absence of the predictors for true positives, or the presence of different predictors of a lack of outcome (such predictors are analogous to protective factors). These "true" outcomes (positive and negative), are generally known as "hits". On the other hand, a *false positive* arises when despite the presence of the predictors the outcome does not arise; while a *false negative* is found when in the absence of predictors the criterion of risk actually occurs. "False" outcomes are generally called "misses".

Consider the decision to release a person with a history of violence and mental disorder from conditions of security. The role of forensic practitioners is to assess the risk of future violence, so informing the process of decision-making regarding the individual's release into the community or his continued detention.

Suppose the prediction is Yes, there is an unacceptable level of risk and, indeed, if the individual had been released into the community there would have been victims (actual Yes). The decision to detain in security is correct (a Hit) and the public will continue to be protected. (The real-life problem here, of course, is that there is no "actual" outcome against which to judge the accuracy of the decision-making.)

However, suppose the prediction is Yes but in fact the individual would *not* have been a danger to the public (actual No). In this case the person will wrongly be detained in security (a Miss), with all the attendant issues with respect to human rights and public spending. Alternatively, the prediction might be No so that the person is not detained in security, however on release he commits violent offences in the community (actual Yes). In this event (a Miss), of which there have been several cases widely reported in the media, there are all the ingredients for a public inquiry into clinical decision-making. Finally, the prediction may be No and the individual returns to the community and does not commit violence (actual No): obviously, this is a good decision (a Hit).

How are assessments of risk carried out? The classic distinction is between *clinical* prediction and *actuarial* (or *statistical*) prediction. The clinical method of risk prediction is based on professional judgement and decision-making. The judgement of risk in a given case may be made by an individual practitioner, or by a clinical team, or by a case conference. There is a long-running debate in the human sciences literature, not just the criminological literature, regarding the relative merits and accuracy of clinical and actuarial risk assessment. The generally accepted position, dating from Meehl's (1954) seminal text, is that statistical prediction is superior to clinical prediction (e.g. Gottfredson, 1987). The finer points of this debate are covered in a searching article by Grove and Meehl (1996). Given recent developments in practice, this chapter will be concerned with actuarial methods of risk assessment in working with offenders.

ACTUARIAL PREDICTION

The actuarial method of risk prediction relies on the use of statistical methods to identify the risk factors for a given criterion of risk. These statistically identified risk factors may then be combined into an algorithm to give a standardized risk assessment. In developing an actuarial algorithm for risk assessment, it is necessary to conduct thorough research to identify the risk predictors. Typically, an appropriate sample population and criterion are identified, say car drivers for risk of accidents, and measures are taken of potential risk factors. The sample of car drivers is then monitored over a period of time (typically years) to establish statistically which potential risk factors actually best predict accidents. These risk factors—say age, type of car, number of previous accidents—are then used to set the premiums for drivers applying for insurance.

It is plain that in risk assessment the stakes can be high for all concerned: in working with offenders assessment of risk can influence sentencing decisions, type of disposal, appropriate level of security, parole, breach of probation order, and level and intensity of interventions. As shown by generations of research, the accurate prediction of criminal behaviour has long been a Holy Grail in criminological research. The search for a valid and reliable method by which to estimate with accuracy the likelihood of an individual re-offending depends in essence on measurement of two variables. The first is accurate measurement of offending which can take many forms as, for example, with self-reported re-offending, arrest record, court appearances, officially recorded reconviction, a reconviction resulting in a return to prison, or parole violation. In addition, types of offending and time to re-offending may be important dimensions of the offending variable. The second requirement is for accurate measurement of the predictors of risk, whatever they may be for type of offence under consideration. It follows that accurate assessment of the risk of re-offending relies upon the identification of efficient predictors that will produce a high number of hits and a low number of misses.

What form might predictors of risk take? Again, a classic distinction is drawn between static and dynamic predictors.

Static and Dynamic Predictors

Static risk predictors are historical or background factors, which, by definition, cannot change, and the presence of which is known to elevate the risk of a given criterion. Thus, for example, in predicting risk of heart disease, a family history of heart disease would be a static risk predictor. It should be noted that static predictors do not predetermine an event: the presence of static predictors simply raises the probability of the event occurring in the future.

On the other hand, dynamic risk factors are aspects of an individual's current functioning related to the occurrence of the risk. Thus, smoking, an unhealthy diet, a high cholesterol level, and a stressful job are all dynamic risk factors in relation to heart disease. In practice, it is often a combination of static and dynamic predictors that gives the strongest basis by which to predict risk. The important point, particularly with regard to practice, is that dynamic factors such as psychological functioning and social and situational conditions are open to change. This potential for change with dynamic risk factors presents possibilities for risk management. So, to follow the example above, risk of heart disease can be managed by stopping smoking, changing diet, improving exercise routines, and so on.

Moving from the general to the specific, interest now turns to the risk assessment and criminal behaviour. Where do we stand with respect to the prediction of offending?

PREDICTING OFFENDING

The first attempts at prediction of re-offending were made by criminologists in the 1920s (e.g. Burgess, 1928; Hart, 1923). These early efforts at prediction mainly relied on measurement of a range of potential static risk factors for re-offending, such as information gleaned from demographic and criminological records, followed by statistical calculations to determine the factors that best predicted the outcome (i.e. recidivism). This tradition has continued into more recent times with the development of several actuarial prediction instruments based on static factors for use with more general offender populations.

Actuarial Scales: Focus on Static Predictors

The list of actuarial scales used to predict offending includes the California Base Expectancy Scale (Gottfredson & Ballard, 1965), the Salient Factor Scale (Gottfredson, Wilkins & Hoffman, 1978), the Wisconsin Juvenile Probation and Aftercare Instrument (Ashford & LeCroy, 1988), and the Recidivism Prediction Score (Nuffield, 1982). Specifically for young offenders, Ashford and LeCroy (1990) describe three prediction instruments: the Contra Costa Risk Assessment Instrument, the Orange County Risk Assessment Instrument, and the Arizona Juvenile Risk Assessment Form. Ashford and LeCroy suggest that across the instruments which, like some of the adult scales, use both actuarial and clinical predictors, criminal history variables were the best predictors of recidivism. It is probably more than coincidence that two criminal history variables—number of prior arrests and decision to detain prior to court appearance—are the best predictors of disposition in juvenile courts (Niarhos & Routh, 1992).

The Salient Factor Score is a good example of an actuarial scale containing only static risk factors. Developed and refined in a string of studies within the US Parole Commission (Gottfredson, Wilkins & Hoffman, 1978; Hoffman, 1983; Hoffman & Stone-Meierhoefer, 1979), a 5-year follow-up study has shown that the Salient Factor Score is predictive of recidivism among released prisoners (Hoffman & Beck, 1985).

The Salient Factor Score is a simple six-item checklist that produces a score from 0 to 10 points: the higher the score, the lower the likelihood of reconviction. Bands of scores are used to categorize risk: 0–3 poor risk, 4–5 fair risk, 6–7 good risk, 8–10 very good risk. The salient factor score protocol is shown in Table 12.1. Hoffman (1994) has reported a long-term follow-up of the Salient Factor Score on three samples of prisoners released from prison and concludes that:

> The Salient Factor Score has retained predictive accuracy over the seventeen-year period in which the three samples were released. These findings add to the evidence that the Salient Factor Score is able to separate prisoners into categories having significantly different probabilities of recidivism, and that its predictive accuracy has not diminished over time. (p. 485)

Table 12.1 Salient Factor Score (after Hoffman & Beck, 1985)

Item A: *Prior Convictions/Adjudications*
None = 3; one = 2; two or three = 1; four or more = 0

Item B: *Prior Commitment(s) of More than 30 Days*
None = 2; one or two = 1; three or more = 0

Item C: *Age at Current Offence/Prior Commitments*
Age at commencement of current offence: 26 years of age or more = 2;
20–25 years of age = 1; 19 years of age or less = 0

Item D: *Recent Commitment Free Period (Three Years)*
No prior commitment of more than 30 days (adult or juvenile), or released
to the community from last such commitment at least 3 years prior to the
commencement of the current offense = 1; otherwise = 0

Item E: *Probation/Parole/Confinement/Escape Status Violator This Time*
Neither on probation, parole, confinement, or escape status at the time of
the current offence; nor committed as a probation, parole, confinement, or
escape status violator this time = 1; otherwise = 0

Item F: *Heroin/Opiate Dependence*
No history of heroin or opiate dependence = 1; otherwise = 0

The Reconviction Prediction Score (RPS) was devised by Nuttall (1977) to estimate on a case by case basis the probability of reconviction of male prisoners within two years of their discharge from prison. The purpose of the scale was to provide cogent information on risk of re-offending to assist in making decisions regarding parole. As shown in Table 12.2, the RPS relies on a range of static demographic and criminological information.

Each factor is then given a weighting, as illustrated in Table 12.3, and the total raw score is obtained simply by adding the relevant sub-score for the individual factors. Finally, the raw scores, which can range from −31 to +31, are directly converted to RPS values on a scale from 0 to 100: as the figure on the RPS increases, so the chance of reconviction rises accordingly. Ward (1987) carried out a large-scale validation study of the RCS and concluded that:

> The present study demonstrates a useful relation between the RPS and the reconviction rate, which differs between parolees and those not paroled. For parolees in the sample the RPS overestimates the reconviction rate by 11 percentage points; for those in the sample not paroled it overestimates the reconviction rate by 4 percentage points. (p. 1)

Table 12.2 Predictors in the RPS (Ward, 1987)

Main offence	Interval at risk since last release
Age at offence	Juvenile custodial treatment
Value of property stolen	Probation history
Number of associates	Prison offences
Offences during current sentence	Occupation (Registrar-General's class)
Number of previous convictions	Employment at time of offence
Age at first conviction	Time in last job
Number of previous imprisonments	Living arrangements at time of offence

Table 12.3 Illustration of RPS Weighting Scheme (Ward, 1987)

Time in Last Job	
Short or casual	+3
No job for 5 years since release	+2
Less than 1 month	+3
1 month but less than 6 months	Nil
6 months but less than 1 year	−1
1 year but less than 3 years	−4
3 years but less than 5 years	−5
5 years or more	−6

Ward suggested that minor statistical and methodological modifications could be made to the RPS to improve its accuracy. However, the general conclusion stands that the RPS is a relatively robust tool for the purpose for which it is designed. In the early 1990s changes in legislation in England and Wales brought about changes in procedures for parole, necessitating the development of a new prediction scale. Accordingly, the Risk of Reconviction scale was developed by Copas, Marshall and Tarling (1996).

The Risk of Reconviction scale was based on an analysis of a range of demographic, socio-economic, and criminal characteristics of a sample of 1247 prisoners released from custody. (As most prisoners are male, this is reflected by the figures of 1191 men and 56 women in the sample.) Statistical analysis showed that there were six strong predictors of re-offending for this population: Copas et al. identify these factors as "age at first conviction, number of youth custody sentences, number of adult custodial sentences, number of previous convictions, type of offence committed and sex of the offender" (p. vii). As with the RPS, a series of weightings is applied to these six factors to produce a risk score in an individual case. In the practical application of the scale, information is entered into a computer program to allow scores on individual prisoners to be calculated for use by the Parole Board.

A similar exercise with respect to informing probation officers in writing pre-sentence reports for court saw the development of the Offender Group Reconviction Scale (OGRS). As noted by Copas and Marshall (1998), OGRS contains familiar variables (age, gender, number of youth custody sentences, total number of court appearances, time since first conviction, and type of offence) and an accompanying weighting system.

The point to take from the actuarial research with a focus on static predictors is that reasonably accurate prediction of recidivism is possible using this type of predictor. There are two broad points to make about this statement. First, as expressed by Wormith and Goldstone (1984), caution should be taken with regard to the generalization of findings from predictive studies across offender samples. Similarly, the same point applies in attempting to generalize findings across both countries and cultures. Indeed, Salts et al. (1995) found some marked differences in predictive variables of violent behaviour in African American and Caucasian male adolescents: for example, Salts et al. reported that age was not a significant predictor of violent behaviour for the African Americans but did predict violence for the Caucasians.

Secondly, it is important to note that scales such as the OGRS are not designed with the intention of making a prediction about an individual offender. Rather, they suggest the predicted rate of reconviction for offenders who match that individual on the sampled predictive factors. As Copas and Marshall (1998) suggest, OGRS gives "Quite a comprehensive coverage of criminal history indicators, and so if the actual risk for an offender differs substantially from the OGRS percentage we should expect this to be on account of social, behavioural or psychological factors rather than any further information on the criminal record" (p. 170). For practitioners, it is precisely those social, behavioural or psychological dynamic factors that are of immediate concern. It is self-evident that the commission of an offence must be explicable through understanding dynamic risk factors set against the relevant static factors.

The potential predictive power of dynamic factors is an important issue, as Hoffman and Stone-Meierhoefer (1979, pp. 210–211) recognize:

> It is to be noted that the possible effects of parole supervision (i.e., deterrent or rehabilitative) have not been considered in this analysis [of the Salient Factor Score]. That is, all cases have been used in the preceding tabulations regardless of whether they were released to a long period of supervision, a short period, or no supervision at all. Clearly, it is possible that the presence or absence, intensity, or style of supervision could affect the rates shown. If further research, preferably using random allocation of cases to different supervision treatments, establishes the existence of specific relationships among the above variables, this knowledge could be used to facilitate cost-benefit analyses and enable development of more sophisticated policy matrices.

Hoffman and Stone-Meierhoefer pinpoint the issue: are there dynamic factors that, alongside established static predictors, might be used to predict which offenders (and under what conditions) are most likely to re-offend? Further, are there dynamic factors that might show which offenders respond best, in terms of reduced re-offending, to which criminal justice sanctions? The thorny issue of different outcomes from the offender–sentence interaction is a very real concern as recognized by Lloyd, Mair and Hough (1994) in their study of reconviction rates following community service orders, probation orders, and imprisonment. While finding no major differences in reconviction following these different sanctions, Lloyd et al. make the important point that their findings reflect national averages. Whether there are different success and failure rates, perhaps related to dynamic factors, nested within these averages is a tantalizing question.

Actuarial Scales: Focus on Static and Dynamic Predictors

Several studies have looked to see if the addition of dynamic factors enhances significantly the efficacy of actuarial scales based on static factors. Early investigations of this type consistently reported little significant impact of clinical information on overall predictive accuracy (e.g. Hassin, 1986; Wormith & Goldstone, 1984). In a typical comparative study, Gendreau, Madden and Leipciger (1980) compared the effectiveness of social history information and personality data gathered using a psychometric inventory (Minnesota Multiphasic Personality Inventory; MMPI) as predictors of reconviction. In keeping with earlier studies (Cowden & Pacht, 1967; Smith & Lanyon, 1968), the social history information predicted recidivism better than the psychometric data. Combining the social history information and the psychometric data did, however, increase the accuracy of prediction of recidivism, but only by a minimal degree. Similar findings have been reported by Gough, Wenk and Rozynko (1965) who found that MMPI scores did increase the accuracy of prediction of recidivism from social history information alone, but only by a few percentage points.

Another approach in searching for dynamic predictors of re-offending has been to investigate the predictive power of individual psychological factors.

'Simple' Dynamic Predictors

At its most basic, the search for dynamic predictors looks for a relationship between recidivism and a single psychological construct. There is a substantial literature given to attempts at "simple" dynamic prediction of recidivism: such putative predictors include personality variables, psychometric scales, and intelligence tests. Some typical examples of this line of research are given below.

Roberts et al. (1974) found limited support for measures of impulsiveness and ability to delay gratification as predictors of recidivism. McGurk, McEwan and Graham (1981) also found some evidence that personality type was related to recidivism. McGurk and colleagues administered a battery of psychometric tests—the Hostility and Direction of Hostility Questionnaire (Caine, Foulds & Hope, 1967), the Psychological Screening Inventory (Lanyon, 1973), and the 16 Personality Factor Questionnaire, Form E (Cattell, Eber & Tatsuoka, 1970)—to imprisoned young offenders. Cluster analysis revealed four personality clusters: an "anxious" type, a "normal" type, a "disturbed" type, and a "truculent" type. Those young offenders in the anxious group showed the lowest rate of recidivism; those in the truculent group the highest.

Ingram and colleagues (1985) continued a long line of research (with very mixed findings) looking at the predictive validity of the MMPI. There were indications that some MMPI scales did distinguish recidivists from non-recidivists, although there was limited continuity with previous findings. Ingram et al. also found that recidivists were more impulsive than non-recidivists, as assessed using the Problem Solving Inventory (Heppner & Petersen, 1982). Finally, Byrd et al. (1993) looked at the utility of self-concept as a predictor of juvenile recidivism. Using the Role Construct Repertory Grid (Kelly, 1955) and the Self-Consciousness Scale (Fenigstein, Scheier & Buss, 1975), Byrd et al. report the remarkable finding that "...many youths who identify with juvenile delinquency were somewhat less prone toward delinquent behavior" (p. 199).

As noted by other reviewers (e.g. Andrews & Bonta, 1998), taken overall there is only very weak evidence that "simple" clinical measures are reliably associated with recidivism. There are several reasons for this weakness: there are too many inconsistent findings, particularly with the MMPI; too many unreplicated studies; and too many studies limited by small sample size.

There is also a conceptual issue with regard to "simple" prediction in that, given the complexity of human behaviour, it seems unlikely that a limited range of factors will predict criminal conduct. Can greater success in the search for dynamic predictors of re-offending be achieved with more complex predictors?

"Complex" Predictors

Historically, there have been many attempts, particularly with young offenders, to devise classification (or typology) schemes, and then to relate these classifications to the risk of recidivism (for reviews, see Andrews & Bonta, 1998; Andrews, Bonta & Hoge, 1990). These classification schemes include Quay's Behavioural Typology (Quay, 1964, 1984), the I-Level (Interpersonal Maturity) system (Sullivan, Grant & Grant, 1957) and the allied Jesness Inventory (Jesness, 1971, 1988), and CL (Conceptual Level) classification (Brill, 1979; Leschied, Jaffe & Stone, 1985).

The evidence regarding the effectiveness of the "personality-based" classification systems (MMPI, Quay, I-Level and Conceptual Level) is limited with respect to prediction of future offending. Andrews and Bonta (1994, p. 163) make the judgement that:

> Research on these classification systems needs to explore their predictive validity. Almost all the studies of predictive validity have as their criteria institutional or in-program adjustment, and when these systems are compared they are able to predict (Van Voorhis, 1988). However, although having quiet and well behaved prisoners may be important for the management of a correctional facility, it does not necessarily follow that inmates will transfer this behavior to the community (Bonta & Gendreau, 1992). What is sorely lacking is evidence on the ability of the systems to predict recidivism; what little data does exist has not been impressive.

However, there are three complex predictors for which the recent data are more impressive.

The Violence Prediction Scheme

The Violence Prediction Scheme is based on Canadian research concerned with the development of an actuarial prediction scale for violent recidivism in male mentally disordered offenders after release from a maximum security psychiatric institution. The cohort in the original research, reported by Harris, Rice and Quinsey (1993), was a sample of more than 600 males treated in a maximum security psychiatric hospital. After a mean time at risk of almost seven years, the cohort was then divided into two groups according to whether or not there was a record of violent recidivism. The two groups could then be compared across a range of demographic, clinical, and offence-related measures, with an aim of determining statistically what particular factors differentiated the two groups and hence predicted violent recidivism.

Using multivariate statistical techniques, Harris and co-workers were able to isolate from a large array of demographic, psychometric, and offence characteristics a total of 12 factors predictive of violent re-offending (see Table 12.4). These factors are efficient in the sense that they maximize the likelihood of making a "hit" and minimize the likelihood of a 'miss'.

Table 12.4 Predictors for Violent Recidivism (Harris, Rice & Quinsey, 1993)

Psychopathy Checklist (Revised) score	Female victim-index offence*
Separation from parents under age 16	Failure on prior conditional release
Victim injury in index offence*	Property index offence history
DSM-III schizophrenia*	Age at index offence
Never married	Alcohol abuse history
Elementary school maladjustment	DSM-III personality disorder

*These factors are contra-indicative of recidivism: i.e. their presence suggests that violent recidivism is *less* likely.

In practice, the individual's score on each of the 12 variables is converted to a standard score and an overall score is than calculated by simply summing the 12 standard scores. Harris and colleagues showed that the probability of violent recidivism increased steadily as scores on the prediction instrument increased. A more complex style of analysis is empirically to assign weights to scores on the different variables. However, Harris, Rice and Quinsey found that weighting scores had absolutely no effect on the predictive accuracy of the 12 variables. Overall, the predictor variables "translate into a classification accuracy of about 75%" (pp. 330–331).

Inspection of the 12 variables in Table 12.4 shows that there are several measures associated with psychological and behavioural functioning: specifically, these are the Psychopathy Checklist (Revised) (PCL-R) score, DSM-III diagnoses of schizophrenia and personality disorder, and childhood variables. (Scores on the PCL-R give a measure of the disorder termed psychopathy, see below; DSM-III refers to the third edition of the *Diagnostic and Statistical Manual*, published by The American Psychiatric Association, and in common use in North America.) Harris, Rice and Quinsey recomputed the statistics solely for the seven static variables that remain when the clinical variables are removed. They report that the resulting predictions were less accurate than with the clinical variables included, but that the loss of sensitivity was not of a substantial magnitude.

With the publication of the *Violence Risk Appraisal Guide* (VRAG), Webster et al. (1995) developed this research into a format that presents practitioners with full details on assessing the various predictors. Indeed, risk assessment for violence in mentally disordered offenders continues to develop with other instruments such as the HCR-20 (Douglas & Webster, 1999; Webster et al., 1997) continuing to inform that particular corner of the forensic field. However, it is important to note that scales such as the VRAG may lose their predictive power when applied to other populations than those for which they are intended (Hart, 1998).

The Psychopathy Checklist

The Psychopathy Checklist (PCL) is currently attracting a great deal of attention in the literature (for lengthy reviews see Hare, 1998; Hare & Hart, 1993; Hare, Strachan & Forth, 1993; Hart, Hare & Harpur, 1992). Initially developed by Hare (1980) as a 22-item Checklist, which systematically assesses an amalgam of demographic, criminological, social, and psychological information, the length was subsequently shortened by removing two items to produce a revised 20-item version, the PCL-R. The PCL-R has satisfactory psychometric properties with respect to reliability and validity (Hare, 1991). Administration of the PCL-R requires a

Table 12.5 Synopsis of the Hare Psychopathy Checklist—Revised (after Hare, 1992)

1. Superficial charm	12. Early behaviour problems
2. Grandiose sense of self-worth	13. Lack of long-term planning
3. Need for stimulation/easily bored	14. Impulsive
4. Pathological lying	15. Irresponsible
5. Manipulative	16. Failure to accept responsibility for own
6. Lack of remorse or guilt	actions
7. No emotional depth	17. Frequent marital failures
8. Callous	18. Delinquent as a juvenile
9. Parasitic lifestyle	19. Poor record on probation or other conditional
10. Poor behavioural control	release
11. Promiscuous sexual behaviour	20. Versatile as acriminal

semi-structured interview, typically lasting 90 to 120 minutes, and access to detailed case history notes and files. Hart, Hare and Forth (1994) note that a full PCL-R assessment, by a trained assessor, is a lengthy affair demanding several hours of intensive work. A summary of the items in the PCL-R is shown in Table 12.5.

To produce an assessment measure that requires minimal time, effort and training to use, Hart, Hare and Forth (1994) report the development of the *Psychopathy Checklist: Screening Version* (PCL: SV). As reported by these researchers, this is a robust measure, with satisfactory psychometric properties, and serves as a useful screening instrument for clinicians and researchers with limited time and case history information.

The evidence strongly suggests that the PCL-R assesses a lifestyle that is parasitic and antisocial along with the personal, cognitive and emotional traits—e.g. habitual lying, lack of empathy and remorse, and guiltlessness—that combine to produce the psychopathic individual (Cooke, Forth & Hare, 1998).

While there is continuing debate regarding the concept of psychopathy (Blackburn, 1993), it is clear that the PCL-R is strongly associated with criminal behaviour. For example, Hare, McPherson, and Forth (1988) note from their study that: "Psychopaths generally had significantly more convictions for assault, theft, robbery, fraud, possession of a weapon, and escaping custody than did non psychopaths" (p. 711). With respect to their offence patterns, Hare, McPherson and Forth (1988) conclude that male psychopaths engage in a far wider range of types of criminal behaviour than most offenders, attract more convictions, and spend more time in prison than other offenders.

After conditional release from prison, psychopaths are likely to present with the greatest supervisory problems and to be reconvicted with in one year (Hart, Kropp & Hare, 1988). The PCL-R has been shown in several studies to relate strongly to offending after release from prison. Hart, Hare and Forth (1994, pp. 83–84) make the following observations:

> Following release [from prison], offenders in the top third of the PCL distribution were almost three times more likely to violate the conditions of release, and almost four times more likely to commit a violent crime, than were those in the bottom third. Similar results were obtained by Serin, Peters, and Barbaree (1990) and Serin (1991) who found a strong association between the PCL-R

and outcome following release from prison on unescorted temporary absence and parole. The PCL-R predicted both violent and nonviolent outcome better than did a combination of criminal-history and demographic variables, and several standard actuarial risk instruments, including the Base Expectancy Scale (Gottfredson and Bonds 1961), the Recidivism Prediction Scale (Nuffield 1982), and the Salient Factor Score (Hoffman and Beck 1974). Psychopathy also predicts violent recidivism in male young offenders. Forth, Hart, and Hare (1990) found that PCL-R scores in a sample of 75 young offenders were significantly correlated with the number of charges or convictions for violent offenses after release.

A body of evidence has now accumulated that shows that psychopaths are persistent and serious offenders and that, for both mentally disordered and general offender populations, the PCL-R has significant predictive power with respect to recidivism (Hemphill, Hare & Wong, 1998).

The Level of Supervision Inventory

The *Level of Supervision Inventory* (LSI) was originally developed by Andrews (1982) as a quantitative measure of both risk assessment and needs assessment. Founded on a social learning theory, rather than personality based approach to understanding human behaviour, the LSI offers a means by which to gather risk and needs information for planning treatment and assigning the level of supervision. The most recent, revised version of the LSI, the LSI-R, was published by Andrews and Bonta (1995) and renamed the *Level of Service Inventory* (*Raised*) (LSI-R).

As shown in Table 12.6, the LSI-R is composed of 10 subcomponents, with different numbers of items per subcomponent. There is a total of 54 items, answered with "Yes–No" or a rating from 0 to 3, that address both static and dynamic factors. Completed through file review and interview, the LSI-R assesses a range of criminogenic factors, including "static" factors such as previous convictions, and "dynamic" factors such as drink problems and employment. The pattern of scores identifies specific areas of offender risk and need, while the total score can be translated into a risk band for future offending (Andrews & Bonta, 1995).

Concerning its psychometric properties, there is ample evidence that the LSI-R is both valid and reliable. Andrews (1982) showed that the LSI had satisfactory reliability, as assessed by both inter-rater and test–retest methods. With regard to validity, LSI-R findings typically correspond with other measures of risk, criminality, and rule violation (Andrews et al., 1986; Bonta & Motiuk, 1985; Gendreau, Goggin & Law, 1997; Loza & Simourd, 1994; Simourd & Malcolm, 1998; Zamble &

Table 12.6   Sub components in the LSI–R (Andrews & Bonta, 1995)

Criminal History (10)	Leisure/Recreation (2)
Education/Employment (10)	Companions (5)
Financial (2)	Alcohol/Drug problems (9)
Family/Marital (4)	Emotional/Personal (5)
Accommodation (3)	Attitudes/Orientation (4)

Note: Number of items per subcomponent are shown in parentheses.

Quinsey, 1997). Yet further, LSI-R scores correlate highly with PCL-R scores (Loza & Simourd, 1994).

Andrews and Bonta (1995) note that the LSI-R provides specific criteria for the following: for identifying treatment targets and monitoring offender risk while under supervision and/or treatment services; for making probation supervision decisions; for making decisions regarding placement into halfway houses; for deciding appropriate security level classification within institutions; and for assessing the likelihood of recidivism. Thus, in practice, the LSI has been applied to a range of tasks. With sentenced offenders from various institutions, as Andrews and Bonta (1995) note, LSI-R scores are predictive of granting of parole, parole violation, and re-incarceration within one year. A string of studies has shown that LSI scores are good predictors of successful placement of imprisoned offenders in correctional halfway houses, a diversionary alternative to imprisonment in the Canadian system (e.g. Bonta & Motiuk, 1985, 1987, 1990, 1992). With regard to sentenced offenders from various institutions, LSI-R scores are predictive of prison misconducts (Gendreau, Goggin & Law, 1997), granting of parole, parole violation, and re-incarceration within one year of discharge (Andrews & Bonta, 1994; Gendreau, Little & Goggin, 1996); a finding that holds for female as well as male offenders (Coulson et al., 1996).

The LSI has also been shown to be sensitive to criminogenic factors, as Andrews and Bonta (1994, pp. 173–174) note:

> Studies have found considerable empirical support for the predictive validity of the LSI with general inmate populations...For example, LSI scores have predicted prison misconduct, assaults and recidivism one year after release from prison (Bonta & Motiuk, 1987, 1992). Finally, support of the predictive validity of the LSI also has been found among female offenders (Coulson, Nutbrown & Giulekas, 1993) and young offenders (Shields, 1993; Shields & Simourd, 1991).

A recent study has extended the use of the LSI-R to assess the non-sexual criminogenic needs of sex offenders (Simourd & Malcolm, 1998).

In summary, the LSI has been shown to be an effective and practical instrument in predicting and *monitoring* offender risk. While the LSI-R includes items that relate to both static and dynamic predictors, Andrews and Bonta (1995) note the "dynamic validity" of change scores on the LSI. Bonta (1996) discusses a small number of studies that show that reduction in risk, as measured by the LSI, is associated with lower rates of future criminal behaviour. Similarly, with imprisoned offenders, Hollin, Palmer and Clark (in press) found evidence of significant change on the dynamic items of the LSI-R over the period of a prison sentence. The collection of recidivism data will then allow a test of the hypothesis that a change in dynamic risk score is related to a change in offending.

The final approach to predicting the risk of recidivism, appropriate for imprisoned offenders, lies in the use of institutional measures.

Institutional Behaviour

Is it possible to predict recidivism on the basis of behaviour while imprisoned? Certainly, Zamble and Porporino (1988) suggest that behavioural measures can predict disciplinary offences over a sentence. Similarly, Berecochea and Gibbs (1991) describe an inmate classification system based on two predictors—inmate background, and behaviour during previous incarcerations—that provides a reasonably effective assessment of institutional misbehaviour. Berecochea and Gibbs note that this classification system can be used to inform decisions regarding the appropriate level of security for individual prisoners.

However, turning to the possibility of using institutional behaviour to predict recidivism, the issue hinges on the degree of continuity of behaviour. In other words, does *offending* behaviour prior to imprisonment predict institutional (mis)behaviour? Then, does institutional behaviour predict recidivism post release?

A study reported by Clark, Fisher and McDougall (1993) addressed the issue of continuity of offending behaviour between community and prison. Clark and colleagues were concerned to develop a risk assessment methodology based on the relationship between indices of offending behaviour and functionally similar behaviours observed in a prison environment. Detailed behavioural coding of the recorded details of the events leading up to an offence, and the behaviour during the offence, was used to define the risk factors associated with a given offence. These risk factors were then translated into types of predicted behaviour that could reasonably be expected to be displayed in prison in that they would produce functionally similar outcomes to the offence. A unique set of predicted behaviours could therefore be generated for each prisoner.

The next stage in the analysis was a further detailed behavioural coding of the prisoner's institutional (i.e. actual) behaviour. Finally, the degree of association between predicted and actual prison behaviour was calculated. Clark, Fisher and McDougall report a high degree of correspondence between predicted and actual behaviour leading to the conclusion that: "It is possible accurately to predict offence-related behaviour in the prison environment on the basis of an objective, behavioural analysis of the offence" (p. 444).

The Clark et al. study provides an answer to the first part of the equation: that is, there is demonstrable continuity between offending behaviour and institutional behaviour. The second part of the question is concerned with the relationship between institutional behaviour and recidivism. Hill (1985) provides a comprehensive review of the literature, stretching back to the 1920s, concluding that:

> Institutional misconduct seems to be the most reliable institutional predictor of recidivism...More research is clearly needed to establish the extent to which institutional variables, such as disciplinary infractions, add to known predictors of recidivism, such as previous criminal record. (p. 114)

Zamble and Porporino (1990) looked at a range of predictors of recidivism after imprisonment. They found that, as anticipated, criminal history variables were the strongest predictors of recidivism. However, Zamble and Porporino (p. 59) also note that, with respect to assessment in prison:

> A variety of current behavioral or cognitive measures were also reasonably predictive of reoffending. Prisoners who had little respect for the legal system, who gave little thought to their past or future, and who socialized extensively with other others in prison rather than spending time in their cells were the most likely to become recidivists.

There are practical difficulties in the assessment of institutional behaviour. As Hill notes, any study of institutional behaviour can only be as good as the institutional recording procedures. This same issue has also been noted by McDougall, Clark and Woodward (1995) as causing problems with their evaluation of prison-based behaviour change programmes. McDougall and co-workers found that disciplinary reports for interpersonal conflicts were ineffective as measures of behavioural change because of a low base rate of reporting. Nonetheless, the strands in the literature can be read as telling a consistent story. There is evidence for a continuity of offence-related behaviour and behaviour in prison (Clark, Fisher & McDougall, 1993), and evidence that prison behaviour contributes to prediction of recidivism (Hill, 1985; Zamble & Porporino, 1990). What is lacking, however, is a study that looks systematically at the whole sequence of events using fine-grained behavioural measures: Zamble and Porporino, for example, did not base their measures of institutional behaviour on an analysis of previous offending behaviour. It is arguable that had they done so, along the lines used by Clark and colleagues, then the strength of the predictive value of their institutional measures would have been increased. Similarly, there are no follow-up data from the Clark et al. study to show the strength of the relationship between their individually focused behavioural measures and recidivism. Clearly more research of this type is needed not only to enhance our understanding of the continuity of offending behaviour across different settings but to increase the accuracy of risk assessment.

RISK: A SUMMARY

The force of the discussion so far has been to suggest that the evidence for the power of actuarial scales based on static predictors is reasonably strong. Further, there is a reasonable consensus on the predictive factors: that is, age, number of previous offences, number of custodial sentences, and so on. None of these predictors is surprising and, indeed, the factors are consistent with some of the types of demographic variables seen as predictors of persistent offending in the longitudinal research (e.g. Farrington, 1995). Conversely, it is also plain with the benefit of hindsight that the research looking for "simple" dynamic predictors of re-offending was not likely to be productive. The "second generation" of "complex" actuarial scales, incorporating measures of static and dynamic risk factors, are outperforming their predecessors. The key question with respect to the power of these scales is whether their power is due in the main to the static items or whether the dynamic factors add significantly to their predictive power. Theoretically, the position can be formed that the dynamic variables in, say, the PCL-R will add to the predictive power of the scale precisely because they are demonstrably criminogenic, which perhaps was not always the case in the "simple" measures. In keeping with this theoretical position, Gendreau, Little and Goggin (1996) note the finding from their meta-analysis of the literature on prediction of adult recidivism that dynamic predictors perform as well as static predictors.

For the future, it is likely that research will increasingly focus on age, gender, and cultural issues with respect to risk–needs analysis (Funk, 1999; Jung & Rawana, 1999). Technically, researchers will capitalize on improved statistical methods such as generation of survival models (Visher, Lattimore & Linster, 1991) and the use of hazard analysis (Lattimore, Visher & Linster, 1995). Further, specific attention will continue to be devoted to "specialist prediction", such as violent offenders (Douglas, Cox & Webster, 1999; Ward & Dockerill, 1999), violent conduct and mental disorder (Monahan & Steadman, 1994), and sexual offences (Quinsey et al., 1995; Quinsey, Rice & Harris, 1995). Parenthetically, it is interesting to note that a meta-analysis of criminal and violent recidivism among mentally disordered offenders, reported by Bonta, Law and Hanson (1998), suggested that the strong predictors with this population were similar to those that might be found in general offender populations.

The immediate concern, however, is with the application of risk assessment methods to inform the analysis of need and, hence, allocation of services to meet the identified need.

RISK INTO NEED

At this point it is worth recalling the position articulated by Andrews and Bonta (1994) that criminogenic needs are an integral part of an offender's risk level (see also Zamble & Quinsey, 1997). Specifically, criminogenic needs are the dynamic aspects of an offender's risk level. It follows from this position that strategies to bring about change in criminogenic need will reduce the risk of offending and therefore lead to a reduction in the probability of recidivism. Thus, accurate assessment of criminogenic need is essential for targeting: in other words, the assessment of criminogenic need will allow accurate decisions to be made about the allocation of offenders to programmes.

In total, the effective deployment of resources to reduce offending relies on assessment of criminogenic need. If we consider the risk assessment research discussed above, then scales based on static predictors are not helpful when allocating offenders to programmes. By definition, static predictors cannot change and, as such, programmes are redundant in this respect. This is not to say that scales based on static risk predictors have no practical application with respect to programmes. Scales based on static predictors give information about the risk band into which an offender falls—information that is certainly relevant for programme allocation (consider the risk principle). For example, greater concern would be shown over a violent offender with a higher static risk score than a similar offender with a lower score.

"Simple" dynamic predictors have little support with regard to their effectiveness for prediction of risk, which in turn suggests that they will not perform effectively with respect to identification of criminogenic need. There is evidence to suggest that "complex" predictors do have predictive accuracy and that the inclusion of dynamic predictors (i.e. criminogenic needs) allows the use of these complex predictors as risk–needs assessments. The evidence supporting the LSI as a measure of risk and needs is strong: indeed, Gendreau, Little and Goggin (1996) conclude their review of predictors of adult recidivism with the view that the LSI-R "... appears to be the current measure of choice" (p. 590). The PCL-R is a powerful predictor of risk of re-offending (and correlates highly with LSI-R), although it is perhaps less firmly established with respect to assessment of criminogenic need. However, there is evidence that clinical change is mediated by an individual's PCL-R score (Hughes et al., 1997). This suggests that LSI-R and PCL-R will function effectively as predictors of risk of re-offending; while PCL-R scores may indicate "treatability" with respect to the criminogenic needs identified by the LSI-R.

While the development of complex predictors is an important advance, the critical step lies in the use of risk–needs assessment for effective programme allocation. How might effective allocation be achieved?

CLIENT MANAGEMENT CLASSIFICATION

The strategy embodied in *Client Management Classification* (CMC)—which in Canada is known as *Case Management Strategies* (CMS)—was developed by the Wisconsin Bureau of Community Corrections for planning treatment with prisoners and managing supervision of parolees and probationers (Dhaliwal, Porporino & Ross, 1994; Lerner, Arling & Baird, 1986). The CMC approach has three components: (1) a semi-structured interview with offenders to gather background information; (2) an assessment of 12 criminogenic factors (see Table 12.7), with four nominated as key factors in an offender's criminal behaviour; (3) a correctional treatment plan to address the key factors.

Several American studies have examined the relationship between the CMC approach and recidivism: all reported positive results with respect to reduced recidivism when the approach was adopted (e.g. Eisenberg & Markley, 1987; McManus, Stagg & McDuffie, 1988). However, a Canadian study reported by Dhaliwal, Porporino and Ross (1994) was less enthusiastic about the long-term effects of a CMS approach. These authors reported that prison-based programmes that followed the CMS approach did not impact significantly upon recidivism at 18-month follow-up. However, as Dhaliwal and colleagues note, there was in practice a lack of consistent application of the principles of this approach, and a low completion rate. Yet further, no attempt was made to match level of risk of re-offending with programme intensity. It appears that Dhaliwal and colleagues are pointing to organizational shortcomings in making the system operational, rather than to a failure of the approach per se. Of course, organizational factors are critical in both the overall delivery of the programme (Hollin, Epps & Kendrick, 1995) and in the maintenance of programme integrity (Hollin, 1995).

The promise of the CMC approach lies in taking into consideration a range of background, social, criminogenic, and psychological factors. A similar project

Table 12.7 The 12 criminogenic factors in the CMC

Academic/Vocational skills	Emotional stability
Employment pattern	Alcohol usage
Financial management	Mental ability
Marital/Family relations	Health (physical)
Companions	Sexual behaviour
Drug usage	Values/Attitudes

aimed at the resettlement of prisoners into the community, designed by Michael Cope and his colleagues, is currently beginning in County Durham Probation Service in the north-east of England. In this work the LSI-R will be used to complete the initial risk–needs assessment. The broad areas of need identified by the LSI-R will then be subject to in-depth assessment in order that services can be delivered in order to meet the appropriate level of need. For example, if the LSI-R identifies education as a criminogenic need for a given offender, then detailed assessment of that offender's educational level and ability will follow in order that educational services can be configured to meet the offender's exact needs. One of the demanding aspects of this project is that it will seek to span prison and community, attempting to ensure continuity of service across the two settings. Organizational issues aside, this project faces a formidable logistical task in seeking to coordinate tightly focused in-house programmes, such as parenting skills, with the broader range of community services. There is a network of community services, such as alcohol and drug specialists, housing schemes, educational projects and so on, that are available to discharged prisoners. The effective targeting of these community services so that they are used appropriately (and in sympathy with traditional behaviour change programmes) to meet the offender's needs is the key to the project. Without an effective form of risk–needs assessment such a project would be extremely difficult, if not impossible.

CONCLUSION

The impact of the meta-analyses and the associated "What Works" agenda continues to reach increasingly further into practice with offenders (Hollin, 1999). As services strive to deliver more effective services, they will need to face the practical implications of making operational the risk and need principles. These practicalities include not only preparing and training staff and the development of service delivery systems but also, crucially, the adoption of a risk–needs assessment procedure to inform programme allocation. As discussed here, there are several such assessment procedures available, although the LSI-R has the strongest research pedigree. It can be anticipated that the future will see an increasing emphasis on this element of effective practice in efforts to prevent criminal behaviour and reduce victimization.

Finally, it should not be thought that any of this is new. In discussing radical penal organisation, Radzinowicz (1999) details the development of a comprehensive system of offender assessment, leading to "a blue-print for a differentiated penitentiary organization, a veritable network of specialized institutions or wings with varying regimes" (p. 62). In other words, this is a plan for a system of penal regimes tailored to address the assessed needs of prisoners. The place and time of this revolutionary penal blue-print? Belgium, circa 1930.

REFERENCES

Andrews, D. A. (1982) *The Level of Supervision Inventory (LSI): The First Follow-up*. Toronto: Ontario Ministry of Correctional Services.

Andrews, D. A. & Bonta, J. (1994) *The Psychology of Criminal Conduct*. Cincinnati, OH: Anderson Publishing.

Andrews, D. A. & Bonta, J. (1995) *LSI-R: The Level of Service Inventory-Revised*. Toronto: Multi-Health Systems.

Andrews, D. A. & Bonta, J. (1998). *The Psychology of Criminal Conduct* (2nd edn.). Cincinnati, OH: Anderson Publishing.

Andrews, D. A., Bonta, J. & Hoge, R. D. (1990) Classification for effective rehabilitation: Rediscovering psychology. *Criminal Justice and Behavior, 17*, 19–52.

Andrews, D. A., Kiessling, J. J., Mickus, S. & Robinson, D. (1986) The construct validity of interview-based risk assessment in corrections. *Canadian Journal of Behavioural Science, 18*, 460–471.

Ashford, J. B. & LeCroy, C. W. (1988) Predicting recidivism: An evaluation of the Wisconsin Juvenile Probation and Aftercare Risk Instrument. *Criminal Justice and Behavior, 15*, 141–151.

Ashford, J. B. & LeCroy, C. W. (1990) Juvenile recidivism: A comparison of three prediction instruments. *Adolescence, 25*, 441–450.

Berecochea, J. E. & Gibbs, J. L. (1991) Inmate classification: A correctional program that works? *Evaluation Review, 15*, 333–363.

Blackburn, R. (1993) *The Psychology of Criminal Conduct*. Chichester: Wiley.

Bonta, J. (1996) Risk–needs assessment and treatment. In A. T. Harland (Ed.) *Choosing Correctional Options that Work: Defining the Demand and Evaluating the Supply*. Thousand Oaks, CA: Sage Publications.

Bonta, J. & Gendreau, P. (1992) Coping with prison. In P. Suedfeld & P. E. Tetlock (Eds.) *Psychology and Social Policy*. New York: Hemisphere Publishing.

Bonta, J., Law, M. & Hanson, R. K. (1998) The prediction of criminal and violent recidivism among mentally disordered offenders: A meta-analysis. *Psychological Bulletin, 123*, 123–142.

Bonta, J. & Motiuk, L. L. (1985) Utilization of an interview-based classification instrument: A study of correctional halfway houses. *Criminal Justice and Behavior, 12*, 333–352.

Bonta, J. & Motiuk, L. L. (1987) The diversion of incarcerated offenders to correctional halfway houses. *Journal of Research in Crime and Delinquency, 24*, 302–323.

Bonta, J. & Motiuk, L. L. (1990) Classification to halfway houses: A quasi-experimental evaluation. *Criminology, 28*, 497–506.

Bonta, J. & Motiuk, L. L. (1992) Inmate classification. *Journal of Criminal Justice, 20*, 343–353.

Brill, R. (1979) Implications of the conceptual level matching model for treatment of delinquents. *Journal of Research in Crime and Delinquency, 15*, 229–246.

Burgess, E. W. (1928) Factors determining success or failure on parole. In A. A. Bruce, A. J. Harno, E. W. Burgess & J. Landesco (Eds.) *The Workings of the Indeterminate Sentence Law and the Parole System in Illinois*. Springfield, IL: Illinois State Board of Parole.

Byrd, K. R., O'Connor, K., Thackrey, M. & Sacks, J. M. (1993) The utility of self-concept as a predictor of recidivism among juvenile delinquents. *Journal of Psychology, 127*, 195–201.

Caine, T. M., Foulds, G. A. & Hope, K. (1967) *Manual of the Hostility and Direction of Hostility Questionnaire*. London: University of London Press.

Cattell, R. B., Eber, H. W. & Tatsuoka, M. M. (1970) *Handbook for the Sixteen Personality Factor Questionnaire*. Windsor: NFER.

Clark, D. A., Fisher, M. J. & McDougall, C. (1993) A new methodology for assessing the level of risk in incarcerated offenders. *British Journal of Criminology, 33*, 436–448.

Cooke, D. J., Forth, A. E. & Hare, R. D. (Eds.) (1998) *Psychopathy: Theory, Research and Implications for Society*. Dordrecht, The Netherlands: Kluwer.

Copas, J. & Marshall, P. (1998) The offender group reconviction scale: A statistical reconviction score for use by probation officers. *Applied Statistics, 47*, 159–171.

Copas, J., Marshall, P. & Tarling, R. (1996) *Predicting Reoffending for Discretionary Conditional Release*. Home Office Research Study No. 150. London: Home Office.

Cowden, J. E. & Pacht, A. R. (1967) Predicting institutional and post release adjustment of delinquent boys. *Journal of Consulting Psychology, 31*, 377–381.

Coulson, G., Nutbrown, V. & Giulekas, D. (1993) Using the Level of Supervision Inventory in placing female offenders in rehabilitation programs or halfway houses. *IARCA Journal*, 5, 12–13.

Coulson, G., Ilacqua, G., Nutbrown, V., Giulekas, D. & Cudjoe, F. (1996) Predictive utility of the LSI for incarcerated female offenders. *Criminal Justice & Behavior*, 23, 427–439.

Dhaliwal, G. K., Porporino, F. & Ross, R. R. (1994) Assessment of criminogenic factors, program assignment, and recidivism. *Criminal Justice and Behavior*, 21, 454–467.

Douglas, K. S., Cox, D. & Webster, C. D. (1999) Violence risk assessment: Science and practice. *Legal and Criminological Psychology*, 4, 149–184.

Douglas, K. S. & Webster, C. D. (1999) The HCR-20 violence risk assessment scheme: Concurrent validity in a sample of incarcerated offenders. *Criminal Justice and Behavior*, 26, 3–19.

Eisenberg, M. & Markley, G. (1987) Something works in community supervision. *Federal Probation*, 51, 28–32.

Farrington, D. P. (1995) The development of offending and antisocial behaviour from childhood: Key findings from the Cambridge Study in Delinquent Development. *Journal of Child Psychology and Psychiatry*, 36, 929–964.

Fenigstein, A., Scheier, M. F. & Buss, A. H. (1975) Public and private self-consciousness: Assessment and theory. *Journal of Consulting and Clinical Psychology*, 43, 522–527.

Forth, A. E., Hart, S. D. & Hare, R. D. (1990) Assessment of psychopathy in male young offenders. *Psychological Assessment: A Journal of Consulting and Clinical Psychology*, 2, 342–344.

Funk, S. J. (1999) Risk assessment for juveniles on probation: A focus on gender. *Criminal Justice and Behavior*, 26, 44–68.

Gendreau, P., Goggin, C. E. & Law, M. A. (1997) Predicting prison misconducts. *Criminal Justice and Behavior*, 24, 414–431.

Gendreau, P., Little, T. & Goggin, C. (1996) A meta-analysis of predictors of adult offender recidivism: What works! *Criminology*, 34, 401–433.

Gendreau, P., Madden, P. G. & Leipciger, M. (1980) Predicting recidivism with social history information and a comparison of their predictive power with psychometric variables. *Canadian Journal of Criminology*, 22, 328–326.

Gottfredson, D. M. & Bonds, J. A. (1961) *A Manual for Intake Base Expectancy Scoring*. San Fransciso, CA: California Division of Corrections.

Gottfredson, S. D. (1987) Statistical and actuarial considerations. In F. Dutile & C. Foust (Eds.) *The Prediction of Violence*. Springfield, IL: C. C. Thomas.

Gottfredson, S. D. & Ballard, K. B. (1965) *The Validity of Two Parole Prediction Scales: An Eight Year Follow-up Study*. Vacaville, CA: Institute for the Study of Crime and Delinquency.

Gottfredson, S. D., Wilkins, L. T. & Hoffman, P. B. (1978) *Guidelines for Parole and Sentencing: A Policy Control Method*. Toronto: Lexington Books.

Gough, H. G., Wenk, E. A. & Rozynko, V. V. (1965) Parole outcome as predicted from the CPI, MMPI, and a base expectancy table. *Journal of Abnormal Psychology*, 70, 432–441.

Grove, W. M. & Meehl, P. E. (1996) Comparative efficiency of informal (subjective impressionistic) and formal (mechanical, algorithmic) prediction procedures: The Clinical–Statistical Controversy. *Psychology, Public Policy, and Law*, 2, 293–323.

Hare, R. D. (1980) A research scale for the assessment of psychopathy in criminal populations. *Personality and Individual Differences*, 1, 111–119.

Hare, R. D. (1991) *The Hare Psychopathy Checklist (Revised)*. Toronto: Multi-Health Systems.

Hare, R. D. (1998) The Hare PCL-R: Some issues concerning its use and misuse. *Legal and Criminological Psychology*, 3, 99–119.

Hare, R. D. & Hart, S. D. (1993) Psychopathy, mental disorder, and crime. In S. Hodgins (Ed.) *Mental Disorder and Crime*. Newbury Park, CA: Sage.

Hare, R. D., McPherson, L. M. & Forth, A. E. (1988) Male psychopaths and their criminal careers. *Journal of Consulting and Clinical Psychology*, 56, 710–714.

Hare, R. D., Strachan, C. E. & Forth, A. E. (1993) Psychopathy and crime: A review. In K. Howells & C. R. Hollin (Eds.) *Clinical Approaches to the Mentally Disordered Offender*. Chichester: John Wiley & Sons.

Harris, G. T., Rice, M. E. & Quinsey, V. L. (1993) Violent recidivism of mentally disordered offenders: The development of a statistical prediction instrument. *Criminal Justice and Behavior, 20,* 315–335.

Hart, H. (1923) Predicting parole success. *Journal of Criminal Law and Criminology, 14,* 405–413.

Hart, S. D. (1998) The role of psychopathy in assessing risk for violence: Conceptual and methodological issues. *Legal and Criminological Psychology, 3,* 121–137.

Hart, S. D., Hare, R. D. & Forth, A. E. (1994) Psychopathy as a risk marker for violence: Development and validation of a screening version of the Revised Psychopathy Checklist. In J. Monahan & H. J. Steadman (Eds.) *Violence and Mental Disorder: Developments in Risk Assessment.* Chicago, IL: The University of Chicago Press.

Hart, S. D., Hare, R. D. & Harpur, T. J. (1992) The Psychopathy Checklist: An overview for clinicians and researchers. In J. Rosen & P. McReynolds (Eds.) *Advances in Psychological Assessment* (Vol. 8). New York: Plenum Press.

Hart, S. D., Kropp, P. R. & Hare, R. D. (1988) Performance of male psychopaths following conditional release from prison. *Journal of Consulting and Clinical Psychology, 56,* 227–232.

Hassin, Y. (1986) Two models for predicting recidivism. *British Journal of Criminology, 26,* 270–286.

Hemphill, J. F., Hare, R. D. & Wong, S. (1998) Psychopathy and recidivism: A review. *Legal and Criminological Psychology, 3,* 139–170.

Heppner, P. P. & Petersen, C. H. (1982) The development of a personal problem-solving inventory. *Journal of Counseling Psychology, 29,* 66–75.

Hill, G. (1985) Predicting recidivism using institutional measures. In D. P. Farrington & R. Tarling (Eds.) *Prediction in Criminology.* New York: State University of New York Press.

Hoffman, P. B. (1983) Screening for risk: A revised salient factor score (SFS 81). *Journal of Criminal Justice, 11,* 539–547.

Hoffman, P. B. (1994) Twenty years of operational use of a risk prediction instrument: The United States Parole Commission's salient factor score. *Journal of Criminal Justice, 22,* 477–494.

Hoffman, P. B. & Beck, J. L. (1974) Parole decision-making: A Salient Factor Score. *Journal of Criminal Justice, 2,* 195–206.

Hoffman, P. B. & Beck, J. L. (1985) Recidivism among released federal prisoners: Salient factor score and five year follow-up. *Criminal Justice and Behavior, 12,* 501–507.

Hoffman, P. B. & Stone-Meierhoefer, B. (1979) Post release arrest experiences of federal prisoners: A six-year follow-up. *Journal of Criminal Justice, 7,* 193–216.

Hollin, C. R. (1995) The meaning and implications of "programme integrity". In J. McGuire (Ed.) *What Works: Reducing Re-offending.* Chichester: Wiley.

Hollin, C. R. (1999) Treatment programmes for offenders: Meta-analysis, "what works", and beyond. *International Journal of Law and Psychiatry, 22,* 361–372.

Hollin, C. R., Epps, K. & Kendrick, D. (1995) *Managing Behavioural Treatment: Policy and Practice With Delinquent Adolescents.* London: Routledge.

Hollin, C. R., Palmer, E. J. & Clark, D. (in press) The Level of Supervision Inventory—Revised profile of English prisoners: A needs analysis. *Criminal Justice & Behavior.*

Hughes, G. V., Hogue, T. E., Hollin, C. R. & Champion, H. J. (1997) First-stage evaluation of a treatment programme for personality disordered offenders. *Journal of Forensic Psychiatry, 8,* 515–527.

Ingram, J. C., Marchioni, P., Hill, G., Caraveo-Ramos, E. & McNeil, B. (1985) Recidivism, perceived problem-solving abilities, MMPI characteristics, and violence: A study of black and white incarcerated male adult offenders. *Journal of Clinical Psychology, 41,* 423–432.

Jesness, C. F. (1971) The Preston Typology Study: An experiment with differential treatment in an institution. *Journal of Research in Crime and Delinquency, 8,* 38–52.

Jesness, C. F. (1988) The Jesness Inventory classification system. *Criminal Justice and Behavior, 15,* 78–91.

Jung, S. & Rawana, E. P. (1999) Risk and need assessment of juvenile offenders. *Criminal Justice and Behavior, 26,* 69–89.

Kelly, G. A. (1955) *The Psychology of Personal Constructs*. New York: Norton.

Lanyon, R. I. (1973) *Manual of the Psychological Screening Inventory*. New York: Research Psychologists Press.

Lattimore, P. K., Visher, C. A. & Linster, R. L. (1995) Predicting rearrest for violence among serious youthful offenders. *Journal of Research in Crime and Delinquency, 32,* 54–83.

Lerner, K., Arling, G. & Baird, S. C. (1986) Client management strategies for case supervision. *Crime and Delinquency, 32,* 254–271.

Leschied, A. W., Jaffe, P. G. & Stone, G. L. (1985) Differential response of juvenile offenders to two different environments as a function of conceptual level. *Canadian Journal of Criminology, 27,* 467–476.

Lloyd, C., Mair, G. & Hough, M. (1994) *Explaining Reconviction Rates: A Critical Analysis.* London: HMSO.

Loza, W. & Simourd, D. J. (1994) Psychometric evaluation of the Level of Supervision Inventory (LSI) among male Canadian federal offenders. *Criminal Justice and Behavior, 21,* 468–480.

McDougall, C., Clark, D. A. & Woodward, R. (1995) Application of operational psychology to assessment of inmates. *Psychology, Crime and Law, 2,* 85–99.

McGuire, J. (Ed.) (1995) *What Works: Reducing Re-offending.* Chichester: Wiley.

McGurk, B. J., McEwan, A. W. & Graham, F. (1981) Personality types and recidivism among young delinquents. *British Journal of Criminology, 21,* 159–165.

McManus, R. F., Stagg, D. I. & McDuffie, C. R. (1988) CMC as an effective supervision tool: The South Carolina perspective. *Perspectives, 4,* 30–34.

Meehl, P. E. (1954) *Clinical Versus Statistical Predictions: A Theoretical Analysis and a Review of the Evidence.* Minneapolis, MN: University of Minnesota Press.

Monahan., J. & Steadman, H. J. (Eds.) (1994) *Violence and Mental Disorder: Developments in Risk Assessment.* Chicago, IL: The University of Chicago Press.

Niarhos, F. J. & Routh, D. K. (1992) The role of clinical assessment in the juvenile court: Predictors of juvenile dispositions and recidivism. *Journal of Clinical Child Psychology, 21,* 151–159.

Nuffield, J. (1982) *Parole Decision-Making in Canada: Research Towards Decision Guidelines.* Ottawa: Minister of Supply and Services Canada.

Nuttall, C. P. (1977) *Parole in England and Wales.* London: HMSO.

Quay, H. C. (1964) Psychopathic personality as pathological stimulus-seeking. *American Journal of Psychiatry, 122,* 180–183.

Quay, H. C. (1984) *Managing Adult Inmates: Classification for Housing and Program Assignments.* College Park, MD: American Correctional Association.

Quinsey, V. L., Lalumiere, M. L., Rice, M. E. & Harris, G. T. (1995) Predicting sexual offenses. In J. C. Campbell (Ed.) *Assessing Dangerousness: Violence by Sexual Offenders, Batterers, and Child Abusers.* Thousand Oaks, CA: Sage.

Quinsey, V. L., Rice, M. E. Harris, G. T. (1995) Actuarial prediction of sexual recidivism. *Journal of Interpersonal Violence, 10,* 85–105.

Radzinowicz, L. (1999) *Adventures in Criminology.* London: Routledge.

Roberts, A. H., Erikson, R. V., Riddle, M. & Bacon, J. G. (1974) Demographic variables, base rates, and personality characteristics associated with recidivism in male delinquents. *Journal of Consulting and Clinical Psychology, 42,* 833–841.

Salts, C. J., Lindholm, B. W., Goddard, H. W. & Duncan, S. (1995) Predictive variables of violent behavior in males. *Youth and Society, 26,* 377–399.

Serin, R. C. (1991) Psychopathy and violence in criminals. *Journal of Interpersonal Violence, 6,* 423–431.

Serin, R. C., Peters, R. D. & Barbaree, H. E. (1990) Predictors of psychopathy and release outcome in a criminal population. *Psychological Assessment: A Journal of Consulting and Clinical Psychology, 2,* 419–422.

Shields, I. W. (1993). The use of the Young Offender Level of Service Inventory (YO-LSI) with adolescents. *IARCA Journal, 5,* 10–26.

Shields, I. W. & Simourd, D. J. (1991) Predicting predatory behaviour in a population of incarcerated young offenders. *Criminal Justice and Behavior, 18,* 180–194.

Simourd, D. J. & Malcolm, P. B. (1998) Reliability and validity of the Level of Service Inventory–Revised among federally incarcerated sex offenders. *Journal of Interpersonal Violence, 13*, 261–274.

Smith, J. & Lanyon, R. I. (1968) Prediction of juvenile probation violators. *Journal of Consulting and Clinical Psychology, 32*, 54–58.

Sullivan, C., Grant, M. Q. & Grant, J. D. (1957) The development of interpersonal maturity: Application to delinquency. *Psychiatry, 20*, 373–385.

Van Voorhis, P. (1988) A cross classification of five offender typologies: Issues of construct and predictive validity. *Criminal Justice and Behavior, 15*, 109–124.

Visher, C. A., Lattimore, P. K. & Linster, R. L. (1991) Predicting the recidivism of serious youthful offenders using survival models. *Criminology, 29*, 329–366.

Ward, A. & Dockerill, J. (1999) The predictive accuracy of the violent offender treatment program risk assessment scale. *Criminal Justice and Behavior, 26*, 125–140.

Ward, D. (1987) *The Validity of the Reconviction Prediction Score.* London: HMSO.

Webster, C. D., Douglas, K. S., Eaves, D. & Hart, S. D. (1997) *HCR-20: Assessing Risk for violence (Version 2).* Vancouver: Simon Fraser University.

Webster, C. D., Harris, G. T., Rice, M. E., Cormier, C. & Quinsey, V. L. (1995) *The Violence Prediction Scheme: Assessing Dangerousness in High Risk Men.* Toronto: Centre of Criminology, University of Toronto.

Wormith, J. S. & Goldstone, C. S. (1984) The clinical and statistical prediction of recidivism. *Criminal Justice and Behavior, 11*, 3–34.

Zamble, E. & Porporino, F. (1988) *Coping, Behavior, and Adaptation in Prison Inmates.* New York: Springer-Verlag.

Zamble, E. & Porporino, F. (1990) Coping, imprisonment, and rehabilitation: Some data and their implications. *Criminal Justice and Behavior, 17*, 53–70.

Zamble, E. & Quinsey, V. L. (1997) *The Criminal Recidivism Process.* Cambridge: Cambridge University Press.

Chapter 13

THE POLICY IMPACT OF A SURVEY OF PROGRAMME EVALUATIONS IN ENGLAND AND WALES

Towards a New Corrections-Industrial Complex?

TOM ELLIS AND JANE WINSTONE

Institute of Criminal Justice Studies, University of Portsmouth, UK

This chapter outlines the development of the application of research and evaluation findings to government policy in England and Wales,[1*] with specific reference to a key survey of probation programme intervention. First, we contextualise the recent development of the probation service in England and Wales. Next, we provide a brief picture of how community disposals managed by the probation service fit into sentencing in general in England and Wales. We then outline the results and issues posed by a key survey of intervention programmes run by probation services. Finally we offer a discussion of the current position and difficult issues that lie ahead for the probation service if it is to ensure effective intervention with offenders.

BACKGROUND AND CONTEXT

Throughout the 1990s there was increasing pressure on the probation services of England and Wales to demonstrate an improvement in effectiveness. This pressure came from a number of sources, but it was a politically driven imperative based on research evidence that there were models of intervention that could reduce recidivism and could be delivered through the structures of the existing probation service (Home Office Circular, 35/98).

Rehabilitative treatment has always been one of the key aims of the probation service in England and Wales (Bottoms, Gelsthorpe & Rex, 2001), although there

---

[*] Notes are presented at the end of the chapter.

Offender Rehabilitation and Treatment: Effective Programmes and Policies to Reduce Re-offending. Edited by James McGuire.
© John Wiley & Sons, Ltd.

had been little emphasis, historically, on establishing its effectiveness. This aim was increasingly called into question from the mid-70s when Martinson (1974) produced research evidence to suggest that none of the treatment interventions available was effective in reducing recidivism. The subsequent "nothing works" pessimism characterised both academic and government thinking from the mid-70s onwards. The assumption was that any sort of intervention by the criminal justice system was unlikely to affect future offending behaviour. This substantially undermined internal professional confidence within the probation service, and also, external political confidence in community disposals.

Although the negative results of Martinson and others (Brody, 1976; Lipton, Martinson & Wilks, 1975) continued to affect the thinking of many in the criminal justice field well into the 1990s (McGuire & Priestley, 1995), the "nothing works" idea was challenged almost immediately by Palmer (1975) and Gendreau and Ross (1980). However, this countervailing evidence was slow to gain currency in England and Wales.

From the mid-1970s there was little pressure on resources and the probation service tended to refocus its efforts towards providing practical help rather than rehabilitation. As attention turned to cost rationing in the 1980s, central government initially placed increasing emphasis on "diversion from custody", given that community sentences were no less effective than prison and far cheaper. This resulted in budgetary expansion for the probation service throughout the 1980s, although with this came increasing demands for "efficiency" gains, foreshadowed by the 1984 Statement of National Objectives and Priorities. The need to demonstrate "value for money" led to a sudden reversal of budgetary expansion in the early 1990s, a subsequent increase in caseloads, and the need to demonstrate "effectiveness" in reducing re-offending.

The shift in policy emphasis in the 1990s was inextricably linked to international research developments. In particular, meta-analysis has been increasingly used to re-evaluate existing data from disparate interventions and generate firmer conclusions around effective intervention (Garrett, 1985; Izzo & Ross, 1990). In 1991, the first "What Works" conference was convened to consolidate existing and promising evidence with regard to effective methods to reduce re-offending. Much of this was based on re-analysis of "nothing works" data and new evidence, gathered during the 1980s, yielding positive results (e.g. Andrews et al., 1990; Lipsey, 1992). The conference papers delivered evidence that cognitive-behavioural programmes are most likely to have an impact on a range of target behaviours, including criminal behaviour (Hollin, 1991) and are thus likely to achieve a reduction in future offending. Many of the concepts and strategies debated at this conference are now part of the general vocabulary of the probation service and the Home Office at the beginning of the 21st century, e.g.: Reasoning and Rehabilitation (Ross & Fabiano, 1990); multimodal programmes (Hollin, 1991); community based programmes, structured programmes and high "treatment integrity" (McGuire, 1995) were concepts and strategies debated within the theme of "what works".

These developments, which in England and Wales have become known variously and at different times as "What Works" (with or without a question mark) and "Effective Practice", represent an unprecedented governmental willingness to produce research-led policy and practice. Given the research and theory base for models of intervention, it is arguably the largest psychological experiment ever conducted to manipulate behavioural change (Winstone & Dixon, 2000).

Compliance to what works policy initiatives has been increasingly linked to funding and a rapidly changing political and legislative framework. These changes are aimed at transforming the original "social work" philosophy and value base of the probation service "to advise, assist and befriend", into an attempt to provide "an effective service making a genuine impact on the behaviour of offenders" (Gendreau & Ross, 1987, p. 48). The emphasis is now on protection of the public, prevention of re-offending and rehabilitation (Nellis, 1996). These changes in the probation arena also dovetail with wider initiatives to reform the criminal justice system more generally, starting with the Criminal Justice Act in 1991, and the ensuing development of punishment in the community. This was akin to bringing politics into the community, but, nevertheless, the notion of just deserts, commensurate sentencing and effective rehabilitation have attained much greater political focus and currency in the last decade.

The cumulative effect of the developments of the 1990s, is that the probation service in the early 2000s has a much more selective strategy with regard to the programmes of intervention it now undertakes. Indeed, the government voiced an official agenda for the probation service requiring that the service ensure that "every aspect of work with offenders should be focused on those methods which have been proven to reduce re-offending" (Boateng, Home Office, 2000d, p. 1).

This focus has been sharpened by very recent changes in governance and by the earlier changes to funding arrangements for intervention programmes in England and Wales, known as the *Pathfinder* scheme. Since April 2001, the semi-autonomous status of the individual local probation services has been replaced by direct governmental control. The new national probation service is run directly from the Home Office through the national probation directorate, and formerly independent chief probation officers in each area are now effectively civil servants and have re-emerged as "chief officers". The new-style chiefs are now fully constrained by a funding arrangement which ensures that only those structured intervention programmes that can demonstrate that they adhere to accredited "what works principles" are viable.

Within this context, the results of two key information-gathering exercises on "effective practice", that took place in tandem, had a profound effect on subsequent domestic government policy in England and Wales. The Home Office carried out a survey of 191 cognitive-behavioural programmes (Hedderman & Sugg, 1997). At the same time, Her Majesty's Inspectorate of Probation (HMIP) carried out a survey of all structured programmes run by the probation service (Ellis & Underdown, 1998) to produce what the (then) Chief Inspector of Probation described as "one of the most important reports it has ever produced" (Smith, 1998, p. iii). Despite the positive gloss presented in this report and its subsequently produced companion guide (Chapman & Hough, 1998), the results confirmed that the probation service had failed to improve its historically poor record of properly evaluating interventions with offenders (see, for instance, Fischer, 1978;

Sheldon, 1994). The general lack of evaluation for most interventions identified by Ellis and Underdown (1998), along with a general lack of rigour in ensuring programme integrity, formed a catalyst for change in Home Office policy initiatives for the probation service. The publication of the HMIP report was followed by a major national conference attended by all chief officers and other agencies (Chapman & Hough, 1998). Following this, in early 1998, HMIP, Home Office, Probation Unit and ACOP committed themselves to implementing the findings of the report (Probation Circular 35/98) and lessons learned from such effective local practice as could be demonstrated (see examples from the HMIP survey below).

This chapter focuses in detail on the evidence from the HMIP survey. However it is important to bear in mind that the lack of evaluative effort on the part of the probation service has had a large part to play in the subsequent direction it has taken. This is largely because they failed to collect any systematic evidence that methods other than cognitive-behavioural approaches "work" with offenders, while proponents of cognitive-behavioural interventions are able to marshall ample evidence (see, for instance, Sheldon, 1994; MacDonald, Sheldon & Gillespie, 1992; Merrington & Stanley, 2000).

HOW COMMUNITY PENALTIES FIT INTO SENTENCING IN ENGLAND AND WALES

It is important, in the international context, to provide a brief outline on some key concepts of probation work in England and Wales. Most of the 1.4 million offenders sentenced in 1994[2] by English and Welsh courts received one of the following sentences: custody (5%); community sentence (9%); fine (75%); or discharge (9%). This means that around 130 000 offenders were sentenced to some form of community disposal, and two-thirds of these sentences were for more serious "indictable" offences (Home Office, 1995b, p. 37). As Figure 13.1 shows, around 90% of criminal

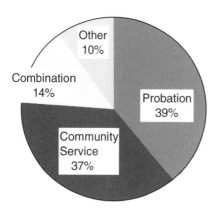

Figure 13.1   Persons commencing orders supervised by the probation service: 1996

supervision orders overseen by the probation service fell into just three categories: probation orders; community service orders; or combination orders[3] (Home Office, 1997, p. 17).

Community service orders (now community punishment orders) require the offender to perform unpaid work of between 40 and 240 hours within one year of conviction at a minimum rate of five hours per week. Work placements are intended to ensure some level of community reparation and integration of the offender. Probation orders (now community rehabilitation orders) require the offender to be supervised by the probation service for a period that may vary between six months and three years. The purpose of these orders is to rehabilitate the offender, protect the public and prevent the offender from committing further offences. Such orders may have additional requirements attached, such as attending programmes to tackle the causes of offending behaviour, but can also include residing at a specified address, and other restrictions. Within the terms of seriousness outlined in the Criminal Justice Act 1991, additional requirements are normally made only for more serious cases, although there is some recent evidence that such conditions are more likely to be attached where sentencers are simply made more aware of the possibility of using them (Hedderman, Ellis & Sugg, 1999). Combination orders are simply a combination of both probation and community service orders into a single sentence and were originally intended for use in only the most serious cases where custody is a distinct possibility. Additional requirements can be attached to the probation element of the order, further increasing the demands made upon the offender.

In 1996, just over 30% of probation orders and 21% of combination orders had additional requirements attached to them. However, the relationship between additional requirements and structured programmes is a loose one. The best proxy for this is "specified activities". Only around 8000 (55%) probation orders and 2500 (67%) combination orders with additional requirements actually required specified activities (Home Office, 1997, pp. 30–31). It is therefore important to bear in mind that most of the programmes evaluated below by Ellis and Underdown (1998) were directed at this relatively narrow band of orders. It is also important to remember that, with an increased emphasis on partnership and case management within the modern probation service, those officers who are in overall charge of an order may not personally deliver the programmes themselves, but will "subcontract" offenders either to specialist officers or outside agencies for the duration of programme intervention.

National Standards

National Standards were introduced in England and Wales for community service orders in 1989 and extended to most community disposals in October 1992 (Home Office, 1992b). They were revised and reissued in 1995 (Home Office, 1995a) and in 2000 (Home Office, 2000d). The standards were conceived as a way of developing and spreading good practice, accommodating changes in relevant legislation, demonstrating effectiveness and providing a public statement of the common requirements and values for all probation services (Home Office, 1992a). They are also intended to ensure that the public could have confidence that community disposals are an effective punishment and a way of ensuring offenders become responsible members of the community (Home Office, 1995a).

The standards set out the requirements for preparing pre-sentence reports (PSRs). These are reports submitted to the courts to assist them in determining "the most suitable method of dealing with an offender which imposes a restriction on liberty commensurate with the seriousness of the offence" (Home Office, 1995a, p. 7). They also provide detailed requirements for the different community orders (and supervision on release from custody), including: assessment and management of risk, public protection; timing and frequency of attendance; supervision plans; enforcement; and record keeping (Home Office, 1995a). Her Majesty's Inspectorate of Probation (HMIP) routinely monitors compliance with these standards.

THE HMIP SURVEY

Prior to the development of the *Pathfinder* scheme, HMIP decided that it was important to measure to what extent probation services in England and Wales were conforming to the "what works" principles in their programmes of intervention for offenders. Therefore, HMIP, in collaboration with the Central Probation Council (CPC), the Association of Chief Officers of Probation (ACOP) and the National Probation Research and Information Exchange (NPRIE) commissioned the investigation the aims of which were:

> To prepare an occasional paper providing the best practice guidance to probation areas to identify effective types of programming appropriate for supervising offenders in the community and to advise on the management arrangements needed to promote and support their effective provision. (HMIP, 1996)

The resulting occasional paper covered all key areas of what works issues, including: service and programme design; targeting and assessment of offenders; programme delivery; case management; organisational development; and evaluation evidence (HMIP, 1998). However, this chapter focuses specifically on the evaluation evidence, since this proved to be such major area of weakness in probation service programme provision. As Perry (1999, p. 15) notes: "The evaluation of outcomes determines the effectiveness of the programme and ultimately is judged by reconviction data."

This is particularly important, since even if all of the other elements of programme design are in place and are satisfactory, a programme's worth in terms of its effectiveness can only be measured by adequate outcome data. In 1980, Blackburn published the results of his re-examination of a series of programmes carried out in the 1970s, using methodological tests proposed by Logan (1972). He found that only five of the studies had actually satisfied adequate criteria on which they could reliably be evaluated, although all of them achieved a reduction in re-offending. As the results of the HMIP survey show, the situation with regard to outcome evaluation within the probation service had improved little since the 1970s. HMIP had originally envisaged that the evaluation survey would produce an analysis of how many of the returned programmes were effective. In fact, we ended up having to ask a much more basic question first: "In how many cases was sufficient evaluation carried out?" Not many programmes progressed beyond this point!

The HMIP survey consisted of three strands. The first two strands concentrated on the management arrangements to introduce effective supervision, and a scrutiny of programme definition and integrity for general offending programmes. However, this section of the chapter focuses on the third strand—the evaluation survey, which was the first of its kind to be carried out nationally in England and Wales. It was designed to identify:

(a) the number of probation programmes evaluated by the Probation Service;
(b) which of these programmes were carrying out adequate outcome evaluation; and
(c) the characteristics of the best-evaluated programmes.

Selecting Programmes from the Returns

In February 1996, HMIP requested information on both programme evaluation and general programme management arrangements. In total, 267 replies on programme outcome evaluation were returned from 43 (78%) of the (then) 55 probation services in England and Wales. Of these 267 programmes we selected 210 potentially suitable programmes that were either still running or had finished recently enough to be of interest. Thirty-four sex offender programmes were excluded since they have been well evaluated elsewhere (see Barker & Morgan, 1993; Beckett et al., 1994; Hedderman & Sugg, 1996).

An increasing number of research studies suggest that the probation service needs to pay more attention to collecting adequate data on programme outcome measures (see, for instance, Lösel, 1995; Vennard, 1996; Hedderman, 1998). For our survey, we asked areas to supply outcome data on all forms of evaluation commonly used to measure the effectiveness of probation programmes: reconvictions; changes in offenders' attitudes or behaviour; changes in social circumstances; levels of completion and compliance; offender feedback; and independent qualitative evaluation. There are more serious difficulties involved with using qualitative data (Antonowicz, Izzo & Ross, 1995) and offender feedback (McIvor, 1995) and we therefore limited our final analysis to the first four measures of programme effectiveness. This is not to say that these measures do not present their own difficulties, as will be seen below.

In order to maximise the chances of finding good practice in the detailed follow-up exercise, all programmes which examined outcome on at least three of the four main evaluation criteria were included. Table 13.1 shows the programmes selected and their combinations of evaluation measures.

Eighty of the 210 programmes considered for this study appeared to have achieved an adequate level of evaluation for our follow-up questionnaires. We

Table 13.1   Selection of programme returns by combinations of evaluation

No. of types of evaluation	Number of programmes (%)
4 main types or more	35 (44%)
Completion/compliance; reconviction; attitudinal	25 (31%)
Reconviction; attitudinal; social situation	2 (2%)
Completion/compliance; attitudinal; social situation	16 (20%)
Completion/compliance; reconviction; social situation	2(2%)
Total	80

also decided to include another 29 programmes which either entailed reconviction analyses, or were likely to be able to produce them in time for our follow-up questionnaire. As Lösel (1995) notes, although "official recidivism" is not a highly reliable and sensitive outcome measure, it continues to be of central importance for practical work. It also continues to be the measure by which the Home Office will judge the effectiveness of *Pathfinder* programmes and of the probation service overall. In sum, we concluded at this first stage of the survey that 109 (52%) of the 210 programmes considered seemed to have carried out adequate outcome evaluation.

It was clear from initial responses that different areas had often interpreted questions on outcome evaluation in different ways. We therefore asked the 109 'surviving' programme respondents to be more explicit about evaluation on the one hand, and other forms of data collection and monitoring on the other (see Vennard, 1996, p. 20). The responses from the 109 selected programmes justified our caution. Indeed, 22 of the 109 selected programmes had, in fact, carried out no evaluation. Only 50 programmes were eventually selected for the detailed follow-up questionnaire and fell into the three categories outlined in Table 13.2.

Programmes in the final category were included only to round out the full study. Of the 48 follow-up returns, we excluded 15 from further analysis either due to poor completion or very recent start dates (and therefore no evaluation results) leaving 33 for further examination. Two of these programmes did not complete

Table 13.2   Selection of programmes for detailed follow-up questionnaire

Had evaluated at least three of our four main outcome criteria	30
Had carried out at least a reconviction evaluation	12
Had been included in the scrutiny strand of the full investigation but had not met our full evaluation criteria	8
Total	50

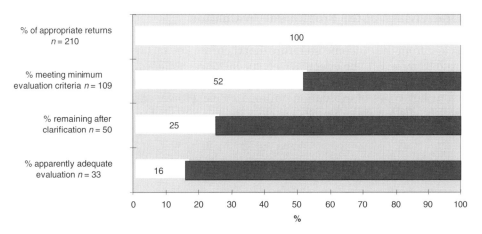

Figure 13.2 Attrition rate of programmes included in the final analysis by stage of selection

the evaluation section of the questionnaire and, instead, supplied only their own evaluation reports. Although these were of a good standard, it was not possible to extract the general information in the form required, and these programmes were, reluctantly, rejected. However, one of these programmes, the Ilderton motor project, has been included in the section on lessons for good practice below, due to the quality of the evaluation report.

Figure 13.2 summarises the attrition rate of programmes and the reasons for exclusion, through selection by our evaluation criteria.

As Table 13.3 shows, programmes targeting general offending behaviour were the largest single category of programmes evaluated to a minimum standard. Most of these programmes were aimed at those convicted of serious offences or with a high risk of re-offending. One programme was for women offenders only, but was otherwise general in scope. Among the programmes which targeted particular offences, the majority were aimed at motoring offences: taking and driving away (TDA); taking without owners consent (TWOC); irresponsible driving and drinking and driving. The remainder of the programmes targeted specific behaviour or circumstances associated with offending: domestic violence; anger management; alcohol and drugs problems; and unemployment.

Table 13.3   Programme targeting

General offending	13 (39%)
Offence specific programmes	11 (33%)
Behaviour associated with offending	7 (21%)
Circumstances associated with offending	2 (6%)
Total	33

Characteristics of the Programme Evaluation

It is clear from the outcome literature that there are key factors that must be present if a programme is to be effective (see, for instance, Vennard, Sugg & Hedderman, 1997; Chapman & Hough, 1998). Here we concentrate on the characteristics of the four key types of evaluation outlined above. However, it is also important to establish whether programmes are clear in their aims before it can be established whether their research designs are appropriate.

Reconvictions Evaluation

At the time the study was carried out, there was no Home Office or probation service standard for evaluating reconvictions for offenders on programmes. However, it is worth noting that the Home Office supplied the Offender Group Reconviction Scale (OGRS)—a computerised actuarial risk of reconviction predictor—to all probation services as both an assessment and research tool in 1996 and this is being superseded by the current roll-out of the new combined assessment tool, the *Offender Assessment System* (OASys: Home Office, 1999a).

Of course, reconvictions are not the only way to gauge programme success, but they are a key measure despite the widely recognised limitations of reconviction rates (see Lloyd, Mair & Hough, 1995; Vennard, 1996; Rex, 1999; Palmer, 1995). There is, moreover, little doubt that reconvictions are considered an essential outcome evaluation component by most policy-makers, practitioners and managers and this is the main thrust of the Home Office's current effectiveness initiative which will be discussed below. This is also reflected by the fact that 25 of the 33 selected programme returns ranked reducing re-offending as their primary aim, and all but one of the 33 programmes attempted some form of reconviction analysis. It was important, therefore, to establish what form reconviction evaluation took and how appropriate this was to the stated aims of the programmes.

As Vennard (1996) points out, there remains a lack of clarity concerning the "correct" follow-up period for reconvictions (Lösel, 1995; Lloyd, Mair & Hough, 1995; Vennard, Sugg & Hedderman, 1997) and the difficulty in choosing appropriate starting points from which to count reconvictions. Both of these points are reflected in the findings from the survey. Of the 26 programmes for which information was available, the period covered by reconvictions analysis varied from 4 to 24 months, with an average of 16 months.

The point from which reconvictions were measured varied enormously between programmes. Both Lloyd, Mair and Hough (1995) and the Home Office (through OGRS) recommend carrying out reconvictions analysis "24 months from point of sentence" as originally recommended by Logan (1972). However, only three programmes (from the same area) appeared to be using this method. Fourteen programmes started their reconviction period from the date an offender completed the programme, five took their starting point from the beginning of the programme, and one from the end of the order. Two measured reconvictions "during the order" and one "on receipt of the appropriate forms"!

The source of the reconviction data also varied enormously. In the 28 cases where this was stated, only two programmes used the Home Office Offenders Index option (as required by OGRS). By far the most popular source was recorded as "probation service" with or without reference to local police or court records: 18 of the programmes cited this as their source of reconviction data. Among the other options were the Criminal Records Office, Police National Computer, interviews with victims of domestic violence and the local police Domestic Violence Unit. Only 5 of these 28 programmes mentioned or provided evidence of the use of expected reconviction figures (three of them using OGRS) and only two programmes mentioned the use of a control sample or quasi-experimental design.

There was considerable variation too in the extent to which certain categories of offenders had been excluded from programme evaluation. For the most part, evaluative work only managed to include offenders who had completed a programme, and there were very few cases where it proved possible to exclude pseudo-reconvictions (see Lloyd, Mair & Hough, 1995).

Evaluating Changes in Attitude/Behaviour

"Changing attitudes towards offending" was ranked in the returns as one of the three main aims of 30 programmes, although in the majority of cases (22) this was ranked second. Twenty-six of the 33 programme returns included some attempt to measure whether offenders' attitudes had changed as a result of attending the programme. Again, there was some variability in the details provided and the type of attitudinal measures used. Five of these 26 programmes did not stipulate the period of analysis.

Twelve programmes used CRIMEPICS/II (Frude, Honess & Maguire, 1990, 1994) to evaluate changes in offenders' attitudes, and two of these used a number of other recognised instruments. One programme used the Rotter locus of control measure alone and three used alcohol knowledge tests. Ten programmes used "home made" self-completion and self-perception questionnaires of varying quality.

Changes in Social Circumstances

Only three programmes included "changing an offender's social circumstances" as a main aim. However, 16 of the 33 programmes included some type of evaluation of changes in this key factor. In 12 cases, this was the CRIMEPICS problem inventory, although the programmes themselves did not always recognise this as a potentially separate evaluation component from the attitudinal scale. Three programmes followed-up the offenders' employment, accommodation and health circumstances by checking with local agencies, while one programme had developed a self-completion questionnaire with the help of an independent consultant.

Completion and Compliance

Completion of the programme was a main aim in only five programme returns, and completion of the order was judged to be a principal feature for only three.

This perhaps reflects the dubious value of relying on completion and compliance as a measure of effectiveness, since it does not measure any effective change. The survey returns indicate that there is no common standard for recording completion and compliance data. The variation in the quality of the returns made it impossible to carry out analysis on this component with any certainty (see also Vennard, Hedderman & Sugg, 1997, for similar findings). For 21 of the returns, respondents had to collate some information specifically for this survey. This, plus one of the author's direct experience of trying to carry out a reconviction follow-up on an "offenders into employment initiative" (carried out by Roberts et al., 1996) suggest that once an offender has completed a programme and the programme staff have moved on, it is often impossible to establish who has been on the programme. While this may, in part, be explained by the greater complexity of probation orders with requirements, there is also an underlying casework-centred cultural bias (Colin Roberts, 1995) against designing-in evaluation from the start of a programme (see McIvor, 1995). For example, one questionnaire noted that completion and compliance data were not available, "since the groupwork providers did not hold responsibility for the total order".

SELECTIVITY

A key "what works" principle for effectiveness is to ensure that offenders are selected appropriately for the type of intervention provided. Areas were, therefore, asked to provide information on the type of offenders they targeted in these selected programmes. Half (17) of the 33 programmes operated a lower age limit, which varied from 16 to 21. Three of these programmes also included an upper age limit. Offenders were selected by gender on only 9 programmes (27%): 8 selected men only and 1 programme was run for women offenders. There were no programmes specifically for minority ethnic groups.

The majority of the selected programme returns (25) claimed that some attempt had been made to match offenders' characteristics with the type of supervision or intervention available on the programme. In 8 of these cases, it was difficult to discern how this selection process differed from a standard PSR interview. Of the other 17 programmes: 2 relied solely on previous offending history or seriousness of current offence; 3 based all assessments on cognitive deficits, motivation levels, social maturity, etc.; 9 combined assessments of previous offending and/or seriousness with other elements, typically involving risk assessment; 2 relied solely on whether the offender was unemployed or not; and 1 also selected offenders on employment and previous history of serious offences.

EVALUATION EVIDENCE OF EFFECTIVENESS

Many of the returns in both stages of the HMIP survey showed that services often did not fully appreciate the distinction between data collection, monitoring and evaluation. Indeed, many of the "evaluation" reports attached to the returns were, in reality, monitoring or progress reports rather than full programme evaluations.

To some extent, it is likely that National Standards' emphasis on monitoring, as opposed to outcome evaluation, has been reflected until recently in the probation service's practices. However, in order to measure the effectiveness of programmes, monitoring information must be of the right type (i.e. not relying on offender feedback) and must be systematically analysed so that impact or outcome can be clearly measured.

This section summarises the main characteristics of the four better-evaluated programmes[4] in England and Wales that had demonstrably effective outcomes, and ends with a discussion of the main difficulties which probation services need to overcome when undertaking programme evaluations. The reports which provided the best evaluation tended to include the following categories of information:

- descriptive information on the offenders and the programmes covered;
- completion and compliance data;
- repeated use, where appropriate, of attitudinal and problem measures;
- adequate reconviction studies, which use predictive scores and control groups;
- qualitative information and offenders'/professionals' views on the adequacy of the programme design.

Some the evaluations included here are comprised of some or all of these elements and a number of positive findings emerge from them.

Mid-Glamorgan Straight Thinking on Probation (STOP)

This programme utilises the *Reasoning and Rehabilitation* cognitive-behavioural approach developed in Canada (see Ross & Fabiano, 1985). The programme is based on a building block approach to teaching cognitive behavioural skills including: self-control; social and thinking skills; values enhancement; critical reasoning; and emotional management.

The aims of the programme are to teach offenders to:

- Stop and think before acting
- Consider the consequences of their behaviour
- Develop alternative ways of responding to personal problems
- To consider the impact of their actions on others (especially victims).

Researchers evaluated a number of aspects of this programme (based on offenders attending the first 10 months of the programme up to April 1992—see Lucas, Raynor & Vanstone, 1992). The completion rate for the evaluation period was 75% when 'dropouts' for legitimate reasons, such as health and employment, were accounted for (Raynor & Vanstone, 1996).

Reconvictions analyses have now been carried out over various periods (including the most commonly specified 24 months) and using a number of different types of comparison groups, including a subgroup of "STOP completers only" (Raynor & Vanstone, 1996). Parole predictor scores were calculated (see Copas, Ditchfield &

Marshall, 1994) for each group. The results show that those who completed the STOP programme had better than predicted reconvictions at 12 months, although results were similar to other community penalty disposals at 24 months (Raynor & Vanstone, 1996). However, the evaluation showed more promising results when looking at the seriousness of reconvictions, and Raynor and Vanstone (1996) concluded that there was a lasting and substantial reduction in the incidence of offences serious enough to attract a custodial sentence. They also added the warning that this positive effect was partly offset by a high reconviction and incarceration rate for those who failed to complete the programme.

Researchers have also carried out two analyses of attitudinal change using CRIMEPICS (see Lucas, Raynor & Vanstone, 1992; Raynor & Vanstone, 1997). The results of the more recent analysis indicate that STOP participants showed more positive change in crime-prone attitudes than offenders on Community Service and more improvement in self-reported problems than was shown either in Community Service or other probation orders.

The evaluation also covered implementation issues (including programme integrity), staff feedback and offender feedback. The latter was notable in that it concentrated on programme impact (unlike many of the offender feedback reports supplied with the returns, which concentrated solely on offender satisfaction). Two weeks after completing the programme, the rusults showed that it had positively affected the thinking, in problem situations, of 91% of the 64 offenders concerned (Raynor & Vanstone, 1996).

Of all the returns made to the HMIP study, this programme was the most extensively evaluated. Part of the evaluation's strength lies in its continuing use of external researchers who reanalyse data and refine their methods. The evaluation concludes with a number of points that are likely to be pursued in the next analysis. For example, it recommends a tightening up of the selection process, perhaps by introducing attitudinal measures into the initial assessment of offenders, and this can be done in various ways—see, for instance, Roberts et al. (1996), Aubrey and Hough (1997) or NPRIE (1997). The intention here is not to weed out offenders with the highest risk factors (and thereby skew the results) but to ensure that those offenders who are selected are likely to respond to the cognitive-behavioural approach. Indeed, Raynor and Vanstone (1997) presciently suggest the need to develop a range of programmes for offenders who are not responsive to Reasoning and Rehabilitation style treatments.

Inner London Probation Service (ILPS) Ilderton Motor Project

The community-based Ilderton Motor Project targeted young offenders previously convicted of vehicle crime. Its intention was to allow these offenders to pursue their interest in cars in a constructive and responsible way. Those on whom the analysis was carried out were on probation orders and were attending the programme on either a mandatory or a voluntary basis. The programme focused on two key outcomes: to reduce offending in general; to reduce motor vehicle offending in particular. The evaluation of this programme was, therefore, limited solely to an analysis of reconvictions.

The assumption made in the programme design is that some offenders do specialise to an extent in vehicle crime (see Harraway, 1986). While the evaluators recognised that there is evidence that a high level of specialisation is unlikely for most offenders (see Farrington, 1992; Tarling, 1994), they found that offenders selected for the Ilderton motor project had 74% of previous offences for Taking and Driving Away (TDA). The study also made use of a control group which showed a 46% Taking and Driving Away (TDA) rate.

The reconvictions analysis (see Wilkinson & Morgan, 1995) was carried out on all project participants over a 7-year period, ending in 1994. The evaluators chose to use arrest data, since they are likely to provide a truer picture of 're-offending' before prosecution and sentencing processes have their effect on the officially recorded "reconviction rate" (see also Lloyd, Mair & Hough, 1995; Vennard, 1996; Vennard, Sugg & Hedderman, 1997). They also applied a PSR predictor (see Wilkinson, 1994) to both the offenders on the motor project and a matched control group.

The reconvictions analyses (at 12, 24 and 36 months) showed that offenders who had attended the Ilderton project were significantly less likely to re-offend than those in the control group. They also found that after two years, the offenders who had attended the Ilderton project were three times less likely to be sentenced to custody than those in the comparison group; and after three years, the difference was even more marked (Wilkinson & Morgan, 1995). Clearly, the indications are that this programme successfully reduces further offending, but, as with many studies, the number of offenders included in this evaluation is too small to be fully conclusive.

One innovation included in the evaluation was an estimation of the financial costs to the community saved by the Ilderton Motor Project, which concluded that the project saved three times what it cost to run.

Camberwell Probation Centre

The Camberwell Probation Centre (CPC) programme, like the STOP programme above, was based on the Reasoning and Rehabilitation approach, with the accompanying aim to "reduce offending by changing the way offenders think" (Wilkinson, 1995a). The evaluation was designed to capture the changes that were brought about in offenders' thinking and re-offending behaviour.

Reconvictions, based on data obtained from the Offenders' Index, were measured (at 6, 12 and 18 months) from 1993, although it is worth noting that the evaluators experienced some difficulty in identifying convictions for offenders in almost half of the cases submitted. Data were collected for those who attended the CPC compared with a similar size control group who did not. The results show that although the CPC appears to reduce reconvictions (and reconvictions for serious offences in particular) compared to the comparison group, the results generally did not attain statistical significance (Wilkinson, 1995a). Despite this, the evaluation is impressive in the number of "intermediate" outcome measures evaluated, including a battery of psychometric tests that foreshadow the Home Office's *Offender Assessment System* (OASys) which has been piloted and is imminently scheduled for 'roll-out'.

Inner London Demonstration Project with Burglars

The ILPS Demonstration Unit was set up in 1981, ran for four years, and was aimed primarily at increasing sentencers' confidence in probation disposals. It was one of the first UK-based projects to run offence-specific courses. The programme used social skills exercises in both one-to-one and individual supervision (see Priestley et al., 1978) to challenge offending behaviour and had affinities, on a theoretical level, with the Reasoning and Rehabilitation approach. One aspect of this course was run for offenders convicted of burglary.

A long-term reconvictions analysis was carried out on 112 offenders, comparing those burglars who were targeted and attended the Demonstration Unit with those who were targeted but did not attend. The criminogenic characteristics of the two groups, including risk of reconviction, were largely similar. Although the numbers involved are small, the analysis shows a significantly lower reconviction rate for the burglars attending the Demonstration Unit than for the control group after one year. However, this effect all but disappeared at the two-year point, indicating a strong but temporary effect (Wilkinson, 1995a).

In contrast to the evaluation of the Ilderton Motor Project and the STOP projects above, reconviction rates did not distinguish between burglary and other offences, partly because offenders attending the Unit could not be classified as specialist burglars. This said, the project is an early example of using a convincing evaluation approach.

THE CURRENT PICTURE AND FUTURE CONSIDERATIONS

The nature and direction of programmatic intervention by the probation service has changed radically since the results of the HMIP survey were first published. Obviously, there were many types of intervention, often on a small scale, and often only in isolated services. Equally obviously, very few of these programmes could produce any evidence that they were effective in achieving their aims—aims which generally included reducing re-offending or reconvictions. The four programmes briefly outlined above were the only evidence of any systematic proof of the value of probation interventions, and all of them were variations on cognitive behavioural approaches.

Given the results of the HMIP survey, one possible direction that could have been taken was to carry out simple outcome evaluations of all, or most, of the existing programmes identified. This would have involved some centralised pre-scription of the type of instruments used: for instance, *Offender Group Reconviction Scale* (OGRS-2; Taylor, 1999) for reconvictions and CRIMEPICS (II) or LSI-R (see Andrews & Bonta, 1995) for attitudes, behaviour, social and other problems. Some of these discussions were held, but inevitably foundered on issues such as the applicability or completeness of OGRS in all cases, local variations and other problems that we return to below. Many of these objections were well-founded. For instance, it is clear that domestic violence programmes cannot measure recidivism using OGRS, but other methods exist which could be agreed upon as equally standardised (see Dobash et al., 1996). Simple evaluations could have been used to justify continuation or discontinuation of existing programmes, especially those aimed at general offending. Programmes that had been found to work could have been investigated further to look at what combination of selectivity, implementation and integrity were present. As Palmer (1995) notes, having established *whether* a form of intervention works it is then important to ascertain *why* it works, in order to avoid sweeping generalisations—something that is perhaps more difficult to achieve with large-scale, national implementations. Unfortunately, as the HMIP survey showed, the individual probation services were not able to coordinate and agree sufficiently on this concept and, as a consequence, have now lost all independent control of their programme provision.

The policy path subsequently taken is one based on recognition of the international research findings, especially the meta-analyses, as providing a blueprint for the content and style of all effective probation programme provision. Given the overwhelming international body of evidence regarding the success of cognitive-behavioural approaches (Reid & Hanrahan, 1981; Sheldon, 1994; MacDonald, Sheldon & Gillespie, 1992; Merrington & Stanley, 2000), which is also mirrored in the limited results of the HMIP study, it is not surprising that this approach also dominates the new, centralised intervention agenda of the national probation service.

In 1998 Lipton presented a paper at conference entitled *Stop and Think* organised by the Prison Service in England and Wales. This paper was titled "How do cognitive skills training programs for offenders compare with other modalities: A meta-analytic perspective". This exemplifies the type of research that supported political decision-making to establish the criteria, implement and fund the roll-out of the *Pathfinder* initiative upon which the accredited programmes would be established and which underpinned the brief when the Joint Prison/Probation Accreditation Panel was set up in 1999 to assess programmes.

The current funding of structured intervention is tied to the implementation of *Pathfinder* programmes, which were initially identified from existing probation service delivery following the HMIP survey. The *Pathfinder* scheme subjects existing and new programmes to a process of joint probation/prison service accreditation to ensure that all funded programmes conform to the "what works" principles (most notably the inclusion of appropriate evaluation of outcomes and programme integrity in terms of content and delivery). In this way, for the first time, the probation service is required to deliver a national agenda of intervention, eradicating, perhaps permanently, the independence of individual probation areas in the decision-making process underpinning provision and any local community biases in provision that had previously existed in a less-regulated climate.

The current crop of accredited programmes that have been rolled out following the *Pathfinder* initiative are unsurprising in their reliance on cognitive-behavioural methods. Accredited status has been achieved for "general offending" programmes such as "Think First", "Enhanced Thinking Skills", "Reasoning and Rehabilitation" and the Priestley One-to-One programme. The other programmes to have achieved this status are "offence specific" programmes and include one on drinking and driving and one for sex offenders. Others are being developed for accreditation are targeted at: violent offenders, sex offenders, acquisitive crime, irresponsible driving, racially motivated offending, domestic violence and women offenders. Some have achieved an intermediate "recognised" status.

The political agenda appears to be veering towards managerialist output-focused targets which may, ultimately, undermine the accompanying outcome focus on reducing reconvictions. The Home Office has set a target of 60 000 offenders (Home Office, 2000a) to pass through accredited programmes in the first five years of the national roll-out. This is supported by a more severe enforcement regime in the revised 2000 issue of national standards and will shortly be enhanced by a new range of "seamless" sentences (see Home Office, 2000b). However, the managerialist appeal of uniform delivery by a uniformly structured probation service has, inevitably, been challenged on two main fronts: doubts about the reliability of the underpinning research; and doubts about provision and implementation.

The Joint Prison/Probation Accreditation Panel (2000), in its first published report on "What Works", had already publicly debated the difficulties involved on both fronts. First they recognised that most of the research evidence is from overseas and may not be strictly transferable to the British context. Further, they noted that some aspects of offending are still under-researched, as are some design and implementation issues. Second, a number of doubts were raised about implementation and provision on such a large scale, from assuring adequate staff training, quality assurance of intensity, sequencing and duration, to the need to ensure constant review provision in the light of experience and emerging evidence. The Panel also noted that the differences between community-based and institution-based approaches had not been adequately analysed and, as is becoming increasingly apparent, neither had the difficulties linked to offender compliance with the long-term interventions.

The publication of a retrospective study of the *Thinkfirst* programme (Home Office, 2000c), could be interpreted as lending weight to some of the concerns expressed by the panel. Data for the first 18–24 months, based on reconviction rates, must be treated cautiously, partly due to dropout rates. This, in itself, is a concern as research suggests that short interventions in isolation, which is the type of dosage associated with dropout, are rarely effective and can be counterproductive (Joint Prison/Probation Accreditation Panel, 2000). Those most likely to drop out had accommodation difficulties and a number of projects have experienced high dropout rates due to the stricter application of enforcement rules in such circumstances. Uncertain accommodation status can be linked to criminal lifestyles (Walters, 1990) and is recognised as a criminogenic need and dynamic risk factor, which is unlikely to simply vanish because the offender is participating in a long-term structured programme. The results of the *Thinkfirst* programme suggest that offenders are faring better in the longer term (as would be expected from the theoretical principles underpinning the model). However, the programme is likely to suffer from integrity threats caused by individual issues such as accommodation and enforcement effects.

It is intended that such personal issues should be resolved through case management. However, as Rex (2001) points out, specifying the requirement and even the arrangements is not the same as ensuring delivery on the ground. Rex suggests that competing priorities, pressures on staff resources and offender non-compliance may interact to produce a reality of delivery that is far from the ideal set out in the manual. This will come as no surprise to professional practitioners who have long recognised that responsivity, in terms of establishing a relationship which the offender perceives as useful and pertinent, is a key factor in drawing the individual into and maintaining the established compliance required for offence-focused work (Winstone & Dixon, 2000). In this context, securing stable accommodation and finding more creative ways of ensuring compliance than applying a rigid "two-strikes" enforcement policy are required (Ellis, 2000) if programmes are to avoid simply treating those offenders who were most likely to improve without assistance.

The *Thinkfirst* programme is not alone in producing less than convincing interim evidence. Merrington and Stanley (2000) have reviewed both published and unpublished evaluations of a range of programmes and conclude that the reconviction rates achieved in North America (see Vennard, Sugg & Hedderman, 1997) have yet to be emulated in the UK despite the more modest Home Office expection of a reduction of 5% across all forms of probation supervision (Home Office, 2000a). One reason for this mismatch between expectations and reality may be that there is a methodological flaw in replicating, on a large scale, results derived from a series of smaller studies (Fraser, 2000), notwithstanding the exacerbating issues of transposing research across cultures and continents. Indeed, the difficulties posed in ensuring national programme integrity and replicability from small-scale studies mitigates against responsivity within programme delivery and the "culture of curiosity, innovation and trust" (Chapman & Hough, 1998) which are contributory factors in the success of cognitive-behavioural models.

The most common criticism of the types of programmes accredited so far has always been that they focus on the individual to the exclusion of socio-economic, political and cultural contexts (Neary, 1992; Pitts, 1992; Vanstone, 2000).[5] The importance of local community factors which are key in the success of delivery (Dixon, 2000; Gendreau, Goggin & Smith, 1999; Paley, 1987) is well documented. Rex (1999, 2001) brings environmental factors to the fore and points to the considerable weight of evidence (Raynor & Vanstone, 1997; May, 1999; Shover, 1996; Farrall & Bowling, 1999) supporting the need to take account of the social environments in which offenders are taking decisions and acting upon them in designing effective rehabilitiative programmes (Rex, 2001). The conclusion could be drawn that lessons have not yet been sufficiently learned from previous studies which demonstrated deterioration in the positive impact on offending rates (Vanstone, 2000) or from studies demonstrating that contributory factors in offender compliance are linked to offender perceptions of relevance and legitimacy of the sentence (Whitfield, 1995; Rex, 2001). Contributory factors of perceptions of relevance and legitimacy could be embraced under the umbrella of the responsivity principle. An example of this is pro-social modelling (Bottoms & Rex, 1998) which promotes changes in individual perceptions of identity that can lead to desistance from offending (Biernacki, 1986; Devlin & Turney, 1999; Graham & Bowling, 1995; Rex, 2001).

A further criticism that has been levelled at this particular stage of the roll-out of the programmes is that a significant proportion of the offender population, such as low or very high risk offenders is being excluded (Gadd, cited in Andrews et al., 2001). Suggestions that the parameters of the criteria for suitability (Probation Circular 96/2000: Home Office, 2000e) be widened would be likely to exacerbate the problems experienced in the McGuire study where the inclusion of high-risk offenders merely increased the dropout rate with all the issues attendant upon that for both recidivism rates and evaluation validity. On the other hand, inclusion of low-risk offenders increases the risk of too high a "dose" of intervention and a potential increase in offending (see Vennard, Sugg & Hedderman, 1997). Hollin (2001) also demonstrates that provision for female offenders is patchy. At least one *Pathfinder* programme has been dropped and others are not yet ready for accreditation. Women therefore continue to be placed in general offending programmes despite the mixed evidence for this practice (Hollin, 2001). A *Pathfinder* programme is being developed to explore the applicability of programmes for minority ethnic groups, but at the time of writing this is still at the research and development phase. Furthermore, differences in provision across the probation areas is likely to be sustained by the programme selection that probation services were required to make (Probation Circular 64/99: Home Office, 1999b).

Much of this reflects the Joint Prison/Probation Accreditation Panel initial concerns. That is not to say that the cognitive-behavioural programmes are not effective, but that there are limitations around the flexibility of implementation, both resource and programme based, which impede the overall effectiveness of probation intervention. While national provision remains uncertain and patchy for a wide group of offenders who fall outside the category of white, male, medium risk, it could be suggested that the competition for resources and prioritising of the *Pathfinder* and accredited programme delivery will sustain the dubious allocation of offenders into potentially unsuitable groups. This is a practice that may alleviate the strain on the probation service to supervise all who come within its remit (efficiency), but it is unlikely to promote the principles of assessment of suitability and programme integrity upon which the evaluations will rely (effectiveness).

There is already some evidence within one probation service that existing short basic skills programmes, which were not evaluated but appealed to sentencers, have been replaced by a single cognitive-behavioural programme of several months' duration. With the new funding structure, this is the only type of programme that is financially viable for that service. This inevitably leads to low-risk offenders being put onto a high-intensity course to satisfy the demands of sentencers for some form of structured intervention in addition to straight probation orders (see Hedderman, Ellis & Sugg, 1999). This is the type of scenario, we would argue, that will be repeated throughout England and Wales through the new national probation service. It is a direct result of the failure (with some notable exceptions evidenced above) of the former local probation services to develop an evaluation culture (hence no evidence of the worth of existing programmes) and of the pressing need for government to establish central control in order to impose the "what works" agenda directly so that it can demonstrate that community intervention is effective.

The decision to implement existing, largely overseas, research findings as a template for success may turn out to have been misguided, perhaps confirming the concerns of the Joint Prison/Probation Accreditation Panel as outlined above. By funding the implementation of a national process, rather than funding the evaluation of existing programme outcomes, the Home Office is, in effect, taking a large gamble on the outcome of the international research findings, but with no guarantee of success in the English and Welsh context. As noted above, the interim evidence suggests that the odds on failure are shortening.

Finally, it is likely that there will be changes to the sentencing structure if the proposals put forward by Halliday (see Home Office, 2000b) are adopted in any significant form. The most radical element of the suggested changes is that "seamless sentences" may involve both community and custodial elements. This is likely to present new problems for evaluators in establishing the relative effectiveness of community disposals compared to custodial sentences.

For the future, it seems clear that the new national probation service itself is "on probation". Despite recent funding increases, the probation service budget is insignificant in relation to either prisons or policing, with the corollary that its power within the criminal justice system is relatively weak. The Prisons–Probation review (Home Office, 1999c) established the new national probation service and also established a new regional structure which matches that of the prison service. Several other, more radical changes, were mooted but not implemented—not least of which was the potential merging of prisons and probation into a single corrections agency. Thus far, the local probation areas, in failing to engage adequately with the effectiveness agenda, have been coerced into a centralised, national structure. If the new national service fails to deliver sufficient reductions in offending, its role (rather than the centralised implementation of accredited programmes) will again come into question and many of the suggestions in the Prisons–Probation review (Home Office, 1999c) are therefore likely to be revisited. The service will then face further coercion to perform with the threat of being amalgamated with the prison service (effectively signifying absorption, given the difference in size and power between the two agencies). In turn, this is likely to lead to greater inroads by private security companies who are now managing several technocratised disposals using electronic tags (including home detention curfew as part of custodial sentences), as well as managing a handful of private prisons. What this will achieve is the further congruence between policy and practice, which is already at its closest historically (Vanstone, 2000). However, the danger is that none of the expected effectiveness (even in the narrow terms defined by the Home Office) will be delivered through the roll-out of accredited programmes. If this happens, we may return to the "nothing works" pessimism of the 70s and 80s, with a managerial emphasis on efficient management of offender populations, but this time through a centralised and increasingly privatised corrections service: as Nils Christie (2000) might put it, a new corrections-industrial complex.

NOTES

1. For historical reasons, Britain has no single equivalent to what would normally be termed the "ministry of the interior". In relation to England and Wales, these responsibilities are assumed by the Home Office. Scotland, which now has devolved powers, has always had separate legal and ministerial status, as has Northern Ireland. Scotland has no probation service and supervision of offenders in the community is carried out by Social Services. While Wales now has devolved powers, the situation with regard to the probation service remains linked to that of England. Probation initiatives in Wales necessarily involve the Welsh Office, but for reasons of brevity and style, we have used "Home Office" as shorthand for "Home Office and Welsh Office". Similarly, Her Majesty's Inspectorate of Probation (HMIP) has jurisdiction in England and Wales only.

2. These figures are cited as those most relevant for the time period covered by the HMIP survey.
3. These orders have been respectively renamed, as a result of the recent Criminal Justice and Court Services Act (2000), as: community rehabilitation orders; community punishment orders; and community punishment and rehabilitation orders.
4. For more detail on these programmes and on the other "promising" programmes captured by the survey, see Ellis and Underdown (1998).
5. However, it should be noted that most "cognitive-behavioural" programmes are based on a model in which offences are conceptualised as the result of a conjunction of personal and situational factors. Programmes, therefore, are often designed specifically to prepare individuals who participate in them to identify and alter the situational or wider external factors that contribute to their difficulties.

REFERENCES

Andrews, D. A. & Bonta, J. (1995) *LSI-R: The Level of Service Inventory—Revised: Manual*. New York, NY and Toronto: Multi-Health Systems, Inc.

Andrews, D. Hollins, C. Raynor, P. Trotter, C & Armstrong, B. (Eds.) (2001) *Sustaining Effectiveness in Working with Offenders: Conference Papers*. Cardiff: The Cognitive Centre Foundation.

Andrews, D. A., Zinger, I., Hoge, R. D., Bonta, J., Gendreau, P. & Cullen, F. T. (1990) Does correctional treatment work? A clinically relevant and psychologically informed meta-analysis. *Criminology, 28*, 369–414.

Antonowicz, D. H., Izzo, R. L. & Ross, R. R. (1995) Characteristics of effective offender rehabilitation programmes. In Ross, R. R. & Ross, R. D. (Eds.) *Thinking Straight: The Reasoning and Rehabilitation Programme for Delinquency Prevention and Offender Rehabilitation*. Ottawa: Air Training and Publications.

Aubrey, R. & Hough, M. (1997) *Assessing Offenders' Needs: Assessment Scales for the Probation Service*. Home Office Research Study 166. London: Home Office.

Barker, M. & Morgan, R. (1993) *Sex Offenders: A Framework for the Evaluation of Community-Based Treatment*. Research and Planning Unit Occasional Paper. London: Home Office.

Beckett, R., Beech, A., Fisher, D. & Fordham, A. S. (1994) *Community-Based Treatment for Sex Offenders: An Evaluation of Seven Treatment Programmes*. Research and Planning Unit Occasional Paper. London: Home Office.

Biernacki, P. (1986) *Pathways from Heroin Addiction: Recovery Without Treatment*. Philadelphia, PA: Temple University Press.

Blackburn, R. (1980) *Still not working? A look at some recent outcomes in offender rehabilitation*. Paper presented to the Scottish Branch of the British Psychological Society, Conference on Deviance, University of Stirling.

Bottoms A., Gelsthorpe L. & Rex S. (2001) *Community Penalties: Change and Challenges*. Cullompton: Willan.

Bottoms, A. & Rex S. (1998) Pro-Social Modelling and Legitimacy: Their potential Contribution to Effective Probation Practice. In S. Rex & A. Matravers (Eds.)*Pro-Social Modelling and Legitimacy: The Day Conference*. Cambridge: Institute of Criminology.

Brody, S. (1976) *The Effectiveness of Sentencing*. Home Office Research Study 35. London: HMSO.

Chapman, T. & Hough, M. (1998) *Evidence Based Practice: A Guide to Effective Practice*. London: HMIP.

Christie, N. (2000) *Crime Control as Industry: Towards GULAGS, Western Style*, (3rd edition). London: Routledge.

Copas, J., Ditchfield, J. & Marshall, P. (1994) *Development of a new reconviction prediction score*. Research Bulletin No. 36. Home Office Research and Statistics Department.

Devlin, A. & Turney, B. (1999) *Going Straight: After Crime and Punishment*. Winchester: Waterside Press.

Dixon, L. (2000) Punishment and the question of owndership: Groupwork in the criminal justice system. *Groupwork, 12*, 6–25.

Dobash, R., Dobash, R. E., Cavanagh, K. & Lewis, R. (1996) *Research Evaluation of Programmes for Violent Men*. Central Research Unit: Scottish Office.

Ellis, T. (2000) Enforcement policy and practice: Evidence-based or rhetoric-based? *Criminal Justice Matters*, No. 39, Spring 2000.

Ellis, T. & Underdown, A. (1998) "Evaluation Survey" and the "Evidence Base" (Chapters 2 and 9) in *Strategies for Effective Offender Supervision*. Report of the HMIP What Works Project. London: HMIP.

Farrall, S. & Bowling, B. (1999) Structuration, human development and desistance from crime.*British Journal of Criminology, 39*, 252–267.

Farrington, D. P. (1992) Criminal career research in the United Kingdom. *British Journal of Criminology, 32* (4), 521–536.

Fischer, J. (1978) Does anything work? *Journal of Social Service Research, 3*, 213–243.

Fraser, D. (2000) A critique of research related to "what works" in reducing offending. *Justice of the Peace, 164*, 356–358.

Frude, N., Honess, T. & Maguire, M. (1990) *CRIME-PICS Handbook*. Cardiff: Michael & Associates.

Frude, N., Honess, T. & Maguire, M. (1994) *CRIME-PICS II Manual*. Cardiff: Michael & Associates.

Garrett, C. J. (1985) Effects of residential treatment on adjudicated delinquents: A meta-analysis. *Journal of Research in Crime and Delinquency, 22*, 287–308.

Gendreau, P., Goggin, C. & Smith P. (1999) The forgotten issue in effective correctional treatment: Program implementation. *International Journal of Offender Therapy and Comparative Criminology, 43*, 180–187.

Gendreau P. & Ross R. R. (1980) Effective correctional treatment: bibliotherapy for cynics. In R. R. Ross & P. Gendreau (Eds.) *Effective Correctional Treatment*. Toronto: Butterworths.

Gendreau, P. & Ross, R. R. (1987) Revivification of rehabilitation: Evidence from the 1980s. *Justice Quarterly, 4*, 349–407.

Graham, J. & Bowling, B. (1995) *Young People and Crime*. Home Office Research Study No. 145. London: Home Office.

Harraway, P.C. (1986) The Driver Retraining Scheme: Towards managing autocrime. In J. Pointing (Ed.) *Alternatives to Custody*. Oxford: Blackwell.

Hedderman, C. (1998) *A Critical Assessment of Probation Research*. Home Office RDS Research Bulletin, No. 39: 1–8.

Hedderman, C. & Sugg, D. (1996) *Does Treating Sex Offenders Reduce Offending?* Research Findings No.45. London: Home Office.

Hedderman, C. & Sugg, D. (1997) *The Influence of Cognitive Approaches: a Survey of Probation Programmes. Changing Offenders Attitudes and Behaviours*. Home Office Research Study No. 171, Part II. London: Home Office.

Hedderman, C., Ellis, T. & Sugg, D. (1999) *Increasing Confidence in Community Sentences: the Results of two Demonstration Projects*. Home Office Research Study No. 194. London: Home Office.

HM Inspectorate of Probation (June 1994) *Inspecting Quality and Effectiveness in the Probation Service: The Manual* (Version 2). London: HMIP.

HM Inspectorate of Probation (1996) Letter to Chief Probation Officers, No. 1/96.

HM Inspectorate of Probation (1998) *Strategies for Effective Offender Supervision*. Report of the HMIP What Works Project. London: Home Office.

Hollin C. (1991) *Rehabilitation with offenders-still not working?* What Works: effective methods to reduce re-offending. Conference Proceedings 18–19 April 1991.

Hollin, C. R. (2001) *Managing Effective Practice*. In Sustaining Effectiveness in Working with Offenders – Paper presented at the Cognitive Centre Foundation Conference. Cardiff: The Cognitive Centre Foundation.

Home Office (1992a) *Draft Probation Service National Standards*. CPO 13/92. London: Home Office, Department of Health and Welsh Office.

Home Office (1992b) *National Standards for the Supervision of Offenders in the Community*. London: Home Office, Department of Health and Welsh Office.

Home Office (1995a) *National Standards for the Supervision of Offenders in the Community*. London: Home Office, Department of Health and Welsh Office.

Home Office (1995b) *Digest 3: Information on the Criminal Justice System in England and Wales*. London: Home Office.

Home Office (1997) *Probation Statistics England and Wales 1996*. London: Home Office.

Home Office (1998) *Effective Practice Initiative: National Implementation Plan for the Supervision of Offenders* (Home Office Circular 35) London: HMSO.

Home Office (1999a) *The Offender Assessment System (OASys) Manual*. Version 3, September 1999. London: Home Office.

Home Office (1999b) Probation Circular 64/1999.

Home Office (1999c) Management Summary, Prison-Probation Review. http://www. homeoffice.gov.uk/cpu/pprapo.htm. [Accessed: 17 March 2001].

Home Office (2000a) *Probation Circular 60/2000: What Works Strategy for the Probation Service*. London: Home Office.

Home Office (2000b) *Making Punishments Work: Overview*. Report of a review of the sentencing Framework for England and Wales. London: Home Office. (Circulated at the launch of the National Probation Service Conference, 4–5 July 2001, London.)

Home Office (2000c) *Research Briefing: a Retrospective Study of the McGuire Programme*. The Probation Studies Unit, Centre for Criminology Research, University of Oxford. Home Office Probation Unit, London.

Home Office (2000d) *National Standards for the Supervision of Offenders in the Community 2000*. London: Home Office.

Home Office (2000e) *What Works: Implementation of Accredited Programmes*. London: Home Office.

Izzo, R. L. & Ross, R. R. (1990) Meta-analysis of rehabilitation programs for juvenile delinquents: A brief report. *Criminal Justice and Behavior, 17*, 134–142.

Joint Prison/Probation Accreditation Panel (2000)*What Works. First Report from the Joint Prison/Probation Accreditation Panel: 1999–2000*. Home Office Communication Directorate.

Lipsey, M. W. (1992) Juvenile delinquency treatment: A meta-analytic inquiry into the variability of effects. In T. Cook, D. Cooper, H. Corday, H. Hartman, L. Hedges, R. Light, T. Louis and F. Mosteller (Eds.) *Meta-Analysis for Explanation: A Casebook*. New York, NY: Russell Sage Foundation.

Lipton, D., Martinson, R. & Wilks, J. (1975) *The Effectiveness of Correctional Treatment: A Survey of Treatment Evaluation Studies*. New York, NY: Praeger.

Lloyd, C., Mair, G. & Hough, M. (1995) *Explaining Reconviction Rates: a Critical Analysis*. Home Office Research Study 136. London: HMSO.

Logan, C. H. (1972) Evaluation research in crime and delinquency: A reappraisal. *Journal of Criminal Law, Criminology and Police Science, 63*, 378–387.

Lösel, F. (1995) The efficacy of correctional treatment: A review and synthesis of meta-evaluations. In J. McGuire (Ed.) *What Works: Reducing Re-offending*. Chichester: Wiley.

Lucas, J., Raynor, P. & Vanstone, M. (1992) *Straight Thinking on Probation: One Year On*. Mid Glamorgan Probation Service.

MacDonald, G., Sheldon, B. & Gillespie, J. (1992) Contemporary studies of the effectiveness of social work. *British Journal of Social Work, 22*, 615–643.

Martinson, R. (1974) What works? Questions and answers about prison reform. *The Public Interest, 10*, 22–54.

May, C. (1999) *Explaining Reconviction Following a Community Sentence: The Role of Social Factors*. Home Office Research Study No. 192 Home Office.

McGuire, J. (1995) Community based Reasoning and Rehabilitation Programmes in the UK In Ross, R. R. & Ross, R. D. (Eds.) *Thinking Straight: The Reasoning and Rehabilitation Programme for Delinquency Prevention and Offender Rehabilitation*. Ottawa: Air Training and Publications.

McGuire, J., Broomfield, D., Robinson, C. & Rowson, B. (1995) Short-term effects of probation programmes: An evaluative study. *International Journal of Offender Therapy and Comparative Criminology, 39*, 23–42.

McGuire, J. & Priestley, P. (1995) Reviewing "what works": Past, present and future. In J. McGuire (Ed.) *What Works: Reducing Re-offending*. Chichester: Wiley.

McIvor, G. (1995) Practitioner evaluation in probation. In McGuire, J. (Ed.) *What Works: Reducing Re-offending*. Chichester: Wiley.

Merrington, S. & Stanley, S. (2000) Doubts about the What Works Initiative. *Probation Journal*, 47 (4), 272–275.

Neary, M. (1992) Some academic freedom, Probation Journal, 39, 200–202. In M. Vanstone (2000) *Cognitive-Behavioural Work with Offenders in the UK: A History of Influential Endeavour*. Howard Journal, 39(2), 171–183.

National Probation Research and Information Exchange (1997) *Risk and needs assessment scales: summary of a one day conference*.

Nellis, M. (1996) Probation training: the links with social work. In T. May & A.A. Vass (Eds.) *Working with Offenders: Issues, Contexts and Outcomes*. London: Sage.

Palmer, T. (1975) Martinson re-visited. *Journal of Research in Crime and Delinquency*, 12, 133–152.

Palmer, T. (1995) Programmatic and Non-Programmatic Aspects of Successful Intervention: New directions for research. *Crime and Delinquency*. 41, 100–131.

Paley, J. (1987) *Somerset one-to-one project: a cognitive behavioural experiment*. Unpublished report cited in S. Merrington & S. Stanley (2000) Doubts about the What Works Initiative. *Probation Journal*, 47, 272–275.

Perry, D. (1999) *What Works initiative crime reduction programme*. Probation Pathfinder Project: Provisional Community Programme Accreditation Criteria, Version 3: 23.6.99. Unpublished paper: Home Office, HMIP, ACOP.

Pitts, J. (1992) The end of an era. *Howard Journal*, 31, 133–149.

Priestley, P., McGuire, J., Flegg, D., Welham, D. and Hemsley, V. (1978) *Social Skills and Personal Problem Solving: A Handbook of Methods*. London: Tavistock.

Raynor, P. (1998) Pro-social approaches and Legitimacy: Implication from Research in Mid-Glamorgan and Elsewhere. In S. Rex & A. Matravers (Eds.) *Pro-Social Modelling and Legitimacy: The Clarke Hall Day Conference:* Cambridge: Institute of Criminology.

Raynor, P. & Vanstone, M. (1996) Reasoning and Rehabilitation in Britain: The Results of the Straight Thinking on Probation (STOP) Programme. *International Journal of Offender Therapy and Comparative Criminology*, 40 (4), 272–284.

Raynor, P. & Vanstone, M. (1997) *Straight Thinking on Probation (STOP): The Mid-Glamorgan Experiment*. Probation Studies Unit Report No. 4. University of Oxford, Centre for Criminological Research.

Reid, W. J. & Hanrahan, P. (1981) The effectiveness of social work: recent evidence. In E. M. Goldberg & J. Connelly (Eds.) *Evaluative Research in Social Care*. London: Heinemann.

Rex, S. (1999) Desistance from offending: experiences of probation. *Howard Journal*, 38, 366–383.

Rex, S. (2001) Beyond cognitive-behaviouralism? Reflections on the effectiveness literature. In A. Bottoms, L. Gelsthorpe & S. Rex, *Community Penalties: Change and Challenges:* Cullompton: Willan.

Roberts, C. (1995) Effective practice and service delivery. In J. McGuire (Ed.) *What Works: Reducing Re-offending*. Chichester: Wiley.

Roberts, C., Burnett, R., Kirby, A. & Hamill, H. (1996) *Evaluating Supervision Practice*. Probation Studies Unit, University of Oxford.

Roberts, K., Barton, A., Buchanan, J. & Goldson, B. (1996) *Evaluation of a Home Office Initiative to Help Offenders Into Employment*. London: Home Office Research and Statistics Directorate.

Ross, R. R. & Fabiano, E. A. (1985) *Time to Think: A Cognitive Model of Delinquency Prevention and Offender Rehabilitation*. Johnson City, Tennessee: Institute of Social Sciences and Arts.

Ross, R. & Fabiano, E. A. (1990) *Reasoning and Rehabilitation: Instructor's Manual*. Ottawa: Cognitive Station.

Sheldon, B. (1994) Social work effectiveness research: implications for probation and juvenile justice services. *Howard Journal*, 33, 218–235.

Sheldon, B. (1996) *Cognitive-Behaviour Therapy*. New York, NY: Routledge.

Shover, N. (1996) *Great Pretenders: Pursuits and Careers of Persistent Thieves.* Oxford: Westview Press.

Smith, G. (1998) Foreword. In T. Chapman & M. Hough (Eds.) *Evidence Based Practice. A Guide to Effective Practice.* London: HMIP.

Tarling, R. (1994) *Analysing Offending: Data Models and Interpretations.* London: Home Office.

Taylor, R. (1999) *Predicting reconvictions for sexual and violent offences using the revised offender group reconviction scale.* Research Findings No.104. London: Home Office Research, Development and Statistics Directorate.

Vanstone, M. (2000) Cognitive-behavioural work with offenders in the UK: A history of influential endeavour. *Howard Journal, 39,* 171–183.

Vennard, J. (1996) Evaluating the effectiveness of community programmes with offenders. *Vista, 2,* 15–27.

Vennard, J., Hedderman, C. & Sugg, D. (1997) *Changing Offenders' Attitudes and Behaviour: What Works? The Use of Cognitive-Behavioural Approaches with Offenders: Messages from the Research.* Home Office Research Study 171. London: Home Office.

Vennard, J., Sugg, D. & Hedderman, C. (1997) *Changing Offenders' Attitudes and Behaviour: What Works?* Home Office Research Study No. 171, Part I. London: Home Office.

Walters, G. (1990) *The Criminal Lifestyle: Patterns of Serious Criminal Conduct.* London: Sage.

Whitfield, D. (1995) Punishment as a Component of Community Service. In J. McGuire & B. Rowson (Eds.) *Does Punishment Work?* London: Institute for the Study and Treatment of Delinquency.

Wilkinson, J. (1994) Using a reconviction predictor to make sense of reconviction rates in the Probation Service. *British Journal of Social Work, 24,* 461–475.

Wilkinson, J. (1995a) *Camberwell Probation Centre (CPC) evaluation.* Unpublished paper: Inner London Probation Service.

Wilkinson, J. (1995b) Programme evaluation using reconviction data. In S. Stanley (Ed.) *Probation Service Quality and What Works Conference 1995.* Inner London Probation Service.

Wilkinson, J. & Morgan, D. (1995) *The Impact of Ilderton Motor Project on Motor Vehicle Crime and Offending.* Inner London Probation Service.

Winstone, J. & Dixon, C. (2000) *Strategies for Tackling Offending Behaviour.* Distance Learning Course Manual. Portsmouth: Institute of Criminal Justice Studies, University of Portsmouth.

Chapter 14

THE COMMON-SENSE REVOLUTION AND CORRECTIONAL POLICY

PAUL GENDREAU,[1] CLAIRE GOGGIN,[1] FRANCIS T. CULLEN[2] AND
MARIO PAPAROZZI[3]

[1] Centre for Criminal Justice Studies, University of New Brunswick, Canada
[2] Dept. of Criminal Justice, University of Cincinnati, USA
[3] Dept. of Law and Justice, College of New Jersey, USA

> There is nothing more uncommon than
> common sense.
> FRANK LLOYD WRIGHT (1868–1959)

INTRODUCTION

Have you ever wondered why the criminal justice system, and more specifically corrections, has historically been rife with panaceaphilia (see Gendreau & Ross, 1979) and prey to more than its fair share of what can only be charitably described as eccentric ideas? We attribute these problems largely to the common-sense revolution.[1*]

Let us clarify at the outset that we do not believe that common sense is invariably an incarnation from the dark side. Common-sense notions form the basis of highly rewarding social intercourse in the same way, for example, as does gossip.[2] Common sense helps us to organize our world and confers a sense of control over our lives. Thankfully, at one level, common-sense perceptions can be accurate reflections of reality. We do not advocate an uncompromising form of "scientism" that denies the validity of common-sense observations of frequent, concrete, and replicable events (e.g. touching a stove's hot element will burn). Nor do we deny that behavioural explanations can be correct under certain conditions (Kelley, 1973).[3] We willingly concede that people can be fairly consistent in their decisions when

---

[*] Notes are presented at the end of the chapter.

Offender Rehabilitation and Treatment: Effective Programmes and Policies to Reduce Re-offending. Edited by James McGuire.
© John Wiley & Sons, Ltd.

examining the same facts under simple circumstances (Arkes & Hammond, 1986). Given such conditions, randomized experiments or exhaustive meta-analyses are typically not required to confirm the truth of a matter. In addition, common sense and qualitative knowledge, regardless of the social context, can provide the basis from which scientific knowledge proceeds (Campbell & Kenny, 1999).

Given these caveats, what then is this egregious type of common sense to which we take such exception? By way of answer, we first define our terms and then describe how common-sense behaviour is reinforced, particularly within the field of corrections. Finally, we suggest some prophylactic methods that might keep the most virulent forms of ideological common sense from becoming full-blown epidemics.

COMMON SENSE: THE BAD KIND

Some History and Characteristics

One of the earliest descriptions of common sense can be found in Francis Bacon's seventeenth-century writings (Bacon, 1994, pp. 57–58). His conceptualization was prescient; indeed, he may even merit the distinction of being the first social psychologist.[4] Bacon stated that people adopt beliefs which satisfy their prejudices or are based on the fashion of the day. In so doing, they are selective in choosing their evidence. Information that is contradictory is ignored and facile distinctions are made in order to preserve one's existing belief system. Bacon also asserted that this type of reasoning accounted for the prevalence of superstitious beliefs (e.g. astrology, dreams, omens, etc.) during his era.[5]

Approximately a century after Bacon, common-sense notions were elevated to a school of philosophy, the prime motivator being the Scottish philosopher Thomas Reid (see Fieser, 2000; Grave, 1967a, b; McCosh, 1996). In reaction to the scepticism of philosophers such as David Hume, Reid posited a theory with a strong biological flavour. That is, everyone is imbued with common-sense intuitions that are the foundations of truth. Moreover, judgements arising from common sense are never in error.[6]

During the next one hundred years, the influence of common sense was widely felt in France and North America where it "established a way of thinking" (Grave, 1967a, p. 121). One can readily appreciate the seductive appeal of the common-sense doctrine during the nineteenth century. Now wisdom was conferred upon all—everyone could be an expert, not just the educated elite or those privileged through birth. Indeed, even in the present day it is not uncommon to hear the view expressed that the social sciences only prove what common sense tells one in the first place (Murphy, 1990). What need then for evidence derived from rigorous empirical examinations?

Indisputably, common sense has now become the *magna carta* of the political *cognoscenti*. Starobin (1997, p. 103) quotes one of the leading intellectuals in the Beltway[7] who purports that, since politics is a political rather than an intellectual exercise, common sense should prevail in setting policy. A number of political parties[8] in the UK and North America have triumphantly proclaimed that "common sense" is the driving force behind many of their policies, particularly those in the area of the economy, health, education, and corrections. Indeed, who can withstand the allure of "common sense" as public policy? The Conservative Party in the UK claims its common-sense revolution will empower communities, make them more secure, release the potential of the country, increase its integrity and independence, etc., not to mention some 46 other benefits (Hague, 1999).

Let us now fast forward from the Bacon and Reid eras by summarizing the enormous gains in knowledge that have been made in the last quarter century regarding how cognitive processes operate within the common-sense schema. The evidence is less than flattering; common sense can lead to "profound, systematic and fundamental errors in judgement" (Nisbett & Ross, 1980, p. 6).[9] To illustrate the basis of Nisbett and Ross's conclusions, in Table 14.1 we present a list of scientific versus common-sense interpretations of phenomena along the dimensions of knowledge sources, analytical processes, and evidence integration. The source material for the table comes from selected readings across a vast and varied psychological literature (see Grove & Meehl, 1996; Kimble, 1994; Matlin, 1988; Myers, 1996; Paulos, 1988; Stanovich, 1992; Tversky & Kahneman, 1974; Vyse, 1997).[10] For the reader unfamiliar with some of the psychological shorthand, brief definitions are provided. In short, regardless of the validity of the information source, when people are faced with interpreting facts that are even moderately complex, especially when numbers are involved, they make sweeping generalizations based on subjective observations of single events, inevitably leading to gross errors in judgement. Furthermore, even well-trained professionals and individuals who depend on numbers for their livelihood are not immune.

For example, in estimating the incidence of a particular phenomenon, base rates are invariably misinterpreted or ignored. Consider the case of the Harvard Medical School staff presented with the following problem (Casscells, Schoenberger & Graboys, 1978). Assume the incidence of AIDS in the population is 1/1000 people. A test is available that is 100% accurate in detecting AIDS, although the test is also known to have a 5% false positive rate. One person, chosen at random from among 1000 people, is tested and found to be positive. What is the probability that that person has AIDS? The most common answer among the Harvard staff was 95%. The correct answer is 2%! The key to the solution lies in knowledge of the phenomenon's base rate. Of the original 1000 people, 999 do not have the disease but, recall, the condition will be mis-diagnosed in 50 of 1000 people. When combined with the single *bona fide* case of AIDS, of the 51 patients testing positive, only 2% (or 1/51) will actually have the disease.

Then there is the representative fallacy; experienced gamblers frequently make the mistake of assuming that if several consecutive coin tosses yield "heads", the odds are much greater than chance that the next toss will result in "tails". Under these conditions, the odds of such an occurrence are in fact always 50%! When making predictive calculations people typically fail to account for the distortion inherent in unrepresentative data from small samples.

Finally, an enormous clinical versus statistical prediction literature exists which clearly demonstrates that the common-sense judgements of even "experts" is

Table 14.1 Scientific versus common sense interpretations

Common sense	Empiricism
Sources of knowledge	
• Qualitative: based on authority, testimonials, anecdotes, intuition, superstition, prejudices, ethnocentrism, morally superior visions, and the media.	• Quantitative: based on evidence derived from the scientific literature.
Analytical processes	
• Judgemental heuristics: anchoring, availability, representative, simulation and hindsight heuristics/base rates and conjoint possibilities.[a] • Co-variation/opinion molecules.[b] • Fundamental attribution.[c] • Illusory correlates.[d] • False consensus/uniqueness/self-serving explanations.[e]	• Data collected from case histories, surveys, correlational studies, quasi- and experimental designs. More confidence placed on results from studies that best control threats to validity (i.e. maturation, history, selection, regression, testing, instrumentation). • Quantitative summaries of large bodies of scientific studies (i.e. meta-analysis).
Integration of Evidence	
• Simple: "Tell it like it is", "what everybody knows" declarations, explanation by naming, exceptions prove the rule, simple causality with little recognition of co-variation and iatrogenic consequences, absence of theory to guide explanation. • Idiographic focus.[f]	• Causality is complex, results described in probabilistic terms, expectations are that the theory guiding the explanation will be revised as more research uncovers new and unanticipated findings. • Nomothetic focus.

Notes:
(a) Over-reliance on the single—often vivid and unusual—case/stereotypical thinking, "I knew it all along"/inability to deal with probabilities.
(b) Inability to appreciate the interrelationship among factors/failure to comprehend the lack of consistency of one's attitudes.
(c) Ascribes causality to dispositional factors while discounting the powerful effects of situations on behaviour.
(d) One sees structure or causal relationships where none exists or discounts the fact that things happen simply by coincidence.
(e) Overestimates the popularity of one's opinions/inflated view of one's abilities which one also assumes to be unique/"How do I love me? Let me count the ways"/not my fault, I didn't make a mistake!
(f) Generalize laws from the facts of an individual case.

decidedly inferior to scientific-based actuarial methods of predicting behaviour (Grove et al., 2000) particularly criminal behaviour (Gendreau, Goggin & Paparozzi, 1996). Next we turn to some instances of BAD common sense.

Common-sense Examples

There are scores of examples to be found that illustrate the disjunction between common-sense beliefs and empirically derived evidence (see Box 14.1).[11] Turning our attention to the field of corrections, we present a classic example of the 'common sense' phenomenon. When boot camp programmes were fashionable, the following comment was made in response to the results of a study of a Georgia programme which failed to reduce recidivism rates (see Cullen, 1994):

Box 14.1   "Common sense" beliefs not supported by data

1. *Education/psychology*
   (a) The "whole language" approach is the superior method of teaching reading.
   (b) Homework assignments produce better grades.
   (c) Throwing money at schools is a waste of time.
   (d) There is a grade inflation crisis in universities.

2. *Health*
   (a) AIDS is a gay plague.
   (b) Injecting more money into the health care system will improve it.
   (c) US doctors and nurses believe a full moon correlates with busier emergency rooms.
   (d) 95% of people who lose weight regain it.
   (e) 150 000 US females die of anorexia each year.

3. *Sports*
   (a) Having a professional sports franchise substantially benefits local economies.
   (b) There is such a thing as a clutch hitter.
   (c) Accuracy in calling balls and strikes is not related to where the umpire stands.
   (d) The major predictor of a sports riot is alcohol abuse.
   (e) Wife battering increases by 40% during football broadcasts.

4. *Miscellaneous*
   (a) Crop circles are the result of alien spacecraft landings.
   (b) Subliminal advertising is effective.
   (c) Dolphin therapy.

> A spokesman for Governor Zell Miller said that "we don't care what the study thinks"—Georgia will continue to use its boot camps. Of note, Governor Miller is an ex-Marine, and says that the Marine boot camp he attended changed his life for the better; and he believes that the boot camp experience can do the same for wayward Georgia youth. Allen Ault, Georgia's Commissioner of Corrections, also joined the chorus of condemnation, saying that academics were too quick to ignore the experiential knowledge of people "working in the system" and rely on research findings. (Vaughn, 1994, (pp. 6–7)

It would appear that the Georgian bureaucracy did not bother to consult World War II evidence from the US military which found that enlisted delinquent youths were three times more likely to commit crimes during their tenure and seven times more likely to receive dishonourable discharges than were their non-delinquent peers (Cullen, 1994). Interestingly, a recent meta-analysis of the boot camp literature reports no effect of this type of sanction on recidivism (Gendreau et al., 2000).[12]

Table 14.2   Some BAD ideas for correctional policy

Policy	Strategy
1. "Getting tough"	• Brain injury reality. • Public shaming/humiliation (e.g. sandwich board justice, road gangs, John TV, cross-dressing therapy, the Uncle Miltie treatment, sitting in a corner). • Making an apology. • Various intermediate sanctions (e.g. electronic monitoring, drug testing, increased surveillance). • Scared Straight. • No frills prisons (e.g. no TV, reintroduce the lash).
2. Not "getting tough"	• Acupuncture. • Karaoke singing. • Better diet and haircuts. • Finger painting. • Healing lodges for females. • Having a pet in prison. • "Leave delinquents alone, they just get labelled incorrectly by the oppressors." • Any treatment programme that targets behaviours that are weak predictors of criminal behaviour (e.g. self-esteem, anxiety, depression). • "Let offenders design the treatments; they are the experts."
3. Miscellaneous	• Prisons pay for themselves. • Prisons are potent schools of crime. • Prisons as tourist attractions. • Sharing and hugging stuffed animals. • Increasing funding for prisons (30%) while decreasing funding for universities (18%) in the US from 1987–1995 is an overall benefit to American society. • It is difficult to predict criminal behaviour (e.g. offenders are similar to non-offenders; dynamic predictors are unstable). • "I can look 'em in the eye to determine who gets paroled." • Accuracy of eyewitness line-up judgements.

Table 14.2 summarizes a list of other BAD common-sense ideas that are prolific in corrections (references available upon request) but have little if any theoretical or empirical justification (Andrews & Bonta, 1998; Andrews, Dowden & Gendreau, 1999; Baird, 1993; Cullen & Gendreau, 2000; Dowden & Andrews, 1999; Gendreau, Goggin & Fulton, 2000; Gendreau, Little & Goggin, 1996; Gendreau, Goggin & Cullen, 1999; Wells, 1993).

For those readers nonplussed by some of the items listed in Table 14.2, we can only say that we share their bewilderment. Consider the "get-tough" strategies, for example. These ideas could certainly not have come out of the 25 000 or so studies published in the last 25 years in the learning and behaviour modification literatures and the social psychology research on resistance processes in attitude change and persuasion (see Gendreau, 1996a, pp. 128–129).[13] Even a casual reading of these literatures would clearly indicate that the "get-tough" strategies described in Table 14.2 could have no hope of reducing recidivism.

Nor could such notions have been derived from psychodynamic, phenomenological, dispositional, behavioural, or social cognitive theories of behaviour which each have something profound to say about the aetiology of behaviour change. Included within these areas are some 40 major theorists (see Liebert & Liebert, 1998), none of whom who, from our reading, are advocates of humiliation or threats and the like as effective therapies.[14] Of course, what do Freud, Skinner, Rogers, Bandura, Meichenbaum, and the rest of this inconsequential lot know about changing behaviour!

Despite our carping, the ubiquity of common sense tells us that "common sense" thrives elsewhere, as in corrections. Why is this the case? We now offer as reasons: how the public thinks, the role of the media, the rise of the new management class, and academia itself.

MAINTAINING BAD COMMON SENSE

The Public and the Media

While Thomas Reid's account of common sense had a strong intuitive flavour, it is more likely that common-sense thinking is learned through social influences (e.g. conformity to authority) and contingent learning procedures (Schwartz & Robbins, 1995, pp. 210–214). Throughout their early years, children have rich and active mental lives, full of irrational, sometimes fantastical beliefs about their world (Opie & Opie, 1959).[15] Should we really be surprised then, that there is a strong residue of such thinking in adulthood? Surveys indicate that between 40% and 90% of American adults believe in miracles, the devil, UFOs, and alien abduction. Furthermore, 93% believe in some paranormal phenomena (Barry, 1997; Vyse, 1997). Even among university students enrolled in "research methods" courses, surveys find that 30% to 90% or more believe that the soul exists after death, that individuals can levitate, that some people are just "born" lucky, that knocking on wood improves one's luck, that black magic exists, and that lucky charms and ritualistic behaviours enhance exam performance (see Vyse, 1997).

And why would people not continue to harbour such beliefs when the media reinforces them with steadfast alacrity? Witness the increase in the frequency of books about the occult and psychic phenomena published between 1964 ($n = 131$) and 1994 ($n = 2859$), the proliferation of astrological charts in daily newspapers, television programmes focusing on "unsolved mysteries", etc. (Kaminer, 1999; Vyse, 1997).

There may be nothing inherently wrong with such widely held beliefs; after all, they do bring a measure of comfort to some people. It becomes problematic, however, when a propensity for "common-sense" pseudo-science begins to permeate decision-making in the public domain, particularly as regards issues such as crime, the environment, health care, etc. (see Kaminer, 1999). It is frightening to know that only 5% of the public have an understanding of science stories appearing in weeklies such as *Time*, and retention of scientific information is very brief (Public Information and Communication Committee, 1993).[16]

The problem lies in the way in which the media presents information, and is one that dates back to the nineteenth century (e.g. Murphy, 1973). With respect to crime issues, the print media has resorted to cheap, Peeping-Tom sensationalism (Chermak, 1994; Krajicek, 1998).[17] Even the "elite" print media (e.g. *Time*, *Newsweek*, *New Republic*, *Nation*, *Atlantic Monthly*, etc.) has gotten into the act and dramatically increased their coverage of crime stories over the last two decades (Clifford, 1995; Dykeman, 1998–99). As for television, the lead news stories from WSOC in Charlotte, North Carolina, for one evening in 1995 says it all for that medium (see Lauren, 1997, p. 39): murder suspect arrested, drive-by shooting at church, armed robbery, truck slams into Pizza Hut, truck slams into Wendy's, truck crash on highway, and truck crash spills glue (what is it with truck drivers in Charlotte!). Sadly, television rejoices over crime stories. Recall television networks celebrating the whopping ratings increases as a result of the Littleton, Colorado, shootings (e.g. "If only the shootings would never stop"; Saunders, 1999, p. A17).

The manner in which the media so easily manipulates public opinion[18] is equally distressing, albeit one cannot help but laud their effective use of some subtle and interesting social psychology principles of persuasion in doing so (see Anastasio, Rose & Chapman, 1999). With regard to crime issues, Garland (1995, p. 38) noted that a single headline in a London tabloid had more pervasive influence than research from the Home Office, and this during a period when the Home Secretary was a veritable rationalist, for a politician that is. When information is overwhelmingly skewed in favour of a particular point of view (i.e. these days the "get-tough" agenda; see Elias, 1994) either by wildly misrepresenting crime statistics (Lauren, 1997), by presenting the views of so-called "experts"[19] or combat intellectuals (Starobin, 1997), through government purchase of stories favourable to White House crime policies (Saunders, 2000), or through simple fabrication (Glass, 1999),[20] this constitutes a serious problem. Indeed, most people are unaware that about 40% of all news, at least a portion of which one may assume to be about crime, is unverified information from 'PR' flacks (i.e. former journalists or political aids) representing vested political interests (Crittenden, 1998).

The conclusion towards which we are heading should be self-evident, and appears to apply to most western countries (Roberts & Stalan, 1997). An overwhelming majority of the public receives its information about crime from the media. Furthermore, public opinions[21] are woefully inaccurate and, not surprisingly, tend to be aligned with the "get-tough" orientation of the media. Thus, the public mistakenly believes that prisons (the harsher the better) deter criminal behaviour, that parole rates and parole violations are far too high, that Canada's incarceration rates are lower than those of other countries and our sentencing policies are soft on crime, recidivism rates are sky high, and violent crime is epidemic[22] (Roberts, 1994, 2000).

Since public opinion has both direct and indirect tangible effects on crime policy (Roberts, 2000), the common sense views of the public regarding corrections policy may make good common sense but may also result in their political masters generating BAD common-sense policies.

Academia

The general public's predilection for BAD common-sense thinking may be defensible. When it comes to academia and its denizens, however, we are less generous, as our fraternity should be well aware of the literature. In our opinion, more than a few academics and their institutions are busy promulgating bafflegab of the highest quality in four different ways. Reflect upon the following developments:

1. Shoddy social science remains common. Consider one research area: the effects of parental divorce on offspring. Common sense is no doubt correct in suggesting that divorce may have some negative consequences but not necessarily to the extent that it produces permanent and catastrophic effects, as some would claim (see Wallerstein, Lewis & Blakeslee, 2000). Not surprisingly, Wallerstein's research has attracted enormous publicity in the socio-political area, particularly among proponents of family violence prevention. What evidence have they presented? Unfortunately, their results were based on a small ($n = 131$) and unrepresentative sample of referrals to a private psychotherapy clinic in Marin County, north of San Francisco! Amazingly, at follow-up the sample consisted of just 5 children (now adults) whose results were not representative of their outcomes as individuals but as "composites". As to the comparison group, it was chosen years after the inception of the project and the selection process was rife with bias. Further, the study reported no statistical analysis.

2. Academia is plagued by internecine warfare. Influential segments of the disciplines of anthropology, art history, criminology, English, history, philosophy, political science, and sociology have rejoiced in the death of positivism and the rise of theoreticism. The new philosopher-kings, as Gross and Levitt (1994) grumpily refer to them, assert that all knowledge is partial, relative, socially constructed, and political.[23] It presents a fanciful perspective on the world, as one is then at liberty to choose the facts one likes and denigrate those that are personally inconvenient (Crews, 1986).[24] Moral superiority is the steadfast trump card.

There is a rich history of this type of thinking, known as knowledge destruction, in criminology (Andrews & Bonta, 1998). Knowledge destruction has been used to counter the notions that criminal behaviour can be predicted, that individual differences are important in criminological theories, that correctional treatment is effective, and that incarceration may not be profoundly psychologically destructive (Andrews & Bonta, 1998; Andrews & Wormith, 1989; Binder & Geis, 1984; Cullen & Gendreau, 2001; Gendreau & Bonta, 1991; Gottfredson, 1979; Hirschi, 1973; Hirschi & Hindelang, 1977).

Basically, there are two knowledge destruction genres: methodological and philosophical (Gendreau, 1995, pp. 202–203): the former attacks research by finding fault with the theory, treatment modalities, statistical accumulation of knowledge (i.e. meta-analysis) and the size of the effect (i.e. never large enough); the latter dismisses research findings as being morally untenable, naïve, purely situational, and ignorant of centuries of human experience. For the interested reader, Andrews

(1989) has summarized most of the knowledge destruction techniques used by criminologists. The following includes some of the classic examples. One researcher dismissed the entire positive effects treatment literature as fraudulent because the conclusions were written by the authors of the reports themselves (so much for Scott Henggeler's research on the effectiveness of MST treatment). Another has concluded that no matter what offenders said and did, they kept on recidivating, the experience of "arrest" was justifiable because it was humiliating, degrading and shameful, and its effects would last a lifetime. A third researcher tried to attribute the failure of a famous "get-tough" programme to problems in balancing fear and anger (sometimes fear wears off, then anger takes over, and then memories surface to challenge the system and prove one's toughness, etc.). This desperate, indeed, bizarre ad hoc theorizing is reminiscent of the phenomenon heretofore used to justify punishment approaches (Andrews et al., 1990) which, moreover, has absolutely no theoretical or empirical support in the punishment literature (e.g. Matson & DiLorenzo, 1984; Schwartz & Robbins, 1995).

3. Some researchers may be "unconsciously" producing results that please their funding agencies. For example, Stelfox et al. (1998) reported a strong association (which we have calculated to be $r = 0.61$!) between authors' published position on the safety of specific drugs and their financial relationship with various drug companies. And there have been similar accusations made in the addictions research area (see Peele, 1992). Might such a phenomenon be occurring in corrections where much research is contract-based and can be quite lucrative? The first two authors have coded authors' conclusions on the effects of intermediate sanctions. As noted previously, this is a literature that produces minuscule reductions, or even slight increases, in recidivism yet authors have repeatedly rationalized the failure of such programmes, while, in some instances, recommending their continuance. Here are some of the classic comments on the effects of intermediate sanctions (with what was left unsaid in brackets):[25]

(a) less costly than prison (but much more costly than the probation comparison groups)
(b) restores principles of just deserts (is it a good principle to inflict an ineffective programme on offenders and taxpayers?)
(c) offers more sentencing options (one should encourage the use of ineffective sentencing options meanwhile discouraging the use of those which employ certain types of treatment known to reduce recidivism)
(d) provides opportune work experiences for dedicated staff to test progressive treatment strategies and develop collaboration with other agencies (no comment needed)
(e) jail doesn't deter, it's only the experience of prosecution that is terrifying and abusive (so let's just prosecute and save some money).

4. Universities are implementing curricula that, on the surface, seem superficial and trite. Consider the following "innovations". Universities are grooming the leaders of tomorrow, our future "back-room boys and girls, policy-makers, pollsters, political leaders and bureaucrats" (Galt, 1999, p. A3) through course work in (no doubt) well-established scientifically grounded areas such as strategic public

opinion and policy analysis, international studies, information technology policy, global cross-cultural perspectives of leadership, enhancing personal well-being, the power of images and images of power.[26] As to "pop science" courses, the kind despised by some scholars (see Levitt, 1999), one can take solace in the fact that the full spectrum of scientific, mathematical, and economic approaches to problem-solving can be covered in two one-term credit courses.[27] Such curricular innovations elevate Fussell's (1991, p. 64) observations (i.e. "Americans set out to experience higher learning but after a brief trial found they did not like it") to the realm of prophecy.

5. No matter what their stripe, some academics are potentially embarrassing in another way—we suspect the public picks up on this a good deal of the time, thereby fuelling their mistrust of science and reinforcing their reliance on common sense—by promulgating nonsense (e.g. cold fusion), if not outright hoaxes (Gardner, 2000; Park, 2000). Occasionally, esteemed scientists move into realms about which they know very little and, subsequently, fall flat on their faces. Recall Linus Pauling's claims regarding the effects of vitamin C on longevity. Somehow he missed a few studies that countermanded his theory (see Knipschild, 1994). We predict that the same will happen for James (DNA) Watson's claims that those people who are sexually the "hottest" are fat white people who spend their time getting sun-burned (i.e. sunlight increases the amount of melanocyte-stimulating-hormone) (McVeigh, 2000).[28]

In corrections, we have a flagrant example of nonsense masquerading as science emanating from the evolutionary theorizing of Thornhill and Palmer (2000) who advocate the following while blithely ignoring the sexual offender literature about what works: (a) build male and female summer camps further apart, (b) have women dress less provocatively and reassure them that, if raped, the resultant trauma is adaptive, and (c) counsel sociopathic rapists to understand their evolutionary history—it's all in their genes (sexual sociopaths have been known to wholeheartedly embrace this excuse!). Also see Coyne (2000) for another critique of Thornhill and Palmer (2000).

In conclusion, academics should not be surprised when politicians characterize them as members of self-serving special-interest groups (Brown, 1991).

The New Management Class

In the "good old days" of the civil service, in Canada as elsewhere, it was not unusual to find senior level policy-makers whose considerable academic credentials were specific to the fields they were administering (Gendreau, Goggin & Smith, 2000; Granatstein, 1982; Osbaldeston, 1989). Moreover, they remained in their portfolios for periods long enough (in excess of 6 years, see Osbaldeston, 1989) to obtain a thorough grasp of the complexities of the issues at hand and provide continuity in policy. How times have changed! We are now in the era of the new management class, endearingly known as fartcatchers (Gendreau, 1999; Gendreau, Goggin & Smith, 2000; Latessa & Holsinger, 1998) which, let us reassure our more sensitive readers,[29] is a legitimate eighteenth-century North American word referring to a gentleman's footman (Bryson, 1994) and accepted terminology among the Canadian media (see *Frank* magazine).

How has the fartcatcher class risen to such prominence? Canadian[30] data provides evidence attesting to this depressing reality. In the 1960s the federal government set out to achieve two management goals. First, it embarked upon a super rational approach to management or what Gendreau (1996b) and Shichor (1997) have labelled the MBA management syndrome and McDonaldization, respectively.[31] In our view these documents have promoted a plethora of management fads such as Theory Z, value chain analysis, quality circles, excellence, restructuring portfolio management, management by walking around, metric management, one-minute managing (see Hammer & Champy, 1993). In these systems the buzz words are efficiency, accountability, and predictability while detailed knowledge of a content area is secondary. A McDonald's manager moves readily from franchise to franchise or, in the case of government, from portfolio to portfolio, fisheries one year, external affairs the next, then followed by corrections, and is deemed to be equally competent in each ministry.[32] Ironically, this management *modus operandi* is no longer *de rigueur* in the eyes of the leading management theorists (Drucker, 1998; Mintzberg, personal communication, April, 1999; Fulford, 1995).

In addition, the Canadian federal government endeavoured to gain more political control over the bureaucracy, a goal which has been accomplished in recent years (Hunter, 2000; Savoie, 1999). Thus, in Canada the most senior policy-makers (Deputy Ministers) now spend less than two years in any one position, few Deputy Minister appointees receive clear directions upon taking up their posts, and the pairings of Deputy Ministers with Ministers, so crucial for establishing coherent and consistent policies, generally run to less than one year (Osbaldeston, 1989; White, 1998). Sadly, some of the senior members of many crown corporations (food safety inspection, nuclear reactor monitoring) use intuition as their principal analytical tool, and credit their positions to political party allegiance and geographical origins (see Jack & Bellavance, 2001).

Our contention is that the fartcatcher phenomenon is very much alive and well in corrections,[33] an area uniquely vulnerable to political manipulation (Blumstein, 1997; Lyons & Scheingold, 2000). If one's goal is the running of cost-effective services that reduce recidivism, the end result of this de-professionalization is disastrous policies (Cerrato, 1982; Gendreau, 1996b; Struckoff, 1978). Consider parole board appointments, one of the most visible and important functions in corrections. Paparozzi and Lowenkamp (2000) surveyed the parole boards in some 20 states. With regard to appointments, four states had very general educational guidelines and nine had vague requirements for criminal justice work experience. All states made appointments through a political process. Other evidence comes from audits of treatment programmes (Gendreau & Goggin, 1997). Some programme administrators (as well as front-line staff) may be admirable "McDonald's" managers but are woefully ignorant of the theory and practice of offender assessment and treatment. As a consequence, it comes as no surprise to encounter correctional programmes whose targets for change are weak predictors of criminal behaviour, and which employ treatments of questionable validity and ethical integrity (Andrews, Dowden & Gendreau, 1999; Gendreau & Goggin, 1997; Gendreau, Goggin & Smith, 2001).

Finally, we offer some common-sense observations as to why the fartcatcher phenomenon persists in light of the repeated failure of so many of the correctional philosophies they have promulgated recently.[34] First, fartcatcher behaviour is rewarded both in terms of the exercise of power (perhaps the most compelling aphrodisiac of them all?) and financial remuneration. Secondly, common sense says that most fartcatchers must have educational backgrounds in those disciplines that eschew traditional scientific values or in new wave leadership-type curricula where the expectation is that "a little dab o' science will do ya". How frequently does one encounter fartcatchers who have been successful in science courses or excelled at quantitative assessments.

Thirdly, we are willing to bet that most fartcatchers have much in common with the participants in Kruger and Dunning's (1999) research[35] which found that people who performed poorly assumed otherwise. Moreover, they had few meta-cognitive skills.[36] They also could not recognize their own incompetencies, akin to the neu-rologically impaired who fail to recognize their own paralysis (i.e. anosognosia). Characteristically, such people lack a sense of humour, employ poor grammar (have you ever wondered where all the new buzz words such as "effectuate", "calcula-bility", and "empower" come from? See Gendreau, 1999), utilize poor logical rea-soning, and have a minimal knowledge of issues which, when combined with their ignorance, makes them truly dangerous. Dear reader, search your own repressed memories and ponder on the fartcatchers you have encountered in your career! Were the above criteria not representative of them? Case closed unless fartcatchers who disagree can empirically demonstrate otherwise! The situation, fortunately, can be rectified. Deficits in meta-cognitive skills are due in part to a lack of negative feedback (no one stays in the job long enough to face the consequences), a lack of opportunity to witness successful policy-making, and attributional ambiguity (Kruger & Dunning, 1999), all of which are mutable conditions.

COMBATING COMMON SENSE

Given the foregoing, anyone with common sense would immediately abandon attempts at rectifying such a bleak situation. Being educators, however, we cannot resist trying to change behaviour. Our standards are modest; we feel it would be a blow for freedom if at least 20% to 40% of correctional policies were based on what we know works (Gendreau, 1999).[37] We now suggest three common-sense credentials to realize this goal.

The Three Credentials

Essentially, one needs to insist that correctional policy-makers and their employers are sufficiently credentialled and have access to, and make use of, credentialled knowledge (see Gendreau, Goggin & Smith, 2000; Meehl, 1997). As to the former, it behoves those tasked with the development of correctional policy to be appro-priately and sufficiently schooled in the correctional literature.

Credentialled People

Firstly, correctional agencies should establish credentialling standards for the ap-pointment of senior managers similar to those within a service of which we are aware that mandates a university degree in an appropriate area (e.g. psychology, criminology) as a requisite eligibility criterion for senior policy-makers (Belanger, 1995).[38] Dare we suggest that hiring decisions also be based, at least in part, upon those characteristics that have been found to be good predictors of job success (and which are probably also predictive of the "good" kind of common sense discussed above in note 6)? The most powerful predictor of occupational success is intelligence (i.e. r values of 0.40 are not uncommon), as measured in the conventional academic manner (linguistic, mathematical, performance items, e.g. *General Aptitude Test Battery*) (Schmidt & Hunter, 1981). Also recommended are promising measures that attempt to assess "practical" intelligence (Sternberg et al., 1995; for a brief review as applied to corrections see Cullen et al., 1997). Subscribing to such a model might increase the probability of hiring more people with better meta-cognitive skills.[39]

Common sense tells us that one should be able to teach scientific thinking (see Arkes, 1981; Sleek, 1996). Individuals, in this case clinicians, who have the ability to integrate large amounts of information, take a multi-dimensional view, and consider a wide range of hypotheses—in other words, those who avoid using judgemental heuristics and fundamental attribution biases—tend to make more accurate judgements than do their less capable peers (Spengler & Strohmer, 1994). Therefore, as part of the credentialling process, the system should operate under the presumption that people can learn such skills and, indeed, the data does tend to support this contention.

Nisbett (1993) reported on several attempts to teach reasoning with some considerable success, and concluded (see p. 11) that an awareness of the rules of reasoning fosters better inferences. Moreover, where individuals are differentially skilled at grasping such rules, the margin of difference can be narrowed through appropriate instruction in abstract reasoning skills and these rules can be made more accessible by teaching examples of their use, especially how to decode the world in ways that make it more amenable to the rule system. By way of caution, training people to reason differently can be quite arduous. It takes repeated re-training (Baron, 1994) and many people may remain resistant.[40] For example, psychologists and physicians are routinely drilled in the use of empirically based actuarial diagnostic systems. Regrettably, only a fraction systematically apply them to their practices,[41] with most continuing to ignore the relevant data on the best predictors in their respective fields (e.g. Paré & Elan, 1999; Peruzzi & Bongar, 1999) by citing justifications ranging from philosophical identification with idiographic ways of thinking, a (mis-placed) sense of ethics, concern for their phenomenological self-worth, or the de-humanization of statistical approaches, among others (see Gendreau, Goggin & Paparozzi, 1996, for corrections-based examples; Grove & Meehl, 1996).[42]

Credentialled Organizations

Secondly, in the present climate of McDonaldization (Ritzer, 1993), we find it intriguing that accountability is a one-way street. That is, one expects offenders to be accountable but not so the correctional agencies which provide service to them.[43] At a minimum, correctional agencies should have a mission statement based on the concepts of fairness, justice, and the improvement of lives through

Table 14.3   A code of conduct for rational discussion

Principle	Action
1. Fallibility	Confess to being fallible, willing to change one's mind.
2. Truth seeking	Examine alternative perspectives, look for insights.
3. Burden of proof	Responsibility to support one's claim with evidence.
4. Charity	Ethical requirement to be fair.
5. Clarity	Focus on real issue, don't obfuscate, special hell for people who say disagreement is semantics.
6. Relevance	On topic, directly related to the merit of the position.
7. Acceptability	Use mutually acceptable premises.
8. Sufficient grounds	Reasons should be sufficient in number, kind and weight.
9. Rebuttal	Encourage challenges to argument.
10. Resolution	Define what is acceptable to settle the issue.
11. Suspend judgement	Wait for more data if necessary.
12. Reconsideration	Re-open the issue.

ethically defensible means rather than one derived from a host of quick-fix panaceas based solely on emotional responses such as anger and punishment (Ingstrup & Crookall, 1998; also see Motiuk, 2000). In this regard, a pro-active administration should establish a code of conduct for rational, truth-seeking discussions when generating policy[44] (Damer, 1995; see Table 14.3 for our summary of his results).

Elsewhere we have suggested (Gendreau, Goggin & Smith, 1999; Gendreau, Goggin & Smith, 2001) a number of "implementation" guidelines that could be used as auditing criteria to test whether correctional agencies satisfy the principal goals of corrections, that is, the provision of effective programmes that reduce offender recidivism, which, ultimately makes its institutions safer to work in, and enhances public protection. Among these guidelines, the interested reader will find the organizational "risk" items to be the most germane. There is tentative evidence to suggest that organizations whose programmes receive a passing grade on quality of implementation are more effective (Gendreau, Goggin & Smith, 1999, p. 181; see Paparozzi, 1994).

Credentialled Knowledge

Thirdly, even though an organization may have a plethora of credentialled staff, elegant mission statements, and use thorough auditing criteria to assess service quality, all is for naught unless the "system" is fuelled by credentialled knowledge. At first glance this seems to be an odd statement. Most organizations would feel they have their houses in order when they meet the first two criteria and be pleased to call it a day. Unfortunately, the evidence they work with may well be confounded, not only for some of the reasons mentioned heretofore, but also by the manner in which knowledge they use is cumulated We have addressed this matter in detail elsewhere (Gendreau, Goggin & Smith, 2000). What follows is a brief synopsis of the main points of the argument.

Two factors operate in tandem to obfuscate research findings and make it difficult to formulate useful policies: information overload and the narrative review process. For example, until the mid-1970s it was possible to achieve a reasonably comprehensive and accurate impression of various facets of the corrections literature (Gendreau, 1996b) simply by consulting several seminal texts and periodically reviewing 10 to 15 journals. Now it is necessary to keep track of several dozen journals in the fields of criminology, economics, management, psychology, and sociology, as well as a similar number of texts. Gone are the days when researchers (e.g. Gendreau & Ross, 1979) rummaged around a small area of the library stacks, recorded a few notes on index cards, and produced a review paper.

In addition, research literatures, even in fairly circumscribed areas, can be daunting and, are at times, in disarray. This scenario is not surprising as each discipline and the researchers within it have different theoretical orientations, employ diverse methodologies, and often use complex statistical analyses. The results that are forthcoming from reviews are often highly variable and sometimes contradictory. This problem, it must be emphasized, is one endemic to the social sciences and medicine (Hunt, 1997).

Put oneself in the shoes of a policy-maker who wants to craft sound policies. How tempting it would be to become disillusioned and resort to common-sense solutions as a consequence of striving to make sense of a literature reviewed in the traditional narrative style. By a narrative review we mean the procedure whereby an author tries to provide a definitive resolution to a policy issue such as what type of treatment produces the greatest reductions in recidivism or which measure is the best predictor of recidivism by reading the pertinent theoretical articles and sifting through the available quantitative evidence.

The conclusions from narrative reviews may be "accurate" when research literatures are small (e.g. several studies) but not when, and this is almost always the case, there are numerous studies that vary in quality, design, and study characteristics and frequently produce more than one outcome of interest. Invariably, in such circumstances the judgements of narrative reviews are imprecise, lack clarity, miss key data, and are subject to the whims and prejudices of the reviewer. Moreover, replications of narrative reviews are rare; what mostly results is a bun fight of words between competing authors (e.g. "You misinterpreted me", "No I did not", *ad nauseam*). Attempts at resuscitating narrative reviews by resorting to box-score analyses (which tabulate the number of significant results) are often fruitless because significance testing provides such misleading conclusions about the magnitude of an effect.[45]

A superior method for cumulating knowledge is to review literatures using quantitative methods, commonly known as meta-analysis.[46] Comparisons between the results of meta-analytic and narrative reviews have reported that the former outperform the latter by about 50% in describing study characteristics, the magnitude of the results, and the effects of moderators (Beaman, 1991). Narrative summaries may underestimate the magnitude of an effect (Cooper & Rosenthal, 1980), which is understandable since many reviewers wish to be cautious in their conclusions when they do not have exact numerical effect size estimates.

Thus, uncertainty in a particular literature can be clarified by using meta-analysis or other quantitative methods such as signal detection (Hammond, Harvey & Hastie, 1992). What a relief for correctional policy-makers to know from meta-analysis that certain types of offender treatments will reduce recidivism by 26%

with a 95% confidence interval of 21% to 31% (Andrews, Dowden & Gendreau, 1999), or that one measure of recidivism will make more accurate predictions than another 78% of the time (Gendreau, Little & Goggin, 1996).

In keeping with the practice/protocols that have been suggested for medicine (Berg, 1998) and clinical psychology (Task Force on Promotion and Dissemination of Psychological Procedures, 1995; Chambless & Hollon, 1998),[47] we are hopeful that if the three credentials are taken seriously, more often than not, rational, empirically based policies will guide correctional practices. We are gratified to report that the federal prison systems in both the UK and Canada have recently established accreditation standards (e.g. Evans, 2000) for implementation, maintenance, and evaluation of correctional programmes based largely on the recent meta-analyses (see Cullen & Gendreau, 2000).

In closing, one may wonder if it is good common sense to be optimistic that correctional policies will come to reflect rational empiricism with greater frequency. We think so. Like crime rates, which rise and fall within a certain bandwidth, we are of the opinion (more erroneous common sense?) that the rampant neo-conservative panaceaphilia that has generated so many costly, ineffective policies in corrections in recent years has finally plateaued (Watson, 2001). The forces of accountability, which are embraced by all political ideologies, will likely spark an increased demand for the three credentials so necessary to the provision of better, more cost-effective services to the public.

NOTES

1. In so doing, the reader is forewarned that we are members in good standing of that professional corrections association loosely known as "hypocrites flourishing under a cloak of benevolence". This is one of the most severe forms of censure one can receive in criminal justice circles. It was put forth by justice model proponents (Gaylin & Rothman, 1976) to describe the intellectually bankrupt ideology and nefarious deeds of rehabilitation proponents, a group in which we were granted platinum card status years ago. We readily acknowledge our hypocrisy in employing common-sense rationales as convenient justifications for some of our viewpoints. We sincerely hope that those who take umbrage with some of our more contentious positions will generate the necessary empirical evidence to demonstrate that we are wrongheaded and misguided (or, indeed, just plain cranky and in need of a new avocation).
2. We can testify firsthand to the value of gossip masquerading as common sense in maintaining "order" in academia (e.g. decisions for tenure, promotions in administration, and, most importantly, livening up social occasions).
3. We may be being a bit generous here. People are great armchair quarterbacks, given their tendency for post hoc confirmation of common-sense observations. It is well documented in the social psychology literature that we routinely deceive ourselves by thinking we know much more, and are more accurate in that knowledge, than is supported by the data (Myers, 1994).
4. An honorific which he might refuse to acknowledge had he any common sense.
5. Paul Fussell (1991) has extended Bacon's reasoning to the present by remarking that such thinking leads to non-substantive grand theories or just plain BAD ideas (e.g. "Americans think death is optional", p. 100) which he maintains have contributed mightily to the dumbing down of his fellow citizens. For whatever reason, Fussell considers the US to be the apogee of BAD ideas, an assumption which has been seconded by none other than Ted Turner (Corporate Culture, 1996). Obviously, neither man has ever spent much time in Canada.

6. Not all philosophers agreed with Reid's propositions. James McCosh (1996), the acknowledged expert on Reid, claimed that the Scot made a crucial mistake in not distinguishing between "good" versus "practical" common sense. McCosh purported that the former is uncommon, found only in those few people (like ourselves and those readers who agree with us) who are careful observers of phenomena and rational in their thinking. Furthermore, good common sense in science and philosophy guards against accepting beliefs until inductive proof is generated. According to McCosh, adherents of "practical sense" in Reid's day tended to deny the existence of New Zealand and Australia, the Earth's rotation, philanthropy, to ridicule the suffering of martyrs, and—this is truly inexplicable—the poetry of Tennyson and Wordsworth! Had Reid any common sense he would surely have opted for "good" sense, but was prevented from doing so by the limitations of his own philosophy. Note that in the early twentieth century, another important philosopher of the common-sense school, G. E. Moore, opined that "common sense" was not infallible (Grave, 1967b).

7. If the Washington, DC, media are to be believed, one could only conclude, supported by common sense of course, that 94.8% of all US intellectuals are located within this circumscribed geographical area (whose parameters obviously do not include two of the authors).

8. As a case in point, consider Ontario, economically the most powerful province in Canada. Under the banner of "common sense", the then newly-elected (1995) Conservative government brought forth various neo-conservative policies that were distinctly punitive towards particular groups (e.g. the poor, offenders, educators). In the Premier's view, his common sense was of the "practical" kind (Jeffrey, 1999). As far as we can ascertain from reading official party documents (e.g. The Progressive Conservative Party of Ontario, 1994), the use of the phrase "common sense" in the Ontario context arose through happenstance and was not derived from any learned reference to the term's philosophical roots or the social psychology literature (also see Jeffrey, 1999, p. 166). Rather, Ontario's common-sense policies were apparently heavily influenced by the policies of US governors such as Engler, Pataki, and Whitman, and, former Republican House Leader Newt Gingrich's *Contract with America* manifesto. An example of common (practical?) sense *chez* the Ontario Conservatives was the appointment of a high school dropout as Minister of Education and Training (who claimed his lack of credentials to be an asset) (McMurtry, 1995) and a car dealer as Minister of Transportation. In New Brunswick, while we have not elevated ourselves to the pantheon of common sense, we take pride in noting that one of our sitting Conservative members of the provincial Legislature credits her career as a Tupperware salesperson as having prepared her for her rôle in developing helpful social policies, while another, Tanker by name, who has spent only two days out-of-province in his life (and those in the neighbouring province of Nova Scotia, a place not to be taken seriously), commented that government work has him busier "than a three-peckered billy goat" (Kaufield, 2000, p. 15). The reader should note that about half of the neo-conservative politicians in Canada have no post-secondary education nor any professional credentials (Jeffrey, 1999).

9. Nisbett and Ross were attacked by academics who declared that if mankind "was so stupid how come we put a man on the moon" (Nisbett & Ross, 1980, p. 249). Their response was that progress in scientific endeavours comes about through the collaboration of *idiots savants* or very knowledgeable people with *specific* skills working towards specific goals. We tend to agree. The *idiots savants* who have authored this paper know how to design effective correctional rehabilitation programmes, but still maintain a host of irrational common-sense beliefs (i.e. the Red Sox will win the World Series, Woody Allen's impressions of New Jersey are not true, the Maritime provinces will become prosperous, etc.).

10. Interestingly, a remarkable parallel with the psychological literature on cognitive thinking errors can be found in the field of philosophy (see Damer, 1995). Damer outlined nine frequently-used fallacious arguments (each with several corollaries). Most of these (fallacies of irrelevance, emotional appeals, begging the question, unwarranted assumptions,

missing evidence, causal and counter evidence) are mirror images of the information presented in Table 14.1.

11. We reckon that this eccentric list, representing the pathological obsessions of the first author, is just the tip of the iceberg.

12. We are frequently surprised at how often these results are not believed by some members of the audiences to whom we present this data, even after pointing out that the values which boot camps try to inculcate—fitness, good hygiene, domestic tidiness, discipline, obedience to higher authority—are not empirically validated predictors of criminal behaviour! In fact, many criminals have these qualities in spades, at least as much as the average student or faculty member. Take it from the "common sense" clinical experience of two of the authors (70 years combined): most higher risk offenders are disciplined, organized, dedicated, and hardworking when it comes to stealing, substance abusing, fighting, denigrating traditional educational and vocational values, disliking authority, etc. Where they differ from non-criminals is in their system of values.

13. The first two authors have coded almost all published "get-tough" outcome studies for our meta-analysis and have found no reference to these literatures.

14. Unfortunately, there are some unscrupulous individuals who falsely claim to be following the theories of some of the leading theorists.

15. Many of these beliefs are a normal, healthy part of the developmental process.

16. This source also cites data that university science majors had difficulty defining the difference between Astrology and Astronomy. Common sense tells us this cannot be true!

17. Blame it on Rupert! Krajicek (1998) and others (Dupré, 2000) lay some of the blame for this on Rupert Murdoch whose television programme A Current Affair changed the face of crime reporting, among other things. And there has been a spate of spin-off "real life" crime programmes on television. Fussell (1991) commented that reading some newspapers is like watching television ("you can have your tube and read it too", p. 133).

18. Stocking and Gross (1989) have outlined how journalists think about issues. They employ many of the techniques described in Table 14.1 (analytical process, column 1). The media also often deliberately misuses statistics by employing samples with built-in biases, conveniently forgetting data, using "gee-whiz" graphics, and the ubiquitous "average" (see Huff, 1954; Kimble, 1978).

19. Dykeman (1998–99) found only 1 of 150 crime articles among the "elite" Canadian print media (Maclean's and Saturday Night) was written by an acknowledged expert/scholar. Combat intellectuals are a fascinating species camouflaging their no-holds-barred ideological fanaticism under an academic or think-tank affiliation.

20. Consider the now infamous retraction of critiques of the D.A.R.E. drug abuse prevention programme published in The New Republic ("Don't you D.A.R.E.", March 3, 1997) and Rolling Stone ("Truth and D.A.R.E.", March 5, 1998). Notwithstanding the Glass controversy, it should be noted that the long-term effectiveness of the D.A.R.E. programme has not been substantiated (Lynam et al., 1999).

21. The public opinion literature is admittedly complex. Support for rehabilitative practices remains strong (see Cullen, Fisher, and Applegate, 2000), with the direction of responses dependent, in part, upon how the questions are phrased. What does seem to be clear is that many politicians choose to focus on the "get-tough" perspective.

22. One survey conducted in Saint John, New Brunswick (an urban area of about 70,000 people) found that university students, the great majority of whom had no personal or familial history of being victims of serious crime, over-estimated the violent crime rate in their city by a factor of 10 (Fox, 1995). Also see Jeffrey and Pasewark (1983) for another example of the public's dramatic over-estimates of crime data.

23. For example, were you aware that Einstein's theory of relativity was a product of cultural factors and bourgeois consciousness, that Newton's theorizing was influenced by seventeenth century mercantilism (Ferguson, 1990), or that his Principia Mathematica has been construed as a rape manual (Harding, 1991; also see Gross and Levitt, 1994)? And did you know that some serious illnesses (e.g. AIDS, drug abuse, etc.) are attributable to the corporate élite (see Satel, 2000)?

24. There are some interesting riffs on this theme. Grounded theory (e.g. Glaser and Strauss, 1967) affirms that there is little point in conducting literature reviews (what a break for two of us, no further need to produce 76 page eye-glazers, see Cullen and Gendreau, 2000), that theory somehow "emerges" from the data. Then there is the curious statement from the president of the American Sociological Association (Portes, 2000) that it is virtually impossible to predict the behaviour of individuals and groups, so sociology should study the *unexpected* which, we can only presume, is somehow more predictable. Finally, there is the belief in the law of small numbers (e.g. Potter and Wetherell 1987, p. 161) that asserts that sample sizes need to be smaller; for example, ten subjects may provide more valid information than does hundreds.

25. References are available upon request for any interested and truly misanthropic readers. If one were to be generous it could be argued that the positive slant on unpopular results may be due to "pressures" from stakeholders, a common problem in evaluation research (Morris & Cohn, 1993; Newman & Brown, 1992).

26. Source material supplied upon request.

27. Some of the course descriptions are priceless. In one "science" course, 12 two-hour lectures cover the great ideas of natural science and their impact on thinking, technologies, society...topics covered include the scientific method and ways of knowing about the world, the philosophical implications of science, the scientific basis of important technological innovations, etc. Indeed, let us not fail to acknowledge the most recent fad: ethnomathematics (Kesterton, 2000).

28. Posh Spice, Calista Flockhart, Kate Moss, and thin people in general are included in his database to support his premise that being thin equates with being discontented. Hey, at least two of us should be gloriously happy!

29. We have at the ready a number of less scatological substitute terms garnered from the great Bard himself (e.g. fawning, flap-mouthed footlicker; mewling, motley-minded moldwarp, etc.).

30. We do not have US data although the fourth author attests under oath that whenever he presents the fartcatcher thesis to US audiences there are immediate signs of recognition.

31. Here is a delightful example of McDonaldization at work in health care (Coutts, 1996). A new system put in place for patient care teams used videos from Disney World and grocery stores as training aids. Patients were treated as customers (even though they would obviously have preferred to be elsewhere and knew nothing of what treatments would work). Staff were instructed to tell severely ill patients to "have a nice day". They reported feeling ill at ease in their jobs; with only 50–60 hours of training staff were carrying out tasks previously assigned to professionals with several years of training. According to Shichor, McDonaldization has led to mandatory sentences in the US which have turned out to be irrational in practice (also see Gendreau, Goggin & Cullen, 1999).

32. We've done at least one thing right in academia by not requiring that fine arts professors teach physics.

33. As of this writing, we have managed to dodge the fartcatcher bullet in Canadian corrections, at least at the federal level. Serendipitously, the system has been led for over a decade by an appropriately qualified, experienced, and well-respected senior manager. He has recently been replaced by a qualified administrator who has considerable experience in corrections.

34. No doubt, existing fartcatchers will deny any responsibility for the mess in which we find ourselves; see the "Mr. Nobody" theory of avoiding blame in corrections (Andrews et al. 1990).

35. Two of the authors are expert fartcatcher-detectors, having themselves acted in the rôle for many years within their respective prison and parole services (see also Dunning & Beauregard, 2000).

36. Here are two general examples of fartcatchers with meta-cognitive deficits. The head of the North Dakota prison system recently applied to be president of the state university citing the fact that both are institutions that run 24 and 7 and both have a rehabilitative philosophy (Wheeler, Suggs & Basinger, 1999). A political supporter of the Premier of

Ontario received a consultation fee of $136 000 for a 2½ page fax (the only evidence on file, by the way) that concluded that the way to change Ontario Hydro's monopoly, the result of 60 years of provincial statues and regulations, was to change the laws (Mittlestaedt, 1999).

37. These percentages represent the optimal results in offender treatment programmes (Andrews, Dowden & Gendreau, 1999). Our common sense tells us that we should not expect any better results (maybe even worse?) in attempting to rehabilitate policy-makers who espouse BAD "common sense".

38. In the agency in question, two thirds of senior staff have at least an M.A. degree (Hale et al., 1992). It is probably no coincidence that it also has a well-deserved reputation as a pro-active service which attempts to generate policies based on the current state of knowledge in the field of corrections. It is also the only correctional agency of which we are aware that publishes a research journal containing articles by leading corrections practitioners and scholars.

39. In the interests of enlivening the debate, there is research indicating which of a variety of individual differences are associated with a greater degree of non-rational thinking (e.g. superstition). These include: having an overprotective father, being poorly educated or educated in the humanities, being rejected by peers, being non-religious, having conservative values, being suggestible, being personally inadequate, having an external locus of control, or being female (Epstein, 1991; Vyse, 1997). Mind you, anyone incorporating these findings (this area cries out for a meta-analysis!) as exclusionary managerial hiring criteria would be faced with a lawsuit in jig time.

40. A classic example comes from the research of Hilton and Simmons (2001). They found that clinical judgements regarding disposition decisions in a forensic setting ignored actuarial data on the V-RAG, a measure that has very good predictive validities and was developed within the facility. In their study, the testimony of senior clinicians, as well as other factors such as patients' physical attractiveness, influenced clinical judgements.

41. The rule of thumb among correctional professionals, be they psychologists or not, is to borrow someone else's instrument and never, ever generate local norms for risk classifications.

42. The first author's experience, based on a long history of conducting service audits and training sessions, is that less than 10% of psychologists or the systems they work in employ actuarial prediction systems based on their own client population norms.

43. Two of the authors remember participating in a planning session for developing state-of-the-art probation services in the US and listening to a senior official from Texas waxing enthusiastically about making the offender accountable for services by paying for them, as if he/she were being offered the chance to buy a television. Unlike probation services, however, the retail market at least affords one the opportunity to choose from among several quality items, complete with warranty!

44. None of us can even imagine what such a meeting would be like in that we have never worked within an organisation that followed even a quarter of the aforementioned criteria during its policy meetings.

45. We realize that this will be a provocative statement for some readers. Please see Gendreau, Goggin & Smith (2000, pp. 55–58), Harlow, Muliak and Steiger (1997), and Hunter and Schmidt (1996) for a detailed explanation.

46. For readers unfamiliar with this attitude towards data analysis, meta-analysis essentially attempts to accomplish the following: (a) to group studies and the variables of concern along certain specified dimensions; (b) to express the outcomes of interest (e.g. recidivism) from these studies in a common metric known as an effect size, most often Pearson r; (c) to average the effect sizes obtained, and (d) to statistically analyse these effect sizes to determine if variations in the magnitude of effect size are correlated with study characteristics (e.g. design quality, risk level of subjects, etc.).

47. It has been recommended that for a treatment to be accredited it must be replicable across studies using between group/single subject designs as well as by different researchers. An extensive treatment manual must be provided.

REFERENCES

Anastasio, P. A., Rose, K. C. & Chapman, J. (1999) Can the media create public opinion? A social-identity approach. *Current Directions in Psychological Science, 8*, 152–155.

Andrews, D. A. (1989) Recidivism is predictable and can be influenced: Using risk assessments to reduce recidivism. *Forum on Corrections Research, 1*, 11–18.

Andrews, D. A. & Bonta, J. (1998) *The psychology of criminal conduct* (2nd edition). Cincinnati, OH: Anderson Press.

Andrews, D. A., Dowden, C. & Gendreau, P. (1999) *Clinically relevant and psychologically informed approaches to reduced re-offending: A meta-analytic study of human service, risk, need, responsivity, and other concerns in justice contexts.* Unpublished manuscript, Carleton University, Ottawa, Ontario.

Andrews, D. A. & Wormith, J. S. (1989) Personality and crime: Knowledge destruction and construction in criminology. *Justice Quarterly, 6*, 289–309.

Andrews, D. A., Zinger, I., Hoge, R. D., Bonta, J., Gendreau, P. & Cullen, F. T. (1990) A human science approach or more punishment and pessimism: A rejoinder to Lab and Whitehead. *Criminology, 49*, 323–330.

Arkes, H. R. (1981) Impediments to accurate clinical judgment and possible ways to minimize their impact. *Journal of Consulting and Clinical Psychology, 49*, 323–330.

Arkes, H. R. & Hammond, K. R. (Eds.) (1986) *Judgement and decision making: An interdisciplinary reader.* London, UK: Cambridge University Press.

Bacon, F. (1994) *Novum organum.* (P. Urbach & J. Gibson, Eds. and Trans.) Chicago, IL: Open Court. (Original work published 1620.)

Baird, C. (1993) The "prisons pay" studies: Research or ideology. *NCCD Focus*, 204–210.

Baron, J. (1994) *Thinking and deciding* (2nd edition). New York, NY: Cambridge University Press.

Barry, E. (1997, August 15) Team dubious. *Styles, The Boston Phoenix*, pp. 6–7.

Beaman, A. L. (1991) An empirical comparison of meta-analytic and traditional reviews. *Personality and Social Psychology Bulletin, 17*, 252–257.

Belanger, J.-P. (September, 1995) Senior staff will need degrees. *Let's Talk, 20*, 1.

Berg, M. (1998) Order(s) and disorder(s) of protocoled medical practices. In M. Berg and A. Mol (Eds.) *Differences in Medicine* (pp. 226–246). Durham, NC: Duke University Press.

Binder, A. & Geis, G. (1984) *Ad populum* argumentation in criminology: Juvenile diversion as rhetoric. *Crime and Delinquency, 30*, 624–647.

Blumstein, A. (1997) Interaction of criminological research and public policy. *Journal of Quantitative Criminology, 12*, 349–361.

Brown, G. E. Jr. (1991) *Federation News special supplement: Address by Congressman George E. Brown Jr.* Washington, DC: Federation of Behavioral, Psychological and Cognitive Sciences.

Bryson, B. (1994) *Made in America.* London, UK: Minerva.

Campbell, D. T. & Kenny, D. A. (1999) *A Primer on Regression Artifacts.* New York, NY: Guilford.

Casscells, W., Schoenberger, A. & Graboys, T. (1978) Interpretation by physicians of clinical laboratory results. *New England Journal of Medicine, 299*, 999–1001.

Cerrato, S. (1982) Politically appointed administrators: An empirical perspective. *Federal Probation, 46*, 22–28.

Chambless, D. L. & Hollon, S. D. (1998) Defining empirically supported therapies. *Journal of Consulting and Clinical Psychology, 66*, 7–18.

Chermak, S. (1994) Body count news: How crime is presented in the news media. *Justice Quarterly, 11*, 561–582.

Clifford, D. (1995) *Technology transfer in criminal justice: What the North American "culturally elite" news magazines say about crime.* Unpublished manuscript, Centre for Criminal Justice Studies, University of New Brunswick at Saint John.

Cooper, H. & Rosenthal, R. (1980) Statistical versus traditional procedures for summarizing research findings. *Psychological Bulletin, 87*, 442–449.

Corporate Culture (1996) *The Nation, 262, 3*.

Coutts, J. (1996, May 9) Business theory seen as failure in hospitals: Telling sick 'clients' to have a nice day seems nonsensical to staff, study finds. *The Globe and Mail*, p. A6.

Coyne, J. A. (2000, April 3) The fairy tales of evolutionary psychology. Of vice and men. *The New Republic, 27–34*.

Crews, F. (1986) In the big house of theory. *The New York Review of Books, 29, 36, 41*.

Crittenden, G. (1998, October 31) Flack attack. *The Globe and Mail*, pp. D1, D3.

Cullen, F. T. (1994, October) *Crime and punishment*. Presentation to the Civic Forum, Cincinnati, OH.

Cullen, F. T. Fisher, B. & Applegate, B. (2001) Public opinion about punishment and corrections. In M. Tonry (Ed.) *Crime and Justice: A Review of Research* (pp. 1–79). Chicago, IL: University of Chicago Press.

Cullen, F. T. & Gendreau, P. (2000) Assessing correctional rehabilitation: Policy, practice, and prospects. In J. Horney (Ed.) *Changes in Decision Making and Discretion in the Criminal Justice System* (vol. 3, pp. 109–175). Washington, DC: National Institute of Justice.

Cullen, F. T. & Gendreau, P. (2001) From nothing works to what works: Changing professional ideology in the 21st century. *The Prison Journal, 81*, 313–338.

Cullen, F. T., Gendreau, P., Jarjoura, G. R. & Wright, J. P. (1997) Crime and the bell curve: Lessons from intelligent criminology. *Crime and Delinquency, 43*, 387–411.

Damer, T. E. (1995) *Attacking Faulty Reasoning: A Practical Guide to Fallacy-Free Arguments* (3rd edition). Belmont, CA: Wadsworth Publishing Company.

Dowden, C. & Andrews, D. A. (1999) What works for female offenders: A meta-analytic review. *Crime and Delinquency, 45*, 438–452.

Drucker, P. (1998, October 5) Management's new paradigms. *Forbes*, pp.152–154, 156, 158–159, 161–162, 164, 166, 168–170, 172–174, 176–177.

Dunning, D. & Beauregard, K. S. (2000) Regulating impressions of others to affirm images of the self. *Social Cognition, 18*, 198–222.

Dupré, F. (2000, March/April) The fight for science and reason. *The Sciences, 40*, 40–45.

Dykeman, E. (1998–99) *A replication and extension of technology transfer in criminal justice: What North American "elite" news magazines say about crime*. Unpublished manuscript, Centre for Criminal Justice Studies, University of New Brunswick at Saint John.

Elias, R. (1994) Official stories: Media coverage of American crime policy. *The Humanist, 54*, 3–8.

Epstein, S. (1991) Cognitive-experiential self theory: Implications for development psychology. In M. Gunnar & L. A. Sroufe (Eds.) *Minnesota Symposia on Child Psychology: Vol. 23. Self-Processes and Development* (pp. 79–123) Hillsdale, NJ: Erlbaum.

Evans, D. G. (2000) Actualizing probation in an actuarial age. *Corrections Management Quarterly, 4*, 17–22.

Famous Quotations Network. (2000) [On-line]. Available: http://www./famous-quotations.com

Ferguson, H. (1990) *The Science of Pleasure*. London, UK: Routledge.

Fieser, J. (Ed.) (2000) A bibliography of Scottish philosophers. In *Scottish Common Sense Philosophy: Sources and Origins* [On-line]. Available: *http://www.thoemmes.com/scottish/sense.htm*

Fox, K. (1995) *Changes in the estimations of violent crime and media influences*. Unpublished manuscript, Centre for Criminal Justice Studies, University of New Brunswick at Saint John.

Fulford, R. (1995) Regarding Henry. *Report on Business Magazine, October*, 67–74, 91.

Fussell, P. (1991) *BAD or The Dumbing of America*. New York, NY: Summit Books.

Galt, V. (1999, May 27) Carleton U to offer degree in public affairs, policy: Jobs opening up in civil service, corporations and non-profit organizations, university says. *The Globe and Mail*, p. A3.

Gardner, M. (2000) *Did Adam and Eve Have Navels? Discourses on Reflexology, Numerology, Urine Therapy and Other Dubious Subjects*. Scranton, PA: Norton Press.

Garland, D. (1995) Does punishment work? Does the evidence matter? In J. McGuire & B. Rowson, (Eds.) *Does punishment work?* London, UK: Institute for the Study and Treatment of Delinquency.

Gaylin, W. & Rothman, D. J. (1976) Introduction. In A. Von Hirsch (Ed.) *Doing Justice: The Choice of Punishments* (pp. xxi–xli). New York, NY: Hill & Wang.

Gendreau, P. (1995) Technology transfer in the criminal justice field: Implications for substance abuse. In T. E. Backer, S. L. David & G. Soucy (Eds.) *Reviewing the Behavioral Science Knowledge Base on Technology Transfer* (pp. 198–208). Rockville, MD: National Institute on Drug Abuse Research Monograph #155.

Gendreau, P. (1996a) The principles of effective intervention with offenders. In A. T. Harland (Ed.) *Choosing Correctional Interventions that Work: Defining the Demand and Evaluating the Supply* (pp. 117–130) Newbury Park, CA: Sage.

Gendreau, P. (1996b) Offender rehabilitation: What we know and what needs to be done. *Criminal Justice and Behavior 23*, 144–161.

Gendreau, P. (1999) Rational policies for reforming offenders. *The ICCA Journal of Community Corrections 9*, 16–20.

Gendreau, P. & Bonta, J. (1991) Boats against the current: A rebuttal. *Law and Human Behavior, 15*, 563–565.

Gendreau, P. & Goggin, C. (1997) Correctional treatment: Accomplishments and realities. In P. Van Voorhis, Braswell, M. & Lester, D. (Eds.) *Correctional Counseling and Rehabilitation* (3rd edition) (pp. 271–279) Cincinnati, OH: Anderson.

Gendreau, P., Goggin, C. & Cullen, F. T. (1999) *The Effects of Prison Sentences on Recidivism* (Cat. #J42-87/1999E). Ottawa, Ontario: Corrections Research and Development and Aboriginal Policy Branch, Solicitor General of Canada.

Gendreau, P., Goggin, C., Cullen, F. T. & Andrews, D. A. (2000) Does "getting tough" with offenders work? The effects of community sanctions and incarceration. *Forum on Corrections Research, 12*, 10–13.

Gendreau, P., Goggin, C. & Fulton, B. (2000) Intensive supervision in probation and parole. In C. R. Hollin (Ed.), *Handbook of Offender Assessment and Treatment* (pp. 195–204). Chichester, UK: John Wiley & Sons.

Gendreau, P., Goggin, C. & Paparozzi, M. (1996) Principles of effective assessment for community corrections. *Federal Probation, 60*, 64–70.

Gendreau, P., Goggin, C. & Smith, P. (1999) The forgotten issue in effective correctional treatment: Programme implementation. *International Journal of Offender Therapy and Comparative Criminology, 43*, 180–187.

Gendreau, P., Goggin, C. & Smith, P. (2000) Generating rational correctional policies: An introduction to advances in cumulating knowledge. *Corrections Management Quarterly, 4*, 52–60.

Gendreau, P., Goggin, C. & Smith, P. (2001) Implementation guidelines for correctional programmes in the "real world". In G. A. Bernfeld, A. W. Leschied & D. P. Farrington (Eds.) *Offender Rehabilitation in Practice: Implementing and Evaluating Effective Programmes* (pp. 247–268). Chichester: John Wiley & Sons.

Gendreau, P., Little, T. & Goggin, C. (1996) A meta-analysis of the predictors of adult offender recidivism: What works? *Criminology, 34*, 575–607.

Gendreau, P. & Ross, R. (1979) Effective correctional treatment: Bibliotherapy for cynics. *Crime and Delinquency 25*, 463–489.

Glaser, B. G. & Strauss, A. L. (1967) *The Discovery of Grounded Theory: Strategies for Qualitative Research*. Chicago, IL: Aldine Publishing Co.

Glass, S. (1999) Apology from Stephen Glass. *DARELINE International* [On-line], 7. Available: http://www.dare.com//D_FEAT/apology.htm

Gottfredson, M. R. (1979) Treatment destruction techniques. *Journal of Research in Crime and Delinquency, 16*, 39–54.

Granatstein, J. L. (1982) *The Ottawa Men: The Civil Service Men, 1937–1957*. Toronto, Ontario: Oxford Press.

Grave, S. A. (1967a) Reid, Thomas. In P. Edwards (Ed.) *The Encyclopedia of Philosophy* (vol. 7, pp. 118–121) New York, NY: The Macmillan Company and The Free Press.

Grave, S. A. (1967b) Common sense. In P. Edwards (Ed.) *The Encyclopedia of Philosophy* (vol. 2, pp. 155–160) New York, NY: The Macmillan Company and The Free Press.

Grove, W. M. & Meehl, P. E. (1996) Comparative efficiency of informal (subjective, impressionistic) and formal (mechanical, algorithmic) prediction procedures: The clinical-statistical controversy. *Psychology, Public Policy, and Law, 2,* 293–323.

Grove, W. M., Zald, D. H., Lebow, B. S., Snitz, B. E. & Nelson, C. (2000) Clinical versus mechanical prediction: A meta-analysis. *Psychological Assessment, 12,* 19–30.

Gross, P. & Levitt, N. (1994) *Higher Superstition: The Academic Left and its Quarrels with Science.* Baltimore, MD: Johns Hopkins University Press.

Hague, W. (October, 1999) *The common sense revolution.* Speech made at the Conservative Party Conference, Blackpool, UK.

Hale, M., Stuart, C., Carleton, D. & Fisher, B. (1992) Studying senior managers' career paths. *Forum on Corrections Research, 4,* 28–30.

Hammer, M. & Champy, J. (1993) *Re-engineering the Corporation: A Manifesto for Business Revolution.* New York, NY: Harper Business.

Hammond, K. R., Harvey, L. O., Jr. & Hastie, R. (1992) Making better use of scientific knowledge: Separating truth from justice. *Psychological Science, 3,* 80–87.

Harding, S. (1991) *Whose Science? Whose Knowledge? Thinking from Women's Lives.* Ithaca, NY: Cornell University Press.

Harlow, L. L., Muliak, S. A. & Steiger, J. H. (Eds.) (1997) *What if There Were no Significance Tests?* Mahwah, NJ: Lawrence Erlbaum Associates.

Hilton, N. Z. & Simmons, J. L. (2001) The influence of actuarial risk assessment and clinical judgements in tribunal decisions about mentally disordered offenders in maximum security. *Law and Human Behavior, 25,* 393–408.

Hirschi, T. (1973) Procedural rules and the study of deviant behaviour. *Social Problems, 21,* 159–173.

Hirschi, T. & Hindelang, M. J. (1977) Intelligence and delinquency: A revisionist review. *American Sociological Review, 42,* 571–587.

Huff, D. (1954) *How to Lie with Statistics.* New York, NY: W. W. Norton.

Hunt, M. (1997) *How Science Takes Stock: The Story of Meta-Analysis.* New York, NY: Russell Sage Foundation.

Hunter, J. (2000, October 20) PM's cadre more influential than Cabinet: Critics. *National Post,* p. A7.

Hunter, J. E. & Schmidt, F. L. (1996) Cumulative research knowledge and social policy formulation: The critical role of meta-analysis. *Psychology, Public Policy, and Law, 2,* 324–347.

Ingstrup, O. & Crookall, P. (1998) The three pillars of public management: Applications in corrections. *Corrections Management Quarterly, 22,* 1–9.

Jack, I. & Bellavance, J.-D. (2001, February 7) Audit slams Ottawa's cronyism. *The National Post,* pp. A1, A6.

Jeffrey, B. (1999) *Hard Right Turn: The New Face of Neo-Conservatism in Canada.* Toronto, Ontario: Harper Collins.

Jeffery, R. & Pasewark, R. (1983) Altering opinions about the insanity plea. *Journal of Psychiatry and Law, 11,* 29–40.

Kaminer, W. (1999) *Sleeping with Extra-Terrestrials: The Rise of Irrationalism and Perils of Piety.* Westminster, NY: Pantheon Books.

Kaufield, K. (2000, March 25) Tanker goes to the legislature: A new breed of MLAs hits Fredericton. *The New Brunswick Reader,* pp. 14–19.

Kelley, H. H. (1973) The process of causal attribution. *American Psychologist, 28,* 107–128.

Kesterton, M. (2000, October 18) PC math. *The Globe and Mail,* p. A20.

Kimble, G. A. (1978) *How to Use (and Misuse) Statistics.* New York, NY: Prentice-Hall.

Kimble, G. A. (1994) A frame of reference for psychology. *American Psychologist, 49,* 510–519.

Knipschild, P. (1994) Some examples. *British Medical Journal, 309,* 719–721.

Krajicek, D. J. (1998) *Scooped! Media Miss Real Story on Crime While Chasing Sex, Sleaze, and Celebrities.* New York, NY: Columbia University Press.

Kruger J. & Dunning, D. (1999) Unskilled and unaware of it: How difficulties in recognizing one's own incompetence lead to inflated assessments. *Journal of Personality and Social Psychology, 77,* 1121–1134.

Latessa, E. J. & Holsinger, A. (1998) The importance of evaluating correctional programmes: Assessing outcome and quality. *Corrections Management Quarterly, 2,* 22–29.

Lauren, R. J. (1997) *Positive Approaches to Corrections: Research, Policy, and Practice.* Lanham, MD: American Correctional Association.

Levitt, N. (1999) *Prometheus Bedeviled: Science and the Contradictions of Contemporary Culture.* New York, NY: Rutgers University Press.

Liebert, R. M. & Liebert, L. L. (1998) *Personality: Strategies and Issues* (8th edition). Pacific Grove, CA: Brooks/Cole.

Lynam, D. R., Milich, R., Zimmerman, R., Novak, S. P., Logan, T. K., Martin, C., Leukefeld, C. & Clayton, R. (1999) Project DARE: No effects at 10-year follow-up. *Journal of Consulting and Clinical Psychology, 67,* 590–593.

Lyons, W. & Scheingold, S. (2000) The politics of crime and punishment. In G. LaFree (Ed.) *Criminal Justice: Vol.1. The Nature of Crime: Continuity and Change* (pp. 103–150). Washington, DC: US Department of Justice, NIJ.

Matlin, M. W. (1998) *Cognition* (4th edition). Fort Worth, TX: Harcourt Brace.

Matson, J. & DiLorenzo, T. (1984) *Punishment and its Alternatives: A New Perspective for Behavior Modification.* New York, NY: Springer.

McCosh, J. (1996) The Scottish Philosophy. In *The Internet Encyclopedia of Philosophy* [On-line]. Available: http://www.utm.edu/research/iep/text/mccosh/mc-26.htm. (Original work published 1875.)

McMurtry, J. (1995) The iconoclast: The common sense revolution. *Canadian Social Studies, 30,* 50–52.

McVeigh, T. (2000, July 4) Fat people happier, says Nobel laureate. *The National Post,* p. A13.

Meehl, P. E. (1997) Credentialled persons, credentialled knowledge. *Clinical Psychology: Science and Practice, 4,* 91–98.

Mittlestaedt, M. (1999, May 28) The $136,000 fax: And other tales of how little some of Mike Harris's friends and supporters supplied to Ontario Hydro – and for how much. *Report on Business Magazine, 15,* pp. 45–46.

Morris, M. & Cohn, R. (1993) Programme evaluators and ethical challenges: A national survey. *Evaluation Review, 17,* 621–642.

Motiuk, L. L. (2000) Public administration and management of adult correctional services in Canada. In J. A. Winterdyk (Ed.) *Corrections in Canada: Social Reactions to Crime* (pp. 65–80). Toronto, Ont.: Prentice Hall.

Murphy, C. (1990) New findings: Hold on to your hat. *The Atlantic, 265,* 22–23.

Murphy, E. F. (1973) *The Black Candle.* Toronto, Ontario: Coles Publishing Company.

Myers, D. G. (1994) *Exploring Social Psychology.* New York, NY: McGraw-Hill.

Myers, D. G. (1996) *Social Psychology* (6th edition). Boston, MA: McGraw-Hill.

Newman, D. L. & Brown, R. D. (1992) Violations of evaluation standards: Frequency and seriousness of occurrence. *Evaluation Review, 16,* 219–234.

Nisbett, R. E. (Ed.) (1993) *Rules for Reasoning.* Hillsdale, NJ: Lawrence Erlbaum Associates.

Nisbett, R. & Ross, L. (1980) *Human Inference: Strategies and Shortcomings of Social Judgement.* Englewood Cliffs, NJ: Prentice Hall.

Opie, I. & Opie, P. (1959) *The Lore and Language of School Children.* London, UK: Oxford University Press.

Osbaldeston, G. (1989) *Keeping Deputy Ministers Accountable.* Whitby, Ontario: McGraw-Hill.

Paparozzi, M. A. (1994) *A comparison of the effectiveness of an Intensive Parole Supervision Programme with traditional parole supervision.* Unpublished doctoral dissertation, Rutgers University, New Brunswick, New Jersey.

Paparozzi, M. & Lowenkamp, C. (2000) To be or not to be - a profession - that is the question for corrections. *Corrections Management Quarterly, 4,* 9–16.

Paré, G. & Elan, J. J. (1999) Physicians' acceptance of clinical information systems: An empirical look at attitudes, expectations and skills. *International Journal of Healthcare Technology and Management, 1,* 46–61.

Park, R. (2000) *Voodoo Science: The Road from Foolishness to Fraud.* New York, NY: Oxford University Press.

Paulos, J. A. (1988) *Innumeracy: Mathematical Illiteracy and its Consequences*. New York, NY: Vintage Books.

Peele, S. (1992) Why is everybody always pickin' on me? A response to comments. *Addictive Behaviors, 17*, 83–93.

Peruzzi, N. & Bongar, B. (1999) Assessing risk for completed suicide in patients with major depression: Psychologists' views of critical factors. *Professional Psychology, Research, and Practice, 30*, 576–580.

Portes, A. (2000) The hidden abode: Sociology as analysis of the unexpected. *American Sociological Review, 65*, 1–18.

Potter, J. & Wetherell, M. (1987) *Discourse and Social Psychology: Beyond Attitudes and Behaviour*. London, UK: Sage.

Progressive Conservative Party of Ontario (1994) *The Common Sense Revolution* (7th edition) [Brochure]. Toronto, Ontario: Author.

Public Information and Communication Committee (1993) Science and the public: Surviving the media. *Psynopsis, 15*, p. 10.

Ritzer, G. (1993) *The McDonaldization of Society*. Newbury Park, CA: Pine Forge.

Roberts, J. (1994) *Public Knowledge of Crime and Justice: An Inventory of Canadian Facts* (Technical Report No. TR1994-15e). Ottawa, Ontario: Research, Statistics and Evaluation Directorate, Department of Justice, Government of Canada.

Roberts, J. (2000) Corrections in Canada: Public knowledge and public opinion. In J. Winterdyk (Ed.) *Corrections in Canada: Social Reaction to Crime* (pp. 49–64). Scarborough, Ontario: Prentice-Hall.

Roberts, J. V. & Stalan, L. S. (1997) *Public Opinion, Crime and Criminal Justice*. Boulder, CO: Westview Press.

Satel, S. (2000) *PC, M.D.: How Political Correctness is Corrupting Medicine*. New York, NY: Basic Books, Inc.

Saunders, D. (1999, April 29) Rampage leads to ratings bonanza: Littleton was made for TV networks eager to cover the bloody drama. But do they have to brag about it? *The Globe and Mail*, p. A17.

Saunders, D. (2000, April 1) Editors made deals on antidrug articles. *The Globe and Mail*, p. A2.

Savoie, D. J. (1999) *Governing from the Center: The Concentration of Power in Canadian Politics*. Toronto, Ontario: University of Toronto Press.

Schmidt, F. L. & Hunter, J. E. (1981) Employment testing: Old theories and new research findings. *American Psychologist, 36*, 1128–1137.

Schwartz, B. & Robbins, S. J. (1995) *Psychology of Learning and Behavior* (4th edition). New York, NY: W. W. Norton and Company.

Shichor, D. (1997) Three strikes as a public policy: The convergence of the new penology and the McDonaldization of punishment. *Crime and Delinquency, 43*, 470–492.

Sleek, S. (1996) Ensuring accuracy in clinical decisions. *Monitor: American Psychological Association, 26*, 30–31.

Spengler, P. M. & Strohmer, D. C. (1994) Clinical judgmental biases: The moderating roles of counselor cognitive complexity and counselor client preferences. *Journal of Counseling Psychology, 41*, 8–17.

Stanovich, K. E. (1992) *How to Think Straight about Psychology* (3rd edition). New York, NY: Harper Collins Publishers.

Starobin, P. (1997) Word warriors. *The Washingtonian, 32*, 48–51, 101–103.

Stelfox, H. T., Chua, G., O'Rourke, K. & Detsky, A. S. (1998) Conflict of interest in the debate over calcium-channel antagonists. *New England Journal of Medicine, 338*, 101–106.

Sternberg, R. J., Wagner, R. K., Williams, W. M. & Horvath, J. A. (1995) Testing common sense. *American Psychologist, 50*, 912–927.

Stocking, H. & Gross, P. H. (1989) *How do Journalists Think?* Bloomington, IN: Smith Research Center, Indiana University.

Struckoff, D. R. (1978) Deprofessionalizing corrections is a bad idea. *Offender Rehabilitation, 2*, 333–338.

Task Force on Promotion and Dissemination of Psychological Procedures (1995) Training in and dissemination of empirically-validated psychological treatments: Report and recommendations. *The Clinical Psychologist*, *48*, 3–23.

Thornhill, R. & Palmer, C. (2000) *A Natural History of Rape: Biological Bases of Sexual Coercion*. Boston, MA: MIT Press.

Tversky, A. & Kahneman, D. (1974) Judgement under uncertainty: Heuristics and biases. *Science*, *185*, 1123–1131.

Vaughn, M. (1994) Boot camps. *The Grapevine*, *2*, 2.

Vyse, S. A. (1997) *Believing in Magic: The Psychology of Superstition*. New York, NY: Oxford University Press.

Wallerstein, J. S., Lewis, J. M. & Blakeslee, S. (2000) *The Unexpected Legacy of Divorce: A 25 Year Landmark Study*. New York, NY: Hyperion Press.

Watson, W. (2001, April 10) Neo-conservatism: An idea that didn't take. *The National Post*, p. A18.

Wells, G. L. (1993) What do we know about eyewitness identification? *American Psychologist*, *48*, 553–571.

Wheeler, D. L., Suggs, W. & Basinger, J. (1999, February 5) Peer Review. *The Chronical of Higher Education*, p. A47.

White, G. (1998) Shorter measures: The changing ministerial career in Canada. *Canadian Public Administration*, *41*, 369–394.

INDEX